Divine Love
and
Wisdom

Divine
Providence

The New Century Edition
of the Works of Emanuel Swedenborg

Angelic Wisdom about

DIVINE LOVE

and about

DIVINE WISDOM

Angelic Wisdom about

DIVINE
PROVIDENCE

EMANUEL SWEDENBORG

Translated from the Latin by George F. Dole

With an Introduction by Gregory R. Johnson

Annotated by George F. Dole, Gregory R. Johnson,
and Jonathan S. Rose

With Additional Notes by Reuben P. Bell, Glen M. Cooper,
and Stuart Shotwell

SWEDENBORG FOUNDATION

West Chester, Pennsylvania

Printed in the United States of America

ISBN (hardcover) 0-87785-480-7
ISBN (paperback) 0-87785-481-5 (*Divine Love and Wisdom* only)
ISBN (paperback) 0-87785-505-6 (*Divine Providence* only)

Library of Congress Cataloging-in-Publication Data

Swedenborg, Emanuel, 1688–1772.
    [Sapientia angelica de divino amore. English]
    Angelic wisdom about divine love and about divine wisdom ; and, Angelic wisdom about divine providence / Emanuel Swedenborg ; translated from the Latin by George F. Dole ; with an introduction by Gregory R. Johnson ; annotated by George F. Dole, Gregory R. Johnson, and Jonathan S. Rose ; with additional notes by Reuben P. Bell, Glen M. Cooper, and Stuart Shotwell.
        p. cm.— (The new century edition of the works of Emanuel Swedenborg)
    Includes bibliographical references and indexes.
    ISBN 0-87785-480-7 (alk. paper)
    1. God—Love. 2. God—Wisdom. 3. Providence and government of God. I. Title: Angelic wisdom about divine love and about divine wisdom ; and, Angelic wisdom about divine providence. II. Dole, George F. III. Johnson, Gregory R. IV. Rose, Jonathan S. V. Bell, Reuben P. VI. Cooper, Glen Michael. VII. Shotwell, Stuart, 1953–. VIII. Swedenborg, Emanuel, 1688–1772. Sapientia angelica de divina providentia. English. IX. Title. X. Series: Swedenborg, Emanuel, 1688–1772. Works. English. 2000.

BX8712 .D4 2002
231'.6—dc21

2002013696

Cover designed by Caroline Kline
Text designed by Joanna V. Hill
Ornaments from the first Latin editions, 1763 and 1764
Indexes by Bruce Tracy
Typeset by Nesbitt Graphics

For information contact:

    Swedenborg Foundation
    320 North Church Street
    West Chester PA 19380 USA

DIVINE LOVE
AND
WISDOM

Contents

Part 1

Part 2

Part 3

Part 4

brings forth nothing. Divinity brings forth everything from
itself, and does so through the spiritual world.   199

Part 5

Notes and Indexes

Translator's Preface

IN 1745, at the age of fifty-seven, Emanuel Swedenborg (1688–1772) had an experience that radically changed the course of his life. Much later, he would describe it as a vision of Jesus Christ commissioning him to "open to people the spiritual meaning of Scripture"[1] and initiating years of regular experiences of the spiritual world. Soon after this vision, he resigned from his post on the Swedish Board of Mines and spent the remainder of his years writing and publishing the theological works for which he is now best known.

The Genesis of *Divine Love and Wisdom*

Divine Love and Wisdom and its sequel, *Divine Providence,* were published in 1763 and 1764 respectively, a little more than halfway through Swedenborg's theological career. He had begun that career by taking his commission quite literally. Between 1749 and 1756 he produced a work titled *Secrets of Heaven* (traditionally known by its Latin title, *Arcana Coelestia*) consisting of eight substantial volumes on the spiritual meaning of Genesis and Exodus. He then altered his course, and in 1758 published five much smaller works (two being little larger than leaflets) on specific religious topics; much of the material was drawn from *Secrets of Heaven*.[2]

Once these were in print, he returned to his exegetical task and drafted most of a substantial work on the spiritual meaning of the Book of Revelation, a work that was never published and in fact never quite completed: *Revelation Explained* (traditionally titled *Apocalypse Explained*).[3] His intent to publish is clear from his draft of a title page to the projected first volume, including the proposed place and date of publication (London, 1759) and his preparation of a fair copy, including instructions in the

---

1. See Hjern 1989, 26–65. For secondary accounts, see Acton 1927, 40–47; Sigstedt 1981, 197–199; and Benz 2002, 193–200.

2. See Dole 2000, 1–3 for further detail.

3. See Swedenborg 1997.

margins concerning typography. Furthermore, at the close of his treatment of chapter 6 he inserted a note that read *Finis Voluminis Primi,* "End of Volume One." However, the mere fact that he did not publish the completed first volume of *Revelation Explained* indicates the extent of his uncertainty about it. This can be seen by a contrast with his publication process for *Secrets of Heaven.* When he had been writing that work, he had not felt it necessary to finish the entire work before commencing publication; he had sent it to press as each volume was complete.

After the first volume, the manuscript of *Revelation Explained* shows internal signs of indecision about publication. He did not prepare a title page for a second volume, and although from the close of chapter 9 onwards he made his accustomed indications of the end of each chapter, often with flourishes of the pen to emphasize the point of division, he made no further note of volume divisions. Nevertheless, the persistence of his intent to publish seems clearly indicated by the fact that he continued the painstaking labor of making a fair copy to within three relatively brief paragraphs from the end.[4]

While Swedenborg has left us no account of his reasons for abandoning a work so clearly intended for publication and so near to completion, there are indications in it that issues dealt with in the present volume were calling for attention. Early in his treatment of chapter 15, he began to insert material on various theological topics at the close of virtually every numbered section.[5] At the close of §1136, he introduced ten so-called laws of divine providence, and proceeded in subsequent sections to deal with them in some detail. Then in §1217 he introduced a series of propositions concerning the Lord's omnipresence, ending with one that attributes omnipresence primarily to divine love, and omniscience primarily to divine wisdom.

He then drafted what are evidently sketches for further work. He began with the heading "On Divine Love" and after twenty-one sections

---

4. See also Dole 1988.

5. These sections constitute paragraphs by the conventions of eighteenth-century page design, though in some works such "paragraphs" cover several pages (see, for example *Revelation Explained* [= Swedenborg 1997] §1042). Both punctuation and substance, however, often indicate subdivisions equivalent to modern paragraphs, and the effort has been made in the present edition to heed these indications. As is customary in Swedenborgian studies, citations of Swedenborg's works in the present volume refer not to page numbers but to these numbered sections of Swedenborg's text, as the numbering is uniform in all editions.

on this topic inserted the heading "On Wisdom," crossed it out, and wrote "On Divine Wisdom," a heading followed by twelve sections on the topic. The sections in each case have roman rather than arabic numerals, giving the appearance of an outline.[6] While the material covered is clearly anticipatory of the present work, both the sequence of presentation and the relative emphasis on particular subjects are quite different.[7]

Before publishing *Divine Love and Wisdom* and its sequel publication, *Divine Providence* (1764), Swedenborg published four brief works on specific teachings for "the New Jerusalem."[8] In the preface to the first of these, *The Lord,* he noted the previous publication of the 1758 works (making no mention of *Secrets of Heaven*) and listed nine titles to be published "by command of the Lord," including the four brief treatises just mentioned as well as *Divine Love and Wisdom* and *Divine Providence.*[9] It is worth noting that once these were in print, he returned to his exegetical task and published a very concise and tightly organized commentary on the Book of Revelation, *Revelation Unveiled.*[10]

---

6. A photolithographic reproduction of the manuscript appears in Swedenborg 1870, as volume 8 of a series.

7. The treatment of divine love, for example, emphasizes from the outset the human form of love and the importance of our having a focus on service (Latin *usus*) if we are to be truly human.

8. In *Last Judgment* 45, Swedenborg spoke of witnessing the establishment of a new church in the heavens and identified it with the New Jerusalem of Revelation 21:2. In his preface to *The Lord,* the first of the four treatises mentioned here, he stated that this new church was being established, evidently on earth, "at this day."

9. The remaining three titles he had been commanded to produce met various fates. The first, *Supplements,* an addendum to his work on the Last Judgment, was in fact published in 1763. The substance of the second, the proposed book on divine omnipotence, omnipresence, omniscience, infinity, and eternity, was worked into other material, as he explained in a letter of February 1767 to his friend Gabriel Beyer (see Tafel 1877, 1:261; and endnote 14 to the translation below). This may account for much of the substantial difference between the published *Divine Love and Wisdom* and the outlines "Divine Love" and "Divine Wisdom" mentioned above—that is, Swedenborg wove in material he had not originally thought to include in these volumes. As for the third, *Angelic Wisdom Concerning Life,* there is no ready explanation for its absence. It may be noted, however, that the "angelic wisdom about life" he had been enjoined to write may be represented by the extended treatment of service (*usus,* see note 7 above) in *Divine Love and Wisdom* 296–348.

10. The careful and consistent structuring of this work is in sharp contrast to the discursive nature of *Revelation Explained* (= Swedenborg 1997).

Form and Content

The original title page of *Divine Love and Wisdom* is graced with a large ornament bearing a Latin motto, CURA ET LABORE, "with care and work." In its position above a cherub watering potted plants in a country garden, the motto seems to suggest that careful attention and hard work are required to make things grow; it calls to mind such themes in the *Georgics,* the didactic poem about farming by the Roman poet Vergil (70–19 B.C.E.).[11] The same ornament appears on the title pages of seven other works published by Swedenborg between 1763 and 1766: *The Lord, Sacred Scripture, Life, Faith, Supplements, Divine Providence,* and *Revelation Unveiled.*[12]

The five parts of *Divine Love and Wisdom* are very clearly demarcated in the first edition. In each case, the first page is headed by a full-width ornament, and the words "Angelic Wisdom about Divine Love," in large type, precede the denotation of the part. This means that the parts are not given individual titles. However, we may refer to §284, or better still, to *Divine Providence* 155 for an indication of their intent. There part 1 is said to be "about the Lord's divine love and wisdom," part 2 "about the sun of the spiritual world and the sun of the physical world," part 3 "about levels" (see also *Divine Providence* 32:1), part 4 "about the creation of the universe" (see also *Divine Providence* 56:1), and part 5 "about our own creation" (see also *Divine Providence* 8). The running heads in the present edition have been adapted from this brief topical summary.

Over the course of the publications of 1763, we can see a new development in the way Swedenborg presents his theology: he begins to use a style and structure of exposition that he had previously reserved for his scientific works alone. In §§8, 23, 29, 37, 45, and 46 of *The Lord,* Swedenborg subdivides the chosen topic into a sequence of propositions, listing them in a group. In subsequent sections, he restates each proposition individually and gives a full explanation.[13] In §§29, 45, and 46, he im-

---

11. Among the many instances of these themes are *Georgics* 1:145, "Labor conquers all," and 4:118–119, "I would sing about the care of cultivation that adorns the rich gardens."

12. On the ornaments in Swedenborg's theological first editions in general and for evidence that Swedenborg may have engraved this specific ornament himself, see Rose 1998.

13. Quite often the wording of the initial statement of the proposition differs somewhat from that of its later restatement. These minor variations have not been flagged in the endnotes to the translation here, as doing so would have added considerably to the bulk of the annotations without adding much value for the reader.

proves on this organization further by numbering the propositions.[14] The same device of listing propositions is used in §§4, 42, and 50 in *Sacred Scripture,* in §23 of *Life,* and in §62 of *Faith.* It is not found in *Divine Love and Wisdom* until §250, but thereafter it becomes more and more frequent. It is used throughout *Divine Providence* and becomes the dominant style in *Marriage Love* (1768) and *True Christianity* (1771).[15]

In the present edition, the general topics into which each of the five parts is divided are presented in italics that begin a new, unindented line after a space.[16] Where a general topic is divided into propositions, these are again set off on a new line in italics, but in this case the first line is indented and the propositions are given arabic numerals.[17] Occasionally (see §§257, 310, 365) the text is subdivided still further. These subdivisions are indicated by lowercase letters in parentheses.[18]

As to content, *Divine Love and Wisdom* and its companion work, *Divine Providence,* explore the counterintuitive claim that life is not inherent in us, that we are essentially "life-receivers." It is my own conviction that what distracted Swedenborg from his exegetical task as he approached the end of *Revelation Explained* was a growing awareness of the radical implications of this claim and the need to deal with it openly and at length.

This conviction of mine is in no way inconsistent with the statement in the preface of *The Lord* that these two works were to be written "by

---

14. To be precise, in §45 he numbers the propositions only when he restates the propositions and develops them more fully.

15. The antecedents of this style of exposition can be seen in the *Elements,* the classic work on geometry by Euclid (flourished around 300 B.C.E.), in which propositions are stated and proved one after another. Enlightenment thinkers were deeply impressed by this method, to this day called the "geometrical style," and when they insisted that humankind must proceed in its acquisition of knowledge through the use of "geometry," they generally meant that theories should be supported by reasoning in the geometrical style. Thus the French philosopher René Descartes (1596–1650) wrote a short essay titled "Arguments Demonstrating the Existence of God and the Distinction between Soul and Body, Drawn up in Geometrical Fashion" (Descartes [1641] 1952, 130–133). It contains no circles, squares, or lines, but definitions, postulates, axioms, and propositions instead, the propositions being followed by proofs. The Dutch philosopher Benedict de Spinoza (1632–1677) likewise describes his *Ethics* as a treatment of the topic "by geometrical method" (Spinoza [1677] 1952, 395).

16. For an example, see the opening of the general topic covered in §§4–6.

17. For an example, see the numbered points that are taken up in §§251–255, which were first presented as a list in §250.

18. The first edition uses roman numerals for propositions and arabic numerals for subdivisions.

command of the Lord." The fact that he published only seven of the nine titles there listed suggests that the "command" was in some way interactive with his own judgment (see his letter of February 1767 to Gabriel Beyer in Tafel 1877, 1:261); and we may suspect that the growing importance of the topic in Swedenborg's consciousness was experienced as a dimension of that command.[19]

Of the works published in 1763, *Divine Love and Wisdom* stands out in one significant respect. Each of the so-called four doctrines—*The Lord, Sacred Scripture, Life,* and *Faith*—is copiously supplied with supporting references to Scripture. *The Lord* in particular may best be regarded as an effort to show that the teachings on this topic are solidly based in the literal meaning of the Bible. In contrast, references to Scripture in *Divine Love and Wisdom* are few and far between, and those that do occur often serve more to explain the meaning of the biblical passages cited than to support the theological point under discussion. In the main, the "authorities" appealed to are human experience and human reason, suggesting an address more to the scientific temper of the Enlightenment than to the orthodox concerns of the church. The reader may compare part 1 of *Divine Love and Wisdom* with chapter 1 of *True Christianity,* where the argument for many of the same points is based on an abundance of biblical references, persuasive to the theologian but not to the scientist.

The contrast between the two treatments may well be illustrated by the experience of the British poet William Blake (1757–1827). He read *Divine Love and Wisdom* with evident interest; a copy with his annotations is in the library of the British Museum. He is also known to have attended a meeting held in London in 1789 to consider the establishment of an ecclesiastical body based on Swedenborg's teachings; he and his wife Catherine Sophia Boucher Blake (1762?–1831) signed the register. Yet apparently Blake experienced the meeting as nothing but the establishment of new fetters of orthodoxy to replace the old. Its primary business consisted of reviewing forty-two theological propositions in support of the establishment of a separate church, and it is significant to an understanding of Blake's response that the propositions were drawn

---

19. See especially *Secrets of Heaven* 5121, where "perception" is identified as a contemporary form of revelation in which the Lord leads recipients to think in accord with the way things actually are. This seems to the recipients of the revelation to be nothing more than the functioning of their own minds.

overwhelmingly from *True Christianity,* with no reference whatever to *Divine Love and Wisdom.*[20]

In *Divine Love and Wisdom,* the reader encounters Swedenborgian theology in its most universalistic form. The work offers a picture of a God who is utterly loving, a God who is equally present with and in everyone on earth and who condemns no one. *Divine Providence* will go on to reconcile this idealistic picture with the actualities of a divided and warring world, making it possible for Swedenborg as an ardent Christian to say that heaven "cannot be made up of the people of one religion only. It needs people from many religions; so all the people who make these two universal principles of the church central to their own lives have a place in that heavenly person, that is, in heaven."[21]

This universalistic focus may be the reason for a significant change in terminology. In *Divine Love and Wisdom,* Swedenborg's use of *Dominus,* "the Lord" in reference to Deity is far more sparing than it is in the rest of his theological works. Especially in part 1, the neuter adjective *Divinum,* here generally translated "Divinity," comes into prominence, and for the first time we find *Deus Homo,* literally, "God-Person." The phrase may be regarded as another form of the far more frequent substantival phrase *Divinum Humanum,* "Divine-Human One," preserving the reference to God incarnate without the use of traditional Christian terminology. It is intriguing in this regard that the one excursus into explicitly Christian theology does not occur until §221, the middle of the book.

The physicist and philosopher David Bohm (1917–1992) writes of "a kind of thought that treats things as inherently divided, disconnected, and 'broken up.'" He argues that this inevitably leads to individuals and groups defending their own needs against the needs of others. He proposes that instead we "include everything coherently and harmoniously in an overall whole that is undivided, unbroken, and without a border" (Bohm 1980, xi). *Divine Love and Wisdom* and *Divine Providence* propose a similar reversal of conventional modes of thinking. Rather than looking at the immense and often conflicting variety of things and trying to see how they fit together, we are to start with the underlying oneness of the

---

20. An account of this meeting was published in Hindmarsh 1861, 79–84, 97, and 101–108. This material was reprinted in Bellin and Ruhl 1985, 121–131.

21. *Divine Providence* 326:10. The "two universal principles" are belief in God and a life of obedience to God's commandments.

God who is their source, and see how and why this multiplicity comes into being. This shift of perspective is by no means easy to make, but the locus of these works in the total theological corpus suggests that it may be pivotal to understanding the theological system as a whole. If we could see everything *sub specie aeternitatis,* "in the light of eternity," it would all look very different.

Editions and Translations of *Divine Love and Wisdom*

The present translation is based on the first edition of the work. I am deeply indebted to Je Hyung Bae of the Bayside Korean Church for sponsoring the scanning of the first editions, to Junchol Lee for the painstaking labor of scanning them in admirably high resolution, and to Philip Kyung Bae for providing compact disks that yielded eminently readable printouts. It has been an invaluable help to have before me hard copies that I could take wherever I wished and annotate to my heart's content.

A second Latin edition was published by the indefatigable Johann Friedrich Immanuel Tafel in Stuttgart in 1843, and a third, edited by Samuel H. Worcester, in New York by the Swedenborg Printing and Publishing Society in 1890. In the same year, the latter text was published together with the English translation of John C. Ager as one of a series of Latin-English volumes. In 1999 a fourth Latin edition was issued in Bryn Athyn, Pennsylvania, under the editorship of N. Bruce Rogers.

In surveying the history of translation of the work, it should first be noted that in both Britain and the United States, reprints were made on demand with considerable frequency. The first English translation, that of Nathaniel Tucker, was published in London in 1788 and was subsequently reprinted in both Britain and America. A revision by Tilly B. Hayward appeared in 1835, and one by James John Garth Wilkinson in London in 1843. An independent translation by George Harrison, studiously avoiding the use of Latinate terminology, was published in London in 1860, and a translation by R. Norman Foster was issued by J. B. Lippincott in Philadelphia in 1868. A further revision of the Tucker translation, by William Bruce, was published in London in 1873 and in New York in 1875.

In the next decade, a fresh translation by Wilkinson and Rudolph L. Tafel was issued in London in 1883, followed in 1885 by the version of John C. Ager, which has for over a century been the standard in this country. In 1913, a translation by Frank Bayley was published in the Everyman's Library Series, and a British pocket edition, the work of H. Goyder Smith, appeared in 1937. The version of Clifford Harley and Doris H. Harley was published in London in 1969, and my own translation in New York in 1986. The present version, it should be noted, is in no way a revision of the 1986 effort. While I regard myself as responsible for it, I do not regard myself as responsible to it, but only to the Latin text itself. Most recently, the work was translated by N. Bruce Rogers and published in Bryn Athyn, Pennsylvania, in 1999.[22]

The work has also been translated into Danish, Dutch, French, German, Hindi, Icelandic, Italian, Japanese, Korean, Portuguese, Swedish, Tamil, and Russian.

Issues in Translating *Divine Love and Wisdom*

The work presents few difficulties to the Latin reader. The language is extraordinarily straightforward, and as anyone knows who has tried to write about profound matters, such simplicity is not easily come by. It is in fact this simplicity that presents the translator with the greatest difficulty, since it would be absurdly simple to translate it quite literally into awkward and difficult English. It is my hope that this translation will convey some of the accessibility that we may be sure Swedenborg labored so diligently to offer.

Recognizing the fact that the vocabularies of different languages do not exactly coincide, I have sacrificed word-for-word consistency in favor of sensitivity to context. Swedenborg rarely offers definitions of his terms and does not always seem to feel bound by such definitions as he does provide. In any case, it is surely of less moment to gain control of a particular vocabulary than to encounter the meaning that vocabulary is intended to convey. The profound coherence and consistency of thought in the many volumes of Swedenborg's theological works may in fact be more obscured than illuminated by efforts at consistency in terminology. It is perhaps a peculiar weakness of translators to try to make every sentence self-explanatory and to achieve in a few words what can result only from the cumulative effect of more extensive reading.

---

22. Information on editions previous to 1913 has been drawn from Hyde 1906. I am indebted to William Ross Woofenden for much of the information concerning subsequent editions.

Acknowledgments

My gratitude is due to David Eller for his initiative in creating the New Century Edition and his ongoing support and guidance.[23] Working with fellow translators Lisa Hyatt Cooper, Jonathan Rose, and Stuart Shotwell has been constantly enlightening and refreshing; and I owe an immense debt of gratitude to Jonathan and Stuart in particular for their patience in seeing to all the myriad details of publication. My primary consultants, Wendy Closterman and Kristin King, have given the first draft exemplary attention, and their contributions are invisibly present on virtually every page. I am grateful as well to Carolyn Andrews and Claudia Paes York for the painstaking labor of verifying references. The entire project would be impossible without the support of a number of interested foundations, including the Swedenborg Foundation. I share with my colleagues the hope that the results will justify their extraordinary generosity.

I also share with my fellow translators the realization that we are learning a great deal as we proceed and that there is a great deal more still to learn. Releasing this for publication feels like choosing a single frame from a movie; the translation is offered not as "the definitive version," but as the best that we can offer at this point in the process.

GEORGE F. DOLE
Bath, Maine
September, 2002

---

23. The need for an annotated edition of Swedenborg's theological works was noted by the Swedenborgian scholar John Faulkner Potts (1838–1923) as early as 1902 (Potts 1902, 859), and the hope kept alive in our own times particularly by William Ross Woofenden.

Works Cited
in the Translator's Preface

Acton, Alfred. 1927. *Introduction to the Word Explained.* Bryn Athyn, Pa.: Academy of the New Church.

Bellin, Harvey F. and Darrell Ruhl, eds. 1985. *Blake and Swedenborg: Opposition Is True Friendship.* New York: Swedenborg Foundation.

Benz, Ernst. 2002. *Emanuel Swedenborg: Visionary Savant in the Age of Reason.* Translated by Nicholas Goodrick-Clarke. West Chester, Pa.: Swedenborg Foundation.

Bohm, David. 1980. *Wholeness and the Implicate Order.* London: Routledge.

Descartes, René. [1641] 1952. *Objections against the Meditations and Replies.* Translated by Elizabeth S. Haldane and G.R.T. Ross. In vol. 31 of *Great Books of the Western World.* Chicago: Encyclopedia Britannica.

Dole, George F. 1988. "A Rationale for Swedenborg's Writing Sequence." In *Emanuel Swedenborg: A Continuing Vision.* Edited by Robin Larsen. New York: Swedenborg Foundation.

———. 2000. Preface to *Heaven and Its Wonders and Hell,* translated by George F. Dole. West Chester, Pa.: Swedenborg Foundation.

Hindmarsh, Robert. 1861. *The Rise and Progress of the New Jerusalem Church in England, America, and Other Parts.* London: Hodson & Son.

Hjern, Olle. 1989. *Carl Robsahm: Anteckningar om Swedenborg.* Stockholm: ABA Cad/Copy & Tryck.

Hyde, James. 1906. *A Bibliography of the Works of Emanuel Swedenborg, Original and Translated.* London: Swedenborg Society.

Potts, John Faulkner. 1902. *The Swedenborg Concordance.* Vol. 6. London: Swedenborg Society.

Rose, Jonathan S. 1998. "The Ornaments in Swedenborg's Theological First Editions." *Covenant: A Journal Devoted to the Study of the Five Churches* 1.4:293–362.

Sigstedt, Cyriel Odhner. 1981. *The Swedenborg Epic: The Life and Works of Emanuel Swedenborg.* New York: Bookman Associates, 1952. Reprint, London: Swedenborg Society.

Spinoza, Benedict de. [1677] 1952. *Ethics.* Translated by W. H. White, revised by A. H. Stirling. In vol. 31 of *Great Books of the Western World.* Chicago: Encyclopedia Britannica.

Swedenborg, Emanuel. 1870. *Emanuelis Swedenborgii, Servi Domini Jesu Christi, Miscellanea Theologica.* Edited by Rudolph L. Tafel. Vol. 8. Stockholm: Societas Photo-Lithographica.

————. 1997. *Apocalypse Explained.* 6 vols. Translated by John C. Ager, revised by John Whitehead, edited by William Ross Woofenden. West Chester, Pa.: Swedenborg Foundation.

Tafel, Rudolph L. 1877. *Documents Concerning the Life and Character of Emanuel Swedenborg.* Vol. 2, parts 1–2. London: Swedenborg Society.

Selected List of Editions
of *Divine Love and Wisdom*

1. Latin Editions

Swedenborg, Emanuel. 1763. *Sapientia Angelica de Divino Amore et de Divina Sapientia.* Amsterdam.

———. [1763] 1843. *Sapientia Angelica de Divino Amore et de Divina Sapientia.* Edited by Johann Friedrich Immanuel Tafel. Stuttgart: Ebner and Seubert.

———. [1763] 1890. *Sapientia Angelica de Divino Amore et de Divina Sapientia.* Edited by Samuel H. Worcester. New York: Swedenborg Printing and Publishing Society.

———. [1763] 1999. *Sapientia Angelica de Divino Amore et de Divina Sapientia.* Edited by N. Bruce Rogers. Bryn Athyn, Pa.: Academy of the New Church.

2. English Translations

Swedenborg, Emanuel. [1763] 1788. *The Wisdom of Angels Concerning Divine Love and Divine Wisdom.* [Translated by Nathaniel Tucker.] London: W. Chalklen.

———. [1763] 1860. *Angelic Wisdom Concerning Divine Love and Concerning Divine Wisdom.* [Translated by George Harrison.] London: Longman, Green, Longman, and Roberts.

———. [1763] 1868. *Angelic Philosophy of the Divine Love and Wisdom.* Translated by R. Norman Foster. Philadelphia: J. B. Lippincott.

———. [1763] 1883. *Angelic Wisdom Concerning the Divine Love and Concerning the Divine Wisdom.* Translated by J. J. Garth Wilkinson and Rudolph L. Tafel. London: Swedenborg Society.

———. [1763] 1885. *Angelic Wisdom Concerning the Divine Love and the Divine Wisdom.* [Translated by John C. Ager.] New York: American Swedenborg Printing and Publishing Society.

———. [1763] 1937. *Angelic Wisdom Concerning the Divine Love and the Divine Wisdom.* Translated by H. Goyder Smith. London: Swedenborg Society.

———. [1763] 1969. *Angelic Wisdom Concerning the Divine Love and Wisdom.* Translated by Clifford Harley and Doris H. Harley. London: Swedenborg Society.

———. [1763] 1986. *Angelic Wisdom Concerning Divine Love and Wisdom.* Translated by George F. Dole. New York: Swedenborg Foundation.

———. [1763] 1999. *Angelic Wisdom Regarding Divine Love and Divine Wisdom.* Translated by N. Bruce Rogers. Bryn Athyn, Pa.: General Church of the New Jerusalem.

On *Divine Love and Wisdom*

Swedenborg's Metaphysics of Creation

GREGORY R. JOHNSON

Outline

IN *Divine Love and Wisdom* Swedenborg explains the nature of God, creation, and humankind in terms of divine love and wisdom, which are two fundamental aspects of God's nature and two fundamental cosmic forces. This makes *Divine Love and Wisdom* the most abstract and philosophical of Swedenborg's mature theological writings. Yet the central ideas of *Divine Love and Wisdom* are quite clear, simple, and illuminating in themselves. The aim of this introduction is to explain some of the book's philosophical abstractions and ease the reader's approach to the text.

    Divine Love and Wisdom falls into five parts. Part 1 deals with three main topics: the nature of love and wisdom, the nature of God, and the nature of space and time. Part 2 treats three topics as well: the correspondences between the spiritual world and the material world, along with the respective suns that illuminate each; how the universe and everything in it was created by God by means of these two suns; and the ultimate aim of creation. Part 3 begins with a discussion of the different types of levels of reality and how they are related to one another. It then discusses the place of humankind in the cosmos in relation to these levels and offers an account of the origin of evil. Part 4 deals first with God's creation of the universe. Swedenborg then discusses his concept of "uses," or useful functions, and ends again with an account of evil. Part 5 discusses human nature, specifically the human faculties of volition and discernment, which are vessels for receiving divine love and divine wisdom respectively. In this part of the book, Swedenborg devotes a good deal of space to the correspondence of volition to the heart and discernment to the lungs. Part 5 also extensively discusses the relationship of love and wisdom. The following introduction only roughly follows Swedenborg's outline and puts the greatest emphasis on the foundational concepts in parts 1 through 3.

I. What Are Divine Love and Divine Wisdom?

What does Swedenborg mean by "love" and "wisdom" and how are they related? It is helpful to think of love and wisdom as functions or powers of the soul, both human and divine, that are correlated with certain faculties. Swedenborg uses "love" to refer to the vital, valuing, and active powers of the soul. Vitality is the principle of life. Values are the principles of action, the purposes for which we act. Swedenborg calls the faculty through which these powers are exercised "volition," the power of choosing or making a decision. He uses "wisdom" to refer to the cognitive powers of the soul and to technical or instrumental reason. He calls the faculty through which these powers are exercised "discernment." The cognitive faculties determine the nature of what is, whereas our valuing faculty deals with what ought to be. Technical-instrumental reason is the ability to determine the proper means to achieve one's ends, whereas our valuing faculty sets our ends and insures that means are used rightly.

Throughout *Divine Love and Wisdom* and his other writings, Swedenborg stresses the primacy of love over wisdom, that is, the primacy of the vital, valuing, active functions of the soul over its cognitive and technical-instrumental functions. Love should rule over wisdom, rather than wisdom over love. Knowledge and technical skills should serve life, values, and action. Swedenborg recognizes that, on its own, love is blind. Its access to reality is through the faculty of discernment. But although love depends upon discernment for its access to reality, love still sets the ultimate aims of thought and action, and wisdom is the means by which love brings its aims about.

This is in marked contrast to much of ancient and medieval philosophy, which stresses the primacy of the theoretical life over the practical life, holding that action is merely a means to cognition, specifically to contemplation. But Swedenborg's view is wholly in accord with the central thrust of modern philosophy, which stresses the subordination of the theoretical life to the practical life, contemplation to action. This is true of other modern religious thinkers such as Blaise Pascal (1623–1662), Gottfried Wilhelm Leibniz (1646–1716), Jean-Jacques Rousseau (1712–1778), Immanuel Kant (1724–1804), Ralph Waldo Emerson (1803–1882), and William James (1842–1910). It is also true of secular thinkers such as Francis Bacon (1561–1626), René Descartes (1596–1650), Thomas Hobbes (1588–1679), and Benedict de Spinoza (1632–1677), though their ultimate aims are not spiritual but secular: the mastery of nature and the liberation of humankind.

Divine Love and Wisdom begins by discussing the ordinary uses of the word "love" to refer to things that we value. When Swedenborg speaks of love, he often means values. When he speaks of an individual's "ruling love" he refers to the core values that in large part constitute the individual's character. But there is a deeper sense of "love": Love is "our very life" (§1).[1] Love is the vital force that pervades the soul and the body, both in general and in every particular. Those who define life in terms of action or in terms of cognitive powers like thought and sensation fail to see that these are not life itself, but merely effects of life. Life gives rise to thought, and thought in turn gives rise to sensation and action. The deepest level of thought is the perception of "ends" or purposes of action. This is a clear indication of the ultimate subordination of the cognitive to the active powers. This all-important power of love is why Swedenborg claims that there is a correspondence between the vivifying power of

---

1. As is common in Swedenborgian studies, text citations to Swedenborg's works refer not to page numbers, but to Swedenborg's section numbers, which are uniform in all editions. In this introduction, section numbers where no work is specified should be understood to refer to *Divine Love and Wisdom*. Thus "§1" here means section 1 of *Divine Love and Wisdom*.

love in the soul and the vivifying power of the sun's warmth in the material world.[2]

According to Swedenborg, God is love itself and life itself. This means that God is the source of his own love and life. All other creatures, by contrast, receive their life and love from outside themselves, ultimately from God. This is a truth that angels appreciate but humans do not. Angels actually *see* how love and wisdom flow into them from God. In heaven, there is a correspondence between divine love and the heavenly (spiritual) sun, specifically between divine love and the *warmth* of this sun, and between divine wisdom and the *light* of this sun. Human beings receive divine love and wisdom from the same spiritual source. Both angels and humans receive divine love and wisdom only to the extent that they are receptive to them. One's soul becomes receptive to the extent that it opens itself through love for God and love for one's neighbor. Swedenborg remarks that the sun of the spiritual world does not create human beings directly; instead it creates them out of material substances and forms them to be capable of receiving the influence of divine love and wisdom. The conceiving of a body is not the conceiving of a living thing, but the conceiving of a material vessel into which life can flow.

II. The Nature of God

Swedenborg's concept of God lies very much within the Christian tradition. God is the creator of the world; yet he himself is uncreated. From God all created beings borrow their being—their sustained, active existence.[3] God, however, does not borrow his existence from outside himself, but contains it within himself.

Swedenborg argues that God is one, because the universe is one, and the universe could not be one if it did not have a single creator and sus-

---

2. Swedenborg says that the spiritual world contains a parallel for each thing in the material world (and more besides). Each thing in the material world can thus be said to "correspond" or "be responsive" to some specific thing in the spiritual world, and vice versa. Thus as noted here, the warmth of the material sun, a material thing, corresponds to love, a spiritual thing. This theory or teaching about the relationship between what is material and what is spiritual is traditionally known as the *doctrine of correspondence;* it is discussed at length in Swedenborg's 1758 work *Heaven and Hell* 87–102.

3. This concept of existence is called *Esse* in Latin, literally the "to be"; in the present translation it has been rendered "reality."

tainer (§§23–27). If there were more than one God, then the universe would be a house divided, and manifestly it is not. Yet the universe does contain an infinity of different kinds of things, and these things are God's creation. Thus Swedenborg also emphasizes that an infinity of things are distinguishable within God in thought. God does not contain the *actual* universe, for that would be pantheism and would make God spatial, both of which positions Swedenborg rejects. But God contains the potential for each thing. God contains an infinity of ideas or archetypes of created beings. This infinity of ideas or archetypes is, "so to speak *reflected* in heaven, in angels, and in us" (§21, emphasis added; see also §155). This account of the unity and the multiplicity of God is very much in the spirit of Plato (427–347 B.C.E.) and Plotinus (204–270 C.E.). The oneness of the world is explained by the influence of a primal unity, and the multiplicity of kinds in the world is explained by the influence of a plurality of archetypes.[4]

According to Swedenborg, God is a "human" or "person" (Latin *homo*). This follows quite logically from a literal interpretation of the claim in Genesis that God made human beings in his own image, which implies that we may understand God in our own image. The human microcosm is the key to the divine macrocosm. Not only is God a person, he is the essential or archetypical person, and we are but imitations of him.

Heaven too is an imitation of God. It appears as a person (§288). This is Swedenborg's doctrine of the *Maximus Homo,* or "Universal Human," which holds that heaven appears as a vast human, whose limbs, organs, and tissues are made up of different angelic communities, each angelic cell of which is also a person. Swedenborg's Universal Human is similar to the Kabbalistic doctrine of Adam Kadmon, the heavenly exemplar of the created Adam. According to the Kabbalists, this heavenly *arcanum* or secret is hidden in the very name of God, the Hebrew Tetragrammaton, which, when turned on its side, looks like a stick figure of a human being. Now, Adam Kadmon is not God himself, but he is God's first creation, who remains with God in heaven while God remains hidden above and beyond him. Thus the Kabbalists claim that there is a giant human in heaven, while Swedenborg claims that heaven simply *is* a giant human.

---

4. On the unity of creation in Plato, see *Timaeus* 31a–b. On the necessity of positing the One, see Plotinus *Enneads* 5:4.

Swedenborg asserts that it is impossible for angels to conceive of God in any other way. There is an "idea" of the divine person built right into our cognitive faculties, so we are incapable of apprehending God in any other fashion. In Swedenborg's words, "thinking proceeds in keeping with heaven's form [that is, in keeping with the Universal Human], so it is not possible for angels to think about God in any other way" (§11).

In §§14–16, Swedenborg explains the personhood of God in terms of the distinction between reality and manifestation. The personhood of God is his manifestation, which is distinguishable in thought, but not in fact, from his reality: "Wherever there is reality, there is its manifestation: the one does not occur without the other. In fact, reality *exists* through its manifestation, and not apart from it" (§14). There is no reality without manifestation, and no manifestation without reality. The two terms imply one another. Thus reality and manifestation can be distinguished in thought, but not in fact. Hence they are "distinguishably one." Swedenborg also claims that love corresponds to reality and wisdom to manifestation, and just as reality and manifestation are distinguishably one, so are love and wisdom. This is also true of the soul and the body. They can be separated in thought but not in reality (see §369). This implies that spiritual beings are not incorporeal, but have a suitably spiritual form of embodiment: "Every soul is in a spiritual body" (§14). In fact, God's manifestation as person can be understood as his spiritual embodiment. In §16, Swedenborg makes the puzzling assertion that God is manifest as a person, "not manifest from himself, but manifest in himself." I take this to mean that God, whole and complete in himself, does not merely take on the external form of a person. Instead, God becomes himself fully by taking on the form of a person. God is fully real by being manifest as a person.

III. Space and Time

God is omnipresent, yet God is one and undivided. These two statements seem hard to reconcile, for if something is everywhere, then it would seem to be divided up and scattered to the farthest reaches of space. But this is inconsistent with being one. In agreement with Plato and Plotinus, Swedenborg claims that this is a pseudo-problem generated by thinking of the divine unity as being in space. Like Plato and Plotinus, Swedenborg claims that the divine unity lies outside of space. Its presence is not spatial; therefore it can be omnipresent without losing its integral nature.[5]

Swedenborg claims that God and the spiritual world lie outside of time as well as space. This too is consistent with Platonism and Neoplatonism. Only material beings in the physical world are differentiated from one another by spans of space and time. In the spiritual world, entities are differentiated in terms of "states" of moral and spiritual development and perfection measured ultimately by their proximity to or remoteness from God.[6] The spatial and temporal order of the material world must be judged inadequate from a moral point of view. In the material world, people who are morally very different are forced to live at the same time and in the same place, while people who are morally similar are widely separated by space and time. In the spiritual world, this inadequacy does not exist. The spiritual world is ordered in terms of moral and spiritual, rather than spatial and temporal, differences. Those who are morally and spiritually similar live together in spiritual communities, and all spiritual communities are ordered in terms of their moral and spiritual proximity to or distance from the Divine.

Swedenborg holds that space and time are real features of the material world. They are as real as the material world itself: "Nature has two basic properties: space and time" (§69). Furthermore, as inhabitants of the material world, we perceive it in terms of the "ideas" of space and time. These ideas are intrinsic features of our cognitive faculties: "In this physical world, we use them [space and time] to form the concepts of our thinking and . . . the way we understand things" (§69). Because of this, when we pass into the spirit world, we take the ideas of space and time with us. Thus when one passes from one's worldly existence into the spiritual world, where space and time are unreal, one still sees a world of spatiotemporally differentiated objects. Spiritual things, although they exist outside of space and time, still appear *as if* they are in space and time, because the only way they can be given to a human knower is in the form of spatiotemporally differentiated objects. The spiritual world appears as spatiotemporal in order to accommodate itself to the spatiotemporal

---

5. See Plato *Parmenides* 130e–131e; Plotinus *Enneads* 6:4–5.

6. In English usage the word *perfect* frequently denotes absolute excellence in every quality, and a reference to something as "more perfect" is seen as a misuse of the term. In Swedenborg's terminology, however, "perfection" as applied to humans or angels denotes their relative approach to the absolute perfection of God.

ideas of finite, created intellects. It is only by means of such an accommodation that it can be given at all. However, once newly arrived spirits become acclimated to their new surroundings, they learn the intelligible correspondences that exist between spatiotemporal appearances and the moral and spiritual states in terms of which spiritual beings are actually differentiated. Once spirits learn these correspondences, they can read true inner moral and spiritual states off of false external spatiotemporal appearances.

Swedenborg departs from Platonism and Neoplatonism with this notion that we perceive both the material and the spiritual world in terms of "ideas" of space and time, which, because they are intrinsic to our cognitive faculties, cause the spiritual world to appear as spatial and temporal even though it is not. I have argued at length elsewhere that this conception of space and time is quite similar to Immanuel Kant's, and that Swedenborg's conception was a decisive influence on Kant's (Johnson 2001, 167–173). I have argued, furthermore, that there is some reason to think that Kant read *Divine Love and Wisdom,* although he could just as easily have encountered Swedenborg's ideas of space and time in *Secrets of Heaven,* which we know he read (Johnson 2001, 37–41). Swedenborg's account of space and time differs from Kant's insofar as Swedenborg claims that space and time are *both* real features of the material world *and* ideas intrinsic to the human subject. Kant claims that if space and time are ideas intrinsic to the human subject, then the world will appear as spatial and temporal whether it is or not. We cannot determine if the world really is as it appears, he claims, and this possibility does not make any practical difference, since the world would appear just the same either way.

Swedenborg's doctrine of space and time is crucial for understanding the senses in which God is eternal and infinite. There are two senses of eternity. The first sense is the endlessness of time extending to infinity backwards into the past and forwards into the future. The second sense is that which lies outside of time entirely. Eternity in the latter sense is not boundless time, but what lies beyond all time.[7] Swedenborg calls this "a spiritual or angelic concept of eternity, one that does not involve time" (§76). There are also two analogous senses of spatial infinity: the boundlessness of space going off in all directions to eternity, and that which lies outside of space entirely. Swedenborg denies that space and time are

---

7. On differing conceptions of eternity, see Sherover 2003, especially chapter 1, "The Concept of Time in Western Thought."

boundless (§156). Therefore, God's eternity and infinity cannot be understood in terms of boundless space and time.

Swedenborg does not deny that God is somehow present in space and time. God, after all, is omnipresent. But the proper sense of divine eternity and infinity is that which lies outside space and time altogether. In Swedenborg's words, "We must say that it [creation] happened from eternity and from infinity, and not from an eternity of time, since there is no such thing, but from a nontemporal eternity that is the same as Divinity, and not from an infinity of space, since there is no such thing, but from a nonspatial infinity that is also the same as Divinity" (§156).

It should be noted that Swedenborg's claim that God is infinite insofar as he is entirely outside of space does not exhaust his conception of divine infinity. In particular, Swedenborg accepts the traditional theological conception of divine infinity as God's possession of all positive attributes to the highest degree. He readily affirms God's omniscience, omnipotence, omnibenevolence, and omnipresence (see §§9 and 130).

IV. The Nature of Creation

Swedenborg conceives of God as containing within himself an infinity of archetypes that are distinguishable in thought yet one in being. Like Plato and Plotinus, he speaks of the created world as the "reflection" (§64) and the "image" of these archetypes: "The universe, from beginning to end and from first to last, is so full of divine love and wisdom that you could call it divine love and wisdom in an image" (§52). These created images of the divine are not themselves divine, but share in the divinity of God. The simultaneous identity and difference of God and creation is expressed with the metaphor of the mirror: "What is created . . . is an analog; and because of the union, it is like an image of God in a mirror" (§56) and "While the created universe is not God, it is from God; and since it is from God, his image is in it like the image of a person in a mirror" (§59). Swedenborg speaks of creatures as "vessels" into which divine love and wisdom flow. The divine nature, although shared among an infinity of different creatures, "is not different in one subject than it is in another" (§54). The divine nature is present in all things, even in opposites like light and dark, but it remains one.

In keeping with his teachings on the nature of space and time, Swedenborg cautions against thinking of creation as beginning in a particular place and time and then expanding to other places and times: "We cannot say that the creation of the universe and everything in it happened from one place to another or from one moment in time to another, that is, gradually and sequentially" (§156). Creation did not begin a long time ago. Creation takes place outside of time altogether, and we see its effects not at one time, then another, but at all times at once. Creation did not begin in one location. Creation takes place outside of space, but we see its effects in all locations at once. Like God himself, his creative activity is outside space and time, but omnipresent in space and time.

But if we cannot ask when and where creation first takes place we can at least ask how and why creation comes about.

Every account of creation must deal with the question, "Why did God choose to create the world rather than remain alone?" There are two basic answers to this question: God creates out of *need* or out of *abundance*.[8]

If God creates out of need, this implies that God alone is not perfect and self-sufficient and that the net amount of being and goodness is increased by the creation of the world. Expressed mathematically, God plus creation is greater than God alone. In the Hermetic tradition, for instance, God creates the world because he lacks self-consciousness. Self-consciousness can only come by the recognition of oneself in another who is capable of recognizing one in turn. God, therefore, must create another being who can know him. He cannot create another God, for a god is uncreated. But he can create a mortal being who is capable of knowing him. This is the human being. Once the human comes to know God, God comes to know himself and is complete. Creation is thus a circular process in which God goes out of himself and then returns to himself by beholding himself in the mirror of his creation.[9]

If on the other hand God creates out of abundance, this implies that God alone is perfect and does not need creation to augment his being and goodness. This means that all the goodness and being of the created world is a *gift* of God, that God *shares* his superabundant being and goodness by creating beings that can receive them. The created world has no being and goodness of its own. Therefore, in terms of being and

---

8. My formulation of the difference between creation out of need and creation out of abundance owes much to Sokolowski 1995, 1–10.

9. Copenhaver 1992, 20, 30, 56. For a most lucid exposition of this dimension of Hermeticism, see Magee 2001, 8–14.

goodness, God plus creation is not greater than God alone. There are different models for understanding creation out of abundance. Plotinus, for example, resists ascribing any human traits to his concept of the One from which all beings emanate. The One gives rise to the world simply as an expression of its infinite creative power (Plotinus *Enneads* 6:8). Christianity, by contrast, understands the creation of the world as an act of love, and not a selfish love that seeks something in return, but an unselfish love, a love that arises not out of neediness but out of the fullness of the soul (Sokolowski 1995, 31–40).

Swedenborg's account of creation is complex because it contains elements of both creation from need and creation from abundance. On the one hand, it is apparent throughout *Divine Love and Wisdom,* from the title on, that Swedenborg casts his account of creation in the Christian language of love. Yet his account of the workings of divine love quickly becomes expressed in the language of need. In §§47–49, under the proposition "Divine love and wisdom cannot fail to be and to be manifested in others that it has created," Swedenborg argues that "the hallmark of love is not loving ourselves but loving others and being united to them through love." Self-love is a matter of "feeling our joy in others . . . and not theirs in ourselves." Swedenborg argues that by contrast unselfish love involves mutuality, that is, feeling our joy in others and feeling the joy of others in ourselves. "What is loving ourselves alone, really, and not loving someone else who loves us in return? This is more fragmentation than union. Love's union depends on mutuality, and there is no mutuality within ourselves alone" (§48). Because God loves, and love requires mutuality, God must create an "other" to love. This other cannot be another God, for even if it were possible for God to create another God, the love that would exist between them would be more like self-love than love for one's neighbor. Thus God requires the existence of finite beings—humans and angels—whom he can love and who can love him in return. In §170, Swedenborg claims that the ultimate goal of creation, the "eternal union of the Creator with the created universe," cannot happen "unless there are subjects in which his divinity can be at home, so to speak, subjects in which it can dwell and abide." Although Swedenborg speaks of God's need of other beings to love and be loved by in return, his position does not ultimately reduce to creation out of lack or imperfection. God loves out of abundance, not out of lack. But once he loves, the nature of love requires beings who can reciprocate.

Creation out of need seems to be implied in *Divine Love and Wisdom* 167, where Swedenborg makes a threefold distinction between "first end," "mediate end," and "final end." He also speaks of the first end merely as the "end," the mediate end as the "cause," and the final end as the "effect."[10] An end is abstract. It is a goal, a plan, a blueprint. It exists merely as an idea. An effect is an end that has been transformed into concrete reality. It is a realized idea. A cause is the mechanism by which an abstract end is transformed into a concrete effect. Swedenborg emphasizes that all three elements must be present in a thing for it to be something at all. It is easy to see that there cannot be an effect without a cause. It is also relatively easy to accept that there can be no cause without an effect. Even if the cause somehow goes astray and does not give rise to the intended effect, it gives rise to an unintended one. It is more controversial to claim that there cannot be a cause and an effect without an end that guides the process. This is what Aristotle (384–322 B.C.E.) called "final causation."[11] Most surprising, however, is the claim that there cannot be an end (purpose) without a cause (means) and an effect (result): "No purpose occurs apart from its means and result" (§167); "A purpose cannot exist in itself alone, but must exist in something that takes place because of it, something in which it can dwell with its total being, something which it can accomplish by its effort as long as it lasts. The reality in which it 'lasts' is that final end that is called its result" (§168). Every abstract possibility must become a concrete actuality. There is no such thing as an unrealized potentiality. If something can be, it will be, it *must* be, it *is*. This is the position that philosopher Arthur O. Lovejoy (1873–1962) called "the principle of plenitude" (Lovejoy 1936, 52).

This implies that God needs creation. Before the act of creation, the created world exists merely as an abstract "end," an "idea" in the divine mind. But Swedenborg tells us that an end *cannot* exist in abstraction. It is inadequate on its own. An end *must* become a concrete effect through a causal process. In this case, the causal process is creation itself. Therefore, God must create. This means that God plus creation is greater than God alone. This compulsion to create is, furthermore, inconsistent with the idea that creation is an act of a divine will that is free to create or not to create as it chooses.

---

10. In the present translation, the terms "end" (Latin *finis*), "cause" *(causa),* and "effect" *(effectus)* have for the sake of clarity generally been translated "purpose," "means," and "result" respectively.

11. Aristotle discusses the "four causes"—formal, efficient, material, and final—in his *Physics* 2:3.

V. The Source of Creation

Another question connected with creation is: "From where or what does creation come?" There are three basic answers to this question. First, God creates the world out of nothing. This is known as creation *ex nihilo,* "from nothing." This is the Mosaic interpretation of the Creation story in the book of Genesis. This implies that God was entirely alone before the Creation. Second, God creates the world out of a pre-existing material. This implies that God is not alone before the Creation. Some material exists alongside him from which he shapes the world. This is the account of creation given in Plato's *Timaeus* (28a–29d, 31b–32c), in which the divine "craftsman" *(demiurge)* shapes a pre-existing matter after the model of pre-existing forms. This is known as creation *ex possibili,* "from possibility." Third, God creates the world out of himself, out of his divine substance. This is known as creation *ex Deo,* "from God." This is the account of creation given by the sixteenth-century Kabbalist Isaac Luria (1534–1572), who claimed that God created the world by withdrawing and opening up a space within his own substance, then projecting an ordering ray of divine light within it.[12]

Swedenborg unequivocally denies creation *ex nihilo:* "Nothing comes from 'absolutely nothing,' and nothing can"; and "To speak of creating something that exists from a 'nothing' that does not exist is a plain contradiction of terms" (§55; see §283). Instead, Swedenborg affirms creation *ex Deo* in such passages as the following: "The universe, being an image of God and therefore full of God, could be created by God only *in* God. God is reality itself, and everything that exists must come from that reality"; "What is created by God *in* God . . ." (§55, emphasis added; see §56); "The Lord from eternity . . . created the universe and everything in it not from nothing but from himself" (§282); and "God did create the universe and everything in it out of himself" (§283).

Swedenborg's language of creation *"in* God" brings to mind Luria's picturesque doctrine. Swedenborg would, of course, deny that there is literally a space in God, just as he denies that God is in space. But Luria too would probably admit the metaphorical nature of his language.[13]

---

12. See Scholem 1974, 129, and Scholem 1946, 261.

13. Like Swedenborg, Luria describes created beings as "vessels." Luria speaks of vessels (כלים, *kēlîm*) of divine light, whereas Swedenborg speaks of vessels *(continentia)* of divine love and wisdom.

Swedenborg cautions against interpreting creation *ex Deo* as pantheism: "Everyone should beware not to slip into the terrible heresy that God pours himself into us and is in us and no longer in himself" (§130; see §283). Creation *from* God does not mean that creation *is* God. To identify God and creation is to make the mistake of placing God in space and time.

VI. The Goal of Creation

Swedenborg's account of creation can be depicted as a circle. God goes out of himself, creating the world out of his own substance. But God implants in creation a desire to circle back and return to himself. According to Swedenborg, the goal of creation is "that everything should return to the Creator and that there should be a union" (§167; see §§327–329); "The grand purpose, or the purpose of all elements of creation, is an eternal union of the Creator with the created universe" (§170). This circular conception of creation is present in Judaism, Christianity, and Islam, as well as in Neoplatonism and Hermeticism.

Creation, according to Swedenborg, is hierarchically ordered. He affirms the classical doctrine of the "Great Chain of Being," stretching from inanimate matter at the bottom through the plant and animal kingdoms to human beings and angels, with God at the top: "There is a ladder of all created things to that First [that is, God] who alone is life" (§66).[14] Angels and human beings are the most accurate reflections of God's nature as a person, but Swedenborg claims that all of creation is a reflection of God's nature as a person, including the animal, plant, and mineral kingdoms. Animals, plants, and even minerals resemble the divine person not in their form, but in their functions: "In every seed . . . there is an image of something infinite and eternal, an inherent effort to multiply and bear fruit without limit, to eternity" (§60). This is true of all animals as well. Furthermore, even the smallest animals have organs that perform functions analogous to those of the Divine human body: "They contain sensory organs, brains, hearts, lungs, and the like" (§60). Plants, too, have analogous functions. Minerals also display crystalline structures that are analogous to flowers. The fact that minerals seem to be inert is not a disanalogy, for Swedenborg holds that all created beings, including plants and animals,

---

14. On the Great Chain of Being, see Lovejoy 1936, 3–23 and 144–226.

are in themselves inert. God alone is intrinsically alive, and created beings are vivified through divine inflow (§§66, 68). Furthermore, Swedenborg thinks that minerals are not inert. The minerals of the soil nurture plant life and thus display a striving "toward becoming plant life and thereby performing a useful function" (§61).

Swedenborg claims that all levels of reality have interlocking functions or uses and display an upward striving. Minerals function to nourish plants. Plants function to nourish animals. There are three levels of the animal kingdom: worms and insects, birds and animals, and humans (§65). Herbivores function to nourish carnivores. And the whole system functions to nourish humankind: "In the last analysis everything has been created for our sake" (§170; see §§329–330). Minerals, plants, and animals are recipients of the natural inflowings of life, minerals receiving one kind, plants an additional kind, and animals a third kind in addition to the first two.

Human beings receive not only the inflow of the three levels of the material world, but also inflow from the spiritual world. Just as there are three ascending levels of the material world, there are three ascending levels of the spiritual world. Because human beings receive inflow from the spiritual world, we can rise above the material world. We do not have to be guided merely by natural drives; instead we can "think analytically and rationally about civil and moral issues within the material world and also about spiritual and heavenly issues that transcend the material world. We can even be lifted up into wisdom to the point that we see God" (§66).

We rise through three levels. First, we are born with the power of perception. On the basis of perception, we then gain factual information. On the basis of factual information, we then develop our ability to reason. These three cognitive levels correspond to the three kingdoms of nature. The three levels of the spiritual world become visible only when we leave our bodies. The first level is visible as soon as we enter the spiritual world. Some then ascend to the second level, and some of these go on to the third where they become heavenly angels and enjoy a vision of God (§67). When heavenly angels behold God, the circle of creation is complete.

VII. The Spiritual Sun and the Material Sun

According to Swedenborg, in the spiritual world divine love and wisdom have the appearance of a sun. This sun and its properties correspond to the sun of the material world. The warmth of this sun is "the good that thoughtfulness does" and the light of this sun is "the truth that faith perceives" (§83). The sun of the spiritual world appears to be the same size as the sun of the material world, but it is redder. Furthermore, the spiritual sun always appears in a fixed place, in the east, about forty-five degrees above the horizon, which provides for equal perceptions of love and wisdom and creates a perpetual springtime in heaven (§105). The angels of the third and highest heaven are closest to the spiritual sun and bask constantly in its glow, while the angels of the second heaven are more distant and see it less often, and the angels of the first heaven are more distant still and see it only occasionally, in proportion to the angels' openness and receptivity to divine love and wisdom (§85). Swedenborg reminds us that there are no real distances in the spiritual world, but merely the appearances of spiritual states (§§108–111). No matter which way the angels turn, the spiritual sun is always in front of them, in the east (§105). In the spiritual world, the four regions—east, west, south, and north—are based upon different levels of spiritual receptivity to divine love and wisdom (§§120–124). Because they always face the sun in the east, the north is to their left, the south is to their right, and the west is behind them (§129).

Swedenborg cautions us not to identify the sun of the spiritual world with God himself. The spiritual sun is merely the appearance of the divine love and wisdom emanating from God (§§86, 97). It is "that first emanation from [God]" (§93). Swedenborg does, however, identify the divine love and wisdom that appear as the spiritual sun with the Holy Spirit of the Trinity: "The divine love and wisdom that emanate from the Lord as the sun and constitute heaven's warmth and light is the emanating Divinity that is the Holy Spirit" (§146). It is natural that divine love and wisdom should appear as a sun, since love and wisdom correspond to fire (§§87, 93). This spiritual fire is traditionally represented as the halo around the head of God and the heads of those closest to him (§94). There are also correspondences between love and warmth and between wisdom and light (§95). Just as the warmth and light that emanate from the material sun are two aspects of the same reality, so divine love and wisdom—the warmth and light of the spiritual sun—are two aspects of the same reality (§101).

God is both the creator and the sustainer of all things. But God uses tools to perform these tasks. The material sun is both the creator and the sustainer of life and motion on earth (see §152). But the material sun, like the rest of nature, is in itself dead. Its life is infused into it from the sun of the spiritual world (§§157–158). The sun of the spiritual world is both the creator and the sustainer of the spiritual and the material worlds (§153). Its power is propagated through the different "atmospheres" of the spiritual world, just as the power of the material sun is propagated through the atmospheres of the material world (§§173–175). These atmospheres serve to hold together beings in the spiritual and material worlds, beings that would dissipate if these atmospheric pressures were removed (§176). In terms of the threefold distinction between end, cause, and effect, the sun of the spiritual world is the end or purpose of everything, the spiritual world is the cause or means by which the end is realized concretely, and the material world is the concrete effect or result.

If the material world is but a concrete effect of spiritual causes, then all "naturalistic" viewpoints that treat the material world as an ultimate explanation are profoundly mistaken.[15] Naturalism is not just a theoretical error, it is a spiritual and moral disease. Because of naturalism, "our minds are closed upward [to spiritual things] and open downward [to material things] and we become focused on nature and our senses— spiritually dead" (§162). The ultimate result of naturalism is the denial of God, the severance of our union with heaven, and a concomitant union with hell. In this condition, we do not lose our ability to think and to act. Instead, we lose the divine guidance that allows us to use those faculties wisely for good purposes, and under the guidance of our lower nature we begin to use them for evil purposes (§162).

VIII. Two Kinds of Difference

In his discussion of the spiritual and material suns, Swedenborg emphasizes that they are different from one another, yet united by correspondence, and therefore constitute a whole. In part 3, he clarifies the two senses in which things differ from one another. He stresses that understanding the two kinds of difference is necessary for understanding the nature of causality. There are differences of *kind* and differences of *degree*. In Swedenborg's language, differences of kind are "vertical levels" or "distinct levels," and differences of degree are "horizontal levels" or "gradual levels." Gradual or horizontal differences are "declines or decreases from coarser to finer or denser to rarer" and "gains and increases from finer to coarser or from rarer to denser" (§184). In the case of gradual or horizontal

---

15. In Swedenborg's day the entire material world was often referred to simply as "nature." Thus "naturalism" here means the belief in exclusively material as opposed to divine or "supernatural" causation.

differences there is a single underlying kind of stuff that varies in terms of degree. Wool or flour can vary from coarse to fine. Water can become denser or rarer as its temperature changes from freezing to melting to boiling, or vice versa. In the case of vertical or distinct differences, we do not move from one degree to another degree of the same underlying kind. Instead, we move from one kind of thing to a distinctly different kind of thing. Swedenborg's example is the threefold distinction between end, cause, and effect. These are different kinds of things, not merely degrees of the same kind of thing. Swedenborg calls the dimension constituted by vertical levels "height" and the dimension constituted by horizontal levels "width," and he adds that their position relative to our viewpoint does not change their labels (§185). Within vertical levels, the best is the highest and the worst the lowest. Within horizontal levels, the best is the center and the worst the periphery. The "center" here is not necessarily the geometrical center, but the spiritual center: that part of an entity that most closely approaches the spiritual world (§205).

The distinction between vertical and horizontal levels is useful for understanding the relationship between the material and spiritual worlds and between the different levels of the spiritual world. Swedenborg uses the example of the three angelic heavens: "There are three heavens marked off by vertical levels so that one is underneath another" (§186). Because of the discontinuity between the different heavens, one might ask how they are unified. Swedenborg's answer is that they are unified in terms of correspondences. In the language of the Emerald Tablet of Hermes Trismegistus, "As above, so below."[16] This principle is true of all levels of reality, not just the heavens. One might also wonder how discontinuous levels of reality communicate, if they communicate at all. Swedenborg's answer is, "The only way they communicate is by an inflow that comes from the Lord through the heavens in sequence down to the lowest, but not the other way around" (§186). This principle too applies to all levels of reality, not merely to the heavens.

Swedenborg's account of the relationship of cause and effect, particularly the causal relationships that exist between levels of reality, is complex. On the one hand, he affirms that causes are more perfect than their effects because they are closer to God:

> The antecedent things that give rise to subsequent ones are more perfect, as are the constituents from which compounds are formed. This is

16. The Emerald Tablet is reproduced in Fideler 1993, 233.

because the antecedent or constituent things are less covered, less shrouded by lifeless substances and materials. They are more divine, so to speak, and as such are closer to the spiritual sun where the Lord is. (§204)

On the other hand, Swedenborg reaffirms that unrealized ends, no matter how close to the divine they may be, are mere abstractions unless they become concretely embodied by giving rise to effects. In Swedenborg's words, "The final level [the effect] is the composite, vessel, and foundation of the prior levels" (§209). Swedenborg claims that this applies "not only [to] physical phenomena but also [to] societal, moral, and spiritual ones" (§209). Although we can discuss all things in the abstract, nothing truly exists that is not concrete. The effect is the "composite" because effects are composed of relatively simpler elements that serve as their cause. It is the "vessel" in the sense that it is the place where the end concretely dwells. It is the "foundation" in the sense that the end depends on the effect for its concrete being just as much as the effect depends upon the end for setting in motion the causal process that gives rise to the effect. Swedenborg also speaks of the effect as the "organ" of the end. Sight is just an abstraction without the concrete organ of the eye. Hearing is an abstraction without the concrete organ of the ear. This is particularly illuminating, as it emphasizes that the end dwells in the effect dynamically, not merely as form, but as living, functioning form.

Swedenborg uses this doctrine to illuminate the nature of Scripture, or the Word. According to Swedenborg, the Word has three distinct levels. In descending order, they are a heavenly meaning, a spiritual meaning, and a material or literal meaning. Each of these distinct levels is unified by correspondences. If the final level is the "composite, vessel, and foundation" of the prior levels, then the heavenly and spiritual meanings of Scripture are fully realized in the material or literal meaning. As Swedenborg puts it, "the Word finds its fullest expression and power in its literal meaning" (§221). This should suffice to dispel the common misimpression that Swedenborg disdains and dismisses the literal meaning of Scripture in his pursuit of its inner meanings.

IX. The Nature of Uses

The concept of "use" (*usus*) is so important to *Divine Love and Wisdom* that if Swedenborg had chosen a longer title, it probably would have been *Divine Love, Divine Wisdom, and Use*. So what is "use"? *Usus* is a

complex and polyvalent term; hence it is rendered in the present translation variously as "use," "function," "useful function," and "service." Swedenborg employs the word *usus* to refer both to things that have uses and
to the uses that things have. He speaks of uses primarily as the con-
cretization of divine love and wisdom. According to Swedenborg, divine
love corresponds to ends (purposes), divine wisdom to causes (means),
and use corresponds to concrete effects. Therefore, use is the "composite,
vessel, and foundation" of divine love and wisdom (§213). It is the "total
presence" of divine love and wisdom (§213). Furthermore,

> unless volition and discernment, or desire and thought, or charity and
> faith, devote themselves to involvement in works or deeds whenever
> possible, they are nothing but passing breezes, so to speak, or images in
> the air that vanish. They first take on permanence in us and become
> part of our life when we perform and do them. (§216)

This means that divine love and wisdom become fully realized when they
give rise to, enter into, and dwell within their effects.

Use is not confined to human action. It is found throughout creation. It is a common structure of all created beings, unifying the great
chain of being from the lowest to the highest. Swedenborg sees the cosmos as an encompassing system of interacting uses (§327). Thus it would
be a mistake to reduce Swedenborg's conception of use to mere instrumental usefulness, particularly purely mechanical usefulness, although
instrumental usefulness is certainly a part of the phenomenon of use.
The core meaning of Swedenborg's concept of use is organic, not mechanical. Recall his use of the eye and the ear as examples of the concrete
embodiment of abstract ends. An organ is not merely a form embodied
in matter. It is an active, functioning form. This is the core of what Swedenborg means by use. Thus Swedenborg's concept of use is very close to
an *entelechy* as defined by Aristotle and Leibniz: the ongoing active embodiment of a functioning form.[17] An entity's use can be described as its
actively being itself, its *functioning as the kind of being that it is.*

Swedenborg does not, however, hold that entities are fully autonomous and self-contained, able to carry on their functions in
isolation from one another. Instead, Swedenborg holds that *to be* is *to be
related,* to be connected with other beings, and ultimately with the whole

---

17. On entelechies in Aristotle, see Lear 1998, 59–71; on entelechies in Leibniz, see Klein 1985,
197–217.

of creation and with God. The uses of beings are, therefore, other-regarding as well as self-regarding. Indeed, it could be said that for Swedenborg, the use of each being is a microcosmic analog of the drama of creation, whereby God realizes himself through his relatedness with the other whom he creates. Each individual being likewise realizes itself—performs its function or use—through its relationship with other beings, which in turn perform their functions through it. For Swedenborg, then, each being is other-fulfilling precisely insofar as it is self-fulfilling and self-fulfilling precisely insofar as it is other-fulfilling.

In the human realm, one attains one's use by pursuing the perfection of one's nature through mutually beneficial interactions with others. Such interactions include trade, but Swedenborg gives far greater emphasis to *charity,* that is, care for the other, whether the other be one's spouse, one's child, one's parent, or one's neighbor; whether it be the church, the state, or the whole human race. The other who is the object of ultimate concern is, of course, God. Swedenborg's notion of use is also similar to the idea of a *Beruf* or a *Bestimmung,* a "calling" or a "vocation," a way of life pursued as an end in itself and endowed with qualities of freedom, nobility, and beauty, as opposed to something pursued merely as a means for other ends.[18] Such callings are, however, useful for others as well. They are, furthermore, providentially organized and harmonized in such a way that the pursuit of individual ends contributes to the order, the perfection, and the good of the whole.

X. The Nature of Evil

Swedenborg claims that "the origin of evil is in the abuse of the abilities proper to us called rationality and freedom" (§264). Rationality is the ability to discern what is true and what is false, what is good and what is evil. Freedom is the ability to "think, intend, and do such things" (§264). But what is evil itself? Evil is the turning of the soul inwards toward selfish desires and the closing of the soul off to God and one's neighbor. The freedom of humankind is its capacity to choose between two fundamentally different forms of life, the heavenly or the hellish. The soul has the

---

18. On this dimension of use, see the superb essay of Henry James, Sr., "A Scientific Statement of the Christian Doctrine of the Lord, or Divine Man," printed under the title "The Perfect Man," in James [1850] 1974, 123–133, especially pages 130–131.

capacity to look upwards and to be guided by the better angels of our nature, or the soul can look downwards and be guided by the promptings
of hellish desires and impulses flowing into it.

The soul that looks upwards also looks outwards. The soul opens itself to God and gratefully acknowledges its absolute dependence upon
him. The soul opens itself to its neighbor and treats that neighbor with
charity and kindness.

The soul that looks downwards also looks inwards. It closes itself off
to God and its neighbor and delights in its sense of autonomy. But its autonomy is illusory. Its freedom is merely a form of slavery to the lower
part of the soul, to selfish desires. Ultimately, it is a descent into hell. The
closed soul may, of course, be aware of God and its neighbor, but does
not see them for what they are. Instead, it sees only the projections of its
needs and fantasies. It has fundamentally domineering and manipulative
relationships to God and its neighbor.

This account of evil throws light on a puzzling section of part 4
(§§336–348). Here Swedenborg anticipates a central topic of *Divine
Providence,* namely the problem of evil: If God is good, then how do we
explain evil? Two kinds of evils need to be explained: natural evils and
moral evils. Natural evils, such as diseases and disasters, are natural phenomena that thwart our well-being. Moral evils, such as crimes and sins,
are products of human freedom that thwart our well-being. Swedenborg
faces the problem of moral evil in *Divine Providence.* In *Divine Love and
Wisdom* he discusses the problem of natural evil. This task is particularly
necessary for Swedenborg because he holds that all the functions of the
natural world were created with our benefit in mind. How then do we
explain rabid dogs and bed bugs? Swedenborg flatly denies that evil uses
come from God. Instead, he claims that they come from hell. All of nature is constantly in contact with the spiritual world. Evil uses are merely
inflowings from hell.[19]

XI. The Necessary Illusion of Autonomy

Swedenborg denies that "we ourselves climb up to God on our own
power. It is done by the Lord" (§68). Our ability to ascend from one

---

19. Swedenborg's account of natural evil is essentially the same as that of Augustine (354–430) in
his *Civitas Dei* (City of God) 11:22.

physical level to the next and one spiritual level to the next depends on our receptivity to divine love and wisdom. This receptivity is not, however, something we control. All created beings are, in themselves, dead and inert. All their vital and active powers are infused into them by God, who is the only intrinsically alive and active being. God is at work in our inmost thoughts and feelings, always guiding us toward him: "The Lord exercises an inner guidance of [angels'] feelings and thoughts and constantly turns them toward himself" (§130). We are unaware of this fact, because nothing seems more our own than our lives: "Angels, like us, simply feel as though they participate in love and wisdom on their own, and therefore that love and wisdom are theirs, their very own" (§115).

This delusory sense of self-reliance plays a complex and ambiguous role in Swedenborg's thought. On the one hand, persistence in this attitude is *the* source of evil, of rebellion against and ingratitude toward God. On the other hand, this attitude is a necessary stage in both the development of the human personality and the realization of the ultimate goal of creation: the loving reciprocal union of God and humankind. Consider the following passage:

> If they [the angels] did not feel this way there would be no union, so the Lord would not be in them, nor they in the Lord. It cannot happen that the Lord is in any angels or people unless they, as subjects of his presence in love and wisdom, sense and feel this as their own. This enables them not only to accept but also to retain what they have accepted, and to love in response. This, then, is how angels become wise and remain wise. Can people decide to love God and their neighbor, can people decide to gain wisdom, unless they feel and sense that what they love, learn, and gain is their own? Can they retain anything in themselves otherwise? If it were not for this, then the inflowing love and wisdom would have no seat. They would flow right through without making any difference; and as a result angels would not be angels and people would not be human. They would be virtually lifeless. (§115)

Swedenborg's point is that the reciprocal union between God and human beings is a relationship between persons, between selves. So human beings must have a sense of self. For a human being to say, "I love God," that individual must first be able to say "I." Since the development of human selfhood is a necessary part of the divine plan, human selfhood as such is not evil.

The human self cannot develop, however, if it does not have the illusion of freedom and self-reliance. Since the relationship of parent to child corresponds in many ways to the relationship of God and humankind, this point can be illustrated with an example from child development.

In his *Émile, or On Education* ([1762] 1979), Jean-Jacques Rousseau frames the central problem of education as how to guide children, who by nature are entirely insecure and dependent upon their parents, so that they develop into secure and independent adults. Rousseau thought that the hallmark of psychological health is self-esteem *(amour de soi-même)*, which presupposes well-defined ego boundaries and allows the individual a certain independence from external things and the opinions of others. The hallmark of psychological illness is "love of one's own" *(amour propre)*, which involves poorly defined ego boundaries, psychological dependency on external things, such as property and the good opinion of others, and a constant gnawing insecurity.[20] *Amour-propre* arises when parents and educators constantly remind the child of the insecurity and dependency that are natural to childhood until these become the core of the adult personality. *Amour de soi-même* arises when parents and educators create an environment that both conceals the insecurity and dependency of childhood and heightens the child's sense of efficacy and independence so that these latter characteristics become the core of the adult personality. Only people of genuine self-esteem can love another person in a reciprocal and "unselfish" way—that is, they can love the other person, including God, as that person really is, as opposed to loving a projection of their own needs, and they can love the other person while respecting his or her freedom, as opposed to manipulating, dominating, and competing with him or her. Furthermore, only those who possess genuine self-esteem are capable of feeling gratitude toward their parents upon reaching maturity and recognizing their dependence upon them. For people with weak ego boundaries, gratitude to their parents is impossible because they are still in the throes of psychological dependence and feel dominated and smothered by them.

Swedenborg holds that union with God is achieved only when we recognize our complete dependence upon him and respond with appropriate gratitude and humility. Only a strong and well-developed self is

---

20. On the distinction between *amour propre* and *amour de soi-même*, see Rousseau [1754] 1992, 91–92.

capable of recognizing this fact, however. But a strong self only develops through the ignorance of this fact and the illusion of freedom and self-sufficiency. The self becomes evil only when, although it is capable of acknowledging its dependence upon God, it refuses to do so and clings to its illusory freedom and self-sufficiency.

XII. On *Divine Providence* as a Companion Piece

Divine Love and Wisdom has generally been published by itself. However, there is another book that might well be considered its companion volume, *Divine Providence.*

At first glance it might seem odd to pair these two volumes. One obvious reason for this pairing, however, is that the two books were published one directly after the other—*Divine Love and Wisdom* in 1763 and *Divine Providence* in 1764. A second reason is that they are two of the most involved and philosophical of Swedenborg's mature theological works. They are strong medicine, meant to be downed all at once. A third reason is on its own sufficiently compelling: Swedenborg reports, in an account of one of his experiences in the spiritual world that appears in his 1766 work *Revelation Unveiled* 875:15, that in heaven he saw a single book on a cedar table under an olive tree: "I looked more closely and saw that it was a book that I had been the means of writing, a book called *Angelic Wisdom about Divine Love and Wisdom and also about Divine Providence.*"

An interesting historical footnote is that these are the first two books by Swedenborg that Henry James, Sr. (1811–1882), read after experiencing his famous "vastation" in Windsor, England, in the spring of 1844. Psychologists today would probably classify James's experience as a pathological anxiety attack. But a woman he met at an English spa where he sought a water cure informed him that Swedenborg gave the term *vastation* to what he was undergoing. This news inspired in James "an immediate hope, amounting to an almost prophetic instinct, of finding . . . some diversion to [his] cares, and [he] determined instantly to run up to London and procure a couple of Swedenborg's volumes." He reports the results of his search thus:

> From the huge mass of tomes placed by the bookseller on the counter before me, I selected two of the least in bulk—the treatise on the *Divine Love and Wisdom,* and that on the *Divine Providence.* I gave them,

after I brought them home, many a random but eager glance, but at last my interest in them grew so frantic under this tantalizing process of reading that I resolved, in spite of the doctors, that, instead of standing any longer shivering on the brink, I should boldly plunge into the stream, and ascertain, once and for all, to what undiscovered sea its waters might bear me. . . . I read from the first with palpitating interest. My heart divined, even before my intelligence was prepared to do justice to the books, the unequalled amount of truth to be found in them. Imagine a fever patient, sufficiently restored of his malady to be able to think of something beside himself, suddenly transported where the free airs of heaven blow upon him, and the sound of waters refreshes his jaded senses, and you have a feeble image of my delight in reading. Or, better still, imagine a subject of some petty despotism condemned to die, and with—what is more and worse—a sentiment of death pervading all his consciousness, lifted by a sudden Miracle into felt harmony with universal man, and filled to the brim with the sentiment of indestructible life instead, and you will have a true picture of my emancipated condition. (James 1879, 51–53)

After reading *Divine Love and Wisdom* and *Divine Providence,* Henry James, Sr., went on to read all of Swedenborg's works. His exploration of Swedenborg helped him to understand and to overcome his psychological crisis. And what is more, although he never joined a Swedenborgian church, he became one of the most original and prolific theologians to have been influenced by Swedenborg. It is my hope that *Divine Love and Wisdom* and its companion, *Divine Providence,* will provide many future readers with as auspicious an introduction to Swedenborg's works.

Works Cited
in the Introduction

Copenhaver, Brian, trans. 1992. *Hermetica*. Cambridge: Cambridge University Press.

Fideler, David. 1993. *Jesus Christ, Sun of God: Ancient Cosmology and Early Christian Symbolism*. Wheaton, Ill.: Theosophical Publishing House.

James, Henry, Sr. 1879. *Society the Redeemed Form of Man and the Earnest of God's Omnipotence in Human Nature: Affirmed in Letters to a Friend*. Boston: Houghton, Osgood.

———. [1850] 1974. "A Scientific Statement of the Christian Doctrine of the Lord, or Divine Man" [printed under the title "The Perfect Man"]. In *Henry James, Senior: A Selection of His Writings,* edited by Giles Gunn. Chicago: American Library Association.

Johnson, Gregory R. 2001. *A Commentary on Kant's* Dreams of a Spirit-Seer. Diss. The Catholic University of America, Washington, D.C.

Klein, Jacob. 1985. "Leibniz: An Introduction." In *Lectures and Essays.* Edited by Robert Williamson and Elliot Zuckerman. Annapolis: Saint John's College Press.

Lear, Jonathan. 1998. *Aristotle: The Desire to Understand*. Cambridge: Cambridge University Press.

Lovejoy, Arthur O. 1936. *The Great Chain of Being: A Study of the History of an Idea*. Cambridge: Harvard University Press.

Magee, Glenn Alexander. 2001. *Hegel and the Hermetic Tradition*. Ithaca: Cornell University Press.

Rousseau, Jean-Jacques. [1762] 1979. *Émile, or On Education*. Translated by Allan Bloom. New York: Basic Books.

———. [1754] 1992. *Discourse on the Origins of Inequality*. Translated by Roger D. Masters. In *Discourse on the Origins of Inequality (Second Discourse), Polemics, and Political Economy*. Vol. 3 of *The Collected Writings of Rousseau*. Edited by Roger D. Masters and Christopher Kelly. Hanover, N.H.: Dartmouth University Press.

Scholem, Gershom. 1946. *Major Trends in Jewish Mysticism*. New York: Schocken.

———. 1974. *Kabbalah*. New York: New American Library.

Sherover, Charles M. 2003. "The Concept of Time in Western Thought." In *Are We In Time? And Other Essays on Time and Temporality*. Edited by Gregory R. Johnson. Evanston: Northwestern University Press.

Sokolowski, Robert. 1995. *The God of Faith and Reason: Foundations of Christian Theology*. 2nd ed. Washington, D.C.: The Catholic University of America Press.

Trismegistus, Hermes. See Copenhaver, Brian.

Short Titles and Other Conventions
Used in This Work

AS is common in Swedenborgian studies, text citations of Sweden-borg's works refer not to page numbers but to Swedenborg's section numbers, which are uniform in all editions. Thus "*Secrets of Heaven* 29" refers to section 29 (§29) of Swedenborg's *Secrets of Heaven*. A reference such as "29:2" indicates subsection 2 of section 29. In the text of the section itself, this subsection would be marked [2].

Swedenborg made extensive cross-references within *Divine Love and Wisdom,* but often did not cite the number of the section or sections to which he was referring. These omitted cross-reference numbers have been inserted in brackets in this edition.

In a few cases Swedenborg supplied the section numbers, but they are obviously in error. Where a plausible correction has been found, it has been inserted in square brackets. These corrections have, further-more, been italicized as an indication that they are intended to replace the preceding entry, not augment it.

This system has also been applied to citations of the Bible and of Swedenborg's works that appear in the main text of the translation: that is, italicized brackets indicate a correction and roman brackets indicate an addition. Words not corresponding to the Latin original but necessary for the understanding of the text also appear in roman brackets; this de-vice has been used sparingly, however, even at the risk of some inconsis-tency in its application.

Comments on the text are printed as endnotes, referenced by super-script numbers appearing in the main text. The initials of the writer or writers of each note are given in square brackets. Translations of material quoted in the endnotes are those of the indicated writer, except in cases in which the cited source is a translated text.

Swedenborg numbered the parts of *Divine Love and Wisdom* but did not number the "chapters" within those parts. His decision not to do so seems to have been deliberate, and in accord with it chapter numbers are not included in the text. However, the table of contents provides such numbers in square brackets for the convenience of readers.

References to Swedenborg's works in this volume accord with the short titles listed below, except where he gives his own version of a title in the text of the translation, or where other translations are cited by the annotators. In this list, the short title is followed by the traditional translation for the title; by the original Latin title, with its full translation; and finally by the place and date of original publication if Swedenborg published it himself, or the approximate date of writing if he did not. The list is chronological within each of the two groups shown—the published theological works, and the nontheological and posthumously published works. The titles given below as theological works published by Swedenborg are generally not further referenced in lists of works cited in the preface, introduction, and endnotes.

Theological Works Published by Swedenborg

Secrets of Heaven
Traditional title: *Arcana Coelestia*
Original title: *Arcana Coelestia, Quae in Scriptura Sacra, seu Verbo Domini Sunt, Detecta: . . . Una cum Mirabilibus Quae Visa Sunt in Mundo Spirituum, et in Coelo Angelorum* [A Disclosure of Secrets of Heaven Contained in Sacred Scripture, or the Word of the Lord, . . . Together with Amazing Things Seen in the World of Spirits and in the Heaven of Angels]. London: 1749–1756.

Heaven and Hell
Traditional title: *Heaven and Hell*
Original title: *De Coelo et Ejus Mirabilibus, et de Inferno, ex Auditis et Visis* [Heaven and Its Wonders and Hell: Drawn from Things Heard and Seen]. London: 1758.

New Jerusalem
Traditional title: *New Jerusalem and Its Heavenly Doctrine*
Original title: *De Nova Hierosolyma et Ejus Doctrina Coelesti: Ex Auditis e Coelo: Quibus Praemittitur Aliquid de Novo Coelo et Nova Terra* [The New Jerusalem and Its Heavenly Teaching: Drawn from Things Heard from Heaven: Preceded by a Discussion of the New Heaven and the New Earth]. London: 1758.

Last Judgment
Traditional title: *The Last Judgment*

Original title: *De Ultimo Judicio, et de Babylonia Destructa: Ita Quod Omnia, Quae in Apocalypsi Praedicta Sunt, Hodie Impleta Sunt: Ex Auditis et Visis* [The Last Judgment and Babylon Destroyed, Showing That at This Day All the Predictions of the Book of Revelation Have Been Fulfilled: Drawn from Things Heard and Seen]. London: 1758.

White Horse

Traditional title: *The White Horse*

Original title: *De Equo Albo, de Quo in Apocalypsi, Cap. XIX: Et Dein de Verbo et Ejus Sensu Spirituali seu Interno, ex Arcanis Coelestibus* [The White Horse in Revelation Chapter 19, and the Word and Its Spiritual or Inner Sense (from *Secrets of Heaven*)]. London: 1758.

Other Planets

Traditional title: *Earths in the Universe*

Original title: *De Telluribus in Mundo Nostro Solari, Quae Vocantur Planetae, et de Telluribus in Coelo Astrifero, deque Illarum Incolis, Tum de Spiritibus et Angelis Ibi: Ex Auditis et Visis* [Planets or Worlds in Our Solar System, and Worlds in the Starry Heavens, and Their Inhabitants, as Well as the Spirits and Angels There: Drawn from Things Heard and Seen]. London: 1758.

The Lord

Traditional title: *Doctrine of the Lord*

Original title: *Doctrina Novae Hierosolymae de Domino* [Teachings for the New Jerusalem on the Lord]. Amsterdam: 1763.

Sacred Scripture

Traditional title: *Doctrine of the Sacred Scripture*

Original title: *Doctrina Novae Hierosolymae de Scriptura Sacra* [Teachings for the New Jerusalem on Sacred Scripture]. Amsterdam: 1763.

Life

Traditional title: *Doctrine of Life*

Original title: *Doctrina Vitae pro Nova Hierosolyma ex Praeceptis Decalogi* [Teachings about Life for the New Jerusalem: Drawn from the Ten Commandments]. Amsterdam: 1763.

Faith

Traditional title: *Doctrine of Faith*

Original title: *Doctrina Novae Hierosolymae de Fide* [Teachings for the New Jerusalem on Faith]. Amsterdam: 1763.

Supplements
Traditional title: *Continuation Concerning the Last Judgment*
Original title: *Continuatio de Ultimo Judicio: Et de Mundo Spirituali* [Supplements on the Last Judgment and the Spiritual World]. Amsterdam: 1763.

Divine Love and Wisdom
Traditional title: *Divine Love and Wisdom*
Original title: *Sapientia Angelica de Divino Amore et de Divina Sapientia* [Angelic Wisdom about Divine Love and Wisdom]. Amsterdam: 1763.

Divine Providence
Traditional title: *Divine Providence*
Original title: *Sapientia Angelica de Divina Providentia* [Angelic Wisdom about Divine Providence]. Amsterdam: 1764.

Revelation Unveiled
Traditional title: *Apocalypse Revealed*
Original title: *Apocalypsis Revelata, in Qua Deteguntur Arcana Quae Ibi Praedicta Sunt, et Hactenus Recondita Latuerunt* [The Book of Revelation Unveiled, Uncovering the Secrets That Were Foretold There and Have Lain Hidden until Now]. Amsterdam: 1766.

Marriage Love
Traditional title: *Conjugial Love*
Original title: *Delitiae Sapientiae de Amore Conjugiali: Post Quas Sequuntur Voluptates Insaniae de Amore Scortatorio* [Wisdom's Delight in Marriage Love: Followed by Insanity's Pleasure in Promiscuous Love]. Amsterdam: 1768.

Survey
Traditional title: *Brief Exposition*
Original title: *Summaria Expositio Doctrinae Novae Ecclesiae, Quae per Novam Hierosolymam in Apocalypsi Intelligitur* [Survey of Teachings for the New Church Meant by the New Jerusalem in the Book of Revelation]. Amsterdam: 1769.

Soul-Body Interaction
Traditional title: *Intercourse between the Soul and Body*
Original title: *De Commercio Animae et Corporis, Quod Creditur Fieri vel per Influxum Physicum, vel per Influxum Spiritualem, vel per Harmoniam Praestabilitam* [Soul-Body Interaction, Believed to Occur Either by a Physical Inflow, or by a Spiritual Inflow, or by a Preestablished Harmony]. London: 1769.

True Christianity

Traditional title: *True Christian Religion*
Original title: *Vera Christiana Religio, Continens Universam Theologiam Novae Ecclesiae a Domino apud Danielem Cap. VII:13–14, et in Apocalypsi Cap. XXI:1, 2 Praedictae* [True Christianity: Containing the Whole Theology of the New Church Predicted by the Lord in Daniel 7:13–14 and Revelation 21:1, 2]. Amsterdam: 1771.

Nontheological and Posthumously Published Works by Swedenborg Cited in This Volume

The Fiber

Traditional title: *The Fiber*
Original title: *Oeconomia Regni Animalis. Transactio Tertia: De Fibra, de Tunica Arachnoidea, et de Morbis Fibrarum* [Dynamics of the Soul's Domain, Part 3: The Fiber, the Arachnoid Mater, and Diseases of the Fibers]. 1738–1740.

Dynamics of the Soul's Domain

Traditional title: *Economy of the Animal Kingdom*
Original title: *Oeconomia Regni Animalis in Transactiones Divisa* [Dynamics of the Soul's Domain: Divided into Treatises]. Amsterdam: 1740–1741.

The Soul's Fluid

Traditional title: *Animal Spirit(s)*
Original title: *De Spiritu Animali* [The Soul's Fluid]. 1741.

The Soul's Domain

Traditional title: *The Animal Kingdom*
Original title: *Regnum Animale, Anatomice, Physice, et Philosophice Perlustratum* [The Soul's Domain Thoroughly Examined by Means of Anatomy, Physics, and Philosophy]. The Hague: 1744–1745.

The Old Testament Explained

Traditional title: *The Word Explained*
Original title: *Explicatio in Verbum Historicum Veteris Testamenti* [The Historical Word of the Old Testament Explained]. 1745–1747.

Spiritual Experiences

Traditional title: *The Spiritual Diary*
Original title: *Experientiae Spirituales* [Spiritual Experiences]. 1745–1765.

Revelation Explained
Traditional title: *Apocalypse Explained*
Original title: *Apocalypsis Explicata secundum Sensum Spiritualem, Ubi Revelantur Arcana, Quae Ibi Praedicta, et Hactenus Recondita Fuerunt* [The Book of Revelation Explained as to Its Spiritual Meaning, Which Reveals Secret Wonders That Were Predicted There and Have Been Hidden until Now]. 1757–1759.

Sketch for Supplement to Last Judgment
Traditional title: *Last Judgment (Posthumous)*
Original title: *De Ultimo Judicio* [Last Judgment]. 1762–1763.

Sketch for Divine Love
Traditional title: *On Divine Love*
Original title: *De Divino Amore* [Divine Love]. 1762–1763.

Sketch for Divine Wisdom
Traditional title: *On Divine Wisdom*
Original title: *De Divina Sapientia* [Divine Wisdom]. 1763.

Biblical Titles

Swedenborg referred to the Hebrew Scriptures as the Old Testament; his terminology has been adopted in this edition. As was the custom in his day, he referred to the Pentateuch (Genesis, Exodus, Leviticus, Numbers, and Deuteronomy) as the books of Moses; to the Psalms as the book of David; and occasionally to the Book of Revelation as John.

DIVINE LOVE
AND
WISDOM

ANGELIC WISDOM
ABOUT
DIVINE LOVE

PART 1

L OVE is our life. For most people, the existence of love is a given, but the nature of love is a mystery.[1] As for the existence of love, this we know from everyday language. We say that someone loves us, that monarchs love their subjects, and that subjects love their monarch. We say that a husband loves his wife and that a mother loves her children, and vice versa. We say that people love their country, their fellow citizens, their neighbor. We use the same language about impersonal objects, saying that someone loves this or that thing.

Even though the word "love" is so commonly on our tongues, still hardly anyone knows what love is. When we stop to think about it, we find that we cannot form any image of it in our thoughts, so we say either that it is not really anything or that it is simply something that flows into us from our sight, hearing, touch, and conversation and therefore influences us. We are wholly unaware that it is our very life—not just the general life of our whole body and of all our thoughts, but the life of their every least detail. Wise people can grasp this when you ask, "If you take away the effects of love, can you think anything? Can you do anything? As the effects of love lose their warmth, do not thought and speech and action lose theirs as well? Do they not warm up as love warms up?" Still, the grasp of these wise people is not based on the thought that love is our life, but on their experience that this is how things happen.

2 We cannot know what our life is unless we know what love is. If we do not know this, then one person may believe that life is nothing but sensation and action and another that it is thought, when in fact thought is the first effect of life, and sensation and action are secondary effects of life. Thought is the first effect of life, as just noted, but there are deeper and deeper forms of thought as well as more and more superficial ones. The deepest form of thought, the perception of ends,[2] is actually the first effect of life. But more on this below [§§179–183][3] in connection with levels of life.

3 We can get some idea that love is our life from the warmth of the sun in our world. We know this warmth acts like the life shared by all earth's plants because when it increases in the spring, plants of all kinds sprout from the soil. They dress themselves in their leafy finery and then in their blossoms and eventually in fruit. This is how they "live." When the warmth ebbs away, though, as it does in fall and winter, they are stripped of these signs of life and they wither. Love works the same way in us because love and warmth correspond[4] to each other. This is why love makes us warm.

4 *God alone—the Lord[5]—is love itself, because he is life itself. Both we on earth and angels are life-receivers.* I will be offering many illustrations of this in works on divine providence and life.[6] Here I would say only that the Lord, who is the God of the universe, is uncreated and infinite, while we and angels are created and finite. Since the Lord is uncreated and infinite, he is that essential reality[7] that is called Jehovah[8] and is life itself or life in itself. No one can be created directly from the Uncreated, the Infinite, from Reality itself and Life itself, because what is divine is one and undivided. We must be created out of things created and finite, things so formed that something divine can dwell within. Since we and angels are of this nature, we are life-receivers. So if we let ourselves be misled in thought so badly that we think we are not life-receivers but are actually life, there is no way to keep us from thinking that we are God.

Our sense that we are life and our consequent belief that we are life rests on an illusion: in an instrumental cause, the presence of its principal cause is only felt as something identical to itself.[9] The Lord himself teaches that he is life in itself in John: "As the Father has life in himself, so too he has granted the Son to have life in himself" (John 5:26); and again in John (11:25 and 14:6) he teaches that he is life itself.[10] Since life and love are one and the same, as we can see from the first two sections above, it follows that the Lord, being life itself, is love itself.

If this is to be intelligible, though, it is essential to realize that the Lord, 5
being love in its very essence or divine love, is visible to angels in heaven as
a sun; that warmth and light flow from that sun; that the outflowing
warmth is essentially love and the outflowing light essentially wisdom; and
that to the extent that angels are receptive of that spiritual warmth and
spiritual light, they themselves are instances of love and wisdom—
instances of love and wisdom not on their own, but from the Lord.

Spiritual warmth and spiritual light flow into and affect not only angels but also us, precisely to the extent that we become receptive. Our receptivity develops in proportion to our love for the Lord and our love for
our neighbor.

That sun itself, or divine love, cannot use its warmth and light to create anyone directly from itself. If it did, the creature would be love in its
essence, which is the Lord himself. It can, however, create people out of
material substances so formed as to be receptive of its actual warmth and
light. In the same way, the sun of our world cannot use its warmth and
light to bring forth sprouts in the earth directly. Rather, the sun uses substances in the soil in which it can be present through its warmth and
light to make plants grow. (On the Lord's divine love being seen as the
sun in the spiritual world, with spiritual warmth and light flowing from
it, giving angels their love and wisdom, see *Heaven and Hell* 116–142.)[11]

Since we are life-receivers, not life, it follows that our conception 6
from our parents is not the conception of life but simply the conception
of the first and purest forms that can accept life. These forms serve as a
nucleus or beginning in the womb, to which are added, step by step, material substances in forms suited, in their various patterns and levels, to
the reception of life.

Divinity[12] *is not in space.* Given the divine omnipresence—presence with 7
everyone in the world, with every angel in heaven, and with every spirit
under heaven—there is no way a merely physical image can compass the
thought that Divinity, or God, is not in space. Only a spiritual image will
suffice. Physical images are inadequate because they involve space. They
are put together out of earthly things, and there is something spatial
about absolutely every earthly thing we see with our eyes. Everything
that is large or small here involves space, everything that is long or wide
or high here involves space—in a word, every measurement, every shape,
every form here involves space. This is why I said that a merely physical
image cannot compass the fact that Divinity is not in space when the
claim is made that it is everywhere.

Still, we can grasp this with our earthly thinking if only we let in a little spiritual light. This requires that I first say something about spiritual concepts and the spiritual thinking that arises from them. Spiritual concepts have nothing to do with space. They have to do solely with state, state being an attribute of love, life, wisdom, desires, and the delights they provide—in general, an attribute of what is good and true. A truly spiritual concept of these realities has nothing in common with space. It is higher and looks down on spatial concepts the way heaven looks down on earth.

However, since angels and spirits see with their eyes the way we do on earth, and since objects can be seen only in space, there does seem to be space in the spiritual world where angels and spirits are, space like ours on earth. Still, it is not space but an appearance of space. It is not fixed and invariant like ours. It can be lengthened and shortened, changed and altered; and since it cannot be defined by measurement, we here cannot grasp it with an earthly concept, but only with a spiritual one. Spiritual concepts are no different when they apply to spatial distances than when they apply to "distances" of what is good and "distances" of what is true, which are agreements and likenesses as to state.

8   It stands to reason, then, that with merely earthly concepts we cannot grasp the fact that Divinity is everywhere and still not in space, and that angels and spirits understand this quite clearly. This means that we too could understand if we would only let a little spiritual light into our thinking. The reason we can understand is that it is not our bodies that think but our spirits; so it is not our physical side but our spiritual side.

9   The reason so many people do not grasp this is that they love what is earthly and are therefore reluctant to lift their thinking above it into spiritual light. People who are reluctant can think only spatially, even about God; and thinking spatially about God is thinking about the extended size of nature.[13]

This premise is necessary because without a knowledge and some sense that Divinity is not in space, we cannot understand anything about the divine life that is love and wisdom, which are our present topic. This means there can be little if any understanding of divine providence, omnipresence, omniscience, omnipotence, infinity, and eternity, which are to be dealt with in sequence.[14]

10   I have stated that in the spiritual world, just as in this physical world, we can see space and therefore distances as well, but that they are appearances, dependent on spiritual likenesses of love and wisdom, or of what is good and true. This is why even though the Lord is with angels

everywhere in heaven, he still appears high overhead, looking like a sun. Further, since it is the acceptance of love and wisdom that causes likeness to him, if angels have a closer resemblance because of their acceptance, their heavens appear to be closer to the Lord than those of the angels whose resemblance is more remote. This is also why the heavens (there are three of them) are marked off from each other, as are the communities of each heaven. It is also why the hells underneath them are farther away in proportion to their rejection of love and wisdom.

It is the same for us. The Lord is present in us and with us throughout the whole world; and the reason for this is simply that the Lord is not in space.

God is the essential person. Throughout all the heavens, the only concept of God is a concept of a person. The reason is that heaven, overall and regionally, is in a kind of human form, and Divinity among the angels is what makes heaven. Further, thinking proceeds in keeping with heaven's form, so it is not possible for angels to think about God in any other way. This is why all the people on earth who are in touch with heaven think about God in the same way when they are thinking very deeply, or in their spirit.

It is because God is a person that all angels and spirits are perfectly formed people. This is because of heaven's form, which is the same in its largest and its smallest manifestations. (On heaven being in a human form overall and regionally, see *Heaven and Hell* 59–87 *[59–86]*, and on thought progressing in keeping with heaven's form, see §§203–204 there.)

It is common knowledge that we were created in the image and likeness of God because of Genesis 1:26, 27 and from the fact that Abraham and others saw God as a person.

The early people, wise and simple alike, thought of God only as a person. Even when they began to worship many gods, as they did in Athens and Rome, they worshiped them as persons. By way of illustration, here is an excerpt from an earlier booklet.

Non-Christians[15]—especially Africans—who acknowledge and worship one God as the Creator of the universe conceive of that God as a person. They say that no one can have any other concept of God. When they hear that many people prefer an image of God as a little cloud in the center, they ask where these people are; and when they are told that these people are among the Christians, they respond that this is impossible. They are told, however, that Christians get this idea from

the fact that in the Word[16] God is called a spirit; and the only concept
they have of spirit is of a piece of cloud. They do not realize that every
spirit and every angel is a person. However, when inquiry was made to
find out whether their spiritual concept was the same as their earthly
one, it turned out that it was not the same for people who inwardly
recognized the Lord as the God of heaven and earth.

I heard one Christian elder say that no one could have a concept of a
being both divine and human; and I saw him taken to various non-
Christians, more and more profound ones. Then he was taken to their
heavens,[17] and finally to a heaven of Christians. Through the whole process
people's inner perception of God was communicated to him, and he
came to realize that their only concept of God was a concept of a person
—which is the same as a concept of a being both divine and human.[18]

12 The ordinary concept of God among Christians is a concept of a person because God is called a person in the Athanasian doctrine of the
Trinity. The better educated, though, claim that God is invisible. This is
because they cannot understand how a human God could have created
heaven and earth and filled the universe with his presence, along with
other things that pass the bounds of understanding as long as people do
not realize that Divinity is not in space. Still, people who turn to the
Lord alone think of one who is both divine and human, and therefore
think of God as a person.

13 We may gather how important it is to have a right concept of God
from the fact that this concept is the very core of the thinking of anyone
who has a religion. All the elements of religion and of worship focus on
God; and since God is involved in every element of religion and worship,
whether general or particular, unless there is a right concept of God there
can be no communication with heaven. This is why every nation is allot-
ted its place in the spiritual world according to its concept of a human
God. This [understanding of God as human] is where the concept of the
Lord is to be found, and nowhere else.

We can see very clearly that our state after death depends on our
avowed concept of God if we consider the opposite, namely that the denial of God, and in the Christian world, a denial of the Lord's divinity,
constitutes hell.

14 *In the Divine-Human One,[19] reality and its manifestation are both distinguishable and united.* Wherever there is reality, there is its manifestation:

the one does not occur without the other. In fact, reality *exists* through its manifestation, and not apart from it. Our rational capacity grasps this when we ponder whether there can be any reality that does not manifest itself, and whether there can be any manifestation except from some reality. Since each occurs with the other and not apart from it, it follows that they are one entity, but "distinguishably one."

They are distinguishably one like love and wisdom. Further, love *is* reality and wisdom is its manifestation. Love occurs only in wisdom, and wisdom only from love. So love becomes manifest when it is in wisdom. These two are one entity in such a way that although they can be distinguished in thought they cannot be distinguished in fact; and since they can be distinguished in thought and not in fact, we refer to them as "distinguishably one."

Reality and its manifestation are also distinguishably one in the Divine-Human One the way soul and body are. A soul does not occur without its body, nor a body without its soul. The divine soul of the Divine-Human One is what we mean by the divine reality, and the divine body of the Divine-Human One is what we mean by the divine manifestation.

The notion that a soul can exist and think and be wise without a body is an error that stems from deceptive appearances. Every soul is in a spiritual body after it has cast off the material skin that it carried around in this world. **15**

The reason reality is not reality unless it is manifested is that before that happens it has no form, and if it has no form it has no attributes.[20] Anything that has no attributes is not really anything. Whatever is manifest on the basis of its reality is one with that reality because it stems from that reality. This is the basis of their being united into a single entity, and this is why each belongs to the other reciprocally, with each being wholly present in every detail of the other, as it is in itself.

It therefore stands to reason that God is a person and in this way is God manifest—not manifest from himself, but manifest in himself. The one who is manifest in himself is the God who is the source of all. **16**

In the Divine-Human One, infinite things are distinguishably one. It is recognized that God is infinite: he is in fact called the Infinite One. But he is called infinite because he is infinite. He is not infinite simply because **17** he is intrinsically essential reality and manifestation, but because there are infinite things in him. An infinite being without infinite things within it would be infinite in name only.

The infinite things in him should not be called "infinitely many" or "infinitely all," because of our earthly concepts of "many" and "all." Our earthly concept of "infinitely many" is limited, and while there is something limitless about our concept of "infinitely all," it still rests on limited things in our universe. This means that since our concept is earthly, we cannot arrive at a sense of the infinite things in God by some process of shifting it to a higher level or by comparison. However, since angels enjoy spiritual concepts they can surpass us by changing to a higher level and by comparison, though they cannot reach infinity itself.

18   Anyone can come to an inner assurance about the presence of infinite things in God—anyone, that is, who believes that God is a person; because if God is a person, he has a body and everything that having a body entails.[21] So he has a face, torso, abdomen, upper legs, and lower legs, since without these he would not be a person. Since he has these components, he also has eyes, ears, nose, mouth, and tongue. He also has what we find within a person, such as a heart and lungs and the things that depend on them, all of which, taken together, make us human. We are created with these many components, and if we consider them in their interconnections, they are beyond counting. In the Divine-Human One, though, they are infinite. Nothing is lacking, so he has an infinite completeness.

We can make this comparison of the uncreated Person, who is God, with us who are created, because that God is a person. It is because of [his being a person] that we earthly beings are said to have been created in his image and in his likeness (Genesis 1:26, 27).

19   The presence of infinite things in God is even more obvious to angels because of the heavens where they live. The whole heaven, made up of millions[22] of angels, is like a person in its overall form. Each individual community of heaven, large or small, is the same; and therefore an angel is a person.[23] An angel is actually a heaven in its smallest form (see *Heaven and Hell* 51–87 [51–86]).

Heaven is in this form overall, regionally, and in individuals because of the divine nature that angels accept, since the extent to which angels accept the divine nature determines the perfection of their human form. This is why we say that angels are in God and that God is in them, and that God is everything to them.

The multiplicity of heaven is indescribable; and since it is Divinity that makes heaven, and therefore Divinity is the source of that indescribable multiplicity, we can see quite clearly that there are infinite things in that quintessential Person who is God.

We can draw the same inference from the created universe if we turn our attention to its functions and the things that answer to them.[24] However, this will not be comprehensible until some examples have been offered.

20

Since there are infinite things in the Divine-Human One, things that are so to speak reflected in heaven, in angels, and in us, and since the Divine-Human One is not in space (see §§7–10 above), we can see and understand to some extent how God can be omnipresent, omniscient, and omniprovident, and how, even as a person, he could have created everything, and how as a person he can forever keep everything he has created in its proper order.

21

Further, if we look at ourselves we can see a kind of reflection of the fact that these infinite things in the Divine-Human One are distinguishably one. There are many things within us—countless things, as already noted [§18]; yet we feel them as one. On the basis of our feelings, we have no sense of our brain or heart or lungs, of our liver or spleen or pancreas, of the countless components of our eyes, ears, tongue, stomach, sexual organs, and so on; and since we are not aware of them, we sense them as all one.

22

The reason is that all these organs are gathered into a form that precludes the absence of any one of them. It is a form designed to receive life from the Divine-Human One, as explained in §§4–6 above. The organization and connection of all these elements in this kind of form give rise to the feeling and therefore to the image of them not as many or countless but as one.

We may therefore conclude that the innumerably many components that constitute a kind of unity in us are distinguishably one—supremely so—in that quintessential Person who is God.

There is one human God who is the source of everything. All the elements of human reason unite in, and in a sense center on, the fact that a single God is the Creator of the universe. As a result, rational people, on the basis of their shared understanding, neither do nor can think in any other way. Tell people of sound reason that there are two creators of the universe and you will feel within yourself how they recoil from this notion,

23

perhaps simply from the tone of their voice in your ear. This enables us to see that all the elements of human reason unite and center on the oneness of God.

There are two reasons for this. The first is that in its own right, our very ability to think rationally is not our own property. It is a property of God within us. Human rationality in general depends on this fact, and this general property causes our reason more or less spontaneously to see the oneness of God. The second is that through our rational ability either we are in heaven's light or we draw from it some general quality of its thought, and the all-pervading element of heaven's light is that God is one.

This is not the case if we have used our rational ability to skew our lower understanding. In this case we still possess the ability, but by the distortion of our lower abilities we have steered it off course, and our rationality is not sound.

24   We may not be aware of it, but we all think of an aggregation of people as a single individual. So we understand right away when someone says that monarchs are the head and that their subjects are the body, or when someone says that this or that individual has some particular role in the body politic, that is, in the realm. It is the same with the spiritual body as with the civil. The spiritual body is the church,[25] whose head is the Divine-Human One. We can see from this what kind of person a church would look like under this construct if we were to think not of one God as creator and sustainer of the universe but of many gods instead. We would apparently be envisioning a single body with many heads on it—not a human being, then, but a monster.

If we were to claim that these heads have a single essence that made them all one head, then the only possible image would be either of a single head with many faces or of many heads with one face. In our perception, then, the church would look grotesque. In fact, one God is the head, and the church is the body that acts at the bidding of the head and not on its own, as is true of us as well.

This is also why there is only one monarch per realm. More than one would pull it apart; one holds it together.

25   It would be the same in the church that is spread throughout the world, which is called a communion because it is like a single body under a single head.[26] It is recognized that the head governs the body beneath itself at will. The head is after all the locus of our discernment and our volition,[27] and the body acts at the behest of our discernment and volition to the point that the body is pure obedience. The body is incapable

of doing anything except at the behest of the discernment and volition in the head; and in similar fashion we of the church can do nothing apart from God. It does seem as though the body acts on its own—as though hands and feet move of their own accord when we do something, as though mouth and tongue vibrate of their own accord when we say something—and yet nothing whatever is done "on its own." It is prompted by the stimulus of our volition and the consequent thinking of the discernment in the head.

Just think. If one body had many heads, and each head had its own agenda based on its mind and its volition, could the body survive? There could be no unanimity among them the way there is with a single head.

It is the same in the heavens, which consist of millions of angels, as it is in the church. Unless every single angel focused on one God, one angel would move away from another and heaven would fall apart. So an angel who even thinks about many gods instantly disappears, exiled to the very edge of heaven, and collapses.

Since the whole heaven and everything in it depend on a single God, it is the nature of angelic speech to come to a close in a particular harmony that flows from heaven's own harmony. This is a sign that it is impossible for angels to think of more than one God. Their speech follows from their thought. **26**

Surely everyone of sound reason perceives the fact that Divinity is not divisible, that there is not a multiplicity of infinite, uncreated, omnipotent beings, or gods. Suppose some irrational soul were to say that there could be a multiplicity of infinite, uncreated, omnipotent beings, or gods, if only they had a single "same essence," and that this would result in one being who was infinite, uncreated, omnipotent, and god. Would not that single same essence have one "same identity"? And it is not possible for many beings to have the same identity. If this individual were to say that one is derived from the other, then the one that is derived from the other is not God in and of himself; yet God in and of himself is the source of all (see §16 above). **27**

The true divine essence is love and wisdom. If you gather together everything you know, focus your mind's insight on it, and look through it carefully from some spiritual height to discover what is common to everything, the only conclusion you can draw is that it is love and wisdom. These two are essential to every aspect of our life. Everything we deal with that is civic, everything moral, and everything spiritual depends on these two things. Apart from them, there is nothing. The **28** same holds true for everything in the life of that composite person who is (as already noted [§24]) our larger and smaller community, our monarchy or empire, the church, and also the angelic heaven. Take love and wisdom away from these collective bodies and ask whether there is anything left, and you will be struck by the fact that without love and wisdom as their source, they are nothing.

29   No one can deny that in God we find love and wisdom together in their very essence. He loves us all out of the love that is within him, and he guides us all out of the wisdom that is within him.

Further, if you look at the created universe with an eye to its design, it is so full of wisdom from love that you might say everything taken all together is wisdom itself. There are things without measure in such a pattern, both sequential and simultaneous,[28] that taken all together they constitute a single entity. This is the only reason they can be held together and sustained forever.

30   It is because the very essence of the Divine is love and wisdom that we have two abilities of life. From the one we get our discernment, and from the other volition. Our discernment is supplied entirely by an inflow of wisdom from God, while our volition is supplied entirely by an inflow of love from God. Our failures to be appropriately wise and appropriately loving do not take these abilities away from us. They only close them off; and as long as they do, while we may call our discernment "discernment" and our volition "volition," essentially they are not. So if these abilities really were taken away from us, everything human about us would be destroyed—our thinking and the speech that results from thought, and our purposing and the actions that result from purpose.

We can see from this that the divine nature within us dwells in these two abilities, in our ability to be wise and our ability to love. That is, it dwells in the fact that we are capable of being wise and loving. I have discovered from an abundance of experience that we have the ability to love even though we are not wise and do not love as we could. You will find this experience described in abundance elsewhere.[29]

31   It is because the divine essence itself is love and wisdom that everything in the universe involves what is good and what is true. Everything that flows from love is called good, and everything that flows from wisdom is called true. But more on this later [§§83–102].

32   It is because the divine essence itself is love and wisdom that the universe and everything in it, whether living or not, depends on warmth and light for its survival. Warmth in fact corresponds to love and light corresponds to wisdom, which also means that spiritual warmth is love and spiritual light is wisdom. But more on this as well later [§§83–84, 89–92].

All human feelings and thoughts arise from the divine love and wisdom that constitute the very essence that is God. The feelings arise from divine love and the thoughts from divine wisdom. Further, every single bit of our being is nothing but feeling and thought. These two are like the springs of everything that is alive in us. They are the source of all our life experiences of delight and enchantment,[30] the delight from the prompting of our love and the enchantment from our consequent thought.   33

Since we have been created to be recipients, then, and since we are recipients to the extent that we love God and are wise because of our love for God (that is, the extent to which we are moved by what comes from God and think as a result of that feeling), it therefore follows that the divine essence, the Creatress,[31] is divine love and wisdom.

Divine love is a property of divine wisdom, and divine wisdom is a property of divine love. On the divine reality and the divine manifestation being distinguishably one in the Divine-Human One, see §§14–16 above. Since the divine reality is divine love and the divine manifestation is divine wisdom, these latter are similarly distinguishably one.   34

We refer to them as "distinguishably one" because love and wisdom are two distinguishable things, and yet they are so united that love is a property of wisdom and wisdom a property of love. Love finds its reality in wisdom, and wisdom finds its manifestation in love. Further, since wisdom derives its manifestation from love (as noted in §15 *[14]* above), divine wisdom is reality as well. It follows from this that love and wisdom together are the divine reality, though when they are distinguished we call love the divine reality and wisdom the divine manifestation. This is the quality of the angelic concept of divine love and wisdom.

Because there is such a oneness of love and wisdom and of wisdom and love in the Divine-Human One, the divine essence is one. In fact, the divine essence is divine love because that love is a property of divine wisdom, and it is divine wisdom because that wisdom is a property of divine love. Because of this oneness, the divine life is a unity as well: life is the divine essence.   35

The reason divine love and wisdom are one is that the union is reciprocal, and a reciprocal union makes complete unity. But there will be more to say about reciprocal union later [§§115–116].

36   There is a union of love and wisdom in every divine work as well. This is why it endures, even to eternity. If there were more divine love than divine wisdom or more divine wisdom than divine love in any created work, nothing would endure in it except what was equal. Any excess would pass away.

37   As divine providence works for our reformation, regeneration, and salvation, it shares equally in divine love and divine wisdom. We cannot be reformed, regenerated, and saved by any excess of divine love over divine wisdom or by any excess of divine wisdom over divine love. Divine love wants to save everyone, but it can do so only by means of divine wisdom. All the laws that govern salvation are laws of divine wisdom, and love cannot transcend those laws because divine love and divine wisdom are one and act in unison.

38   In the Word, "justice" and "judgment" mean divine love and divine wisdom, "justice" meaning divine love and "judgment" meaning divine wisdom; so in the Word justice and judgment are ascribed to God. For example, we read in David,[32] "Justice and judgment are the foundation of your throne" (Psalms 79:15 *[89:14]*); and again, "Jehovah will bring out his justice like light and his judgment like noonday" (Psalms 37:6); in Hosea, "I will betroth myself to you forever in justice and judgment" (Hosea 2:19); in Jeremiah, "I will raise up a just branch for David who will rule as king and make judgment and justice in the land" (Jeremiah 23:5); in Isaiah, "He will sit on the throne of David and over his kingdom, to make it secure in judgment and in justice" (Isaiah 9:6 *[9:7]*); and again, "Let Jehovah be extolled, because he has filled the earth[33] with judgment and justice" (Isaiah 33:5); in David, "When I shall have learned the judgments of your justice . . . seven times a day I will praise you over the judgments of your justice" (Psalms 119:7, 164). "Life" and "light" in John mean the same: "In him was life, and the life was the light of humanity" (John 1:4). "Life" here means the Lord's divine love, and "light" his divine wisdom. "Life" and "spirit" mean the same in John as well: "Jesus said, 'The words that I speak to you are spirit and life'" (John 6:63).

39   Even though love and wisdom seem to be two separate things in us, essentially they are distinguishably one. This is because the quality of our love determines the quality of our wisdom and the quality of our wisdom the quality of our love. Any wisdom that is not united to our love seems like wisdom, but it is not; and any love that is not united to our wisdom seems like wisdom's love even though it is not. Each gets its essence and its life from the other in mutual fashion.

The reason the wisdom and love within us seem to be two separate things is that our ability to understand can be raised into heaven's light, while our ability to love cannot, except to the extent that we act according to our understanding. So any trace of apparent wisdom that is not united to our love for wisdom relapses into the love with which it is united. This may not be a love for wisdom, and may even be a love for insanity. We are perfectly capable of knowing, from our wisdom, that we ought to do one thing or another, and then of not doing it because we have no love for it. However, to the extent that we do the bidding of our wisdom, from love, we are images of God.

Divine love and wisdom is substance and is form.[34] The everyday concept **40**
of love and wisdom is that they are something floating around in, or breathed out by, thin air or ether.[35] Hardly anyone considers that in reality and in function they are substance and form.

Even people who do see that love and wisdom are substance and form sense them as something outside their subject, flowing from it; and they refer to what in their perceptions is outside the subject and flowing from it as substance and form even though they sense it as floating around. They do not realize that love and wisdom are the actual subject, and that what they sense as floating out from the subject is only the appearance of the inherent state of the subject.[36]

There are many reasons why this has not come to light before. One of them is that appearances are the first things the human mind draws on in forming its understanding, and the only way to dispel these appearances is through careful probing into cause. If a cause is deeply hidden, we cannot probe into it unless we keep our discernment in spiritual light for a protracted period of time; and we cannot hold it there for a long time because of the earthly light that keeps pulling us back.

Still, the truth is that love and wisdom are the real and functional substance and form that make up the very subject.

Since this truth is counter to appearance, though, it may seem **41**
unworthy of credence unless some evidence is supplied; and since the only way to supply evidence is with the kinds of thing we perceive with our physical senses, that is what I need to draw on.

We have five external senses, called touch, taste, smell, hearing, and sight. The subject[37] of touch is the skin that envelops us: the very substance and form of the skin make it feel what comes into contact with it. The sense of touch is not in the things that come into contact with it but in the substance and form of the skin. That is the subject, and the sense itself is simply the way it is affected by contact.

It is the same with taste. This sense is simply the way a substance and form, this time of the tongue, are affected. The tongue is the subject. It is the same with smell. We recognize that odors affect the nostrils and are in the nostrils, and that smell is the way impinging aromas affect them. It is the same with hearing. It seems as though hearing were in the place where the sound originates, but hearing is in the ear and is the way its substance and form are affected. It is only an appearance that hearing happens at a distance from the ear.

This is true of sight as well. When we see objects at a distance, it seems as though our sight were where they are. However, sight is in the eye, which is the subject; and sight is the way the eye is affected, too. Distance is simply what we infer about space on the basis of intervening objects or on the basis of reduced size and consequent loss of clarity of an object whose image is being presented within the eye according to its angle of incidence. We can see from this that sight does not go out from the eye to the object, but that an image of the object enters the eye and affects its substance and form. It is the same for both sight and hearing. Hearing does not go out of the ear to seize on the sound, but the sound enters the ear and affects it.

It stands to reason, then, that the affecting of substance and form that constitutes a sense is not something separate from the subject. It is simply the effecting of a change within the subject, with the subject remaining the subject throughout and thereafter. It then follows that sight, hearing, smell, taste, and touch are not things that go floating out from their organs. They are the organs themselves, in respect to their substance and form. Sensation happens when they are affected.

42 It is the same with love and wisdom, the only difference being that the substances and forms that are love and wisdom are not visible to our eyes as are the organs of our external senses. Still, no one can deny that those matters of love and wisdom that we call thoughts, perceptions, and feelings are substances and forms. They are not things that go floating out from nothing, remote from any functional and real substance and form that are their subjects. There are in fact countless substances and forms in the brain that serve as the homes of all the inner sensation that involves our discernment and volition.

What has just been said about our external senses points to the conclusion that all our feelings, perceptions, and thoughts in those substances and forms are not something they breathe out; they themselves are functional and substantial subjects. They do not emit anything, but simply undergo changes in response to the things that touch and affect them. There will be more later [§§210, 273] on these things that touch and affect them.

This brings us to the point where we can see that divine love and wisdom in and of themselves are substance and form. They are essential reality and manifestation, and unless they were as much reality and manifestation as they are substance and form, they would be only theoretical constructs that in and of themselves are nothing.[38]

Divine love and wisdom are substance and form in and of themselves, and are therefore wholly "itself" and unique.[39] I have just given evidence that divine love and wisdom is substance and form, and I have also said that the divine reality and its manifestation is reality and manifestation in and of itself. We cannot say that it is reality and manifestation derived from itself, because that would involve a beginning, a beginning from something else that had within it some intrinsic reality and manifestation; while true reality and its manifestation in and of itself exists from eternity. Then too, true reality and manifestation in and of itself is uncreated; and nothing that has been created can exist except from something uncreated. What is created is also finite; and what is finite can arise only from what is infinite.

Anyone who can pursue and grasp inherent reality and its manifestation at all thoughtfully will necessarily come to grasp the fact that it is wholly itself and unique. We call it wholly itself because it alone exists; and we call it unique because it is the source of everything else.

Further, since what is wholly itself and unique is substance and form, it follows that it is the unique substance and form, and wholly itself; and since that true substance and form is divine love and wisdom, it follows that it is the unique love, wholly itself, and the unique wisdom, wholly itself. It is therefore the unique essence, wholly itself, and the unique life, wholly itself, since love and wisdom is life.

All this shows how sensually people are thinking when they say that nature exists in its own right, how reliant they are on their physical senses and their darkness in matters of the spirit.[40] They are thinking from the eye and are unable to think from the understanding. Thinking from the eye closes understanding, but thinking from understanding opens the eye. They are unable to entertain any thought about inherent reality and manifestation, any thought that it is eternal, uncreated, and infinite. They can entertain no thought about life except as something volatile that vanishes into thin air, no other thought about love and wisdom, and no thought whatever about the fact that they are the source of everything in nature.

The only way to see that love and wisdom are the source of everything in nature is to look at nature on the basis of its functions in their sequence and pattern rather than on the basis of some of nature's forms, which register only on our eyes. The only source of nature's functions is life, and the only source of their sequence and pattern is love and wisdom. Forms, though, are vessels of functions. This means that if we look only at forms, no trace is visible of the life in nature, let alone of love and wisdom, and therefore of God.[41]

47 *Divine love and wisdom cannot fail to be and to be manifested in others that it has created.* The hallmark of love is not loving ourselves but loving others and being united to them through love. The hallmark of love is also being loved by others because this is how we are united. Truly, the essence of all love is to be found in union, in the life of love that we call joy, delight, pleasure, sweetness, blessedness, contentment, and happiness.

The essence of love is that what is ours should belong to someone else. Feeling the joy of someone else as joy within ourselves—that is loving. Feeling our joy in others, though, and not theirs in ourselves is not loving. That is loving ourselves, while the former is loving our neighbor. These two kinds of love are exact opposites. True, they both unite us; and it does not seem as though loving what belongs to us, or loving ourselves in the other, is divisive. Yet it is so divisive that to the extent that we love others in this way we later harbor hatred for them. Step by step our union with them dissolves, and the love becomes hatred of corresponding intensity.

48 Can anyone fail to see this who looks into the essential nature of love? What is loving ourselves alone, really, and not loving someone else who loves us in return? This is more fragmentation than union. Love's union depends on mutuality, and there is no mutuality within ourselves alone. If we think there is, it is because we are imagining some mutuality in others.

We can see from this that divine love cannot fail to be and to be manifested in others whom it loves and who love it. If this is characteristic of all love, it must be supremely characteristic, infinitely characteristic, of love itself.

49 In regard to God, loving and being loved in return are not possible in the case of others who have some share of infinity or anything of the

essence and life of intrinsic love or of Divinity. If there were within them any share of infinity or anything of the essence and life of intrinsic love—of Divinity, that is—it would not be *others* who would be loving God. He would be loving *himself.* What is infinite or divine is unique. If it were in others, it would still be itself; and it would be pure love for itself, of which there cannot be the slightest trace in God. This is absolutely opposite to the divine essence. For love to be mutual, then, it needs to be a love for others in whom there is nothing of intrinsic Divinity; and we will see below [§§55, 305] that it is a love for others who were created by Divinity.

For this to happen, though, there must be an infinite wisdom that is at one with infinite love. That is, there must be the divine love of divine wisdom and the divine wisdom of divine love discussed above (§§34–39).

On our grasping and knowing this mystery depends our grasping and knowing God's manifestation or creation of everything and God's maintenance or preservation of everything—that is, all the acts of God in the created universe that I will be talking about in the following pages. **50**

Please, though, do not muddle your concepts with time and space. To the extent that there is time and space in your concepts as you read what follows, you will not understand it, because Divinity is not in time and space. This will become clear in the sequel to the present book, specifically on eternity, infinity, and omnipresence.[42] **51**

Everything in the universe was created by the divine love and wisdom of the Divine-Human One. The universe, from beginning to end and from first to last, is so full of divine love and wisdom that you could call it divine love and wisdom in an image. This is clearly evidenced by the way everything in the universe answers to something in us. Every single thing that comes to light in the created universe has such an equivalence with every single thing in us that you could call us a kind of universe as well. There is a correspondence of our affective side and its consequent thought with everything in the animal kingdom, a correspondence of our volitional side and its consequent discernment with everything in the plant kingdom, and a correspondence of our outermost life[43] with everything in the mineral kingdom. **52**

This kind of correspondence is not apparent to anyone in our physical world, but it is apparent to observant people in the spiritual world. We find in this latter world all the things that occur in the three kingdoms of our physical world, and they reflect the feelings and thoughts of the people who are there—the feelings that come from their volition and the thoughts that come from their discernment—as well as the outermost aspects of their life. Both their feelings and their thoughts are visible around them looking much like the things we see in the created universe, though we see them in less perfect representations.

From this it is obvious to angels that the created universe is an image depicting the Divine-Human One and that it is his love and wisdom that are presented, in image, in the universe. It is not that the created universe is the Divine-Human One: rather, it comes from him; for nothing whatever in the universe is intrinsic substance and form or intrinsic life or intrinsic love and wisdom. We are not "intrinsic persons." It all comes from God, who is the intrinsic person, the intrinsic wisdom and love, and the intrinsic form and substance. Whatever has intrinsic existence is uncreated and infinite; while what comes from it, possessing nothing within itself that has intrinsic existence, is created and finite. This latter presents an image of the One from whom it derives its existence and manifestation.[44]

53 Created, finite things may be said to have reality and manifestation, substance and form, life, and even love and wisdom, but all of these are created and finite. The reason we can say they have these attributes is not that they possess any divinity but that they are in Divinity and there is Divinity in them. Anything that has been created is intrinsically without soul and dead, but it is given a soul and brought to life by the presence of Divinity in it, and by its dwelling in Divinity.

54 The divine nature is not different in one subject than it is in another. Rather, one created subject is different from another: there are no two alike, so each vessel is different. This is why the divine nature seems to differ in appearance. I will be talking later [§275] about its presence in opposites.

55 *Everything in the created universe is a vessel for the divine love and wisdom of the Divine-Human One.* We acknowledge that everything in the universe, great and small, has been created by God. That is why the universe and absolutely everything in it is called "the work of Jehovah's hands" in the Word.

People do say that the whole world was created out of nothing, and they like to think of "nothing" as absolutely nothing. However, nothing comes from "absolutely nothing" and nothing can.[45] This is an abiding truth. This means that the universe, being an image of God and therefore full of God, could be created by God only in God. God is reality itself, and everything that exists must come from that reality. To speak of creating something that exists from a "nothing" that does not exist is a plain contradiction of terms.

Still, what is created by God in God is not a continuation of him, since God is intrinsic reality and there is no trace of intrinsic reality in anything created. If there were any intrinsic reality in a created being, it would be a continuation of God, and any continuation of God is God.[46]

The angelic concept involved is that anything created by God in God is like something within ourselves that we have put forth from our life, but the life is then withdrawn from it. It then agrees with our life, but still, it is not our life. In support of this, angels cite many things that happen in their heaven, where they say that they are in God and that God is in them, and yet that they have in their being no trace of God that is actually God. This may serve simply as information; more of the angels' evidence will be offered later [§116].

Everything created from this source is in its own nature suited to be receptive of God not by continuity but by contact. Union comes through contact, not through continuity. What is created is suitable for this contact because it has been created by God in God. Because it has been created in this way, it is an analog; and because of the union, it is like an image of God in a mirror. **56**

This is why angels are not angels in their own right but are angels by virtue of their union with the Divine-Human One; and their union depends on their acceptance of what is divinely good and what is divinely true. What is divinely good and what is divinely true are God, and seem to emanate from him even though they are within him. Their acceptance depends on the way angels apply the laws of his design, which are divine truths, to themselves, using their freedom to think and intend according to their reason,[47] a freedom given them by God as their own possession. This is what enables them to accept what is divinely good and divinely true in apparent autonomy; and this in turn is what makes possible the mutual element in their love, for as already noted [§48], love is not real unless it is mutual. It is the same with us here on earth. **57**

All this enables us finally to see that everything in the created universe is a vessel for the divine love and wisdom of the Divine-Human One.

There are many things that need to be said about levels of life and levels of vessels of life before I can give an intelligible explanation of the fact that other things in the universe, things that are not like angels and people, are also vessels for the divine love and wisdom of the **58**

Divine-Human One—for example, things below us in the animal kingdom, things below them in the plant kingdom, and things below them in the mineral kingdom. Union with them depends on their functions. All useful functions have their only source in a related union with God that is, however, increasingly dissimilar depending on its level. As we come down step by step, this union takes on a nature in which there is no element of freedom involved because there is no element of reason. There is therefore no appearance of life involved; but still these are vessels. Because they are vessels, they are also characterized by reaction. It is actually by virtue of their reactions that they are vessels.

I will discuss union with functions that are not useful after I have explained the origin of evil [§§264–270].

59 We can conclude from this that Divinity is present in absolutely everything in the created universe and that the created universe is therefore the work of Jehovah's hands, as it says in the Word. That is, it is a work of divine love and wisdom, for this is what is meant by "Jehovah's hands." Further, even though Divinity is present in all things great and small in the created universe, there is no trace of intrinsic divinity in their own being. While the created universe is not God, it is from God; and since it is from God, his image is in it like the image of a person in a mirror. We do indeed see a person there, but there is still nothing of the person in the mirror.

60 I once heard a number of people around me in the spiritual world talking and saying that they did in fact want to recognize that there was something divine in absolutely everything in the universe because they saw God's wonders there, and the deeper they looked, the more wonderful were the things they saw. However, when they heard someone say that there actually *was* something divine in absolutely everything in the created universe, they resented it. This was a sign that they claimed the belief but did not actually believe it.

They were therefore asked whether they could not see this simply in the marvelous ability in every seed of generating its growth in sequence all the way to new seeds. In every seed, then, there is an image of something infinite and eternal, an inherent effort to multiply and bear fruit without limit, to eternity.

Or they might see this in even the tiniest animals, realizing that they contain sensory organs, brains, hearts, lungs, and the like, along with arteries, veins, nerve fibers, muscles, and the activities that arise from them, to say nothing of incredible features of their basic nature that have had whole books written about them.[48]

All these wonders come from God, though the forms that clothe them are of earthly matter. These forms give rise to plant life and, in due sequence, to human life. This is why humanity is said to have been created out of the ground, to be the dust of the earth with the breath of life[49] breathed in (Genesis 2:7). We can see from this that the divine nature is not our possession but is joined to us.

All the things that have been created reflect the human in some respect. There is evidence for this in every detail of the animal kingdom, in every detail of the plant kingdom, and in every detail of the mineral kingdom.   **61**

We can see ourselves reflected in every detail of the animal kingdom from the fact that all kinds of animal have in common with us members for locomotion, sensory organs, and the inner organs that support these activities. They also have their impulses and desires like our own physical ones. They have the innate knowledge proper to their desires, with an apparently spiritual element visible in some of them, more or less obvious to the eye in the beasts of the earth, the fowl of the heavens, bees, silkworms, ants, and the like.[50] This is why merely earthly-minded people regard the living creatures of this kingdom as much like themselves, lacking only speech.

We can see ourselves reflected in every detail of the plant kingdom in the way plants grow from seeds and go through their successive stages of life. They have something like marriages with births that follow. Their vegetative "soul" is the function to which they give form. There are many other ways in which they reflect us, which some writers have described.[51]

We can see ourselves reflected in every detail of the mineral kingdom simply in its effort to produce the forms that reflect us—all the details of the plant kingdom, as I have just noted—and to perform its proper functions in this way. The moment a seed falls into earth's lap, she nurtures it and from all around offers it resources from herself for its sprouting and emerging in a form representative of humanity. We can see this effort in solid mineral materials if we look at deep-sea corals[52] or at flowers in mines, where they spring from minerals and metals. This effort toward becoming plant life and thereby performing a useful function is the outermost element of Divinity in created things.

Just as there is an energy in earth's minerals toward plant growth, there is an energy in plants toward movement. This is why there are various kinds of insect that are responsive to the fragrances they give off. We   **62** will see later [§§157–158] that this is not caused by the warmth of our world's sun but comes through it, from life, according to the recipient vessels.

63   What has been cited thus far tells us that there is some reference to the human form in everything in the created universe, but it enables us to see this fact only obscurely. In the spiritual world, though, people see this clearly. Everything in the three kingdoms exists there as well, surrounding each angel. Angels see these things around themselves and also are aware that they are pictures of their own selves. In fact, when the very heart of their understanding is opened, they recognize themselves and see their own image in their surroundings, almost like a reflection in a mirror.

64   We can be quite certain, on the basis of all this and of many other things consistent with it (which it would take too long to include) that God is a person and that the created universe is an image of him. The overall totality offers a reflection of him, just as specific aspects offer reflections of us.

65   *The useful functions of everything created tend upward, step by step, from the lowest to us, and through us to God the Creator, their source.* As already stated [§52], these "lowest things" are all the elements of the mineral kingdom—various forms of matter, some stony substances, some saline, some oily, some mineral, some metallic, with the constant addition of a humus composed of plant and animal matter reduced to minute particles. Here lie hidden the goal and the beginning of all the functions that arise from life. The goal of all useful functions is the effort to produce [more] functions; the beginning of all functions is an active force that comes out of that effort. These are characteristics of the mineral kingdom.

The intermediate things are all the elements of the plant kingdom—grasses and herbs of all kinds, plants and shrubs of all kinds, and trees of all kinds. Their functions are in support of everything in the animal kingdom, whether flawed or flawless. They provide food, pleasure, and life. They nourish [animal] bodies with their substance, they delight them with their taste and fragrance and beauty, and they enliven their desires. This effort is inherent in them from their life.

The primary things are all the members of the animal kingdom. The lowest of these are called worms and insects, the intermediate ones birds and animals, and the highest humans; for there are lowest, intermediate, and highest things in each kingdom. The lowest are for the service of the intermediate and the intermediate for the service of the highest. So the useful functions of all created things tend upwards in a sequence from the lowest to the human, which is primary in the divine design.

There are three ascending levels in the physical world and three ascending levels in the spiritual world. All animals are life-receivers, the more perfect ones receiving the life of the three levels of the physical world, the less perfect receiving the life of two levels of that world, and the least perfect the life of one level. Only we humans are receptive of the life not only of the three levels of the physical world but also of the three levels of the spiritual world. This is why we, unlike animals, can be lifted up above the physical world. We can think analytically and rationally about civil and moral issues within the material world and also about spiritual and heavenly issues that transcend the material world. We can even be lifted up into wisdom to the point that we see God. I will discuss in their proper place, though, the six levels by which the functions of all created things rise up all the way to God, their Creator.[53]

66

This brief summary enables us to see that there is a ladder of all created things to that First who alone is life and that the functions of all things are the actual vessels of life, and so too, therefore, are the forms of those functions.

I need also to explain briefly how we climb—or rather, are lifted—from the last level to the first. We are born on the lowest level of the physical world, and are lifted to the second level by means of factual knowledge. Then as we develop our discernment through this knowledge, we are lifted to the third level and become rational. The three ascending levels in the spiritual world are within this, resting on the three physical levels, and do not become visible until we leave our earthly bodies. When we do, the first spiritual level is opened for us, then the second, and finally the third. However, this last happens only for people who become angels of the third heaven.[54] These are the ones who see God.

67

Angels of the second heaven and of the lowest heaven are people in whom the second and the lowest level can be opened. The opening of each spiritual level within us depends on our acceptance of divine love and wisdom from the Lord. People who accept some of this love and wisdom reach the first or lowest spiritual level; people who accept more reach the second or intermediate spiritual level; and people who accept a great deal reach the third or highest level. However, people who do not accept any divine love and wisdom stay on the physical levels, deriving from the spiritual levels only enough to allow them to think and therefore to talk and to intend and therefore to act—but not intelligently.

68   There is something else that we need to know about this lifting of the inner levels of our minds. Reaction is characteristic of everything created by God. Only life is action, while reaction is prompted by the action of life. This reaction seems to be proper to the created being because it becomes perceptible when that being is stirred; so when it happens in us, it seems to be our own. The reason is that even though we are only life-receivers, we have no sense that our life is anything but our own.

This is why we react against God as a result of our inherited evil. However, to the extent that we believe that all our life comes from God and that everything good about it comes from an act of God and everything bad about it from our own reaction, our reaction becomes a property of the action and we are then acting with God with apparent autonomy. The equilibrium of all things comes from action and immediate reaction, and everything must necessarily be in an equilibrium.

I mention these things to prevent any belief that we ourselves climb up to God on our own power. It is done by the Lord.

69   *Divinity fills all space in the universe nonspatially.*[55] Nature has two basic properties: space and time. In this physical world, we use them to form the concepts of our thinking and therefore the way we understand things. If we stay engaged with them and do not raise our minds above them, there is no way we can grasp anything spiritual and divine. We entangle such matters in concepts drawn from space and time, and to the extent that we do, the light of our discernment becomes merely earthly. When we use this light to think logically about spiritual and divine matters, it is like using the dark of night to figure out things that can be seen only in the light of day. Materialism comes from this kind of thinking.

However, when we know how to raise our minds above images of thought derived from space and time, we pass from darkness into light and taste things spiritual and divine. Eventually we see what is inherent in them and what they entail; and then we dispel the darkness of earthly lighting with that [new] light and dismiss its illusions from the center to the sides.

People who possess discernment can think on a higher level than these properties of nature—can think realistically, that is—and see with assurance that Divinity, being omnipresent, is not within space. They can also see with assurance the other things already mentioned. If they deny divine omnipresence, though, and attribute everything to nature, then they do not want to be lifted up even though they could be.

These two properties of nature—the space and time just men- 70
tioned—are left behind by everyone who dies and becomes an angel. At
that time, people come into a spiritual light in which the objects of their
thought are truths, and the objects of their vision—even though those
objects look like things in this physical world—are actually responsive to
their thoughts.

The objects of their thought, which as just noted are truths, are not
at all dependent on space and time. While the objects of their sight do
seem to be in space and in time, angels do not use them as the basis for
their thinking. The reason is that in the spiritual world intervals of space
and time are not fixed the way they are in our physical world, but are
changeable in response to their states of life. This means that states of life
take the place of space and time in the concepts of their thinking. Issues
related to states of love are in place of spatial intervals and issues related
to states of wisdom are in place of temporal intervals. This is why spiritual thought and the consequent spiritual speech are so different from
earthly thought and its speech that they have nothing in common. They
are alike only as to the deeper aspects of their subject matter, which are
entirely spiritual. I need to say more about this difference later [§§163,
295, and 306].

Since angels' thoughts do not depend at all on space and time, then,
but on states of life, we can see that angels do not understand when
someone says that Divinity fills space. They do not know what spatial intervals are. They understand perfectly, though, when someone says that
Divinity fills everything, with no reference to any image of space.

The following example should illustrate how merely earthly people 71
think in spatial terms about matters spiritual and divine, while spiritual
people do so without reference to space. When merely earthly people
think, they use images they have garnered from things they have seen.
There is some shape to all of these involving length, breadth, and height,
some angular or curved form bounded by these dimensions. These dimensions are clearly present in the mental images people have of visible,
earthly things; and they are present as well in their mental images of
things they do not see, such as civic and moral matters. They do not actually see these dimensions, but they are still present implicitly.[56]

It is different for spiritual people, and especially for heaven's angels.
Their thinking has nothing to do with form and shape involving spatial
length, breadth, and height. It has to do with the state of the matter as
it follows from a state of life. This means that in place of length they

consider how good something is as a result of the quality of the life from which it stems; in place of breadth they consider how true something is because of the truth of the life from which it stems; and in place of height they consider the level of these qualities. They are thinking on the basis of correspondence, then, which is the mutual relationship between spiritual and earthly things. It is because of this correspondence that "length" in the Word means how good something is, "breadth" means how true it is, and "height" means the level of these qualities.

We can see from this that the only way heaven's angels can think about divine omnipresence is that Divinity fills everything, but nonspatially. Whatever angels think is true, because the light that illumines their understanding is divine wisdom.

72   This is a foundational thought about God, since without it, while readers may understand what I am going to say about the creation of the universe by the Divine-Human One and about God's providence, omnipotence, omnipresence, and omniscience, they still will not retain it. This is because even when merely earthly people do understand these things, they still slip back into the love of their life that is their basic volition. This dissipates their previous thought and plunges their thinking into space, where they find the light that they call "rational." They do not realize that to the extent that they deny what they have understood, they become irrational.

You may confirm the truth of this by looking at the concept of the truth that God is human. Please read carefully what I wrote above in §§11–13 and thereafter, and you will understand that it is true. Then bring your thoughts back into the earthly lighting that involves space. Will these things not seem paradoxical to you? And if you bring your thoughts all the way back, you will deny them.

This is why I said that Divinity fills all space in the universe and did not say that the Divine-Human One does. If I were to say this, merely earthly light would not accept it, though it can accept the notion that Divinity fills all space because this agrees with the standard language of theologians. They say that God is omnipresent, and hears and knows everything. There is more on this subject in §§7–10 above.

73   *Divinity is in all time, nontemporally.*[57] Just as Divinity is in all space nonspatially, it is in all time nontemporally. Nothing proper to the physical world can be attributed to Divinity, and space and time are proper to the

physical world. Space in the physical world can be measured, and so can time. Time is measured in days, weeks, months, years, and centuries; days are measured in hours; weeks and months in days; years in the four seasons; and centuries in years. The physical world gets these measurements from the apparent circuit and rotation of earth's sun.[58]

It is different in the spiritual world. Life does seem to go on in time there in much the same way. People live with each other the way we do on earth, which cannot happen without some appearance of time. However, time there is not divided into segments the way it is in our world because their sun is always in its east. It never moves. It is actually the Lord's divine love that angels see as their sun. This means that they do not have days, weeks, months, years, or centuries, but states of life instead.[59] It provides them with divisions that cannot be called divisions into time segments, only divisions of state. This is why angels do not know what time is, and why they think of state when time is mentioned. Further, when it is state that determines time, time is only an appearance. A pleasant state makes time seem brief, and an unpleasant one makes it seem long. We can therefore see that time in the spiritual world is simply an attribute of state.

This is why hours, days, weeks, months, and years in the Word mean states and their sequences, viewed either serially or comprehensively. When the church is described in terms of time, its morning is its initial state, its noon is its fulfillment, its evening is its decline, and its night is its end. The same holds true for the four seasons of the year: spring, summer, fall, and winter.

We can see from this that time is the equivalent of thought from feeling. This is in fact the source of our basic quality as people. **74**

There are many examples of the fact that as people move through space in the spiritual world, distances are equivalent to progress through time. Paths there are actually or correspondingly lengthened, in response to eagerness, which is a matter of thought from affection. This is also why we speak of "stretches of time." In other situations, though, such as in dreams, where thought is not coordinated with our actual feelings, time is not in evidence.

Now, since the segments of time that are proper to nature in its world are nothing but states in the spiritual world, and since these states come to view sequentially because angels and spirits are finite, it stands to reason that they are not sequential in God, because God is infinite. The infinite things in God are all one, in keeping with what has been **75** explained above in §§17–22. It then follows from this that Divinity is present in all time, nontemporally.

76　　If people do not know about God beyond time, if they cannot think about such a God with some insight, then they are totally incapable of seeing eternity as anything but an eternity of time. They cannot help getting caught in crazy thoughts about God from eternity, thinking about some beginning; and a beginning has to do with nothing but time. This leads to the fantasy that God emerged from himself, and promptly degenerates into nature originating from itself.[60] The only way out of this notion is through a spiritual or angelic concept of eternity, one that does not involve time. Once time is excluded, eternity and Divinity are one and the same; Divinity is Divinity in and of itself, and not from itself. Angels say that while they can conceive of God from eternity, there is no way they can conceive of nature from eternity, let alone nature from itself; by no means whatever can they conceive of nature that is intrinsically nature. This is because anything that has intrinsic existence is the reality itself that is the source of everything else. That intrinsic reality is the "life itself" that is the divine love that belongs to divine wisdom and the divine wisdom that belongs to divine love.

This, for angels, is eternity, which transcends time the way the Uncreated transcends the creature or the Infinite one transcends the finite. There is no ratio whatever between them.

77　　*Divinity is the same in the largest and smallest things.* This follows from the two preceding sections, from Divinity being nonspatially present in all space and nontemporally present in all time. There are larger and larger and smaller and smaller spaces; and since as already noted [§74] space and time are indistinguishable, the same holds true for segments of time. The reason Divinity is the same in all of them is that Divinity is not changeable or inconsistent like everything that involves space and time, or nature. It is constant and unchanging, so it is everywhere and always the same.

78　　It does seem as though Divinity were not the same in one person as in another, as though it were different in a wise person than in a simple one, for example, or different in an elderly one than in a child. This is just the deceptive way things seem, though. The person may be different, but Divinity within is not. The person is a receiver, and the receiver or vessel will differ. A wise person is a more adequate receiver of divine love and wisdom than a simple one, and therefore a fuller receiver. An elderly and wise individual is more receptive than a child or youth. Still, Divinity is the same in the one as in the other.

Outward appearance also gives rise to the illusion that Divinity is different in heaven's angels than it is in people on earth because heaven's angels enjoy indescribable wisdom and we do not. However, this apparent difference is in the subjects and depends on their openness to Divinity. It is not in the Lord.

We may also use heaven and an individual angel to illustrate the fact that Divinity is the same in the largest and smallest things. Divinity in the whole heaven and Divinity in an individual angel is the same. This is why all heaven can be seen as a single angel. [79]

The same holds true for the church and for the individual member of it. The largest entity in which Divinity is present is all of heaven and the whole church together; the smallest is an individual angel or an individual member of the church. On occasion I have seen a whole heavenly community as a single angelic person, and I have been told that this may look like an immense, gigantic individual or like a little, childlike one. This is because Divinity is the same in the largest and smallest things.

Divinity is also the same in the largest and smallest of inanimate created things. It is actually present in every benefit of the function that they serve. The reason they are not alive is that they are forms of functions rather than forms of life, and the form will vary depending on the benefit of the function. I will be explaining how Divinity is present in them later,[61] when we get to the subject of creation. [80]

Take away space and absolutely rule out vacuum, and then think about divine love and wisdom as ultimate essence once space has been taken away and vacuum has been ruled out. Then think in terms of space, and you will see that Divinity is the same in the largest and the smallest instances of space. Once you remove space from essence, there is no "large" or "small." It is all the same. [81]

I need to say something about vacuum at this point. I once heard some angels talking with Newton[62] about vacuum, saying that they could not stand the notion of vacuum. This was because in their world, which is a spiritual one, within or above the space and time of our earthly world, they were still feeling, thinking, being moved, loving, intending, and breathing, and still talking and acting, which could not possibly happen in a vacuum that was "nothing" because nothing is nothing, and we cannot attribute anything to nothing. [82]

Newton said he knew that Divinity, the One who is, fills everything, and that he was aghast at the notion of a vacuum as nothing because this was a totally destructive notion.[63] He urged the angels who were discussing vacuum with him to beware the notion of nothing, calling it a fantasy because there is no mental activity in nothing.

ANGELIC WISDOM
ABOUT
DIVINE LOVE

PART 2

IN the spiritual world, divine love and wisdom look like a sun. There are 83 two worlds, one spiritual and one physical; and the spiritual world does not derive anything from the physical one, nor does the physical one derive anything from the spiritual one. They are completely distinct from each other, communicating only by means of correspondence, whose nature has been amply explained elsewhere.[64] The following example may be enlightening. Warmth in the physical world is the equivalent of the good that thoughtfulness does in the spiritual world, and light in the physical world is the equivalent of the truth that faith perceives in the spiritual world. No one can fail to see that warmth and the goodness of being thoughtful, and light and the truth of faith, are completely distinct from each other.

At first glance, they seem as distinct as two quite different things. That is what comes to the fore when we start thinking about what the goodness of being thoughtful has in common with warmth and what the truth of faith has in common with light. Yet spiritual warmth is that very "goodness," and spiritual light is that very "truth."

In spite of the fact that they are so distinct from each other, though, they still make a single whole by means of their correspondence. They are so united that when we read about warmth and light in the Word, the spirits and angels who are with us see thoughtfulness in the place of warmth and faith in the place of light.

I include this example to make it clear that the two worlds, the spiritual one and the physical one, are so distinct from each other that they have nothing in common, and that still they have been created in such a way that they communicate with each other and are actually united through their correspondences.

84 Because these two worlds are so distinct from each other, it is quite obvious that the spiritual world is under a different sun than is the physical world. There is just as much warmth and light in the spiritual world as there is in the physical world, but the warmth there is spiritual and so is the light. Spiritual warmth is the good that thoughtfulness does and spiritual light is the truth that faith perceives.

Now, since the only possible source of warmth and light is a sun, it stands to reason that there is a different sun in the spiritual world than there is in the physical world. It also stands to reason that because of the essential nature of the spiritual world's sun, spiritual warmth and light can come forth from it, while because of the essential nature of the physical world's sun, physical warmth [and light] can come forth from it. The only possible source of anything spiritual—that is, anything that has to do with what is good and true—is divine love and wisdom. Everything good is a result of love and everything true is a result of wisdom. Any wise individual can see that this is their only possible source.

85 People have not realized before that there is another sun besides the sun of our physical world. This is because our spiritual nature has become so deeply involved in our physical nature that people do not know what the word "spiritual" means. So they do not realize that there is a spiritual world other than and different from this physical one, a world where angels and spirits live.

Because that spiritual world has become so completely hidden from people in this physical world, the Lord has graciously opened the sight of my spirit so that I can see things in that world just the way I see things in this physical world, and then provide descriptions of that spiritual world.[65] This I have done in the book *Heaven and Hell,* which has a chapter on the sun of the spiritual world.[66] I have in fact seen it, and it seemed about the same size as the sun of this physical world. It had a similar fiery look, but was more reddish. I was given to understand that the whole angelic heaven lies beneath this sun and that angels of the third heaven see it constantly, angels of the second heaven often, and angels of the first or most remote heaven occasionally.

It will be made clear in what follows that all their warmth and all their light—everything people see in that world—comes from that sun.

That sun is not the Lord himself, though it is from the Lord. What 86
looks like the sun in the spiritual world is the emanating divine love and
wisdom. Since love and wisdom are one in the Lord (see part 1), we say
that this sun is divine love. Divine wisdom is actually an attribute of divine love, so it too is love.

The reason that sun looks like fire to angels' eyes is that love and fire 87
are interactive. Angels cannot see love with their eyes, but instead of love
they see what answers to it. They have inner and outer natures just as we
do. It is their inner self that thinks and is wise, that intends and loves,
and their outer self that feels, sees, speaks, and acts. All these outer functions of theirs are responsive to the inner ones, but the responsiveness is
spiritual and not earthly.

To spiritual beings, divine love feels like fire. This is why fire means
love when it is mentioned in the Word. That is what "sacred fire" used
to mean in the Israelite church, and that is why we often ask in our
prayers to God that heavenly fire (meaning divine love) should kindle
our hearts.

Since there is the kind of distinction described in §83 between what 88
is spiritual and what is physical, not a trace of anything from the sun of
the physical world can cross over into the spiritual world—that is, not a
trace of its light and warmth or of any object on earth. The light of the
physical world is darkness there, and its warmth is death there. Still, our
world's warmth can be brought to life by an inflow of heaven's warmth,
and our world's light can be brightened by an inflow of heaven's light.
This inflow happens by means of correspondences, and cannot happen
as a result of continuity.

Warmth and light emanates[67] *from the sun that arises from divine love* 89
and wisdom. In the spiritual world where angels and spirits live, there is
just as much warmth and light as there is in the physical world where
we live. The warmth feels just like warmth and the light looks just like
light, as well. Still, the warmth and light of the spiritual world and the
warmth and light of the physical world are so different that they have
nothing in common, as I have already mentioned [§83]. They are as
different as life and death. The warmth of the spiritual world is essentially alive, and so is the light; while the warmth of the physical world
is essentially dead, and so is the light. The warmth and the light of the
spiritual world come from a sun that is nothing but love, while the
warmth and light of the physical world come from a sun that is nothing but fire. Love is alive, and divine love is life itself. Fire is dead, and

solar fire is death itself. We may call it that because it has absolutely no life in it.

90 Since angels are spiritual beings, they cannot live in any warmth or any light that is not spiritual. We, on the other hand, cannot live in any warmth or any light that is not physical. This is because what is spiritual suits what is spiritual, and what is physical suits what is physical. If angels were to depend on physical warmth and light to even the least extent, they would be destroyed. It is absolutely wrong for their life.

Each of us is a spirit, as far as the inner levels of our minds are concerned. When we die, we leave this world of nature completely behind. We give up everything it has to offer and enter a world that contains nothing proper to the world of nature. In that world we live so completely distanced from nature that there is no communication along a continuum, that is, nothing like degrees of purity or coarseness. It is a case of before and after, with no communication except by correspondences.

It stands to reason, then, that spiritual warmth is not a purer form of physical warmth, that spiritual light is not a purer form of physical light, but that they are completely different in essence. Spiritual warmth and light derive their essence from a sun that is nothing but love, a sun that is life itself, while physical warmth and light derive their essence from a sun that is nothing but fire, containing no life whatever, as I have already stated [§89].

91 Given this kind of difference between the warmth and light of the two worlds, it is obvious why people who live in one of the worlds cannot see people who are living in the other. Our eyes, which see in physical light, are made of substances of their own world, and angels' are made of substances of their world. In other words, in each case they are designed for adequate sensitivity to their own light.

We can see from this what ignorance underlies the thinking of people who exclude from their faith any notion that angels and spirits are people, simply because they do not see them with their own eyes.

92 It has not been known before that angels and spirits are in a completely different light and warmth than we are. It has not even been known that there was a different light and warmth. Human thought has not penetrated beyond the deeper or purer aspects of nature. As a result, many people have located the dwellings of angels and spirits in the ether or even in the stars—within nature, that is, and not above or beyond it. In fact, though, angels and spirits are wholly above or beyond nature. They are in their own world, one that is under a different sun. Further,

since spatial intervals are only apparent in that world, as I have explained
earlier [§7], we cannot say that they are in the ether or in the stars. They
are right with us, united to our own spirits in feeling and thought. Each
of us is a spirit. That is the source of our thinking and intending. This
means that the spiritual world is right where we are, not distanced from
us in the least. In short, as far as the deeper levels of our minds are concerned we are all in that world, surrounded by angels and spirits there.
We think because of the light of that world and love because of its
warmth.

That sun is not God. Rather, it is an emanation from the divine love and   **93**
wisdom of the Divine-Human One. The same is true of warmth and light
from that sun. "The sun that angels see" (the sun that gives them warmth
and light) does not mean the Lord himself. It means that first emanation
from him that is the highest form of spiritual warmth. The highest form
of spiritual warmth is spiritual fire, which is divine love and wisdom in
its first correspondential form. This is why that sun looks fiery and also is
fiery for angels, though it is not for us. What we experience as fire is not
spiritual but physical, and the difference between these two is like the
difference between life and death. The spiritual sun, then, brings spiritual people to life with its warmth and maintains spiritual things, while
the physical sun does the same for physical people and things. It does not
do this with its own power, though, but by an inflow of spiritual warmth
that provides it with effective resources.

    The spiritual fire where light dwells in its origin becomes a spiritual   **94**
warmth and light that decrease as they emanate, with the decrease occurring by levels that will be discussed later.[68] The ancients pictured this as
brightly gleaming circles of reddish fire around the head of God, a form
of representation that is still common today when God is portrayed as
human in paintings.

    It is obvious from actual experience that love generates warmth and   **95**
wisdom generates light. When we feel love, we become warmer, and
when we think from wisdom, it is like seeing things in the light. We can
see from this that the first thing that emanates from love is warmth and
that the first thing that emanates from wisdom is light.

    We can also see that these are correspondences, since the warmth
does not occur within the love itself but as a result of it, in our volition
and therefore in our bodies. The light does not occur within the wisdom,
but in the thinking of our discernment and therefore in our speaking.
That is, love and wisdom are the essence and life of warmth and light;

and warmth and light are emanations from love and wisdom. Because they are emanations from them, they are also responsive to them.

96   If you observe carefully the thoughts of your own mind, you can recognize that there is a spiritual light completely distinct from physical light. When a mind is thinking, it sees its objects in light, and people who think spiritually see truths as readily at midnight as in daytime. This is why we attribute light to our discernment and talk about "seeing." One person may hear what someone else says and say, "I see that this is true," meaning "I understand." Since this understanding is spiritual, it cannot see by physical light. Physical light does not last, but departs with the sun. We can see from this that our discernment enjoys a light other than that of our eyes, and that this light comes from a different source.

97   Take care not to think that the spiritual world's sun is actually God. The real God is a person. The first emanation from his love and wisdom is something fiery and spiritual that looks like a sun to angels. When the Lord makes himself visible to angels in person, then, he does so in human form, sometimes within the sun, sometimes outside it.

98   It is because of this correspondence that in the Word the Lord is called not only the sun but also fire[69] and light.[70] "The sun" refers to him as divine love and wisdom together; "the fire" refers to him as divine love, and "the light" refers to him as divine wisdom.

99   *The spiritual warmth and light that result from the emanation from the Lord as the sun form a single whole just as his divine love and wisdom do.* Part 1 explains how divine love and wisdom form a single whole in the Lord. Warmth and light form a similar whole because they are emanations, and emanations constitute a whole by reason of their correspondence. The warmth answers to love, and the light to wisdom.

It therefore follows that since divine love is the divine reality and divine wisdom is the divine manifestation (see §§14–16 above), spiritual warmth is Divinity emanating from the divine reality and spiritual light is Divinity emanating from the divine manifestation. This means that just as divine love is a property of divine wisdom and divine wisdom is a property of divine love because of this union (see §§34–39 above), spiritual warmth is a property of spiritual light and spiritual light is a property of spiritual warmth. As a result of this kind of oneness, it follows that warmth and light are a single whole as they emanate from the Lord as the sun.

We will see later, though [§125], that they are not accepted as a single whole by angels or by us.

The warmth and light that emanate from the Lord as the sun are $\quad$ **100**
what we call "spiritual"; and they are referred to as spiritual in the singular because they are a single whole. In the following pages, therefore,
when it says "spiritual" it will mean both as a single whole. It is because
of this spiritual [energy] that the whole other world is called "spiritual."
Everything in that world has its source in that spiritual [energy] and
takes its name from it as well.

The reason the warmth and light are called "spiritual" is that God is
called "the Spirit," and God as the Spirit is that emanation. As to his very
essence, God is called Jehovah; but he enlightens and gives life to
heaven's angels and to us of the church through that emanation. This is
why it is said that giving life and bringing about enlightenment are acts
performed by the spirit of Jehovah.[71]

The oneness of [spiritual] warmth and light (that is, of the spiritual $\quad$ **101**
[energy] that emanates from the Lord as the sun) can be illustrated by the
warmth and light that emanate from the sun of our physical world.
These "two" are also a single whole as they radiate from the sun. The reason they are not a single whole on earth is to be found in the earth itself,
not in the sun. The earth rotates daily on its axis and follows its annual
ecliptic orbit. This is why its warmth and light do not seem to be a single
whole, why there is more warmth than light in midsummer and more
light than warmth in midwinter. The same thing happens in the spiritual
world. While the earth there does not rotate or follow an orbit, angels do
turn more and less toward the Lord. The ones who turn more toward
him accept more of the warmth and less of the light; while the ones who
turn less toward the Lord accept more of the light and less of the
warmth. This is why the heavens, which are made up of angels, are
marked off into two kingdoms, one called "heavenly" and the other
called "spiritual." Heavenly angels accept more of the warmth and spiritual angels accept more of the light.

The regions where angels live also look different depending on their
acceptance of the warmth and light. The correspondence is exact, provided we think of angels' change of state instead of earthly motion.

We will see later [§124] that in their own right, all the spiritual phe- $\quad$ **102**
nomena that stem from the warmth and light of their sun constitute a
single whole in the same way, though they do not do so if we regard them
as coming from the feelings that angels have. When the warmth and light
are a single whole in the heavens, it is like springtime for angels. When
they are not a single whole, it is like either summer or winter—not like
winter in cold latitudes but like winter in warm latitudes. The essence of

angelic nature is a balanced acceptance of love and wisdom, so angels are angels of heaven depending on the oneness of their love and wisdom. The same holds true for us of the church, if our love and wisdom, or charity and faith, are fully united.

103 *The sun of the spiritual world is seen at a middle elevation, as far from angels as our physical world's sun is from us.* Many people bring with them from our world an image of God as high overhead and of the Lord as being in heaven among its angels. The reason they bring an image of God as high overhead is that God is called "most high" in the Word, and it says that he lives "on high."[72] This is why we lift up our eyes and our hands when we pray and worship, unaware that "highest" means "inmost."

The reason people bring along an image of the Lord as being in heaven among its angels is that they think of him only as being like any other individual, or like an angel. They do not realize that the Lord is the real and only God, the one who rules the universe. If he were living in heaven among the angels, he could not keep the universe under his sight and hold it in his care and keeping. If he were not shining like the sun on the people in the spiritual world, angels could not have any light. Angels, that is, are spiritual beings, so only spiritual light is suited to their essence. When I discuss levels later [§182], we will see that there is a light in the heavens that is far, far greater than our light on earth.

104 As for the sun that is the source of angels' warmth and light, they see it at about a forty-five degree angle above the lands where they live, at a middle elevation. It also seems to be about as far from angels as this world's sun is from us.

They see the sun at that height and distance constantly; it does not move. This is why angels do not have stretches of time marked off into days and years or any daily progression from morning through noon to evening and on into night. They do not have a yearly sequence from spring through summer to autumn and on into winter, either.[73] Instead, they have a constant daylight and constant springtime; which means that instead of "times" they have states, as already noted [§§70, 73].

105 The following are the primary reasons why the sun of the spiritual world is seen at a middle elevation. First, this means that the warmth and light that emanate from that sun are at their median level—they are of equal proportions, therefore, and appropriately moderate. That is, if the sun appeared above that middle elevation, angels would perceive more warmth than light, while if it appeared lower, they would perceive more light than warmth, as happens on earth when the sun is above or

below the middle of the sky. When it is above, the warmth increases more than the light; and when it is below, the light increases more than the warmth. The light actually stays the same in summer and winter, but the warmth increases or decreases depending on the degree of the sun's height.

A second reason that the spiritual world's sun appears at a middle height above the angelic heaven is that this results in a constant springtime for all the angelic heavens. Consequently, angels are in a state of peace, for this state corresponds to springtime on earth.

A third reason is that it enables angels to turn their faces toward the Lord constantly and to see him with their eyes. For angels, the east—and therefore the Lord—is in front of them no matter which way they turn their bodies, which is a unique feature of their world. This would not happen if the sun of their world were above or below middle height, and it would be absolutely impossible if it were directly overhead.

If the spiritual world's sun did not seem to be as far from angels as the physical world's sun is from us, the whole angelic heaven, the hell underneath it, and our globe of lands and seas below them could not be under the Lord's watchful guidance, omnipresence, omniscience, omnipotence, and providence. In the same way, if our world's sun were not at the distance from the earth where we see it to be, it could not be present and effective with its warmth and light in all our lands, so it could not provide its subsidiary resources to the spiritual world's sun. 106

It is of critical importance to realize that there are two suns, a spiritual one and a physical one, the spiritual sun for people who are in the spiritual world and the physical sun for people who are in the physical world. Unless this is recognized, there can be no real comprehension of creation or of humanity, subjects we are about to deal with. True, some effects can be seen, but unless the causes behind the effects are seen at the same time, it is like looking at the effects in the night. 107

The distance between the sun and angels in the spiritual world is an apparent distance that depends on their acceptance of divine love and wisdom. All the illusions that are prevalent among evil people and simple people come from appearances that have been taken as facts. As long as appearances remain appearances, they are virtual truths, and it is all right for anyone to think and talk in terms of them. However, when they are taken to be actual truths, which happens when they are defended as facts, then the virtual truths become falsities and fallacies. 108

For example, it seems as though the sun travels around the earth every day and also follows its yearly ecliptic path. As long as this is not taken as fact, this is a virtual truth, and anyone may think and talk in such terms. We can say that the sun rises and sets, causing morning, noon, evening, and night. We can say that the sun is at this or that point on the ecliptic, or at this or that elevation, causing spring, summer, autumn, and winter. However, when these appearances are defended as the real truth, then the person who defends them is thinking and speaking falsity based on illusion.

The same holds true for countless other appearances, not only in earthly, civic, and moral matters, but also in spiritual ones.

109 It is the same with the distance of the spiritual world's sun, the sun that is the first emanation of the Lord's divine love and wisdom. The truth is that there is no distance. Rather, the distance is an appearance that depends on angels' acceptance of divine love and wisdom on their own level. It makes sense that distances in the spiritual world are appearances when we consider what has been presented already, like the material in §§7–9 [7–10] on Divinity not being in space and in §§69–72 on Divinity filling all space nonspatially. If there are no segments of space, then there are no distances either; or in other words, if segments of space are appearances, so are distances, since distances are a matter of space.

110 The reason the spiritual world's sun appears at a distance from angels is that they accept divine love and wisdom at an appropriate level of warmth and light. Since angels are created and finite, they cannot accept the Lord at the prime level of warmth and light, as it is in the sun. That would mean being totally consumed; so they accept the Lord at the level of warmth and light that matches their own love and wisdom.

The following may serve to illustrate. Angels of the lowest heaven cannot rise up to angels of the third heaven. If they were to rise up and enter their heaven, they would collapse in a kind of faint, as though their life were struggling against death. This is because their love and wisdom is at a lower level, and so is the warmth of their love and the light of their wisdom. What would happen, then, if an angel were to rise up toward the sun and enter its fire?

As a result of the differences in angels' acceptance of the Lord, the heavens appear to be marked off from each other. The highest heaven, called the third heaven, seems to be over the second, and the second over the first. It is not that the heavens *are* distant from each other, but that they seem to be. In fact, the Lord is just as present with people in the most remote heaven as he is with people in the third heaven. What causes the appearance of distance is in the subjects, the angels, and not in the Lord.

It is almost impossible to grasp this in any earthly image, since that would involve space. It can be grasped in a spiritual image, though, since there is no space involved. That is the kind of image angels have.

This much can be grasped in an earthly image, though—love and wisdom, or in other words the Lord who is divine love and wisdom, cannot move through space but is with every one of us depending on our acceptance. The Lord teaches in Matthew 28:20 that he is with everyone; and in John 14:21 *[14:23]* he says that he makes his home with those who love him.

This may seem like a matter of higher wisdom since it is being supported by reference to heavens and angels. However, the same holds true for us. As far as the deeper levels of our minds are concerned, we are warmed and enlightened by that same sun, warmed by its warmth and enlightened by its light, to the extent that we accept love and wisdom from the Lord. The difference between angels and us is that angels are under that [spiritual] sun only, while we are not only under that sun but also under the sun of our world. Our bodies could not take form and endure if they were not under both suns. It is different for angels' bodies because they are spiritual.

Angels are in the Lord and the Lord is in them; and since angels are vessels, the Lord alone is heaven. Heaven is called God's dwelling and God's throne, so people think that God lives there like a monarch in a realm. However, God—that is, the Lord—is in the sun above the heavens and is in the heavens by means of his presence in warmth and light, as I have explained in the last two sections. Further, even though the Lord is present in heaven in this apparently distant way, he is still also intrinsically present there, so to speak, since as I have just explained in §§103–112 the distance between the sun and heaven is not a distance but a virtual distance. Given the fact that this distance is only apparent, then, it follows that the Lord himself is in heaven. He is in the love and wisdom of heaven's angels; and since he is in the love and wisdom of all the angels and the angels make up heaven, he is in all of heaven.

The reason the Lord is not only *in* heaven but actually *is* heaven itself is that love and wisdom make an angel, and these two are properties of the Lord in the angels. It therefore follows that the Lord is heaven.

Angels are not angels because of anything that belongs to them. What belongs to them is just like what belongs to us—evil. The reason this is what belongs to angels is that all angels were once earthly people, and this attribute clings to them from their birth. It is simply moved aside, and to the extent that it is, they accept love and wisdom, or the Lord, into themselves.

With a little elevation of understanding, everyone can see that it is quite impossible for the Lord to dwell with angels in anything but what is his, that is, what belongs to him, which is love and wisdom. He cannot dwell in anything that belongs to the angels, which is evil. This is why the Lord is in them, and they are angels, to the extent that evil is moved aside. The actual angelic essence of heaven is divine love and wisdom. This divine reality is called "angelic" when it is in angels; so again we can see that angels are angels because of the Lord and not on their own. The same therefore holds true for heaven as well.

115   Still, there is no understanding how the Lord is in an angel and an angel is in the Lord except through knowing what kind of union is involved. It is a union of the Lord with the angel and of the angel with the Lord, so it is a reciprocal union. On the angel's side, it is like this. Angels, like us, simply feel as though they participate in love and wisdom on their own, and therefore that love and wisdom are theirs, their very own. If they did not feel this way there would be no union, so the Lord would not be in them, nor they in the Lord. It cannot happen that the Lord is in any angels or people unless they, as subjects of his presence in love and wisdom, sense and feel this as their own. This enables them not only to accept but also to retain what they have accepted, and to love in response. This, then, is how angels become wise and remain wise. Can people decide to love God and their neighbor, can people decide to gain wisdom, unless they feel and sense that what they love, learn, and gain is their own? Can they retain anything in themselves otherwise? If it were not for this, then the inflowing love and wisdom would have no seat. They would flow right through without making any difference; and as a result angels would not be angels and people would not be human. They would be virtually lifeless.

It makes sense, then, that if there is to be union, there must be reciprocity.

116   However, this calls for an explanation of how angels can feel and sense this as their own and so accept and retain it when in fact it is not theirs, given the statement that angels are not angels on their own but by virtue of what is within them from the Lord. The essence of the matter is this. There is freedom and rationality in every angel.[74] These two qualities are there so that angels can be open to love and wisdom from the Lord. Neither of these, though—neither the freedom nor the rationality—

belongs to the angels. They are in them but belong to the Lord. However, since these two elements are intimately united to angels' life, so intimately united that you could call them linked to their life, it seems as though they belong to the angels.[75] Freedom and rationality enable them to think and intend and to speak and act; and what they think, intend, speak, and act as a result seems to be done on their own. This gives rise to the reciprocal element that is the means to union.

Still, the more that angels believe that love and wisdom are within them and claim them for themselves as their own, the more there is nothing angelic within them. To the same extent, then, there is no union with the Lord for them. They are outside the truth; and since truth is identical with heaven's light, they are correspondingly unable to be in heaven. This leads to a denial that they live from the Lord and a belief that they live on their own and therefore that they possess some divine essence. The life called angelic and human consists of these two elements—freedom and rationality.

This leads to the conclusion that angels have a reciprocal ability for the sake of their union with the Lord, but that the reciprocal element, seen as an ability, is the Lord's and not theirs. As a result, angels fall from angelhood if they abuse this reciprocal element that enables them to feel and sense what is the Lord's as their own by actually claiming it for themselves. The Lord himself teaches us in John 14:20–24 and 15:4, 5, 6 that union is reciprocal, and in John 15:7 that the Lord's union with us and ours with him occurs in things that belong to him, things called "his words."

There are people who think that Adam had a kind of freedom or ability to choose that enabled him to love God and be wise on his own, and that this freedom to choose was lost in his descendants. This, however, is wrong. We are not life, but life-receivers (see §§4–6 and 54–60 [55–60] above); and people who are life-receivers cannot love and be wise from their own resources. So when Adam wanted to love and be wise from his own resources, he fell from wisdom and love and was cast out of the garden.[76]

We can say much the same about the heaven that is made up of angels as we have said about individual angels, since Divinity is the same in the largest and smallest things (see §§77–82 above). What we have said about angels and heaven needs to be said about us and the church as well, since angels of heaven and we of the church act in consort because of our union. Further, as to the inner reaches of our minds, we of the church are angels—but "we of the church" means people who have the church within themselves.

119 *The east in the spiritual world is where the Lord is seen as the sun, and the other directions follow from that.* Now that I have discussed the spiritual world's sun and its essence, its warmth and light, and the Lord's consequent presence, I need to talk as well about the regions of that world. The reason for talking about the sun and that world is that our subject is God, and love and wisdom. To discuss these apart from their *origin* would be to start from effects and not from their causes. Yet effects teach us nothing but effects. When only they are highlighted, they do not show us any cause; rather, causes show us effects. Knowing about effects on the basis of their cause is being wise, but exploring causes on the basis of their effects is not being wise; because when we do, various illusions present themselves that we as investigators identify as causes. To do this is to make foolishness of wisdom. Causes precede and effects follow. We cannot see preceding things from following things, but we can see following things from preceding things. That is the pattern.

This is why we are dealing with the spiritual world first here. That world is where all the causes are. Later [§§134, 154] we will discuss the physical world, where everything we see is an effect.

120 At this point, then, we need to discuss the regions in the spiritual world. There are regions there just as there are in the physical world; but the regions of the spiritual world, like that world itself, are spiritual, while the regions of the physical world, like this world itself, are physical. This means that they are so different that they have nothing in common.

There are four regions in each world, called the east, the west, the south, and the north. In the physical world, these four regions are static, determined by the sun in the south. The north is behind, with the east on one side and the west on the other. These regions are determined by the south wherever you go, since the sun's position at noon is always the same and therefore static.[77]

It is different in the spiritual world. There the regions are determined by the sun, which always appears in its own place; and where it appears is the east. So the assignment of regions in that world is not from the south as it is in the physical world but from the east. The west is behind, with the south on one side and the north on the other. We will see below, however, that the regions are not caused by its sun but by the inhabitants of that world, the angels and spirits.

Since these regions are spiritual because of their source (the Lord as the sun), the places where angels and spirits live are spiritual as well, since the places all depend on these regions. The places are spiritual because their locations depend on the angels' acceptance of love and wisdom from the Lord. People who are at a higher level of love live in the east, while people who are at a lower level of love live in the west. People who are at a higher level of wisdom live in the south, while people who are at a lower level of wisdom live in the north.   **121**

This is why "the east" in the Word, in its highest sense, means the Lord, while in a secondary sense it means a love for him, while "the west" means a waning love for him. "The south" means wisdom in the light and "the north" wisdom beclouded. There are some variations of these meanings as they relate to the state of the people under discussion.

Since the east is the basis on which all the regions in the spiritual world are laid out, and since the east in the highest sense means the Lord and divine love, we can see that the Lord and love for him is the source of everything. We can also see that to the extent that people do not share in that love, they are far from him and live either in the west or in the south or in the north, with the distance depending on their openness to love.   **122**

Since the Lord as the sun is always in the east, early people[78]—for whom all the elements of worship were symbolic of spiritual realities—faced the east when they worshiped. Further, to be sure that they did this in all their rituals, they faced their temples in the same direction. This is the reason churches are built in the same way at present.   **123**

The regions in the spiritual world are not caused by the Lord as the sun but by the angels, depending on their receptivity. I have stated that angels live in distinct regions, some in the east, some in the west, some in the south, and some in the north. I have also stated that the ones who live in the east are engaged in a higher level of love, those in the west in a lower level of love, those in the south in the light of wisdom, and those in the north in the shadow of wisdom.   **124**

This variation of place seems to be caused by the Lord as the sun, yet it is actually caused by the angels. The Lord is not at a greater or lesser degree of love and wisdom; as the sun, he is not at a greater or lesser level of warmth and light for one person than for another. He is everywhere the same. However, he is not accepted at the same level by one person as by another, and this makes it seem as though they are more or less distant from each other, in a variety of regions. It follows from this that the regions in the spiritual world are simply variations in the receptivity of love and wisdom and therefore of the warmth and light of the Lord as the sun. If you look at what was explained in §§108–112 about distances in the spiritual world being apparent only, you will see that this is true.

125   Since the regions are variations in the way angels accept love and wisdom, I need to say something about the variety that gives rise to the appearance.

As I explained in the preceding section, the Lord is in each angel, and each angel is in the Lord. However, since it looks as though the Lord as the sun were outside angels, it also looks as though the Lord is seeing them from the sun and that they are seeing the Lord in the sun. This is much like seeing an image in a mirror. So if we talk on the basis of the way things seem, that is how it is. The Lord sees and examines angels face to face, but angels do not see the Lord in the same way. When they are engaged in the love for him that comes from him, they do see him straight ahead, so they are in the east or the west. When they are more engaged in wisdom, though, they see the Lord off to the right, and when they are less engaged in wisdom they see him off to the left, so they are respectively in the north or the south.

The reason they have an oblique view is that love and wisdom emanate from the Lord as a single whole, but they are not accepted that way by angels, as I have already noted [§99]. Any wisdom that goes beyond love may look like wisdom, but it is not, since there is no life from love in that excess wisdom.

We can see from this where the differences in receptivity come from, the differences that cause the appearance that angels live in the different regions in the spiritual world.

126   It makes sense that a particular openness to love and wisdom establishes a region in the spiritual world, given the fact that angels change their location in response to any increase or decrease of love in them. We can see from this that the location is not caused by the Lord as the sun but by angels, according to their receptivity.

The same holds true for us as far as our spirits are concerned. In spirit, each of us is in some particular region of the spiritual world no matter where we may be in the physical world. That is, the regions of the spiritual world have nothing in common with those of the physical world, as already stated [§120]. We are in the one as to body and in the other as to spirit.

127   For love and wisdom to be a single whole in angels and in us, there are pairs throughout our bodies. Our eyes, ears, and nostrils are paired,

our hands, sides, and feet are paired, our brains are divided into two hemispheres, our heart into two chambers, our lungs into two lobes, and so on. So for both angels and for us there is a right side and a left side; and all the right side parts have to do with the love that gives rise to wisdom, while all the left side parts have to do with the wisdom of that love. We could also say, which amounts to the same thing, that all the right side parts have to do with the good that gives rise to the true and all the left side parts with what is true because of that goodness.

Both we and angels have these pairs so that love and wisdom, or what is good and what is true, may act in unison and focus on the Lord in unison—but there will be more on this later [§§384, 409].

We can see from this how caught up in illusion and consequent distortion people are if they think that the Lord parcels heaven out arbitrarily, or arbitrarily enables one person to be wiser and more loving than another. No, the Lord intends that one person should be just as wise and just as saved as another. He offers all of us the means. To the extent that we accept them and live by them, we are wise and we are saved, because the Lord is the same with one person as with another. The receivers, though, the angels and the people on earth, are different because of their differing receptivity and life. **128**

This fits with what has already been said [§124] about the regions and about the way angels' locations depend on them, namely that the differences stem from the recipients and not from the Lord.

Angels always face the Lord as the sun, so south is on their right, north on their left, and west behind them. All these statements about angels and the way they face the Lord as the sun should also be understood as applying to us spiritually, since we are spirits as to our minds, and angels if we are engaged in love and wisdom. So after death, when we shed the outer forms we have derived from the physical world, we become spirits or angels. Since angels do constantly face the sunrise (the Lord), we say of people who are engaged in love and wisdom from the Lord that they see God, that they look to God, and that they have God before their eyes, meaning that they are living like angels. We say these things in this world both because that is what is really happening in heaven and because that is what is actually happening in our spirits. Do we not all look straight ahead at God when we pray, no matter which way we are facing? **129**

The reason angels constantly face the Lord as the sun is that angels are in the Lord and the Lord is in them. The Lord exercises an inner guidance of their feelings and thoughts and constantly turns them **130** toward himself. This means that they cannot help but look toward the east where they see the Lord as the sun. We can see from this that angels do not turn themselves toward the Lord—the Lord turns them toward himself. When angels are thinking about the Lord inwardly, they think of him simply as in themselves. This deeper thought itself does not create any distance, while more outward thought does, the thought that acts in unison with eyesight. The reason is that the outward thought is in space, while the inward thought is not, though even when it is not in space (as in the spiritual world) it is still in an appearance of space.

It is hard for people to understand this, though, if they think spatially about God. God is actually everywhere and yet not in space. So he is both within and outside angels, which enables them to see him both inside and outside themselves—inside themselves when they are thinking from love and wisdom, and outside themselves when they are thinking about love and wisdom. This topic will be discussed in greater detail, though, in works on the Lord's omnipotence, omniscience, and omnipresence.[79]

Everyone should beware not to slip into the terrible heresy that God pours himself into us and is in us and no longer in himself.[80] God is everywhere, within us and outside us, being in all space nonspatially, as I have already explained in §§7–10 and 69–72. That is, if he were in us he would be not only divided up but enclosed in space, and we could then even think that we were God. This heresy is so loathsome that in the spiritual world it stinks like a corpse.

131 Angels' turning toward the Lord is like this: no matter which way they turn their bodies, they are looking at the Lord as the sun in front of themselves. Angels can turn this way and that and can thus see the various things that surround them, but still the Lord as the sun seems to be constantly in front of them.

This may seem remarkable, but it is the truth. I too have been allowed to see the Lord as the sun like this. I have been seeing him in front of me for a number of years; whatever direction I turned to, I saw him like this.

132 Since the Lord as the sun and therefore the east is in front of all heaven's angels, it follows that the south is to their right, the north to their left, and the west behind them, again no matter which way they turn their bodies. That is, all the regions in the spiritual world are based on the east, as already stated [§120]. This means that people who have the east before their eyes are in those very regions and actually set their boundaries; since, as I have just explained in §§124–128, the regions are not caused by the Lord as the sun but by the angels, according to their receptivity.

Now, since heaven is made up of angels, and since this is what angels are like, it follows that the whole heaven faces the Lord and that because it does, heaven is governed by the Lord as though it were a single individual—which is what heaven looks like in the Lord's sight. On heaven looking like a single individual in the Lord's sight, see *Heaven and Hell* 59–87 *[59–86]*. This is the cause of heaven's regions as well.   133

Since these regions are virtually written on each angel and on all of heaven, angels, unlike us in our world, know their homes and houses no matter where they travel. The reason we do not know our homes and houses instinctively, from their regions, is that we are thinking in terms of space and therefore in terms of this physical world's geography, which has nothing in common with the geography of the spiritual world.   134

However, birds and animals have this kind of knowledge by instinct. They know their homes and dwellings instinctively, as much experience testifies. This is a clue to the nature of the spiritual world, since everything that happens in the physical world is an effect and everything that happens in the spiritual world is a cause of such effects. Nothing happens in nature that does not have its cause in the spiritual realm.

Everything in the deeper reaches of angels' minds and bodies alike is turned toward the Lord as the sun. Angels have discernment and volition, and they have faces and bodies. Further, there are deeper levels of discernment and volition and deeper contents of their faces and bodies. The deeper levels of their discernment and volition are activities of their deeper feeling and thought. The deeper contents of their faces are their brains, and the contents of their bodies are their viscera, headed by heart and lungs. In a word, angels have everything we on earth have. This is what makes them human. An outward form apart from these inner elements would not make them human; only an outward form with its inner elements and even constituted by them would do so. Otherwise they would be only images of people with no life in them because there was no form of life within.   135

It is recognized that volition and discernment control the body completely. The mouth says what discernment thinks and the body does what volition intends. We can see from this that the body is a form responsive to discernment and volition. Further, since we attribute form to discernment and volition, we can say that the body's form is responsive to the form of discernment and volition. This is not the place, however, to describe the nature of either form. There are countless components in each, and those countless components act in unison in each because they are responsive to   136 each other. This is why the mind (or volition and discernment) controls the body completely, just as though it were controlling itself.

It follows from this that the deeper levels of the mind act in unison with the deeper levels of the body, and that the outer levels of the mind act in unison with the outer levels of the body. I need to discuss the deeper levels of the mind later, when we deal first with levels of life, and then in the same vein with the deeper levels of the body [§§236–241 and 277–281].

137   Given the fact that the deeper levels of the mind act in unison with the deeper levels of the body, it follows that when the deeper levels of the mind turn toward the Lord as the sun, the deeper levels of the body do the same. Further, since the outer levels of both body and mind depend on their inner levels, they behave in the same way. The outer does what it does at the prompting of the inner, since a collective body derives its whole nature from its specific components. We can see from this that because an angel is turning face and body toward the Lord as the sun, the inner levels of that angel's mind and body have been turned in that direction as well.

It is the same with us. If we constantly keep the Lord before our eyes (which happens if we are engaged in love and wisdom), then it is not only our eyes and face that turn to him, it is our whole mind and our whole heart. That is, it is everything in our intention and mind and everything in our body at the same time.

138   This turning toward the Lord is an active turning—it is a kind of lifting up. We are actually lifted into heaven's warmth and light, and this is accomplished by an opening of our inner reaches. When these have been opened, love and wisdom flow into the deeper reaches of our minds and heaven's warmth and light flow into the deeper reaches of our bodies. This results in a lifting, as though we were brought out of the mist into clear air, or out of the air into the ether. Further, love and wisdom, together with their warmth and light, are the Lord with us, the Lord who, as already noted [§130], turns us toward himself.

The opposite holds for people who are not engaged in love and wisdom, and all the more for people who resist love and wisdom. The deeper reaches of their minds and bodies alike are closed; and when they are closed, then their outer natures resist the Lord because this is their inherent nature. This is why such people turn away from the Lord, and this "turning away" is a turning toward hell.

139   This active turning toward the Lord comes from love and wisdom together, not from love alone or wisdom alone. Love alone is like a reality with no manifestation, since love makes itself manifest in wisdom; and wisdom without love is like a manifestation with no reality, since wisdom is the manifestation of love.

There is actually a kind of love apart from wisdom, but it is ours and not the Lord's. There is also wisdom apart from love, but while it comes from the Lord, it does not have the Lord within it. It is like sunlight in winter that does of course come from the sun but does not have within it the essence of the sun, its warmth.

Every kind of spirit turns toward her or his ruling love in the same way. First I need to define "angel" and "spirit." Immediately after death we come into a world of spirits[81] that is halfway between heaven and hell. There we work through our stretches of time, or our states, and are prepared either for heaven or for hell, depending on the way we have lived. As long as we stay in this world, we are called "spirits." Anyone who has been brought up from this world into heaven is called an angel, and anyone who has been cast into hell is called a satan or a devil.[82] As long as we are in the world of spirits, people who are being readied for heaven are called angelic spirits, and people who are being readied for hell are called hellish spirits. All the while, angelic spirits are united to heaven and hellish spirits to hell.

140

All the spirits who are in the world of spirits are together with us because we are similarly between heaven and hell as to the deeper levels of our minds. Through these spirits we are in touch with either heaven or hell, depending on the way we are living.

It should be clear that "the world of spirits" is not the same thing as "the spiritual world." The world of spirits is the one I have just been talking about, while the spiritual world includes that world, heaven, and hell.

Something also needs to be said about loves, since we are talking about how angels and spirits turn toward their loves because of their loves.

141

Heaven as a whole is laid out in communities depending on all the differences in loves. So is hell, and so is the world of spirits. Heaven, though, is laid out in communities according to differences in heavenly loves, while hell is laid out in communities according to differences in hellish loves, and the world of spirits is laid out in communities according to differences in both heavenly and hellish loves.

There are two loves that are at the head of all the rest, and two loves that lie behind all the rest. The head of all heavenly loves, the love basic to them all, is love for the Lord. The head of all hellish loves, or the love that underlies them all, is a love of controlling prompted by self-love. These two loves are absolute opposites.

Since these two loves—love for the Lord and love of controlling prompted by self-love—are absolute opposites, and since everyone who

142

is caught up in love for the Lord turns toward the Lord as the sun, as explained in the preceding section, it stands to reason that everyone who is caught up in a love of controlling prompted by self-love turns away from the Lord. The reason people turn in opposite directions is that those who are caught up in love for the Lord love being led by the Lord more than anything else, and want the Lord alone to be in control. In contrast, if people are caught up in a love of controlling prompted by self-love, there is nothing they love more than leading themselves. They want to be the *only* ones who are in control.

The reason we refer to "a love of controlling prompted by self-love" is that there is a love of controlling out of a love of service. Since this love acts in unison with love for our neighbor, it is a spiritual love. In fact, it cannot truly be called a love of being in control: it should be called a love of service.

143 The reason spirits of all kinds turn toward their ruling loves is that for all of us, love is life (as explained in §§1–3 of part 1), and life turns its vessels, called members, organs, and viscera—the whole person, therefore—toward the particular community that is engaged in a similar love, the community where our own love is.

144 Since a love of controlling prompted by self-love is the absolute opposite of love for the Lord, spirits caught up in this love of controlling turn away from the Lord. So their eyes are looking toward that world's west; and since their bodies are turned around, the east is behind them, the north is on their right, and the south is on their left. The east is behind them because they harbor a hatred of the Lord; the north is on their right because they love illusions and the consequent distortions; and the south is on their left because they have no use for the light of wisdom. They can turn this way and that, but still everything they see around themselves looks like their love.

They all are oriented toward outward nature and their senses. They are the kind of people who think they are the only ones who are really alive and who see others as unreal. They think they themselves are wiser than anyone else, even though they are insane.

145 In the spiritual world, you can see roads laid out like roads in our physical world. Some of them lead to heaven and some to hell. The roads that lead to hell are not visible to people who are going to heaven, and the roads that lead to heaven are not visible to people who are going to hell. There are more such roads than you can count, roads leading to each heavenly community and to each hellish community. Each individual spirit sets out on the road that leads to the community of his or her own love and does not even see the roads that lead in other directions. As a result, when spirits turn toward their ruling love, they also travel.

The divine love and wisdom that emanate from the Lord as the sun and constitute heaven's warmth and light is [83] *the emanating Divinity that is the Holy Spirit.* I explained in *Teachings for the New Jerusalem on the Lord* [84] that God is one in both person and essence, consisting of a trinity, and that this God is the Lord. I also explained that his trinity is called Father, Son, and Holy Spirit. Divinity as source is the Father, Divinity as human is the Son, and Divinity as emanating is the Holy Spirit. [85]   **146**

We say "Divinity as emanating," and yet no one knows why we say "emanating." The reason for this ignorance is that people have not known before that the Lord looks like a sun to angels and that from that sun there issues a warmth that is essentially divine love and a light that is essentially divine wisdom. As long as this remains unknown, people cannot help "knowing" that Divinity as emanating is intrinsic Divinity because it says in the Athanasian doctrine of the Trinity that the Father is one Person, the Son another, and the Holy Spirit another. Now that we know that the Lord looks like a sun, though, we can have an appropriate image of the "Divinity as emanating" that is called the Holy Spirit. We can realize that while it is one with the Lord, it emanates from him the way warmth and light emanate from the sun. This is also why angels are in divine warmth and light to the extent that they are caught up in love and wisdom.

Without this recognition that the Lord looks like a sun in the spiritual world and that his Divinity emanates from him in this way, there is no way for anyone to know what "emanating" means—whether it means simply sharing what belongs to the Father and the Son or simply enlightening and teaching. However, it does not come from enlightened reason if we acknowledge the Holy Spirit as intrinsic Divinity, call it "God," and draw boundaries around it when we know as well that God is both one and omnipresent.

I explained above [§126] that God is not in space and is therefore omnipresent and that Divinity is everywhere the same, but that there is an apparent variation of divinity in angels and in us because of our differences in receptivity. Since divinity as emanating from the Lord as the sun takes place in light and warmth, then, and since light and warmth flow first of all into those universal vessels that are called "atmospheres" in our world, and since these are what contain clouds, it stands to reason that the way the deeper levels of angels' minds, or of our own, are veiled by   **147** such clouds determines how open we are to Divinity as emanating. By these "clouds," I mean spiritual clouds. These are thoughts that are in harmony with divine wisdom if they are based on true perceptions and that disagree if they consist of false ones. So when they are represented visually in the spiritual world, thoughts based on true perceptions look like bright clouds and thoughts based on false perceptions look like black clouds.

We may therefore conclude that Divinity as emanating is actually within all of us, but that it is variously veiled by us.

148 Since Divinity itself is present with angels and with us through its spiritual warmth and light, we look at people who are caught up in the truth of divine wisdom and the goodness of divine love, who are moved by them, and who are therefore in heartfelt thought, and we say that they are being "warmed by God." Sometimes this happens so openly that it can be noticed and felt, as when a preacher speaks with passion. We also say of such people that they are being "enlightened by God" because with his emanating divinity, the Lord not only kindles human intentions with spiritual warmth but also floods human minds with spiritual light.

149 We can see from the following passages in the Word that the Holy Spirit is the same as the Lord and is the very truth that is the source of our enlightenment. "Jesus said, 'When the spirit of truth has come, he will lead you into all truth. He will not speak on his own, but will say what he has heard'" (John 16:13). "He will glorify me because he will receive from me and will proclaim to you" (John 16:14, 15). He will be with the disciples and in them (John 15:26 *[14:17]*).[86] "Jesus said, 'The things I am telling you are spirit and life'" (John 6:63).[87] We can see from these passages that the very truth that emanates from the Lord is called the Holy Spirit, which enlightens us because it is in the light.[88]

150 While the enlightenment attributed to the Holy Spirit actually comes from the Lord, it happens through the agency of spirits and angels. I cannot yet describe what kind of agency it is, but can say only that in no way can angels and spirits enlighten us on their own because they, like us, are enlightened by the Lord. Since they are enlightened in this same way, it follows that all enlightenment is from the Lord alone. It happens through angels and spirits because when we are receiving enlightenment we are surrounded by the angels and spirits who are receiving more enlightenment than others from the Lord alone.

151 *The Lord created the universe and everything in it by means of that sun that is the first emanation of divine love and wisdom.* "The Lord" means God from eternity or Jehovah, who is called the Father and the Creator, because as explained in *Teachings for the New Jerusalem on the Lord*, the Lord and the Father are one.[89] When I return to the topic of creation below [§§282–357], therefore, I will refer to "the Lord."

I gave ample evidence in part 1 that everything in the universe was created by divine love and wisdom (see particularly §§52–53 *[52–54]*). The point here is that this was done by means of the sun that is the first emanation of divine love and wisdom.

152

No one who can see how effects follow from causes and how causes lead to effects in due order and sequence can deny that the sun is the beginning of creation. Everything in our world is sustained by it, and because everything is sustained by it, everything arose from it—the one fact follows from the other and bears witness to it. Everything, that is, is watched over by the sun because the sun has determined its being, and the act of watching over it is an ongoing determination of that thing's being. This is why we say that being sustained is a constant coming into being.[90] If anything were totally removed from the inflow of the sun through our atmospheres, it would instantly dissipate. It is the atmospheres with their different degrees of purity, empowered by the sun, that hold everything together. Since the universe and everything in it is sustained by the sun, then, we can see that the sun is the beginning of creation, the source.

We say "by the sun" but we mean "by the Lord through the sun," since the sun too was created by the Lord.

There are two suns by means of which the Lord created everything, the sun of the spiritual world and the sun of the physical world. The Lord created everything by means of the spiritual world's sun, but not by means of the physical world's sun, since this latter sun is far beneath the former one. The spiritual sun is at a midpoint, with the spiritual world above it and the physical world below it.[91] The physical world's sun was created to play a supporting role, a role that will be discussed below [§157].

153

The reason the Lord created the universe and everything in it by means of the spiritual world's sun is that this sun is the first emanation of divine love and wisdom, and as explained above (§§52–82), everything comes from divine love and wisdom.

154

There are three components of everything that has been created, no matter how large or how small it is: a purpose, a means, and a result.[92] There is nothing created that lacks these three components. In the largest instance, the universe, these three components arise in the following pattern: the purpose of everything is in that sun that is the first emanation of divine love and wisdom; the means of everything is in the spiritual world; and the result of everything is in the physical world. I will describe below [§§167–172] how these three components occur in both first and last forms.

Since there is nothing created that lacks these three components, it follows that the universe and everything in it has been created by the Lord by means of the sun where the purpose of everything resides.

155   Creation itself cannot be described intelligibly unless you banish space and time from your thoughts; but it can be understood if you banish them. If you can, or to the extent that you can, banish them and keep your mind on an image that is devoid of space and time. If you do, you will notice that there is no difference between the largest expanse and the smallest, and you will inevitably have the same image of the creation of the universe and of the creation of any particular feature of the universe. You will see that the diversity in created things arises from the fact that there are infinite things in the Divine-Human One and therefore unlimited things in that sun that is the first emanation from him, and those unlimited things emerge in the created universe as their reflections, so to speak. This is why there cannot be one thing identical to another anywhere. This is the cause of that variety of all things that meet our eyes in the context of space in this physical world, and in the appearance of space in the spiritual world. The variety is characteristic of both aggregates and details.

I presented the following points in part 1: Infinite things are distinguishably one in the Divine-Human One (§§17–22); everything in the universe was created by divine love and wisdom (§§52–53 [52–54]); everything in the created universe is a vessel for the divine love and wisdom of the Divine-Human One (§§54–60 [55–60]); Divinity is not in space (§§7–10); Divinity fills all space nonspatially (§§69–72); and Divinity is the same in the largest and smallest things (§§77–82).

156   We cannot say that the creation of the universe and everything in it happened from one place to another or from one moment in time to another, that is, gradually and sequentially. We must say that it happened from eternity and from infinity, and not from an eternity of time, since there is no such thing, but from a nontemporal eternity that is the same as Divinity, and not from an infinity of space, since there is no such thing, but from a nonspatial infinity that is also the same as Divinity.

I know that all this transcends any mental images that arise in physical light, but they do not transcend mental images that arise in spiritual light. There is no trace of space and time in these latter images. Actually, this does not completely transcend images that arise in physical light, since everyone would agree on the basis of reason that there is no such thing as an infinity of space. The same holds for eternity, which is an infinity of time. If you say "to eternity," this can be understood in temporal terms; but if you say "from eternity," that is incomprehensible unless you banish time.

The physical world's sun is nothing but fire and is therefore dead; and since **157** *nature has its origin in that sun, nature is dead.* In no respect whatever can creation itself be attributed to the physical world's sun: it is due entirely to the spiritual world's sun. This is because the physical world's sun is totally lifeless, while the spiritual world's sun is alive, being the first emanation of divine love and wisdom. Anything that is lifeless does not effect anything on its own, but is activated; so to attribute any aspect of creation to a lifeless sun would be to attribute the work of an artisan to the tool in the artisan's hand.

The physical world's sun is nothing but fire, with all its life removed. The spiritual world's sun is a fire that has divine life within it.

The angelic concept of the fire of the physical world's sun and the fire of the spiritual world's sun is like this: divine life is internal to the fire of the spiritual world's sun and external to the fire of the physical world's sun. We can see from this that the activity of our physical sun is not autonomous but stems from a living force[93] that emanates from the spiritual world's sun. Consequently, if the living force of that sun were withdrawn or removed, our sun would fail. This is why the worship of the sun is the lowest of all forms of worship of God. It is just as dead as the sun itself; so in the Word it is called an abomination.[94]

Since the physical world's sun is nothing but fire and is therefore life- **158** less, the warmth that emanates from it is also lifeless, and so is the emanating light. By the same token, the atmospheres called ether and air that receive this sun's warmth and light and bring them down into our embrace are lifeless as well. Since all these are lifeless, absolutely all the earthly things beneath them called soils are lifeless. However, they are all surrounded by spiritual realities that emanate and flow out from the spiritual world's sun. If they were not surrounded in this way, soils could not be activated to bring forth the forms of use called plants and the forms of life called animals, and they could not provide the substances that enable us to come into being and to survive.

Now since nature begins from this sun, and since everything that **159** arises from it and is sustained by it is called "natural," it follows that nature and absolutely everything in it is dead. Nature seems to be alive in us and in animals because of the life that visits it and animates it.

160 Since the lowest elements of nature that constitute our soils are dead and not varied and changeable in response to our states of feeling and thought the way they are in the spiritual world, but are unchangeable and stable, we have space and various spatial distances here. They have this stable nature because this is where creation comes to a close and remains at rest. We can see from this that space is proper to nature; and since space here is not an appearance of space responsive to states of life, the way it is in the spiritual world, we can refer to it as "dead."

161 Since times are similarly stable and constant, they too are proper to nature. The length of a day is always twenty-four hours and the length of a year is always three hundred and sixty-five days. The actual states of light, darkness, warmth, and cold that make these differences are constantly returning as well. The states that return every day are morning, noon, evening, and night; the states of the year are spring, summer, fall, and winter. Then too, the states of the year are constantly altering the states of the days. All of these states, since they are not states of life like the ones in the spiritual world, are lifeless. That is, in the spiritual world there is a constant light and a constant warmth. The light is responsive to the state of wisdom among the angels, and the warmth to the state of their love. As a result, these states are alive.

162 From this we can see the folly of people who attribute everything to nature. If we decide in nature's favor, we adopt a state in which we no longer want to raise our minds above nature. So our minds are closed upward and open downward, and we become focused on nature and our senses—spiritually dead. Further, since all we can think about is based on the kind of information we get through our physical senses, or from the world through those senses, at heart we deny God.

The result is a union with hell because our union with heaven has been broken. All we have left is the ability to think and intend—the ability to think coming from our rationality and the ability to intend coming from our freedom, two abilities the Lord gives every one of us and never takes away. Demons and angels alike have these abilities, but demons use them for madness and malice, while angels use them for wisdom and good.

163 *There would be no creation if it were not for this pair of suns, one living and one dead.* Generally speaking, the universe is divided into two worlds, a spiritual one and a physical one. Angels and spirits are in the spiritual world, and we are in the physical world. These two worlds are exactly alike in outward appearance, so much alike that there is no way to tell them apart; but as to inner appearance, they are completely different. The very people who are in the spiritual world (who are called angels and spirits, as I have just said) are spiritual beings; and since they are spiritual beings, they think spiritually and talk spiritually. On the other hand, we who are in the physical world are physical, so we think physically and talk physically. Spiritual thought and speech and physical thought and speech have nothing in common. We can see from this that the two worlds, the spiritual one and the physical one, are completely distinct from each other, so much so that there is no way for them to be in the same place.

Since these two worlds are so distinct, then, it is necessary that there be two suns, one the source of everything spiritual and the other the source of everything physical. Further, since everything spiritual is alive in origin and everything physical is dead in origin, and the suns are the origins, it follows that the one sun is alive and the other dead, and that the sun that is actually dead was created by the Lord by means of the sun that is living. **164**

The reason for the creation of the dead sun is so that in final forms everything may be set and stable and lasting, so that it can give rise to things that last through the years. This is the only way creation can have a foundation. Our globe of lands and seas, with things like this in and on and around it, is like a solid base, since it is the final work in which everything comes to a close, on which everything rests. I will discuss later [§171] how it is also a kind of matrix from which are produced the effects that are the goals of creation. **165**

As evidence that everything was created by the Lord by means of the living sun and nothing by means of the dead sun, there is the fact that what is living arranges what is dead as it pleases. It shapes it for the forms of service that are its goals. The process does not happen the other way around. **166**

Only someone deprived of reason can think that everything comes from nature, that it is even the source of life. People like this do not know what life is. Nature cannot arrange life for anything. In its own right, nature is completely lifeless. It is totally contrary to the design for something dead to activate something living, for a dead force to activate a living one,[95] or—which amounts to the same thing—for something physical to activate something spiritual. Thinking along such lines is therefore contrary to the light of sound reason.

True, something dead or physical can be distorted or changed in many ways by external impingements, but it still cannot activate life. Rather, life activates it according to any change of form that has been imposed on it. The same holds for any physical inflow into the spiritual workings of the soul. We realize that this does not happen because it cannot happen.

167 *The goal of creation—that everything should return to the Creator and that there should be a union—becomes manifest in outermost forms.* First of all, I need to say something about "ends." There are three, which follow in sequence: They are called the first end, the mediate end, and the final end; and they are also called the purpose, the means, and the result.[96] These three must all be present in anything in order for it to be something, since no first end occurs without an intermediate end and a final one at the same time. This is the same as saying that no purpose occurs apart from its means and result, or no means by itself, without a purpose as its source and a result that contains it, or no result by itself without a means and a purpose.

You can see the truth of this if you consider that a purpose apart from its result or separated from its result is nothing that in fact comes into being, so it is nothing but a word. For a purpose effectively to be a purpose, that is, it must be defined, and it finds its definition in its result. That is where it is first called a purpose, because this is its purpose. It looks as though the active or effective element arose spontaneously, but this is an appearance caused by the fact that it is in its result. If it is separated from its result, though, it promptly dissipates.

We can therefore see that this trio of purpose, means, and result needs to be in every entity if it is to be anything.

168 We also need to realize that the purpose is the sum and substance of the means and also the sum and substance of the result. This is why we call the purpose, the means, and the result the first, intermediate, and final ends. For the purpose to be the sum and substance of the means, though, there needs to be something from the purpose in which it exists; and for it to be the sum and substance of the result there must be something from the purpose through the means in which it exists. A purpose cannot exist in itself alone, but must exist in something that takes place because of it, something in which it can dwell with its total being, something which it can accomplish by its effort as long as it lasts. The reality in which it "lasts" is that final end that is called its result.[97]

Throughout the created universe, in its largest and smallest instances alike, we find these three—purpose, means, and result. The reason we find them in the largest and smallest instances of the created universe is that these three are in God the Creator, who is the Lord from eternity. Since he is infinite, though, and since in one who is infinite there are infinite things in a distinguishable oneness (as explained in §§17–22 above), these three are a distinguishable oneness in him and in the infinite things that belong to him. This is why the universe, being created from his reality and (if we look at its functions) being an image of him, retains these three in each of its constituent details.   **169**

The grand purpose, or the purpose of all elements of creation, is an eternal union of the Creator with the created universe. This does not happen unless there are subjects in which his divinity can be at home,[98] so to speak, subjects in which it can dwell and abide. For these subjects to be his dwellings and homes they must be receptive of his love and wisdom apparently of their own accord, subjects who will with apparent autonomy raise themselves toward the Creator and unite themselves with him. In the absence of this reciprocity, there is no union.   **170**

We are those subjects, people who can raise themselves and unite with apparent autonomy. I have already explained several times [§§4–6, 57, 68, 116] that we are subjects of this sort and that we are receptive of Divinity with apparent autonomy.

Through this union, the Lord is present in every work he has created, since in the last analysis everything has been created for our sake. As a result, the functions of all created things rise level by level from the lowest things to us, and through us to God the Creator, their source, as explained in §§65–68 above.

Creation is constantly pressing toward this final goal by means of this trio of purpose, means, and result, because these three elements are in God the Creator, as just stated. Further, Divinity is in all space nonspatially (§§69–72) and is the same in the largest and smallest things (§§77–82). We can see from this that the entire creation, in its general tending toward its final goal, is the intermediate end, relatively speaking. God the Creator is constantly drawing up out of the earth forms of service in their sequence, a sequence that culminates in us, who are from the earth as far as our bodies are concerned. By accepting love and wisdom from the Lord, we are then raised up and furnished with all the means for the acceptance of love and wisdom. Moreover, we are so created that we can accept them if we are only willing to.   **171**

What has now been said enables us to see, if only in a general way so far, that the goal of creation becomes manifest in final things, the goal being the return of all things to their Creator, and union.

172   The presence of this trio of purpose, means, and result in absolutely everything created is evidenced also by the fact that all the results that we call final goals become fresh new goals in an endless series, from the First, who is the Lord the Creator, to the last, which is our union with him. We can see that all final goals become fresh new goals from the fact that there is nothing so lifeless and dead that it has no trace of effectiveness in it. Even from sand there breathes something that provides a resource for accomplishing something, and therefore for having some effect.

ANGELIC WISDOM
ABOUT
DIVINE LOVE

PART 3

THERE are atmospheres, liquids, and solids[99] *in the spiritual world just as there are in the physical world, but they are spiritual, while ours are physical.* I have already noted (and in the book *Heaven and Hell* illustrated)[100] the fact that the spiritual world and the physical world are similar to each other, the only difference being that every single thing in the spiritual world is spiritual and every single thing in the physical world is physical. Because these two worlds are similar to each other, there are atmospheres, liquids, and solids in each. These are the general elements that provide the means and substances for all the infinite variety of phenomena that arise.

As for the atmospheres that we refer to as "ethers" and "airs,"[101] there are similar forms in each world, the spiritual and the physical, the difference being that in the spiritual world they are spiritual, while in the physical world they are physical. They are spiritual because they come from a sun that is the first emanation of the Lord's divine love and wisdom and accept into themselves the divine fire from him that is love and the divine light from him that is wisdom, bringing each down to the heavens where angels live. They bring about the presence of that sun in everything there, from the largest things to the smallest.

The spiritual atmospheres are distinct substances or elemental forms that arise from the sun. Since they accept the sun individually, the sun's

115

fire becomes a warmth that is ultimately adapted to the love of angels in heaven and spirits under heaven by being separated into a corresponding number of substances, enfolded in them, and tempered by being enfolded. The same holds true for the sun's light.

In this respect, our physical atmospheres are like the spiritual ones. They too are distinct substances and elemental forms, arising from the physical world's sun. They too accept the sun individually and conceal its fire within themselves, temper it, and bring it down as warmth to earth where we are; and the same holds true for light.

175 The difference between spiritual atmospheres and physical atmospheres is that spiritual atmospheres are vessels of divine fire and light, of love and wisdom, then. They bear these things within themselves. Physical atmospheres, though, are not vessels of divine fire and light; they are vessels of the fire and light of their own sun, which is intrinsically dead, as explained above [§§89, 157–159]. As a result, there is nothing from the spiritual world's sun within them. However, they are surrounded by the spiritual atmospheres that come from that sun.

This differentiation between spiritual atmospheres and physical atmospheres is a matter of angelic wisdom.

176 It stands to reason that there are atmospheres in the spiritual world just as there are in the physical world, given the fact that angels and spirits breathe and talk and hear just the way we do in this physical world. Breathing involves that lowest atmosphere that we call "air," as do speech and hearing. We may also cite the fact that angels and spirits see just as we do in this physical world, and sight would not be possible without a medium purer than air. Then there is the fact that angels and spirits think and are moved just as we are in this physical world, and thought and feeling would not be possible without the aid of still purer atmospheres. Finally, there is the fact that every part of angels' and spirits' bodies, both the inner and the outer parts, is held closely together, the outer parts by an airlike medium and the inner parts by ethereal ones. Clearly, if it were not for the active pressure of these atmospheres, the inner and outer forms of their bodies would disintegrate.

Since angels are spiritual beings, then, and since everything about their bodies is held together, given form, and organized by these atmospheres, it follows that the atmospheres are spiritual. They are spiritual too because they come from the spiritual sun that is the first emanation of the Lord's divine love and wisdom.

177 I have already presented (and in *Heaven and Hell* illustrated)[102] the fact that there are bodies of water and there are lands in the spiritual

world just as there are in the physical world, with the difference that the
bodies of water and lands in the spiritual world are spiritual. Because
they are spiritual, they are moved and affected by the warmth and light
of the spiritual sun through its atmospheres just as the bodies of water
and lands in our physical world are moved and affected by the warmth
and light of the sun of our world through its atmospheres.

We speak of atmospheres, liquids, and solids here because these are
the three basics through which and from which everything arises, with
infinite variety. The atmospheres are active factors, the liquids intermediate factors, and the solids passive factors from which all results arise. The
arrangement of three such factors in this sequence comes solely from
the life that emanates from the Lord as the sun and enables them to be
active.

178

There are levels of love and wisdom, consequent levels of warmth and light,
and also levels of atmosphere. Without a knowledge that there are levels,
what they are and what they are like, what is to follow will be incomprehensible, since there are levels in everything that has been created; therefore they exist in every form. Consequently, I need to discuss levels in
this part of *Angelic Wisdom.*[103]

179

We can tell clearly from the angels of the three heavens that there are
levels of love and wisdom. Angels of the third heaven so surpass angels of
the second heaven in love and wisdom, and these in turn so surpass angels of the farthest heaven, that they cannot live in the same place. Their
levels of love and wisdom mark them off and separate them. This is why
angels of the lower heavens cannot climb up to angels of the higher heavens, and why if they are allowed to climb up they do not see anyone or
anything around them. The reason they do not see anyone is that the
love and wisdom of the higher angels is on a higher level, a level beyond
their perception. Every angel actually is her or his love and wisdom; and
love together with wisdom is human in form because God, who is love itself and wisdom itself, is human.

Occasionally I have been allowed to see angels of the farthest heaven go
up to angels of the third heaven. When they managed to get there, I heard
them complain that they could not see anyone; and yet they were surrounded by angels. They were afterwards told that these angels had been
invisible to them because they could not perceive their love and wisdom,
and it is love and wisdom that give angels their human appearance.

It is even clearer that there are levels of love and wisdom if
we compare angels' love and wisdom with our love and wisdom. It is

180

generally acknowledged that the wisdom of angels is unutterable, relatively speaking. You will see later [§§267, 416] that it is also incomprehensible to us when we are wrapped up in our earthly love. The reason it
seems unutterable and incomprehensible is that it is on a higher level.

181   Since there are levels of love and wisdom, there are levels of warmth
and light—warmth and light here meaning spiritual warmth and light as
angels experience them in the heavens and as they exist for us in the
deeper levels of our minds. This is because we do have a warmth of love
and a light of wisdom like that of angels.

It is like this in the heavens. The quality and amount of angels' love
determines the quality and amount of their warmth, with the same relationship between their wisdom and their light. This is because there
is love in their warmth and wisdom in their light, as I have already described [§§5, 32, 84]. The same holds true for us on earth, but with the
difference that angels feel the warmth and see the light, while we do
not, the reason being that we are focused on physical warmth and light;
and as long as we are, we feel spiritual warmth only as a kind of pleasure of love and see spiritual light only as a kind of sense of what is
true.

Since people know nothing about the spiritual warmth and light
within them as long as they are focused on physical warmth and light,
and since they can know about this only through experience offered by
the spiritual world, I need first of all to talk about the warmth and light
that surround angels and their heavens. This is the one and only way to
shed some light on this matter.

182   However, the levels of spiritual warmth cannot be described on the
basis of experience because the love to which spiritual warmth corresponds does not fit into the images of our thought. Still, the levels of
spiritual light can be described because light does fit. It is actually an attribute of thought. On the basis of levels of light, we can understand levels of spiritual warmth, since warmth and light are on comparable levels.

As for the spiritual light that surrounds angels, I have been allowed
to see this with my own eyes. For angels of the higher heavens, the light
is so brilliant that it is indescribable, even by comparison with the brilliance of snow; and it also has a glow that defies description, even by
comparison with the radiant glory of our world's sun. In short, this light
is a thousand times greater than the light at noon on earth. The light of
angels of the lower heavens can in some measure be described by
comparisons, though. Even so, it surpasses the highest level of light
on earth.

The reason the light of angels of the higher heavens defies description is that this light is integral to their wisdom. Since their wisdom, relative to ours, is inexpressible, so is their light.

We can tell from these few facts that there are levels of light; and since wisdom and love occur on comparable levels, it follows that there are similar levels of warmth.

Since the atmospheres are what receive and hold warmth and light, it follows that there are as many levels of atmosphere as there are of warmth and light—as many, that is, as there are levels of love and wisdom. An abundance of experience in the spiritual world has shown me that there are several atmospheres, distinguished from each other by level. One kind of experience was especially convincing, namely that angels of lower heavens cannot breathe in the realm of higher angels. They seem to labor for breath like creatures taken out of the air into the ether, or like creatures taken out of the water into the air. Then too, the spirits below heaven look as though they were in a cloud.

On the existence of several atmospheres distinguished from each other by levels, see §176 above.

There are two kinds of levels, vertical levels and horizontal levels. Knowing about levels is a kind of key to unlocking the causes of things and probing into them. In the absence of this knowledge, hardly anything can be known about causes. In the absence of this knowledge, the objects and subjects of both worlds look so simple that there seems to be nothing within them beyond what meets the eye. Actually, though, in comparison to what lies hidden within, this surface is like one feature compared to a thousand or ten thousand.

There is no way to uncover these deeper, invisible features without a knowledge of levels. We move from outer to inner and then to inmost by levels, and not by gradual levels but by distinct ones. "Gradual levels" is the name we give to declines or decreases from coarser to finer or denser to rarer, or better, to gains or increases from finer to coarser or from rarer to denser. They are just like going from light to darkness or from warmth to cold.

In contrast, distinct levels are totally different. They are like antecedent, subsequent, and final events, or like the purpose, the means, and the result.[104] We refer to them as "distinct" because the antecedent event exists in its own right, the subsequent event in its own right, and the final event in its own right; and yet taken together they constitute a single whole.

Our atmospheres from top to bottom, from sun to earth, the atmospheres called ethers and airs, are marked off in levels of this kind. They are like the elements, compounds, and compounds of compounds that, taken all together, constitute a complex entity. These levels are distinct because they arise separately. They are what we mean by "vertical levels." The other levels, though, are gradual because they increase evenly. These are what we mean by "horizontal levels."

185   Absolutely everything that happens in the spiritual world and in the physical world results from a confluence of distinct and gradual levels, or of vertical and horizontal levels. We call the dimension constituted by distinct levels "height" and the dimension constituted by gradual levels "width." Their position relative to our eyesight does not change their labels.

Without a recognition of these levels, nothing can be known about the differences between the three heavens or about the differences of the love and wisdom of angels there, nothing about the differences of the warmth and light that surround them, nothing about the differences of the atmospheres that encompass and envelop them. Without a recognition of these levels, nothing can be known about differences of the inner abilities of our own minds, which means that nothing can be known about our states of reformation and regeneration,[105] nothing about the differences of the outer, bodily abilities of both us and angels, nothing whatever about the difference between what is spiritual and what is physical and nothing therefore about correspondences, nothing about any difference between the life of humans and that of animals or between higher and lower animals, nothing about differences in the forms of the plant kingdom or the substances of the mineral kingdom.

We can tell from this that people who do not know about these levels do not see causes clearly and fairly. They see only effects and form judgments about causes on that basis—usually by tracing a string of effects. Yet causes produce effects not by simple continuity but by a distinct step. The cause is one thing and the effect another, and the difference between them is like the difference between an antecedent event and a subsequent one, or like the difference between what forms and what is formed.

186   The angelic heavens may serve as an example for better comprehension of the reality and nature of distinct levels and of how they differ from gradual levels. There are three heavens marked off by vertical levels so that one is underneath another. The only way they communicate is by an inflow that comes from the Lord through the heavens in sequence down to the lowest, and not the other way around.

Each heaven on its own, though, is marked off not by vertical levels but by horizontal ones. The people in the middle or center are in the light of wisdom, while those around them all the way to the borders are in the shadow of wisdom. That is, wisdom wanes all the way to ignorance as the light declines into shadow, which happens gradually.

It is the same with us. The inner realms of our minds are marked off into as many levels as are the angelic heavens, with one level over another. So the inner realms of our minds are marked off in distinct or vertical levels. This is why we can be engaged in the lowest level, a higher level, or the highest level depending on the level of our wisdom. It is why the higher level is closed when we are exclusively engaged in the lowest one, and why the higher one is opened as we accept wisdom from the Lord. There are also gradual or horizontal levels in us just as there are in heaven.

The reason we resemble the heavens is that we are miniature heavens as to the deeper realms of our minds when we are engaged in love and wisdom from the Lord. (On our being miniature heavens as to the deeper realms of our minds, see *Heaven and Hell* 51–58.)

We can tell from this sample that people who know nothing about 187 distinct or vertical levels cannot know anything about our state when it comes to reformation and regeneration, processes that are effected by our acceptance of love and wisdom from the Lord and a consequent opening of the deeper levels of our minds in due sequence. They cannot know, either, about the inflow through the heavens from the Lord or about the design into which they themselves were created. Anyone who ponders these subjects on the basis of gradual or horizontal levels rather than distinct or vertical ones can see them only in terms of effects and not at all in terms of causes. Seeing things solely in terms of effects is basing thought on illusions, which leads to one error after another. By inductive reasoning we can multiply these errors so much that ultimately grotesque distortions are labeled truths.

I am not aware that anything about distinct or vertical levels has yet 188 come to people's attention—only things about gradual or horizontal levels. Yet nothing about causes can come to light in truth without familiarity with both kinds of level. That is why this whole part is devoted to this subject. After all, the purpose of this modest work is to uncover causes and to see effects on that basis, thereby dispelling the darkness that envelops people in the church concerning God, the Lord, and the divine matters in general that we refer to as "spiritual."

This I can relate, that angels are struck with sorrow at the darkness on earth. They say that they hardly see any light anywhere and that people are latching onto illusions and "proving" them so that they pile distortion on distortion. In order to prove their distortions, they use reasoning based on illusions and on distorted truths to investigate things that cannot be cleared up because of the darkness that surrounds causes and because of their ignorance of truths. Angels expressed the greatest grief over their "proof" of faith separated from charity and over justification by faith, as well as over [mistaken] concepts of God, angels, and spirits, and over ignorance of the nature of love and wisdom.

189 *Vertical levels are matched in kind, with one following from another in sequence like a purpose, a means, and a result.* Since horizontal or gradual levels are like levels of light to shade, warmth to cold, hard to soft, dense to sparse, coarse to fine, and so on, and since we are familiar with these levels from our sensory and visual experience while we are not familiar with vertical or distinct levels, I need to give particular attention to these latter in this part. Without familiarity with these levels, that is, we cannot see causes.

It is in fact recognized that a purpose, a means, and a result follow in sequence like antecedent, subsequent, and final events. It is recognized that the purpose produces the means and then produces the result through the means so that the purpose can be realized; and much more is recognized along the same lines. Knowing such things without seeing them by applying them to actual events, however, is only abstract knowledge. It lasts only as long as we are engaged in analytical thought on the basis of metaphysical principles. As a result, even though a purpose, a means, and a result do progress by distinct levels, still there is little if any knowledge of those levels in the world. Thinking only about abstractions is like something ethereal that dissipates; but if these abstract principles are applied to things of an earthly nature, then they are like something we see with our own eyes on earth, and they stay in our memory.

190 Everything in the world characterized by three dimensions, that is, everything we call a compound, is constituted by three vertical or distinct levels. Some examples may make this clear. We know from visual experience that every muscle in the human body is made up of tiny fibers and that these, gathered into bundles, make up the larger fibers we call motor fibers. From these bundles come that compound entity called a muscle.

It is the same with our nerves. The smallest fibers in them are woven together into larger ones that look like threads, and gatherings of these are woven together into nerves. It is the same with the rest of the weavings, bundlings, and gatherings that make up our organs and viscera. They are compounds of fibers and vessels in various arrangements, depending on similar levels.

It is the same as well in all the members of the plant kingdom and all the members of the mineral kingdom. There are threefold gatherings of filaments in wood and threefold conglomerates of elements in metals and rocks as well.

We can see from this what distinct levels are like, namely that one level is made from another and a third from the second, the third being called a compound. Each level is distinct from the other.

On this basis we can draw conclusions about things not visible to our eyes, since their arrangement is similar—for example about the organized substances that are the vessels and dwellings of the thoughts and feelings in our brains, about the atmospheres, about warmth and light, and about love and wisdom. The atmospheres are vessels of warmth and light, and warmth and light are vessels of love and wisdom. So if there are levels of the atmospheres, then there are similar levels of warmth and light and similar levels of love and wisdom. There is not one set of relationships in one case and a different set in another. **191**

We can tell from what has just been said that these levels are consistent, of the same character and nature. The smallest, larger, and largest motor fibers of our muscles have the same basic nature. The smallest, larger, and largest nerve fibers match; the woody filaments match from their smallest forms to their compounds; and the parts of rocks and metals match in the same way. The organized substances that are vessels and dwellings of our thoughts and feelings match, from the very simplest to their overall compound, the brain. The atmospheres match, from pure ether to air. The levels of warmth and light that parallel those of the atmospheres in their sequence match; and therefore so do the levels of love and wisdom. **192**

Things that are not of the same character and nature do not match and do not harmonize with things that do. This means that they cannot combine with them to make up distinct levels. They can combine only with their own kind, with things of the same character and nature, things that match.

Clearly, these levels are in a sequence like that of a purpose, a means, and a result, since the first or smallest promotes its cause through the intermediate and achieves its result through the last. **193**

It is important to realize that each level is delineated from the other by its own membrane, with all the levels together being delineated by a **194** common membrane. This common membrane communicates with the deeper and deepest levels in proper sequence, which is what makes possible the union and concerted action of all of them.

195 *The first level is the sum and substance of all the levels.* This is because the levels of every subject and every object are matched in kind, and they are matched in kind because they have been produced by the first level. The way they are formed is that the first level produces a second by folding together or congregating—in short, by gathering; and through this second level, it produces a third. Further, it marks each level off from the other by a surrounding membrane.[106] We can see from this that the first level is in primary and sole control of the subsequent ones, and that in fact the first level is the sum and substance of all the levels.

196 While we talk about the relationships of the levels to each other, this principle really applies to the substances that exist on their levels. The language of levels is an abstract language that is universal and therefore applicable to any subject or object that may have levels in its own particular way.

197 We can apply this principle to everything that was listed in the previous section—to muscles and nerves, for example, to the substances and components of both the plant and mineral kingdoms, to the organized substances that are the subjects of our own thoughts and feelings, to the atmospheres, to warmth and light, and to love and wisdom. In each instance the first is the only controlling reality in things subsequent and is in fact their only content; and since it is their only content, it is all there is to them.

We can see the truth of this from what we have already recognized, namely that the purpose is the whole of the means and through the means is the whole of the result. This is why we refer to a purpose, a means, and a result as a first end, an intermediate end, and a final end. It is why the cause of a cause is also the cause of what is caused. It is why there is nothing essential within the means except the purpose and nothing essential in motion except energy. It is also why there is only one substance that is substance in its own right.

198 This makes it clear that Divinity, being substance in its own right or the unique and sole substance, is the source of absolutely everything that has been created. This means that God is the sum and substance of the universe, in accord with what was presented in part 1: divine love and wisdom is substance and form (§§40–43); divine love and wisdom is substance and form in its own right, and is therefore wholly itself and

unique (§§44–46); everything in the universe was created by divine love and wisdom (§§54–60 *[52–60]*); the created universe is therefore an image of him (§§61–65 *[61–64]*); and [in part 2,] the Lord alone is the heaven where angels live (§§113–118).

All processes of perfection increase and rise by and according to levels. I have already explained that there are two kinds of level, horizontal and vertical, in §§184–188 above. I have explained that the horizontal levels are like levels of light tending toward darkness or wisdom tending toward ignorance, while vertical levels are like those of a purpose, a means, and a result, or like something antecedent, something subsequent, and something final. These latter levels are described as rising and falling, since they involve height; while the former are described as waxing and waning because they involve width.

199

These levels are so different from each other that they have nothing in common; so they need to be grasped clearly and not confused with each other in any way.

The reason all processes of perfection increase and rise by and according to levels is that all attributes are secondary to their substances, and perfection and imperfection are general attributes. We attribute them to life, to events, and to forms.

200

Perfection of life is perfection of love and wisdom, and since volition and discernment are their vessels, perfection of life is also perfection of volition and discernment and therefore of feelings and thoughts. Further, since spiritual warmth is the vehicle of love and spiritual light is the vehicle of wisdom, their perfection too can be traced back to perfection of life.

Perfection of events is perfection of everything that is activated and set in motion by life, though life is not inherent in the events. Such events are the atmospheres in regard to what they do, also our own inner and outer organized substances and those of all kinds of animal. Such events also are all the things in the physical world that get their activities directly or indirectly from its sun.

Perfection of forms and perfection of events constitute a single entity, since the nature of the events determines the nature of the forms. The only difference is that the forms are forms of substance while the events are what the substances do. Consequently, the two have similar levels of perfection. Even forms that are not doing anything at a given time have their kinds of perfection according to levels.

There is no need at this point to discuss the way processes of perfection of life, events, and forms rise and fall by horizontal or gradual

201

levels because these levels are familiar in our world. There is, however, a need to discuss the way processes of perfection of life, events, and forms rise and fall by vertical or distinct levels, because these levels are not familiar in our world. From what we can see in this physical world, it is almost impossible to understand how these processes rise and fall by distinct levels, but it is quite clear in what we can see in the spiritual world. All we discover from what we see in the physical world is that the deeper we look, the more wondrous are the things we run into—in our eyes, for example, or our ears, tongue, muscles, heart, lungs, liver, pancreas, kidneys, and the rest of our internal organs, as well as in seeds, fruits, and flowers and even in metals, minerals, and rocks. It is widely known that we run into more wondrous things in all these phenomena the deeper we probe; but little attention has been paid to the fact that the deeper perfection increases by vertical or distinct levels. Our ignorance of these levels has kept this hidden.

Since these levels are openly visible in the spiritual world, though, with that whole world clearly marked off by them from top to bottom, we can gain familiarity with these levels on that basis and then draw conclusions about the processes of perfection of events and forms that occur on comparable levels in this physical world.

202 There are three heavens in the spiritual world, arranged by vertical levels. The angels in the highest heaven are better in every respect than those of the intermediate heaven, and the angels in the intermediate heaven are better in every respect than those of the lowest heaven. Because of these levels of perfection, angels of the lowest heaven cannot even approach the threshold of the perfection of angels of the intermediate heaven, and these latter in turn cannot approach the threshold of the perfection of angels of the highest heaven. This may appear paradoxical, but it is the truth. The reason is that they are grouped by distinct levels and not by gradual ones.

Experience has taught me that there is such a difference between angels of the higher and lower heavens in feelings and thoughts and therefore in speech that they have nothing in common. Communication happens only by the correspondences that arise through the Lord's direct inflow into all the heavens and the indirect inflow through the highest heaven to the lowest.

Because of the nature of these distinctions, they cannot be expressed in earthly language, so I cannot describe them. Angels' thoughts do not fit into earthly concepts because they are spiritual. They can only be expressed and described by angels in their own language and words and writing, but not in human ones. This is why it says that people have heard and seen indescribable things in the heavens.

The following may afford some understanding of these differences. The thoughts of angels of the highest or third heaven are thoughts of purposes; the thoughts of angels of the intermediate or second heaven are thoughts of means; and the thoughts of angels of the lowest or first heaven are thoughts of results. It is important to realize that it is one thing to think on the basis of purposes and another to think about purposes, one thing to think on the basis of means and another to think about means, one thing to think on the basis of results and another to think about results. Angels of the lower heavens do think about means and about purposes; but angels of the higher heavens think on the basis of means and on the basis of purposes. Thinking on the basis of such things comes from a higher level of wisdom, while thinking about them comes from a lower level. Thinking on the basis of purposes comes from wisdom; thinking on the basis of means comes from intelligence; and thinking on the basis of results comes from being informed.

We can see from this that all processes of perfection rise and fall by and according to levels.

Since the deeper reaches of our own minds, of our volition and discernment, are like the heavens as far as levels are concerned (we are actually miniature heavens as to the deeper reaches of our minds), their processes of perfection are similar. However, these processes are not perceptible to any of us as long as we are living in this world, since we are then on the lowest level; and the higher levels are unrecognizable from the lowest level. After death, though, we can identify them, since then we are on whatever level answers to our love and wisdom. Then we become angels and think and say things that are indescribable to our physical self. The raising up of everything in our minds then is not by some simple ratio but by the threefold ratio that is the ratio of vertical levels. The simple ratio applies to horizontal levels. **203**

The only people who rise or are brought up to those levels, though, are the ones who have been attentive to truths in this world and have applied them to their lives.

It may seem as though antecedent things are less perfect than subsequent ones and constituent things are less perfect than compounds, but in fact the antecedent things that give rise to subsequent ones are more perfect, as are the constituents from which compounds are formed. This is because the antecedent or constituent things are less covered, less shrouded by lifeless substances and materials. They are more divine, so to **204** speak, and as such are closer to the spiritual sun where the Lord is. Perfection itself is in the Lord and therefore in the sun that is the first emanation of his divine love and wisdom. It comes from there into things that are next in sequence, and so on in order down to the lowest things, which are more imperfect as they are more remote.

If it were not for this supreme perfection in things antecedent and constituent, neither we nor any living creature could arise from seed and then continue in existence. The seeds of trees and shrubs could not sprout and spread, either. The more antecedent a thing is, or the more whole it is, the more immune it is to harm because of its greater perfection.

205 *In a sequential arrangement, the first level is the highest and the third the lowest, while in a simultaneous arrangement, the first level is the center and the third level is the circumference.* There is a sequential arrangement and a simultaneous one. The sequential arrangement of these levels is from highest to lowest or from top to bottom. This is the arrangement of the angelic heavens, with the third heaven as the highest, the second in between, and the first as the lowest. These are their relative locations.

The same sequential arrangement applies to states of love and wisdom among angels in heaven, to warmth and light, and to spiritual atmospheres. The same arrangement applies to all the processes of perfection of events and forms there.

When the vertical or distinct levels are in this sequential arrangement, they are like a tower divided into three floors so that one can go up or down. The most perfect and lovely things are on the top floor, less perfect and lovely things on the middle floor, and still less perfect and lovely things on the lowest floor.

In a simultaneous arrangement of the same levels, though, it looks different. Then the highest elements of the sequential arrangement—as I have mentioned, the most perfect and lovely ones—are in the center, the lower ones in an intermediate region, and the lowest on the outside. It is as though there were a solid object made up of these three levels with the finest substances in the middle or center, less fine particles around that, and on the outside, forming a kind of envelope, parts composed of these and therefore coarsest. It is as though the tower we were talking about had settled into a plane, with the top floor becoming the center, the middle floor an intermediate region, and the lowest floor the outside.

206 Since the highest thing in sequential arrangement is the central thing in simultaneous arrangement and the lowest is the outermost, "higher"

in the Word means more internal and "lower" means more external. The same holds for "upward" and "downward" and for "high" and "low."

In every final form there are distinct levels in simultaneous arrange- **207** ment. This is the arrangement of the motor fibers in every muscle, the fibers in every nerve, the fibers and tiny vessels in all our viscera and organs. At the heart of each are the simplest and most perfect substances, while the outside is formed from their compounds.

The same arrangement of these levels is found in every seed, every fruit, even in every metal and rock. This is the nature of the parts that constitute their totality. Their central, intermediate, and outermost parts are on these levels, and they themselves are successive compounds, aggregates, or masses of these simple components that are their primary substances and materials.

In short, there are levels like this in every final form and therefore **208** in every effect, since every final form consists of antecedents that in turn consist of things primary to them. Likewise every result comes from a means and every means from a purpose, the purpose being the whole essence of the means and the means the whole essence of the result, as I have just explained [§§168, 197]. Further, the purpose constitutes the center, the means the intermediate, and the result the final outcome.

We will see later [§§224, 231, 232, 235, 236–241] that the same holds for levels of love and wisdom, warmth and light, and for the organized forms of feelings and thoughts within us. I have discussed the sequence of these levels in sequential and simultaneous arrangements in *Teachings for the New Jerusalem on Sacred Scripture* 38[107] and elsewhere, showing that there are similar levels in all the details of the Word.

The final level is the composite, vessel, and foundation of the prior levels. Ex- **209** amples of the principle of levels that is under discussion in this part have thus far been drawn from various things that occur in our two worlds— levels of the heavens where angels live, for example, levels of the warmth and light that surround them, of the atmospheres, of various parts of the human body, and of things in the animal and mineral kingdoms. The principle of levels has a wider range, though. Its range includes not only physical phenomena but also societal, moral, and spiritual ones in all their detail.

There are two reasons why the principle of levels includes such matters. The first is that there is a trine in everything that can be said to have attributes, a trine called purpose, means, and result; and these three are related to each other by vertical levels. The second reason is that no societal, moral, or spiritual phenomenon is abstract or disembodied. They are matters of substance, for just as love and wisdom are not abstractions but substances (as I have explained above in §§40–43), so are all the things we refer to as societal, moral, and spiritual. We can of course think about them in the abstract, as disembodied, but in their own right they are not abstractions. Take feeling and thought, for example, or charity and faith, or volition and discernment. What applies to love and wisdom applies to them as well, namely that they do not happen apart from subjects that are substantial. They actually have to do with the state of those subjects or substances. We will see later [§§273, 316] that they are shifts of state that give rise to change. "Substance" means form as well, since there is no such thing as a formless substance.

210   Since we can think about volition and discernment, about feeling and thought, and about charity and faith apart from the substantial realities that are their subjects, and since we have thought about them in this way, we have lost any appropriate concept of them, any realization that they refer to the states of substantial realities or forms. Exactly the same principle applies to sensations and actions, which are not things in the abstract apart from our sensory and motor organs. In the abstract, or apart from their organs, they are theoretical constructs only. They[108] are like sight with no eye, hearing with no ear, taste with no tongue, and so on.

211   Since all societal, moral, and spiritual events, like all physical ones, happen not only by gradual levels but also on distinct levels, and since processes on distinct levels are like the processes of purpose to means and means to result, I should like to illustrate and demonstrate the present topic (that the final level is the composite, vessel, and foundation of the prior levels) by what I have just mentioned, namely instances of love and wisdom, of volition and discernment, of feeling and thought, and of charity and faith.

212   We can tell quite clearly that the final level is the composite, vessel, and foundation of the prior ones by looking at the way purpose and means progress to result. Enlightened reason can grasp the fact that the effect is the composite, vessel, and foundation of the means and the purpose, but cannot grasp as clearly the fact that the purpose in all fullness and the means in all fullness are actively present in the result, with the result being completely inclusive of them.

This follows from what has already been said in this part, especially from the fact that one level comes from another in a three-stage sequence and that a result is simply a purpose in its final form. Since the final form is this kind of composite, it follows that the final form is their vessel and also their foundation.

As for love and wisdom, love is the purpose, wisdom the means, and service the result. Further, service is the composite, vessel, and foundation of wisdom and love, such a composite and such a vessel that every bit of love and every bit of wisdom is actively present in it. It is their total presence. We need to be absolutely clear, though, that in keeping with what was presented in §§189–194 above, what are present in service are all the elements of love and wisdom that are of the same kind, harmonious.

Desire, thought, and act occur on a sequence of similar levels, since every desire has to do with love, every thought with wisdom, and every act with service. Charity, faith, and good works occur on the same sequence of levels, since charity is a matter of desire, faith of thought, and good works of act. Volition, discernment, and practice occur on the same sequence of levels as well, since volition is a matter of love and therefore of desire, discernment of wisdom and therefore of faith, and practice of service and therefore of deeds. Just as all the elements of wisdom and love dwell within service, all the elements of thought and desire dwell within act, and all the elements of faith and charity dwell within deeds, and so on. This means all the elements that are of the same kind, that are harmonious.

People have not yet recognized that the last member of each sequence—service, act, deed, and practice—is the composite and vessel of all the earlier members. It seems as though there were nothing more within service, act, deed, or practice than there is within motion. However, all these prior stages are actively present within, so completely present that nothing is missing. They are enclosed within it the way wine is enclosed in a bottle or furnishings in a house.

The reason this is not noticed is that we look at acts of service from the outside only, and things seen from the outside are simply events and motions. It is like seeing our arms and hands move and not knowing that a thousand motor fibers are cooperating in each movement, with a thousand elements of thought and desire answering to those thousand motor fibers and stimulating them. Since these things are happening far inside, they are not visible to any of our physical senses. This much is known, that nothing is done in or through the body except from volition and through thought; and since these two are acting, every element of volition and thought must necessarily be present within the act. They cannot be separated. This is why we draw conclusions on the basis of deeds or works about each other's purposeful thought, which we refer to as "intent."

I have learned that angels can sense and see from someone's single deed or work everything about the intention and thought of the one who is doing it. From the person's volition, angels of the third heaven see the purpose for which it is being done, and angels of the second heaven see the means through which the purpose is working. This is why deeds and works are so often mandated in the Word, and why it says that we are known by our works.

216 According to angelic wisdom, unless volition and discernment, or desire and thought, or charity and faith, devote themselves to involvement in works or deeds whenever possible, they are nothing but passing breezes, so to speak, or images in the air that vanish. They first take on permanence in us and become part of our life when we perform and do them. The reason is that the final stage is the composite, vessel, and foundation of the prior stages.

Faith apart from good works is just this kind of airy nothing or image, and so are faith and charity apart from their practice. The only difference is that people who put faith and charity together know what is good and are able to intend and do it, but not people who are devoted to faith apart from charity.

217 *The vertical levels find their full realization and power in their final form.* I explained in the preceding section that the final level is the composite and vessel of the prior levels. It follows from this that the prior levels find their full realization in their final level. That is where they are in their effect, and every effect is a summary of its causes.

218 Everything I have already cited from what we can sense and perceive may be used in support of the proposition that the rising and falling levels, the ones we call antecedent and subsequent or vertical and distinct levels, find their power in their final stage. At this point, though, I want to cite only energy, force, and motion in lifeless and living entities.

It is common knowledge that energy does not accomplish anything by itself, but only through forces responsive to it, using them to cause motion. This is why energy is the whole essence of force, and through force, the whole essence of motion.[109] Since motion is the final stage of energy, energy exercises its power through motion. The only way energy, force, and motion are united is by vertical levels, a union that is not one of continuity, since the levels are distinct, but of responsiveness. Energy, that is, is not force, and force is not motion. Rather, force is produced by energy, and force is energy being exercised; and motion is produced by force. This means that there is no power in pure energy or pure force, but in the motion that they produce.

The truth of this may appear debatable because I have not illustrated it by application to things we can sense and perceive in the physical world.[110] Still, this is the nature of stages that culminate in power.

Let me apply these principles to living energy, living force, and living motion. Living energy in us, who are the living subjects, is our volition in union with our discernment. The living forces in us are what make up the inner parts of our bodies, throughout which there are motor fibers interconnected in various ways. Living motion in us is the action that is produced by volition in union with discernment through the agency of these forces. The deeper levels of volition and discernment constitute the first level, the inner parts of the body constitute the second level, and the whole body, their composite, constitutes the third level. It is common knowledge that the deeper levels of the mind are not empowered except through forces in the body, and that the forces become powerful and effective only through the action of the body.

219

These three stages do not act by continuity but by distinct levels, and acting by distinct levels is acting by responsiveness. The deeper levels of the mind answer to the inner parts of the body and the inner parts of the body answer to those outer parts that give rise to actions; so the two prior stages are empowered through the outer parts of the body.

It might seem as though our inner energy and forces had some power even in the absence of action—in dreams, for example, or when we are at rest—but at such times the energy and forces find definition in our general physical motions, those of heart and lungs. Once these stop, however, the forces stop as well, and with them the energy.

Since the whole being or body focuses its powers primarily in the arms and hands, which are the extremities, arms and hands in the Word mean power, with the right hand meaning the greater power. Since this is how the levels unfold and express themselves in power, the angels who are with us and are sensitive to everything in us can tell simply from a single action of our hand what we are like in discernment and intent, in charity and faith, and therefore in the inner life of our minds and the outer life in our bodies, which comes from the inner life.

220

I have often been astounded by the kind of recognition angels have simply from the physical action of a hand, but it has been shown to me often enough and by personal experience. I have also been told that this is why induction into ministry is done by the laying on of hands and why touching with the hand means sharing, among other things. This leads to the conclusion that the whole of charity and faith is in works and that charity and faith without works are like halos around the sun that dissipate and vanish when a cloud passes by. So time after time the Word talks about works and doing and says that our salvation depends on such things. Then too, the one who does something is called wise and the one who does not is called foolish.[111]

We should realize, though, that "works" means deeds of service that are put into action. The whole of charity and faith is in them and depends on them. The correspondence is with acts of service because while the correspondence is spiritual, it happens through the substances and materials that are its subjects.

221   I am now allowed to disclose two secrets that can be brought within comprehension through what has just been said.[112]

The first is that the Word finds its fullest expression and power in its literal meaning. There are three meanings in the Word answering to the three levels—a heavenly meaning, a spiritual meaning, and an earthly meaning. Since the Word contains these three meanings by the three vertical levels and their union is through correspondence, the final meaning, the earthly one that we call the literal meaning, is not only the composite, vessel, and foundation of the deeper, corresponding meanings, it is also the Word in its fullest expression and its full power. There is an abundance of evidence and support for this in *Teachings for the New Jerusalem on Sacred Scripture* 27–35 *[27–36]*, 36–49 *[37–49]*, 50–61, and 62–69.

The second secret is that the Lord came into the world and took on a human nature in order to gain access to the power to conquer the hells and bring everything in the heavens and on earth back into order. He put on this human nature over the human nature he had before. The human nature he put on in the world was like our own worldly nature, but each nature was still divine and therefore infinitely transcendent of our own and angels' finite human nature. Further, since he completely transformed his physical human level all the way to its limits, he, unlike anyone else, rose from death with his whole body. By taking on this human nature he clothed himself with a divine omnipotence not only for the conquest of the hells and the reordering of the heavens but also for keeping the hells subject forever and saving us. This power is what is meant by his sitting at the right hand of the power and might of God.

Since the Lord made himself divine truth in ultimate form by taking on a physical human nature, he is called "the Word," and it says that the

Word was made flesh.[113] Divine truth in its ultimate form is the Word in its literal meaning. He made himself that Word by fulfilling everything about himself in the Word, in Moses and the prophets.[114]

Everyone is his or her own good and true nature. Nothing else makes us human. Because he took on a physical human nature, the Lord is divine good and divine truth itself, or in other words, divine love and divine wisdom itself, in both their primal and their ultimate forms. This is why he looks like a sun in the angelic heavens with greater glory and fuller brilliance after his coming into the world than before his coming. This is a secret that can be brought within comprehension by the principle of levels.

I will be discussing later [§233] his omnipotence before his coming into the world.

There are levels of both kinds in everything that has been created, no matter how large or small. There is no way to offer visible examples of the fact **222** that the largest and smallest things of all are made up of distinct and gradual, or vertical and horizontal, levels, because the smallest things that occur are not visible to our eyes and the largest do not seem to be marked off into levels. The only available way to explain this principle, then, is by looking to universal phenomena; and since angels are engaged in wisdom on the basis of universal principles and derive knowledge about details on that basis, I may offer some of the things they have said on the subject.

Angelic pronouncements on the subject are as follows. There is no **223** thing so small that it does not contain levels of both kinds—not the smallest thing in any animal, not the smallest thing in any plant, not the smallest thing in any mineral, not the smallest thing in the ether or the air. Further, since the ether and air are vessels of warmth and light, this holds for the smallest trace of warmth and light, and since spiritual warmth and spiritual light are vessels of love and wisdom, there is not the smallest bit of these in which there are not levels of both kinds.

Another pronouncement of angels is that every least bit of desire, every least bit of thought, even every least bit of a mental image, is made up of levels of both kinds, and that any least thing that is not made up of these levels is actually nothing. It has no form, so it has no characteristics, no state that can shift and change so that it becomes manifest.[115]

Angels support this by the truth that the infinite things in God the Creator, who is the Lord from eternity, are "distinguishably one," with infinite things within those infinite things of his and levels of both kinds within those infinitely infinite things that are also distinguishably one in him. Since these are within him, then, and since everything was created by him and everything so created offers a kind of image of what is within him, it follows that there is not the smallest finite thing that does not have these levels in it. The reason these levels are in the smallest and the largest things alike is that Divinity is the same in the largest and smallest things.

On infinite things being distinguishably one in the Divine-Human One, see §§17–22 above; and on Divinity being the same in the largest and smallest things, §§77–82. There are further examples in §§155, 169, and 171.

224   The reason there is not the slightest trace of love and wisdom or of desire and thought or of a mental image that does not have levels of both kinds in it is that love and wisdom, and likewise desire and thought, are substance and form (as I have explained in §§40–43 above). As I have already stated [§223] there is no form that does not involve levels of both kinds. It follows that they involve these same levels. To separate love and wisdom or desire and thought from substance-in-form is to annihilate them, because they do not occur apart from their subjects. They are actually manifested by the states of these subjects as we perceive them when they change.

225   The largest things that involve levels of both kinds include the universe in all its fullness and the physical world in all its fullness. They include the spiritual world in its fullness, every empire and every monarchy in its fullness and their every moral and spiritual feature in its fullness, the whole animal kingdom, the whole plant kingdom, and the whole mineral kingdom, each in all its fullness. Then there are the atmospheres of each world[116] taken as a whole, and their forms of warmth and light. The same holds for less inclusive entities, such as ourselves in our fullness, every animal in its fullness, every tree and shrub in its fullness, even every stone and metal in its fullness.

Their forms are similar in this respect, namely that they are made up of levels of both kinds. This is because the Divinity by which they were created is the same in the largest and smallest things, as noted above in §§77–82. All their details, no matter how minute, resemble their shared aspects—no matter how widely shared those aspects are among them— in being forms made up of levels of both kinds.

226   The fact that the largest and smallest things are forms made up of levels of both kinds results in their being connected from beginning to end; their likeness actually unites them. Still, there is not the least thing that is identical to something else, which is why there is a distinctiveness of everything, down to the least detail.

The reason there are no identical elements in any form or between different forms is that there are the same kinds of levels in the largest entities, and the largest entities are made up of the smallest ones. When the largest entities are made up of these levels, with corresponding constant distinctions from top to bottom and from center to circumference, it follows that there is nothing in them involving these levels, nothing lesser or least, that is identical.

It is also an item of angelic wisdom that the perfection of the created universe comes from a resemblance in regard to levels between inclusive forms and their particular constituents, or between the largest and smallest things. This means that each thing sees the other as a kindred with which it can unite in its whole function and with which it can realize its whole purpose in actual results. 227

All this may seem paradoxical, true, because it has not been presented with application to things we can see. Still, since abstract principles are universal, they are often easier to grasp than the applications. The applications vary constantly, and the variation is confusing. 228

Some people say that there is a substance so simple that it is not a form made up of lesser forms, and that by putting enough of this substance together, secondary substances or compounds come into being, eventually leading to the substances that we refer to as "matter."[117] However, there is no such thing as these "simplest substances." What would a substance be without some form? It would be something without attributes, and nothing can be constituted by putting together things that have no attributes. 229

Later, when I discuss forms,[118] we will see that there are countless elements in the very first created substances, the very smallest and simplest ones.

There are three infinite and uncreated vertical levels in the Lord, and three finite and created levels in us. The reason there are three infinite and uncreated vertical levels in the Lord is that the Lord is love itself and wisdom itself, as explained above [§§28–33]. Since the Lord is love itself and wisdom itself, he is also usefulness itself, since love has useful functions as its goal and puts them into effect by means of wisdom. Apart from usefulness, love and wisdom have no definition or boundary, no dwelling. This means that we cannot say they exist or are present unless there is a useful function in which they occur. 230

These three elements constitute three vertical levels in agents of life. These three are like the first end, the intermediate end that we refer to as the means, and the ultimate end that we refer to as the result. I have already [§§167–169, 184] explained and amply documented the fact that purpose, means, and result constitute three vertical levels.

231   We can tell that there are these three levels in us from the way human minds are raised all the way into those levels of love and wisdom that angels of the second and third heaven enjoy. All those angels were born human; and in regard to the inner reaches of our minds, each of us is a miniature form of heaven. Count the number of heavens and you have the number of vertical levels within each of us, from our creation. Each of us is an image and likeness of God; so these three levels are written into us because they are in the Divine-Human One—that is, in the Lord.

We can tell that these levels in the Lord are infinite and uncreated while ours are finite and created on the basis of what I presented in part 1, for example from the principle that the Lord is intrinsic love and wisdom, that we are recipients of love and wisdom from the Lord, that only what is infinite can be attributed to the Lord, and that only what is finite can be attributed to us.[119]

232   For angels, these three levels are called heavenly, spiritual, and earthly; and for them, the heavenly level is the level of love, the spiritual level the level of wisdom, and the earthly level the level of useful functions. The reason for giving the levels these names is that the heavens are divided into two kingdoms, one called the heavenly kingdom and the other the spiritual kingdom, with a third kingdom added where we in the world are, called the earthly one.[120]

Then too, the angels who make up the heavenly kingdom are focused on love, while the angels who make up the spiritual kingdom are focused on wisdom and we in this world are focused on useful functions. This is why the kingdoms are united. I will be describing in the next part[121] how to understand the statement that we are focused on useful functions.

233   I have received information from heaven that before the Lord from eternity (who is Jehovah) took on a human nature in the world, the first two levels in him were actual while the third level was potential, which is the way things are for angels. After he took on a human nature in our world, though, he clothed himself with that third level as well, the one we call "earthly," and in this way became a human being like us in this world. Still, there was the difference that this level like the others was infinite and uncreated, while in angels and in us the levels are finite and created.

What happened was that although the Divinity that had filled all space without being bound by space (see §§69–72) also penetrated to the most remote elements of nature, before taking on a human nature the divine inflow into the earthly level was indirect, through the angelic heavens. After taking on the human nature it was direct from Divinity itself. This is why all the world's churches[122] before his coming were representative of spiritual and heavenly realities,[123] while after his coming they became spiritual and heavenly on the earthly level and representational worship was done away with. This is also the reason why the sun of the angelic heaven (which as already noted [§93] is the first emanation of his divine love and wisdom) shone out with greater radiance and brilliance after he took on a human nature than before. This is also the meaning of the following words in Isaiah: "In that day the light of the moon will be like the light of the sun, and the light of the sun will be sevenfold, like the light of seven days" (Isaiah 30:25 [30:26]). This is about the state of heaven and the church after the Lord's coming into the world. There is also Revelation 1:16, "the face of the Human-born One looked like the sun shining at full strength";[124] and such other passages as Isaiah 60:20; 2 Samuel 23:3, 4; and Matthew 17:1, 2.[125] We might compare our indirect enlightenment through the angelic heaven, which obtained before the Lord's coming, with the moon's light, which is indirect sunlight. Since this became a direct enlightenment after the Lord's coming, it says in [the passage just cited from] Isaiah that the light of the moon will be like the light of the sun; and it says in David, "Righteous people will blossom in his day, and peace in abundance until the moon is no more" (Psalms 72:7). This too is about the Lord.

The reason the Lord from eternity, or Jehovah, took on this third **234** level by assuming a human nature in the world is that he could not enter this world except through a nature like our own. The coming could not have been accomplished, then, except by conception from his own Divinity and birth by a virgin. This enabled him to take off a nature that was intrinsically dead, and yet receptive of Divinity, and take on a divine nature. This is the meaning of the Lord's two states in the world, called a state of emptying out and a state of transformation, which I have dealt with in *Teachings for the New Jerusalem on the Lord*.

I have said these things about the three-step ladder of vertical levels **235** in generalizations; but since as stated in the preceding section these levels are characteristic of the largest and smallest things, I cannot say anything about them in detail at this point. I can say only that there are levels like this in everything that has to do with love and therefore in everything that has to do with wisdom, and that as a result there are levels like this in everything that has to do with usefulness. However, in the Lord they are all infinite, while in angels and in us they are finite. How these levels exist in love, wisdom, and use, though, can be described and unfolded only at some length.

236 *These three vertical levels exist in each of us from birth and can be opened in sequence. As they are opened, we are in the Lord and the Lord is in us.* The existence of three vertical levels in us has not been widely recognized before. This is because vertical levels themselves have not been identified, and as long as these levels have been unrecognized, the only levels people could know about are the gradual ones. When these are the only levels people know about, they can believe that our love and wisdom increase only gradually.

It needs to be realized, though, that we all have these three vertical or distinct levels in us from our birth, one above or within the other, and that each vertical or distinct level has horizontal or gradual levels by which it increases incrementally. This is because there are both kinds of level in everything, no matter how large or small, as explained above in §§222–229. Neither kind of level can exist apart from the other.

237 As noted in §232 above, these three vertical levels are called earthly, spiritual, and heavenly. When we are born, we come first into the earthly level, which gradually develops within us in keeping with the things we learn and the intelligence we gain through this learning, all the way to that summit of intelligence called rationality. This by itself, though, does not open the second level, the one called spiritual. This level is opened by a love for being useful that comes from our intelligence; but the love for being useful is a spiritual one, a love for our neighbor.

In the same way, this level can develop by incremental steps all the way to its summit; and it does so by our discovering what is true and good, or by spiritual truths. Even so, these do not open that third level that is called heavenly. This is opened by a heavenly love for being useful that is a love for the Lord; and love for the Lord is nothing but applying the precepts of the Word to our lives, these precepts being essentially to abstain from evil things because they are hellish and demonic and to do good things because they are heavenly and divine. This is how the three levels are opened in us sequentially.

238 As long as we are living in this world, we have no knowledge of any opening of levels within us. This is because our attention is focused on the earthly level, which is the most remote. We are thinking, intending, and talking and acting on that basis; and the spiritual level, which is deeper, does not communicate with the earthly level directly, but only by correspondence. Communication by correspondence is imperceptible.

However, as soon as we put off the earthly level, which happens when we die, we come into awareness of whatever level has been opened within us in the world, of the spiritual level if that level has been opened, of the heavenly level if that level has been opened. If we become conscious on the spiritual level after death, then we no longer think, intend, or talk or act in an earthly way, but spiritually. If we become conscious on the heavenly level, then we think, intend, and talk and act on that level. Further, since communication among the three levels occurs only by correspondence, the differences in level of love, wisdom, and useful function are so definite that there is no communication between them by direct contact.

We can see from this that we do have three vertical levels and that these can be opened in sequence.

Because there are within us these three levels of love and wisdom and therefore of usefulness, it follows that there are three levels of volition and discernment and consequent closure, and therefore of concentration within us on usefulness, since volition is the vessel of love, discernment the vessel of wisdom, and closure the usefulness that results from them. We can see from this that there is within each of us an earthly, a spiritual, and a heavenly volition and discernment, potentially from birth, and effectively when they are opened. 239

In short, the human mind, consisting of volition and discernment, has three levels from creation and birth, so we have an earthly mind, a spiritual mind, and a heavenly mind. Consequently, we can be raised into angelic wisdom and possess it even while we are living in this world. Still, we become conscious of it only after death, if we become angels; and then we say inexpressible things, things incomprehensible to an earthly-minded person.

I was acquainted with a moderately educated man in the world and saw him and talked with him in heaven after his death. I sensed very clearly that he was talking like an angel and that what he was saying was beyond the grasp of earthly-minded people. The reason was that in the world he had applied the precepts of the Word to his life and had worshiped the Lord; so the Lord had raised him into the third level of love and wisdom.

It is important to know about this raising up of the human mind, since understanding what follows depends on it.

There are two abilities within us, gifts from the Lord,[126] that distinguish us from animals. One ability is that we can discern what is true and what is good. This ability is called "rationality," and is an ability of our discernment. The other ability is that we can do what is true and what is 240 good. This ability is called "freedom," and is an ability of our volition. Because of our rationality, we can think what we want to think, either in favor of God or against God, in favor of our neighbor or against our neighbor. We can also intend and do what we are thinking, or when we see something evil and are afraid of the penalty, can use our freedom to refrain from doing it. It is because of these two abilities that we are human and are distinguished from animals.

These two abilities are gifts from the Lord within us. They come from him constantly and are never taken away, for if they were taken away, that would be the end of our humanity. The Lord lives in each of us, in the good and the evil alike, in these two abilities. They are the Lord's dwelling in the human race, which is why everyone, whether good or evil, lives forever. However, the Lord's dwelling within us is more intimate as we use these abilities to open the higher levels. By opening them, we come into consciousness of higher levels of love and wisdom and so come closer to the Lord. It makes sense, then, that as these levels are opened, we are in the Lord and the Lord is in us.

241 I have noted above [§§212, 213] that the three vertical levels are like a purpose, a means, and a result, and that the sequence of love, wisdom, and usefulness follows this sequence. I need at this point, then, to say a little about love as the purpose, wisdom as the means, and usefulness as the result.

People who pay attention to their reason when that reason is in the light can see that our love is the purpose of everything we do, since it is what we love that we think about, decide upon, and do, so it is what we have as our purpose. Our reason can also show us that wisdom is the means, since the love that is our purpose gathers in our discernment the means it needs to reach its goal. So it listens to its wisdom, and these resources constitute the means through which it works. We can see without further explanation that usefulness is the result.

Love, though, is not the same in one individual as in another, so wisdom is not the same in one individual as in another, and neither is usefulness. Since these three are matched in kind (as explained in §§189–194 above), the quality of our love determines the quality of our wisdom, and of our usefulness. I say "wisdom," but this means whatever is characteristic of our discernment.

242 [127] *Spiritual light flows in within us through three levels, but not spiritual warmth except to the extent that we abstain from evils as sins and turn to the Lord.* What I have presented thus far indicates that light and warmth emanate from the sun of heaven, that sun, described in part 2, that is the first emanation of divine love and wisdom. The light emanates from his[128] wisdom and the warmth from his love. Further, the light is the vessel of wisdom and the warmth is the vessel of love; and the more we are engaged in wisdom, the more we come into that divine light, and the more we are engaged in love, the more we come into that divine warmth.

We can also tell from what has been presented that there are three levels of light and three levels of warmth, or three levels of wisdom and three levels of love, and that these levels are formed within us in such a way that we are open to divine love and wisdom and therefore to the Lord.

The present task, then, is to show that while spiritual light flows in through these three levels in us, spiritual warmth does not—except to the extent that we abstain from evils as sins and turn to the Lord; or what amounts to the same thing, to show that we can accept wisdom all the way to the third level, but not love—unless we abstain from evils as sins and turn to the Lord; or (what again amounts to the same thing) to show that our discernment can be raised up into wisdom, but our volition cannot be raised up [into love]—except to the extent that we abstain from evils as sins.

It has become abundantly clear to me from my experiences in the spiritual world that our discernment can be raised up into heaven's light, or into angelic wisdom, but that our volition cannot be raised up into heaven's warmth or angelic love unless we abstain from evils as sins and turn to the Lord. I have often seen and sensed that very ordinary spirits who knew only that God exists and that the Lord was born as a human—hardly anything else—understood the mysteries of angelic wisdom completely, almost the way angels do. Nor were they the only ones. Even many members of the demonic mob understood. They understood while they were listening, that is, but not in their private thinking. When they were listening, light flowed into them from above; but in their private thinking the only light that could get in was the light that agreed with their warmth or love. So even after they had heard these mysteries and grasped them, when they turned their hearing away they retained nothing. In fact, the members of the devil's mob spat it out and denied it categorically. The reason was that the fire of their love and its light, being mindless, brought down a darkness that snuffed out the heavenly light that was flowing in from above. **243**

It is the same in this world. Anyone who has any sense at all and has not become inwardly convinced of false principles on the grounds of intellectual pride, on hearing people talk about higher things or on **244** reading about them understands, retains them, and eventually affirms them if there is any desire for learning. This holds true for evil and good people alike. Even evil people who at heart deny the divine gifts of the church can understand, discuss, and preach higher things, and can defend them in scholarly writing. However, when they are left on their own to think about them, their thinking is based on their hellish self-centeredness, and they deny them. We can see from this that our discernment can be in spiritual light even though our volition may not be in spiritual warmth.

It also follows from this that our discernment does not lead our volition, or that wisdom does not give rise to love. It merely teaches and shows the way. It teaches how we should live and shows us the way we should follow. It also follows from this that our volition leads our discernment and gets it to work in unison with itself. The love that is the substance of our volition gives the name of "wisdom" to whatever in our discernment it finds harmonious.

I will be showing below that on its own, apart from discernment, our volition accomplishes nothing. Everything it does, it does in conjunction with our discernment. However, our volition gains the cooperation of our discernment by flowing into it, and not the other way around.

245   Now I need to describe how light flows into the three levels that make up the human mind. From our birth, the forms that are receptive of warmth and light or love and wisdom (which as already noted [§223] are in a threefold pattern or on three levels) are translucent and let spiritual light pass through, the way clear glass lets physical light through. This is why we can be raised up all the way to the third level in respect to our wisdom. These forms are not opened, though, until spiritual warmth, or the love of wisdom, is united to the spiritual light. It is through this union that the translucent forms are opened level by level.

This is like the light and warmth of the world's sun and plant life on earth. The winter light is just as bright as summer light, but it does not open anything in seeds or trees. However, when the warmth of spring is united to that light then things open. The resemblance stems from the fact that spiritual light is analogous to physical light and spiritual warmth is analogous to physical warmth.

246   The only way to gain that spiritual warmth is by abstaining from evils as sins and then turning to the Lord, since as long as we are caught up in evil pursuits we are caught up in a love for them. We are enmeshed in our cravings for them; and that love for what is evil, that craving, is a form of love that is opposed to spiritual love and desire. Further, the only

way to get rid of that love or craving is by abstaining from evils as sins; and since we cannot do that on our own, but only by the Lord's agency, we need to turn to him. When we do abstain from our evils by the Lord's agency, then, our love for evil and its warmth are put aside and a love for what is good, with its warmth, is brought in in its place, enabling a higher level to be opened. The Lord actually flows in from above and opens it and unites the love or spiritual warmth with wisdom or spiritual light. As a result of this union we begin to blossom spiritually like a tree in springtime.

We are differentiated from animals by the inflow of spiritual light into all three levels of our minds; and beyond what animals can do, we can think analytically; we can see things that are true not only on the earthly level but on the spiritual level as well; and when we see them, we can acknowledge them and so be reformed and regenerated. Our ability to accept spiritual light is what we call rationality, already discussed [§240]. It is a gift from the Lord to each one of us, and one that is not taken away, since if it were taken away, we could not be reformed. It is because of this ability called rationality that we not only can think but can say what we are thinking, which animals cannot do. Then because of that second ability called freedom, also discussed above, we can do what we have thought intellectually.

Since I dealt with these two abilities that we claim—rationality and freedom—in §240, there is no need to say more about them here.

If that higher level, the spiritual level, is not opened in us, we become focused on the physical world and our sense impressions. I have just explained that there are three levels of the human mind called earthly, spiritual, and heavenly; that these levels can be opened in us in sequence; that the earthly level is opened first; and that afterward, if we abstain from evils as sins and turn to the Lord, the spiritual level is opened, and ultimately the heavenly level. Since the sequential opening of these levels depends on how we live, it follows that the two higher levels may also not be opened, in which case we stay on the earthly level, which is the most remote.

It is recognized in the world that we have an earthly self and a spiritual self, or an outer and an inner self. It is not recognized that the earthly self becomes spiritual by the opening of a higher level within, and that this opening is accomplished by a spiritual life, a life in accord with divine precepts, and that unless we live by these precepts, we remain centered on the physical world.

249   There are three kinds of earthly-minded people. One kind is made up of individuals who have no knowledge of divine precepts, a second of people who know that such precepts exist but give no thought to living by them, and a third of people who trivialize and deny them. As for the first kind, the ones who have no knowledge of divine precepts, they cannot help remaining earthly-minded because there is no way for them to teach themselves. We all learn about divine precepts from others, who know about them from their religion. We do not gain them by direct revelation (see *Teachings for the New Jerusalem on Sacred Scripture* 114–118).

People of the second kind, the ones who know that divine precepts exist but give no thought to living by them, also remain earthly-minded and are not concerned with anything except what is worldly and physical. After death they become employees and servants of the spiritual-minded, performing for them the functions for which they are fitted. This is because an earthly-minded individual is an employee or servant, while a spiritual-minded one is an employer or householder.

People of the third kind, the ones who trivialize and deny divine precepts, not only remain earthly-minded but even become sense-centered to the extent that they trivialize and deny divine precepts. Sense-centered people are the lowest of the earthly-minded, unable to raise their thoughts above deceptive physical appearances. After death, they are in hell.

250   Since people in this world do not know what a spiritual-minded person is and what[129] an earthly-minded person is, and since many call someone "spiritual" who is merely earthly-minded, and vice versa, I need to say the following things clearly.

1. What an earthly-minded person is and what a spiritual-minded person is.
2. What an earthly-minded person is like whose spiritual level has been opened.
3. What an earthly-minded person is like whose spiritual level has not been opened but is not yet closed.
4. What an earthly-minded person is like whose spiritual level has been completely closed.
5. Lastly, the difference between the life of a wholly earthly-minded person and the life of an animal.

251   1. *What an earthly-minded person is and what a spiritual-minded person is.* We are not human because of our faces and bodies but because of our abilities to discern and intend, so "earthly-minded person" and "spiritual-minded person" refer to our discernment and volition, which can be either earthly or spiritual. When we are earthly-minded, we are like an earthly world in respect to our discernment and volition and can even be called a world or microcosm. When we are spiritual-minded, we are like a spiritual world in respect to our discernment and volition, and can even be called a spiritual world or a heaven.

We can see from this that earthly-minded people, being a kind of image of the earthly world, love whatever has to do with the earthly world, while spiritual-minded people, being a kind of image of the spiritual world, love whatever has to do with that world or heaven. Spiritual-minded people do love the earthly world, it is true, but only the way householders love their servants, who enable them to be of service. In fact, the earthly-minded people become spiritual in a way through their service. This happens when an earthly-minded person feels the joy of service from a spiritual source. This kind of earthly-minded person is called "earthly-spiritual."

Spiritual-minded people love spiritual truths, not only loving to know and understand them but intending them as well; while earthly-minded people love to talk about these truths and carry them out as well. Putting truths into action is being of service. This ranking comes from the way the spiritual world and the earthly world go together, since anything that surfaces and exists in the earthly world has its cause in the spiritual world.

We can tell from this that spiritual-minded people are completely distinct from earthly-minded people, and that the only communication between them is the kind that occurs between a cause and its effect.

2. *What an earthly-minded person is like whose spiritual level has been opened.* This you can see from what has already been said [§251]; but I need to add that an earthly-minded person is a complete person when the spiritual level has been opened within. Once that happens, we are actually in the company of angels in heaven at the same time that we are in the company of people on earth, living under the watchful care of the Lord in both realms. Spiritual-minded people derive their imperatives from the Lord through the Word and carry them out by means of their earthly selves.

Earthly-minded individuals whose spiritual level has been opened do not realize that they are thinking and acting from their spiritual selves. They seem to themselves to be acting on their own, though in fact it is not on their own but from the Lord. Earthly-minded people whose spiritual level has been opened do not realize that they are in heaven

252

because of their spiritual selves, either, even though their spiritual selves are surrounded by heaven's angels. Sometimes such people are even visible to angels, but since they are drawn back to their earthly selves, they vanish in a little while.[130]

Earthly people whose spiritual level has been opened do not realize that their spiritual minds are filled with thousands of hidden treasures of wisdom and with thousands of love's joys as gifts from the Lord. They do not realize that they will begin to participate in this wisdom and joy after they die, when they become angels. The reason earthly-minded people are not aware of all this is that communication between our earthly and our spiritual selves takes place by correspondences, and communication by correspondences is perceived in our discernment only as seeing truths in the light, and in our volition only as being helpful because we enjoy it.

253   3. *What an earthly-minded person is like whose spiritual level has not been opened but is not yet closed.* The spiritual level is not opened in us but is still not closed when we are leading a reasonably thoughtful life but do not know very much real truth. This is because that level is opened by a union of love and wisdom, or of warmth and light. Love alone, or spiritual warmth alone, will not do it, and neither will wisdom alone or spiritual light alone. It takes both together. So if we do not know the real truths that constitute wisdom or light, love cannot manage to open that level. All it can do is keep it able to be opened, which is what "not being closed" means. The same holds true for plant life. Warmth alone will not make seeds sprout or trees leaf out. Warmth together with light is what does it.

We need to realize that everything true is a matter of spiritual light and that everything good is a matter of spiritual warmth, and that what is good opens the spiritual level by means of things true, since goodness does what is helpful by means of truths. Helpful acts are the good that love does, deriving their essence from the union of what is good and what is true.

What happens after death to people whose spiritual level is not opened but still not closed is that since they are still earthly-minded and not spiritual-minded, they are in the lowest parts of heaven, where they sometimes have a hard time of it. Alternatively, they may be around the edges of a somewhat higher heaven, where they live in a kind of twilight. This is because (as already noted [§186]) in heaven and in each distinct community the light decreases from the center to the circumference, with the people who are especially engaged with divine truths in the middle and the people only slightly engaged in truths at the borders.

People are only slightly engaged with truths if all they have learned from their religion is that God exists, that the Lord suffered for their sake, and that charity and faith are the essential qualities of the church, without making any effort to find out what faith is and what charity is. Yet essentially, faith is truth, and truth is complex, while charity is every duty we fulfill because of the Lord. We do things because of the Lord when we abstain from evils as sins.

This is just what I have already said [§§168, 197]. The purpose is the whole substance of the means, and the purpose through the means is the whole substance of the result. The purpose is thoughtful action, or some good, the means is faith, or something true, and the results are good deeds or acts of service. We can see from this that nothing from charity can be instilled into our deeds except to the extent that our charity is united to those truths that we attribute to faith. They are the means by which charity enters into works and gives them their quality.

4. *What an earthly-minded person is like whose spiritual level has been* **254** *completely closed.* The spiritual level is closed in people who are focused on evil in their lives, especially if they are engaged in distortion because of their evils. It is rather like the way our little nerve fibers contract at the slightest touch of anything unsuitable, as does every muscular motor fiber and every muscle and the whole body, at the touch of something hard or cold. This is how the substances or forms of the spiritual level within us react to things that are evil and to the distortions that result— they are unsuitable. The spiritual level, being in the form of heaven, is open only to things that are good and to the truths that result from what is good. These are congenial to it, while evils and the falsities they give rise to are unsuitable.

This level contracts, and closes by contracting, especially in people who are caught up in a love of being in control for selfish reasons in this world, since this love is the opposite of a love for the Lord. It is also closed, though not as firmly, in people who because of their love for this world are caught up in a mindless craving to acquire the assets of others. The reason these loves close off the spiritual level is that they are the sources of our evils.

The contraction or closure of this level is like a coil twisting back on itself, which is why this level deflects heaven's light once it has been closed. This yields darkness in place of heaven's light. Accordingly, the truth that is found in heaven's light becomes sickening.[131]

For these people, it is not just [the spiritual] level itself that is closed. It is also the higher area of the earthly level, the area called "rational."

Eventually, then, only the lowest area of the earthly level stays open, the area we call "sensory." This is right next to the world and to our outward physical senses, which thereafter constitute the basis of our thinking, talking, and rationalizing. In the spiritual world, earthly-minded people who have become sense-centered because of their evils and consequent distortions do not look human in heaven's light. They look grotesque, with flattened noses. The reason they have these concave noses is that the nose corresponds to a perception of what is true. They cannot bear a single ray of heaven's light, either. The only light in their caves is like the light of embers or smoldering charcoal. We can see from this who the people are whose spiritual level has been closed, and what they are like.

255   5. *The difference between the life of an earthly-minded person and the life of an animal.* I need to deal with this difference more specifically later, in discussing life.[132] At this point I need to say only that we humans differ in having three levels of mind or three levels of discernment and volition, and that these levels can be opened in sequence. Since they are translucent, we can be raised in discernment into heaven's light and see things that are not only civically and morally true but spiritually true as well. Once we have seen many such truths, we can on that basis draw a series of true conclusions, and keep perfecting our discernment in this way forever.

Animals, though, do not have the two higher levels, only the earthly levels, and apart from the higher levels the earthly levels have no ability to think about any civic, moral, or spiritual issue. Further, since these earthly levels cannot be opened and therefore raised into higher light, animals cannot think in sequential order. They can think only in a simultaneous pattern, and that is not really thinking. It is simply acting on the basis of the knowledge that answers to their love;[133] and since they cannot think analytically or survey their lower thought from any higher vantage point, they cannot talk. All they can do is make sounds that suit their love's knowledge.

The only difference between sense-centered people (the lowest of the earthly-minded) and animals is that they can fill their minds with information and think and talk on that basis. They get this from an ability we all possess, our ability to understand what is true if we want to. This ability makes the difference. However, many people have made themselves lower than animals by their abuse of this ability.

256   *In its own right, the earthly level of the human mind is a continuum, but because of its responsiveness to the two higher levels, it seems to have distinct*

levels when it is raised up. Even though it is hard for people to understand this if they are not yet familiar with vertical levels, it still needs to be disclosed, since it is a matter of angelic wisdom. While earthly-minded people cannot think about this wisdom the way angels do, they can still grasp it mentally if their minds are raised into the level of light that angels enjoy. Our minds can actually be raised that far and enlightened accordingly. However, this enlightenment of our earthly minds does not happen by distinct levels. There is instead a gradual increase, and in keeping with that increase, our minds are enlightened from within, with the light of the two higher levels.

We can understand how this happens by perceiving that for vertical levels, one is above the other, with the earthly level, the terminal one, acting like an inclusive membrane for the two higher levels. As the earthly level is raised toward a higher level, then, the higher activates that outer earthly level from within and enlightens it. The enlightenment is actually happening because of the light of the higher levels from within, but it is received gradually by the earthly level that envelops and surrounds them, with greater clarity and purity as it ascends. That is, the earthly level is enlightened from within, from the light of the higher, distinct levels; but on the earthly level itself, it happens gradually.

We can see from this that as long as we are in this world and are therefore focused on the earthly level, we cannot be raised into wisdom itself, the way it is for angels. We can be raised only into a higher light at the boundary of angels and receive enlightenment from their light, which flows into us from within and illumines us.

I cannot describe this any more clearly. It is better understood through its effects; for if we have some prior knowledge about causes, their effects embody and present them in the light and thereby make them clear.

The following are "effects." (a) Our earthly mind can be raised as far **257** as the light of heaven that surrounds angels, and can therefore sense on the earthly level what angels sense spiritually—that is, it does not sense so fully. Still, our earthly mind cannot be raised all the way into angelic light itself. (b) With our earthly mind raised as far as heaven's light, we can think and even talk with angels; but when this happens, the thought and speech of the angels are flowing into our earthly thought and speech, and not the other way around. This means that angels talk with us in earthly language, in our native tongues. (c) This happens by a flow of the spiritual level into the earthly, and not by any flow of the earthly level into the spiritual. (d) There is no way for our human wisdom, which is

earthly as long as we are living in the earthly world, to be raised into angelic wisdom, only into some reflection of it. This is because the raising
of the earthly mind is along a continuum, like that of darkness to light,
or coarse to fine. Still, if our spiritual level has been opened, we come
into consciousness of that wisdom when we die, and we can also come
into consciousness of it through the quiescence of our physical senses,
and then through an inflow from above into the spiritual elements of
our minds. (e) Our earthly mind is made up of both spiritual substances
and earthly substances. Our thinking results from the spiritual substances and not from the earthly substances. These latter substances fade
away when we die, but the spiritual substances do not. So when we become spirits or angels after death, the same mind is still there in the
form it had in the world. (f) The earthly substances of our minds
(which fade away after death, as I have just noted) form the skinlike
covering of the spiritual bodies we inhabit as spirits and angels. It is by
means of this covering, taken from the earthly world, that our spiritual
bodies have their stability, the earthly substance being the outermost
vessel.[134] This is why there is no angel or spirit who was not born
human.

These hidden treasures of angelic wisdom are appended at this point
to show the nature of our earthly mind, which will be further discussed
later [§§260–263].

258   Each of us is born with the ability to understand truths even at the
deepest level where angels of the third heaven live. As our human discernment climbs up on a continuum around the two higher levels,[135] it
receives the light of wisdom from those levels in the manner already described in §256. As a result, we can become rational in proportion to its
ascent. If it comes up to the third level, it becomes rational from the
third level; if it comes up to the second level, it becomes rational from
the second level; and if it does not ascend at all, it is rational on the first
level. We say that it becomes rational from those levels because the
earthly level is the general recipient vessel of their light.

The reason we do not become rational to the highest degree we are
capable of is that our love, which is a matter of our intent, cannot be
raised up in the same way as our wisdom, which is a matter of our discernment. The love that is a matter of intent is raised only by abstaining
from evils as sins and then by those good actions of thoughtfulness that
are acts of service, acts that we are then performing from the Lord. So if
the love that is a matter of intent is not raised up along with it, then no
matter how high the wisdom that is a matter of our discernment has

risen, it ultimately falls back to the level of its love. This is why we become rational only on the lowest level if our love is not raised to the spiritual level as well.

We can tell from all this that our rational ability seems to be made up of three levels, one ability from the heavenly level, one from the spiritual level, and one from the earthly level. We can also tell that our rationality, an ability that can be raised, is still with us whether it is raised up or not.

I have stated that everyone is born with this ability, or with rationality, but this means everyone whose outward organs have not been damaged by any external events in the womb, or after birth by illness or some head injury, or by the outburst of a senseless love that lowers all restraints. The rational ability cannot be raised up for people like this. The life of their volition and discernment has no boundaries in which it finds definition, that is, boundaries so arranged that the life can accomplish outward deeds coherently. It does act in keeping with outermost boundaries, but not because of them. On the unavailability of rationality in childhood and early youth, see the close of §266 below.

The earthly mind, being the envelope and vessel of the higher levels of the human mind, is reactive. If the higher levels are not opened, it acts against them; whereas if they are opened, it acts with them. I explained in the last section that since the earthly mind is on the last level, it surrounds and encloses the spiritual mind and the heavenly mind, which are on higher levels. Now we have reached the point where I need to show that the earthly mind reacts against the higher or inner minds. The reason it reacts is that it does surround, enclose, and contain them. This could not happen without that reaction, since if it did not react, the enclosed inner elements would start to spread and force their way out so that they dissipated. It would be as though the coverings of the human body were not reacting, in which case the viscera within the body would spill out and trickle away; or it would be as though the membranes around the motor fibers of our muscles did not react against the forces of those fibers when they were activated. Not only would the action cease, the whole inner weblike structure would unravel as well.

It is the same with any terminal vertical level. So it is the same with the earthly mind relative to the higher levels, since as I have just said, there are three levels of the human mind, earthly, spiritual, and heavenly, and the earthly mind is on the final level.

The earthly mind's reaction against the spiritual mind is also the reason the earthly mind consists of substances from the earthly world as well as substances from the spiritual world, as noted in §257 above. By their very nature, substances of the earthly world react against substances of the spiritual world, since substances of the earthly world are intrinsically dead and are activated from the outside by substances of the spiritual world. Anything that is dead and is activated from the outside resists by its very nature, and therefore reacts by its very nature.

We can tell from this that the earthly self reacts against the spiritual self, and that there is a conflict. It is all the same whether we refer to the earthly self and the spiritual self or to the earthly mind and the spiritual mind.

261 We can tell from this that if the spiritual mind is closed, the earthly mind is constantly resisting whatever comes from the spiritual mind, fearing that something from that source will flow in that will disturb its states. Everything that flows in through the spiritual mind is from heaven because the spiritual mind is a heaven in form; and everything that flows into the earthly mind is from the world because the earthly mind is a world in form. It follows, then, that when the spiritual mind is closed, the earthly mind resists everything that comes from heaven and will not let it in—except to the extent that it may serve as a means for gaining possession of worldly benefits. When heavenly things serve[136] as means for the purposes of the earthly mind, then even though those means seem to be heavenly, they are still earthly. The purpose gives them their quality, and they actually become like items of information for the earthly self, items in which there is no trace of inner life.

However, since heavenly things cannot be united to earthly ones in this way so that they act as one, they distance themselves; and for people who are purely earthly, heavenly things come to rest outside, at the circumference, around the earthly things that are within. As a result, merely earthly people can discuss and preach heavenly things and can even act them out, even though they are thinking the opposite within. They behave one way when they are alone, and another way in public. But there will be more on this later [§§266, 267].

262 Because of an inborn reflex, the earthly mind or self resists what comes from the spiritual mind or self when that mind loves itself and the world above all else. Then it finds delight in all kinds of evil—in adultery, cheating, vindictiveness, blasphemy, and the like; and it also recognizes only nature as the creatress[137] of the universe. It uses its rational ability to find proofs of all this, and once it has these proofs, it distorts or stifles or diverts whatever of the church and heaven is good and true. Eventually it either escapes such things, or rejects them, or hates them. It does this in spirit, and does it also physically whenever it dares to speak with others from its spirit without fear of losing reputation, for the sake of respectability and profit.

When people are like this, then their spiritual mind closes more and more tightly. It is primarily the justifications of evil by falsity that close it, which is why confirmed evil and falsity cannot be rooted out after death. They can be rooted out only in this world, by repentance.

When the spiritual mind is open, though, the state of the earthly mind is entirely different. Then the earthly mind is inclined to obey the spiritual mind and to be subservient. The spiritual mind acts on the earthly mind from above or from within; and it moves aside the things there that are reactive and adapts to its purposes the things that are cooperative. So it gradually eliminates any overpowering resistance.

263

We need to realize that action and reaction are involved in everything in the universe, no matter how large or small, whether alive or lifeless. This yields a balance throughout, which is canceled when action overcomes reaction or vice versa. It is the same for the earthly mind and the spiritual mind. When the earthly mind is acting on the basis of the delights it loves and the fascinations of its thinking (which are intrinsically evil and false), then the reaction of the earthly mind moves aside whatever comes from the spiritual mind and blocks the doors against its entry. As a result, any action is controlled by whatever agrees with the reaction. This is the nature of the action and reaction of the earthly mind, which is the opposite of the action and reaction of the spiritual mind; and this is what causes the closing of the spiritual mind or the reversing of the spiral.[138]

However, if the spiritual mind is open, then the action and reaction of the earthly mind are reversed. The spiritual mind is acting from above or within, and as it does so it is working through whatever in the earthly mind is amenable, whether it comes from within or from the outside. Then it reverses the spiral characteristic of the action and reaction of the earthly mind. This mind has been in opposition to the purposes of the spiritual mind from birth, deriving this by heredity from our parents, as is well known.

This is the nature of that change of state called reformation and regeneration.[139] The state of the earthly mind before its reformation might be compared to a spiral twisted or twisting downward, while after its reformation it might be compared to a spiral twisted or twisting upward. So before our reformation, we are looking down toward hell, while after our reformation we are looking up toward heaven.

264 *The origin of evil is in the abuse of the abilities proper to us called rationality and freedom.* By rationality, I mean the ability to discern what is true and therefore what is false, and to discern what is good and therefore what is evil. By freedom, I mean the ability freely to think, intend, and do such things.

The following conclusions can be drawn from what has already been said, and will be further supported below. We all possess these two abilities from creation and therefore from birth—they are given us by the Lord. They are not taken away from us. They are the source of the appearance that we think and speak and intend and act with what seems to be autonomy. The Lord dwells in these abilities within each of us, and it is from this union that we live to eternity. We can be reformed and regenerated because of these abilities, and not apart from them; and it is by them that we are distinguished from animals.

265 The origin of evil in the abuse of these abilities will be presented in the following sequence.

1. Evil people, like good people, enjoy these two abilities.
2. Evil people misuse them to validate things that are evil and false, while good people use them to validate things that are good and true.
3. The evil and false things that we have validated stay with us, becoming part of our love and therefore of our life.
4. Things that have become part of our love and life are passed on to our offspring.
5. All evil characteristics, whether inherited or acquired, reside in the earthly mind.

266 1. *Evil people, like good people, enjoy these two abilities.* I explained in the preceding section that as far as understanding things is concerned, the earthly mind can be raised all the way to the light that surrounds angels of the third heaven, seeing what is true, acknowledging it, and then talking about it. We can see from this that since the earthly mind can be raised up in this fashion, evil people and good people alike enjoy the ability we call rationality; and since the earthly mind can be raised up that far, it follows that both evil people and good people can think and talk about such matters.

As for their ability to intend and do such things even though they do not actually intend and do them, this is witnessed by both reason and experience. Reason asks whether people are incapable of intending and doing what they think. However, the fact that we do not intend and do particular things is because we do not want to intend and do them. The ability to intend and do is the freedom that the Lord gives everyone. The reason people do not intend and do what is good when they can is found in a love for evil that finds it distasteful. Still, we can resist this, and many people do.

This has been verified for me several times by experience in the spiritual world. I have listened to evil spirits, people who were demons inwardly and who had in the world rejected the truths of heaven and the church. When their desire for learning was aroused (a desire we all enjoy from childhood on) by the glamor that surrounds every love like the radiance of a flame, then they grasped mysteries of angelic wisdom just as clearly as good spirits who were inwardly angels. The demonic spirits even claimed that they were capable of intending them and acting in keeping with them, but that they did not want to. When they were told that they would want to if they were to abstain from evils as sins, they said that they could do that, too, but that they did not want to. I could see from this that evil and good people alike have the ability we call freedom. Anyone who reflects will see that this is true. The reason we are able to want to do things is that the Lord, the source of that ability, is constantly making it possible; for as already noted [§264], the Lord dwells in these two abilities in everyone. The Lord is therefore in that ability, or in the power we have of wanting.

As for the ability to discern that we call rationality, this is not given us until our earthly mind comes of age. Until then, it is like a seed in unripe fruit that cannot break open underground and sprout. This ability is not found in the people mentioned above in §259, either.

2. Evil people misuse these abilities to validate things that are evil and false, while good people use them to validate things that are good and true. The mental ability we call rationality and the volitional ability we call freedom afford us the possibility of validating anything we please. As earthly-minded people, we can raise our discernment to a higher light as far as we want to; but if we are bent on evil and the distortions it causes, we raise it no higher than the upper levels of the earthly mind, rarely to the region of the spiritual mind. This is because we are caught up in the pleasures of our earthly mind's love. If we do rise above that level, the

267

pleasures of its love die away. If we rise even higher and see true things that are contrary to the pleasures of our life or the basic premises of the intellect that we claim as our own, then we either distort them or ignore them, dismissing them as worthless, or we hold them in our memory so that they may be of use as tools to our life's love or our pride in our own intelligence.

It is obvious from the abundance of heresies in Christendom (each one validated by its adherents) that earthly-minded people can validate whatever they please. Can anyone miss the fact that all kinds of evil and false notions can be validated? We can "prove" (and inwardly, evil people do "prove") that God does not exist and that nature is all there is, having created itself;[140] that religion is only a device for holding the minds of the simple in bondage;[141] that our own prudence accomplishes everything; and that divine providence does nothing but maintain the universe in the pattern in which it was created;[142] and even, according to Machiavelli and his followers, that there is nothing wrong with murder, adultery, theft, deception, and revenge.[143]

Earthly-minded people can justify a host of things like this, can fill books with "proofs"; and once they have been justified, we see these false notions in their own illusory light, and true ideas are in such darkness that they are virtually invisible, like ghosts in the night. In brief, take the falsest notion you can think of, frame it as a proposition, and tell someone clever to prove it, and you will find it "proved" to the absolute stifling of any true light. But then step back from those proofs and take a second look at the same proposition from your own rationality, and you will see how grotesquely false it is.[144]

This shows that we are able to misuse the two abilities the Lord instills in us to validate all kinds of evil and false notions. No animal can do this because animals do not enjoy these abilities. So unlike us, animals are born into the complete pattern of their lives, with all the knowledge necessary for their earthly love.

268   3. *The evil and false things that we have validated stay with us, becoming part of our love and therefore of our life.* "Proofs" of what is evil and false are simply motions away from what is good and true; and as they are multiplied, they become rejections, since what is evil distances and rejects what is good, and what is false does the same to what is true. As a result, proofs of what is evil and false amount to closures of heaven because everything good and true flows in from the Lord through heaven. Once heaven is closed, we are in hell, in some community there where congenial forms of evil and falsity hold sway, with no possibility of getting out.

I have been allowed to talk with people who had justified for themselves the false principles of their religion centuries ago, and I saw that they were still centered in the same principles they had adopted in the world. This is because everything we justify internally becomes part of our love and our life. It becomes part of our love because it becomes part of our intentions and our discernment, and intention and discernment constitute our life.[145] When it becomes part of our life, it becomes part not only of our whole mind but of our whole body as well. So we can see that once we have justified ourselves in our evil and false principles, that is what we are from head to toe; and once we are wholly of this nature, there is no kind of inversion or reversal of direction that will bring us back into the opposite state and thereby drag us out of hell.

This, together with what has been said earlier in this section, shows where evil comes from.

4. *Things that have become part of our love and life are passed on to our* **269** *offspring.* It is generally acknowledged that we are born into evil and that we get this as an inheritance from our parents. Some people believe that it is not from our parents, but through them from Adam; but this is a mistake. It comes from the father, from whom we get the soul that is clothed with a body in the mother. The semen that comes from the father is the first vessel of life; but it is the kind of vessel it was in the father. It is actually in the form of his love, and everyone's love is the same in its largest and its smallest forms. There is within it a striving toward the human form, a form into which it gradually develops.[146] It follows, then, that the evils we call hereditary come from our fathers and are therefore handed down from our grandfathers and earlier ancestors to their offspring in sequence.

Experience tells us this, too. There is a likeness of disposition in peoples that comes from their first ancestor, a greater likeness within extended families, and a still greater likeness within individual households. The similarity is so clear that we recognize lineages not only by their dispositions but by their faces as well. There will be more about the way evil love is born into us from our parents later on,[147] when I discuss the way the mind (that is, our volition and discernment) corresponds to the body and its members and organs. At this point I cite only a few things in order to show that evils are handed down from our parents in sequence and that they grow, piling up one generation after another, until we are nothing but evil at birth. The viciousness of evil increases in proportion to the closing of the spiritual mind, with the earthly mind closing to anything from above as well. This is remedied in our descendants only by their abstaining from evils as sins, with the Lord's help. There is no other way to open the spiritual mind and thereby bring the earthly mind back into a corresponding form.

270   5. *All evil characteristics and their consequent distortions, whether inherited or acquired, reside in the earthly mind.* The reason evils and their consequent distortions reside in the earthly mind is that in form, or in image, this mind is an earthly world. The spiritual mind, though, is in form or in image a heaven, and there is no way for evil to find a welcome in heaven. So from birth, this latter mind is not open, only potentially so. The earthly mind derives its form in part from substances of the earthly world, but the spiritual mind derives its form solely from substances of the spiritual world. This latter mind is kept in its wholeness by the Lord so that we can become human. We are actually born animal, but become human.

The earthly mind, with everything in it, turns in spirals from right to left, while the spiritual mind turns in spirals from left to right. So the two minds are turning in opposite directions—a sign that evil is resident in the earthly mind and that on its own, it resists the spiritual mind. Further, turning from right to left is turning downward, toward hell, and turning from left to right moves upward, toward heaven. I have been shown this by the experience that evil spirits cannot turn their bodies from left to right, only from right to left, while good spirits find it hard to turn from right to left and easy to turn from left to right. Their turning follows the flow of the deeper levels of their minds.

271   *Evil and false things are absolutely opposed to good and true things because evil and false things are demonic and hellish, while good and true things are divine and heavenly.* On first hearing, everyone will admit that evil and good are opposites, and that the distortions of evil are opposite to the truth of what is good. However, the whole feeling and consequent sense of people who are engaged in evil pursuits is that evil is good. Evil gratifies their senses, especially sight and hearing, and therefore it also gratifies their thoughts and consequently their perceptions. Because of this, while they do recognize that evil and good are opposites, as long as they are engaged in evil they call evil good and good evil because of their delight.

For instance, if we use our freedom wrongly to think and do evil, we call it freedom; and the opposite, which is thinking what is intrinsically good, we call slavery. Yet this latter is true freedom, and the former is slavery. Again, people who love adultery call adultery freedom, and they call it slavery to be restrained from adultery. They find delight in lasciviousness and discomfort in chastity. People who love power for selfish reasons feel a living delight in that love, a delight that surpasses any other kind of delight. So they call everything associated with that love good and everything that conflicts with it bad, when in fact the opposite is true.

It is the same with every other evil; so even though everyone does admit that evil and good are opposites, people who are engaged in evil pursuits have an opposite picture of this opposition. Only people who are engaged in good pursuits have a fair picture. While involved in evil, no one can see what is good, but people who are involved in something good can see what is evil. It is as though evil were down below in a cave, and good up above on a mountain.

Since most people do not know what evil is and how absolutely opposed it is to good, and since it is important to know this, I need to make this clear in the following sequence. 272

1. An earthly mind engaged in things evil and therefore false is a form and an image of hell.
2. An earthly mind that is a form and image of hell has three descending levels.
3. The three levels of an earthly mind that is a form and image of hell are the opposites of the three levels of a spiritual mind that is a form and image of heaven.
4. An earthly mind that is a hell is absolutely opposed to a spiritual mind that is a heaven.

1. *An earthly mind engaged in things evil and false is a form and an image of hell.* I cannot describe at this point what an earthly mind is like in its substantive form within us, what it is like in the form derived from the substances of the two worlds woven together in our brains,[148] where that mind primarily dwells. A general picture of this form will be offered later, where I will be dealing with the correspondence of the mind and the body.[149] At this point, I need only say something about the states of that form and the changes of state that give rise to perceptions, thoughts, aims, intentions, and what is associated with them, since it is in regard to these that an earthly mind engaged in evil and false pursuits is a form and an image of hell. This form establishes a substantive form as a ground— changes of state cannot occur apart from a substantive form as their ground, just as there can be no sight without an eye and no hearing without an ear. 273

As for the form or image by which the earthly mind reflects hell, that form and image is like this. The dominant love, together with its urges, being the general state of this mind, acts the part of a devil in hell; and the distorted thoughts that arise from that dominant love are like that devil's gang. Nothing more nor less than this is meant in the Word by "the Devil and its cohorts."

The situation is much the same, since the dominant love in hell is a love of power for selfish reasons. That is what is referred to as "the Devil" there; and attractions to what is false, with the thoughts that arise from that love, are referred to as "the Devil's gang." It is the same in each of hell's communities, with differences like individual variations on a single theme.

An earthly mind that is engaged in evil and therefore false pursuits has a similar form; so after death, earthly-minded people of this kind come into a community of hell that resembles themselves. They then behave in unison with that hell in every respect. They are actually coming into their own form, that is, into the state of their own minds.

There is also another love, called satan, secondary to the earlier love called the devil. This is the love of owning the assets of other people, using fair means or foul. Malice, deviousness, and deceit are its gang.

People who are in this hell are called satans collectively, while people in the former hell are called devils collectively. In fact, the ones who do not act in secret do not reject the title. This is why the hells as a whole are called "the Devil" and "Satan."

The reason the two hells are broadly distinguished by these two loves is that all the heavens are distinguished by two loves into two realms, a heavenly one and a spiritual one. The demonic hell is an inverse parallel to the heavenly realm and the satanic hell an inverse parallel to the spiritual one. (On heaven's division into two realms, a heavenly one and a spiritual one, see *Heaven and Hell* 26–28 *[20–28]*.)

The reason this kind of earthly mind is a hell in form is that every spiritual form is the same in its largest and smallest manifestations. This is why every angel is a heaven in smaller form, as has also been explained in *Heaven and Hell*, in §§51–58. It also follows from this that every individual or spirit who is a devil or satan is a hell in smaller form.

274   *2. An earthly mind that is a form and image of hell has three descending levels.* In §§222–229 above, it was explained that there are two kinds of levels, called vertical and horizontal, in the largest and smallest instances of everything. This holds true as well of the earthly mind in its largest and smallest forms. At this point, we are talking about vertical levels.

By virtue of its two abilities, called rationality and freedom, the earthly mind is in a state that allows it to rise up by three levels or descend by three levels. It rises up as a result of good and true actions, and it descends as a result of evil and false actions. Further, when it rises up, the lower levels that tend toward hell are closed off, and when it descends the higher levels that tend toward heaven are closed off. This is because they resist each other.

The three higher and lower levels are neither open nor closed in us when we are first born. This is because at that time we are ignorant of what is good and true and of what is evil and false. However, as we engage ourselves in these things, the levels are opened and closed in one direction or the other.

When they are opened toward hell, then the highest or central place is given to our dominant love, which is a matter of our volition. A second or intermediary place is given to distorted thinking, which is a matter of the discernment derived from that love. The lowest place is given to the realization of our love by means of our thinking, or of our volition by means of our discernment.

All this is like the vertical levels already discussed,[150] which in their sequence are like a purpose, its means, and its result, or like first, intermediate, and final ends.

The downward course of these levels is toward the body; so as they move lower, things become coarser, focused on what is material and bodily.

If truths from the Word are recruited on the second level for its formation, then these truths are distorted because of the first level, which is a love for what is evil. They become servants, slaves. We can tell from this what truths of the church and the Word are like in people who are engaged in a love for what is evil or whose earthly minds are hell in form—that is, since they are serving a devil as its means, these truths are being profaned. The love for evil that takes control in a hellish earthly mind is its devil, as already noted [§273].

3. *The three levels of an earthly mind that is a form and image of hell are the opposites of the three levels of a spiritual mind that is a form and image of heaven.* I have already explained [§§130, 248, 270] that there are three levels of mind called earthly, spiritual, and heavenly, and that a human mind made up of these levels looks and turns toward heaven. We can therefore see that when an earthly mind is looking downward and turning toward hell, it is likewise made up of three levels, with each of its levels the opposite of a level of the mind that is a heaven.

275

This has been made quite clear to me by things I have seen in the spiritual world. I have seen that there are three heavens marked off by three vertical levels and three hells also marked off by three vertical levels, or levels of depth, with the hells opposite to the heavens in every detail. Further, the lowest hell is the opposite of the highest heaven, the intermediate hell the opposite of the intermediate heaven, and the highest hell the opposite of the lowest heaven. It is the same with an earthly mind that is a hell in form. Spiritual forms are in fact consistent in their largest and smallest instances.

The reason the heavens and the hells are in this kind of opposition is that their loves are opposed in this fashion. Love for the Lord and a consequent love for their neighbor constitute the inmost level in the heavens, while love for themselves and love for the world constitute the inmost level in the hells. Wisdom and intelligence from their loves constitute the intermediate level in the heavens, while stupidity and madness from their loves (which put on the appearance of wisdom and intelligence) constitute the intermediate level in the hells. It is the final effects of these two levels, though, either coming to rest in the memory as knowledge or finding definition in the body in actions, that constitute the final level in the heavens; while the realizations of the two levels that become either knowledge or actions constitute the most superficial level in the hells.

The following experience showed me how good and true elements of heaven are changed into evil and false things and therefore into their opposites in the hells. I heard that a divine truth was flowing down from heaven into hell, and heard that on the way down it was transformed step by step into something false, so that when it reached the lowest hell it had turned into its exact opposite. I could see from this that depending on their level, the hells are in opposition to the heavens as far as anything good and true is concerned, and that things become evil and false by flowing into forms that are turned backward. It is recognized, that is, that our perception and sense of anything that flows in depend on the recipient forms and their states.

I was also shown by the following experience that things are turned into their opposites. I was given a view of the hells in their position relative to the heavens, and the people there seemed to be upside down, heads below and feet above. I was told, though, that they seem to themselves to be standing upright. We might compare them to people in the southern hemisphere.[151]

We can tell from this experiential evidence that the three levels of an earthly mind that is a form and image of hell are the opposites of the three levels of an earthly mind that is a form and image of heaven.

4. *An earthly mind that is a hell is absolutely opposed to a spiritual mind that is a heaven.* When loves are opposite, then all perceptive functions are opposite. It is from love, which constitutes our essential life, that everything else flows, like streams from their spring. In the earthly mind, things that are not from that source separate themselves from things that are. What comes from the dominant love is in the center, and everything else is at the sides. If these latter elements are truths of the church drawn from the Word, they are pushed even farther away and eventually are exiled. Then the individual, or the earthly mind, feels evil as good and sees falsity as truth, and vice versa. This is why it believes that malice is wisdom, insanity is intelligence, deviousness is prudence, and evil arts are skillfulness. Then too, it completely trivializes the divine and heavenly things that are proper to the church and its worship and puts supreme value on bodily concerns and the world. By doing this it inverts the state of its life, assigning matters of the head to the soles of the feet and walking all over them, and promoting matters of the soles of the feet to the head. When we do this, we move from life to death. (We may call someone "alive" whose mind is a heaven, and someone "dead" whose mind is a hell.)

Everything in the three levels of the earthly mind is enclosed in the works that are done by our physical actions. The information about levels conveyed in this part may serve to disclose this hidden principle, namely that everything proper to our minds, to our volition and discernment, is enclosed in our actions or deeds, much like the things we can and cannot see in a seed, a piece of fruit, or an egg. The actions or deeds themselves may seem to be nothing but what shows on the surface, but there are countless elements within them. There are the energies of the motor fibers of the whole body that are cooperating; and there are all those actions of the mind that are rousing and directing those energies, actions on three levels, as already explained [§§200–201]. Further, since all the actions of the mind are involved, so are all the actions of volition, all the desires of our love, that make up the first level. So are all the actions of our discernment, all the thoughts that shape our perception, which make up the second level. All the contents of our memory, all the images of our thinking that are closest to our speech, are also drawn from this source; they

276

277

constitute the third level. It is from these, focused into actions, that our deeds arise, deeds in whose outward form the antecedents that actually dwell within are not visible.

On the final level as the composite, vessel, and foundation of the prior ones, see §§209–216 above, and on the vertical levels finding their full realization in their final form, see §§217–221.

278 There is a reason that our physical acts look so simple and plain to the eye, like the outer forms of seeds, fruits, and eggs and like almond nuts in their kernels, when in fact they contain within themselves all the prior elements that have given rise to them. The reason is that every final form is a covering that serves to mark it off from its antecedents. Then too, every level is enveloped with a membrane that serves to mark it off from another. As a result, elements of the first level are unrecognizable to the second level, and elements of this are unrecognizable to the third level. For example, the love of our volition, which is the first level of our mind, is discernible in the wisdom of our discernment, which is the second level of our mind, only by a kind of delight in thinking about something. That first level (the love of our volition, as already noted [§277]) is discernible in the knowledge of our memory, which is the third level, only as a kind of pleasure found in being knowledgeable and in talking.

The obvious conclusion from this is that a deed that is a physical act encloses all these elements, even though it seems as simple as can be in its outward form.

279 In support of this is the fact that the angels who are with us are aware in detail of the actions of our minds within our deeds. Spiritual angels perceive what is enclosed from our discernment, and heavenly angels what is enclosed from our volition. This may seem like a paradox, but it is true. It does need to be realized, though, that the mental elements involved in a contemplated or present deed are in the center, with the rest surrounding in proportion to their relevance.

Angels say that they perceive what someone is like from a single deed, though the image of someone's love will vary depending on the way it finds definition in desires and therefore in thoughts. In brief, every one of the acts or deeds of a spiritual person is like a delicious, nourishing, and beautiful fruit to angels, a fruit that yields flavor, nourishment, and pleasure when it is sliced and eaten.

On angels' having this kind of perception of our actions and deeds, see §220 above.

280 It is the same with our speech. Angels recognize our love from the sound of our speech, our wisdom from the way the sound is articulated, and our knowledge from the meaning of the words. They also tell me that these three elements are in every word, because a word is like a realization that has the sound, the articulation, and the meaning within it. Angels of the third heaven have told me that they sense from any word a speaker says in a sentence the general state of that individual's mind, and some specific states as well.

I have explained at some length in *Teachings for the New Jerusalem on Sacred Scripture* that in the individual words of Scripture there is something spiritual that expresses divine wisdom and something heavenly that expresses divine love, and that angels are aware of these when someone is reading the Word devoutly.

This leads to the conclusion that the deeds of people whose earthly minds are going down to hell by three levels contain everything they have that is evil and therefore false, and that the deeds of people whose earthly minds are moving up into heaven contain everything they have that is good and true, and also that angels perceive both simply from what we say and do. This is why it says in the Word that we are to be judged according to our works and that we will have to give an account of our words.[152]

ANGELIC WISDOM
ABOUT
DIVINE LOVE

PART 4

THE Lord from eternity, who is Jehovah, created the universe and everything in it not from nothing but from himself. It is known worldwide and acknowledged through an inner perception by everyone who is wise that there is one God who is the creator of the universe. Further, the Word informs us that the God who created the universe is called "Jehovah," from "being," because God alone *is*.[153] In *Teachings for the New Jerusalem on the Lord* there is ample evidence from the Word that the Lord from eternity is that Jehovah.[154]

Jehovah is called the Lord from eternity because Jehovah took on a human nature in order to save us from hell. At that time too he commanded his disciples to call him "Lord."[155] So in the New Testament, Jehovah is called "the Lord," as we can tell from [the citation of the verse] "You shall love *Jehovah your God* with all your heart and all your soul" (Deuteronomy 6:5) [as] "You shall love *the Lord your God* with all your heart and with all your soul" in the New Testament (Matthew 22:35 [22:37]). We find the same in other Old Testament[156] passages cited in the Gospels.

People who think rationally and clearly see that the universe was not created from nothing because they see that nothing can arise from nothing. Nothing is simply nothing, and to make something out of nothing

282

283

169

is self-contradictory. Anything that is self-contradictory is in conflict with the light of truth that comes from divine wisdom, and if something is not from divine wisdom, it is not from divine omnipotence either.

Everyone who thinks rationally and clearly also sees that everything has been created out of a substance that is substance in and of itself. This is the essential being from which everything that exists can arise. Since only God is substance in and of itself and is therefore essential being, it follows that there is no other source of the arising of things.

Many people do see this, since reason enables them to. However, they do not dare argue it for fear that they might arrive at the thought that the created universe is God because it is from God—either that, or the thought that nature is self-generated, which would mean that its own core is what we call "God." As a result, even though many people have seen that the only source of the arising of everything is God and God's essential being, they have not dared move beyond the first suggestion of this. If they did, their minds might get ensnared in a so-called Gordian knot with no possibility of escape.[157] The reason they could not disentangle their minds is that they were thinking about God and God's creation of the universe in temporal and spatial terms, terms proper to the physical world, and no one can understand God and the creation of the universe by starting from the physical world. Anyone whose mind enjoys some inner light, though, can understand the physical world and its creation by starting from God, because God is not in time and space.

On Divinity not being in space, see §§7–10 above; on Divinity filling all space in the universe nonspatially, see §§69–72, and on Divinity being in all time nontemporally, see §§72–76 [73–76]. We will see later that even though God did create the universe and everything in it out of himself, still there is not the slightest thing in the created universe that is God. There will be other things as well that will shed an appropriate light on the subject.[158]

284 In part 1 of the present work, I discussed God as divine love and wisdom and as life, and as that substance and form that constitute the one and only reality. In part 2, I dealt with the spiritual sun and its world and with the physical sun and its world, showing that the universe and everything in it was created by God by means of these two suns. Part 3 was about the levels that apply to absolutely everything that has been created. Now in this fourth part, I will be dealing with God's creation of the universe. The reason for presenting all this material is that angels have been expressing their grief to the Lord about seeing nothing but darkness when they look into our world, seeing among us no knowledge about God, heaven, and the creation of nature, knowledge that could serve them as a basis for wisdom.

The Lord from eternity, or Jehovah, could not have created the universe and everything in it except as a person. If people have an earthly, physical concept of the Divine-Human One, they are utterly incapable of understanding how a human God[159] could create the universe and everything in it. They think to themselves, "How can a human God wander from place to place through the universe creating things?" or "How can God speak the word from one place, and things be created as soon as the word is spoken?" Things like this come to mind when people say that God is a person if people are thinking about the Divine-Human One the same way they do about earthly people, and when their thought about God is based on nature and its attributes, time and space. On the other hand, if their thought about God is not based on earthly people, not based on nature and its space and time, they grasp clearly that the universe could not have been created unless God were a person.

285

Focus your thought on the angelic concept of God, of a human God, and as far as you can, eliminate any concept of space, and you will be close to the truth in your thinking.

Some scholars have actually grasped the fact that spirits and angels are not in space because they conceive of spirit as being apart from space. Spirit is like thought. Even though our thought is within us, it enables us to be present somewhere else, no matter how far away. This is the state of spirits and angels, who are people even in respect to their bodies. They seem to be wherever their thought is because in the spiritual world place and distance are apparent only, and are in complete accord with what people are thinking about with interest.

We can tell from this that the God who is visible as a sun far above the spiritual world, who cannot be given any appearance of space, is not to be thought of in spatial terms. In that case, we can understand that the universe was not created out of nothing but out of God, and that God's human body is not to be thought of as large or small or of some particular height because these are matters of space. This means that God is the same from first to last, in the largest and smallest things. It means also that this Person is at the heart of everything created, but nonspatially so.

On Divinity as being the same in the largest and smallest things, see §§77–82 above; and on Divinity as filling all spaces nonspatially, see

§§69–72. Since Divinity is not within space, it is not on the same continuum as the inmost aspect of nature.

286   As for God's inability to create the universe and everything in it except as a person, this is something a discerning individual can grasp very clearly on the following basis. Inwardly, we cannot deny that love and wisdom, mercy and forgiveness exist in God. God, as the source of what is good and true, is their essence. Since we cannot deny this, we cannot deny that God is a person, since none of these things can exist apart from a person. The person is their subject, and to separate them from their subject is to say that they do not exist.

Think of wisdom, and posit it outside a person. Is it anything? Can you conceive of it as something ethereal or flamelike? No, unless perhaps you think of it as within these things; and if it is within them, it must be wisdom in a form like ours. It must be in every aspect of that form. Nothing can be lacking if wisdom is to be within it.

In brief, the form of wisdom is human, and because a person is a form of wisdom, a person is also a form of love, mercy, forgiveness—of whatever is good and true, because these act in complete unison with wisdom.

On the fact that love and wisdom cannot occur except in some form, see above, §§40–43.

287   We can also tell that love and wisdom are human by looking at heaven's angels, who are people in full beauty to the extent that they are caught up in love, and therefore in wisdom, from the Lord. The same conclusion follows from what it says in the Word about Adam's being created in the image and likeness of God (Genesis 1:26), because he was created in the form of love and wisdom.

All earthly individuals are born in the human form as to their physical bodies. This is because our spirit, which is also called our soul, is a person; and it is a person because it is receptive of love and wisdom from the Lord. To the extent that our spirit or soul actually accepts love and wisdom, we become human after the death of these material bodies that we are carrying around. To the extent that we do not accept love and wisdom we become grotesque creatures, retaining some trace of humanity because of our ability to accept them.

288   Since God is a person, the whole angelic heaven, taken as a single unit, presents itself as a single person. It is divided into regions and districts according to our human members, organs, and viscera. There are heavenly communities that make up the district of the brain and all its components, of all the facial parts, and of all our physical internal organs; and these districts are distinguished from each other exactly the way they are in us. In fact, angels know what district of the [heavenly] person they live in.

Heaven as a whole has this appearance because God is a person; and God is heaven because the angels who constitute heaven are recipients of love and wisdom from the Lord, and recipients are images.

I have explained at the close of a series of chapters in *Secrets of Heaven* that heaven is in the human form in all respects.[160]

This shows us the senselessness of concepts people have when they think about God in nonhuman terms and about divine attributes as not being in a human God. Separated from person, these concepts are nothing but theoretical constructs. **289**

On God as the essential person, from whom we are human by virtue of our acceptance of love and wisdom, see §§11–13 above. I stress this here for the sake of what follows, to make it clear that the universe was created by God because God is a person.

The Lord from eternity, or Jehovah, brought forth the sun of the spiritual world out of himself, and created the universe and all its contents from it. **290** Part 2 of the present work dealt with the sun of the spiritual world, and the following points were made there. In the spiritual world, divine love and wisdom look like a sun (§§83–88). Spiritual warmth and spiritual light emanate from that sun (§§89–92). That sun is not God. Rather, it is an emanation from the divine love and wisdom of the Divine-Human One. The same is true of warmth and light from that sun (§§93–98). The sun of the spiritual world is seen at a middle elevation, as far from angels as the physical world's sun is from us (§§103–107). The east in the spiritual world is where the Lord is seen as the sun, and the other directions follow from that (§§119–124 *[119–123]*, 125–128 *[124–128]*). Angels always face the Lord as the sun (§§129–134, 135–139). The Lord created the universe and everything in it by means of that sun that is the first emanation of divine love and wisdom (§§151–156). The physical world's sun is nothing but fire and is therefore dead; and since nature has its origin in that sun, it is dead. Further, the physical world's sun was created so that the work of creation could be finished off and completed (§§157–162).[161] There would be no creation if it were not for this pair of suns, one living and one dead (§§163–166).

One of the things explained in part 2, then, was this: that sun is not the Lord. Rather, it is an emanation from the Lord's divine love and wisdom. It is called an emanation because that sun is brought forth from the **291** divine love and divine wisdom that in and of themselves are substance and form; and Divinity emanates by means of it.

However, our reason by its nature will not consent to anything unless it sees the reason behind it, unless it sees how it has happened. In the present instance, reason needs to grasp how the spiritual world's sun was brought forth, inasmuch as it is not the Lord but an emanation from the Lord, so something must be said about this as well. I have had many conversations with angels about this. They have told me that they grasp it clearly in their spiritual light, but that it is almost impossible for them to present it to us in our earthly light because there is such a difference between the two kinds of light, and therefore between their thoughts and ours.

They did say, though, that it is like the aura of feelings and consequent thoughts that surrounds every angel, through which angels' presence is established for people both nearby and at a distance. This surrounding aura is not the actual angel, but it is derived from every part of the angel's body. Coherent substances flow from it like a river, and the emanations envelop them. These substances bordering angels' bodies, substances constantly energized by the two fountains of their life, the heart and the lungs, stir the atmospheres into their activities, and in this way establish a sense of the angel's virtual presence among others. This means that there is not a separate aura of feelings and consequent thoughts that go forth in connected fashion, even though that is what we call it, because the feelings are simply states of the forms of the mind within.

The angels went on to say that all angels have this kind of aura around them because the Lord does, and that the aura around the Lord is similarly derived from him. This aura is their sun, or the sun of the spiritual world.

292   I have fairly often been allowed to perceive that there is this kind of aura around an angel or spirit and that there is a general aura around groups in community. I have also been allowed to see this aura in various guises, sometimes in heaven looking like a faint flame and in hell like a harsh flame, sometimes in heaven looking like a delicate and bright cloud and in hell like a dense black cloud. I have also been allowed to sense these auras as different kinds of aroma and stench. This has convinced me that everyone in heaven and everyone in hell is surrounded by an aura made up of substances distilled and separated from his or her body.

I have also noticed that an aura flows out not only from angels and **293** spirits but also from absolutely everything you see in that world—from trees and their fruits there, for example, from shrubs and their blossoms, from plants and grasses, even from soils and their particles. I could therefore see that this is a universal characteristic of things both living and lifeless, that everything is surrounded by something resembling what lies within it and that this is constantly breathing forth.

The experience of numerous scholars informs us that something like this happens in the physical world. For example, an outgoing wave is constantly flowing from individuals and from every animal, also from trees, fruits, shrubs, and flowers, and even from metals and stones. The physical world gets this from the spiritual world, and the spiritual world gets it from Divinity.

Since the elements that make up the sun of the spiritual world are **294** from the Lord and are not the Lord, they are not intrinsic life but are devoid of intrinsic life. In the same way, the elements that flow out from angels and from us and form surrounding auras are not the angels or the people. They are derived from them but are devoid of their life. They are part of the angel or person only in the fact that they are in harmony with them because they are derived from those forms of their bodies that are forms of the life within them.

This is a mystery that angels can see in thought and express in speech with their spiritual concepts, while we cannot do the same with our earthly concepts. This is because a thousand spiritual concepts go to make up one earthly one, and we cannot resolve a single earthly concept into any spiritual one, let alone into several. The reason for this is that they differ as to the vertical levels discussed in part 3.

The following experience taught me what kind of difference there is **295** between angels' thoughts and our thoughts. They were told to think about something spiritually and then to tell me what they had been thinking. Once they had done this and tried to tell me, they could not, and they explained that they could not articulate it. The same thing held true for both their spiritual speech and their spiritual writing. There was not a single word of spiritual speech that resembled a word of earthly speech, no element of spiritual writing that resembled earthly writing except the letters, and each of these contained a complete meaning.

Remarkably enough, though, they told me that they seemed to themselves to be thinking and talking and writing in their spiritual state the same way we do in our earthly state even though there is no similarity whatever. I could see from this that what is earthly and what is spiritual differ as to vertical level, and that they communicate with each other only through correspondences.[162]

296 *There are three things in the Lord that are the Lord—a divine element of love, a divine element of wisdom, and a divine element of service. These three things are made visible outside the sun of the spiritual world—the divine element of love through its warmth, the divine element of wisdom through its light, and the divine element of service through the atmospheres that enclose it.* On the emanation of warmth and light from the spiritual world's sun—warmth from the Lord's divine love and light from the Lord's divine wisdom—see §§98–92 *[93–98]*, 99–102, and 146–150. I now need to note that the third thing that emanates from the sun there is an atmosphere that serves as the vessel of warmth and light, and that it emanates from that divine aspect of the Lord that is called "service."

297   Anyone who thinks with some enlightenment can see that love has service as its goal, that love tends toward service, and that love brings about service through wisdom. In fact, love cannot accomplish anything useful by itself, only by means of wisdom. After all, what is love unless there is something that is loved? That "something" is service. Service is what is loved; and since it is brought forth by means of wisdom, it follows that service is the vessel of love and wisdom.

   I explained in §§209–216 above (as well as elsewhere)[163] that these three, love, wisdom, and service, follow in sequence by vertical levels, and that the final level is the composite, vessel, and foundation of the preceding levels. It therefore stands to reason that these three elements—elements of divine love, divine wisdom, and divine service—are in the Lord, and in essence are the Lord.

298   I will be explaining at ample length below [§§319–335] that if you look at both the inner and the outer aspects of humans, we are a form suited to all kinds of service, and that all the useful functions in the created universe have their equivalents in these kinds of service. At this point I need only mention it in order to call attention to the fact that God as a person is the very form suited to all kinds of service, the one in whom all useful functions in the created universe find their source. This means that in terms of its useful functions, the created universe is an image of God.

   By "useful functions," I mean those processes that were created by the Divine-Human One, or the Lord, as part of the design. I do not mean activities that derive from our own self-concern. That concern is hell, and its activities violate the design.

Bear in mind, then, that these three elements—love, wisdom, and 299
service—are in the Lord and are the Lord. Bear in mind also that the
Lord is everywhere, is in fact omnipresent. Then consider that the Lord
cannot make himself manifest to any angel or to us as he really is and as
he is in his sun. This is why he makes himself manifest by means of
things that can be accepted, doing so as to love in the form of warmth, as
to wisdom in the form of light, and as to service in the form of an atmosphere.

The reason the Lord manifests himself as to service in the form of an
atmosphere is that an atmosphere serves as a vessel for warmth and light
the way service serves as a vessel for love and wisdom. The warmth and
light that radiate from Divinity as the sun cannot radiate in nothing, in a
vacuum, but need some vessel as their medium.[164] We call this vessel the
atmosphere that surrounds the sun, takes it in its embrace, and carries it
to the heaven where angels are and from there to the world where we are.
This is how the Lord's presence is made manifest everywhere.

I explained in §§173–178 and 179–183 above that there are atmos- 300
pheres in the spiritual world just as there are in the physical world; and I
noted that the atmospheres of the spiritual world are spiritual, and that
those of the physical world are physical. Given the origin of the spiritual
atmosphere most closely surrounding the spiritual sun, then, it stands to
reason that in all respects it is, in essence, of the same quality as the sun is
in its essence.

With their spiritual concepts, which are nonspatial, angels assert the
truth of this by saying that there is only one single substance underlying
everything and that the spiritual world's sun is that substance. Further,
since Divinity is not in space and since it is the same in the largest and
smallest things, the same holds true for that sun that is the first emanation of the Divine-Human One. They further assert that the one substance, the sun, radiating by its atmospheres, gives rise to the variety of
everything in the created universe, in accord with both the gradual or
horizontal levels and the distinct or vertical ones.[165]

Angels have told me that there is no way to understand such things
unless space is banished from our concepts; that if space is not banished,
superficial appearances will inevitably give rise to illusions. We are not
susceptible to them, though, if we hold in mind the fact that God is the
absolute reality underlying everything.

Further, in the light of angelic concepts, which are nonspatial, it is 301
perfectly clear that in the created universe there is nothing living except
the Divine-Human One—the Lord—alone, that nothing moves except

by life from God, and that nothing exists except by means of the sun from God. So it is true that in God we live and move and have our being.[166]

302   *The atmospheres—three in number in each world, spiritual and physical— in their final forms terminate in the kinds of material substance characteristic of our earth.* In §§173–176 *[173–178]* of part 3, I explained that there are three atmospheres in each world, the spiritual and the physical, distinguished from each other by vertical levels and diminishing as they move downward by horizontal levels. Since the atmospheres do diminish as they move lower, it follows that they are constantly becoming denser and less active, ultimately so dense and inactive that they are no longer atmospheres but inert substances, and in a physical world they become stable, like the substances on earth that we call "matter."

There are three consequences of this origin of material substances.[167] First, material substances also have three levels. Second, they are kept in interconnection by the enveloping atmospheres. Third, they are suited in their forms to the production of all kinds of useful activity.

303   No one who thinks that there are constant intermediate steps between what is first and what is final, and that nothing can come into being except from some antecedent, and ultimately from what is first, can fail to agree that the material substances on earth have been brought forth by the sun by means of its atmospheres. What is first is the spiritual world's sun, and what is first relative to that sun is the Divine-Human One, or the Lord.

Since the atmospheres are those relatively early things by which the sun makes itself present in outermost things, and since those relatively early things are constantly diminishing as they work and extend themselves all the way to their limits, it follows that when their action and expansion come to rest at their limits, they become the kinds of material substance that we find on earth, retaining from the atmospheres that gave rise to them a tendency and effort to produce useful functions.

People who propose a creation of the universe and everything in it with no constant intermediate steps from what is first cannot help but formulate theories that are fragmentary and disconnected from actual causes. When these theories are explored by a mind that probes the matter more deeply, they look not like houses but like a pile of rubble.

304   Because of this common origin of everything in the created universe, its smaller components have a similar characteristic. That is, they go from their beginning to their limits, limits that are in a relatively quiet

state, in order to come to rest and persist. In the human body, this is how the fibers develop from their first forms until they become tendons, and the fibers together with their smaller vessels develop from their beginnings until they become cartilage and bone, where they become stable and durable.

Because there is this kind of process from beginnings to limits for our human fibers and vessels, there is a similar procession of the states of these fibers and vessels, their states being sensations, thoughts, and feelings. These too go through a sequence from their beginnings, where they are in the light, to their limits, where they are in darkness; or from their beginnings, where they are in warmth, to their limits, where they are not. Since they have this kind of progression, there is a similar progression for love and everything involved in it and for wisdom and everything involved in it. In short, this kind of progression is characteristic of everything in the created universe. This is just what I said in §§222–229 above, that there are levels of both kinds in everything that has been created, no matter how large or small.

The reason there are both kinds of level in even the smallest things is that the spiritual sun is the sole substance that gives rise to everything, according to the spiritual concepts of angels (§300).

There is nothing of absolute Divinity in the material substances that make **305** *up earth, but they are still derived from absolute Divinity.* On the basis of the origin of earth as described in the preceding section, we may conclude that there is no trace of absolute Divinity in the earth's material substances; they are completely devoid of absolute Divinity. There are, as already stated [§§184, 189], boundaries and limits of the atmospheres, whose warmth lapses into cold, light into darkness, and activity into torpor. Still, by being connected with their source, the substance of the spiritual sun, they retain something that is in that sun from Divinity. As noted above in §§291–298 *[291–294]*, this was the aura that envelops the Divine-Human One, the Lord. The material substances of earth arise from this aura by extension from the sun, by means of the atmospheres.

There is no other way to describe the origin of earth from the spiritual sun by means of the atmospheres using words that issue from earthly **306** concepts. It can be described differently using words derived from spiritual concepts, though, because these are nonspatial; and since they are nonspatial, they do not fit into any words of an earthly language.

See above (§295) on the fact that spiritual thought, speech, and writing are so different from earthly thought, speech, and writing that they have nothing in common, and communicate only by means of correspondences. It will have to do, then, that we understand the origin of earth to some extent physically.

307   *All useful functions, which are the goals of creation, are in forms, and they get these forms from the material substances characteristic of earth.* All the things I have been talking about so far—the sun, the atmospheres, and the earth—are simply means toward goals, and the goals of creation are what are brought forth from earth by the Lord as the sun, through the atmospheres. These goals are called useful functions, and they include everything involved in the plant kingdom, everything involved in the animal kingdom, and ultimately the human race and the angelic heaven that comes from it.

These are called useful functions because they are receptive of divine love and wisdom and because they focus on God the Creator as their source and thereby unite him with his master work in such a way that they continue to exist through him in the same way they arose. I say "they focus on God the Creator as their source and unite him with his master work," but this is talking in terms of the way things seem. It actually means that God the Creator works it out so that these useful functions seem to focus on and unite themselves to him on their own initiative. I will describe later [§§310–317] how they focus on and thereby unite themselves to him.

I have already dealt with these subjects to some extent in appropriate places; in §§47–51, for example, divine love and wisdom cannot fail to be and to be manifested in others that it has created; in §§54–60 *[55–60]*, everything in the created universe is a vessel of divine love and wisdom; and in §§65–68, the useful functions of every created thing tend upward to us step by step, and through us to God the creator, their source.

308   Can anyone fail to see quite clearly that the goals of creation are useful functions? Simply bear in mind that nothing can arise from God the Creator—nothing can be created, therefore—that is not useful. If it is to be useful, it must be for the sake of others. Even if it is for its own sake, it is still for others, because we are useful to ourselves in order to be fit to be useful to others. Anyone who keeps this in mind can also keep in mind the thought that functions that are truly useful cannot arise from us but must be in us from one who brings forth nothing but what is useful—the Lord.

Since the subject is the forms of useful functions, I need to discuss them in the following sequence.

309

1. Earth has an active tendency to bring forth useful functions in particular forms, or forms of useful functions.
2. In all such forms there is some image of the creation of the universe.
3. In all such forms there is some human image.
4. In all such forms there is some image of what is infinite and eternal.

1. Earth has an active tendency to bring forth useful functions in particular forms, or forms of useful functions. The presence of this tendency in the earth is a corollary of its origin, since the material substances that make up the earth are boundaries and limits of the atmospheres that come from the spiritual sun as useful functions (see above, §§305 and 306). Further, since the material substances that make up the earth are from this source, and since their compounds are constantly held together by the surrounding pressure of the atmospheres, it follows that this gives them a constant active tendency to bring forth forms of useful functions. They derive their very ability to bring these forth from their origin as the boundaries of the atmospheres, with which they are therefore in harmony.

310

I said that this tendency and quality are in the earth, but by this I mean that they are characteristic of the material substances that make up the earth, whether in the earth itself or exhaled by the earth as atmospheres. It is generally recognized that the atmospheres are full of such tendencies.

The presence of this tendency and quality in earth's material substances shows quite clearly in the fact that all kinds of seed are opened to their cores by warmth, are impregnated by substances so subtle that they can only be from a spiritual source, and in this way have the potential of uniting themselves to their function, which is multiplication. After this, they unite with matter of a physical origin to bring forth forms of useful functions, and then, so to speak, bring them forth from the womb so that they emerge into the light, which enables them to sprout and grow.

From then on, this tendency is constantly working from the earth through the roots all the way to the boundaries, and from the boundaries back to the beginning where the function itself dwells in its source. This is how useful functions are transformed into forms, and how as forms develop from their beginnings to their limits and back from their limits to their beginnings, they derive from their function, which is like their soul, a usefulness of each and every component. I am saying that the useful function is like the soul because its form is like its body.

It also follows that there is a still deeper tendency, a tendency to bring forth processes that support the development of the animal kingdom, since all kinds of animal are nourished by plants. It also follows that there is a very deep element in this tendency, a tendency to be of use to the human race. These conclusions follow from the following premises: (a) There are boundaries, and all antecedent things are gathered together in proper sequence within these boundaries, as explained in any number of places above.[168] (b) Each kind of level is found in the largest and smallest instances of everything, as explained in §§222–229 above. The same holds true for their tendency. (c) All useful functions are brought forth by the Lord from outermost things, so there must be an active tendency toward useful functions in outermost things.

311   Still, all these tendencies are not alive. They are tendencies of the energies of the ultimate expressions of life, energies that ultimately have within them, because of the life they come from, a striving to return to their origin by the means at hand. In their final forms, the atmospheres are energies of this sort, energies by which the material substances characteristic of earth are prompted to take form and are maintained in forms both inwardly and outwardly. I am not at leisure to explain this in greater detail, since that would be a major undertaking.

312   The first productive thing earth does when it is still fresh and in all its simplicity is to bring forth seeds. Earth's first tendency could not be anything else.

313   2. *In all such forms there is some image of creation.* There are three kinds of forms of functions: forms of the functions of the mineral kingdom, forms of the functions of the plant kingdom, and forms of the functions of the animal kingdom. The forms of the functions of the mineral kingdom are beyond description because they are not open to our sight. The first forms are the material substances that make up the earth at their most minute. The second forms are compounds of these, which are infinitely varied. The third forms come from decayed vegetation and from dead animals, and from the gaseous vapors they are constantly giving forth, which combine with the earth to form its soil.

These three levels of the forms of the mineral kingdom offer an image of creation in that as they are activated by the sun through its atmospheres and their warmth and light, they do bring forth useful functions in particular forms, functions that are goals of creation. This image of creation in their tendencies (described in §310 above) lies deeply hidden.

We can see how the forms of functions in the plant kingdom offer an image of creation in the way they develop from their beginnings to their limits and from their limits to their beginnings. Their beginnings are seeds, and their limits are their stalks clothed with bark. Through the bark, which is the limit of the stalk, they develop toward seeds, which are their beginnings, as already noted. The stalks clothed with bark echo the planet clothed with soils that give rise to the creation and formation of all its useful functions. There is ample evidence that plant growth takes place through the bark and cortical layers, working through the stalks and branches as extensions of the coverings of the roots into the beginnings of fruits, and in the same way through the fruits into seeds. An image of creation in the forms of functions is offered in the development of their formation from beginnings to limits and from limits to beginnings, as well as in the fact that throughout their development there is the goal of producing fruits and seeds that are useful.

314

We can see from what I have just been saying that the process of creation of the universe goes from its very beginning, the Lord clothed with the sun, to its limit, which is the soil, and from this, through its functions, back to its very beginning, the Lord. We can see also that the goals of the whole creation are useful functions.

We need to realize that the warmth, light, and atmospheres of the physical world contribute absolutely nothing to this image of creation. This image is entirely the work of the warmth, light, and atmospheres of the spiritual world's sun. These bring the image with them and instill it into the forms of the functions of the plant kingdom. All that the warmth, light, and atmospheres of the physical world do is open the seeds, keep their productivity increasing, and provide the matter that gives them solidity.

315

They do not accomplish this with energies from their own sun, though, which are nothing in their own right. They accomplish it with energies from the spiritual sun that is constantly prompting them to do so. They contribute absolutely nothing to the process of giving the forms an image of creation. The image of creation is spiritual; but in order for it to be visible and to function usefully in a physical world, in order for it to be solid and durable, it needs to be "materialized," or filled in with this world's matter.

There is a similar image of creation in the forms of the functions of the animal kingdom. For example, a body is formed from the seed

316

deposited in the womb or egg, a body that is its final form; and when this matures, it produces new seeds. The sequence is like the sequence of forms of functions in the plant kingdom. The seeds are the initial elements; the womb or egg is like the soil; the state before birth is like the state of the seed in the earth while it is making its roots; the state after birth until reproduction is like the sprouting of a tree until its fruit-bearing state.

We can see from this parallelism that there is a likeness of creation in the animal forms just as there is in plant forms. Specifically, there is a sequence from beginnings to limits and from limits to beginnings.

There is a similar image of creation in the details of our own nature, since the sequence of love through wisdom into useful functions is similar, and so therefore is the sequence of intent through discernment into act, and of charity through faith into works. Intent and discernment, charity and faith, are the first and originating elements, while acts and deeds are the final ones. There is a return from these latter, through the delights of being useful, to the first elements, which as noted are intent and discernment, or charity and faith. We can see clearly that the return is by way of the delights we find in being useful from the pleasure we sense in acts and deeds that come from some love. The delights of acts and deeds are the delights we attribute to being useful.

There is a similar sequence from beginnings to limits and from limits to beginnings in the purely organic forms of our desires and thoughts. There are in our brains the star-shaped forms called gray matter, with fibers stretching from them into the medullary matter and through the neck into the body. There they go to their limits, and from these limits they return to their beginnings. The return of the fibers to their beginnings is by way of the blood vessels.

There is a similar sequence of all our desires and thoughts, which are shifts and changes of the states of their forms and substances. The fibers that stretch out from their forms or substances are analogous to the atmospheres that come from the spiritual sun and are vessels of warmth and light. The physical acts are like the things produced from the earth by means of the atmospheres, with the delights of their useful functions returning to their source.

It is scarcely possible, though, to gain a full mental grasp of the nature of their sequence and of the way it embodies an image of creation, since the thousands upon thousands of energies at work in an action seem to be a single event. Further, the delights of useful functions do not give rise to concepts in our thought, but simply affect us without being clearly perceived.

On these matters, see what has already been presented about the way the functions of everything created tend upward by vertical levels to us, and through us to God the creator, their source (§§65–68), and how the goal of creation—that everything should return to the Creator and that there should be a union—becomes manifest in outermost forms (§§167–172).

These matters will be seen in clearer light, though, in the next part [§§371–431], when I discuss the correspondence of volition and discernment with the heart and lungs.

3. I explained above, in §§61–64, that *in all such forms there is some human image.* It will be made clear in the next section that all useful functions from beginnings to limits and from limits to beginnings have a relationship and a responsiveness to everything in humans, so that we are a kind of image of the universe and conversely the universe, from a functional point of view, is in our image.

317

4. *In all such forms there is some image of what is infinite and eternal.* We can see an image of the infinite in these forms from the tendency and potentiality of filling the space of the whole world and even of many worlds, without end. A single seed brings forth a tree, shrub, or plant that takes up its own space. From each tree, shrub, or plant, there come seeds, in some cases thousands of them. Assuming these to be planted and to have sprouted, they take up their spaces; and if from each of their seeds new generations arise again and again, after a few years the whole world is full. If the propagation continues, any number of worlds is filled, and so on to infinity. Figure on a thousand seeds coming from one, and then multiply a thousand by a thousand ten or twenty or a hundred times, and you will see.

318

There is a similar image of eternity in these processes. Seeds reproduce year after year, and the reproductions never cease. They have not paused from the creation of the world to the present, and they will not stop forever.

These two facts are obvious indications and eloquent signs that everything in the universe was created by an infinite and eternal God.

In addition to these images of what is infinite and eternal, there is another image in variety. There can never be a substance, state, or thing in the created universe that is exactly the same as any other. Not in the atmospheres, not on earth, not in the forms that arise from them, and therefore not in any of the things that fill the universe can anything identical ever be brought forth. We can see this very clearly in the variety of all human faces. There is not one identical to another in all the world, and never can be to eternity. This means that there is no human spirit like another, since the face bears the stamp of the spirit.

319   *From a functional point of view, everything in the created universe is in our image; and this testifies that God is human.* The ancients called the individual person a microcosm because each of us reflects the macrocosm, that is, the universe in its entirety.[169] Nowadays, though, people do not know why the ancients gave us this name. Nothing of the universe or the macrocosm is visible in us except that we are nourished by its animal and plant kingdoms and are physically alive, that we are kept alive by its warmth, see by its light, and hear and breathe by its atmospheres. These things, though, do not make us a microcosm the way the universe and everything in it is a macrocosm.

Rather, the ancients learned to call us a microcosm or little universe from the knowledge of correspondences that the earliest people enjoyed and from their communication with angels of heaven. Heaven's angels actually know from what they see around themselves that if we focus on functions, we can see an image of a person in everything in the universe.

320   We are a microcosm or little universe because the created universe has a human image if it is seen in terms of functions. However, this notion remains outside the scope of the thinking we do on the basis of the universe as we see it in this physical world[170] and outside the scope of the knowledge that derives from that thinking. This means that the only way this thought can be established is by an angel who is in the spiritual world or by someone who has been granted entry into that world to see what is there. Since this has been granted to me, I can unveil this mystery from what I have seen there.

321   We need to realize that to all outward appearances, the spiritual world is just like the physical world. You can see lands there, mountains, hills, valleys, plains, fields, lakes, rivers, and springs like the ones in our earthly world; everything, then, that belongs to the mineral kingdom. You can see parks as well, gardens, groves, and woods, with all kinds of trees and shrubs with their fruits and seeds, smaller plants, flowers, herbs, and grasses; everything, then, that belongs to the plant kingdom. You can see all kinds of animals, birds, and fish—everything that belongs to the animal kingdom. The people there are angels and spirits.

This is prefaced to let it be known that the whole spiritual world is just like the whole physical world, the sole difference being that things there are not static and stable the way they are in a physical world because there is nothing of nature there. Everything is spiritual.

There is very solid ground for believing that there is a human image to the universe of the other world in the fact that everything listed in §321 is happening concretely around angels and around angelic communities. It is as though these things were being brought forth or created by them. They persist around them without fading away. You can tell that they are apparently brought forth or created by the angels because when an angel goes away or when a community relocates, these things are no longer visible. Then too, when other angels arrive to take their place, the appearance of everything around them changes. The trees and fruits of the parks change, the blossoms and seeds of the flower beds change, the herbs and grasses of the fields change, and so do the kinds of animals and birds.

322

The reason things occur and change like this is that everything occurs in response to the angels' feelings and consequent thoughts. They are responsive entities, and because the things that respond are integral aspects of that to which they respond, they are their visual images.

The actual image is not visible when the focus is on the forms of anything, but it is visible when the focus is on their functions. I have been allowed to see that when angels' eyes have been opened by the Lord so that they see these things as they answer to functions, the angels recognize and see themselves in their surroundings.

Since the things that occur around angels in response to their feelings and thoughts resemble a kind of universe in being lands, plants, and animals, and since they amount to an image that represents the angels, we can see why the ancients called us a microcosm.

323

There is ample support for the truth of this in *Secrets of Heaven* and also in the book on *Heaven and Hell,* as well as throughout the preceding pages where I have dealt with correspondence [§§52, 83, 87]. I explained there that there is nothing in the created universe that does not answer to something in us, not only to our feelings and consequent thoughts, but also to our physical organs and viscera—not in respect to their substances, but in respect to their functions.

324

This is why when the Word talks about the church and its people, there is such frequent mention of trees like the olive and the vine and the cedar, of gardens and groves and woods, and of the beasts of the field, the fowl of the air, and the fish of the sea. They are mentioned because they correspond and are united by corresponding, as noted. So too, when we are reading things like this in the Word, angels are not conscious of them but of the church in their stead, or of the church's people in regard to their state.

325   Since there is a human image to everything in the universe, Adam's wisdom and intelligence are described by the garden of Eden, where there were trees of every kind, as well as rivers, precious stones, and gold, along with the animals that he named. All of these meant things that were within him and that made him what we call "human."

Quite similar things are said of Assyria in Ezekiel 31:3–9, meaning the church as far as its intelligence is concerned, and about Tyre in Ezekiel 28:12 and 23 [13], meaning the church in regard to its firsthand knowledge of what is good and true.

326   We can tell from all this, then, that if we focus on functions, there is a human image to everything in the universe. We can also tell that this testifies to the fact that God is human, because the things just listed do not come into being around angelic people from themselves, but from the Lord through them. They actually arise from the flow of divine love and wisdom into the angels, who are recipients, and are brought forth to their sight the way the universe is created. So people there know that God is human and that the created universe, functionally viewed, is an image of God.

327   *All of the Lord's creations are useful functions; and they are useful functions in the sequence, on the level, and in the specific way that they relate to humanity and through humanity to the Lord, their source.* I have already made the following points on this subject. Nothing can arise from God the Creator that is not useful (§308). The useful functions of everything created tend upward, step by step, from the lowest to us, and through us to God the Creator, their source (§§65–68). The goal of creation—that everything should return to the Creator and that there should be a union—becomes manifest in outermost forms (§§167–172). They are useful to the extent that they focus on their Creator (§307). Divinity cannot fail to exist in and be manifested in others that it has created (§§47–51). Everything in the universe is a vessel according to its usefulness, and this depends on its level (§38 [58, 66]). Seen in terms of its functions, the universe is an image of God (§39 [169, 298]). There are many other relevant statements as well. These witness to the truth that all the Lord's creations are useful functions, and that they are useful

functions in the sequence, on the level, and in the specific way that they relate to humanity, and through humanity to the Lord, their source. It remains now to say something more detailed about useful functions.

By this "human" to whom useful functions relate, I mean not only an individual but also groups of people and smaller and larger communities such as republics and monarchies and empires and even that largest community that comprises the whole world, since all of these are human. So too in the heavens the whole angelic heaven is like a single individual in the Lord's sight, and so is each individual community of heaven. This is why each individual angel is human. On this subject, see *Heaven and Hell* 68–103 *[68–102]*. This shows what is meant by "human" in the following pages. 328

We can tell what a useful function is from the goal of the creation of the universe. The goal of the creation of the universe is to bring about an angelic heaven; and since an angelic heaven is the goal, so is humanity or the human race, since that is where heaven comes from. It follows, then, that everything that has been created is an intermediate goal, and that the functions are useful in the sequence, on the level, and in the specific way that they relate to humanity, and through humanity to the Lord. 329

Since the goal of creation is a heaven from the human race (and therefore the human race itself), the intermediate goals are everything else that has been created. Because these do relate to us, they focus on these three aspects of us: our bodies, our rational functioning, and, for the sake of our union with the Lord, our spiritual functioning. We cannot be united to the Lord unless we are spiritual; we cannot be spiritual unless we are rational; and we cannot be rational unless we are physically whole. These aspects are like a house, with the body as its foundation, the structure of the house as our rational functioning, and the contents of the house as our spiritual functioning. Living in the house is union with the Lord. 330

This enables us to see the sequence, level, and focus of the relationship to us of the useful functions that are intermediate goals of creation. That is, they are for the support of our bodies, for the development of our rational ability, and for our acceptance of what is spiritual from the Lord.

Useful functions for the support of our bodies have to do with its nourishment, clothing, shelter, recreation and pleasure, protection, and the preservation of its state. The useful things created for physical nourishment are all the members of the plant kingdom that we eat and drink, 331 such as fruits, grapes, seeds, vegetables, and grains. Then there are all the members of the animal kingdom that we eat, such as steers, cows, calves, deer, sheep, kids, goats, lambs, and the milk they give, as well as many kinds of bird and fish.

The useful things created for clothing our bodies also come in abundance from these two kingdoms, as do those for our shelter and for our recreation and pleasure, for our protection, and for the preservation of our state. I will not enumerate these because they are familiar, so listing them would only take up space.

There are of course many things that we do not find useful, but these extras do not prevent usefulness. In fact, they enable useful functions to continue. Then there are abuses of functions; but again, the abuse of a function does not eliminate the useful function, just as the falsification of something true does not destroy the truth except for the people who are doing the falsifying.

332 *Useful functions for the development of our rational ability* are all the ones that teach us what I have just been talking about. These are called academic disciplines and fields of study having to do with nature, economics, politics, and morals, things that we get from parents and teachers, from books, from our dealings with each other, or from ourselves through our inner reflection about these subjects. These develop our rational ability to the extent that they are higher-level functions, and they become secure to the extent that we apply them to our lives.

There is not room to list these useful functions both because there are so many of them and because their relationship to the common good varies.

333 *Useful functions for our acceptance of what is spiritual from the Lord* are all the elements of our religion and its worship, everything, then, that teaches us to recognize and understand God and to recognize and understand what is good and what is true—that therefore teaches us eternal life. These, like academic disciplines, we get from parents, teachers, sermons, and books, and especially by devoting ourselves to living by them. In the Christian world, this comes through teaching and preaching from the Word, and through the Word, from the Lord.

We can describe the range of these functions much as we describe physical functions—in terms of nourishment, for example, clothing, shelter, recreation and pleasure, and protection of our state, as long as we apply them to the soul. We may compare nourishment to the good that love does, clothing to the truth that wisdom provides, dwelling to heaven, recreation and pleasure to life's happiness and heavenly joy,

protection to [safety from] the attacks of evil, and preservation of our
state to eternal life.

The Lord grants all these gifts upon our acknowledgment that everything physical also comes from the Lord and that we are simply like servants or stewards given responsibility for the Lord's goods.

It is abundantly clear that these are for our use and that they are gifts
freely given if we look at the state of angels in the heavens. They have
bodies, rational abilities, and spiritual receptivity just as we on earth do.
They are nourished for free, because they are given their food daily. They
are clothed for free, because they are given their clothing. They are
housed for free, because they are given their homes. They have no anxiety
about any of these things; and to the extent that they are spiritually rational, they enjoy pleasure, protection, and preservation of their state.

The difference is that angels see that these things come from the Lord
because they are created in response to the angels' state of love and wisdom, as explained above in §322, while we do not see this because things
recur according to the calendar and happen not according to our states of
love and wisdom but according to our efforts.

Even though we say that functions are useful because they relate to
the Lord through us, we cannot say that they are from us for the sake of
the Lord. They are from the Lord for our sake because all useful functions are infinitely united in the Lord, and none of them are in us except
as gifts from the Lord. We can actually do nothing good on our own,
only from the Lord, and the good we do is what we are calling useful
functions. The essence of spiritual love is to do good to others for their
sake and not for our own. This is infinitely more so in regard to the
essence of divine love. It is like the love of parents for their children.
They do good for them out of love, for the children's sake, not for their
own sake. We can see this clearly in the love mothers have for their little
ones.

People believe that because the Lord is to be revered, worshiped, and
praised the Lord loves reverence, worship, and praise for his own sake. In
fact, he loves them for our sake, because they bring us into a state where
something divine can flow in and be felt. This is because by these activities we are removing that focus on self[171] that prevents the inflow and acceptance. The focus on self that is self-love hardens and closes our heart.
It is removed by our realization that in our own right we are nothing but
evil and that nothing but what is good comes from the Lord. This yields
the softening of heart and humility from which reverence and worship
flow.

334

335

It follows from this that the purpose of the useful functions the Lord provides for himself through us is that he may bless us out of his love; and since this is what he loves to do, our receiving it is the joy of his love.

No one should believe that the Lord is with people who simply worship him. He makes his home with people who do his commandments—that is, his useful functions—and not with the others. See also what it says about this in §§47, 48, and 49 above.

336 *Evil functions were not created by the Lord. Rather, they came into being along with hell.* All good things that find expression in act are called functions, and all evil things that find expression in act are also called functions. The latter, though, are called evil functions, while the former are called good functions. Since everything good is from the Lord and everything evil from hell, it follows that only good functions have been created by the Lord, and that all the evil ones have come from hell.

The particular functions I am talking about in this section are all the things we see on earth, like all kinds of animal and all kinds of plant. In both instances, the ones that are good for us are from the Lord and the ones that do us harm are from hell. By the same token, "useful functions from the Lord" means all the things that help develop our rational ability and that enable us to be receptive of spiritual gifts from the Lord; while "evil functions" means everything that destroys our rational ability and makes it impossible for us to become spiritual.

The reason harmful things are called "useful functions" is that they are useful to evil people for their evildoing, and also because they serve to soak up malice and therefore lead to remedies. I use "useful functions" in this dual sense, and do the same with "love," speaking of "a good love" and "an evil love." Whatever love brings forth it calls useful.

337 I will use the following sequence to show that good functions are from the Lord and that evil functions are from hell.

1. Which things in our world I mean by "evil functions."
2. Everything that is an evil function exists in hell, and everything that is a good function exists in heaven.
3. There is a constant inflow from the spiritual world into the earthly world.
4. The inflow from hell activates things that are evil functions, in places where there are things that answer to them.

5. The lowest spiritual level, separated from what is higher, is what does this.

6. There are two forms in which activation by inflow occurs, the plant form and the animal form.

7. Each form gets the ability and the means of propagating its own kind.

1. *Which things in our world I mean by "evil functions."* "Evil functions" in our world means everything harmful in both kingdoms, the animal and the plant, and harmful things in the mineral kingdom as well. There is no room to list all the harmful things in these kingdoms, for this would be simply to pile up names; and piling up names with no indication of what kind of harm each species inflicts would bring none of the usefulness this work intends. I may simply name a few by way of information.

338

In the animal kingdom, there are poisonous snakes, scorpions, crocodiles, lizards,[172] owls,[173] mice, locusts, frogs, and spiders, and also flies, wasps, moths, lice, and mites. In short, there is everything that consumes grains, leaves, fruits, and seeds, our food and our drink, and inflicts harm on animals and people. In the plant kingdom there are many herbs that are harmful, poisonous, and lethal, as well as plants and shrubs of the same sort. In the mineral kingdom there are all the toxic substances.

We can see from these few examples what I mean by "evil functions" in this world of ours. "Evil functions" are all the things that conflict with the good functions discussed in the previous section.

2. *Everything that is an evil function exists in hell, and everything that is a good function exists in heaven.* Before we can see that all evil functions that occur on our earth come not from the Lord but from hell, some kind of preface about heaven and hell is needed. Unless this is understood, evil functions may be credited to the Lord just like good ones and thought to be together with them from creation, or they may be credited to nature and thought to originate in its sun. People cannot be rescued from these two errors unless they know that nothing whatever happens in the physical world that does not find its cause and therefore its origin in the spiritual world and that what is good comes from the Lord and what is evil comes from the devil, that is, from hell. "The spiritual world" means both heaven and hell.

339

In heaven, you can see all the good functions described in the preceding section. In hell, on the other hand, you can see all the evil functions just listed in §338—wild animals of every kind like snakes, scorpions, lizards, crocodiles, tigers, wolves, foxes, boars, night birds, owls,[174] bats, mice, rats, frogs, locusts, spiders, and many kinds of harmful insect. You can also see toxic and dangerous things of all kinds, and poisons[175] in both plants and soils—in a word, everything that does injury and that kills people. In the hells, things like this are just as vividly visible as they are on and in the earth.

I say that they are visible there, but they do not exist there the same way they do on earth. They are pure reflections of the cravings that spew from the evils of [demonic spirits'] loves, presenting themselves to others in these forms. Because there are things like this in the hells, foul stenches pour out as well, smells of carrion, feces, urine, and decay that demonic spirits relish, the way animals relish things that contain toxins.

It stands to reason, then, that things like this in the earthly world do not find their source in the Lord, created from the beginning, and that their origin is not from nature through its sun, but that they are from hell. It is abundantly clear that their origin is not from nature, through its sun, from the fact that what is spiritual flows into what is earthly and not vice versa. It is clear that they are not from the Lord from the fact that hell is not from him, so neither is anything in hell that reflects their evils.

340   3. *There is a constant inflow from the spiritual world into the physical world.* Unless people realize that there is a spiritual world and that it is as distinct from the physical world as an antecedent circumstance is from its consequence or a cause from what it causes, they cannot know anything about this inflow. This is why people who have written about the origin of plants and animals have found it necessary to trace them back to nature. If they do trace them back to God, they say that God gifted nature with the ability to bring forth plants and animals in the beginning. They do not realize that nature is not "gifted" with any power. In its own right, it is dead and contributes no more to bringing things forth than a tool contributes to the work of an artisan—if it is to accomplish anything, it needs constantly to be activated. It is spiritual reality, reality that finds its origin in the sun where the Lord is and that goes to the limits of nature, that produces the forms of plants and animals and causes the miracles that we see in both, filling them in with earthly substances so that the forms are stable and enduring.

It is acknowledged, then, that there is a spiritual world, that what is spiritual comes from a sun where the Lord is who is its source, and that this spiritual reality stirs nature into action the way something living stirs something lifeless. It is acknowledged further that there are things in that spiritual world that resemble things in our physical world. We can therefore see that plants and animals have come into being solely from the Lord through that world and that they constantly keep coming into being through it. This means that there is a constant inflow from the spiritual world into the physical one. There will be ample support for this in the next section.

The production of harmful things on earth through an inflow from hell happens by the same law of tolerance that applies to the very evils that flow from hell into people. I will discuss this law in *Angelic Wisdom about Divine Providence*.[176]

4. *The inflow from hell activates things that are evil functions, in places where there are things that answer to them.* The things that answer to evil functions (that is, harmful plants and animals) are characteristic of corpses, decay, feces and manure, spoilage, and urine. As a result, the plants and little creatures like these, the ones just listed, turn up in places where these substances are found. There are more such species in the tropics, where we find snakes, basilisks, crocodiles, scorpions, mice, and the like.

Everyone knows that swamps, marshes, manure piles, and rotten soils teem with creatures like these and that vicious insects fill the air like clouds, and vicious bugs infest the earth like armies and devour plants down to their very roots. I noticed once in my own garden that in the space of a cubit almost all the dust turned into tiny winged creatures, because when I stirred it with my stick they rose up in clouds.

We can see simply from experience that carrion and decay are congenial and close kin to these vicious and useless little creatures. It is particularly clear when we consider the reason, namely that there are foul stenches like these in the hells, where such little creatures are also found. That is why hells are named after their odors, some called morgues, some manure piles, some urinals, and so on. They are all covered, though, so that their exhaust fumes do not escape, for when they are opened a little (which happens when newly arriving demons are let in), it induces vomiting and headaches; while the ones that are also toxic cause a loss of consciousness. The dust itself in hell is like this, so it is known there as "the dust of doom."[177]

We can see from this that these vicious creatures are found where foul substances like this occur because they suit each other.

I need now to deal with the question of whether creatures like this come from eggs brought through the air or in rain or by the devious paths of water, or whether they come from the actual fluids and odors. Experience overall does not support the notion that the vicious little creatures and insects I have been talking about come out of eggs, either borne to their site or hidden in the ground since creation. That is, worms turn up in tiny seeds, in nuts, in pieces of wood, and in stones; they come from leaves; lice and maggots turn up on plants and in plants that are congenial to them. Then there are the flies that show up in houses, fields, and forests in summer where there is no corresponding supply of egglike matter. There are the ones that destroy meadows and lawns, and that fill and infest the air in warm climates, besides the invisible ones that swim and fly in stagnant water, sour wine, and disease-laden air. These experiences support the people who say that the odors, stenches, and vapors themselves, coming from the plants, soil, and ponds, also provide the beginnings of such creatures.[178]

The fact that they multiply by eggs or by a discharge once they have begun does not rule out their spontaneous generation,[179] since every little creature gets organs of generation and propagation along with its other viscera, as discussed below in §347.[180]

There is further support in a previously unknown experience, namely that things like this occur in the hells as well.

343   The hells just mentioned have not only a communication but even a union with similar phenomena on earth. This follows from the fact that the hells are not distant from us but are around us and even in us when we are evil. They are therefore in direct contact with earth. We are surrounded by angels of heaven or by spirits of hell in regard to our desires and consequent thoughts and as to the deeds that result from them both, deeds that are either good or evil functions. Since the same kinds of thing we have on earth exist in the heavens and the hells as well, it follows that the inflow from that source produces such things directly when conditions are right. Everything visible in the spiritual world, whether in heaven or in hell, reflects passions and desires because everything there arises in response to them. As a result, when passions and desires that are intrinsically spiritual find circumstances that are congenial or responsive, there is something spiritual there that provides a soul and something physical that provides a body. There is in everything spiritual an inherent tendency to clothe itself with a body.

The reason the hells are around and are therefore in direct contact with the earth is that the spiritual world is not in space, but is found wherever there is a responsive feeling.

In the spiritual world, I once heard two presidents of the British [Royal] Society, Sir Sloane[181] and Sir Folkes,[182] discussing the origin of seeds and eggs and their propagations on earth. The first attributed all this to nature, saying that from creation they were gifted with a power and energy for propagation by means of the sun's warmth. The second said that this force was continually coming from God the Creator into nature. To resolve the disagreement, Sir Sloane was shown a lovely bird and told to examine it closely to see whether it was at all different from similar birds on earth. He held it in his hand and examined it carefully and said that there was no difference. He knew that it was simply the feeling of a particular angel that was being portrayed outwardly as a bird and that it would vanish or go out of existence along with that feeling, which then happened.

This experience convinced Sir Sloane that nature contributed nothing whatever to the propagation of plants and animals. It is simply what flows into nature from the spiritual world. He said that if that particular bird had been filled in with appropriate earthly matter down to the last detail and so had become stable, it would have been a lasting bird just like our earthly birds, and that the same held true for things that came from hell.

He went on to say that if he had known what he now knew about the spiritual world, he would not have attributed anything to nature except the service it provides to spiritual reality from God, for giving stability to the forces that are constantly flowing into nature.

5. *The lowest spiritual level, separated from what is higher, is what does this.* I explained the following things in part 3.[183] What is spiritual flows from its sun all the way down to the borders of nature by three steps, and these steps are called heavenly, spiritual, and earthly. They are within us from creation and therefore are inherent in us from birth. They are opened in proportion to our lives. If the heavenly level is opened, which is the highest and central one, then we become heavenly. If the spiritual level is opened, which is the intermediate one, then we become spiritual. If only the earthly level, the lowest and most remote, is opened, then we become earthly; and if we become nothing but earthly, we love only what has to do with our bodies and the world. To the extent that this is the case, we do not love things that are heavenly and spiritual and we do not turn toward God; and to that extent we become evil.

We can see from this that the lowest spiritual level, called "the spiritual-earthly level," can be separated from what lies above it and that it is so separated in the people who constitute hell. This lowest spiritual level cannot be separated from what lies above it either in animals or in soils[184] and turn toward hell. This can happen only in humans.

It therefore follows that when the lowest spiritual level is separated from what lies above it the way it is for people in hell, this is what creates those evil functions on earth that I have just been discussing.

As for the claim that the harmful things on earth can be traced back to us and therefore to hell, this is supported by conditions in the land of Canaan described in the Word. When the Israelites lived by the Commandments, the land provided them with food as well as flocks and herds, while when they lived contrary to the Commandments it became barren and cursed, so to speak, bringing forth thorns and briars instead of grain. Their flocks and herds miscarried and wild beasts invaded.[185] We can draw the same conclusion from the locusts, frogs, and lice in Egypt.[186]

346

6. *There are two forms in which activation by inflow occurs, the plant form and the animal form.* It is common knowledge that our earth brings forth only two basic forms, since there are two kingdoms of nature called the animal kingdom and the plant kingdom. All the members of each kingdom have many things in common. In the animal kingdom, for example, all its members have organs of sense as well as organs of motion, members, and viscera that are animated by their brains, hearts, and lungs. As for the plant kingdom, all its members put down roots into the ground and form stems, branches, leaves, flowers, fruits, and seeds. If we look at the way both the animal and the plant kingdoms are brought forth in these forms, the beginning is by a spiritual inflow and a working from heaven's sun, where the Lord is, and not from any inflow and working of nature from its sun. This serves only to stabilize them, as already noted [§§339–340].

All the greater and lesser animals start from something spiritual on the lowest level, the one called "earthly." Only we humans come from all the levels, from the three that are called heavenly, spiritual, and earthly. Since each vertical or distinct step declines gradually from perfection to imperfection the way light declines into darkness, so do animals. The perfect ones are elephants, camels, horses, mules, cattle, sheep, goats, and the other members of flocks and herds. The less perfect are the winged ones, and the imperfect are fish and shellfish. Since they are the lowest of this level, it is as though they were in darkness, while the others are in light.

Still, since these all get their life only from the lowest spiritual level, the one called earthly, the only direction they can look is toward the earth and their food and, for propagation, their kindred. For all of them, their soul is an earthly desire and urge.

The same holds true for members of the plant kingdom. There are complete, less complete, and incomplete ones. The complete ones are fruit trees, the less complete are vines and shrubs, and the incomplete are grains. However, plants derive a usefulness from the spiritual reality that is their source, and animals derive passionate and impulsive natures from the spiritual reality that is their source, as already noted [§§313–316].

[7.][187] *Whenever it occurs, each form gets the means of propagating its own kind.* I explained in §§313–318 above that there is some image of creation, some human image—even some image of what is infinite and eternal—in all the things that the earth brings forth, which as noted belong either to the plant or to the animal kingdom. I also noted that this image of the infinite and eternal shines forth in their capacity for infinite and eternal proliferation. This is why they all get means of propagation, members of the animal kingdom by seeds in eggs or the womb or by a discharge, and members of the plant kingdom by seeds in the ground. We can tell from this that even though the incomplete and harmful animals and plants begin from a direct inflow from hell, from then on they are propagated by the means of seeds, eggs, or grafts. The one source, that is, does not rule out the other.

347

An example may illustrate the fact that both good and evil functions have a spiritual origin, namely the sun where the Lord is. I heard that some good and true gifts had been let down by the Lord through the heavens to hell, and that as they were accepted step by step, all the way to the lowest level of hell, they were turned into the evil and false things that were opposite to the good and true gifts. The reason this happened was that the recipient subjects turn everything that flows in into things that agree with their own forms, just as the pure light of the sun becomes offensive colors or blackness in objects whose inner substances are in the sort of form that stifles light and extinguishes it, and just as swamps, manure piles, and corpses turn the sun's warmth into stenches.

348

We can tell from this that even evil functions come from the spiritual sun, but [they are] good functions turned into evil ones in hell. This shows that the Lord has not created and does not create anything but good functions, while hell brings forth the evil ones.

What we can see in the created universe bears witness to the fact that nature has brought forth nothing and brings forth nothing. Divinity brings forth everything from itself, and does so through the spiritual world. Many people

349

in our world take events at face value and say that the sun produces the
things that we can see in our meadows, fields, gardens, and forests by its
warmth and light, that the sun hatches grubs from eggs by its warmth
and makes the beasts of the earth and the birds in the sky reproduce, and
even that it brings us to life. People can talk this way if they are simply
talking in terms of appearances but are not really ascribing these powers
to nature. They are not actually thinking about it. It is like people talking
about the sun, saying that it rises and sets and makes days and years, that
it is now at one height or another. They are likewise talking in terms of
appearances, and they can do so, without thinking about the sun as sta-
tionary and the earth as revolving.

People who prove to themselves that the sun does produce the things
we see on earth by its warmth and light end up giving nature credit for
everything, even the creation of the universe. They become materialists
and ultimately atheists. They can later say that God created nature and
endowed it with the ability to do all this, but they say this out of fear of
harm to their reputation.[188] All the while, by "God the Creator" they really mean nature—for some of them, its inmost essence—and completely trivialize the divine qualities that the church teaches.

350   Still, we must forgive some people who attribute what they see to nature, and this for two reasons. First, they have had no knowledge of
heaven's sun, where the Lord is, or about the inflow from it. They have
had no knowledge of the spiritual world and its state or of its presence
with us. As a result, they could think of spiritual reality only as a purer
form of earthly reality, so that angels were either in the ether or in the
stars, the devil either was an evil person or, if he were actually to come
into existence, would be in the air or in the depths, and that our own
souls after death were either at the center of the earth or in a mysterious
"elsewhere"[189] until judgment day, along with other notions of the same
sort that give rise to delusions born of their ignorance of the spiritual
world and its sun.

The second reason for forgiving them is that they have had no way to
know how Divinity produces all the things we see on our earth where
there are so many things both good and evil. They have been afraid of
drawing their conclusion, to keep from attributing evil to God or giving
birth to a materialistic concept of God, equating God with nature, and
therefore confusing them.

These are two reasons for forgiving people who believe that nature
brings forth the things we can see by a power instilled at creation. However, we should not forgive people who make atheists of themselves by

"proving" this role of nature, because they could "prove" the same role for Divinity. Ignorance does excuse, true, but it does not cancel deliberate proof of what is false, since this falsity is intimately connected to evil and therefore to hell. As a result, people who opt decisively for nature to the point that they divorce Divinity from it attach no weight to sin, since all sin is against the Divinity they have divorced and thus rejected. If people in spirit attach no weight to sin, then after death, when they become spirits, they rush as captives of hell into the unspeakable consequences of their cravings, cravings whose reins have been loosened.

People who believe that Divinity is at work in the details of nature can prove the role of Divinity for themselves by a host of things they observe in nature—just as fully as and even more fully than people who decide in favor of nature. People who decide for Divinity pay attention to the miracles they see in the way both plants and animals reproduce. In the reproduction of plants, they see that a root goes forth from a tiny seed cast into the ground, with a stem from the root and then twigs, leaves, flowers, fruit, all the way to new seeds. It is exactly as though the seed knew the sequence or the process for its own renovation. What rational person could believe that the sun, which is nothing but fire, knows this, or that it can endow plants with the ability to accomplish this with its warmth and light, that it can work these miracles in plants with the intent to perform some useful function? Anyone whose rational abilities are lifted up, on seeing and pondering such things, can only think that they come from One who has infinite wisdom, from God.

People who acknowledge Divinity see this and think this way. People who do not acknowledge Divinity, though, do not see this or think this way because they do not want to. So they lower their rational abilities down to the sensory level that gets all its concepts from the light that envelops our physical senses. They then "prove" their fallacies by saying, "Can't you *see* the sun making this happen by its warmth and light? What is anything that you cannot see? Is it anything at all?"

People who decide in favor of Divinity pay attention to the miracles they see in the way animals reproduce. At this point I may mention only what happens in eggs. Hidden within the egg is the chick "in seed" or in potential, with everything it needs for coming to hatching and for the whole sequence after hatching until it becomes a bird, a flying creature in the image of its parents. If people pay close attention to the nature of the form involved and think deeply about it, they cannot fail to be stunned. They see, for example, that in the smallest creatures as in the largest, in the invisible ones as in the visible, there are sensory organs for sight,

351

smell, taste, and touch; there are organs of motion called muscles—these creatures actually fly and walk; and they have organs around their hearts and lungs that are activated by their brains. We have been informed by people who have written about their anatomy that even lowly insects enjoy these gifts: see especially Swammerdam's *Book of Nature.*[190]

People who attribute everything to nature do see these things, but they simply think that they happen and say that nature makes them happen; and they say this because they have diverted their minds from thinking about Divinity. If people have diverted their minds from thinking about Divinity, then when they see the miracles in nature they cannot think rationally, let alone spiritually. They think in terms of sensation and matter, and in so doing think about nature from within nature and not from above it. This is just what people in hell do. The sole difference between them and animals is that they have rational capacity; that is, they could understand and think differently if they wanted to.

352   If people turn from thinking about Divinity when they see nature's miracles and therefore become sense-centered, they do not take into account the fact that their eyesight is so crude that they see a host of tiny insects as a single cloud. Yet each one of those insects is designed for sensing and for moving, which means it is equipped with fibers and vessels, with tiny hearts, windpipes, viscera, and brains. These are woven together out of the most delicate substances in nature, and the ways they are woven are responsive to a particular life that activates their smallest elements quite precisely.

If we consider the fact that our eyesight is so crude that a host of such creatures, each one with all its countless complexities, looks to us like a little cloud, and then realize that in spite of this, people who are sense-centered think and judge on the basis of this sight, we can see how coarsened their minds are, and therefore how benighted they are in spiritual matters.

353   Any people who want to can decide in favor of Divinity on the basis of what they can see in nature, and people do so decide who base their thinking about God on life. They do this, for example, when they see the birds of the air. Each species knows its foods and where to find them, recognizes its kindred by sound and sight, and knows which of them are friends and which are hostile. They join in marriage and know how to mate and how to build their nests skillfully. They lay their eggs there and incubate them, knowing how long the incubation should last; and when the time has come they hatch their chicks, love them most tenderly, shelter them under their wings, gather food and nourish them, all this until

the chicks come of age and can do the same, having their own families and thus ensuring the continuance of their kind.

Anyone who wants to think about the divine inflow through the spiritual world into the physical world can see it in these events. Anyone who wants to can say at heart, "Knowledge like this cannot be flowing into them from the sun, through its light rays. The sun, which provides nature with its origin and essence, is pure fire, so its light rays are absolutely lifeless." We can therefore come to the conclusion that things like this come from an inflow of divine wisdom into the very boundaries of nature.

Anyone who looks at larvas can decide in favor of Divinity on the basis of observation of nature. Larvas are moved by the pleasure of some impulse to exchange their earthly state for one that is a parable of heaven. So they crawl off to particular places where they put themselves into a kind of womb in order to be reborn. There they become chrysalises, mature pupas, caterpillars, nymphs, and eventually butterflies. At the close of this transformation they are equipped with beautiful wings according to their species, fly in the air as though it were their heaven, play in it cheerfully, form marriages, lay eggs, and provide themselves with descendants. All the while they are nourishing themselves on sweet, soft food from flowers. **354**

Does anyone who is deciding for Divinity on the basis of observation of nature fail to see a kind of reflection of our earthly state in the caterpillars and of our heavenly state in the butterflies? Yet people who are deciding for nature, since they emphatically reject any "heavenly state," say that these are simply earthly instincts.

Anyone can decide for Divinity on the basis of observations of nature by looking at what we know about bees. Bees know how to collect wax from plants and flowers and how to extract honey, how to build cells like little homes and arrange them in a form like a city, with open spaces for entrance and exit. They scent at a distance the flowers and plants from which they collect wax for their dwellings and honey for their food. Laden with them they fly back to their own territory, to their own hive. In this way, they provide themselves with food and shelter for the coming winter just as though they saw it coming. They appoint a female leader as queen to be the source of their progeny and they build a kind of hall above her, surrounding her with servants; and when the time of birth has arrived, she goes from cell to cell with her retinue of servants and lays her eggs, with the attendant crew sealing the cells to protect them from the air. This provides them with a new generation. **355**

Later, when this generation has reached the age when it can do the same, it is driven out of its home, and once it has been driven out it first gathers itself and then forms a swarm so that its company will not be dispersed, and flies off in search of a home. About autumn, too, the useless drones are taken out and shorn of their wings so that they cannot return and use up food to which they contribute nothing. There is much more, which enables us to conclude that it is for the useful function they perform for the human race and from an inflow from the spiritual world that they have a form of government like ours on earth and even like angels' in heaven. Can anyone furnished with rationality fail to see that things like this do not come from the physical world? What does the sun, the source of nature, have in common with a government that rivals and reflects heavenly government?

On the basis of all this and of other miracles among simple animals, people who acknowledge and worship nature decide for nature, while people who acknowledge and worship God decide for Divinity on the very same basis. That is, a spiritually-minded person sees spiritual forces in these events, and an earthly-minded person sees physical forces in these events. We see [reflections of] our own nature.

As for me, things like this have been testimonies to a spiritual inflow into nature, of the spiritual world into the physical world, an inflow, therefore, from the Lord's divine wisdom. Ask yourself seriously whether you could even think analytically about any form of government, any civil law, any moral virtue, or any spiritual truth unless Divinity were flowing in with its wisdom through the spiritual world. In my own case, I never could and I still cannot. I have actually been constantly watching this inflow perceptibly, tangibly, for nineteen years, so I am saying this on the basis of evidence.

356 Can anything earthly have useful functioning as a goal and arrange functions in sequences and forms? Only someone wise can do this, and only God, who has infinite wisdom, can arrange and form the universe in this way. Who else—or what else—can foresee and make available all the things that serve for our food and clothing, food from the fruits of the earth and from animals, and clothing from both as well?

It ranks among the miracles that the humble insects called silkworms provide splendid, beautiful, silken clothing for both women and men, from queens and kings to maids and servants, and that the humble insects called bees provide wax for the candles that lend their brilliance to temples and courts. These and many other facts are clear evidence that the Lord produces everything that happens in nature from himself through the spiritual world.

I need to add that I have seen people in the spiritual world who, on the basis of their observations of the world, had decided in favor of nature to the point of becoming atheists. In spiritual light, their intelligence seemed to be open downward and closed upward because in thought they were looking down to the earth and not up to heaven. The upper surface of their sensory functioning, which is the lowest level of intelligence, seemed to have a kind of covering on it. For some people, it flashed with hellfire, for some it was black as soot, and for some it was leaden and corpselike. Beware of decisions in favor of nature, then. Decide for Divinity: there is no lack of material.

ANGELIC WISDOM
ABOUT
DIVINE LOVE

PART 5

THE Lord has created and formed within us two vessels and dwellings for himself called volition and discernment. Volition is for his divine love and discernment for his divine wisdom. I have already discussed the divine love and wisdom of God the Creator, who is the Lord from eternity, and I have discussed the creation of the universe. Now I need to say something about our own creation.

We read that we were created in the image of God and according to his likeness (Genesis 1:26). In this passage "the image of God" means divine wisdom and "the likeness of God" means divine love, since wisdom is nothing more than the image of love. Love actually presents itself to view and to recognition in wisdom, and since that is where we see and recognize it, wisdom is its image. Then too, love is the reality of life and wisdom is its consequent manifestation. This "image and likeness" of God is strikingly visible in angels. Love shining from within is in their faces and wisdom in their beauty, with beauty as the form of their love. I have seen this, and I have come to know it.

We could not be images of God according to his likeness unless he were within us and were our life from our very center. God's presence within us and God's being our life from our very center follow from what I explained in §§4–6 above, namely that God alone is life and that we and angels are life-receivers from him.

The Word tells us that God is in us and makes his home with us; and because the Word tells us this, preachers are fond of telling us to prepare ourselves to let God come into our lives so that he may be in our hearts and that our hearts may be his dwelling. The devout say the same in their prayers. Some [preachers] talk and preach more explicitly about the Holy Spirit, who they believe is within them when they are filled with holy zeal as the source of their thought, speech, and preaching. I have explained in §§51–53 of *Teachings for the New Jerusalem on the Lord* that the Holy Spirit is the Lord and not some God who is a separate individual. The Lord actually says, "In that day you will know that you are in me and I in you" (John 14:21 *[14:20]*), and he says similar things in John 15:24 *[15:4]* and 17:23.

360   Since the Lord is divine love and wisdom, then, and these two are he himself in essence, if he is to live within us and give us life he must have created and formed his own vessels and dwellings within us, one for love and one for wisdom. These vessels and dwellings within us are called volition and discernment, volition being the vessel and dwelling of love, and discernment being the vessel and dwelling of wisdom.

We will see below that these two belong to the Lord within us and that these two are the source of all our life.

361   It is both known and unknown in the world that we all have volition and discernment and that they can be distinguished from each other the way love and wisdom can. We know this from common sense, but not from our considered thinking and even less from written works. Judging the matter simply on common sense, would anyone *not* realize that the volition and discernment within us are distinguishable? Everyone grasps this on first hearing. We can say to someone, "That individual means well but does not understand things well," or "That individual understands things well but does not mean well. I like people who understand and mean well but not people who understand well and mean harm." When people start thinking about volition and discernment, though, they do not regard them as two distinguishable functions but mix them together. This is because their thinking is in touch with their physical sight. They understand even less about the distinct difference between volition and discernment when they start writing, which is because then their thinking is in touch with the sensory level that is our own human possession. This is why some people can think and talk well but still not write well, as is frequently the case with the female sex.[191] The same holds in many other cases.

Does anyone fail to realize, simply on the basis of common sense, that people who live good lives are saved and people who live evil lives are damned? That people who live well come to be with angels and see, hear, and talk there like people? Or that the people who have a conscience are the ones who do what is fair because it is fair and what is right because it is right? If people step back from common sense, though, and give the matter serious thought, they do not know what conscience is or that the soul can see, hear, and talk the way we can or that a good way to live is anything more than giving to the poor. Then if you start writing on the basis of this thinking, you support these opinions with superficial and deceptive observations and with words that are all sound and no substance. This is why many of the scholars who have given much thought to this—and even more, the ones who have written about it—have undermined, obscured, and even destroyed their common sense. This is also why simple people see what is good and true more clearly than people who believe they are wiser.

This common sense comes from an inflow from heaven and descends through thought all the way to sight; but thought separated from common sense fades into fantasy based on sight and on self-importance.

You may test the truth of this. Say something true to people who have common sense and they will see it; tell them that we exist and move and live from God and in God[192] and they will see it; tell them that God is living within us in our love and wisdom and they will see it; say even that volition is the dwelling of love, and discernment the dwelling of wisdom, and explain it a little and they will see it; say that God is love itself and wisdom itself and they will see it; ask them what conscience is and they will tell you. But say these same things to scholars who have not been thinking on the basis of common sense but on principles derived either from preconceptions or from what they observe in the world, and they will not see.

Then figure out who are the wiser.

Volition and discernment, the vessels of love and wisdom, are in the whole brain and every part of it and therefore in the whole body and every part of it. This will be explained in the following sequence.

362

1. Love and wisdom, and the volition and discernment that come from them, constitute our very life.
2. Our life is found in its primary forms in our brains and in secondary forms in our bodies.

3. The quality of a life in its primary forms determines its quality overall and in every part.

4. By means of its primary forms, life is in the whole from every part and in every part from the whole.

5. The quality of the love determines the quality of the wisdom and therefore the quality of the person.

363   1. *Love and wisdom, and the volition and discernment that come from them, constitute our very life.* Hardly anyone knows what life is. When people think about it, it seems like something ethereal, something with no specific image. It seems like this because people do not know that only God is life and that his life is divine love and wisdom. We can see from this that the life in us is nothing else and that there is life in us to the extent that we accept it.

We know that warmth and light radiate from the sun and that everything in the universe is a recipient, growing warm and bright in proportion to its receptivity. The same holds true as well for the sun where the Lord is, whose radiating warmth is love and whose radiating light is wisdom, as explained in part 2. It is from these two emanations from the Lord as the sun, then, that life comes.

We can tell that life is love and wisdom from the Lord from the fact that we grow sluggish as love ebbs away from us and dull as wisdom ebbs away; and if they leave us completely, we are snuffed out.

There are many forms of love that have been given their own names because they are derivatives, such as desires, cravings, appetites, and their gratifications and delights. There are many forms of wisdom, too, like perception, reflection, memory, thought, and focus on a subject. Further, there are many forms that come from both love and wisdom, such as agreement, decision, and resolve to act, among others. All of these belong to both [love and wisdom], but they are assigned their names on the basis of what is dominant and nearer to hand.

Finally, our senses are derived from these two, our sight, hearing, smell, taste, and touch, with their own pleasures and satisfactions. The appearance is that our eye is seeing, but our discernment is seeing through our eye, which is why we ascribe sight to our discernment. The appearance is that our ear is hearing, but our discernment is hearing through our ear. This is why we speak of the attentiveness and listening that are actually functions of discernment as "hearing." The appearance is that our nostrils smell and that our tongue tastes, but discernment is smelling with its perceptiveness and is tasting as well; so we refer to perceptiveness as smelling and tasting, and so on. The wellsprings of all these functions are love and wisdom; we can therefore tell that these two constitute our life.

Everyone sees that discernment is the vessel of wisdom, but not many see that volition is the vessel of love. This is because our volition does nothing by itself, but acts through our discernment. It first branches off into a desire and vanishes in doing so, and a desire is noticeable only through a kind of unconscious pleasure in thinking, talking, and acting. We can still see that love is the source because we all intend what we love and do not intend what we do not love.

2. *Our life is found in its primary forms in our brains and in secondary forms in our bodies.* "In its primary forms" means in its beginnings, and "in secondary forms" means in the things that are produced and formed from these beginnings. "Life in its primary forms" means volition and discernment. It is these two functions that occur in their primary forms in our brains and in their derivative forms in our bodies.

We can tell that the primary forms or beginnings are in the brain for a number of reasons. (a) Simply from the feeling we have when we are focusing our minds and thinking, our sense that we are thinking with our brain. We turn our sight inward, so to speak, and furrow the brow with a sense that this concentration is happening inside, especially behind the forehead and a little above it. (b) From the way we are formed in the womb, where the brain or head is formed first and remains larger than the body for some time. (c) The head is above and the body below, and the orderly arrangement is for the higher to activate the lower and not the other way around. (d) If the brains are damaged in the womb by some wound, by disease, or by lack of concentration, thinking becomes uncertain, and sometimes the mind becomes deranged. (e) All the outer senses of the body—sight, hearing, smell, taste, and the all-inclusive sense of touch—as well as speech, are in the front part of the head called the face; and they are in direct touch with the brain through fibers and get their active and sensitive life from it. (f) This is why we can see people's feelings of love in a kind of image in their face and their thoughts of wisdom in a kind of light in their eyes. (g) Anatomy informs us that all the fibers go down from the brains through the neck into the body, and that none go up from the body through the neck into the brain.[193] Where the fibers have their primary forms and beginnings is where life is in its primary forms and beginnings. Can anyone maintain a denial that the origin of life is where the fibers originate? (h) Ask anyone with common sense where thinking happens, or where one thinks, and the answer you will get is "In one's head." But then ask someone who has located the seat of the soul in some little gland or in the heart or somewhere else where desire and its consequent thought begin, whether it is in the brain, and the answer you will get is either "No" or "I don't know."[194] You may find the reason for this uncertainty in §361 above.

366   3. *The quality of a life in its primary forms determines its quality overall and in every part.* For the reader to understand this, I need to say just where these primary forms are in the brains and how they branch off.

We can see from anatomy just where these primary forms are in the brain. This tells us that there are two brains and that these have extensions from the head into the spine. It tells us that the brains consist of two substances called the cortical substance and the medullary substance, with the cortical substance consisting of countless little glandlike things and the medullary substance of countless fiberlike things. Since the little glands are at the heads of the little fibers, then, they are also their primary forms. The fibers begin there and they radiate outward, gradually gathering into nerves; and once they have gathered or formed nerves they go down to the sensory organs in the face and the motor organs in the body and form them. Check with anyone versed in the knowledge of anatomy and you will find this to be true.

This cortical or glandular substance constitutes the surface of the brain and the surface of the corpora striata that make up the medulla oblongata, to link with the cerebellum and through the cerebellum to the spinal cord. Wherever the medullary or fibrous substance is found, however, it begins and goes from the cortical substance. This is the source of the nerves that all the parts of the body come from. This fact is learned from dissection.

If people know this from the science of anatomy or from people versed in that science, they can see that the primary forms of life are nowhere but where the beginnings of the fibers are, and that the fibers cannot radiate from themselves but from the primary forms. The primary forms or beginnings that look like little glands are almost beyond counting. We can compare their abundance to the number of stars in the universe, and the abundance of fibers that come from them to the number of rays that radiate from the stars and bear their warmth and light to the planets.

We may also compare the abundance of these little glands to the abundance of angelic communities in the heavens. These too are beyond counting and are similarly arranged, so I have been told; and the abundance of little fibers radiating from these little glands can be compared to the spiritual good and true activities that flow down like rays in much the same way.

This is why the individual human being is like a universe and like a heaven in miniature, as I have stated and explained throughout what precedes [§§19, 186, 203, 231]. We can tell from this that the quality of life in its primary forms determines its quality in secondary forms, or that the quality of life in its beginnings in the brain determines its quality in the things in the body that originate there.

4. *By means of its primary forms, life is in the whole from every part* **367** *and in every part from the whole.* This is because in terms of its origin, the whole—brain and body together—consists of nothing but the fibers that come from these primary forms in the brains. They have no other source, as we can see from the things just presented in §366. So the whole comes from each part. The reason that life in each part comes through the primary forms from the whole is that the whole provides each part with the share that it needs and thereby makes it a part of the whole. In brief, the whole arises from the parts and the parts are sustained by the whole. We can see from many things in the body that there is this kind of mutual sharing, and through it, a union.

It is much the same in the body as it is in a state, republic, or monarchy. The commonwealth arises from the people who are its parts, and the parts or individuals are sustained by the commonwealth. It is the same in everything that is in some form, especially humans.

5. *The quality of the love determines the quality of the wisdom and* **368** *therefore the quality of the person.* This is because the quality of love and wisdom determines the quality of volition and discernment, volition being the vessel of love and discernment the vessel of wisdom, as already explained [§§358–361]; and these two constitute us as humans and give us our quality.

Love is highly complex, so complex that its various forms are without limit. This we can tell from the human race on earth and in the heavens. There is not a single individual or angel so like another that there is no difference. Love is what makes the difference, each individual being her or his own love. People think that wisdom is what differentiates, but wisdom comes from love. It is love's form, for love is the underlying reality of life and wisdom is the manifestation of life from this underlying reality.

The world believes that intelligence is what makes us human, but people believe this because our discernment can be raised up into heaven's light, as already explained [§§242–243, 255–256, 258], and it can seem as though we were wise. However, any discernment that goes too far, that is, discernment that is not wisdom of love, appears as though it were ours. This makes us seem like intelligent people, but that is only an appearance. The discernment that goes too far is actually a love for knowing and being wise and not at the same time a love for applying our knowledge and wisdom to life. So in this world it either ebbs away over time or waits around temporarily on the edges, outside the contents of memory. After death, then, it is separated from us, and nothing is left but what agrees with the real love of our spirit.

Since love does constitute our life and therefore ourselves, all the communities of heaven and all the angels of those communities are arranged according to the passions that come from their loves. No community and no angel within a community is located by any gift of discernment apart from his or her love. The same holds for the hells and their communities, but that depends on loves that are opposite to heavenly loves.

We can tell from this that the quality of the love determines the quality of the wisdom, and that these determine the quality of the person.

369   It is generally recognized that our quality is determined by the quality of our primary love, but this is applied only to our minds and spirits, not to our bodies, which means that it is not applied to the whole person. However, an abundance of experience in the spiritual world has taught me that from head to toe, from the primary elements in our heads to the very limits of our bodies, our nature is determined by our primary love. All the people in that world are forms of their love, angels forms of heavenly love and demons forms of hellish love. These latter have misshapen faces and bodies, while the former have lovely faces and bodies. Further, when their love is attacked, their faces change; and if it is attacked severely, they disappear completely. This is a distinctive feature of the spiritual world. It happens because their bodies are completely at one with their minds.

We can see why from what has already been said, namely that everything in the body is secondary. That is, it is woven from fibers that come from specific origins that are vessels of love and wisdom; and when the origins have a particular nature, the secondary elements cannot be different. As a result, wherever the origins reach out, the secondary elements follow. They cannot be separated.

This is why people who lift their minds to the Lord are completely lifted to the Lord, and why people who plunge their minds into hell are wholly plunged there. So the whole person comes either into heaven or into hell, depending on the love of her or his life.

It is a matter of angelic wisdom that the human mind is a person because the Lord is a person, and that the body is a covering of the mind that senses and acts. So they are one single being, not two.

We do need to note that while the essential forms of the members, organs, and viscera of the body are basically woven from fibers that begin from primary origins in our brains, still they are stabilized by the kinds of material substance that we find on earth, and from solid substances in the air and the ether. This happens by means of the blood. So if all the parts of the body are to maintain their proper form and hold up in their proper functions, we need to be nourished by material food and constantly reassembled. **370**

There is a correspondence between volition and the heart and between discernment and the lungs.[195] This will be presented in the following series. **371**

1. Everything in the mind goes back to volition and discernment, and everything in the body goes back to the heart and the lungs.
2. There is a correspondence of volition and discernment with the heart and the lungs and a consequent correspondence of everything in our minds with everything in our bodies.
3. Volition corresponds to the heart.
4. Discernment corresponds to the lungs.
5. This relationship enables us to discover many secrets about our volition and discernment and also about love and wisdom.
6. Our mind is our spirit, and the spirit is a person, with the body being a covering through which the mind or spirit senses and acts in its world.
7. The union of the human spirit and body is accomplished through the correspondence of volition and discernment with the heart and lungs, and disunion is caused by a lack of correspondence.

1. *Everything in the mind goes back to volition and discernment, and everything in the body goes back to the heart and the lungs.* "Mind" means simply volition and discernment, which embrace everything that moves us and everything we think. This means that it embraces everything that belongs to our feeling and thinking. The things that move us belong to our volition, and the things we think about belong to our discernment. **372**

We recognize that everything we think belongs to our discernment because discernment is the basis of our thinking. It is not so clear to us, however, that everything that moves us belongs to our volition. This is because when we are thinking, we do not pay attention to our feeling but only to what we are thinking. It is like our listening to someone talk and paying no attention to the tone quality but only to the discourse itself. Yet the feeling within our thinking is like the tone quality within our speech, so that we can tell how people are feeling from their tone of voice and can tell what they are thinking from what they say.

The reason feelings belong to volition is that every feeling is an aspect of love, and as already noted [§§358–361], volition is the vessel of love.

People who do not know that feelings belong to volition confuse feeling with thinking. They actually say that feeling is the same as thinking even though they are not the same but simply act in unison. We can see this confusion in casual speech when someone says "I think I'll do that" meaning "I intend to do that." The fact that they are two things also shows up in casual speech when someone says "I'd like to think about that." When someone does "think about that," there is volition's feeling within discernment's thought just the way there is tone quality within speech, as noted.

It is generally recognized that everything in the body depends on the heart and the lungs; but it is not generally recognized that there is a correspondence of the heart and the lungs with volition and discernment. This matter, then, needs to be dealt with later [§§374–393].

373   Since volition and discernment are vessels of love and wisdom, they are two organic forms, or organized forms made out of the purest substances. They need to be like this in order to be vessels. The fact that their organization is not visible to the eye offers no objection because their organization is finer than eyesight, even when amplified by a microscope. Tiny insects are finer than eyesight, too, insects containing sensory and motor organs, since they feel and crawl and fly. Careful observers of their anatomy have discovered with their microscopes that insects also have brains, hearts, windpipes, and viscera. If these insects are invisible to our eyesight—to say nothing of the tiny inner organs they are made of—and we do not deny that they are organized down to the last detail, how can anyone say that the two vessels of love and wisdom called volition and discernment are not organized forms? How can love and wisdom, which are life from the Lord, act on some nonagent or on something that has no substantial presence? How else could thought have a residence?

Or could someone talk on the basis of thoughts that had no residence? Is the brain where thinking happens not a complete whole, with every single component organized? We can actually see its organized forms with the naked eye, seeing the vessels of volition and discernment in their primary forms quite clearly in the cortical substance, where they look like very small glands (see above, §366).

Please do not think about these matters in terms of a vacuum. A vacuum is nothing, and nothing happens in nothing or comes from nothing. On the concept of a vacuum, see §82 above.

2. *There is a correspondence of volition and discernment with the heart and the lungs and a consequent correspondence of everything in our minds with everything in our bodies.* This is something new, since it has not yet been recognized because people have not known what anything spiritual was or how it differed from what is physical. As a result, they have not known what correspondence is, correspondence being a relationship between spiritual and physical things, and the means of their union.

While I am saying that people have not yet recognized what anything spiritual is or how it corresponds to what is physical, which has left them ignorant of what correspondence is, still they could have known both of these facts. Is anyone unaware that feelings and thoughts are spiritual and that therefore everything that has to do with feelings and thoughts is spiritual? Is anyone unaware that action and speech are physical, and that therefore everything that has to do with action and speech is physical? Is anyone unaware that feelings and thoughts, which are spiritual, impel us to speak and act? Is there anyone who could not learn from this how spiritual and physical things correspond? Is it not thought that impels the tongue to speak and desire combined with thought that impels the body to act? These are two distinguishable activities. I can think and not speak, and I can intend and not act. Further, we know that the body does not think and intend, but that thinking flows into speech and intention into action.

Then too, do not feelings radiate from the face and show their impress there? Everyone recognizes this. Seen in its own right, is not feeling spiritual, while the changes of the face that we call expressions are physical? Can anyone fail to conclude, then, that there is a responsiveness, and therefore that there is a correspondence of everything in the mind with everything in the body? Further, since everything in the mind goes back to feeling and thought (or to volition and discernment, which amounts to the same thing), while everything in the body goes back to the heart

374

and the lungs, can anyone fail to conclude that there is a correspondence of volition with the heart and of discernment with the lungs?

The reason things like this have gone unrecognized, even though they could have been recognized, is that we have become so superficial that we are unwilling to give credence to anything but what is physical. This gratifies our love and therefore gratifies our discernment; so we are uncomfortable raising our thoughts above the physical level toward anything spiritual separated from what is physical. As a result, our physical love and its gratification prevents us from thinking of the spiritual as anything but a purer version of the physical, and of correspondence as anything but a flow along a continuum. In fact, strict materialists cannot conceive of anything separated from what is physical. To them, it is nothing.

Another reason these things have not been seen and therefore recognized is that we have displaced from our field of vision all the matters of religion that we refer to as "spiritual" by the dogma, prevalent throughout Christendom, that theological matters, "spiritual" matters, as defined by the councils and by some primates of the church, are to be believed blindly because (so they say) they transcend understanding. This has led some people to believe that anything spiritual is like a bird that flies beyond the air into the ether, beyond the reach of our eyesight. In fact, though, it is like a bird of paradise flying so close to our eyes that its lovely feathers brush the pupils, willing to be seen. "Our eyesight" means our intellectual sight.

375 The correspondence of volition and discernment with heart and lungs cannot be simply proven, that is, not by rational arguments, but it can be proven by effects. It is much the same as it is with the causes of events. Although we can see them rationally, we see them clearly only through their effects. The causes are in the effects and present themselves to view there. Only then is the mind sure about causes. I will discuss the effects of this correspondence later [§§378–384].

However, to prevent anyone from getting detoured into preconceived theoretical concepts of the soul in the discussion of these correspondences, some of the material presented in the preceding section may be reread: for example, §§363–364, on love and wisdom, and therefore volition and discernment, constituting our essential life; §365, on our life occurring in its fundamental forms in our brains, and secondarily in our bodies; §366, on the quality of our life in its fundamental forms determining its quality throughout and in every part; §367, on the fact that through these fundamental forms there is life in the whole from every part and life in every part from the whole; §368, on the quality of the love determining the quality of the wisdom, and therefore the quality of the person.

In support of this I may include here a portrayal of the correspondence of volition and discernment with the heart and the lungs that I saw in the company of angels in heaven. By a fascinating flowing, spiral movement, beyond words to express, the angels formed an image of a heart and an image of lungs, including all the deeper tissues within them; and they followed the flow of heaven, since heaven tends toward forms like this because of the inflow of love and wisdom from the Lord. In this way they portrayed the union of the heart and the lungs and at the same time their correspondence with volition's love and discernment's wisdom. They call this correspondence and union a "heavenly marriage," and they say that it is the same throughout the body and in its individual members, organs, and viscera, with whatever is in them from the heart and the lungs. Further, anywhere that the heart and the lungs are not active, each in its turn, there can be no motion of life prompted by some voluntary principle and no sensation of life prompted by some cognitive principle.

I am about to discuss the correspondence of the heart and the lungs with volition and discernment. Upon this rests the correspondence of everything in the body, called the members of the body as a whole, the sensory organs, and the body's viscera. Further, the correspondence of physical things with spiritual ones has not been recognized even though it was fully demonstrated in two works, one of which is *Heaven and Hell* and the other of which is on the spiritual meaning of the Word in Genesis and Exodus, titled *Secrets of Heaven.* For all these reasons, I should like now to point out the sections of these two works where I have written explanations of correspondence.

In *Heaven and Hell,* there is material on the correspondence of everything in heaven with everything in us, §§87–102; and on the correspondence of everything in heaven with everything on earth, §§103–115.

In the work on the spiritual meaning of the Word in Genesis and Exodus, titled *Secrets of Heaven,* there is material on the correspondence of the face and its expressions with the feelings of the mind: §§1568, 2988, 2989, 3631, 4796, 4797, 4880 *[4800]*, 5195 *[5165]*, 5168, 5695, 9306; on the correspondence of the body in its motions and actions with matters of discernment and volition: §§2988, 3632, 4215; on the correspondence of the senses in general: §§4318–4330; on the correspondence of the eyes and their sight: §§4403–4420; on the correspondence of the nostrils and smell: §§4624–4634; on the correspondence of the ears and hearing: §§4652–4634 *[4652–4659]*; on the correspondence of the tongue and taste: §§4791–4805; on the correspondence of the hands, arms, legs, and feet: §§4931–4953; on the correspondence of the groin and the reproductive organs: §§5050–5062; on the correspondence of the inner viscera of the body, particularly the stomach, thymus, the cisterna, the chyle and its ducts and the mesentery: §§5171–5180, 5189 *[5181]*; on the correspondence of the spleen: §9698; on the correspondence of the peritoneum, kidneys, and bladder: §§5377–5396 *[5377–5391]*; on the correspondence of the liver and the ducts of the liver, of the bladder, and of the pancreas: §§5183–5185; on the correspondence of the intestines: §§5392–5395, 5379; on the correspondence of the bones: §§5560–5564; on the correspondence of the skin: §§5552–5573; on the correspondence of heaven with a person: §§911, 1900, 1982 *[2162]*, 2996, 2998, 3624–3649, 3741–3745, 3884, 4091 *[4041]*, 4279 *[4280]*, 4423 *[4323]*, 4524, 4525, 6013, 6057, 9279, 9632; on the fact that everything in the physical world and its three kingdoms corresponds to something you can see in the spiritual world: §§1632, 1881, 2758, 2890–2893 *[2990–2993]*, 2897–3043 *[2987–3003]*, 3213–3227, 3483, 3624–3649, 4044, 4053, 4156, 4366 *[4936]*, 4939, 5116, 5377, 5428, 4477 *[5477]*, 8211, 9280; that everything you see in heaven is a correspondence: §§1521, 1532, 1619–1625, 1807, 1808, 1971, 1974, 1977, 1980, 1981, 2299, 2601, 3213–3226, 3348, 3350, 3457 *[3475]*, 3485, 3748 *[3747]*, 9481, 9570, 9576, 9577. The correspondence of the literal meaning of the Word with its spiritual meaning is dealt with throughout, and is also treated in *Teachings for the New Jerusalem on Sacred Scripture* 5–26 and 27–69.[196]

378   3. *Volition corresponds to the heart.* As I mentioned above [§375], this cannot be shown in a clearer and more precise way than by examining the effects of volition. It can be shown in some detail by the fact that all the feelings that arise from love induce changes in the motions of the heart. We can tell this from the arterial pulse that acts synchronously with the heart. It has countless changes and motions in response to feelings that arise from love. The only ones we can detect with the finger are that it may beat slower or faster, boldly or gently, soft or hard, regularly or irregularly, and so on. So it varies from happiness to sorrow, from peace of mind to rage, from courage to fearfulness, from fevers to chills, and so on.

Since the motions of the heart (called systole and diastole) do vary in this way depending on the feelings that arise from someone's love, many of the ancients and some moderns have ascribed feelings to the heart and named it as the home of the feelings.[197] So in common language we have come to speak of a magnanimous heart or a timid one, a happy or a sorrowful heart, a soft or a hard heart, a great or a mean heart, a whole or a broken heart, a heart of flesh or one of stone, of being heavy, soft, or gentle at heart, of putting our heart into a task, of giving our whole heart, giving a new heart, resting at heart, taking to heart, of not laying something to heart, of hardening the heart, of being a friend at heart. We have the words concord and discord and envy[198] and many others that have to do with love and its feelings.

The Word says similar things because it was composed in correspondences. It makes no difference whether you say love or volition, since volition is the vessel of love, as already noted [§§358–361].

It is generally recognized that there is a vital warmth in humans and in all animals, but people do not know where it comes from. People discuss it on the basis of conjecture, so if they do not know anything about the way matter is responsive to spirit, they identify the warmth of the sun as its source, some focusing on the activity of particles and some on life itself. However, since these last do not know what life is, they are just substituting one word for another.

However, once people realize that there is a relationship of responsiveness between love and its feelings on the one hand and the heart and its derivative vessels on the other, they can know that love is the source of our vital warmth. Love radiates as warmth from the spiritual sun where the Lord is and is felt as warmth by angels. This spiritual warmth, which essentially is love, is what flows into the heart and its blood by correspondence and instills both its warmth and its life. We know that we are warmed and virtually kindled by our love, depending on its intensity, and that we become sluggish and cold as that intensity decreases. We feel and see this, feeling it in a warmth throughout our bodies and seeing it as our faces flush. In contrast, we feel its loss as a physical chill and see it as faces turn pale.

Since love is our life, the heart is the beginning and ending of our life; and since love is our life and the soul brings its life through the body in the blood, the blood is called the soul in the Word (see Genesis 9:4 and Leviticus 17:14). I will be explaining later [§383] what "soul" means in its various senses.

It is because of the correspondence of the heart and blood with love and its feelings, too, that blood is red. There are all kinds of colors in the spiritual world, with red and white as the primary ones and the rest deriving their characteristics from these and from their opposites, which are a dark, fiery hue and black. Red corresponds to love there, and white to wisdom.

The reason red corresponds to love is that its source is the sun's fire; and the reason white corresponds to wisdom is that its source is the sun's light. Further, since love corresponds to the heart, blood needs to be red and to point to its source.

This is why the light is flamelike and angels wear reddish-purple in heavens where love for the Lord predominates, while the light is clear and angels wear white linen in heavens where wisdom predominates.

381 The heavens are divided into two realms, one called "heavenly" and the other called "spiritual." In the heavenly realm, love for the Lord reigns supreme, while in the spiritual realm, wisdom from that love reigns. The realm where love reigns is called the heart region of heaven, and the realm where wisdom reigns is called the lung region of heaven.

We need to realize that the whole angelic heaven, all in all, reflects a single person and looks like a single person to the Lord. Consequently, the heart forms one realm and the lungs another. There is actually a general cardiac and pulmonary motion throughout heaven, and a secondary one in every individual angel. The general cardiac and pulmonary motion is from the Lord alone, because he is the sole source of love and wisdom. These two motions occur in the sun where the Lord is, the sun that comes from the Lord, and from there flows into the angelic heaven and into the universe. Cancel out the notion of space and think about omnipresence and you will be assured that this is true.

On the division of heaven into two realms, one heavenly and one spiritual, see *Heaven and Hell* 26–28 *[20–28]*; and on the whole angelic heaven, taken as a unit, reflecting a single individual, see §§59–87 *[59–86]* of the same work.

382 4. *Discernment corresponds to the lungs.* This follows from what has already been said [§§378–381] about volition's correspondence with the heart. There are, that is, two dominant things in the spiritual person or mind, namely volition and discernment, and there are two dominant things in the physical self or the body, namely heart and lungs. There is a correspondence of everything in the mind with everything in the body, as already noted [§§374–377]. It then follows that if volition corresponds to the heart, discernment corresponds to the lungs.

Everyone can observe internally that discernment corresponds to the lungs on the basis of thought and on the basis of speech. On the basis of thought: we cannot think at all without the concurrence and support of the breath of our lungs. So quiet thought is accompanied by quiet breathing, deep thought by deep breathing. We hold and release our breath, we suppress or intensify our breathing, in response to our thinking—in response, then, to the inflow of some feeling related to what we love, breathing slowly, rapidly, eagerly, gently, or intently. In fact, if we suppress our breathing completely, the only way we can think is in the spirit, by its breathing, which is not clearly noticeable.[199]

On the basis of speech: not even the shortest word comes from the mouth without the support of our lungs. The sound that is articulated into words comes entirely from the lungs through the trachea and epiglottis. So depending on the inflation of this bellows and the opening of its passageways, speech is either amplified into shouting or, by their contraction, muted; and if the passage is completely blocked, speech and thought both cease.

Since our discernment corresponds to our lungs, and our thinking therefore to their breathing, "soul" and "spirit" in the Word mean discernment, as in "you shall love the Lord your God with your whole heart and your whole soul" (Matthew 22:35 [22:37]), or "God will give a new heart and a new spirit" (Ezekiel 36:26; Psalms 51:12, 13 [51:10]).[200] I have already explained [§§378–381] that the heart means the love of our volition, so soul and spirit mean the wisdom of our discernment.

383

You may see in *Teachings for the New Jerusalem on the Lord* 50–51 that the spirit of God, also called the Holy Spirit, means divine wisdom and therefore divine truth, the means of our enlightenment.

This is why "the Lord breathed on the disciples and said, 'Receive the Holy Spirit'" (John 20:22). This is also why it says, "Jehovah God breathed the breath of life into Adam's nostrils, and he became a living soul" (Genesis 2:7), and why God said to the prophet, "Prophesy over the spirit and say to the wind, 'Come, spirit, from the four winds and breathe upon these who have been slain, so that they may live'" (Ezekiel 37:9). There are similar statements elsewhere as well. It is why the Lord is called the spirit of the nostrils and also the breath of life.

Since our breathing comes through our nostrils, they are used to mean perception. An intelligent person is referred to as "keen-scented," and a dense person as "dull-scented." This is also why in Hebrew and in some other languages, "spirit" and "wind" are expressed by the same word. In fact, the word "spirit" is derived from [a root that means] breathing;[201] so when people die we speak of their "breathing their last."[202] This is also why people believe that a spirit is a wind or something airy, like the breath that issues from our lungs, and believe the same of the soul as well.

We can tell from this that "loving God with the whole heart and with the whole soul" means with all our love and all our discernment, and that "giving a new heart and a new spirit" means a new volition and a new discernment.

It is because the spirit means discernment that it says of Bezaleel that "he was filled with the spirit of wisdom, intelligence, and knowledge" (Exodus 31:3) and of Joshua that "he was filled with the spirit of wisdom" (Deuteronomy 34:9), and that Nebuchadnezzar said of Daniel that "a superlative spirit, one of knowledge and intelligence and wisdom was in him" (Daniel 6:5 *[5:11, 12, 14]*), and why it says in Isaiah that "those who are wandering in spirit will know intelligence" (Isaiah 29:24). Similar statements may be found in many other places.

384 Since all the elements of the mind have to do with volition and discernment and all the elements of the body with the heart and lungs, there are two brains in our heads, as distinct from each other as volition and discernment. The cerebellum serves volition primarily, and the cerebrum serves discernment primarily. In the same way, heart and lungs are distinct from everything else in the body. They are marked off by the diaphragm and enclosed in their own membrane, the pleura, forming the region of the body known as the chest.

These two aspects are found united in other parts of the body, the ones called members, organs, and viscera; so they too occur in pairs—arms and hands, legs and feet, eyes, and nostrils, for example. Within the body there are the kidneys, the ureters, and the reproductive glands; and the viscera that are not paired are still divided between right and left. Further, the brain itself is divided into two hemispheres, the heart into two ventricles, and the lungs into two lobes. The right side has to do with the good that results from truth and the left to the truth that results from good; or in other words, the right refers to the good that love can do, which leads to the truth of wisdom, while the left refers to the truth of wisdom that results from the good that love can do.[203] Since the union of what is good and what is true is reciprocal, and since they become a virtual single whole by virtue of that union, these pairs within us act together as a unit in our deeds, motions, and sensations.

385 5. *This relationship enables us to discover many secrets about our volition and discernment and also about love and wisdom.* There is little awareness in this world of the actual nature of volition and love because we cannot love deliberately, and intend from love, the way we can apparently think deliberately. In the same way, we cannot deliberately control the motions of our hearts the way we can control the breathing of our lungs. Given, then, the ignorance in this world of the nature of volition and love and our knowledge of the nature of our heart and lungs (since they are present to the examination of our eyesight and have been examined and described by anatomists, while volition and discernment are not present to the examination of our eyesight), once we know that they correspond and act in unison by means of that correspondence, we can discover many secret things about volition and love that otherwise we could not. We can discover things, for example, about the union of volition with discernment and the reciprocal union of discernment with volition, or about the union of love with wisdom and the reciprocal union of wisdom with love. We can discover how love branches off into feelings, how those feelings are associated with each other, and how they flow into our perceptions and thoughts and ultimately, by means of correspondence, into our physical actions and sensations.

These secrets, and many others, can be discovered and explained by examining the way the heart and the lungs are united, how the blood flows from the heart into the lungs and back from the lungs into the heart, and from there through the arteries into all the members, organs, and viscera of the body.

6. *Our mind is our spirit, and the spirit is a person, with the body being a covering through which the mind or spirit senses and acts in its world.* It is hard for people to accept with any trust the notion that our mind is our spirit and that the spirit is a person if they have thought that the spirit is a wind and that the soul is something ethereal, like the breath breathed out from our lungs. They ask how the spirit can be a person when it is a spirit, or how the soul can be a person when it is a soul. They say the same about God because God is called a spirit. `386`

They have gathered these concepts of spirit and soul from the fact that in some languages there is only one word for "spirit" and "wind," so when someone dies, they talk about "the last breath" or "giving up the ghost"[204] and that when someone has suffocated or fainted, life comes back when the spirit or life comes back into the lungs. Since this seems to be nothing but wind and air, they conclude on the basis of their eyes and their physical senses that after death our spirit or soul is not a person.

Various theories have sprouted from this materialistic assessment of the spirit and the soul, resulting in the belief that we are not persons until Judgment Day comes, that until then we are in some undefined place waiting for the reunion [with our bodies]. This is discussed in *Supplements on the Last Judgment [and the Spiritual World]* 32–38.[205]

It is because the human mind is our spirit that angels, who are also spirits, are called "minds."

387   The reason our mind is our spirit and the spirit is a person is that *mind* means everything involved in our volition and discernment, and these are found in their primary forms in our brains and in their derivative forms in our bodies. Consequently, they are everything we have as far as our basic form is concerned. Since this is the case, the mind, or our volition and discernment, activates the body and everything in it at will. Does not the body do whatever the mind thinks and intends? Does not the mind prick up the ear to listen, focus the eye to see, move the lips and tongue to speak, activate the hands and fingers to do what it wants and the feet to walk where it wants to go? Is the body, then, anything but obedience to the mind? Could the body be like this if the mind in its derivative forms were not present in it? Does it make rational sense to believe that the body obediently does what the mind wants as though they were two individuals, one above and the other below, one giving orders and the other submitting? Since this is contrary to all reason, it follows that our life exists in its primary forms in our brains and in derivative forms in our bodies, as explained in §365 above; and that the nature of life in its primary forms determines its nature in the whole body and in every part of it (§366). It follows that through these primary forms life exists from every part in the whole and from the whole in every part (§367).

I have already explained [§§362–370] that everything in the mind goes back to volition and discernment, that volition and discernment are the vessels of love and wisdom from the Lord, and that these two constitute our life.

388   We can also see from what has been said that the human mind is the essential person. The very first impulse toward the human form, or the essential human form, complete in all detail, comes from its primary forms, extended from the brain through its nerves, as already explained [§366].

This is the form we attain after death, the form we call a spirit or an angel, a form that is an absolutely complete person, but a spiritual one. The material form that was added on the outside in the world is not the human form in its own right, but is derived from that form, added on the outside so that we can function usefully in the physical world. It also provides us with a stable vessel for our spiritual natures, a vessel drawn from the purer substances of this world, that we take with us [after death] in order to carry on and continue our lives.[206]

It is an item of angelic wisdom that the human mind, both in a general way and in every least detail, is in a constant effort toward the human form because God is human.[207]

For a person to be a person, no part that occurs in a complete person can be lacking either from the head or from the body, since there is nothing there that does not belong to and constitute that form. It is actually the form of love and wisdom, which in its own right is divine. It contains all the specific forms of love and wisdom that are infinite in the Divine-Human One but finite in his images—in us, in angels, and in spirits. If any part were missing that occurs in that person, then some specific corresponding form of love and wisdom would be missing, some form through which the Lord can be present with us from our core to our boundaries, providing for lives of service in the created world out of his divine love, through divine wisdom. **389**

7. *The union of the human spirit and body is accomplished through the* **390** *correspondence of volition and discernment with the heart and the lungs, and disunion is caused by a lack of correspondence.* It has not yet been realized that our mind, meaning our volition and discernment, is our spirit, and that the spirit is a person. It has also not yet been realized that our spirit has a pulse and breathing just as the body does. As a result, there has been no way to know that the pulse and breathing of the spirit within us flows into the pulse and breathing of our body and causes them.

If our spirit enjoys a pulse and breathing just as our body does, it follows that there is the same kind of correspondence between the pulse and breathing of our spirit and the pulse and breathing of our body. The mind, as already noted [§§386–389], is our spirit; so when the correspondence between these two activities ceases, there is a separation—death.

Separation or death occurs when the body either by disease or by trauma reaches a state when it can no longer act in concert with its spirit. In this way, the correspondence ceases; and when the correspondence ceases, so does the union. This is not when the breathing alone stops, but when the heartbeat stops, since as long as the heart is working, love is still there with its vital warmth, maintaining life. We can see this in cases of fainting or suffocation as well as in the state of the fetus in the womb.

In brief, our physical life depends on the fact that our physical pulse and breathing are responsive to the pulse and breathing of our spirit; and when this responsiveness ceases, physical life ceases and the spirit departs, to continue its life in the spiritual world. This life is so much like our life in the physical world that we do not realize we have died.

Most people are in the spiritual world within two days after leaving their bodies. I have talked with some individuals after two days.

391 Proof that spirits have a pulse and breathing just as we earthly people do in our bodies can come only from spirits and angels themselves when someone is enabled to talk with them. This has been granted to me; so when I have asked them, they have told me that they are just as much people as we are in this world and that they too have bodies, but spiritual ones. They have told me that they too can feel their hearts beating in their chests and in the arteries in their wrists just the way we people in the physical world do. I have asked a good many about this, and they have all said the same thing.

I have been enabled to learn from my own experience that the human spirit is breathing within the body. Occasionally, angels have been allowed to control the extent of my breathing, to diminish it at will and eventually to restrain it to the point that only the breathing of my spirit was left to me, at which point I could actually sense it. The same thing happened to me when I was shown what it is like to die: see *Heaven and Hell* 449.

Sometimes, too, I have been restricted to nothing but the breathing of my spirit, and then was sensibly aware of its harmony with the general breathing of heaven. On any number of occasions, too, I have been in a state like that of angels and have been lifted up to them in heaven; and at times like these I was in the spirit and out of the body, using my breathing to talk with them just as we do in this world.

These and other firsthand proofs have made it clear to me not only that our spirits are breathing within our bodies, but also that they do so after we leave our bodies behind; and also that the breathing of our spirits is so subtle that we do not sense it. It flows into the obvious breathing of our bodies almost the same way a cause flows into an effect or a thought flows into the lungs and through the lungs into speech.

We can also see, then, that the union of spirit and body in us is brought about by the responsive relationship between the motions of the heart and the lungs of the two.

392 The reason these two motions (that of the heart and that of the lungs) happen so reliably is that the whole angelic heaven is engaged in these two life motions both overall and in individual instances. The reason the whole angelic heaven is engaged in them is that the Lord is instilling them from the sun where he is and which comes from him.

This sun causes these two motions at the Lord's behest. Further, since by design all heaven and earth depend on the Lord through that sun, since they are as intimately connected as a work that is linked together from beginning to end, and since the life of love and wisdom comes from him and all the activities in the universe depend on life, we can see that this is their only source. It follows that their variations depend on the way love and wisdom are accepted.

I will be saying more about the correspondence of these motions later [§417], describing what they are like for people who breathe together with heaven and people who breathe together with hell, for example, and what they are like for people whose speech is in touch with heaven but whose thought is in touch with hell—that is, for hypocrites, flatterers, charlatans, and the like.

393

From the correspondence of the heart with volition and the lungs with discernment, we can learn everything that can be known about volition and discernment or love and wisdom—everything, therefore, that can be known about the human soul. A host of people in learned circles have sweated over their research about the soul.[208] However, since they have not known anything about the spiritual world and our state after death, all they have been able to do has been to formulate theories not about the nature of the soul but about how it works in the body.[209] Their only conceivable notion of the nature of the soul was of something supremely pure, something in the ether, with the ether itself as its vehicle.[210] They have not dared publish much about this for fear of attributing something physical to the soul when they knew that the soul was spiritual.

394

Given this concept of the soul as well as the knowledge that the soul is at work in the body producing everything involved in sensation and motion, they have, as I just noted, sweated over their research into the way the soul works in the body. Some have stated that this happens by an inflow, others that it happens by a harmony.[211] However, since this has led to no discoveries satisfactory to a mind that wants to see whether something is true or not, I have been granted the privilege of talking with angels and becoming enlightened on the matter through their wisdom. One item of their wisdom is that the human soul that lives after death is the human spirit and that it is a perfectly formed person. Further, this soul of ours is our volition and discernment, whose soul is love and wisdom from the Lord. It is these two that constitute our life, a life that is from the Lord alone and that is the Lord. To enable us to accept him, he makes us feel as though this life belongs to us; but to prevent us from claiming life as our own possession and thereby undermining our ability to accept him, the Lord teaches us that every element of love that we call good and every element of wisdom that we call true comes from him. Nothing of it comes from us; and since these two are our life, every trace of life that is really alive comes from him.

395   Since in essence the soul is love and wisdom and these two are within us from the Lord, two vessels have been created within us, vessels that are also dwellings for the Lord. One of these is for love and the other is for wisdom. The one for love is called volition, and the one for wisdom is called discernment. Further, since love and wisdom in the Lord are distinguishably one (see §§17–22 above), and since divine love is a property of the Lord's divine wisdom and divine wisdom a property of his divine love (see §§34–39), and since these as well emanate from the Divine-Human One, the Lord—then the two vessels and dwellings within us called volition and discernment have been created by the Lord in such a way as to be distinguishably two but to function as a single unit in everything we do and everything we sense. Volition and discernment cannot be separated in these functions.

However, since we are intended to become vessels and dwellings, our discernment has necessarily been given the ability to be lifted above our own love into some of wisdom's light, which is beyond our own love. This enables us to see and learn how we are to live if we are to attain to heavenly love as well as heavenly light and so enjoy blessedness forever.

Since we have now misused our ability to lift our discernment above our own love, we have destroyed within ourselves the possibility of being the Lord's vessels and dwellings, that is, vessels and dwellings of love and wisdom from the Lord. We have done this by making our volition the dwelling of love for ourselves and love for the world, and our discernment the dwelling of whatever justifies these loves.

This is why these dwellings—our volition and discernment—have become dwellings of hellish love, and by our justification of these loves vessels of that hellish thought that is treasured as wisdom in hell.

396   The reason love for ourselves and love for the world are hellish loves, the reason we could become absorbed in them and thereby destroy our own volition and discernment, is that as created, love for ourselves and love for the world are heavenly loves. They are in fact loves proper to our physical self and of service to our spiritual loves the way foundations are of service to houses. It is love for ourselves and love for the world that prompt us to care about our bodies, to want nourishment, clothing, and

housing, to take care of our homes, to look for jobs in order to be useful, to be granted respect due to the worth of our responsibilities so that people heed us, and even to find delight and recreation in worldly pleasures. All of these activities, however, should be for the sake of usefulness. They bring us into a state of serving the Lord and the neighbor. In contrast, when there is no love for serving the Lord and the neighbor, when there is nothing but love for using the world to suit ourselves, then the love becomes hellish instead of heavenly. It makes us focus our minds and spirits on our self-image, which intrinsically is completely evil.

To make sure that we are not in heaven as to our discernment, which is possible, and in hell as to our volition, which would give us a mind divided against itself, after death any elements of discernment that transcend our own love are taken away. The result is that for everyone, volition and discernment eventually act in unison. For people in heaven, their volition loves what is good and their discernment thinks what is true. For people in hell, their volition loves what is evil and their discernment thinks what is false. **397**

The same holds true for us in this world when we are thinking from the spirit. This happens when we are alone, though many people think differently during their physical lives, when they are not alone. The reason for this difference is that they lift their discernment above the self-concern of their volition, or the love of their spirit.

I mention all this to show that volition and discernment are two distinguishable functions, still created to be one function, and that they are constrained to act in unison after death, if not before.

Now, love and wisdom (and therefore our volition and discernment) are that entity that we call the soul, and we need next to explain how the soul's impulses affect the body and make everything in it work. We can learn about this from the responsive relationship between the heart and volition and between the lungs and discernment. For these reasons, the following matters have been disclosed on the basis of that relationship. **398**

1. Love, or volition, is our essential life.
2. Love or volition is constantly striving toward the human form and toward everything the human form comprises.
3. Unless it is married to wisdom or discernment, love or volition cannot accomplish anything through its human form.
4. Love or volition prepares a home or bridal chamber for its spouse-to-be: wisdom or discernment.

5. Love or volition also prepares everything in its human form so that it can act in unison with wisdom or discernment.

6. After the "wedding," the first union is with a desire for knowing, which gives rise to a desire for what is true.

7. The second union is with a desire for discerning, which gives rise to a sense of what is true.

8. The third union is with a desire to see what is true, which gives rise to thought.

9. Through these three unions, love or volition engages in its life of sensing and its life of acting.

10. Love or[212] volition leads wisdom or discernment into every corner of its house.

11. Love or volition does not do anything without its spouse.

12. Love or volition marries wisdom or discernment to itself and arranges things so that wisdom or discernment marries it willingly.

13. Because of the power given it by love or volition, wisdom or discernment can be raised up, can accept things in heaven's light, and can grasp them.

14. Love or volition can be raised up in the same way and can grasp things in heaven's warmth provided it loves its spouse to that degree.

15. Otherwise, love or volition pulls wisdom or discernment back from its height so that they act in unison.

16. If they are raised up together, love or volition is cleansed by wisdom in our discernment.

17. Love or volition is polluted in and by our discernment if they are not raised up together.

18. Love that has been cleansed by wisdom in our discernment becomes spiritual and heavenly.

19. Love that has been polluted in and by our discernment becomes limited to nature and our senses.

20. There still remain that ability to discern that we call rationality and that ability to act that we call freedom.[213]

21. When love is spiritual and heavenly, it is a love for the Lord and for our neighbor; while when it is limited to nature and our senses, it is a love for the world and for ourselves.

22. It is the same for charity and faith and their union as it is for volition and discernment and their union.

1. *Love, or volition, is our essential life.* This follows from the responsive relationship between the heart and our volition discussed in §§378–381 above; for our volition acts in our mind the same way our heart acts in our body. Further, just as everything in the body depends on the heart for its origin and for its motion, everything in the mind depends on volition for its origin and its life. By "volition" I mean "love," since volition is the vessel of love and love is the essence of life (see §§1–3 above). The love that is the essence of life, further, comes from the Lord alone.

By looking at the heart and its extension in the body through arteries and veins, we can learn that love or volition is our life. This is because things that correspond to each other act in the same way, the only difference being that one is physical and the other spiritual.

The science of anatomy shows us how the heart acts in the body. It shows us, for example, that everything is alive or responsive to life where the heart is at work through the channels it extends from itself, and that everything is not alive where the heart is not at work through its channels. It shows further that the heart is both the first and last thing that acts in the body. We can tell that it is first by looking at embryos, and that it is last by looking at the dying. We can tell that it acts separately from the lungs by looking at people who have suffocated or fainted. This enables us to see that the life of the mind depends entirely on volition just the way the life that supports the body depends entirely on the heart and that our volition remains alive even when thought ceases, just the way the heart does when breathing ceases. This too we can see in embryos, in the dying, and in people who have suffocated or fainted.

It follows from all this that love or volition is our very life.

2. *Love or volition is constantly striving toward the human form and toward everything the human form comprises.* This we can see from the way the heart corresponds to volition, since we know how everything in the body is formed in the womb. We know that everything is formed there by fibers from the brain and by blood vessels from the heart and the fabric of all our organs and viscera are made from these two materials. This enables us to see that everything within us comes into being from the life of our volition, which is love, from beginnings in our brains, through these fibers, with everything in our bodies coming from the heart through its arteries and veins.

Clearly then, life (which is love and its consequent volition) is constantly striving toward the human form; and since the human form comprises everything that is within us, it follows that love or volition is engaged in a constant effort to form all these things. The reason this effort is toward the human form is that God is a Person and divine love and wisdom is[214] the life of that Person. This is the source of every trace of life.

Everyone can see that if the life that is the essential person were not activating something that intrinsically is not life, nothing that is within us could be formed the way it is. There are thousands upon thousands of things within us that are acting in unison, totally united in their effort toward an image of the life that is their source so that we can become his[215] vessel and dwelling.

We can see from this that love—and from love, our volition, and from volition, our hearts—is constantly striving toward the human form.

401   3. *Unless it is married to wisdom or discernment, love or volition cannot accomplish anything through its human form.* This too we can see from the way the heart corresponds to our volition. The human fetus is alive as to its heart but not as to its lungs. Blood is not yet flowing from the heart into the lungs and enabling them to breathe, but is flowing through an opening into the left ventricle of the heart. As a result, the fetus cannot yet move any part of its body, but rests bound; and it cannot sense anything, with its sensory organs closed.

It is the same with the love or volition. [The fetus] is alive because of it, but in darkness. That is, it lacks sensation and action. As soon as the lungs are opened, though, which happens after birth, it begins to sense and to act and at the same time to intend and to think.

We can tell, then, that unless it is married to wisdom or discernment, love or volition cannot accomplish anything through its human form.

402   4. *Love or volition prepares a home or bridal chamber for its spouse-to-be, wisdom or discernment.* In the created universe and in every detail of it there is a marriage between what is good and what is true. This is because what is good is a matter of love and what is true is a matter of wisdom, and these two exist in the Lord, from whom everything was created.

We can see how this marriage happens in us, reflected in the union of our heart with our lungs, since the heart corresponds to love or what is good and the lungs to wisdom or what is true (as explained in §§378–381 and 382–384 above).

We can see from their union how love or volition pledges itself to wisdom or discernment, and later leads it or enters a kind of marriage with it. It pledges itself by preparing a home or room for wisdom, and it leads it by a marriage that takes place through desires. Then it brings wisdom with it into its house.

The only way to verify this would be to use spiritual language because love and wisdom are spiritual, which means that volition and discernment are spiritual as well. They can be presented in earthly language, but only with a hazy perception, because people do not know what love is or what wisdom is or what desires for what is good are or what desires for wisdom are, namely desires for what is true. However, we can see the nature of the pledging and marriage between love and wisdom (or volition and discernment) through the parallelism that obtains because of their correspondence with the heart and the lungs. Things are the same for the one as for the other, so similar that the only difference is that one is spiritual and the other physical.

We can tell from the heart and the lungs, then, that the heart first forms the lungs and then weds itself to them. It forms the lungs in the fetus and weds them after birth. The heart does this in its own home, called the chest, where they gather. This is separated from the rest of the body through the membrane called the diaphragm and the envelope called the pleura.

It is the same with love and wisdom, or with volition and discernment.

5. *Love or volition also prepares everything in its human form so that it can act in unison with wisdom or discernment.* I am talking about volition and discernment, but it needs to be absolutely clear that volition is the whole person. Actually, volition is found with discernment in primary forms in the brain and in derivative forms in the body, so (as explained in §§365, 366, and 367 above) it is found in the whole body and in every part. We can tell from this that volition is the whole person in respect both to overall form and to the particular form of every part. We can tell also that discernment is its partner just as the lungs are the partner of the heart.

People need to guard against entertaining any notion of volition as something apart from the human form: the two are the same.

We can see from this not only how volition prepares a room for discernment but also how it prepares everything in its home, the whole body, so that it can act in unison with discernment. The preparation is like this. The whole body and all its parts are united to discernment just as they are united to volition; or just as the whole body and all its parts are subject to volition, they are subject to discernment.

403

As for how the whole body and all its parts are prepared for a union with discernment like that with volition, this can be seen only as it is reflected or imaged by the science of anatomy in the body. This shows how everything in the body is so connected that when the lungs breathe, the whole body and every part of it is moved by the lungs' breathing just as by the heart's beating. We learn from anatomy that the heart is united to the lungs by its auricles and that these extend into the recesses of the lungs. We learn also that all the viscera of the whole body are connected to the chest cavity by ligaments—so closely connected that when the lungs breathe, the whole body and everything in it, together and individually, receive an impulse from the breathing. When the lungs swell, then the ribs expand the chest, the pleura dilates, and the diaphragm is stretched; and along with them all the lower parts of the body, which are connected to them by ligaments, receive some impulse from the motion of the lungs. Let me say no more, or people who lack anatomical knowledge will find themselves confused because of their unfamiliarity with the terminology of this discipline. Just ask people who are experienced and skilled in anatomy whether everything in the whole body, from the chest on down, is not so tied together that when the lungs swell during breathing, the whole body and everything in it is stirred into motion in time with the lungs.

This enables us to see what kind of union volition prepares for discernment, union with the whole human form and everything it comprises. Just search out the connections and examine them with the eye of the anatomist, and then look at their coordination with the breathing lungs and with the heart in the light of those connections. Then think "discernment" for "lungs" and "volition" for "heart," and you will see.

404   6. *After the "wedding," the first union is with a desire for knowing, which gives rise to a desire for what is true.* "After the wedding" means our state after birth, beginning with a state of ignorance and continuing through a state of discernment all the way to a state of wisdom. The first state, that of pure ignorance, is not what I mean by the wedding, since our discernment has no thought at that point, only a faint impulse of our love or volition. This state is a prelude to the wedding. It is recognized that there is a desire for knowing in the second state, the one characteristic of our childhood. This is what enables little ones to learn to talk and to read and then gradually to learn the kinds of things that constitute discernment. We cannot doubt that love—which is a matter of volition—is doing this, since unless love or volition were the driving force, it would not happen.

Everyone who reflects rationally on experience realizes that after we are born we all have a desire for knowing and that this is the basis of our learning the kinds of things that lead gradually to the formation, development, and attainment of discernment. We can also see that this gives rise to a desire for what is true, since once we have become discerning because of our desire for knowing, we are motivated not so much by a desire for knowing as by a desire for systematic thinking and drawing conclusions about subjects that we love—economics, perhaps, or civic or moral issues. When this desire rises all the way to spiritual concerns, it becomes a desire for spiritual truth. We can see that the first step or prelude was a desire for knowing from the fact that a desire for what is true is a higher level of the desire for knowing. This is because being moved by truths comes from wanting to know them because of our desire and then absorbing them with passionate delight when we find them.

7. *The second union is with a desire for discerning, which gives rise to a sense of what is true.* Anyone can see this who is willing to explore the matter with some rational insight. Rational insight shows that a desire for what is true and a sense of what is true are two abilities enjoyed by our discernment, abilities that merge into one for some people but not for others. They merge into one for people who want to grasp what is true intelligently, but not for people who want only to know about what is true. We can also see that our engagement in the grasp of truth depends on our desire to understand it. If you take away the desire to understand what is true, there will be no grasp of what is true; while if you grant the desire to understand what is true, there will be a grasp of it proportional to the intensity of the desire. This is because no one of sound reason ever lacks a sense of what is true as long as the desire to understand it is present. I have already explained [§162] that everyone has the ability to discern what is true that we call rationality.

8. *The third union is with a desire to see what is true, which gives rise to thought.* A desire for knowing is one thing; a desire for discerning is another thing; and a desire to see something is something else again. We can also say that a desire for what is true is one thing; a grasp of what is true is another thing; and thinking is something else again. If people have no clear grasp of the workings of the mind, they can see this only dimly; but it is clear for people who can grasp them clearly. The reason people see this only dimly if they cannot grasp the workings of the mind clearly is that these activities are all happening at the same time in the thinking of people who are caught up in a desire for what is true and in a grasp of what is true; and when they happen at the same time, they

cannot be distinguished from each other. We are engaged in conscious thinking when our spirit is thinking in the body. This is the case especially when we are in the company of others. However, when we are engaged in a desire for discerning and come thereby into a grasp of what is true, then we are engaged in the thinking of our spirit. This is meditation, which does indeed reach down into our physical thought, but subtly. It is on a higher level and looks into thought processes based on memory as below it, since it is using them either for decision or for support. The actual desire for what is true, though, is felt only as an impulse of our volition stemming from a kind of pleasure. This resides within reflection like its life, and draws little attention.

We may conclude from all this that these three abilities—the desire for what is true, the grasp of what is true, and thought—follow in sequence from love and are nowhere manifest but in our discernment. When love enters discernment (which happens when the union is realized), then it first gives rise to the desire for what is true, then to the desire to understand what it knows, and finally to a desire to see in physical thought whatever it understands. Thinking is actually nothing but an inner sight. Thinking does happen first because it is a function of our earthly mind; but when it comes to thinking on the basis of a grasp of what is true because of a desire for what is true, that happens last. That kind of thinking is the thinking of wisdom, while the other is thinking on the basis of memory, using the sight of our earthly mind.

All the workings of love or volition outside our discernment are based not on desires for what is true but on desires for what is good.

405   Granted, rational people can understand that these three follow sequentially in our discernment from the love that belongs to our volition, but they still cannot see it clearly enough to believe it with confidence. However, since by virtue of correspondence the love proper to volition acts in concert with the heart and the wisdom proper to discernment acts in concert with the lungs, as already explained, there is no better way to see and show what I have just said about the desire for what is true, the grasp of what is true, and thinking (see §404 above) than by looking at the lungs and their construction; so I need to describe this briefly.

After birth, the heart sends blood into the lungs from its right ventricle, and once it has passed through, it sends it into its left ventricle. This is what opens the lungs. The heart does this by means of the pulmonary arteries and veins. The lungs have bronchia that branch off and ultimately turn into the little sacs where the lungs admit air and thereby breathe. There are also arteries and veins (called "bronchial") around the bronchia and their branches. They start from the azyga or vena cava and the aorta, and they are distinct from the pulmonary arteries and veins. This enables us to see that the blood flows into the lungs by two routes and flows out of them by two routes. This is why the lungs can breathe in a different rhythm from the heart. It is widely recognized that the rhythms of the heart and the rhythms of the lungs are not the same.

Now, since the correspondence of the heart and lungs is with our volition and discernment, as already explained [§§371–393], and since union by correspondence means that the one behaves in the same way as the other, we can see from the blood flow from the heart into the lungs how volition flows into discernment and causes the things mentioned in §404 about our desire for what is true, about our grasp of what is true, and about thought. Correspondence has shown me this and even more on this topic, which I cannot describe briefly.

Since love or volition answers to the heart and wisdom or discernment answers to the lungs, it follows that the blood vessels from the heart to the lungs answer to desires for what is true and that the branches of the lungs' bronchia answer to perceptions and thoughts generated by those desires. If you were to look into the way the lungs are woven from these origins and draw the parallel with the love of our volition and the wisdom of our discernment, you could see a kind of image of what I have said in §404 and come to believe it with confidence.

However, since not many people are familiar with the anatomical data about the heart and the lungs, and since supporting a proposition with unfamiliar material yields confusion, I forbear presenting any further instances of the parallelism.

9. *Through these three unions, love or volition engages in its life of sensing and its life of acting.* The reason love can neither sense nor act in the body apart from discernment, or any desire of love apart from the thinking of discernment, is that to all intents and purposes, love without discernment is blind, and desire without thought is in the dark. Discernment is the light that enables love to see. Then too, the wisdom of discernment comes from the light that radiates from the Lord as the sun. If the love of our discernment cannot see anything and is blind apart from the light of discernment, it follows that without discernment's light, our physical senses too would be immersed in blindness and stupidity—not only our sight and hearing, but our other senses as well. The reason this would apply to our other senses is that all our perception of what is true is a property of love within discernment, as already explained

[§404], and all our physical senses derive their sensitivity from the sensitivity of our mind.

The same applies to all our physical actions, since an action that springs from love apart from discernment is like something we do in the night without knowing what it is that we are doing. So there would be no trace of intelligence or wisdom in the act, and the act could not be called a living deed. An action, that is, gets its reality from love and its quality from intelligence.

Further, whatever power anything good has comes by means of truth, so what is good acts in and therefore by means of what is true. What is good is a matter of love and what is true is a matter of discernment.

We may then conclude that it is through the three unions discussed in §404 that love or volition engages in its life of sensing and its life of acting.

407 We can find striking support for this in the union of the heart with the lungs, since it is in the nature of the volition-heart and discernment-lungs correspondence that the heart acts with the lungs on the physical level the way volition acts with discernment on the spiritual level. This enables us to see what I have been talking about in a kind of visual image.

As for our lack of any sensory life, and therefore of any active life, when heart and lungs are not working together, this is evidenced by the state of a fetus or infant in the womb and the state of the same after birth. As long as the individual is a fetus or is in the womb, the lungs are closed. As a result, the individual has no sensation or action. The sense organs are closed, the hands are restrained, and so are the feet.[216] After birth, though, the lungs are opened, and as they are opened we sense and act. The lungs are opened by blood that flows in from the heart.

We can also see from people who have fainted that if the heart and the lungs are not working together we are deprived of both sensory and active life. When people have fainted, only the heart is working, not the lungs—breathing has been taken away. Everyone knows that people who have fainted are deprived of sensation and action.

It is the same with people who suffocate, whether by water or because of something that blocks their windpipe and closes off the lungs' breathing passage. People then seem to be dead, having neither sensation nor action. Yet we know that the heart is still keeping them alive. They in fact return to both sensory and active life as soon as the blockages of the lungs are removed. In the meantime, blood has been making its circuit through the lungs, but only through the pulmonary arteries and veins, not through the bronchial arteries and veins; and these latter give us the ability to breathe.[217]

It is the same with the inflow of love into discernment.

10. *Love or volition leads wisdom or discernment into every corner of its*   408
house. By the "house" of love or volition, I mean the whole person, everything that goes to make up our minds; and since these things correspond to everything in our bodies (as already explained [§§374–377]), the "house" also means the whole [physical] person, everything that goes to make up our bodies, which we refer to as members, organs, and viscera. What has already been presented shows that the lungs are brought into these latter just the way discernment is brought into all the functions of the mind. See, for example, §402, "Love or volition prepares a home or bridal chamber for its spouse-to-be, wisdom or discernment," and §403, "Love or volition also prepares everything in its human form or house so that it can act in unison with wisdom or discernment." We can see from what it says there that the whole body and everything in it is connected by extensions from the ribs, the vertebrae, the sternum, the diaphragm, the peritoneum that is suspended from them, and the ligaments—so closely connected that when the lungs are breathing all the organs are impelled and carried along in a similar rhythmic movement.

Anatomy shows us that this respiratory rhythm penetrates right into the viscera, even to their deepest recesses, since the ligaments already mentioned are connected to the coverings of the viscera, and the coverings reach into the deepest recesses through their extensions just the way the arteries and veins do through their branches. We may conclude, then, that the lungs' breathing is completely united to the heart in the whole body and in all its parts. To make this union complete in all respects, the heart itself is involved in the respiratory motion. It rests in the lung cavity and is connected to it by its auricles, and it rests on the diaphragm, so that its arteries are also involved in the respiratory movement. Further, the stomach is similarly united because of the connection between its esophagus and the windpipe.

I cite these anatomical details to show what the union is like between love or volition and wisdom or discernment, and how the two of them in partnership are united to everything in the mind, since the [spiritual and physical] unions are similar.

11. *Love or volition does not do anything without wisdom or discern-*   409
ment. Since love has neither sensory nor active life apart from discernment, and since love leads discernment into all the functions of the mind (see §§407 and 408 above), it follows that love or volition does not do

anything apart from discernment. What would it be to act from love apart from discernment? We could only call it something senseless. Discernment is what shows us what needs to be done and how it needs to be done. Love does not know this apart from discernment. As a result, there is so full a union between love and discernment that even though they are two functions, they still act as one. There is a similar union between what is good and what is true, since what is good is a matter of love and what is true is a matter of discernment.

There is the same kind of union in everything the Lord has created in the universe. Their function looks to what is good, and the form of their function looks to what is true.

It is because of this union that there is a right and a left to the whole body and everything in it. The right goes back to the good that prompts what is true, and the left to the truth that is prompted by what is good, so they go back to that union. This is why there are pairs in us—two brains [the cerebrum and the cerebellum], two hemispheres of the cerebrum, two ventricles of the heart, two lobes of the lungs, two eyes, ears, nostrils, arms, hands, legs, feet, kidneys, reproductive glands, and so on; and where there are not separate pairs, there is still a right side and a left side. This is because the good looks to the true for its manifestation and the true looks to the good for its existence. The same holds true in the angelic heavens and in the individual communities there.

There is more on this subject in §401 above, where I explained that unless it is married to wisdom or discernment, love or volition cannot accomplish anything through its human form. I will elsewhere[218] discuss the inverse of the union of what is good and what is true, namely the union of what is evil and what is false.

410 12. *Love or volition marries wisdom or discernment to itself and arranges things so that wisdom or discernment marries it willingly.* We can see that love or volition marries wisdom or discernment from their correspondence with the heart and the lungs. Anatomical research teaches that the heart is engaged in its life motion before the lungs are. We learn this by experience from people who have fainted, people who have suffocated, embryos in the womb, and chicks in eggs.

Anatomical research also teaches us that while the heart is acting by itself, it forms the lungs and organizes them so that it can breathe in them, and that it also forms the other viscera and organs so that it can perform its various functions in them. It forms the organs of the face so that it can sense, the organs of motion so that it can act, and the other parts of the body so that it can fulfill the functions that answer to the desires of its love.

The main conclusion we can draw from this is that just as the heart brings forth such organs for the sake of the different functions it is going to undertake in the body, so love does the same in its vessel, which we call volition, for the sake of the different desires that make up its form—which as already noted [§400] is the human form.

Next, since the first and immediately following desires of love are the desire for knowing, the desire for discerning, and the desire to see what we know and discern, it follows that love forms discernment for these desires and actually enters into them when it is beginning to sense and act and when it is beginning to think. We can tell from the parallelism with the heart and lungs just mentioned that discernment makes no contribution to this process.

This in turn shows that love or volition marries wisdom or discernment and that wisdom or discernment does not marry itself to love or volition. We can also look at the knowledge that love gets because of its desire for knowing, the sense of what is true that it gets from its desire for discerning, and the thought it gets from its desire to see what it knows and discerns and conclude that these are products not of discernment but of love. Thoughts and perceptions and consequent knowledge do indeed flow in from the spiritual world, but they are not accepted by our discernment. They are accepted by our love depending on its desires in our discernment. It seems as though discernment were accepting them and not love or volition, but this is an illusion. It also seems as though discernment married itself to love or volition, but this too is an illusion. Love or volition marries itself to discernment and arranges things so that the marriage is mutual. The reason it is mutual lies in the marriage of love with it;[219] so the union seems to be mutual because of the life and consequent power of love.

The same holds true for the marriage of what is good and what is true, since the good is a matter of love and the true is a matter of discernment. The good does everything. It accepts the true into its house and marries it to the extent that it is in harmony. The good can accept truths that are not in harmony, but it does this out of its desire for knowing, understanding, and thinking before it has settled on the functions that constitute its goals and are called its virtues. The reciprocal union—the union of what is true with what is good—is actually nonexistent. The reciprocity of the union comes from the life of what is good.

This is why the Lord looks at everyone, at us, at spirits, and at angels, in regard to our love or good. No one is seen in terms of discernment or of what is true apart from love or what is good. Our life is our love, as already explained [§§1–3]; and we have life insofar as we have lifted up our desires by means of truths, that is, to the extent that we have completed our desires by means of wisdom, since the desires of our love are lifted up and completed by means of truths and therefore by means of wisdom. Then love acts in unison with wisdom just as though it were acting out of wisdom. It is acting out of itself, though, and through wisdom as its form. That form derives nothing whatever from our discernment. It derives everything from some specific instance of love that we call a desire.

411   Love calls "good" everything it has that supports it, and it calls "true" whatever things it has that serve as means to that "good." Since they are means, they are loved and become objects of love's desires; and in this way they become formed desires. Consequently, truth is simply the form of love's desires. Beauty is its intelligence, which it acquires by means of the truths it gains through outer and inner sight or hearing. It is these that love arranges in the form of its desires. There are many variations on this form, but they all take some similarity from their common form, which is the human form. To love, all these forms are beautiful and loveable, but others are ugly and unlovable to it.

It also follows from this that love marries itself to discernment, not the other way around, and that the answering union comes from love as well. This is what it means to say that love or volition arranges things so that wisdom or discernment marries it willingly.

412   We can see and confirm what I have been talking about in a kind of image in the way the heart answers to love and the lungs to discernment as already described [§§371–393], since if the heart answers to love, then its limited forms, its arteries and veins, answer to desires, with the ones in the lungs answering to desires for what is true. Further, since there are other vessels in the lungs (called airways) that make respiration possible, these vessels answer to perceptions.

We need to be fully aware that the arteries and veins in the lungs are not desires and that the breaths are not perceptions and thoughts, but that they are corresponding functions. They are actually responsive or synchronized. It is the same for the heart and the lungs. They are not love and discernment, but are corresponding functions; and since they are corresponding functions, we can see one in the other. Anyone who knows the whole structure of the lungs from anatomy and makes a careful comparison with discernment can see quite clearly that discernment does nothing on its own. It neither senses nor thinks on its own, but does everything because of desires proper to love. The ones in discernment are called the desire already described for knowing, understanding, and seeing [what is true].[220] All the different states of the lungs depend on blood from the heart and from the vena cava and aorta; while the breathing that takes place in the bronchial tube[221] occurs in keeping with their state, since breathing stops when the inflow of blood stops.[222]

I could disclose a great deal more by comparing the structure of the lungs to the discernment that it answers to, but since not many people are familiar with the science of anatomy, and since it beclouds a subject to explain or support it by unfamiliar examples, I may not say more about this. I am wholly convinced by what I know about the structure of the lungs that love marries itself to discernment by means of its desire and that discernment does not marry itself to any desire of love. Rather, it is married willingly by love so that love may have a sensory and active life.

At all costs, we must realize that we have two forms of breathing, one of the spirit and one of the body. The breathing of the spirit depends on the fibers that come from the brain, and the breathing of the body depends on the blood vessels that come from the heart and from the vena cava and aorta.

Clearly, too, it is thought that gives rise to breathing and it is love's desire that gives rise to thought, since thought without desire is exactly like breathing without a heart—impossible. We can therefore see that love's desire marries itself to discernment's thought, as just stated. It is the same with the heart in the lungs.

13. *Because of the power given it by love, wisdom or discernment can be raised up, can accept things in heaven's light, and can grasp them.* I have already and often stated[223] that we can grasp hidden treasures of wisdom when we hear them. This ability of ours is what we call "rationality," and it is ours from creation. This ability to see into things deeply and to form conclusions about what is fair and just, about what is good and true, is what distinguishes us from animals. It is also what I mean by the statement that discernment can be raised up, can accept things in heaven's light, and can grasp them.

We can also see a kind of image of this fact in the lungs, since the lungs correspond to our discernment. Looking at the lungs, we see that their substance comprises little chambers. These consist of the extensions of the bronchia all the way into the tiny sacs where the air is taken in when we breathe. Our thoughts act in unison with them because of their correspondence. It is characteristic of the substance of these little sacs that it has two ways of expanding and contracting, one in unison with

413

the heart and the other almost independent of the heart. Its unison with the heart is because of the pulmonary arteries and veins, which come directly from the heart. Its virtual independence is because of the bronchial arteries and veins, which come from the vena cava and aorta, vessels external to the heart. This happens in the lungs because our discernment can be raised above its own love, which answers to the heart, and accept light from heaven. Even so, when our discernment is raised above its own love it does not leave it completely behind. It takes along some of it, which we can call a desire for knowing and discerning for the sake of promotion, praise, or profit in this world. Some trace of this clings to each love like a coating. This gives the love a superficial glow; but for wise people, there is an actual translucence.

I cite these facts about the lungs to show that our discernment can be raised up and accept and grasp things in heaven's light. There is in fact a complete correspondence. To see from correspondence is to see the lungs reflected in our discernment and our discernment reflected in our lungs, and to find assurance in each at the same time.

414 14. *Love or volition can be raised up in the same way and can grasp things in heaven's warmth provided it loves its spouse, wisdom, to that degree.* I have explained in the preceding section (and often enough before that) that our discernment can be raised into heaven's light and gather in wisdom from it. I have also frequently noted that our love or volition can be raised up as well if it loves the things that are found in heaven's light, things that involve wisdom. However, our love or volition is not raised up by any concern for promotion, praise, or profit, but by a love of service—that is, not for our own sake but for the sake of our neighbor. Since this love is granted us only from heaven by the Lord, and since the Lord gives it to us when we abstain from evils as sins, this is how our love or volition can be lifted up as well; otherwise it cannot happen. Love or volition, though, is raised into heaven's warmth, while discernment is raised into heaven's light. If they are both raised up, a marriage takes place there that we call "the heavenly marriage" because it is a marriage of wisdom and heavenly love.[224] This is why I said that love is raised as well if it loves wisdom, its spouse, to that degree. A love for our neighbor that comes from the Lord is a love for wisdom, or the human mind's real love.

The same thing is true of light and warmth in the world. There is light without warmth and there is light with warmth—without warmth in winter and with warmth in summer. When there is light with warmth, then everything blooms. The light in us that answers to winter light is wisdom apart from its love, and the light in us that answers to summer light is wisdom together with its love.

We can observe this union and separation of wisdom and love virtually imaged in the way the lungs are connected to the heart. The heart can be connected with the clustered little bronchial bladders by blood that comes directly from itself and also by blood that comes not from itself but from the vena cava and aorta. This makes it possible for our physical breathing to be independent of our spiritual breathing; though if the blood is coming only from the heart, the two forms of breathing cannot be separated.

415

Next, since our thoughts act in unison with our breathing because of their correspondence, we can also see from the double nature of the lungs' breathing that we can think one way and speak and act out our thoughts one way when we are with other people, while when we are by ourselves—that is, when we have no fear of damage to our reputation— we think another way and speak and act out our thoughts another way. Then we can both think and say things against God, the neighbor, the spiritual values of the church, and moral and civic values. We can act against these as well by deeds of theft, revenge, blasphemy, and adultery. All the while, when we are in public where we risk loss of reputation, we can talk, preach, and behave exactly as though we were spiritual, moral, and civic individuals.

We can tell from this that love or volition, like discernment, can be lifted up so as to receive things proper to the warmth or love of heaven provided only that it loves wisdom to that degree; while if it does not love it, they can part company.

15. Otherwise, love or volition pulls wisdom or discernment back from its height so that they act in unison. There is earthly love and there is spiritual love. When we are engaged in earthly love and spiritual love together, then we are rational people. When we are engaged solely in earthly love, though, we can think just as rationally as spiritual people, but we are not really rational individuals. We do lift our discernment up into heaven's light, into wisdom, but the matters of wisdom or heaven's light are not objects of our love. It is our love that is making this happen, but behind it is a desire for respect, praise, and profit. However, once we realize that we are not getting any benefit from this elevation (as we do realize when we are thinking to ourselves on the basis of our earthly love), then we have no love for matters of heaven's light or wisdom. So our love then pulls our discernment down from its height so that the two will act in unison.

416

For example, when our discernment is filled with wisdom because it has been lifted up, then our love sees what justice, honesty, and chastity[225] are, even what real love is. Earthly love can see this because of its ability to understand and ponder things in heaven's light. It can even talk about, preach, and describe these as both moral and spiritual virtues. When our discernment is not lifted up, though, then if our love is merely earthly it does not see these virtues. It sees injustice as justice, deception as honesty, lust as chastity, and so on. If we do think about the matters we discussed when our discernment was at its height, then we may make fun of them and think that they serve us only to ensnare people's minds.

We can therefore tell how to understand the statement that unless love loves its spouse, wisdom, to that degree, it pulls it down from its height so that they act in unison. (On love's ability to be lifted up if it does love wisdom to that degree, see §414 above.)

417   Since love corresponds to the heart and discernment to the lungs, what I have just said can be supported by their correspondence. That is, we can see how discernment can be lifted above its own love all the way into wisdom and how if the love is merely earthly it will pull discernment down from its height.

We have two kinds of breathing, one physical and one spiritual. These two kinds of breathing can be independent or coordinated. For people who are completely earthly-minded, especially for hypocrites, they are independent, while for spiritual and honest people they rarely are. This means that once their discernment has been lifted up so that they have a store of elements of wisdom left in their memory, people who are completely earthly-minded and hypocritical can talk wisely in public because their thinking is based on their memory. Still, when they are not in public they base their thinking on their spirit and not on their memory, which means they base it on their love. They breathe in the same way, since thinking and breathing are responsive to each other.

I have already explained [§§405, 415] that the structure of the lungs enables breathing to take place from blood directly from the heart and from blood not directly from the heart.

418   Most people think that wisdom is what makes us who we are; so when they hear someone speaking or teaching wisely, they believe that this is a wise individual. People even believe this of themselves at such times, since when they are speaking and teaching in public they are thinking on the basis of their memory. If they are completely earthly-minded people, then the source is the surface of their love, a desire for respect, praise, and profit. However, when these same people

are by themselves, they think from the deeper love of their spirits—not wisely at all, but at times insanely.

This shows that no one is to be evaluated on the basis of verbal wisdom, but on the basis of life. That is, we are not to rely on verbal wisdom separated from life but on verbal wisdom together with life. Life means love: I have already explained [§§1–3] that love is life.

16. *If they are raised up together, love or volition is cleansed by wisdom in our discernment.* From birth, all we love is ourselves and the world, because this is all that comes into our view. So this is all we think about. This love is on the earthly, physical level: we may call it materialistic. Not only that, this love has become defiled by its separation from heavenly love in our parents.

**419**

This love cannot be separated from its impurity unless we have the ability to lift our discernment into heaven's light and see how we need to live in order to have our love raised up into wisdom along with our discernment. It is through discernment that our love sees—that we, in fact, see—which evils are defiling and polluting our love. This also enables us to see that if we resolutely abstain from those evils as sins, we love the opposites of those evils, which are all heavenly. We also see the means by which we can resolutely abstain from those evils as sins. Love sees all this—that is, we see all this—by using our ability to lift our discernment into heaven's light, which gives us wisdom. Then to the extent that love puts heaven first and the world second, at the same time putting the Lord first and ourselves second, love is cleansed of its pollutants and purified. That is, it is to that extent lifted into heaven's warmth and united to the light of heaven that surrounds discernment. Then the marriage takes place that is called the marriage of the good and the true, the marriage of love and wisdom.

Anyone can grasp mentally and see rationally that to the extent that we resolutely abstain from theft and cheating, we love honesty, integrity, and justice. To the extent that we resolutely abstain from vengefulness and hatred, we love our neighbor. To the extent that we resolutely abstain from adultery, we love chastity, and so on.

However, hardly anyone knows what is heavenly and divine about honesty, integrity, justice, love for our neighbor, chastity, and the other desires of heavenly love until their opposites have been removed. Once their opposites have been removed, we are involved in them, so we recognize and see them from the inside. Until that happens, there is a kind of veil in the way. It does let a little of heaven's light reach our love, but since that love does not love wisdom, its spouse, to that extent, it does not accept the light. It actually criticizes it severely and finds fault with it when it comes back down from its height, though the light is still attractive to it because wisdom in our discernment can be a tool that helps gain us respect, praise, and profit. Then, however, we are putting ourselves and the world first and the Lord and heaven second, and what we put second is loved only as long as it is useful to us. If it is not useful, we renounce and reject it, after death if not before.

This illustrates the truth that love or volition is cleansed in our discernment if they are raised up together.

420   There is an image of the same process in the lungs. Its arteries and veins answer to desires proper to love, and its respiratory motions answer to perceptions and thoughts proper to discernment, as already noted [§§405, 412].

There is ample experience to support the proposition that the heart's blood is purified in the lungs from what it has not digested and that it nourishes itself there with appropriate elements from the air that is drawn in. As for the blood being purified in the lungs from what it has not digested, this we can tell not only from the inflowing blood, which is venous and therefore full of chyle gathered from what we have eaten and drunk, but also from the moist breath we exhale and the odors others can smell. We can also tell from the fact that the blood that flows back into the left ventricle of the heart is diminished in volume.

As for the fact that the blood nourishes itself with appropriate elements drawn from the air, this we can tell from the immense variety of fragrances that are constantly given off by shrubs, flowers, and trees as well as from the immense variety of different kinds of salts and liquids from soils, rivers, and lakes. There is also the immense variety of gaseous emanations that both we and animals give off—the air is full of them. Undeniably, these enter our lungs with our indrawn breaths, so it is also undeniable that our blood absorbs elements that are good for it. The elements that are good for it are the ones that answer to the desires of our love. This is why in the tiny sacs at the center of our lungs there are so many little veins with minute pores that take these substances in. This is why the blood that flows back into the left ventricle of the heart is changed into arterial blood and is brilliant. All this shows that the blood is purifying itself from unsuitable elements and nourishing itself with suitable ones.[226]

Until now, it has not been recognized that the blood purifies and nourishes itself in the lungs in a way that answers to the desires of our own nature, but this is common knowledge in the spiritual world. Angels in the heavens take pleasure only in odors that answer to the love of their wisdom. Spirits in hell, on the other hand, find pleasure only in odors that answer to a love that rejects wisdom. These are foul odors, while the others are fragrant.

It follows that we in this world are saturating our blood with similar elements depending on how those elements answer to the desires of our love. Whatever our spirit loves, our blood seeks out in response, and our breathing draws in.

It flows naturally from this correspondence that we are purified in our love if we love wisdom, and are defiled if we do not love it. All our purification happens by means of truths that constitute wisdom, and all our defilement happens by means of false beliefs that reject the truths of wisdom.

17. *Love or volition is polluted in and by our discernment if they are not raised up together.* This is because if the love is not raised up it remains impure, as noted in §§419 and 420 above. When it remains impure, it loves what is impure. It loves things like vengefulness, hatred, deceit, blasphemy, and adultery. These are what appeal to it then, what we call its cravings; and it rejects whatever springs from thoughtfulness, justice, honesty, truth, and chastity.

I stated that love is polluted in and by discernment. It is polluted in discernment when love is influenced by these impurities. It is polluted by discernment when it makes matters of wisdom its own servants, and even more when it distorts, falsifies, and corrupts them.

There is no need to say more about the way this state answers to the heart or to its blood in the lungs than has already been said in §420. I may add only that the blood is polluted instead of being purified, and that instead of its being nourished by fragrant odors it feeds on stenches, just the way it happens in heaven and in hell.

18. *Love that has been cleansed in our discernment becomes spiritual and heavenly.* We are born earthly, but to the extent that our discernment is raised into heaven's light and our love into heaven's warmth along with it, we become spiritual and heavenly. Then we become like a Garden of Eden, bathed in the light and warmth of springtime.

Our discernment does not become spiritual and heavenly. Our love does, and when it does it makes its spouse, discernment, spiritual and heavenly as well.

Love becomes spiritual and heavenly through a life in accord with the truths of wisdom, truths that discernment teaches and illustrates. Love absorbs these truths not on its own but by means of discernment, since love cannot lift itself up unless it knows truths; and it can know truths only by means of a discernment that has been lifted up and enlightened. Then love is lifted up to the extent that it loves these truths by doing them. It is one thing to discern, that is, and another to intend; or it is one thing to speak and another to act. There are people who understand truths of wisdom and utter them but still do not intend and do them. When love, then, puts into practice the truths of light that it discerns and utters, then it is raised up.

Simple reason shows that this is so. After all, what are we when we discern and utter truths of wisdom while we are living—that is, intending and acting—contrary to them?

The reason love becomes spiritual and heavenly when it has been purified by wisdom is that we have three levels of life, levels called earthly, spiritual, and heavenly. These were discussed in part 3 of the present work [§§236–241]. We can be lifted up from one to the next; but we are not raised simply by wisdom. We are raised by a life in accord with wisdom, because our life is our love. So to the extent that we live in accord with wisdom we love it; and we live in accord with wisdom to the extent that we purify ourselves from those unclean things we call sins; and to the extent that we do this, we love wisdom.

423   It is not that easy to see from the correspondence with heart and lungs how love is purified by wisdom in our discernment and becomes spiritual and heavenly because no one can see what the blood is like that keeps the lungs breathing. The blood can be full of impurities and still be indistinguishable from pure blood. Then too, the breathing of purely earthly-minded people seems very much like the breathing of spiritual-minded people. However, people can tell them apart very clearly in heaven. Individuals there breathe in keeping with the marriage of their love and wisdom; so just as angels can be identified by that marriage, they can be identified by their breathing. This is why when people who are not in that marriage arrive in heaven, they begin to feel chest pains and to struggle for breath like people in the throes of death. As a result, they hurl themselves down headlong and find no rest until they are with people whose breathing is like their own. Then, because of the correspondence, they are with people who feel the way they do and therefore think the way they do.

We can therefore tell that if we are spiritual, it is our purer blood, sometimes called the animal spirit,[227] that is purified, and that it is purified to the extent that we participate in the marriage of love and wisdom. It is that purer blood that most closely answers to this marriage; and since it does flow into our physical blood, it follows that it also purifies that blood. The opposite happens for people whose love is defiled in their discernment.

As I have already noted,[228] though, no one can investigate this by experiments with our blood, only by looking at the desires of our love, since these correspond to our blood.

19. *Love that has been polluted in and by our discernment becomes limited to nature, our senses, and our bodies.* An earthly love separated from spiritual love is opposed to spiritual love. This is because earthly love is love for ourselves and love for the world, and spiritual love is love for the Lord and love for our neighbor. Love for ourselves and for the world looks downward and outward, and love for the Lord looks upward and inward. So when an earthly love is separated from spiritual love, it cannot be raised away from our self-absorption. It remains immersed in it and even mired in it, to the extent that it loves it. If our discernment does rise up and see elements of wisdom in heaven's light, then our love drags it back down and unites it to itself in its self-absorption. There it either discards the elements of wisdom or distorts them or arranges them outside itself so that it can mouth them for the sake of reputation.

424

Just as an earthly love can rise up by levels and become spiritual and heavenly, it can also go down by levels and become sensory and physical. It goes down to the extent that it loves being in control with no love of service, simply for love of ourselves. This is the love that we call demonic.

People involved in this kind of love can talk and behave like people involved in spiritual love, but at such times they are operating either out of memory or out of a discernment that has lifted itself into heaven's light. The things they say and do, though, are like fruit that looks lovely on the outside but is nothing but rot inside, or like almonds whose shells look intact but which have been completely eaten away by worms inside. In the spiritual world they summon up illusions that enable prostitutes (called "sirens" there) to look beautiful and to dress in attractive clothing. Once the illusions are taken away, though, they look like ghosts. They are like demons, too, who make themselves into angels of light; for when that physical love drags its discernment down from its height (which happens when we are alone) and thinks from its own love, then it thinks against God and for nature, against heaven and for the world, against the true and good values of the church and for the false and evil values of hell. That is, it thinks against wisdom.

This shows what the people we call "physical" are like. They are not physical as far as their discernment is concerned, but they are as far as their love is concerned. That is, they are not mentally physical when they speak in public, but they are when they talk with themselves in spirit. Further, since they are like this in spirit, after death they are like this in both respects, in both love and discernment. They become the spirits called "physical spirits." People who in this world absolutely loved being in control because of their self-absorption and were also intellectually a cut above others look physically like Egyptian mummies,[229] and are crude and foolish mentally. Is there anyone in the world these days who knows that this is what this love is really like?

However, there is a love for being in control because of a love of service—a love of service not for the sake of ourselves but for the common welfare. It is hard, though, to tell this from the other kind, even though the difference between them is like the difference between heaven and hell. On the difference between these two kinds of love for being in control, see *Heaven and Hell* 531–565 *[551–565]*.

425   20. *There still remain that ability to discern that we call rationality and that ability to act that we call freedom.* I have discussed these two abilities of ours already in §§264–267. The reason we have these two abilities is so that we can become spiritual instead of earthly, which is being reborn.[230] I have already explained [§§422–423] that it is our love that becomes spiritual and that is reborn; and the only way it can become spiritual or be reborn is by using discernment to learn what is evil and what is good and what is therefore true and what is false. Once it knows this, it can choose either one or the other. If it chooses what is good, then it can use discernment to learn about the means by which it can reach what is good. We are provided with all the means we need to reach what is good. Knowing and discerning these means depends on our rationality, while intending and acting depend on our freedom, freedom being our own intent to know, to discern, and to think about these matters.

People do not know about these abilities called rationality and freedom if they believe, as the church has taught, that spiritual and theological matters transcend understanding and are therefore to be believed without being understood. All they can do is deny the existence of the ability called rationality. Further, if people believe that we cannot do good on our own, as the church has taught, and that therefore we do not need to do anything good voluntarily for the sake of our salvation, they cannot help denying the existence of our other ability because of their religious principles. After death, therefore, people who have convinced themselves of these beliefs lose both abilities because of their beliefs.

They might have been in heavenly freedom, but they are in hellish freedom instead. They might have enjoyed angelic wisdom because of their rationality, but instead they are immersed in the insanity of hell. Strange as it may seem, they still recognize the gift of these two abilities in their evil behavior and their false thinking, not realizing that the freedom of doing evil is slavery and the rationality of thinking falsely is senseless.

However, we need to be quite clear about the fact that neither of these abilities, neither freedom nor rationality, is really ours. They are the Lord's gifts to us, and we are not to claim them as our own. They cannot really belong to us; they are constantly being given to us by the Lord. Still, they are never taken from us because we cannot be saved without them. Without them, that is, we cannot be reborn, as already noted [§264]. This is why the church teaches that we cannot think what is true on our own or do what is good on our own.

However, since our whole perception is that we do think what is true on our own, and that we do do what is good on our own, the idea that we only seem to think what is true on our own and only seem to do what is good on our own is clearly something we need to *believe*. If we do not believe this, then we neither think what is true nor do what is good, and we therefore have no religion whatever. Either that, or we think what is true as well as do what is good with our own strength, which is claiming for ourselves what belongs to Divinity.

On our need to think what is true and do what is good in apparent independence, see *Teachings about Life for the New Jerusalem*[231] from beginning to end.

21. *When love is spiritual and heavenly, it is a love for our neighbor and for the Lord; while when it is limited to nature and our senses, it is a love for the world and for ourselves.* "Love for our neighbor" means a love for acts of service, and "love for the Lord" means a love for doing such acts, as already noted [§237]. The reason these loves are spiritual and heavenly is that loving acts of service and doing them because we love to is divorced from any concern for our own image.[232] That is, when we love acts of service spiritually, we are not focused on ourselves but on others outside ourselves, others for whom we are doing something good. Love for ourselves and for the world are the opposites of these loves because they focus our attention on doing acts of service not for the sake of others but for our own sake. When we do this, we are turning the divine design upside down, putting ourselves in the Lord's place and the world in heaven's place. This means we are looking away from the Lord and heaven, and

426

looking away from them is looking toward hell. There is more about these loves, though, in §424 above.

Still, we do not have the same kind of feeling and sense of love for doing what is useful for its own sake that we have for doing what is useful for our own sake. This also means that when we are doing something useful we do not know whether we are doing it for its own sake or for our own sake. We might know, though, that we do what is useful for its own sake to the extent that we abstain from evils because to the extent that we do, the source of our acts of service is not ourselves but the Lord. Evil and good are opposites, so to the extent that we are not engaged in something evil, we are engaged in something good. No one can be in evil and in good at the same time because no one can serve two masters at the same time.[233]

I mention this because it helps to know that even though we may have no clear sense of whether we are doing acts of service for their own sake or for ours—whether the acts are spiritual, that is, or merely earthly—we could tell by seeing whether we think evil deeds are sins or not. If we think they are sins and therefore do not do them, then our acts of service are spiritual; and once we begin abstaining from sins because they are distasteful to us, then we begin to have an actual sense of loving service for its own sake because there is a spiritual pleasure in service.

427

22. *It is the same for charity and faith and their union as it is for volition and discernment and their union.* There are two loves that are the grounds of a basic distinction in the heavens, namely heavenly love and spiritual love. Heavenly love is love for the Lord and spiritual love is love for our neighbor. The difference between these two loves is that heavenly love is a love for what is good, while spiritual love is a love for what is true. When we are moved by heavenly love, we do our acts of service out of love for what is good; while when we are moved by spiritual love we do them out of love for what is true. The marriage of heavenly love is with wisdom, and the marriage of spiritual love is with intelligence. Wisdom is doing what is good because it is good, and intelligence is doing what is good because it is true. This means that heavenly love acts out what is good, while spiritual love acts out what is true.

The only way I can describe the difference between these two loves is to say that people who are moved by heavenly love have wisdom written not on their memory but on their lives. This is because they do not talk about divine truths, they simply do them. In contrast, people who are moved by spiritual love have wisdom written on their memory, so they talk about divine truths and do them on the basis of the principles they hold in their memory.

Since people who are moved by heavenly love have wisdom written on their lives, whenever they hear something they know immediately whether it is true or not; and when they are asked whether something is true, they say either that it is or that it is not. They are the people referred to by the Lord's words, "Let your speech be 'Yes, yes; no, no'" (Matthew 5:37). Because this is their nature, they do not like it when people talk about faith. They say, "What is faith? Is it not wisdom? And what is charity? Is it not action?" If anyone says that faith is believing what we do not understand, they turn away and say, "That's crazy."

These are the people who live in the third heaven, and they are the wisest of all. People get that way in this world by applying whatever divine principles they hear directly to their lives with an aversion to evils as hellish and a total reverence for the Lord. Because they live in innocence, they look to others like little children; and because they never talk about truths of wisdom and there is no trace of self-importance in their conversation, they seem simple. However, when they hear others talking they can sense their whole love from their tone of voice and their whole intellect from what they are saying.

These are the people who are kept in the marriage of love and wisdom by the Lord. As already mentioned [§381], they also reflect the heart region of heaven.

In contrast, people who are moved by spiritual love, by love for their **428** neighbor, do not have wisdom written on their lives. They do have intelligence, since as already noted [§427] it is characteristic of wisdom to do what is good because we are moved by what is good and characteristic of intelligence to do what is good because we are moved by what is true. People like this do not know what faith is either. If someone mentions faith, they hear "truth," and if someone mentions charity, they hear "doing the truth." If someone says something should be believed, they call it nonsense and say, "Who doesn't believe what is true?" They say this because they are seeing what is true in the light of their heaven. So in their eyes, it is either simplemindedness or folly to believe what we do not see.

These are the people who make up the lung region of heaven, as also noted earlier [§381].

Some people, though, are moved by spiritual love on the earthly **429** level. They do not have either wisdom or intelligence written on their lives, they simply have some element of faith drawn from the Word, to the extent that it is united to charity. Since they do not know what charity is or whether their faith is true, they cannot enjoy the company of people in the heavens, people who are occupied with wisdom and intelligence. They find themselves with people who are occupied simply with information. Still, if they have abstained from evils as sins, they are in the farthest heaven, where the light is like moonlight at night.

Then again, if they have not become set in a faith in the unknown and have felt some attraction to truths, once they have been taught by angels (as far as their openness to truths and to a life by them allows), they are brought up into communities of people who are moved by spiritual love and therefore live intelligently. They become spiritual, while the others remain spiritual only on an earthly level.

However, if people have lived in a faith that is separated from charity, they are sent away and relegated to desolate regions because they are not engaged in anything worthwhile. This means that they do not participate in any marriage of what is good and true, the marriage characteristic of everyone in the heavens.

 430 Everything I have said in this part about love and wisdom could also be said about charity and faith, provided only that charity is understood to mean a spiritual love and faith is understood to mean the truth that leads to intelligence. The same would hold true if we spoke of our volition and discernment, or our love and intelligence, since our volition is the vessel of love and our discernment is the vessel of intelligence.

431 I should like to add a matter of interest. All the people in heaven who are engaged in being of service because they enjoy doing it derive from their collective body a wisdom and happiness greater than that of others. As far as they are concerned, being of service means being honest, fair, proper, and faithful in whatever task is appropriate to their station. This is what they call "charity," and they refer to their acts of formal worship as emblems of charity. Anything else is a duty or a good deed. They say that whenever they do the tasks proper to their station honestly, fairly, properly, and faithfully, the collective body takes on substance and permanence in their good work. This is what it means to be "in the Lord," since everything that flows into them from the Lord has to do with service; and it flows from the members into the collective body and from the collective body into the members. The members there are angels, and the collective body is their community.

432 *The nature of our first stage after conception.* No one can know what our first or primal stage in the womb after conception is like because we cannot see it. Further, it is composed of a spiritual substance that is not visible in physical light. Some people in this world are inclined to focus their minds on our primal stage, the father's semen that is the agent of conception, and many of them have fallen into the error of thinking that we are complete humans from the very first and then reach completeness simply by getting larger.[234] For this reason, some angels to whom the Lord had revealed it showed me what this first or primal stage of ours is like with respect to its form. Since they had made this a matter of their wisdom and since the delight of that wisdom was to share what they knew with others, they were given permission to present a representation of that initial form of ours to my own eyes in heaven's light.

It was like this. I saw what seemed to be a tiny image of a brain with a sort of face drawn faintly on its front, with no appendages. On its upper convex part, this primal form was a composite of closely connected little balls or spheres. Each sphere was made up of still smaller spheres, and each of these of spheres still smaller. This meant that there were three levels. Something that looked like a face was outlined on the front, concave part.

The convex part was enveloped by a very thin, transparent meningeal membrane. The convex part, the miniature image of a brain, was also divided into what seemed to be two lobes the way the full-scale brain is divided into two hemispheres. I was told that the right lobe was the vessel of love and that the left lobe was the vessel of wisdom, and that by some incredibly intricate connections they were like partners or roommates.

In the light of heaven, a radiant light, the angels also showed me that inwardly this composite structure of a miniature brain was in the design and form of heaven with respect to both its setting and its flow, while the outer composite structure was opposed to that design and that form.

Once I had seen what they showed me, the angels said that the two inner levels, the ones that were in the design and form of heaven, were vessels of love and wisdom from the Lord, while the outer level, the one that was opposed to heaven's design and form, was a vessel of hellish love and madness. This is because we are born into all kinds of evil because of our hereditary imperfection, and these evils are located in our outermost natures. These flaws cannot be eliminated unless our higher levels are opened, the levels that are vessels of love and wisdom from the Lord, as already noted. Further, since love and wisdom are the essential person, love and wisdom being the Lord in essence, and since this primal stage of ours is a vessel, it follows that there is in this primal stage a constant striving toward the human form, a form that it gradually takes on.

THE END

NOTES & INDEXES

Notes

Notes to §§1–3

1. The Latin sentence here translated "For most people, the existence of love is a given, but the nature of love is a mystery" is *Homo novit quod amor sit, sed non novit quid amor est,* literally, "People know that love is, but they do not know what love is." [GFD]

2. The Latin term here translated "end," *finis,* is a common philosophical term that includes the ideas both of intent and of result. For example, fresh vegetables are the gardener's "end" both in the sense that they are the purpose, aim, or goal the gardener has in mind from the beginning of the process of growing them and in the sense that the actual vegetables constitute the fulfillment of that intent, the "end" of the process. The phrase "the perception of ends," however, is less common; Swedenborg only uses it here and in §4633 of an earlier work, *Secrets of Heaven,* which was published in eight volumes between 1749 and 1756. (On the use of section numbers to refer to Swedenborg's works, see note 3 below.) On the meaning of this term, see the introduction, page 26 above, and compare the mention in his 1768 work *Marriage Love* 461:3–5 of angels who see things from the perspective of "ends." [GFD, JSR]

3. As is customary in Swedenborgian studies, text citations of Swedenborg's works refer not to page numbers but to Swedenborg's section numbers, which are uniform in all editions. See the list of short titles and conventions on pages 43–48 above. This is the first of a number of passages in the work in which Swedenborg cross-references material elsewhere in his text. Where he himself supplies the section numbers of these cross-references, they generally appear in parentheses; where the editors supply them, they appear in square brackets or, if a correction, in italic square brackets. [JSR]

4. The concept of "correspondence" presented in Swedenborg's works is briefly defined in §71 below as "the mutual relationship between spiritual and earthly things" (see also §374 below). In its full formulation, it holds that there are two separate universes, one spiritual and one physical, that are related to each other through similarity but not through any shared matter or direct continuity. We human beings bridge the two worlds by having both a spiritual aspect and a physical aspect. Love is spiritual; physical warmth corresponds to it. Warmth then has an effect on nature that is similar to that which love has on our mind or spirit. In Swedenborg's terminology, the mutual relationship between love and warmth can be called a "correspondence," and the love and the warmth themselves can also be called "correspondences." See also note 64 below. [JSR]

Notes to §§4–6

5. In Swedenborg's works, "the Lord" refers to Jesus Christ as God. A core concept in Swedenborg's theology is that there are not three persons in the Trinity; there is one person, whose soul is the unknowable divine, whose human manifestation is Jesus Christ, and whose spirit (or influence) is holy. Of the many names and terms from philosophical and biblical backgrounds that Swedenborg uses to denote God (the Divine Being, the Divine, the Divine Human, the One, the Infinite, the First, the

Creator, the Redeemer, the Savior, Jehovah, God Shaddai, and many more), the most frequently occurring term is "the Lord" (Latin *Dominus*), a title rather than a name, meaning "the one in charge," and referring to Jesus Christ as the manifestation of the one and only God. For Swedenborg's brief explanation of his reasons for using "the Lord," see *Secrets of Heaven* 14. [JSR]

6. The projected work on divine providence mentioned here was published in early 1764 immediately after the present work and is so clearly a sequel to it that at one point Swedenborg saw them as a single volume (see Swedenborg's 1766 work *Revelation Unveiled* 875:15). It is referred to in this edition by the short title *Divine Providence*. The work "on life" is presumably *Teachings about Life for the New Jerusalem*, referred to by the short title *Life* in this edition. It is one of four "teachings" published together in 1763 just before *Divine Love and Wisdom*, namely, *The Lord, Sacred Scripture, Life*, and *Faith*. For a fuller discussion of the relationship of *Divine Love and Wisdom* to Swedenborg's other works, see the translator's preface. [GFD]

7. The Latin term here translated "reality" is *Esse*, the infinitive of the verb "to be" used as a noun. It is a philosophical term for basic existence or "is-ness" as an attribute. [GFD]

8. Following a Christian practice of his times, Swedenborg often used "Jehovah" as a rendering of the tetragrammaton, יהוה *(yhvh)*, "YHWH," the four-letter name of God in Hebrew Scriptures. A complex set of circumstances gave rise to the name "Jehovah." The Hebrew alphabet originally consisted only of consonants. It was not until the eighth century of the Common Era that a complete system of diacritical marks for vowel notation was developed. When for any reason the consonantal text was held not to be suitable for reading as it stood, the vowels of an approved reading would be added to the consonants that stood in the text, whether the number of syllables in the two words matched or not. Since the sanctity of the name of God, YHWH, was felt to preclude its being pronounced, the word אֲדֹנָי *(Ǎḏōnāi)*, "Lord," was regularly substituted, and to indicate this, vowels closely resembling those of the name Adonai were added to YHWH: YeHoWaH. This combination of consonants and vowels was transliterated into Latin as "Jehovah." (Some English Bibles since then have adopted the name "Jehovah" while others have rendered the term as "Lᴏʀᴅ," so capitalized.) The currently accepted scholarly reconstruction of the original pronunciation of the name is "Yahweh": see *Theological Dictionary of the Old Testament* under "YHWH." As others have done, Swedenborg relates the name YHWH or Jehovah to the concept of being or "is-ness"; see his 1771 work *True Christianity* 19:1, as well as 9:2–3. [GFD]

9. Here as often Swedenborg assumes that his readers will be familiar with definitions of various kinds of cause developed by the Greek philosopher Aristotle (384–322 B.C.E.) and the medieval Scholastic philosophers. Aristotle introduced the four main categories of cause (*Physics* 2:3); they can be described in simplistic terms with respect to an artifact such as a statue that is being carved from stone. The *material cause* is what the artifact is made of, the stone. The *efficient cause* is the agent that makes the artifact, the sculptor. The *formal cause* is the quality gained by the material that is being made into the sculpture, its "statueness." The *final cause* is the purpose for which the statue is made. Beyond these basic causes the Scholastic philosophers defined many more, including *instrumental cause*, which is an instrument or tool that serves another cause (the hand with which the sculptor works, for example), and *principal cause*, a cause that works through the power of its own form so that the result is in some way like itself (the humanness of a sculptor carving a statue of a human might be an example). Here the

point is that the Divinity that flows into us is the *principal cause* creating something in its own likeness; we, though we are *instrumental causes* (inasmuch as we serve the Creator's end), erroneously see that principal cause as identical to us. In short, God is so present in us that we might mistakenly regard the divine life we experience in ourselves as evidence that we are God. [JSR, SS]

10. The relevant statement in John 11:25 is "I am the resurrection and the life," and in John 14:6, "I am the way, the truth, and the life." [GFD]

11. *Heaven and Hell* is an earlier work by Swedenborg, published in 1758. [GFD]

Notes to §§7–10

12. The Latin word here translated "Divinity" is *Divinum,* a neuter adjective used as a noun to mean "that which is divine." Swedenborg uses it to denote "divineness," that is, the quality of divinity both as it exists in God and as it radiates from God throughout the created universe. [GFD]

13. Among the many senses of the world *nature* (Latin *natura*) in Swedenborg's usage, two stand out. When the word is modified, either with an adjective before, for example "inner nature," or by a prepositional phrase afterward, for example, "the nature of their minds," he means character or quality. When he speaks of "nature" alone without modifying language, as he does here, he means the entire physical universe. Swedenborg's reference here to "the extended size of nature" is reminiscent of *res extensa* ("that which is extended"), the term used by French philosopher René Descartes (1596–1650) to describe the material reality that occupies measurable space. In Descartes's philosophy, it stood in contrast to *res cogitans* ("that which thinks"), the immaterial reality that cannot be quantified. [GFD, JSR]

14. Swedenborg's statement here that "divine providence, omnipresence, omniscience, omnipotence, infinity, and eternity . . . are to be dealt with in sequence" is apparently not fulfilled. It echoes a promise in the preface to *The Lord,* which was also published in 1763—a promise of nine books that Swedenborg was going to publish "by command of the Lord" *(ex mandato Domini),* one of which was to be called *Angelic Wisdom Concerning Divine Omnipotence, Omnipresence, Omniscience, Infinity, and Eternity.* Four years later one of the first avid readers of Swedenborg, Gabriel Beyer (1720–1779), asked Swedenborg what had become of this projected work. Swedenborg replied that there were many things on these subjects in works he had already published (*Divine Love and Wisdom* 4, 17, 19, 21, 44, 69, 72, 76, 106, 156, 318; *Divine Providence* 46–54, 157; *Revelation Unveiled* 961); and that there would be more in the work soon to appear (1768) on marriage love; "for to write a separate treatise on these Divine attributes, without the assistance of something to support them, would cause too great an elevation of the thoughts; wherefore these subjects have been treated in a series with other things which fall within the understanding" (Tafel 1877, 1:261). This change of plans offers a rare glimpse of an interplay between Swedenborg's sense of divine commission and his exercise of his own judgment. [GFD, JSR]

Notes to §§11–13

15. The Latin word here translated "non-Christians" is *gentes.* There does not seem to be any English word that fairly represents what Swedenborg intends by this usage. In

Secrets of Heaven 367, the term clearly means "gentiles" (non-Jews) in contrast to Jews; in *Heaven and Hell* 516, it means certain unspecified non-Christians who are also not Muslims. There does not seem to be any passage in which Swedenborg specifically includes Jews among the *gentes,* so it seems safe to conclude that by this term he generally meant people who were neither Christians nor Jews. The translation "non-Christians" has been adopted primarily to avoid the derogatory connotations of the words "heathen" and "pagan," it being clear from the passage as a whole that Swedenborg intended no derogation whatever. Though the term "non-Christian" might seem inaccurate on the grounds that it does not indicate that the people in question are also not Jews, in fact in at least one passage Swedenborg indicates that he considers Jews to be a category of Christians. This occurs in *Sacred Scripture* 54, where he speaks of the understanding of Scripture "in the Christian world" and goes on to name specifically the Reformed, the Catholics, and the Jews. A parallel can be found in the Qur'an, which speaks of أَهْلُ ٱلْكِتَابِ, *(ahlu-lkitābi),* the "people of the book," meaning "those who have the Torah, the Gospel, or the Qur'an." This delineation corresponds nicely to the definition of *gentes* in *Heaven and Hell* 308 as "people who are outside the church, where the Word is not found." (On the meaning of "the Word," see note 16 below.) [GFD]

16. "The Word" (Latin *Verbum*) refers to the Bible and denotes it as truth revealed by God. It was the common term for the Bible in the Lutheran tradition in which Swedenborg was raised. He indicates elsewhere, however, that by "the Word" he means a smaller set of books of the Bible than are found in the complete Lutheran Bible, specifically the works that he identifies as having a spiritual meaning throughout, namely the Pentateuch (Genesis, Exodus, Leviticus, Numbers, Deuteronomy), some other historical books (Joshua, Judges, 1 and 2 Samuel, 1 and 2 Kings), the Book of Psalms, the major and minor prophets (Isaiah, Jeremiah, Lamentations, Ezekiel, Daniel, Hosea, Joel, Amos, Obadiah, Jonah, Micah, Nahum, Habakkuk, Zephaniah, Haggai, Zechariah, Malachi), the Gospels (Matthew, Mark, Luke, John), and the Book of Revelation. (See *Secrets of Heaven* 10325, and parallel passages in Swedenborg's 1758 works *New Jerusalem* 266, and *White Horse* 16.) It should be noted that in his last work, *True Christianity,* he seems to use the term in the full Lutheran sense, including passages from the epistles of the apostles among citations from "the Word." For his explanation as to why he did not generally include the works of the apostles and Paul in "the Word," see his letter to Gabriel Beyer (April 15, 1766), cited in Acton 1955, 612–613. [GFD, JSR]

17. This movement to the heavens implies that the initial setting of the account is the "world of spirits," the region "halfway between heaven and hell" where people first arrive after death and where they stay until they finally choose either heaven or hell (see *Heaven and Hell* 421–431). Also see note 81 below. On the multiplicity of heavens, see *Heaven and Hell* 29–50. [GFD]

18. The two paragraphs quoted here first appeared in Swedenborg's 1763 work *Supplements* 74, with slight differences in the opening phrase. [JSR]

Notes to §§14–16

19. The Latin term here translated "the Divine-Human One" is *Deus Homo,* literally, "God Human," a term for God that occurs frequently in the present work, four times in *True Christianity,* and nowhere else in Swedenborg's corpus. The name

places two nouns in apposition. It may best be regarded as the noun version of an adjectival form Swedenborg uses much more frequently: *Divinum Humanum,* meaning "that which is both divine and human." See also the translator's preface, page 7. [GFD, JSR]

20. In the Western philosophical tradition, there are two senses of form (Latin *forma*) expressed by the Greek words μορφή *(morphé),* and εἶδος *(eîdos).* Although both of these words can be rendered into English as "form," this is ambiguous, for *morphé* can also be rendered as "shape," meaning the form of concrete things, and *eîdos* as "idea," meaning the abstract form, model, or blueprint of a class of concrete things. Swedenborg's use of "form" here clearly refers to the shape of concretely existing things, since he is talking about the concrete manifestation of the immaterial. Likewise, Swedenborg uses "attributes" (expressed in the singular Latin word *quale*) to refer to a concrete attribute, not to the abstract attribute of an abstract form. [GRJ]

Notes to §§17–22

21. The Latin original of this passage contains no hint of God's being either male or female. Although the identification of Jesus in his transformed state as God is central to Swedenborg's theology, as is the related concept of God's humanity, Swedenborg seems stringently to avoid any indication of masculine or feminine gender in God. He consistently uses the neutral term *homo,* "a human," rather than a gendered term for God's humanity; and where he uses adjectives in the role of nouns as terms for God, such as "the Infinite," "the Divine," "the Divine Human," and "the Human," he casts them as neuter rather than feminine or masculine. (A possible exception to this rule is the use of *Creatrix,* a feminine term for the creator; see note 31 below.) The present edition uses the pronoun "he" for God even though it introduces gender implications that are not present in the original, because (a) the text's strong emphasis on the oneness of God contraindicates the use of plural pronouns; (b) the English language has no established gender-neutral singular third-person pronoun; (c) the text's strong emphasis on the humanness of God contraindicates the use of "it"; and (d) the identification of Jesus with God would make any pronoun but "he" awkward. [JSR]

22. The Latin words here translated "millions" are *myriadibus myriadum,* literally, "ten thousands of ten thousands," an idiom intended to convey not mathematical precision but simply an inconceivably great number. [GFD]

23. Swedenborg introduces rather briefly here a counterintuitive concept discussed in greater detail in *Heaven and Hell* 73, namely, that angels derive their humanity from their communities and from heaven as a whole, rather than the reverse. Our full humanity depends on our being inwardly in harmony with the human community that surrounds us—in contemporary terms, on our "internalizing" it. [GFD]

24. The Latin phrase here translated "to its functions and the things that answer to them" is *ex usibus & eorum correspondentiis. Usus,* traditionally translated "uses," is perhaps best understood as denoting what a thing, a person, or an action is "good for"— much like Aristotle's "final cause" (see note 9 above). The *correspondentiae,* literally, "correspondences," of those useful functions are things that have analogous effects on a spiritual rather than a physical level. The parallels Swedenborg has drawn above between physical and spiritual light (see §5) may serve as examples. [GFD]

Notes to §§23–27

25. Swedenborg uses the word "church" (Latin *ecclesia*) in a variety of senses. Sometimes it refers to a religious approach in the abstract, whether that occurs in an individual or in a group large or small; sometimes it refers more concretely to local or national Christianity, to all Protestantism, or even to Christianity as a whole; sometimes it applies more broadly to all believers on earth of whatever faith; and sometimes it is used historically to mean the core religious approach of a given age or era through which heaven was connected with humankind, of which there have been five in sequence: the earliest (or "most ancient") church, the early (or "ancient") church, the Jewish church, the Christian church, and the new church (see Swedenborg's 1758 work *Last Judgment* 46 and notes; see also *Divine Providence* 328; *True Christianity* 760, 762, 786). Presumably here Swedenborg is using the term to mean Christianity as a whole, because in the following section (§25) it is contrasted with the broader "church that is spread throughout the world," presumably meaning all believers of whatever faith. [JSR]

26. See note 25 just above. [JSR]

27. The Latin terms here translated "discernment" and "volition" are *intellectus* and *voluntas,* traditionally translated "understanding" (or "intellect") and "will." Each term has two basic meanings. "Discernment" means both the mental faculty that enables us to think, reason, and know and also the exercise of that faculty in an act of judging or perceiving. Likewise, "volition" means both the faculty of will or intention that enables us to make choices and also the actual exercise of that faculty in deciding on a given course of action. Swedenborg regards volition and discernment as the two primary characteristics of humanity. As such they are very broad terms. Discernment includes all the cognitive functions by which we apprehend and interpret the world, while volition is correspondingly inclusive of all the feelings that motivate us to respond in specific ways. For Swedenborg, volition is primary and discernment secondary, meaning that the ways we perceive and understand are prompted and significantly shaped by our intentions. [GFD, JSR]

Notes to §§28–33

28. On Swedenborg's concept of sequential and simultaneous arrangement, see §§205–207 below. [GFD]

29. See, for example, §266 below and *Divine Providence* 223. [JSR]

30. Swedenborg's mention of things that are enchanting (Latin *amaena,* which means approximately "things pleasing through their elegance") refers to things that delight us intellectually rather than emotionally. The parallel in modern English is the term "elegant" as used of a mathematical proof or a scientific theory. [GFD]

31. Swedenborg's use here of the feminine noun *Creatrix,* "Creatress," is striking (see note 21 above). While it may be prompted by the fact that *Essentia,* "essence," is a feminine noun, there is no grammatical necessity for a noun to agree in gender with a noun with which it is in apposition. This feminine noun occurs again in §262 and in *True Christianity* 178, in both instances in apposition with *natura,* "nature"; in these instances, it is quite possible that "nature" was visualized in female form. [GFD]

Notes to §§34–39

32. In Swedenborg's time, David's authorship of the Book of Psalms was virtually unchallenged; thus he often uses "in David" to mean "in the Psalms." [GFD]

33. Swedenborg's original here reads *terra,* "the earth," where most Bibles have the word for "Zion." [GFD]

Notes to §§40–43

34. Swedenborg's use of the singular verb *est,* "is," here is striking, and undoubtedly represents his insistence that love and wisdom are only apparently separate entities. Though "substance" *(substantia)* and "form" *(forma)* are technical philosophical terms, here Swedenborg seems to use them merely as contrasts to the popular misunderstanding of divine love and wisdom as a formless and insubstantial "vapor." Substance here connotes enduring presence, as opposed to transience, while form connotes a concrete shape, as opposed to shapeless fluidity. [GFD, GRJ]

35. Swedenborg shared the belief of his times that there is an atmosphere rarer than air, called "ether," that is the medium of light the way air is the medium of sound (see *Secrets of Heaven* 4523:1, 6013:2, 6057:1; *True Christianity* 32:8, 79:2–6). This substance was also considered by some to be the stuff of which souls, angels, and spirits are made, for which reason some people called them "ethers" (see *Marriage Love* 315:11 and note 210 below). [JSR]

36. Here as often Swedenborg uses "subject" (Latin *subjectum*) in the philosophical sense of that which underlies a perceptible process, as a substratum or substance that can be said to have particular attributes or abilities. In this section the "subject" is God. Swedenborg's point is that divine love and wisdom are not emanations *from* God that are somehow separate from God's nature. Instead, divine love and wisdom are emanations *of* God's nature, God's real presence throughout the cosmos. [GFD, GRJ]

37. On the meaning of "subject" here, see note 36 just above. [GFD]

38. Here Swedenborg makes it clear that "substance and form" are like "reality and manifestation" in referring to concrete realities, as opposed to abstract "theoretical constructs that in and of themselves are nothing." [GRJ]

Notes to §§44–46

39. The Latin expression here translated "wholly 'itself' and unique" is *Ipsum et Unicum,* literally, "what is itself and what is unique." In §§44–45 Swedenborg frequently uses singular verbs and pronouns where plurals would be expected, presumably to emphasize God's oneness. See also notes 34, 67, 83, and 214. [GFD]

40. Swedenborg objects to the assertion that nature exists in its own right because such a claim is tantamount to a denial that nature was created by God. This assertion was sufficiently common in Swedenborg's day to provoke his comment, but it can be traced back at least as far as Aristotle, who maintained that the world is uncreated and, as a whole, lies outside of time—that is, it is eternal. See Aristotle *On the Heavens* 1:10–12 and 2:1–7. [GRJ]

41. Here Swedenborg is contrasting static and dynamic perspectives on nature. The static perspective takes a snapshot of nature and studies the inanimate forms that are revealed. The dynamic perspective looks at the functioning of forms in time. The static perspective is clearly inadequate, because it abstracts forms from their living embodiment. [GRJ]

Note to §§47–51

42. See note 14 above. [GFD]

Notes to §§52–54

43. The Latin here translated "outermost" is *ultimae,* literally, "farthest," "most remote." Swedenborg regularly uses this word to refer to what is "farthest" from God and therefore lowest or most external. [GFD]

44. This paragraph is the clearest expression of Swedenborg's conception of the relationship of God and creation. God is not to be identified with creation, for that is pantheism. But God is not wholly cut off from creation either. God and creation are *both* identical *and* different. To express this, Swedenborg likens creation to an image of God. As an image of God, creation shares in God's nature, but is still different from God. If one injures a created being, this is surely an *insult* to God insofar as it is an attack on his image, since there is an identity between image and original. But to injure creation is not to *injure* God, since there is also a difference between image and original. [GRJ]

Notes to §§55–60

45. Swedenborg's comment that "nothing comes from 'absolutely nothing' and nothing can" (Latin *ex plane nihilo nihil fit, nec aliquid fieri potest*) echoes the famous principle of Melissus of Samos (flourished around 444–441 B.C.E.): "In no way could anything come to be from nothing" (οὐδαμὰ ἂν γένοιτο οὐδὲν ἐκ μηδενός, *oudamà àn génoito oudèn ek medenós*). See Kirk, Raven, and Schofield 1983, 393. Melissus uses this principle to deny the existence of change (coming to be and passing away), on the assumption that all change involves the emergence of something from nothing, but nothing comes from nothing. This belief was mentioned by Aristotle (see specifically *Physics* 1:8; *Metaphysics* 11:6; and generally *On Generation and Corruption* 1). In Latin this notion was usually expressed by the Scholastic commonplace *ex nihilo nihil fit,* "from nothing, nothing comes to be"; see the scholastic philosophers Anselm (1033–1109) *Monologium* 8; and Aquinas (1224 or 1225–1274) *Summa Theologiae* 1:45:1 and 2. Swedenborg appeals to this principle to dispute the idea that God created the world out of nothing, *ex nihilo.* [GRJ, SS]

46. Here again Swedenborg is differentiating his position from pantheism; see note 44 above. [GRJ]

47. The wording here anticipates the first "law of divine providence," which is that "we should act in freedom and in accord with reason." See *Divine Providence* 71–99. [GFD]

48. In a similar context in §351 below Swedenborg specifically cites the *Biblia Naturae* (The Book of Nature) of Jan Swammerdam (1637–1680), which was published posthumously in 1737–1738. A groundbreaking work of entomology, it is likely to have been one of the works Swedenborg had in mind here. For more on Swammerdam, see Tafel 1877, 1:233–234, 2:1256–1257. Another great microscopist and writer on insects and other small forms of life was Antonie van Leeuwenhoek (1632–1723), five of whose volumes were in Swedenborg's library upon his death in 1772. [JSR]

49. The Latin phrase here translated "breath of life" is *anima vitarum,* literally, "the soul/breath of lives," reflecting a very literal translation of the Hebrew נִשְׁמַת חַיִּים *(nišmaṯ ḥayyîm)* of Genesis 2:7. [GFD]

Notes to §§61–64

50. The "beasts of the earth" here (Latin *bestiae terrae*) mean domesticated animals. They are contrasted in *True Christianity* 34:2 with wild animals *(ferae)*. Presumably "the fowl of the heavens" *(volucres caeli)* likewise mean domesticated or at least edible birds. Swedenborg generally divides both animals and birds into good kinds that are beneficial to the human race and bad kinds that are harmful to it (see §§331, 338 below). [JSR]

51. This may be a reference to Swedenborg's well-known cousin-in-law Carolus Linnaeus (Karl von Linné, 1707–1778), Swedish botanist and founder of the modern classification system for plants and animals. His works frequently describe plants in anthropomorphic terms. [JSR]

52. In Swedenborg's time, corals were thought to be members of the plant kingdom. A contemporary Latin-English dictionary describes coral as something that "grows in the Sea like a shrub, and taken out waxeth hard as stone" (Littleton 1723, under *coralium*). See also the *Oxford English Dictionary* under "coral." [JSR]

Notes to §§65–68

53. This is the central focus of part 3, §§173–281. [GFD]

54. Swedenborg describes the third heaven, variously referred to as the inmost, highest, or "heavenly" (Latin *coeleste*) one, as the abode of people whose intentions are so purified as to be wholly trustworthy, enabling them to think and act with total spontaneity and innocence. See, for example, *Secrets of Heaven* 4750 and 7877:2; *Heaven and Hell* 33 and 459; and §427 below. [GFD]

Notes to §§69–72

55. The Latin phrase here translated "nonspatially" is *absque spatio,* literally, "without space" or "apart from space." In *Heaven and Hell,* Swedenborg devoted separate chapters to time in heaven (§§162–169) and space in heaven (§§191–199). His basic message in those chapters is that while there is every appearance of space and time in the spiritual world, these are simply products of spiritual consciousness and therefore fluid, changing as our own thoughts and feelings change. By the same token, Deity totally transcends both space and time—everywhere is "here" and all time is "now." Accordingly, neither size nor duration can be predicated of Deity. Note the statement at

the close of this section that Deity is "not within space" (Latin *in spatio*), clearly meaning that it is not confined or limited by it. [GFD]

56. The Latin words here translated "implicitly" are *ut continua,* literally, "as continuations, as extensions." [GFD]

Notes to §§73–76

57. See note 55 above. [GFD]

58. See §108 below. [GFD]

59. The statement that angels do not have days and the like is best understood as meaning that such intervals are subjectively rather than objectively generated, that they are responsive to the "states of life" here mentioned. Like the intervals of space described in §70, they are changeable rather than fixed. For the existence of days in the spiritual world, see, for example, the extended story in *Marriage Love* 11–25, which in §19 mentions an "evening" and a wedding to be celebrated on "the following day." This is actually quite consistent with Swedenborg's view of the life rhythms of angels (see *Heaven and Hell* 154–161). [GFD]

60. The idea that God is his own cause is traditionally referred to with the Latin phrase *causa sui* (literally, "through the cause of himself"). Although this idea is much older than the *Ethics* of the Dutch philosopher Benedict de Spinoza (1632–1677), it figures very prominently in that work in the first line of definition 1 of part 1, "Of God" (Spinoza [1677] 1952, 355). The supposition that Swedenborg is alluding to Spinoza makes sense of his assertion that the *causa sui* doctrine leads to the idea that nature is its own cause, since Spinoza identifies God and nature and was widely seen as advocating, or at least preparing the way for, an atheistic form of naturalism. [GRJ]

Notes to §§77–82

61. See part 4, §§282–357. [GFD]

62. Sir Isaac Newton (1642–1727), English physicist and mathematician, invented the reflecting telescope, discovered the binomial theorem and the integral and differential calculi, established that white light is a compound of all the colors of the spectrum, theorized that light in general is "corpuscular" (composed of particles), and proposed the law of universal gravitation. His principal works are *Mathematical Principles of Natural Philosophy* (1687) and *Optics* (1704, 1717). [GRJ]

63. Whether a true vacuum could exist was a question that had been hotly debated by ancient Greek philosophers. Ultimately Aristotle dismissed the possibility (*Physics* 4:6–9), effectively establishing the principle that "nature abhors a vacuum." When scientists such as Evangelista Torricelli (1608–1647) succeeded in experimentally demonstrating something that appeared to be a vacuum, the debate revived in a new form: Was what Torricelli and others had demonstrated a true vacuum, or only an airless space still replete with some even finer substance? Newton became identified as a believer in the vacuum because he was extremely cautious about postulating a medium by which the force of gravity could work. In a now-famous passage of the general scholium of his *Mathematical Principles of Natural Philosophy* he refuses to hypothesize the cause of the properties of gravity, which by implication include the action of that force over a distance (Newton [1687] 1952, 371). However, in the very next paragraph he does

hypothesize the existence of a "subtle spirit that pervades and lies hid in all gross bodies" (Newton [1687] 1952, 372); and in the *Optics* he further hypothesizes that this substance, otherwise known as ether (see note 35 above), might fill all space (Newton [1704] 1972, 520–521 [3:1, queries 18–21]). Furthermore, he is known from a private letter to theologian Richard Bentley (1662–1742) on February 25, 1693, to have rejected the notion of gravity acting through a vacuum, writing that the idea was "so great an absurdity, that I believe no man who has in philosophical matters a competent faculty of thinking, can ever fall into it" (Newton 1953, 54). [SS]

Notes to §§83–88

64. Correspondence is defined in §71 above; see also §52 above and *Secrets of Heaven* 2987. For one instance of the kind of ample explanation Swedenborg mentions here, see *Heaven and Hell* 87–102, including his notes there, especially the many references to *Secrets of Heaven* in note d on §98. See also note 4 above. [GFD, JSR]

65. Swedenborg lived in an age that was increasingly enamored of empirical observation and inductive reasoning from it. Thus he often backs up his claim to have simultaneous consciousness of the physical world and the spiritual world by asserting that it rests on the evidence of the senses. For example, on the initial occasion when he makes this claim, in the first of his published theological works, *Secrets of Heaven* 68, he observes that he is not deterred by the skepticism his claim will arouse, because he has "seen, heard, and felt" (Latin *vidi, audivi, et sensi*). [GFD, SS]

66. See *Heaven and Hell* 116–125. [GFD]

Note to §§89–92

67. As in the first sentence of §40 (see also the first sentence of note 34), the verb here in Swedenborg's Latin is singular, a reminder of his insistence that love and wisdom are actually one and not two. [GFD]

Notes to §§93–98

68. See part 3, especially §§179–183. [GFD]

69. See, for example, the imagery in Ezekiel 1:4, 27; and Malachi 3:2. [GFD]

70. See, for example, Psalms 27:1; John 1:4–9. It is noteworthy here that Swedenborg is not appealing to Scripture in support of his theological argument, but is using the theology to clarify the meaning of Scripture. In other works, notably *The Lord* and *True Christianity,* he treats Scripture as authoritative and cites it copiously, clearly addressing a readership that accepts the Lutheran insistence on the Bible as the definitive revelation of divine truth. In the present work, however, such appeals are notably absent, and the few references to Scripture have instead the effect of recommending the Bible to secular philosophers as containing unsuspected levels of meaning. [GFD]

Note to §§99–102

71. See, for example, Psalms 104:30; Isaiah 11:2; and Joel 2:28. [GFD]

Notes to §§103–107

72. For Biblical examples of "most high" or "highest" as referring to God, see Genesis 14:18–20; Psalms 9:2; 47:2; 50:14; 87:5; Mark 5:7; Luke 1:32, 35, 76; 6:35; and 8:28; for references to his living "on high," see Psalms 113:5; Isaiah 33:5; and Jeremiah 25:30. [GFD]

73. These statements that angels lack a progression of times of the day and a yearly sequence of seasons seem to be contradicted by *Heaven and Hell* 155: "When they [the angels] are in the highest level of love, they are in the light and warmth of their lives, or in their greatest clarity and delight. Conversely, when they are in the lowest level they are in shadow and coolness, or in what is dim and unpleasant. From this latter state they return to the first, and so on. The phases follow each other with constant variety. These states follow each other like variations of light and shade, warmth and cold, or like the morning, noon, evening, and night of individual days in our world, varying constantly throughout the year." A possible reconciliation of this with the passage at hand is that Swedenborg is here ruling out any such changes that progress mechanically, affecting all angels regardless of their states. (See also note 59 above.) [GFD, JSR]

Notes to §§113–118

74. See note 47 above. [GFD]

75. The paradox of human freedom and divine omnipotence is extensively and forcefully presented in *Divine Providence* 191–213 under the general heading "Our Own Prudence Is Nothing—It Only Seems to Be Something, As It Should. Rather, Divine Providence Is All-Inclusive Because It Extends to the Smallest Details." [GFD]

76. In his *Secrets of Heaven* 64, Swedenborg explains "Adam" not as an individual but as representing an early "church," or religious culture. See note 25 above. [GFD]

Notes to §§119–123

77. This passage is obviously expressed from the point of view of an inhabitant of the northern hemisphere. Not only was such a point of view natural to Swedenborg, but his reasonable expectation would have been that his immediate readers would share it. [GFD]

78. By "early people" here Swedenborg means people in the "early church" (see note 25 above) before the development of Judaism. [JSR]

Notes to §§129–134

79. See note 14 above. [GFD]

80. Swedenborg is referring again here to pantheism, the identification of God and creation and the denial of divine transcendence. See note 44 above. [GRJ]

Notes to §§140–145

81. The "world of spirits" (Latin *mundus spirituum*) is a technical term in Swedenborg's usage throughout his works. It refers to the region "halfway between heaven and hell" in which people spend their "halfway state after death" before going to either

heaven or hell (*Heaven and Hell* 422). As indicated just below in this section, the world of spirits is not to be confused with the spiritual world (*mundus spiritualis*), although the former is part of the latter. When he refers to the spiritual world, Swedenborg means heaven, the world of spirits, and hell. [JSR]

82. Although Swedenborg sometimes briefly follows the general Christian view of his times in referring to "the Devil" as if there were a single evil force opposite God, doing so even in his third of five tenets for the new church (see Swedenborg's 1769 work *Survey* 43; see parallel passages at *Survey* 117; *Marriage Love* 82:1; and *True Christianity* 3:2), in fuller discussions elsewhere he asserts that there is no such thing: "the Devil" is a collective term for hell; nor is there one supreme "Satan." Swedenborg does, however, speak of two classes of people in hell called "satans" and "devils." The distinction is outlined in *Heaven and Hell* 311:2 and in §273 of the present work. In general, "devils" are associated with demonic loves and "satans" with maliciously distorted thoughts, or "devils" with love for oneself and "satans" with love for the world. Swedenborg consistently describes "devils" as more profoundly pernicious than "satans." [GFD, JSR]

Notes to §§146–150

83. The switch in number from the plural verb "emanate" to the singular verb "is" here reflects a shift in the original Latin. For the ambivalence as to whether divine love and wisdom are one thing or two, see note 34 above. [GFD]

84. The work mentioned here was published by Swedenborg in 1763. It is referred to in this edition by the short title *The Lord*. [JSR]

85. See *The Lord* 45–54. [GFD]

86. As is often the case with Swedenborg's first editions and his approach to Scripture quotation, this citation is formatted as a direct quotation but is clearly a modification of John 14:17: "The spirit of truth . . . dwells with you and will be in you." [JSR]

87. This kind of use of Scripture in support of a doctrinal premise, while common elsewhere in Swedenborg's theological works, is unusual in the present one (see note 70 above). Its sudden introduction here may be due to the fact that while Swedenborg can appeal to experience in discussing such subjects as love, Scripture is the only recognized source of information about the Trinity. [GFD]

88. For a more complete explanation of this view of the relationship between the Holy Spirit and Jesus Christ, see *True Christianity* 138–158. [JSR]

Notes to §§151–156

89. On the point at issue here, see particularly *The Lord* 45. [GFD]

90. The Latin phrase here translated "being sustained is a constant coming into being" (*quod subsistentia sit perpetua existentia*) was a common theological maxim (see *Secrets of Heaven* 3483:2, 5084:3; see also *Marriage Love* 380:8; and Swedenborg's 1769 work *Soul-Body Interaction* 4). Swedenborg frequently built on it (see *Secrets of Heaven* 775:2, 3648:2, 4322, 4523:3, 5116:3, 5377, 6040:1, 6482, 9502, 9847, 10076:5, 10152:3, 10252:3, 10266; *Heaven and Hell* 106, 303; *Divine Providence* 3:2; *Soul-Body Interaction* 9:1; *True Christianity* 46, 224:1). The notion is referred to as a commmonplace in part 5 of Descartes's *Discourse on Method* (Descartes [1637] 1952, 55): "It is an opinion commonly received by the theologians, that the action by which [God] now preserves [the

universe] is just the same as that by which He at first created it." Elsewhere Descartes offers this explanation: "The present time has no causal dependence on the time immediately preceding it. Hence, in order to secure the continued existence of a thing, no less a cause is required than that needed to produce it at the first" (Descartes [1641] 1952, 131). Catholic philosopher Thomas Aquinas (1224 or 1225–1274) makes a similar statement about all "creatures," that is, created things: "The being of every creature depends on God, so that not for a moment could it subsist [have independent existence], but would fall into nothingness were it not kept in being by the operation of the Divine power" (*Summa Theologiae* 1:104:1; translation in Aquinas 1952). In support of his position, Aquinas in turn cites another Church Father, Gregory the Great (540–604), specifically his *Moralia in Job* (Ethical Disquisitions on Job) 16:37; he is probably thinking of Gregory's statement there that "All things subsist in him [God]. . . . No created thing avails in itself either to subsist or to move." This Scholastic theory of perpetual creation is also discussed by the Anglo-Irish philosopher George Berkeley (1685–1753) in his work *The Principles of Human Knowledge* (Berkeley [1710] 1952, §46). [JSR, SS]

91. These apparently spatial statements about the location of the spiritual sun should be read in conjunction with the warning to the reader against thinking spatially (see §155 just below). [GFD]

92. The Latin terms here translated "a purpose, a means, and a result" are *finis, causa,* and *effectus,* traditionally translated as "end, cause, and effect." [GFD]

Notes to §§157–162

93. Swedenborg seems here to be using a well-known technical term, though not in its well-known technical meaning. The term "living force" (*vis viva*) was coined by German philosopher and mathematician Gottfried Wilhelm Leibniz (1646–1716) for force "joined to actual motion" (Leibniz [1840] 1959, 318, quoted in Jammer 1962, 164, note 10); Leibniz thus distinguished it from "dead force" (*vis mortua*), a term used by Italian physicist Galileo Galilei (1564–1642) for what we today might call pressure or tension, that is, force without motion. *Vis viva* was also the term used for a specific physical quantity that we would today define as mass times the square of velocity (mv^2). On Swedenborg's predilection for recasting familiar terminology, see Hite [1910] 1988, 411. For some other instances of *vis viva* elsewhere in Swedenborg, see §§166, 219 below; *Soul-Body Interaction* 11, 12; *True Christianity* 576, 607:2. [SS]

94. See Deuteronomy 17:2–4. [GFD]

Note to §§163–166

95. On "living force," see note 93 above. [SS]

Notes to §§167–172

96. See §154 above, and note 92. [GFD]

97. See note 2. [JSR]

98. The Latin phrase here translated "can be at home" is *potest esse sicut in se,* literally, "can be as if in itself." [GFD]

Notes to §§173–178

99. The Latin words here translated "liquids, and solids" are *aquae, et terrae,* literally, "waters, and earths." [GFD]

100. See §§84, 89 above and *Heaven and Hell* 170–176, 582. [GFD]

101. As explained more fully in note 35 above, the "ether" refers to a light-conducting atmosphere rarer than air. The term is usually singular, just as the term for "air" is usually singular. The reason for the unusual plural reference here to "ethers" and "airs" may perhaps be found below in §184, where we read of multiple levels within the ether and multiple levels within the air. Presumably the "ethers" and "airs" mentioned here refer to these many levels and types of atmosphere between the sun and ourselves. Compare also *True Christianity* 186, where the light of the sun is said to pass through the "ethers" and finally progressively through the air to reach us. [JSR]

102. See §173 just above, and *Heaven and Hell* 582, 585. [JSR]

Note to §§179–183

103. Elsewhere when Swedenborg refers exclusively to the present work, he uses the full title *Angelic Wisdom about Divine Love and Wisdom* or the short title *Divine Love and Wisdom.* If "Angelic Wisdom" here is an abbreviated version of this title, it is unique as such. However, from references in Swedenborg's 1763 works *The Lord* 36, *Sacred Scripture* 100, and *Life* 15 and 107 to works under the collective title "Angelic Wisdom," it appears that Swedenborg may be using this title collectively here as well. It would presumably refer then to several projected titles beginning with "Angelic Wisdom about." Just two such titles reached publication: the present work, published in 1763, and *Angelic Wisdom about Divine Providence,* published in 1764. For more on the projected work or works that were not completed, see note 14 above. There is also a reference in Swedenborg's 1766 work *Revelation Unveiled* 434 to a projected work titled *Angelic Wisdom about Marriage,* a title that in fact never reached publication, although the full title of the 1768 work *Marriage Love* does mention wisdom. [JSR]

Notes to §§184–188

104. On the terms "purpose, means, and result," see note 92 above. [GFD]

105. "Reformation" (Latin *reformatio*) is Swedenborg's term for the restructuring of our priorities that is effected by self-discipline; "regeneration" *(regeneratio)* is his term for the deeper transformation made possible by this restructuring but accomplished by the Lord. Swedenborg speaks far more frequently of *regeneratio* than of *renascentia* or "rebirth," with which it is sometimes equated (see note 230 below). On regeneration, see the chapter in *New Jerusalem* 173–186; it includes extensive references to appearances of the topic in his previous work, *Secrets of Heaven.* For an extended discussion of reformation and regeneration, see *True Christianity* 571–620. [GFD]

Note to §§195–198

106. Here Swedenborg describes the relationship of levels to one another in a vocabulary that brings to mind embryonic growth, that is, the emergence of complex biological forms from relatively simple ones, the emergence of multi-leveled systems

from a single-leveled system, through involution or internal complexification. The use of the language of "folding" to describe change is consistent with Swedenborg's denial of the reality of the void and his affirmation that the universe is a plenum, a filled space. The early Greek atomists explained change as the movement and recombination of material particles in a void. If the world is a plenum, then change must be understood as different parts of the plenum sliding past one another or folding in upon themselves to generate new structures. Leibniz shared this conception of change. See Deleuze 1992. [GRJ]

Note to §§205–208

107. The work mentioned here was published by Swedenborg in 1763. It is referred to in this edition by the short title *Sacred Scripture*. [JSR]

Note to §§209–216

108. "They" here refers to volition and discernment, feeling and thought, and charity and faith, when considered apart from the substantial realities that are their subjects. [JSR]

Notes to §§217–221

109. Though this discussion of energy, force, and motion is introduced by the phrase "It is common knowledge that . . . ," the concept of force (Latin *vis*) was defined in various ways in Swedenborg's time and was consequently a source of tremendous controversy (Jammer 1962, 158–182). Swedenborg's purpose is to illustrate his exposition of vertical levels and to lay the groundwork for a discussion of energy, force, and motion in us as living beings in §219 below; "energy" and "force" are therefore not used here in their current scientific definitions. [SS]

110. Obviously motion can be sensed and perceived in the physical world. Presumably what Swedenborg means here is that the other two levels, energy and force, are undetectable in the physical world apart from any motion they cause. [JSR]

111. See Matthew 7:24–27; 25:2–4. [GFD]

112. This section stands out as the book's lone excursus into Christian theology, accomplished by setting two primary doctrines, that of revelation and that of the nature of Christ, in the philosophical framework that is now in place. It should be noted that there is no appeal to Biblical authority and in fact no direct quotation of Scripture whatever, in sharp contrast to accepted Lutheran practice. It is particularly striking that it first occurs so near the middle of the book, and then is not mentioned again. [GFD]

113. See John 1:14. [GFD]

114. "Moses" here, by Jewish and by standard eighteenth-century conventions, refers to the first five books of the Bible (Genesis, Exodus, Leviticus, Numbers, and Deuteronomy), and "the prophets" includes the "former prophets" that we now refer to as the historical books, Joshua through Second Kings, as well as the "latter prophets," Isaiah through Malachi. "Moses and the prophets," then, or "the law and the prophets," means the most essential books of the Hebrew Bible. [GFD]

Notes to §§222–229

115. This may be taken as a reference to the general principle articulated elsewhere that all perception depends on contrast. See, for example, *Secrets of Heaven* 2694:2, 7812; *Divine Providence* 24. [GFD]

116. This line of text in the first edition ends with a word break *(Mun-)* that is not completed in the next line. While the syllable that needs to be supplied is obvious *(-di,* yielding *Mundi,* "of [the] world"), and the text is translatable with this addition, the omission suggests that a line of type may have been lost. [GFD]

117. In his earlier scientific theorizing, Swedenborg had dealt with this problem by positing a "first natural point" of pure but complex motion, whose compounds were characterized by successively simpler forms of motion until they finally yielded the relatively inert form of physical matter. For Swedenborg's original exposition of these concepts, see Swedenborg 1734, 27–122 (= Swedenborg [1734] 1846, 46–208); for a convenient summary, see Sigstedt 1981, 111–114. [GFD]

118. See particularly §§307–318. [GFD]

Notes to §§230–235

119. See §§28–33, 4–5, and 17 and 44, respectively. [GFD]

120. Although these two kingdoms and three levels of heaven clearly relate to the two kingdoms and the three heavens discussed in *Heaven and Hell* 20–28 and 29–40, and although the two kingdoms are a recurring theme throughout Swedenborg's theological works, as are the three heavens, nevertheless the relationship between the kingdoms and the heavens is difficult to establish. One possibility is that the two kingdoms are equivalent to the two higher heavens, as a few passages seem to state directly (*Secrets of Heaven* 5922:2, 6417; see also *Sacred Scripture* 6). However, Swedenborg devotes separate chapters to the two kingdoms and the three heavens in *Heaven and Hell,* and does not mention this identification in either chapter. Another possibility is that the kingdoms constitute a "vertical" division and the heavens a "horizontal" division; that is, each of the two kingdoms has parts of all three heavens within it. This view is suggested by the way they are mapped onto the human body (see *Heaven and Hell* 29, 65, 95), by the statement that each kingdom is partitioned into three (*Secrets of Heaven* 10079:1), by other references to multiple heavens in each kingdom (*Secrets of Heaven* 10068, 10150; *Life* 32), and by the differentiation of the lowest heaven into a spiritual-earthly and a heavenly-earthly section (*Heaven and Hell* 31). The passage at hand contains one of the few explicit references in the theological works to a third kingdom that is "natural" or "earthly." Here and in another passage it is said to consist of people in our world (*Sacred Scripture* 34). However, in Swedenborg's last theological work, *True Christianity* 195, he makes statements that are surprising in light of his previous exposition of this topic. The "earthly kingdom" is said to be a third kingdom in the spiritual world; it is said to be equivalent to the lowest of the three heavens; and individuals in our world are said to belong to any of the three heavenly kingdoms. The novel features in the account in *True Christianity* are especially striking because they occur in a lengthy description otherwise copied quite closely from a passage in an earlier work by Swedenborg, *Sacred Scripture* 6. [JSR]

121. See especially §§319–335. [GFD]

122. For Swedenborg's use of the word "church," see note 25 above. [JSR]

123. See *Secrets of Heaven* 4288:2 for an extended definition of the *ecclesia repraesentativa* or "representational church." It centers in the performance of symbolic acts with a knowledge of their spiritual intent—a kind of self-conscious imaging of the spiritual in the physical, as distinguished from either a spontaneous responsiveness to the inner promptings of the divine presence or an empty, meaningless ritualism. [GFD]

124. While this sentence is set in quotation marks in the first edition, it is a paraphrase rather than a direct quotation, in accordance with the somewhat looser conventions for quotations obtaining during the eighteenth century. [GFD]

125. These passages mention the Lord as "your eternal light" and "the morning light" when "the sun rises, a morning without clouds," and describe Christ's face as "shining like the sun" during his transfiguration. [GFD]

Note to §§236–241

126. In §§115–116 above, Swedenborg has insisted that these abilities, rationality and freedom, are not "ours," but that they must seem to be so if we are to enter voluntarily into a relationship with the Lord. This theme receives concentrated attention in *Divine Providence* 154–213, with the particularly strong statement in §191 that our own prudence is nothing; "it only seems to be something, as it should." See also the statement in §42 of that work that "The more closely we are united to the Lord, the more clearly we seem to have our own identity, and yet the more obvious it is to us that we belong to the Lord." The principle has its most compact and frequent expression in statements that we are to abstain from evils "as if we were doing so on our own" (Latin *sicut a se*), but should acknowledge that this is actually the Lord's work in us. A summary treatment of the principle may be found in *Life* 101–107. [GFD]

Notes to §§242–247

127. In the first edition, this and the next section were both numbered 243. [GFD]

128. The translation here reads "his wisdom" rather than "its wisdom," although the antecedent of the pronoun is "the sun of heaven," because Swedenborg here uses the Latin pronoun *Ipsius*, which is normally reserved for reference to the Lord in human form. In the initial discussion of the sun of the spiritual world, Swedenborg instead regularly uses forms of the Latin pronoun *ille*, meaning roughly "that one." [GFD]

Notes to §§248–255

129. Reading *quid*, "what," for the obviously erroneous *quin*, "rather," of the first edition. [GFD]

130. A slightly more detailed description of this phenomenon of people on earth appearing and then disappearing before angels is offered in *Heaven and Hell* 438. [GFD]

131. The Latin here translated "becomes sickening" is *fit nausea*, literally, "becomes nausea" or seasickness. [GFD]

132. The reference may be to §346. [GFD]

133. On a number of occasions, Swedenborg takes note of how much animals "know"—for instance, birds know how and where to nest, bees know how to construct

and tend their cells, and animals in general know what foods they need. See, for example, §§351–355 below and *Heaven and Hell* 108. Swedenborg also notes what animals generally love: to feed themselves, to live in safety, to propagate their species, and to rear their young (*Secrets of Heaven* 7750:1; see also *Secrets of Heaven* 4776:4, 6323:2). He asserts that love and knowledge are separable in humans but inseparable in animals (see *Marriage Love* 96). [JSR]

Notes to §§256–259

134. For more on the physical "covering" that our spirits have, see §388 below and the discussion in *True Christianity* 103:1 of a permanent physical "border" (Latin *limbus*) that remains around our spirit after death. [JSR]

135. This reference to "climbing" suggests the spiral figure that will be introduced more explicitly in §270 below. [GFD]

Notes to §§260–263

136. The Latin phrase here translated "serve" is *& inserviunt,* "and serve." The *&* (the symbol for Latin *et,* "and") may simply have been inserted by mistake, or it may indicate that some text that was to appear before it has been omitted. [GFD]

137. See note 31 above. [GFD]

138. "The spiral" refers to the shape and orientation of the mind; see further in this section and §270 below. [JSR]

139. On reformation and regeneration, see notes 105 above and 230 below. [GFD]

Notes to §§264–270

140. On nature creating itself, see note 40 above. [JSR]

141. Although it is not certain which particular thinkers Swedenborg had in mind, the notion that religion is a device for repressing the simple people was a philosophical commonplace throughout the Enlightenment period. For example, in the early Enlightenment the English philosopher Thomas Hobbes (1588–1679) describes ancient rulers using religion "to keep the people in obedience and peace" (Hobbes [1651] 1952, 82); and in 1765, shortly after the publication of *Divine Love and Wisdom,* the *philosophe* Voltaire (1694–1778) asserted in his *Dictionnaire philosophique* (Philosophical Dictionary), that the first kings used the superstitions arising from the effects of nature "to cement their power" (Voltaire 1765, under the entry "God"). [SS]

142. It is worth pointing out that Swedenborg does not seem to be referring to the Enlightenment dispute as to whether or not God intervenes in the physical universe to keep it running. He is, rather, referring to the question raised by French philosopher Nicolas de Malebranche (1638–1715) as to whether God's providence is *general* or *particular;* that is, whether all it does is maintain the universe on a large scale (that is, acts in general) or whether it also intervenes in even the smallest matters (acts on particulars). Both Malebranche and other thinkers in the Enlightenment refused to accept particular providence. For example, in the *Philosophical Dictionary* (see note 141 above), Voltaire tells a parable about a Catholic nun who believes she has brought her pet sparrow back to life by saying nine Hail Marys. A figure called "the Metaphysician" tells her: "I

believe in general providence, my dear Sister—that providence from which there has emanated throughout eternity the law that rules all things, as light bursts forth from the sun; but I don't in the least believe that a particular providence tinkers with the plan of the universe for the sake of your sparrow" (Voltaire 1765, under the entry "Providence"). The providential action of God in the world was also called into question by the *philosophes* in their belittling of biblical stories and in the searing irony of such works as Voltaire's *Candide* (1759). See also note 188 below. [GRJ, SS]

143. Niccolò Machiavelli (1469–1527) was a Florentine statesman and writer. In works such as *Il principe* (The Prince, 1513), he proposed what he saw as realistic solutions for the dire political chaos of the Italy of the early *cinquecento*. "A prince," he says, "cannot observe all those things which are considered good in men, being often obliged, in order to maintain the state, to act against faith, against charity, against humanity, and against religion" (Machiavelli [1513] 1950, 65). Such policies were in sharp contrast to the idealism that had pervaded political treatises before his time, and his name quickly became synonymous with the cynical and amoral use of power. [SS]

144. The medieval *disputatio,* "disputation," a system of education by debate, was still utilized in universities in Swedenborg's time, and Swedenborg is known to have participated in it (Broberg 1988, 284). In these disputations, a student defending a point of view would first entertain objections to it; he would then attack the objections and thus vindicate the proposed thesis. Written Scholastic argumentation assumed the same pattern. Students were also required to argue for or against propositions at the whim of their professor; and in some cases, scholars themselves called for *quaestiones quodlibetales,* "questions on any topic you like" (Colish 1997, 272), which inevitably led to showcase defenses of absurd positions. Implicit in these educational methods was the notion that an able scholar should be able to prove anything true. For a detailed argument of this kind, "proving" that crows are white, see *True Christianity* 334:5; compare *Marriage Love* 233:4; *Divine Providence* 318:4; and Swedenborg's unpublished manuscript of 1759, *Revelation Explained* (= Swedenborg 1997a) §824:2. [JSR, SS]

145. The terminology here indicates that for Swedenborg "love" and "life" can be virtually synonymous. For an indication of the importance of this relationship, see §1 above. [GFD]

146. The view that in conception the father contributes the spiritual or formal element of the offspring while the mother contributes only the material element dates back at least as far as Aristotle (*Generation of Animals* 1:20–22). See also Lacus Curtius Pliny (Pliny the Elder, 23/24–79 C.E.) *Natural History* 7:15. This view was widely accepted until the late Renaissance and continued to be a live option in debates about generation well into the eighteenth century. See also Pinto-Correia 1997. [GRJ]

147. The subject is touched on briefly in §419, in the course of Swedenborg's extended exploration of the correspondence of heart and lungs to volition and discernment. [GFD]

Notes to §§271–276

148. On the form derived from the substances of the two worlds woven together in our brains, see §§257 and 260 above. [GFD]

149. In §398 below, Swedenborg introduces a description of the way the soul acts on the body by listing twenty-two statements; these points are then developed sequentially in §§399–429. [GFD]

150. See §§179–263, especially §§184, 189–194. [JSR]

151. See note 77 above. [JSR]

Note to §§277–281

152. For our being judged according to our works, see, for example, Matthew 16:27; Romans 2:6. For our having to give an account of our words, see Matthew 12:36. [GFD]

Notes to §§282–284

153. See Exodus 3:14–15; see also *True Christianity* 9:2–3; 19:1. [JSR]

154. The work mentioned here, *The Lord,* cites scriptural passages on the Lord's existence before incarnation in §37, and passages that equate "Jehovah" and "the Lord" in §38. [GFD]

155. See John 13:13: "You call me 'the teacher' and 'the Lord,' and you speak well, for I am." [GFD]

156. Following a long-standing Christian tradition, Swedenborg referred to the Hebrew Scriptures as "the Old Testament." [JSR]

157. A "Gordian knot" means a complicated, unsolvable tangle or problem. Legend has it that the original Gordian knot was tied by a King Gordius of Phrygia in central Asia Minor. An oracle stated that whoever could untangle the knot would rule Asia. Alexander the Great (356–323 B.C.E.) is said to have discovered a solution to the Gordian knot when he visited Phrygia in 333 B.C.E.: he slashed it in half with his sword. See Arrian *Anabasis of Alexander* 2:3. [JSR]

158. See §§305–306 for specific attention to this subject. What Swedenborg means by "other things" here may remain a matter of conjecture. [GFD]

Notes to §§285–289

159. The Latin phrase here translated "a human God" is *Deus ut Homo,* literally, "God as a human." Subsequently Swedenborg goes back to using the term *Deus Homo,* translated "the Divine-Human One" (see note 19 above). [GFD]

160. The reference is to Swedenborg's work titled *Secrets of Heaven,* originally published in eight volumes between 1749 and 1756. See the list of references to it in §377 below. For a collection of such passages, see Swedenborg 1984. [JSR]

Notes to §§290–295

161. Unlike the preceding sentences in this list, which have been taken word for word or with slight alterations from topic sentences at the places referenced, this sentence is not closely paralleled in the material cited. [GFD]

162. See, for example, Swedenborg's experiments with earthly and spiritual language as reported in *Marriage Love* 326 and the parallel passage *True Christianity* 280. [JSR]

Notes to §§296–301

163. See, for example, §§176, 183, 257, and 260. [GFD]

164. This reflects the logic by which Swedenborg insisted on the existence of an ether. See notes 35, 63, and 101 above. [GFD]

165. Levels are discussed in §§184–188 above. [GFD]

166. The phrase here translated "in God we live and move and have our being" is an allusion to Acts 17:28, where in his speech to the Athenians on Mars Hill, the apostle Paul (possibly quoting Epimenides, a Cretan holy figure of the seventh or sixth century B.C.E.) says, "For in him we live and move and have our being." [GFD]

Note to §§302–304

167. The Latin here translated "material substances" is *substantiarum & materiarum,* literally, "substances and matters." The recurrent phrase is here interpreted as hendiadys (a figure of speech in which one thing is given two names), since in the paragraph immediately preceding, *materia,* "matter," is treated as a synonym of *substantiae,* "substances." [GFD]

Note to §§307–318

168. See especially §§209–221 above. [JSR]

Notes to §§319–326

169. The microcosm-macrocosm analogy apparently originates in Plato's *Timaeus,* in the discourse of the Pythagorean philosopher Timaeus of Locri (who, if he is not an invention of Plato, could be presumed to have lived in the fifth century B.C.E.). There it is claimed that the soul of humankind is made on the same model as the soul of the cosmos, although of inferior materials, and is then encased in a material body. See Plato *Timaeus* 40a–42d. [GRJ]

170. Where this translation reads "in this physical world," the first edition has *in Mundo spirituali,* "in the spiritual world," a reading that offers no basis for the contrast implicit in the following sentence. [GFD]

Note to §§327–335

171. The Latin word here translated "focus on self" is *proprium,* an adjective used as a noun to mean "what is our own." Since Swedenborg insists that in the last analysis nothing is really "our own," *proprium* more precisely denotes what we claim as our own. Swedenborg uses the Latin term with a wide range of meanings that extend from a healthy sense of self to an evil preoccupation with self; see, for example, *Secrets of Heaven* 141, 1937, and 5660. [GFD]

Notes to §§336–348

172. The Latin word here translated "lizards" is *dracones,* which may also mean "dragons" and "serpents." [GFD]

173. The Latin words here translated "owls" are *bubones* and *ululae,* two kinds of nocturnal bird, both of which we now know as owls but which were apparently considered in Swedenborg's time to be categorically different. The two terms appear as

separate items in other general lists at §339 just below and in *Divine Providence* 292:2, 296:2; *Revelation Unveiled* 757:4; and *True Christianity* 78:5, 531. Lexicographers generally render them both as "owls," although *bubones* are sometimes specified as "barn owls" or "tawny owls" and *ululae* as "screech owls." [GFD, JSR]

174. The Latin words here translated "night birds, owls" are *bubones, noctuae, ululae*. *Noctuae* are "night birds." For the reason that *bubones* and *ululae* are translated simply as "owls," see note 173 just above. [JSR]

175. The Latin words here translated "toxic and dangerous things of all kinds, and poisons" are *toxica et cicutae omnis generis, et aconita*, literally, "poisons and all kinds of hemlocks, and aconites." [GFD]

176. This 1764 work by Swedenborg is referred to in this edition by the short title *Divine Providence*. See especially *Divine Providence* 234–274. [GFD]

177. The Latin phrase here translated "the dust of doom" is *pulvis damnatus*, literally, "damned dust." While Swedenborg usually uses *damnatus*, "damned," in the obvious sense of "condemned to hell," he does occasionally use it in ways that suggest connection with *damnum*, "injury," "harm," as in *Secrets of Heaven* 130. A meaning of this sort seems appropriate also in the only other occurrence of the phrase, *Revelation Unveiled* 153:10 (with a parallel passage in *True Christianity* 281:10), where a bed of such dust is clearly a place of particular torment. [GFD]

178. Swedenborg here argues for "spontaneous generation" or "abiogenesis," a concept widely held until the seventeenth century, and still debated in the eighteenth, that under certain circumstances living creatures, especially smaller ones, are spawned by nonliving matter. For a history of the concept, see Farley 1977. [JSR]

179. The Latin phrase here translated "spontaneous generation" is *exortus eorum immediatos*, very literally, "their unmediated arisings." See note 178. [GFD]

180. In the present work, Swedenborg normally refers to passages that appear later in the book by subject rather than by section number, suggesting that he had a reasonably detailed outline before him. Where he does refer to a specific number, as here, we may presume that he inserted it when he made his fair copy for the printer. [GFD]

181. Sir Hans Sloane (1660–1753) was a member of the British Royal Society who invited Swedenborg to become a corresponding member in 1724 (Tafel 1875, 339–340). In 1727 he succeeded Sir Isaac Newton as president of the Society, and remained in that office until 1741. It was his collection that constituted the first phase of the British Museum. [GFD]

182. Martin Folkes (1690–1754), known primarily as a published numismatist, succeeded Sir Hans Sloane as the president of the Royal Society from 1741 to 1752. Swedenborg is incorrect in ascribing a noble title to him. [GFD]

183. See especially §§236–241 and 248–255. [GFD]

184. Swedenborg's uncharacteristic leap here from animals to minerals without any mention of plants suggests that some text may have been omitted. [GFD]

185. See especially the predictions in Deuteronomy 28:15–68. [JSR]

186. For the plague of locusts, see Exodus 10:1–20; for the plague of frogs, see Exodus 8:1–15; for the plague of lice, see Exodus 8:16–19. The listing of these three plagues is probably intended to refer the reader in general to the plagues on the Egyptians described in Exodus 7–12. [JSR]

187. Although it clearly belongs here, the number of the proposition is omitted in the first edition. [GFD]

Notes to §§349–357

188. The theological position Swedenborg describes here holds that God withdrew from further interaction with the universe after creating nature and endowing it with the ability to produce independently the conditions requisite for life. This position was sometimes imputed to adherents of the philosophical school known as Deism. Generally speaking, the Deists held that the most important religious beliefs were innate or natural to humankind—specifically, that there was a Supreme Being and that humans owed worship, an upright moral life, and repentance to that Being. Many Deists also believed in the afterlife. Few would have subscribed to the extreme view described in this passage, though it was imputed to them so effectively that during the nineteenth and early twentieth centuries the term Deism came to refer principally to this position. In this passage Swedenborg asserts that such a position is essentially atheistic, and that it is only professed as a cover to avoid the political or social opprobrium attached to atheism, as well as the legal consequences, which could be considerable in his day. [GFD, SS]

189. The Latin phrase here translated "in a mysterious 'elsewhere'" is *in aliquo ubi seu pu,* literally, "in some where? or where?" *ubi* being the Latin word for "where?" and *pu* (που) being its Greek equivalent. [GFD]

190. See note 48 above. [JSR]

Notes to §§358–361

191. For another seemingly pejorative statement on some women's ability to write, see *Marriage Love* 175:3. The Swiss-born philosopher Jean-Jacques Rousseau voiced a similar opinion (Kleinbaum 1977, 225–226). It should be noted, however, that even those women of this period who were taught to read were often not taught to write more than their signature (Wiesner 2000, 149–150; on women's education in general during this period, see Möbius 1984, 92–109; Sonnet 1993, 101–131; and Porter 2000, 320–338). It should also not be overlooked that women are here credited with the ability to think well, an assertion unrepresentative of the general views of Swedenborg's time (see the discussion in Kleinbaum 1977, 219–230). In practice, Swedenborg supported female authors. Just a few years before writing this statement, he had helped publish a two-volume work written by his friend Elisabet Stierncrona Gyllenborg (1714–1769) on the subject of theology ([Gyllenborg] 1756–1760; see Kirven and Larsen 1988, 44). Much earlier in his life (1710) Swedenborg had written a dedicatory poem praising the writing skills of Sophia Elisabeth Brenner (1659–1730); it was published along with her work (Brenner 1713; for an English translation of and commentary on this poem, see Swedenborg 1995, 67, 152–154). [GFD, SS]

192. See note 166 above. [GFD]

Notes to §§362–370

193. Swedenborg may be referring to the growth of the fibers in the embryo, which occurs from the brain outward ("downward") to the rest of the body. The nerves are only then differentiated into the categories of efferent (nerves bearing output from the brain) and afferent (nerves bearing input to the brain). No nerve growth occurs from the body to the brain ("upward") during the development of the embryo. [RPB]

194. René Descartes argued that the seat of the soul is the pineal gland in the brain (Descartes 1650 [= Descartes [1650] 1985 = Descartes [1650] 1989] articles 31–47). In article 33 of his discussion of the pineal gland, he also disputes the traditional claim that the heart is the seat of the soul, a view that was shared by the ancient Egyptians, Mesopotamians, Hebrews, and Greeks. See Onians 1954, especially 23–65. [GRJ]

Notes to §§371–393

195. Swedenborg held the view that the brain is the seat of the soul, and he included in the soul the faculties of volition and discernment. This view paralleled the findings of contemporary science, which situated conscious thought in the brain. Here, however, Swedenborg claims that there is a further *correspondence* of volition with the heart and of discernment with the lungs. (On correspondence, see notes 4 and 64 above.) Thus in addition to maintaining the scientific view of the brain as the location of the higher faculties, Swedenborg preserves the common identification of the heart as the seat of love, as found in ancient and modern popular thought and poetry. He also preserves the less common identification of the lungs as the seat of discernment. An example of such an identification is the ancient Greek concept of φρήν *(phrén),* the mind as situated in the lungs and/or diaphragm. See Onians 1954, 23–43. [GRJ]

196. The first edition here cites Swedenborg's 1763 work *Teachings for the New Jerusalem on the Lord,* but the reference is clearly to another 1763 work, *Sacred Scripture.* [JSR]

197. For a discussion of this ancient attribution of the feelings to the heart, see Onians 1954, 23–65. [GRJ]

198. In Latin the words here translated "concord and discord and envy" are *concordia, discordia,* and *vecordia* respectively, all compounds of the Latin word *cor,* "heart." [GFD]

199. When Swedenborg was a child, he discovered the correlation of breath and thought and consequently the possibility of controlling thought by controlling the breath; he also noticed at certain points that when he was deep in thought, his breathing virtually ceased (see Swedenborg's 1745–1765 manuscript, *Spiritual Experiences* [= Swedenborg 2002] §§3320, 3321, and *Spiritual Experiences* [= Swedenborg 1889] §3464). This remained characteristic of at least some of his paranormal experiences in later life. However, it should be noted that he describes having conversations in the spirit while conscious in the body and in the company of others (see, for example, Swedenborg's unpublished manuscript of 1745–1747, *The Old Testament Explained* [= Swedenborg 1927–1951] §943), when he was presumably physically active. He is also described by witnesses as speaking audibly in some of his conversations with spirits (Tafel 1875, 39, 41). See also §391 below. [GFD, GRJ]

200. On the identification of spirit and breath, see Onians 1954, 23–65. [GRJ]

201. The Latin word here translated "breathing" is *animatione,* literally, "moving with soul/life/breath." [GFD]

202. The Latin expression here translated "breathing their last" is *emittat animam,* literally, "sending out the soul/life/breath." [GFD]

203. This alternative definition does not seem to accord with its predecessor: the first definition suggests that truth and goodness come from each other, while the second speaks only of goodness yielding truth. [GFD]

204. The Latin idiom here translated "'the last breath' or 'giving up the ghost'" is *emittere spiritum aut animam,* literally, "to send out the spirit or soul/life/breath." [GFD]

205. The work mentioned here was published by Swedenborg in 1763. It is referred to in this edition by the short title *Supplements.* [JSR]

206. For more on this permanent physical vessel for our spirit after death, elsewhere called a "border," see §257 above, with note 134 there. [GFD]

207. See §400 below. [GFD]

Notes to §§394–431

208. As Swedenborg makes clear in the next sentence, the topic over which these people exercised themselves is the interaction of the soul and the body—that is, the question of how a noncorporeal entity, the soul, could act on a material entity, the body. This learned "host" would, then, include the defenders of the major positions on the soul-body interaction in the seventeenth and eighteenth centuries: (1) *preestablished harmony,* defended by Leibniz, which holds that no finite being, spiritual or material, causally interacts with any other being; that all modifications of a substance are produced spontaneously by the substance in accordance with its unique, divinely created and sustained nature; and that all apparent causal interactions between substances are merely apparent, the product of the harmonious coordination of substances and their spontaneous self-modification established at the time of creation; (2) *physical influx,* which holds that bodies affect minds, a theory associated with Aristotle, the Scholastics, and English philosopher John Locke (1632–1704); and (3) *spiritual influx,* which holds that material bodies are inert, and that all motion must, therefore, come from nonmaterial vital or animating principles, such as spirits or minds. When applied to cognition, the spiritual influx theory stresses the importance of the subject's spontaneous and vivifying activity in transforming the inert matter of sensibility into cognition. Spiritual influx was defended by Swedenborg, the Swiss-born philosopher Jean-Jacques Rousseau (1712–1778), and the German philosopher Immanuel Kant (1724–1804). Also classified under spiritual influx is the system of *occasionalism* defended by Nicolas de Malebranche (1638–1715), Géraud de Cordemoy (1626–1684), and Arnold Geulincx (1624–1669), which holds that no finite being, spiritual or material, has any causal efficacy whatsoever, and that God is the sole cause of all interactions, whether between bodies, between minds, or between minds and bodies. René Descartes can be classified both as a physical and a spiritual influx theorist because in truth he defended both positions. Swedenborg classified him as a spiritual influx theorist, in fact as an occasionalist, in *Soul-Body Interaction* 19, where he names particular members of this learned host: Aristotle, Descartes, Leibniz, and Christian Wolff (1679–1754), whom he saw in the spiritual world. [GRJ]

209. Here Swedenborg might be alluding to himself in years past as one such researcher. His spiritual breakthrough came in the course of his lengthy search for the soul in its "kingdom," the human body. This effort had led to the publication in 1740 and 1741 of the two volumes of *Oeconomia Regni Animalis* (traditionally translated as *The Economy of the Animal Kingdom* [= Swedenborg [1740–1741] 1955] but more accurately rendered as *Dynamics of the Soul's Domain*) and in 1744–1745 of three volumes of *Regnum Animale* (again, traditionally *The Animal Kingdom* [= Swedenborg [1744–1745] 1960], more accurately *The Soul's Domain*). Besides these published works, he also

developed a substantial amount of material for projected subsequent volumes. This massive effort must have been in his mind as he began the present paragraph. [GFD]

210. An "ether," "etherical," or "astral" body is a "subtle" material body that serves as the vehicle of the soul. The ether body pervades the gross matter of the living body, infusing it with life and sensation. When the gross material body dies, the ether body remains alive as the vehicle in which the soul departs. The idea of the ether or astral body has ancient origins and is central to theosophical currents of thought to this very day. It can be traced back to Aristotle, and hints can be seen even in Plato (427–347 B.C.E.). Aristotle argued that the heavenly bodies must be composed of a fifth element that is not subject to decay and moves always in a circle (*On the Heavens* 1:2). He called this element ether (*On the Heavens* 1:3). Since ether is the stuff of *stars* (Greek ἄστρα, *ástra*), the terms "ether" and "astral" function as synonyms. Aristotle also argued that ether is present in our sense organs and in semen. In both cases, it plays the same role: as the diaphanous medium for the transmission of form. These elements were synthesized together by later thinkers, from Plotinus (205–270) to Marsilio Ficino (1433–1499) and Paracelsus (Theophrastus Bombastus von Hohenheim, 1493–1541) to Helena Petrovna Blavatsky (1831–1891), into the idea of the ether body. See Peck 1953, 111–121, and Solmsen 1957, 119–123. [GRJ]

211. On the theories of inflow and harmony, see note 208 above and *Soul-Body Interaction* throughout. [GRJ]

212. The first edition here reads *&*, the symbol for *et*, "and," instead of the clearly necessary *seu*, "or." [GFD]

213. Freedom and rationality form a major theme in Swedenborg's immediately subsequent work, *Divine Providence*. The first of the "laws" there presented is that providence acts constantly to enable us to act in freedom according to reason. See especially §§71–99. [GFD]

214. As in §40 above, Swedenborg here again uses a singular verb "is" with the plural subject "divine love and wisdom," perhaps to indicate their underlying unity. See the first sentence of note 34 above. [GFD]

215. The Latin word here translated "his" is *Ipsius*, a pronoun that is usually reserved for referring to the Lord in human form. Its use here suggests that such apparently impersonal words as "love" and "wisdom" are actually intended to convey something personal and human. Compare note 128 above. [GFD]

216. Swedenborg must have been well aware that as infants develop in the womb, they do begin to move. It seems probable that by sensation and action in this context he means conscious or deliberate sensation and action. [GFD]

217. See §405 above for a description of the two components of the circulatory system—the pulmonary and the bronchial—linking the heart and lungs. The notion that bronchial circulation ceases when respiration is forcibly curtailed is consistent with a mechanism for respiration Swedenborg proposes in *The Soul's Domain* (= Swedenborg [1744–1745] 1960) §§2:408–409, 457, in his unpublished manuscript of 1738–1740 *The Fiber* (= Swedenborg 1918) §551, and elsewhere in his scientific works. According to this model, the bronchial arteries run parallel to the pulmonary, and communicate with them at their deepest level; and it is through the bronchial veins that nourishing blood eventually reaches the muscles of respiration. This nourishment is a primary cause of respiration, apart from the secondary local stimulation of bronchial nerves by respiratory motion. In that sense it "gives us the ability to breathe." Interruption of the air

supply would not at first greatly disturb pulmonary circulation, but would immediately degrade the quality of blood going to the muscles of respiration and cause their motion to cease. Though the growth of scientific knowledge since Swedenborg's time has outstripped the factual basis of the illustration he has chosen, the theological exposition remains clear. For further discussion of the theory of bronchial and pulmonary blood in Swedenborg, see Beekman 1902, 16–18. [RPB]

218. The union of what is evil and what is false has been mentioned in previous works, specifically in *Heaven and Hell* 377, 422, and 425 and in *New Jerusalem* 17. An extensive discussion later than the present passage occurs in *True Christianity* 398. [GFD]

219. The pronoun "it" here has no clear antecedent in the original Latin, but its gender in context suggests that it refers to "wisdom." [GFD]

220. While the Latin of the first edition has only *id*, "it," where the translation has "[what is true]," the bracketed phrase is supplied on the basis of propositions 6–8 in §398 above. [GFD]

221. The Latin word here translated "bronchial tube" is *ramis*, literally, "branches." [GFD]

222. On the notion that breathing stops when the inflow of bronchial blood stops, see §407 and note 217 above. [RPB]

223. See, for example, §§243, 266. [JSR]

224. The Latin phrase here translated "wisdom and heavenly love" is *amoris coelestis & sapientiae*, literally, "love heavenly and wisdom." The translation alters the word order to indicate that the adjective "heavenly" modifies "love" but not "wisdom." [GFD]

225. Swedenborg defines chastity not as sexual celibacy or abstinence but as a faithful sexual relationship between husband and wife. See *Marriage Love* 138–155b. [JSR]

226. At the time when Swedenborg wrote *Divine Love and Wisdom* (1763), all that was known about respiration was that through the respiratory process some substance needed by the body is absorbed and a waste product is eliminated. The expository assertions Swedenborg uses in describing the physical function of the lungs ("Undeniably . . . it is undeniable that . . . This is why . . . All this shows . . .") indicate his recognition of the limited nature of contemporary knowledge and of the need to offer a viable theory of respiration to his readers. The specific role of oxygen and carbon dioxide in respiration was not fully recognized until the work of the French chemist Antoine-Laurent Lavoisier (1743–1794), based on an experiment made in 1777, although oxygen had been obtained from mercuric oxide by both the Swedish apothecary Carl Scheele (1742–1786) about 1772 and by the English scientist Joseph Priestley (1733–1804) in 1774. [SS]

227. The term *spiritus animalis*, usually translated "animal spirit(s)," literally means "distilled liquid of the soul." Though the term was widely employed in varying meanings by other philosophers (Odhner 1933, 218–223), in Swedenborg's physical theory it refers to an extremely fine fluid associated with the soul. For a discussion of the term, including references to its occurrences in Swedenborg's scientific works, see Odhner 1933; for a translation of Swedenborg's unpublished work on the topic, see Swedenborg 1917. [GFD, SS]

228. See §420 and earlier in this section itself. [JSR]

229. Swedenborg uses the image of the contrast between the beautiful exterior and

corrupt interior of mummies several times in his theological works; see, for example, *Secrets of Heaven* 876. For his mention of mummies among the sights at the museum in Copenhagen, see the entry in his travel journal for July 23, 1736, in Tafel 1877, 1:79–80. [SS]

230. As is most frequently the case, Swedenborg here uses the verb *regenerari,* traditionally translated "to be regenerated," in preference to other possible ways of expressing the general notion of spiritual renewal. In a number of passages, he treats this verb as a synonym of *renasci,* "to be reborn" (see *Secrets of Heaven* 1255, 3138, 3203, 3860, 4904, 5116:1, 5117:1, 5160, 5236:2, and especially 10367:3–4; *Heaven and Hell* 279; and *Divine Providence* 83). *Renasci* is particularly frequent in the statements of traditional Christian doctrine in *Survey;* and we may assume that it was the term most familiar to Swedenborg from his intense engagement with Lutheran Pietism in his childhood and youth. It may be that the preference for *regenerari* is intended to call attention to the Lord's parental role in the process, a nuance that the English "regenerate" does not convey. It is worth noting also that Swedenborg does on occasion refer to us as being "reborn by the Lord"—see *Secrets of Heaven* 1255, 3138, 3860, and 10367:3, with possible further examples in §§3203:2 and 4925:1. [GFD]

231. The work mentioned here was published by Swedenborg in 1763. It is referred to in this edition by the short title *Life.* [JSR]

232. The Latin word here translated "our own image" is *proprium,* literally, "what is our own." Swedenborg regularly uses the word to denote whatever we claim as our own and associates it with taking credit for whatever good we may do. For more on the meaning of this term, see note 171 above. [GFD]

233. The mention of serving two masters at the same time is a reference to Matthew 6:24 and Luke 16:13. [GFD]

Note to §432

234. Swedenborg refers here to the position known as "preformationism," the view that the human form is fully developed at conception and simply grows larger. "Epigenesis," the opposing position defended by Swedenborg, holds that after conception the human form develops over time. On seventeenth- and eighteenth-century debates on conception, see Pinto-Correia 1997. [GRJ]

Works Cited
in the Notes

Acton, Alfred. 1955. *The Letters and Memorials of Emanuel Swedenborg.* Vol. 2. Bryn Athyn, Pa.: Swedenborg Scientific Association.

Aquinas, Thomas. 1952. *Summa Theologiae.* Translated by the Fathers of the English Dominican Province, revised by Daniel J. Sullivan. Vols. 19–20 of *Great Books of the Western World.* Chicago: Encyclopedia Britannica.

Beekman, Lillian. 1902. "Connection of Respiration with Muscular Control." *The New Philosophy* 5:10–18.

Berkeley, George. [1710] 1952. *The Principles of Human Knowledge.* In vol. 35 of *Great Books of the Western World.* Chicago: Encyclopedia Britannica.

Brenner, Sophia Elisabeth. 1713. *Sophiae Elisabeth Brenners uti åtskillige språk, tider och tillfällen författade poetiske dikter.* [Edited by Urban Hjärne.] Stockholm: Julius Georg Matthiae.

Broberg, Gunnar. 1988. "Swedenborg and Uppsala." Translated by Gunilla Stenman Gado. In *Emanuel Swedenborg: A Continuing Vision.* Edited by Robin Larsen. New York: Swedenborg Foundation.

Colish, Marcia L. 1997. *Medieval Foundations of the Western Intellectual Tradition, 400–1400.* New Haven: Yale University Press.

Deleuze, Gilles. 1992. *The Fold: Leibniz and the Baroque.* Translated by Tom Conley. Minneapolis: University of Minnesota Press.

Descartes, René. 1650. *Les passions de l'âme.* Paris: Augustin Courbé.

———. [1637] 1952. *Discourse on the Method of Rightly Conducting the Reason.* Translated by Elizabeth S. Haldane and G.R.T. Ross. In vol. 31 of *Great Books of the Western World.* Chicago: Encyclopedia Britannica.

———. [1641] 1952. *Objections against the Meditations and Replies.* Translated by Elizabeth S. Haldane and G.R.T. Ross. In vol. 31 of *Great Books of the Western World.* Chicago: Encyclopedia Britannica.

———. [1650] 1985. *The Passions of the Soul.* Translated by Robert Stoothoff. In vol. 1 of *The Philosophical Writings of Descartes.* Cambridge: Cambridge University Press.

———. [1650] 1989. *The Passions of the Soul.* Translated by Stephen H. Voss. Indianapolis: Hackett.

Farley, John. 1977. *The Spontaneous Generation Controversy from Descartes to Oparin.* Baltimore: Johns Hopkins University Press.

[Gyllenborg, Elisabet Stierncrona]. 1756–1760. *Marie bäste del eller Thet ena nödwändiga.* Vol 1. Stockholm: Lorentz Ludwig Grefing. Vol. 2. Stockholm: Lars Salvius.

Hite, Louis. [1910] 1988. "Love: The Ultimate Reality." In *Emanuel Swedenborg: A Continuing Vision.* Edited by Robin Larsen. New York: Swedenborg Foundation.

Hobbes, Thomas. [1651] 1952. *Leviathan.* In vol. 23 of *Great Books of the Western World.* Chicago: Encyclopedia Britannica.

Jammer, Max. 1962. *Concepts of Force: A Study in the Foundations of Dynamics.* New York: Harper and Brothers.

Kirk, G. S., J. E. Raven, and M. Schofield, eds. and trans. 1983. *The Presocratic Philosophers.* 2nd ed. Cambridge: Cambridge University Press.

Kirven, Robert H. and Robin Larsen. 1988. "Emanuel Swedenborg: A Pictorial Biography." In *Emanuel Swedenborg: A Continuing Vision.* Edited by Robin Larsen. New York: Swedenborg Foundation.

Kleinbaum, Abby R. 1977. "Women in the Age of Light." In *Becoming Visible: Women in European History.* Edited by Renate Bridenthal and Claudia Koonz. Boston: Houghton Mifflin.

Leibniz, Gottfried Wilhelm. [1840] 1959. *Opera Philosophica Quae Extant, Latina, Gallica, Germanica Omnia.* Edited by Johan Eduard Erdmann. Facsimile edition. Aalen: Scientia

Littleton, Adam. 1723. *Latin Dictionary in Four Parts.* 5th ed. London.

Machiavelli, Niccolò. [1513] 1950. *The Prince and the Discourses.* New York: Random House.

Möbius, Helga. 1984. *Woman of the Baroque Age.* Translated by Barbara Chruscik Beedham. Montclair, N.J.: Abner Schram.

Newton, Isaac. 1953. *Newton's Philosophy of Nature.* Edited by H. S. Thayer. New York: Hafner.

———. [1687] 1972. *Mathematical Principles of Natural Philosophy.* Translated by Andrew Motte, revised by Florian Cajori. In vol. 34 of *Great Books of the Western World.* Chicago: Encyclopedia Britannica.

———. [1704] 1972. *Optics.* In vol. 34 of *Great Books of the Western World.* Chicago: Encyclopedia Britannica.

Odhner, Hugo Lj. 1933. "The History of the 'Animal Spirits,' and of Swedenborg's Development of the Concept." *The New Philosophy* 36:218–223, 234–249.

Onians, Richard Broxton. 1954. *The Origins of European Thought about the Body, the Mind, the Soul, the World, Time, and Fate.* 2nd ed. Cambridge: Cambridge University Press.

Peck, A. L. 1953. "The Connate *Pneuma:* An Essential Factor in Aristotle's Solutions to the Problems of Reproduction and Sensation." In *Science, Medicine, and History: Essays on the Evolution of Scientific Thought and Medical Practice Written in Honour of Charles Singer.* Edited by E. Ashworth Underwood. Vol. 1. London: Oxford University Press.

Pinto-Correia, Clara. 1997. *The Ovary of Eve: Egg and Sperm and Preformation.* Chicago: University of Chicago Press.

Porter, Roy. 2000. *The Creation of the Modern World: The Untold Story of the British Enlightenment.* New York: W. W. Norton.

Sigstedt, Cyriel Odhner. 1981. *The Swedenborg Epic: The Life and Works of Emanuel Swedenborg.* New York: Bookman Associates, 1952. Reprint, London: Swedenborg Society.

Solmsen, Friedrich. 1957. "The Vital Heat, the Inborn *Pneuma,* and the *Aether." Journal of Hellenic Studies* 77:119-123.

Sonnet, Martine. 1993. "A Daughter to Educate." Translated by Arthur Goldhammer. In *A History of Women in the West,* vol. 3, *Renaissance and Enlightenment Paradoxes.* Edited by Natalie Z. Davis and Arlette Farge. Cambridge, Mass.: Belknap Press.

Spinoza, Benedict de. [1677] 1952. *Ethics.* Translated by W. H. White, revised by A. H. Stirling. In vol. 31 of *Great Books of the Western World.* Chicago: Encyclopedia Britannica.

Swammerdam, Jan. 1737–1738. *Biblia Naturae, sive Historia Insectorum, in Classes Certas Reducta.* Translated into Latin from the Dutch by H. D. Gaubius. Leyden: I. Severinus.

Swedenborg, Emanuel. 1734. *Principia Rerum Naturalium.* Dresden and Leipzig: Frederickus Hekelius.

———. [1734] 1846. *The Principia; or, The First Principles of Natural Things.* Translated by Augustus Clissold. London: W. Newbery.

———. 1917. *The Animal Spirit. The New Philosophy* 20:114–130.

———. 1918. *The Fibre.* Transaction 3 of *The Economy of the Animal Kingdom.* Translated and edited by Alfred Acton. Philadelphia: Swedenborg Scientific Association.

———. 1927–1951. *The Word Explained.* 10 vols. Translated and edited by Alfred Acton. Bryn Athyn: Academy of the New Church.

———. [1740–1741] 1955. *The Economy of the Animal Kingdom.* 2 vols. Translated by Augustus Clissold. London: W. Newbery, H. Bailliere; Boston: Otis Clapp, 1845–1846. Bryn Athyn, Pa.: Swedenborg Scientific Association. A more accurate translation of the title of this work is *Dynamics of the Soul's Domain.*

———. [1744–1745] 1960. *The Animal Kingdom.* 2 vols. Translated by J.J.G. Wilkinson. London: W. Newbery, 1843–1844. Bryn Athyn, Pa.: Swedenborg Scientific Association. A more accurate translation of the title of this work is *The Soul's Domain.*

———. 1984. *Emanuel Swedenborg: The Universal Human and Soul-Body Interaction.* Edited and translated by George F. Dole. New York: Paulist Press.

———. 1995. *Ludus Heliconius and Other Latin Poems.* Edited by Hans Helander. Uppsala.

———. 1997. *Apocalypse Explained.* 6 vols. Translated by John C. Ager, revised by John Whitehead, edited by William Ross Woofenden. West Chester, Pa.: Swedenborg Foundation.

———. 1999. *Emanuel Swedenborg's Diary, Recounting Spiritual Experiences.* Vol. 2. Translated by J. Durban Odhner. Bryn Athyn, Pa.: General Church of the New Jerusalem.

———. 2002. *Emanuel Swedenborg's Diary, Recounting Spiritual Experiences.* Vol. 3. Translated by J. Durban Odhner. Bryn Athyn, Pa.: General Church of the New Jerusalem.

Tafel, Rudoph L. 1875. *Documents Concerning the Life and Character of Emanuel Swedenborg.* Vol. 1. London: Swedenborg Society.

———. 1877. *Documents Concerning the Life and Character of Emanuel Swedenborg.* Vol. 2, parts 1–2. London: Swedenborg Society.

Theological Dictionary of the Old Testament. 1986. Edited by G. Johannes Botterweck and Helmer Ringgren, translated by John T. Willis. Vol. 5. Grand Rapids, Mich.: William B. Eerdmans.

Voltaire. 1765. *Dictionnaire Philosophique.* 5th ed. Amsterdam: Varberg.

———. [1759] 1966. *Candide, or Optimism.* Translated by R. M. Adams. New York: Norton.

Wiesner, Merry E. 2000. *Women and Gender in Early Modern Europe.* 2nd ed. Cambridge: Cambridge University Press.

Index to Preface, Introduction, and Notes

The following index, referenced by page number, covers material in the translator's preface, the introduction, and the scholars' notes. References to the Bible in this material are listed under the heading "Scripture references." (References to the Bible that appear in the translation proper are treated in a separate index.)

Index to Scriptural Passages
in *Divine Love and Wisdom*

The following index refers to passages from the Bible cited in the translation of *Divine Love and Wisdom*. The numbers to the left under each Bible book title are its chapter numbers. They are followed by verse numbers with the following designations: bold figures designate verses that are quoted; italic figures designate verses that are given in substance; figures in parenthesis indicate verses that are merely referred or alluded to. The numbers to the right are section numbers in *Divine Love and Wisdom*. (Passages from the Bible cited in the preface, introduction, and scholars' notes can be found under the heading "Scripture references" in the separate index of those elements.)

Table of Parallel Passages

The following table indicates passages in *Divine Love and Wisdom* that parallel passages in Swedenborg's other theological works. The table draws on John Faulkner Potts's *Swedenborg Concordance* (1902, London: Swedenborg Society) 6:859–864, and on the tables of parallel passages in Emanuel Swedenborg, *Delights of Wisdom Relating to Married Love,* translated by N. Bruce Rogers (1995, Bryn Athyn, Pennsylvania: General Church of the New Jerusalem), *Three Short Works,* translated by N. Bruce Rogers (1997, Bryn Athyn, Pennsylvania: General Church of the New Jerusalem), and *Angelic Wisdom Regarding Divine Love and Divine Wisdom,* translated by N. Bruce Rogers (1999, Bryn Athyn, Pennsylvania: General Church of the New Jerusalem).

Reference numbers in this table correspond to Swedenborg's section numbers; subsection numbers are separated from section numbers by a colon.

Divine Love and Wisdom	Parallel Passage
1	*Marriage Love* 34
6	*Sketch for Divine Love* 4 = II:2
7:1, 2	*True Christianity* 30:1
11:2	*Supplements* 74; *True Christianity* 836
82	*Sketch for Supplement to Last Judgment* 290 = 266
350	*Marriage Love* 422
351	*Marriage Love* 416:1–3; *True Christianity* 12:1–3
352	*Marriage Love* 416:4; *True Christianity* 12:4
353	*Marriage Love* 417; *True Christianity* 12:5
354	*Marriage Love* 418; *True Christianity* 12:6
355	*Marriage Love* 419; *True Christianity* 12:7, 8
356	*Marriage Love* 420; *True Christianity* 12:9; 13:3
357	*Marriage Love* 421; *True Christianity* 12:10
378	*Sketch for Divine Wisdom* 88 = VI:2, 3

Index to *Divine Love and Wisdom*

The following index covers the translation of *Divine Love and Wisdom*. For references to passages from the Bible and to topics treated in the preface, introduction, and scholars' notes, see the separate indexes to those elements.

Reference numbers in this index correspond to Swedenborg's section numbers in *Divine Love and Wisdom*.

DIVINE PROVIDENCE

Contents

Divine Providence

Notes and Indexes

Translator's Preface

I N 1745, at the age of fifty-seven, Swedenborg had an experience that
radically changed the course of his life.[1] Much later, he would describe
it as a vision of Jesus Christ commissioning him to "open to people the
spiritual meaning of Scripture"[2] and initiating years of regular experiences of the spiritual world. Soon after this vision, he resigned from his
post on the Swedish Board of Mines and spent the remainder of his years
writing and publishing the theological works for which he is now best
known.

The Genesis of *Divine Providence*

Divine Providence (1764) and its immediate predecessor, *Divine Love
and Wisdom* (1763), were published a little more than halfway through
Swedenborg's theological career. He had begun that career by taking his
commission quite literally. Between 1749 and 1756 he produced a work
titled *Secrets of Heaven*—eight substantial volumes on the spiritual
meaning of Genesis and Exodus. He then altered his course, and in 1758
published five much smaller works (two being little larger than leaflets)
on specific religious topics; much of the material was drawn from *Secrets
of Heaven.*[3]

Once these volumes were in print, he returned to his exegetical task
and drafted most of a substantial work on the spiritual meaning of the
Book of Revelation, a work that was never published and in fact never
quite completed: *Revelation Explained* (traditionally titled *Apocalypse*

---

1. Because *Divine Providence* is so closely connected to Swedenborg's *Divine Love and Wisdom,*
many of the issues concerning the origin, form, content, and translation of the two works are
similar. Some of the following remarks are therefore adapted from the preface to my 2003 translation of *Divine Love and Wisdom.* The indulgence of the reader is asked for the repetition of this
information.

2. See Hjern 1989, 26–65. For secondary accounts, see Acton 1927, 40–47; Sigstedt 1981, 197–199;
and Benz 2002, 193–200.

3. See Dole 2000, 1–3 for further detail.

Explained).[4] His intent to publish the work is clear from his draft of a title page to the projected first volume, including the proposed place and date of publication (London, 1759) and his preparation of a fair copy, including instructions in the margins concerning typography. Furthermore, at the close of his treatment of chapter 6 he inserted a note that read *Finis Voluminis Primi,* "End of Volume One."

After the first volume, the manuscript of *Revelation Explained* shows internal signs of indecision about publication. He did not prepare a title page for a second volume, and although from the close of chapter 9 onwards he made his accustomed indications of the end of each chapter, often with flourishes of the pen to emphasize the point of division, he made no further note of volume divisions. Nevertheless, the persistence of his intent to publish seems clearly indicated by the fact that he continued the painstaking labor of making a fair copy to within three relatively brief paragraphs from the end.[5]

While Swedenborg has left us no account of his reasons for abandoning a work so clearly intended for publication and so near to completion, there are indications in it that issues dealt with in the present volume were calling for attention. Early in his treatment of chapter 15 of the Book of Revelation, he began to insert material on various theological topics at the close of virtually every numbered section.[6] At the close of §1136 (midway through chapter 18), he introduced ten "laws of divine providence," and proceeded in subsequent sections to deal with them in some detail. This theme of the laws of divine providence is addressed in the present volume as well. Furthermore, in the discussion of Revelation 19:6 that appears in §1217 of *Revelation Explained,* he introduced a series of propositions concerning the Lord's omnipresence, ending with one that attributes omnipresence primarily to divine love and omniscience primarily to divine wisdom, the eponymous themes of *Divine Love and*

---

4. See Swedenborg 1997.

5. See also Dole 1988.

6. These sections constitute paragraphs by the conventions of eighteenth-century page design, though in some works such "paragraphs" cover several pages (see, for example *Revelation Explained* [= Swedenborg 1997] §1042). Both punctuation and substance, however, often indicate subdivisions equivalent to modern paragraphs, and the effort has been made in the present edition to heed these indications. As is customary in Swedenborgian studies, citations of Swedenborg's works in the present volume refer not to page numbers but to these numbered sections of Swedenborg's text, as the numbering is uniform in all editions.

Wisdom. After continuing *Revelation Explained* through the exegesis of only four more verses, thereby reaching a point nearly halfway through the nineteenth chapter out of the total of twenty-two in the Book of Revelation, he abandoned nearly two years' worth of labor and laid the entire massive work aside.

Just before publishing *Divine Love and Wisdom* and *Divine Providence,* Swedenborg published four brief works on specific teachings for "the New Jerusalem."[7] In the preface to the first of these, *The Lord,* he noted the previous publication of the 1758 works (making no mention of *Secrets of Heaven*) and listed nine titles to be published "by command of the Lord," including the four brief treatises just mentioned as well as *Divine Love and Wisdom* and *Divine Providence.*[8] It is worth noting that once these were in print, he returned to his exegetical task and published a very concise and tightly organized commentary on the Book of Revelation, *Revelation Unveiled.*[9]

Divine Providence's companion work, *Divine Love and Wisdom,* is divided into five major parts. These parts are not given formal titles, but we may turn to §155 of the present work for an indication of their intent. Here part 1 of the earlier work is said to be "about the Lord's divine love and wisdom," part 2 "about the sun of the spiritual world and the sun of the physical world," part 3 "about levels" (see also §32:1), part 4 "about the creation of the universe" (see also §56:1), and part 5 "about our own creation" (see also §8). The basic motion of *Divine Love and Wisdom,* then, is from the absolute universality of Divinity to the particularity of humankind.

---

7. In *Last Judgment* 45, Swedenborg spoke of witnessing the establishment of a new church in the heavens and identified it with the New Jerusalem of Revelation 21:2. In his preface to *The Lord,* the first of the four treatises mentioned here, he stated that this new church was being established, evidently on earth, "at this day."

8. The remaining three titles he had been commanded to produce met various fates. The first, *Supplements,* an addendum to his work on the Last Judgment, was in fact published in 1763. The substance of the second, the proposed book on divine omnipotence, omnipresence, omniscience, infinity, and eternity, was worked into other material, as he explained in a letter of February 1767 to his friend Gabriel Beyer (see Tafel 1877, 1:261). As for the third, *Angelic Wisdom Concerning Life,* there is no ready explanation for its absence. It may be noted, however, that the "angelic wisdom about life" he had been enjoined to write may be represented by the extended treatment of service *(usus)* in *Divine Love and Wisdom* 296–348.

9. The careful and consistent structuring of this work is in sharp contrast to the discursive nature of *Revelation Explained* (= Swedenborg 1997). For a more detailed examination of this publishing sequence, see Dole 1988.

Divine Providence follows directly from this sequence. One need only look at the first statement in the present work, "Divine providence is the form of government exercised by the Lord's divine love and wisdom," to suspect the connection. The remainder of the present work's introductory section is composed of references to points made in the earlier work. The gulf between the transcendent vision of a perfectly loving and infinitely wise Creator and the world we live in, so often unloving and unwise, may seem unbridgeable; but bridging it is precisely the task that *Divine Providence* undertakes.

Divine Love and Wisdom and *Divine Providence* combined may well be regarded as exploring the basis and implications of the radically counterintuitive claim that life is not inherent in us, that we are not intrinsically alive. It is my own conviction that what distracted Swedenborg from his exegetical task as he approached the end of *Revelation Explained* was a growing awareness of the centrality of this issue and the need to deal with it openly and explicitly.

Form and Content

The original title page of *Divine Providence* is graced with a large ornament bearing a Latin motto, CURA ET LABORE, "with care and work." In its position above a cherub watering potted plants in a country garden, the motto seems to suggest that careful attention and hard work are required to make things grow; it calls to mind such themes in the *Georgics,* the didactic poem about farming by the Roman poet Vergil (70–19 B.C.E.).[10] The same ornament appears on the title pages of seven other works published by Swedenborg between 1763 and 1766: *The Lord, Sacred Scripture, Life, Faith, Supplements, Divine Love and Wisdom,* and *Revelation Unveiled.*[11]

While the five parts of *Divine Love and Wisdom* are clearly demarcated in the first edition, each beginning with a major ornamental heading, a striking feature of *Divine Providence* is that its eighteen substantive

---

10. Among the many instances of these themes are *Georgics* 1:145, "Labor conquers all," and 4:118–119, "I would sing about the care of cultivation that adorns the rich gardens."

11. On the ornaments in Swedenborg's theological first editions in general and for evidence that Swedenborg may have engraved this specific ornament himself, see Rose 1998.

segments are set in virtual continuity, with their headings (centered and in large type) generally occurring in the middle of a page. Unlike *Divine Love and Wisdom,* then, *Divine Providence* is presented as a single grand unit of text.

A second hallmark of *Divine Providence* is the care with which this continuity is structured. The eighteen labeled but unnumbered segments into which the work is divided are almost always subdivided into numbered propositions.[12] Quite frequently these propositions are given still further subdivisions (indicated in the present edition by lowercase letters in parentheses).[13] Furthermore, there is a structurally complex passage in the middle of the work in which virtually all the sentences in four continuous sections (§§236–239) are subsequently (§§241–274) developed into numbered sets of propositions, though the original sentences are unnumbered. Organizational features such as this suggest that Swedenborg was working from a carefully developed outline.

Divine Providence ends with what can be described as a major stylistic innovation in Swedenborg's works: the use of a narrative account of one of Swedenborg's experiences in the spiritual world as a separate element

12. The antecedents of this style of exposition can be seen in the *Elements,* the classic work on geometry by Euclid (flourished around 300 B.C.E.), in which propositions are stated and proved one after another. Enlightenment thinkers were deeply impressed by this method, to this day called the "geometrical style," and when they insisted that humankind must proceed in its acquisition of knowledge through the use of "geometry," they generally meant that theories should be supported by reasoning in the geometrical style. Thus the French philosopher René Descartes (1596–1650) wrote a short essay titled "Arguments Demonstrating the Existence of God and the Distinction between Soul and Body, Drawn up in Geometrical Fashion" (Descartes [1641] 1952, 130–133). It contains no circles, squares, or lines, but definitions, postulates, axioms, and propositions instead, the propositions being followed by proofs. The Dutch philosopher Benedict de Spinoza (1632–1677) likewise describes his *Ethics* as a treatment of the topic "by geometrical method" (Spinoza [1677] 1952, 395).

13. A secondary structure within the text are the subsection numbers indicated by bracketed arabic numbers: [1], [2], and so on. These were introduced by the Swedenborgian scholar John F. Potts (1838–1923) in the course of editing his massive six-volume concordance to Swedenborg's theological works (Potts 1888–1902). In order to be able to indicate locations within the text more precisely, Potts divided the longer sections of those works into subsections. (On the use of sections in Swedenborg's works, see note 6 above.) His subsection numberings have since become standard, although current translators may take some license to adjust them to better fit the sense. It is instructive to contrast *Divine Love and Wisdom* and *Divine Providence* with respect to Potts's subsections. *Divine Love and Wisdom* has 432 sections, none of which the concordancer found long enough to divide; *Divine Providence,* however, which is almost half again as long, has only 340 sections, and thus Potts felt the need to create many subsections—in one case (§296) no fewer than fifteen.

of composition. Up to this time, Swedenborg has related such spiritual experiences often, but has not marked them off as a distinct component of the text. Here in §340:6 he provides just such an account after a row of floral ornaments and the comment, "Forgive me for adding the following to fill out the rest of the page." Just two years later, in writing *Revelation Unveiled,* he no longer seems apologetic about such separate accounts of spiritual experiences: he includes them at the end of every chapter, now explicitly calling them "memorable occurrences" (Latin *memorabilia*) and again using floral ornaments to set them off.[14] Thereafter these distinct narrative accounts are a regular element of his theological writings.

As for content, *Divine Love and Wisdom* and *Divine Providence* together present Swedenborgian theology in its most universalistic manifestation. The former offers a picture of a God who is utterly loving, a God who is equally present with and in everyone on earth and who condemns no one. The latter reconciles this idealistic picture with the actualities of a divided and warring world, making it possible for Swedenborg as an ardent Christian to say that heaven "cannot be made up of the people of one religion only. It needs people from many religions; so all the people who make these two universal principles of the church central to their own lives have a place in that heavenly person, that is, heaven."[15]

Editions and Translations of *Divine Providence*

The present translation is based on the first edition of the work. I am deeply indebted to Je Hyung Bae of the Bayside Korean Church for sponsoring the scanning of the first editions, to Junchol Lee for the painstaking labor of scanning them in admirably high resolution, and to Philip Kyung Bae for providing compact disks that yielded eminently readable printouts. It has been an invaluable help to have before me hard copies that I could take wherever I wished and annotate to my heart's content.

---

14. In sharp contrast to his apologetic presentation of the memorable occurrence at the end of *Divine Providence,* Swedenborg sent cover letters advertising the presence of such elements in *Revelation Unveiled* (Acton 1955, 610, 612). He apparently created a flyer in England listing the narrative accounts by section number and giving some idea of their content (Hyde 1906, 455).

15. *Divine Providence* 326:10. The "two universal principles" are belief in God and a life of obedience to God's commandments.

A second Latin edition of *Divine Providence* was published by Johann Friedrich Immanuel Tafel in London in 1855. A third edition, edited by Samuel H. Worcester, was published in New York in 1899; the same year saw the publication of a Latin-English edition using Worcester's Latin text and an English translation by John C. Ager. A fourth Latin edition is forthcoming in Bryn Athyn, Pennsylvania, under the editorship of N. Bruce Rogers.

The first English translation, that of Nathaniel Tucker, was published in London in 1790. An American edition of the same translation appeared in Boston in 1796, and a revision of it by A. Maxwell in Manchester in 1833. In 1840, a translation by Tilly B. Hayward was published in Boston. George Harrison's translation, studiously avoiding Latinate vocabulary, was published in London in 1860. A further revision of the Tucker translation, this time by J. B. Keene, appeared in London in 1862 and a still further revision, by Jonathan Bayley, in 1873.

J. B. Lippincott published R. Norman Foster's translation in Philadelphia in 1868. The Rotch Edition version of 1877 was a revision by Samuel H. Worcester of the Hayward translation of 1840. In 1892, the Swedenborg Society in London published a further revision of the Foster translation, begun by J. Presland and completed by J. B. Keene; in this country the translation of John C. Ager was published in 1899.

In 1949, a fresh translation by William C. Dick and E. J. Pulsford appeared in London, followed in 1961 by that of William F. Wunsch in New York. As of this writing, a new translation is forthcoming from N. Bruce Rogers, to be published in Bryn Athyn, Pennsylvania.[16]

The work has also been translated into Danish, Dutch, French, German, Italian, Japanese, Korean, Latvian, Polish, Portuguese, Swedish, and Tamil.

Issues in Translating *Divine Providence*

The work presents few difficulties to the Latin reader. The language is extraordinarily straightforward; and as anyone knows who has tried to write about profound matters in simple language, this does not happen

---

16. Information on editions and translations from the eighteenth and nineteenth centuries has been drawn from Hyde 1906. Hyde is also the source of much of the information concerning the identity of translators and revisers, as their names are often not given in the translations. William Ross Woofenden furnished the twentieth-century items in the publishing history.

by accident. It is in fact this simplicity that presents the translator with the greatest difficulty, since it would be absurdly simple to translate it quite literally into awkward and difficult English. It is my hope that this translation will convey some of the accessibility that we may be sure Swedenborg labored so diligently to offer.

Recognizing the fact that the vocabularies of different languages do not exactly coincide, I have sacrificed word-for-word consistency in favor of sensitivity to context. Swedenborg rarely offers definitions of his terms and does not always seem to feel bound by such definitions as he does provide. In any case, it is surely of less moment to gain control of a particular vocabulary than to encounter the meaning that vocabulary is intended to convey. The profound coherence and consistency of thought in the many volumes of Swedenborg's theological works may in fact be more obscured than illuminated by efforts at consistency in terminology. It is perhaps a peculiar weakness of translators to try to make every sentence self-explanatory, and to achieve in a few words what can result only from the cumulative effect of more extensive reading.

Acknowledgments

My gratitude is due to David Eller for his initiative in creating the New Century Edition and his ongoing support and guidance.[17] Working with fellow translators Lisa Hyatt Cooper, Jonathan Rose, and Stuart Shotwell has been constantly enlightening and refreshing; and I owe an immense debt of gratitude to Jonathan and Stuart in particular for their patience in seeing to all the myriad details of publication. My primary consultants, Wendy Closterman and Kristin King, have given the first draft exemplary attention, and their contributions are invisibly present on virtually every page. I am also grateful to Carolyn Andrews, Jenica Holmes, Janna King, and Claudia Paes York for the painstaking labor of verifying references. The entire project would be impossible without the support of a number of interested foundations, including the Swedenborg Foundation. I share with my colleagues the hope that the results will justify their extraordinary generosity.

---

17. The need for an annotated edition of Swedenborg's theological works was noted by John Faulkner Potts as early as 1902 (Potts 1888–1902, 6:859), and the hope kept alive in our own times particularly by William Ross Woofenden.

I also share with my fellow translators the realization that we cannot possibly represent in English all the values that we find in the Latin. The decision to give priority to simplicity and clarity over more pedantic concerns has not been made lightly, and should not be regarded as a concession to the reader. It is rather an effort to adopt Swedenborg's own priorities, as evidenced not only by the simplicity and clarity of the texts themselves but also by the self-editing witnessed in his manuscripts. It is our hope and prayer that this may widen the doorway to a quite extraordinary world of meaning.

GEORGE F. DOLE
Bath, Maine
September, 2002

Works Cited
in the Translator's Preface

Acton, Alfred. 1927. *Introduction to the Word Explained.* Bryn Athyn, Pa.: Academy of the New Church.

———. 1955. *The Letters and Memorials of Emanuel Swedenborg.* Vol. 2. Bryn Athyn, Pa.: Swedenborg Scientific Association.

Benz, Ernst. 2002. *Emanuel Swedenborg: Visionary Savant in the Age of Reason.* Translated by Nicholas Goodrick-Clarke. West Chester, Pa.: Swedenborg Foundation.

Descartes, René. [1641] 1952. *Objections against the Meditations and Replies.* Translated by Elizabeth S. Haldane and G.R.T. Ross. In vol. 31 of *Great Books of the Western World.* Chicago: Encyclopedia Britannica.

Dole, George F. 1988. "A Rationale for Swedenborg's Writing Sequence." In *Emanuel Swedenborg: A Continuing Vision.* Edited by Robin Larsen. New York: Swedenborg Foundation.

———. 2000. Preface to *Heaven and Its Wonders and Hell,* translated by George F. Dole. West Chester, Pa.: Swedenborg Foundation.

Hjern, Olle. 1989. *Carl Robsahm: Anteckningar om Swedenborg.* Stockholm: ABA Cad/Copy & Tryck.

Hyde, James. 1906. *A Bibliography of the Works of Emanuel Swedenborg, Original and Translated.* London: Swedenborg Society.

Potts, John Faulkner. 1888–1902. *The Swedenborg Concordance.* 6 vols. London: Swedenborg Society.

Rose, Jonathan S. 1998. "The Ornaments in Swedenborg's Theological First Editions." *Covenant: A Journal Devoted to the Study of the Five Churches* 1.4:293–362.

Sigstedt, Cyriel Odhner. 1981. *The Swedenborg Epic: The Life and Works of Emanuel Swedenborg.* New York: Bookman Associates, 1952. Reprint, London: Swedenborg Society.

Spinoza, Benedict de. [1677] 1952. *Ethics.* Translated by W. H. White, revised by A. H. Stirling. In vol. 31 of *Great Books of the Western World.* Chicago: Encyclopedia Britannica.

Swedenborg, Emanuel. 1997. *Apocalypse Explained.* 6 vols. Translated by John C. Ager, revised by John Whitehead, edited by William Ross Woofenden. West Chester, Pa.: Swedenborg Foundation.

Tafel, Rudolph L. 1877. *Documents Concerning the Life and Character of Emanuel Swedenborg.* Vol. 2, parts 1–2. London: Swedenborg Society.

Selected List of Editions
of *Divine Providence*

1. Latin Editions

Swedenborg, Emanuel. 1764. *Sapientia Angelica de Divina Providentia.* Amsterdam.

———. [1764] 1855. *Sapientia Angelica de Divina Providentia.* Edited by Johann Friedrich Immanuel Tafel. Tübingen: Verlags-Expedition.

———. [1764] 1899. *Sapientia Angelica de Divina Providentia.* Edited by Samuel H. Worcester. New York: American Swedenborg Printing and Publishing Society.

———. [1764] forthcoming. *Sapientia Angelica de Divina Providentia.* Edited by N. Bruce Rogers. Bryn Athyn, Pa.: Academy of the New Church.

2. English Translations

Swedenborg, Emanuel. [1764] 1790. *The Wisdom of Angels Concerning the Divine Providence.* [Translated by Nathaniel Tucker.] London: R. Hindmarsh.

———. [1764] 1840. *Angelic Wisdom Concerning the Divine Providence.* [Translated by Tilly B. Hayward.] Boston: Otis Clapp.

———. [1764] 1860. *Angelic Wisdom Concerning Divine Providence.* [Translated by George Harrison.] London: Longman, Green, Longman, and Roberts.

———. [1764] 1868. *Angelic Wisdom Concerning the Divine Providence.* Translated by R. Norman Foster. Philadelphia: J. B. Lippincott.

———. [1764] 1899. *Angelic Wisdom Concerning the Divine Providence.* Translated by John C. Ager. New York: American Swedenborg Printing and Publishing Society.

———. [1764] 1949. *Angelic Wisdom Concerning the Divine Providence.* Translated by William C. Dick and Edward J. Pulsford. London: Swedenborg Society.

———. [1764] 1961. *Angelic Wisdom about Divine Providence.* Translated by William F. Wunsch. New York: Swedenborg Foundation.

———. [1764] forthcoming. *Angelic Wisdom Regarding Divine Providence.* Translated by N. Bruce Rogers. Bryn Athyn, Pa.: General Church of the New Jerusalem.

On *Divine Providence*

Swedenborg's Metaphysics of Freedom

GREGORY R. JOHNSON

Outline

SWEDENBORG'S *Divine Providence* (1764) is the sequel to *Divine Love and Wisdom* (1763).[1] *Divine Love and Wisdom* discusses God's love and wisdom in themselves and the creation of the world out of divine love by means of divine wisdom. *Divine Providence* discusses the ongoing governance of creation by divine love and divine wisdom. "Divine providence" is the name given to this ongoing governance.

---

1. For the original Latin titles of these works, see the list of short titles on pages 39–44.

I. Providence as a Theological Problem

There are two main philosophical issues connected with divine providence: divine foreknowledge versus human freedom, and the problem of
evil.

Divine foreknowledge seems incompatible with human freedom. A
human act is free if we face a range of real options and choose among
them, but could have chosen otherwise. Divine foreknowledge means
that while we are weighing our options, God already knows what choice
we are going to make. But if God already knows that we are going to
choose *X,* then do we really have the option of choosing *Y?* Could we really do otherwise? Could we really prove God wrong?[2]

The problem of evil was first formulated by Epicurus (341–270
B.C.E.), in a fragment preserved by the Christian apologist Lucius Caecil-
ius Firmianus Lactantius (about 240 to about 320 C.E.), who quotes it in
his *De Ira Dei* (On the Wrath of God) 13:20–22:

> God either wants to eliminate bad things and cannot, or can but does
> not want to, or neither wishes to nor can, or both wants to and can. If
> he wants to and cannot, then he is weak—and this does not apply to
> God. If he can but does not want to, then he is spiteful—which is
> equally foreign to God's nature. If he neither wants to nor can, he is
> both weak and spiteful and so not a god. If he wants to and can, which
> is the only thing fitting for a god, where then do bad things come
> from? Or why does he not eliminate them?[3]

The classic formulation is given by David Hume (1711–1776) in his
Dialogues Concerning Natural Religion: "Epicurus' old questions are yet
unanswered. Is he [God] willing to prevent evil, but not able? Then he is

---

2. Aristotle (384–322 B.C.E.) does not formulate the problem of free will and divine foreknowledge
as such, but the starting point of most subsequent debates on this topic is chapter 9 of his *On Interpretation,* which contains his discussion of the relationship of necessity and contingent future
events. The classic early formulations of the problem of free will and divine foreknowledge are
found in the treatise *On Free Choice of the Will* by Augustine (354–430), and book 5 of *The Consolation of Philosophy* by Boethius (480–524).

3. Epicurus 1994, 97. Other early formulations of the problem of evil are found in *Outlines of
Pyrrhonism* 3:3 by Sextus Empiricus (flourished at the end of the second century C.E.). Another,
roughly contemporary, formulation is attributed to the Gnostic Marcion (flourished early in the
second century C.E.) by the Church Father Tertullian (Quintus Septimus Florens Tertullian,
about 160 to about 240). See Tertullian *Adversus Marcionem* 2:5. Marcion appealed to the problem of evil to establish that the creator God of the Old Testament is actually the evil Demiurge.

impotent. Is he able, but not willing? Then he is malevolent. Is he both able and willing? Whence then is evil?" (Hume 1992, 261). In both formulations, God's omnipotence and benevolence are shown to be irreconcilable with the existence of evil. If God is incapable of preventing evil, then he is not all-powerful. If God is uninterested in preventing evil, then he is not good. One can also make the same argument regarding God's omniscience: If evil happens behind God's back, then he is not all-knowing. If he knows of it but does nothing, he is not good. If he knows, but cannot do anything, then he is not all-powerful. So what is God's justification for the presence of evil in his world? The project of vindicating the justice of divine providence is called "theodicy," from the Greek θεός, *theós* ("God"), and δίκη, *díke* ("justice"). A theodicy is an answer to the problem of evil. The tradition of theodicy distinguishes between natural and moral evils. Natural evils are natural phenomena, like earthquakes and plagues, which harm human beings. Moral evils are human phenomena, like crimes and sins, arising from the abuse of our freedom.

In Christianity, the problems of evil and of divine foreknowledge versus human freedom are given a more specific focus because the Bible claims both that God wants all people to be saved and that some will not be saved, but will be condemned to eternal punishment.[4] But if God wants to save all, then how is it that some are not saved? Either God does not want to save all, in which case he is not good, or he does want to save them, but cannot, and is therefore not all-powerful. The problem of evil acquires an added dimension from the doctrine of eternal predestination. If God is all-knowing, then he knows from eternity which people are going to be saved and which are going to be damned. This means that we have no real power to affect our ultimate destiny, even though we are held responsible for the result. This means that God destines some to eternal punishment for offenses they cannot avoid. And God destines others for a life of eternal bliss that they do not really earn. But how is such an order consistent with the idea of a just and loving God?[5]

It should be no surprise, therefore, that divine providence has been debated for millennia in the Western philosophical and theological tradi-

---

4. For the notion that God wants to save all, see, for example, Ezekiel 18:23, 32; Romans 5:18; 1 Corinthians 15:22. For the idea that some will be saved, but not all, see Luke 13:23–28, among other passages.

5. For an excellent introduction to the debates surrounding predestination, with special reference to Jansenism and Blaise Pascal (1623–1662), see Kolakowski 1995.

tions, monotheist and polytheist, biblical and pagan.[6] The Book of Job raises the problem of evil in the most humanly compelling terms: Why does evil befall the innocent? Why *me?* Socrates (469–399 B.C.E.) is one of the earliest Western philosophers whose reflections on providence have been preserved, by Xenophon (430–354 B.C.E.) and Plato (427–347 B.C.E.), both of whom apparently subscribed to Socrates' views.[7] Socrates defended a form of "optimism," the view that providence orders everything for the best. Aristotle denies the existence of providence, arguing instead for a God concerned only with himself.[8] Epicurus too posits gods unconcerned with human affairs.[9] Providence was a central concept of the Stoics, who based their own form of optimism on that of Socrates, particularly Xenophon's account of Socrates.[10] In the early centuries of the Christian era, the religious movements known as "Gnosticism" split into an optimistic minority (the so-called Hermeticists) who affirmed the albeit incomplete goodness of creation, and a pessimistic majority who regarded the created world as evil.[11] The great Neoplatonist Plotinus (205–270 C.E.) also defended a form of optimism, authoring a treatise on

---

6. For a useful anthology surveying discussions from ancient times to the present day, see Larrimore 2001.

7. Xenophon *Memorabilia* 1:4, 4:3; and Plato *Phaedo* 96a–100b. In *Timaeus* 27c–31b, 41a–42e, Plato also presents views of providence ascribed to the Pythagorean thinker Timaeus of Locri, who may or may not be fictitious.

8. Aristotle *Metaphysics* 11:7 (1072b:15–30). Aristotle does occasionally use metaphors that seem to imply a providential relationship between God and the world, but as W. D. Ross argues, "It is remarkable how little trace there is of this way of thinking, if we discount passages where Aristotle is probably accommodating himself to common opinions; he never uses the word 'providence' [Greek πρόνοια, *prónoia*] of God as Socrates and Plato had done; he has no serious belief in divine rewards and punishments; he has no interest as Plato has in justifying the ways of God to man [theodicy]." See Ross 1959, 181–182.

9. Epicurus 1994, 16–17 ("Letter to Herodotus"), 22–23 ("Letter to Pythocles"). The longest extant exposition of Epicurean thought is by the Roman poet Titus Lucretius Carus (about 94 to 55 or 51 B.C.E.). On the denial of providence, see Lucretius *De Rerum Natura* (On the Nature of Things) 2:168–184, 646–660; 5:146–234; 6:49–79, 380–423.

10. The writings of the Greek Stoics are almost entirely lost, but some of their opinions on providence are preserved by Marcus Tullius Cicero (106–43 B.C.E.); see his *De Natura Deorum* (On the Nature of the Gods) book 2. For the best statement of Roman Stoicism on providence, see Lucius Annaeus Seneca (4 B.C.E.–65 C.E.) *De Providentia* (On Providence).

11. On the distinction between optimistic and pessimistic forms of Gnosticism, see Versluis 1992, 307–320.

providence that remains unsurpassed as a purely philosophical treatment of the topic. Plotinus also disputed the Gnostic pessimists' denial of the goodness of the created world.[12] Providence is a central issue in the tradition of Christian philosophy from *The City of God* and *On Free Choice of the Will* by Augustine (354–430) through *The Consolation of Philosophy* by Boethius (480–524) to the great systems of speculative theology of the High Middle Ages, epitomized by the *Summa Theologiae* (Summary of Theology) of Thomas Aquinas (1224 or 1225–1274). Providence is also a central theme of the Jewish traditions of philosophy, theology, and esoteric spirituality running from the Book of Job and Philo of Alexandria (about 25 B.C.E.–50 C.E.) in the ancient world through Moses Maimonides (1135–1204) and the Kabbalists in the Middle Ages, up to a host of twentieth-century Holocaust theologians.[13] In the seventeenth and eighteenth centuries, revolutions in Christian theology combined with revolutions in science, technology, and exploration made providence an important topic of thought with such thinkers as Antoine Arnauld (1612–1694), Blaise Pascal (1623–1662), Nicolas de Malebranche (1638–1715), Pierre Bayle (1647–1706), Giovanni Battista Vico (1668–1744), Gottfried Wilhelm Leibniz (1646–1716), Shaftesbury (Anthony Ashley Cooper, 1671–1713), Christian Wolff (1679–1754), Alexander Pope (1688–1744), David Hume (1711–1776), Jean-Jacques Rousseau (1712–1778), Gotthold Ephraim Lessing (1729–1781), Moses Mendelssohn (1729–1786), and Immanuel Kant (1724–1804).

The thesis of "optimism" associated with Leibniz and Pope—that "This is the best of all possible worlds,"[14] that "Whatever is, is right"[15]—

---

12. Plotinus *Enneads* 3:2–3 *(Providence)*; 2:9 *(Against the Gnostics)*.

13. For an overview of much of this tradition, see Leaman 1995.

14. This is Voltaire's pithy summation in *Candide* (Voltaire [1759] 1966, 12) of Leibniz's more prolix statement: "It follows from the supreme perfection of God that he has chosen the best possible plan in producing the universe, a plan which combines the greatest variety together with the greatest order; with situation, place, and time arranged in the best way possible; with the greatest effect produced by the simplest means; with the most power, the most knowledge, the greatest happiness and goodness in created things which the universe could allow. For as all possible things have a claim to existence in God's understanding in proportion to their perfections, the result of all these claims must be the most perfect actual world which is possible. Without this it would be impossible to give a reason why things have gone as they have rather than otherwise" (Leibniz [1714] 1989, §10, page 639).

15. Pope 1958, epistle 1, line 294.

seemed to perfectly capture the temperament of the Enlightenment. Thus Voltaire (François-Marie Arouet, 1694–1778) ignited a storm of controversy with his attacks on optimism, prompted by the great Lisbon earthquake of 1755 and expressed in his poem *"Sur le désastre de Lisbonne"* ("On the Lisbon Disaster," 1755) and most trenchantly in his satire *Candide* (1759).[16] Optimism lost its status as a serious intellectual option not by refutation but by mere ridicule. A far more substantive and serious blow against speculative theories of providence was Kant's *Critique of Pure Reason* (1781, 1787). Although Kant argued that providence was a defensible article of "rational faith," he denied that anything could be learned about it by pure reason.[17] After Kant, providence faded as a topic of philosophical speculation, although it remained in the background of German Idealism, particularly the philosophies of history of Kant and G.W.F. Hegel (1770–1831). Throughout the nineteenth and twentieth centuries, the idea of providence is conspicuous primarily for the denial of the concept, whether in the pessimism of Arthur Schopenhauer (1788–1860), the aestheticism of Friedrich Nietzsche (1844–1900), or the postmodern philosophies of contingency. Indeed, in the nineteenth and twentieth centuries, the only serious attempt to revive the concept of optimism was made by William James (1842–1910). Following the lead of Kant, James argues for optimism on pragmatic rather than speculative grounds.[18]

II. Swedenborg and the Tradition

Swedenborg's *Divine Providence* was published in Amsterdam in the first half of 1764. Thus it is tempting—indeed, it is necessary—to read *Divine Providence* against the backdrop of the Western philosophical and theological tradition in general and of seventeenth- and eighteenth-century

---

16. Both texts may be found in Voltaire 1949, 560–569 and 229–328, respectively; *Candide* alone in Voltaire [1759] 1966.

17. See Kant [1781, 1787] 1929. Kant expands his thoughts on theodicy in his *Critique of Practical Reason* (Kant [1788] 1996), and "On the Miscarriage of All Philosophical Trials in Theodicy" (Kant [1791] 1996).

18. See especially his essay "The Dilemma of Determinism," in James [1897] 1956, 145–183. The overall argument of James's *Varieties of Religious Experience* (James [1902] 1994) can also be read as a defense of a kind of chastened and realistic optimism.

debates on providence in particular. Swedenborg does deal with such traditional questions as freedom and foreknowledge, the problem of evil, predestination, and eternal punishment. We know, furthermore, that Swedenborg had extensive knowledge of the writings of Malebranche, Leibniz, and Wolff. He read Malebranche's work with care as early as 1710 (Dole and Kirven 1992, 87). He also devoted considerable space to their ideas in notes dating from 1740–1741, where their names appear along with Plato, Aristotle, Augustine, Hugo Grotius (1583–1645), and René Descartes (1596–1650) in a list of important thinkers to be quoted.[19] Thus it is not remarkable to encounter occasional phrases in *Divine Providence* that call to mind the ideas and language of Malebranche, Leibniz, Wolff, and other thinkers.

What is remarkable is the almost complete independence of *Divine Providence* from its intellectual context. This is not the spurious independence of thinkers who hide their sources to create a false impression of originality. It is the genuine independence of a thinker who has thoroughly assimilated and then transcended his intellectual context.[20] What sets Swedenborg's account of providence apart is his focus on the inner life of the individual. Swedenborg offers an account of how our emotional lives and inner struggles for wholeness and meaning are connected to heaven, hell, and the laws of divine providence. The healthy soul is a miniature heaven, the sick soul a miniature hell. Since the microcosm mirrors the macrocosm, the individual can look to the cosmic whole for a key to decipher the mysteries of his or her own inner life. This in large part explains Swedenborg's enduring appeal to serious spiritual seekers over the centuries, including such great and turbulent souls as William Blake (1757–1827), Ralph Waldo Emerson (1803–1882), Henry James, Sr. (1811–1882), William James, Charles S. Peirce (1839–1914), August Strindberg (1849–1912), and William Butler Yeats (1865–1939). Swedenborg reveals the guiding star of providence in the darkest night of the soul.

---

19. These notes have been published under the title *A Philosopher's Note Book: Excerpts from Philosophical Writers and from the Sacred Scriptures on a Variety of Philosophical Subjects; Together with Some Reflections, and Sundry Notes and Memoranda by Emanuel Swedenborg* (Swedenborg 1931); for the list of influences, see page 10 there.

20. For two useful recent discussions of Swedenborgian theodicy, see Fox 2000, ix–l, and Dole 2001.

III. *Divine Love and Wisdom* and *Divine Providence*

Swedenborg divided *Divine Providence* into eighteen parts under separate headings. Under the heading "Divine Providence Is the Form of Government Exercised by the Lord's Divine Love and Wisdom" (§§1–26),[21] he treats the relationship of *Divine Love and Wisdom* to *Divine Providence*. God creates the world out of divine love by means of divine wisdom. Divine providence is the ongoing governance of creation by divine love and divine wisdom. A central theme of this discussion is the role of divine providence in preserving the unity of divine love and divine wisdom in the created world. In God, divine love and divine wisdom are one: Love without wisdom is not true love. Wisdom without love is not true wisdom.

In the act of creation, divine love and divine wisdom proceed as one from God into the created world. The unity of divine love and wisdom is, therefore, reflected in every created thing. But this unity is reflected to lesser and lesser degrees as we descend down the "great chain of being" from spirituality to materiality, from perfection to imperfection.[22] Here Swedenborg offers a metaphysical explanation for the existence and nature of evil. Evil is, in essence, otherness from God. If God is perfectly good, then anything other than God is imperfectly good. To the extent that beings diverge more and more from God, they become less and less perfect, more and more evil. This is not to say that creation is entirely evil. Creation is good insofar as it borrows or reflects, to varying degrees, the goodness of God. Creation can be said to be evil only insofar as it is not perfect, and insofar as its goodness is not its own, but merely borrowed and reflected.

The most grievous form of metaphysical imperfection is the sundering of the original unity of divine love and divine wisdom by humankind. We have two faculties by which we can receive and appreciate divine love and divine wisdom: rationality, through which we know the truth, and freedom, through which we choose the good. The primary

---

21. As is common in Swedenborgian studies, text citations to Swedenborg's works refer not to page numbers, but to Swedenborg's section numbers, which are uniform in all editions.

22. The term "great chain of being" refers to the universe as "composed of an immense or . . . infinite number of links ranging in hierarchical order from the meagerest kind of existents, which barely escape non-existence, through 'every possible' grade up to the *ens perfectissimum* [most perfect being]" (Lovejoy 1936, 59). For the history of this idea, see Lovejoy 1936; on its origin, see pages 24–66 there.

faculty is freedom. Freedom is not just receptive of divine love, but disposed by our own human love, our values, our sense of what is good. Each human character is most fundamentally defined by its central love, its core values, not by its beliefs. These core values direct the operation of the rational faculty. Rationality and freedom can exist in disharmony. People can be good while living in falsehood, and they can be evil while knowing the truth. The emergence of this state of internal division and disharmony can be understood as the fall of humankind. The persistence of this disharmony from generation to generation can be understood as original sin.[23] Humankind's internal division can also be understood as a state of spiritual sickness. The role of divine providence is to restore the unity of divine love and divine wisdom in the created world. This requires that divine providence heal the human soul, that it raise humankind up from its fallen state. The cosmos is healed through the salvation of humanity.

This healing cannot, however, take place by abrogating human reason and human freedom, for these faculties are essential to humankind, and thus their destruction would mean our destruction. Therefore divine providence works through human reason and freedom. Our freedom consists in the fact that we are suspended between heaven and hell. By this, Swedenborg means that we can choose between two masters: God and "the devil."[24] We can follow the path of heaven to the unification, healing, and salvation of our soul. Or we can follow the path of hell, closing the soul in upon itself, living life according to our evil desires, and falling into greater and greater spiritual division and discord.

The existence of hell does not merely establish human freedom. Swedenborg also argues that the influences of hell teach us the nature of what is good. He claims that good and evil exist on a continuum. Our knowledge of each point on the continuum is mediated by our knowledge of the others. Our knowledge of the good is therefore mediated by our knowledge of the evil. Without hellish influences, therefore, we would be unable to appreciate heavenly influences, and vice versa. Furthermore, Swedenborg claims that divine providence uses hellish influences for our

---

23. In Swedenborg, the term "original sin" does not refer to the notion that Adam's misdeeds plague us all, but to the idea that we do inherit evil from our immediate ancestors, which can have a cumulative effect. See *Divine Providence* 277a.

24. Swedenborg does not believe in an individual Devil or Satan. Rather, he claims that hell is populated by many devils and satans, who are the spirits of human beings whose spiritual corruption has caused them to gravitate toward hell.

purification. First, by combating temptation, we purify ourselves. Second, God uses evils and falsehoods like yeast, to leaven and ferment society and individual souls, separating things in discord and uniting things in concord.

IV. The Ultimate Aim of Providence

Under the heading "The Lord's Divine Providence Has as Its Goal a Heaven from the Human Race" (§§27–45), Swedenborg discusses the ultimate goal of divine providence. Swedenborg denies that angels, demons, and other spiritual beings are specially created. Instead, heaven, hell, and the intermediate world of spirits are populated entirely by the embodied and departed spirits of human beings. (Swedenborg also holds that there are human beings on other planets. These human beings may be rather different in appearance and habits than earthlings, but in his terminology, they are human beings nonetheless.) The ultimate goal of divine providence is that all of these spiritual beings become angels and dwell in heaven in the presence of the Lord.

Angels are in heaven insofar as they dwell in unity with God. This unity is reciprocal. Divine love flows into the angels, and the angels reciprocate with wisdom. This wisdom is not, however, the wisdom of the angels, but divine wisdom imparted by God. Divine wisdom flows into the angels, and the angels reciprocate with love—with divine love imparted by God. Humankind is by nature capable of different degrees of union with God. There are three discrete degrees of human proximity to God: the physical, the spiritual, and the heavenly, and within each of these degrees there is continual variation. Although a spiritual being may become closer and closer to God, she or he will never actually be one with him, since God is infinite and all created beings are finite, and there is no way for a finite being to bridge that gap. Swedenborg also reminds us that all talk of the distance and proximity of spiritual beings in relation to God should not be understood in spatial terms, for space and time per se do not exist in the spiritual world. Instead, spiritual distance and proximity is a matter of the degree of harmony between the individual spirit's love and wisdom and divine love and wisdom. The closer a spirit is to God, the wiser and the happier he or she becomes.

Swedenborg also claims that despite opinions to the contrary, as spirits become closer to God, they become freer as well. Here Swedenborg adverts to a distinction between two kinds of freedom that is at least as old as Plato's *Gorgias* (466d–469b). The freedom to choose evil and the freedom to choose good both appear to be forms of freedom. But the freedom to do evil is actually a form of slavery, because it leads to unhappiness, whereas choosing the good leads to happiness. Likewise for Swedenborg, the freedom to do evil is not true freedom, but slavery to the influences of hell and a cause of misery, whereas the freedom to do good is true freedom, because it leads to our happiness. Furthermore, the freedom to do evil is frustrated by God's opposition to evil, whereas the freedom to do good is helped, not hindered, by God. Therefore, as spirits we simultaneously become both better and freer as we join ourselves to God and bring our own love and wisdom into harmony with divine love and wisdom.

This distinction between the freedom to choose evil and the freedom to choose good helps to resolve an apparent contradiction in Swedenborg's statements on freedom. On the one hand, Swedenborg claims that we are free insofar as we can choose good or evil, the way of heaven or the way of hell. It seems clear that Swedenborg is talking about a real freedom, a real capacity to choose good or evil. On the other hand, Swedenborg speaks of this freedom as merely "apparent." Since appearance is often contrasted to reality, it is quite natural to interpret the claim that freedom is apparent as the denial that it is real. This reading means that Swedenborg is contradicting himself, asserting that freedom is both real and unreal at the same time and in the same respect. In fact, however, Swedenborg is not contradicting himself. In saying that the freedom to choose evil is merely "apparent," he is not claiming that this faculty is not real *at all,* that is, that it does not exist. Instead, he is merely claiming that it is not real *freedom.* When one wants what is good, one has complete freedom to pursue it. When one wants what is evil, one is restricted in one's pursuit of it by laws and restraints in this world and by punishments in the other world. Therefore, real freedom is the power to choose good, not the power to choose evil. The freedom to choose evil exists, but it is not real freedom. In fact, it is a form of bondage to the influence of hell.

V. The Relationship of the Eternal and the Temporal

Under the heading "In Everything That It Does, the Lord's Divine Providence Is Focusing on What Is Infinite and Eternal" (§§46–69), Swedenborg discusses two main topics. First he treats the relationship of God, who is infinite and eternal, to creation, which is finite and temporal. Second, he treats the form of heaven. Heaven takes the form of a giant human, the *Maximus Homo* or Universal Human, which is an image of God, the parts of which consist of communities of angels. The connection between the two topics seems to be the principle that God can relate to finite beings only insofar as they reflect his nature. This is true both inwardly and outwardly. In the inner or spiritual realm, God relates to human beings only insofar as their souls are open to the influence of divine love and wisdom. God does not relate to the human self, which is closed in upon itself and closed off to God. Because it is involuted and aims at self-sufficiency, the self is evil. And even if the self were good, its goodness would be merely material and closed off to the good influences of the higher order. In the outer realm, the realm of appearances, God relates to the communities of angels only insofar as they allow themselves to be organized into the Universal Human, a finite image of God. The Universal Human is not, of course, actually shaped like a human being, for shape is spatial, and heaven exists outside of space and time. Rather, heaven takes on the spatial *appearance* of a Universal Human.

VI. The Five Laws of Divine Providence

The next six parts (§§70–190) constitute the core of the book. Here Swedenborg sets forth the five laws of divine providence. Here he shows his greatest psychological acuity. He also demonstrates how uniquely adapted his theology is to the Enlightenment, with its central emphases on critical reason as opposed to blind faith, freedom as opposed to force, and natural law as opposed to miracles and visions.

The first law of divine providence is that we should use our faculties of reason and freedom. We should act freely according to reason; we should exercise our power of choice rationally. Reason and freedom are essential characteristics of humankind. We cannot be reformed and regenerated by destroying our essential characteristics. Thus we must be reformed and regenerated through our reason and freedom. Our freedom is our faculty of choosing the good. It corresponds to divine love. Our reason is our faculty of knowing the true. It corresponds to divine wisdom. By using these faculties, therefore, we become closer and closer to God.

Swedenborg sets out three main steps of the spiritual journey. First is the state of *damnation,* the sin that we inherit from our parents. This

state is characterized by love for ourselves and the world. People in the
state of damnation may sincerely believe that they love God and their
neighbor, but these beliefs remain peripheral to their lives, which are centered on self-love and love for the world. Second is the state of *reformation,* in which we begin to turn away from self-love and love for the
world to love for God and for our neighbor, albeit motivated primarily
by our selfish desire for the joys of heaven. The state of reformation is
characterized by an awareness of sin and the desire to be free from it.
Third is the state of *regeneration,* which begins when we fight against and
abstain from our sins, and culminates when our lives are recentered
around love for God and for our neighbor, rather than self-love and love
for the world.

Regeneration also requires that we recognize that what is good in our
reason and freedom comes from divine influence. Reason and freedom
operate through divine influence, and recognizing this fact turns reason
and freedom back toward God, completing the circle. But if our reason
and freedom operate through divine influence, then we do not act autonomously. Swedenborg accepts this fact forthrightly. And if we are
saved through faculties of reason and freedom that are really operated by
God, not by our selves, then we are not ultimately responsible for our
own salvation. Swedenborg also accepts this, although he also asserts that
we are responsible for our own damnation. Swedenborg insists that although we do not act autonomously, it is a law of divine providence that
we should think and act *as if* we were autonomous. Swedenborg's insistence on the necessity of the illusion of freedom is a sign of his psychological acuity. If people knew that they were not autonomous, then they
would become passive and fatalistic. They would not work for their reformation and regeneration, but would instead passively await it, all the
while sinking deeper and deeper into sin. God, however, desires that people take an active role in their reformation and regeneration, and this requires the illusion of autonomy.

The second law of divine providence is that we should work to remove the evils and sins of the outer self, thereby making us receptive to
God's removal of the evils and sins of the inner self as well as the outer
self. By the "outer" and "inner" self, Swedenborg does not mean the body
and the soul, but different levels of the soul. He parses this distinction in
different ways. The inner soul can be our true self, the outer the false
impression we give to others. The inner soul can be our innate propensities and deeply ingrained habits, the outer the particular behaviors that
arise from our propensities and reinforce our habits. The inner soul can

be our ruling love, our core values; the outer can be our ephemeral fixations. The inner soul can be our fixed and core beliefs, the outer less fundamental and fixed ones. The inner soul can be our ultimate ends, the outer the means by which we pursue them and the satisfactions we gain from the pursuit. Swedenborg stresses that the outer self is determined by the inner.

But if this is the case, then why reform the outer first? Swedenborg's answer is that God "cannot" reform the inner self before the outer self reforms itself. But what does it mean to say that God "cannot" do anything? Furthermore, how is this consistent with the view that we do nothing autonomously? Swedenborg's answer is that, although we do nothing autonomously, God can choose to use us as the means to our own salvation. Thus the sense in which God "cannot" reform the inner self before the outer is simply that God has chosen this course of action; God has imposed this limit upon himself.

The second law also displays great psychological insight in two areas. First, if people have a strong desire to commit adultery and have become habitual adulterers, then adultery has become a flaw of their inner nature. Their actual acts of adultery and the pleasure they take in those acts reside in their outer nature. It is simply not realistic to expect their adulterous propensities and habits to be reformed before they actually give up committing adultery. Each outward act of adultery and the pleasure they derive from it simply reinforce their inner tendencies. Only when they cease to reinforce those tendencies is there any chance of their reformation. Second, Swedenborg has a very realistic sense of the limits of human self-knowledge. Although we may attain some lucidity about the outer surfaces of the self, our inmost depths are hidden to us. Swedenborg is one of the first to discuss the mysteries of the unconscious mind. Thus if we are to change ourselves at all, we must work from the outside in. By reforming our outer selves, we might set in motion mysterious processes of inner reform as well.

The third law of divine providence is that in matters of religion, we should not be compelled by external means to believe and to love. Instead, each of us should persuade and at times compel ourselves to do so. By external force, Swedenborg does not simply mean threats of physical harm, whether from nature or from human beings. He also includes miracles, signs, visions, and conversations with the dead, because such uncanny events constrain and bewitch our thought processes.

Swedenborg rejects force for several reasons. First, we are free and rational beings. We cannot be saved by any means that would destroy our humanity. External force attacks both reason and freedom, which are our essential human traits. Swedenborg is indeed careful to note that some aspects of our inner nature can be controlled by external forces. He hastens to add, however, that these aspects are not distinctly human, but are shared with the beasts. Second, all attempts to compel belief are not only futile but also counterproductive. We value our freedom. When it is taken away, even for our own good, we reassert it by rejecting what is foisted upon us. Third, forced worship simply leads people to hide their sins inside, which causes inner corruption. Fourth, the inner self is attracted toward belief and love not by the threat of pain, but by the promise of pleasure. Swedenborg also adds a very important point that the pleasures of freedom rule over the pleasures of reason, meaning that what we love or value rules over our thoughts, not vice versa. This means that we cannot be reformed by faith (belief) alone, but only through a transformation of our core values. Fifth, the inside is not reformed by the outside (through factors such as externally applied force), but the outside is reformed by the inside. This principle seems to contradict the second law, that reform of the outer self must come before reform of the inner. But in fact there is no contradiction. In his discussion of the second law, Swedenborg makes it clear that the outer self can only be known because there is an inner one. We can know ourselves because we can split our egos into an inner subject that knows and an object that is known. Likewise, we can work to reform ourselves only by splitting the self into an outer self that is reformed and an inner self that reforms. Swedenborg adds that this self-compulsion is not a form of force, but an exercise of freedom. He also makes clear that the scriptural "fear" of God is not fear of force, but a corollary of love. We fear to offend those whom we love.

The fourth law of divine providence is that we are led toward salvation by the Lord alone, through the Word of God,[25] and teaching and preaching derived from the Word, and not by ourselves alone, although this appears to be the case. Swedenborg's main point here is that God is just as much at work in the Word and the theology and sermons that expound it as he is elsewhere. We are no more autonomous in our encounters with the Word than we are anywhere else.

The fifth law of divine providence is that we should not perceive the operation of divine providence, but that we should know that it exists

---

25. Following common practice in his day, Swedenborg referred to the Bible as "the Word."

and acknowledge it. Swedenborg gives four reasons why the workings of divine providence should be hidden from us. First, if we were aware of providence, we would be denied the illusions of autonomy and personal responsibility and thus stripped of our humanity. Second, if we knew the workings of providence, we would try to interfere with them and thus corrupt and destroy them. Swedenborg's explanation is most interesting. He makes it clear that he is talking about the workings of providence in the inner soul. He draws an analogy between the soul and the body. Certain physiological functions are automatic and involuntary and most of us are unaware of their very existence. That is for the best. If we became aware of them, we might try to assert volitional control over them and cause them to malfunction. The same goes for the automatic and unconscious processes of the inmost soul, where divine providence does its work. Here Swedenborg makes very clear that he not only grasps that there is an unconscious mind, but he has an explanation for why it is best that it remain unconscious. Third, Swedenborg claims that if we knew the workings of providence we would rebel against God. We would do this because naturally we love our selves and the world. God's providence leads us away from these loves. If we were aware of this, we would hate God and deny his existence. Finally, we are allowed to see the workings of divine providence only in retrospect, after they have already happened, not before they have been carried out. And we are allowed to see this only when we adopt a spiritual rather than a materialistic point of view.

VII. Prudence and Particular Providence

Under the heading "Our Own Prudence Is Nothing—It Only Seems to Be Something, As It Should. Rather, Divine Providence Is All-inclusive Because It Extends to the Smallest Details" (§§191–213), Swedenborg deals with two issues. First, he denies the secular-naturalistic claim that human prudence is a self-sufficient guide to life. This claim is a manifestation of self-love and love for the world over love for God and one's neighbor. It is an attempt to close us off to divine influence and to encompass the world in the control of our conscious mind. Swedenborg's critique is profoundly psychological. The core of the human personality, and the source of all our thoughts, is our "life's love"—our set of core values—that lies in our inmost soul. The inmost soul, however, is a mystery to us. We know *from* it, but we do not know *of* it. Thus human prudence cannot be our guide. Only God knows our inmost soul. Thus only God can guide us. God guides the life's love in each of us, giving rise to our thoughts and to our prudence. Prudence, therefore, is not a self-sufficient guide, but merely a tool of divine providence.

Second, Swedenborg raises the question: Does divine providence frame only the universal laws of nature and leave the details to our prudence? In this way, he broaches an issue in seventeenth- and eighteenth-century discussions of providence and eternal damnation, namely, the question of universal versus particular providence. In scholastic terminology, God's "antecedent will" is that all people be saved; however, after the Fall, God's "consequent will" is that only some people be saved. The Jansenist theologian Antoine Arnauld coined the phrases "general will" *(volonté générale)* for God's antecedent will and "particular will" *(volonté particulière)* for his consequent will (Riley 1986, 4). The general will is the moral order of the cosmos, God's providential plan of salvation and damnation. The theological terminology of the general and particular will was taken up and applied in moral and political contexts by Pascal, by Malebranche, and most famously by Rousseau. Pascal, in his posthumously published *Pensées* (Thoughts), identifies the general will with the collective good of a corporate entity, be it an individual body or a body politic (Pascal 1914, 381–385). Malebranche, in his *Treatise on Nature and Grace* (1680),[26] associates the general will not only with the antecedent will to universal salvation, but also with the eternal order of natural law. This innovation provides the foundation of a theodicy harmonizing the justice of God with the existence of earthly evils and the apparent scandal of eternal damnation. God supposedly establishes the providential order through *volontés générales,* "acts of general will," which aim at the good of the whole in the kingdom of nature (the material world) and at universal salvation in the kingdom of grace (the spiritual world). But in the kingdom of nature, the good of the whole permits the suffering of particular individuals, even though this suffering is not willed by God, just as in the kingdom of grace, the antecedent will to universal salvation is consistent with the consequent will that some will suffer eternal damnation.

Why does God's consequent will diverge from his antecedent will? According to Malebranche, God's antecedent or general will consists of certain simple, universal, and impartial laws, laws that are no respecters of

---

26. Malebranche [1680] 1958. For a translation of the first of the seven editions of the *Traité* with some supplementary materials from the later editions, see Malebranche [1680] 1992.

persons or particular situations, and therefore condemn countless people to hell. In order to save such people, God would have to contravene his general providence with innumerable *volontés particulières,* "particular acts of will." But, Malebranche argues, such a course of action would call into question the wisdom of God's initial general will. Malebranche thought the hallmark of divine wisdom was "to establish general laws, and to choose the simplest ones which are at the same time the most fruitful, [which] is a way of acting worthy of him whose wisdom has no limits,"[27] whereas, "to act by *volontés particulières* shows a limited intelligence which cannot judge the consequences or the effects of less fruitful causes."[28]

During his journeyman years, Swedenborg had great respect for Malebranche. But Swedenborg categorically rejected Malebranche's denial of particular providence. Indeed, in *Secrets of Heaven,* Swedenborg attacks this idea as "idiotic" (Latin *stupidum*):

> When angels have a comprehensive or universal picture, they also have the individual images that the Lord arranges within the overall picture, each distinct from the next. The comprehensive and universal levels are nothing unless they contain the particulars, down to the smallest details, that go to make them up and that allow them to be called comprehensive or universal. The more detail they contain, the more comprehensive and universal they are. Obviously, then, the Lord's universal providence is absolutely nothing without the smallest, most specific providences that enter into it and make it universal. It is idiotic to assert that something universal exists in the Deity and then rob it of any particulars.[29]

For Swedenborg, therefore, the general will is God's providential order, his divine design, which is framed in terms of universal and general laws that the wise strive to know and live by. But those who do not live in accordance with general providence require particular providence:

> The Lord, working through the spiritual world, exerts a *general influence* and a *particular influence* on the objects of the material world. His general influence affects things that follow the divine order; his

---

27. Malebranche [1680] 1958, 147, 148, in the translation of Riley 1986, 29.

28. Malebranche [1680] 1958, 166, in the translation of Riley 1986, 29.

29. *Secrets of Heaven* 4329:4; translation by Lisa Hyatt Cooper. See also *Secrets of Heaven* 5850, 5993, 6481–6482, 6489–6494, and 10773.

particular influence acts on those that do not. . . . Humans . . . do not follow the divine order or any law of that order, so it is the Lord's particular influence that acts on them. In other words, angels and spirits are present with us to act as a conduit for the Lord's influence. Without them, we would plunge into every unspeakable crime and quickly throw ourselves headlong into the deepest hell. Through those spirits and angels, the Lord watches over and guides us. . . . Since our lives are diametrically opposed to the order of heaven, then, the Lord controls us through separate spirits and angels.[30]

Particular providence is needed by humans to ensure their salvation. As we shall see, Swedenborg holds that all are predestined to heaven and none are predestined to eternal damnation. He who wills the end must will the means, and the only means of assuring universal salvation is particular providence. Thus divine providence is present even in the tiniest details of the soul and the world. Swedenborg suggests that a visible sign of this fact is the view that luck plays a role in even the smallest of events.

VIII. Providence as Divine Influence

Under the heading "Divine Providence Focuses on Eternal Matters, and Focuses on Temporal Matters Only As They Coincide with Eternal Ones" (§§214–220), Swedenborg reduces all temporal matters to eminence and wealth. In themselves, these are morally neutral. They are curses if their use is guided by a self-love and love for the world, by a merely human prudence. They are blessings if their use is guided by love for God and our neighbor, gifts of divine influence. It is the tendency of fallen humans to embrace temporal things, separating them from eternity, which leads to their misuse. It is the work of divine providence to unite the temporal with the eternal, ensuring that they are rightly used. This chapter can be read as a critique of classical pagan moral philosophers, such as Plato, Aristotle, and the Stoics. These figures held that ordinary things are neither intrinsically good nor intrinsically bad, but are in themselves morally neutral. Their goodness or badness is derived entirely from the wisdom with which they are used. The same thing may be good if used wisely, bad if used foolishly. Wisdom, on this account, is the ability to make right use

---

30. *Secrets of Heaven* 5850; translation by Lisa Hyatt Cooper.

of all things.[31] This wisdom is, however, a merely human form of prudence, which can be gained by merely human means, independent of divine providence. Swedenborg, therefore, regards it as just another form of folly. True wisdom—the true ability to make right use of all things—is divine, not human. It is a divine influence, not the product of human reason. It is a divine gift, not our private property. It is cause for gratitude and humility, not for the storied pride of the philosophers.

Under the heading "We Are Not Granted Inner Access to the Truths That Our Faith Discloses and the Good Effects of Our Caring Except As We Can Be Kept in Them to the End of Our Life" (§§221–233), Swedenborg deals with the condition under which we can receive the truths of faith and the goodness of charity. As free and rational beings, we are capable of receiving them at any time. But if we receive them at the wrong time, we can backslide from them. This is the worst possible form of profanity. Therefore, we receive them only when we are able to resist backsliding and hold onto them for the rest of our days. Backsliding takes place because good and evil, truth and falsehood cannot exist within the same part of the soul at the same time. Truth and goodness can only enter where evil and falsehood have been banished. It is possible, however, for reason to absorb truths while our wills are evil. When this happens, however, our evil wills profane and adulterate the truth. Therefore, providence does not allow us to absorb the truths of faith inwardly until our wills are sufficiently reformed.

IX. The Problem of Evil

Under the heading "Laws of Permission Are Also Laws of Divine Providence" (§§234–274) Swedenborg offers his answer to the problem of evil and extensive casuistic explanations of particular evils. Here he deals specifically with the problem of moral evil. His discussion of natural evil is found in *Divine Love and Wisdom,* part 4 (§§336–348). God is not the author of moral evil. Human beings are. God permits moral evil, not because he wants it to happen in itself, but because it is a necessary means to his ultimate goal, which is our salvation. If we are to be saved as humans, we must be saved as free and rational beings. That means that we must have the genuine option of falling into evil and error.

---

31. The classic source of this viewpoint is Plato *Euthydemus* 278e–283b.

Under the heading "Evils Are Permitted for a Purpose: Salvation" (§§275–284), Swedenborg explains precisely why evils have to be permitted by God. All human beings are involved in evil—self-love and love for the world—from the moment of birth. Divine providence works to lead us away from these evils so that we can be reformed. In order for evils to be set aside, they have to come to light. This does not necessarily mean that we must do evil. It is enough to examine ourselves and discover our propensities to evil. We can examine our selves because the self has different levels. We can examine the outer self by means of the inner self, the inner self by still more inward levels of the self, and so forth. Once we understand our evils and set them aside, we can be forgiven. Swedenborg then deals with some common misconceptions about reformation. First, evils that are set aside do not disappear. Instead, they move from the center of the self to the periphery, while the center is occupied by goodness. Second, our lives cannot be changed instantaneously from good to evil. Good and evil are opposite ends of a continuum. To move from one to the other, we must pass through all the degrees in between, which requires a lifetime of slow spiritual progress. Third, people think that evil impulses are relatively simple, but they are actually quite complex and interconnected and thus require time to change. Fourth, Swedenborg observes that mental states are correlated to brain states, which are enormously complex. The brain cannot be transformed instantaneously from one state to another. Therefore neither can the mind.

Under the next heading, "Divine Providence Is for Evil People and Good People Alike" (§§285–307), Swedenborg focuses on the nature of spiritual evil. Under the previous heading, Swedenborg had given his most succinct definitions of good and evil: "Evil is the pleasure we find in the urge to act and think in violation of the divine pattern, and . . . goodness is the pleasure we feel when we act and think in harmony with the divine pattern" (§279:5). Swedenborg's accounts of good and evil are very similar to Aristotle's accounts of virtue (ἀρετή, areté) and vice (κακία, kakía) in his *Nicomachean Ethics*.[32] Both Swedenborg and Aristotle use the distinction between reason and the will in constructing their accounts. Aristotle defines virtue as a combination of knowing and loving the good. Thus the virtuous take pleasure in doing what they know to be right. Likewise, for Swedenborg, the good do not merely know the divine pattern, they also love it and take pleasure in acting accordingly.

---

32. Aristotle *Nicomachean Ethics* 7:1. For a lucid exposition see Sokolowski 1995, 53–68.

Aristotle defines vice as not merely thinking that bad things are good, but actually loving them as good and taking pleasure in them. Vice is a perversion not just of the will but of the cognitive faculty. The same is true for Swedenborg, who describes how evil people not only love evil things but also experience them as if they were good. Good people, by contrast, hate the same things and experience them as bad.

If, as Swedenborg claims, divine providence is at work in every nook and cranny, then it is at work in evil people as well. Is God, therefore, responsible for their evils? Swedenborg's answer is insightful. Divine providence is a continuous outflowing of goodness that reaches the farthest corners of creation. Divine providence is the same everywhere. What changes are the recipients. What is received from God is modified according to the nature of the recipient. Good people receive divine goodness and truth without distortion. Evil people distort and corrupt divine goodness into evil, divine truth into falsehood.

How does divine providence work to reform evil people? First, as just noted, Swedenborg makes it clear that this is a lifelong process. Evil is not simple, but enormously complex and multifaceted. Because of this, it can only be changed step by step, bit by bit, over the whole span of a lifetime. Second, evil people are constantly working themselves further and further into evil because they take pleasure in it. Third, providence sorts through these evils and allows only those that it can use to draw the person toward the good. This process takes place in the unconscious mind—in the inmost recesses of the will and reason—and is essentially mysterious. Fourth, one way that providence reforms evil people is by exploiting the pleasure they take in the activities of contemplation, thought, and reflection that they use as means to their evil ends. In a complex metaphor, Swedenborg claims that these pleasures can break up and transmute the evils of the inner soul just as digestive juices break up and transmute food in the stomach. Fifth, evil people cannot be led away from evil as long as they think that their prudence is sufficient and deny the workings of providence. The soul has to open itself to the workings of providence, then God can do the rest. Finally, Swedenborg again stresses the primacy of will over intellect. As long as our will is evil, whatever truths we hold will be corrupt and ineffectual. Thus providence must reform the will before the intellect.

Under the heading "Divine Providence Does Not Charge Us with Anything Evil or Credit Us with Anything Good; Rather, Our Own Prudence Claims Both" (§§308–321), Swedenborg elaborates the distinction between those who claim that their prudence is sufficient and those who recognize their dependence on divine providence, illustrating the distinction with many accounts from the spiritual world. Swedenborg also elaborates on the power of ill will to corrupt reason.

X. Predestination and Universal Salvation

Under the heading "Everyone Can Be Reformed, and There Is No Such Thing as Predestination" (§§322–330), Swedenborg deals with the question of predestination and eternal punishment: How just is it for God to predestine some to eternal punishment they cannot avoid and others to eternal bliss they do not earn? Swedenborg's answer is essentially identical to Leibniz's in his *Theodicy* ([1710] 1985, §§266 and 268). All human beings can be saved and none are predestined to eternal punishment. The only people who suffer eternal punishment are those who choose it by refusing God's help. But it is hard to see how anyone could or would choose eternal damnation in light of Swedenborg's teachings that all people are imbued with the desire for salvation, a desire for the good, a desire for God—a desire that does not seem to be completely corruptible by hereditary evil; that those who are in hell choose hell only because of the perversion of their desires, a perversion that causes them to experience hellish torments as ecstasies; and that God works even through these hellish pleasures to turn those who suffer them toward salvation. It seems doubtful that anyone could slip through such a finely meshed providence and fall into eternal damnation.

Swedenborg also deals with a number of the Enlightenment's objections to Christian revelation.[33] How can a just God condemn to hell those people who never had a chance to become Christians—for example, small children, those who lived before the time of Christ, and those who have never heard of Christianity? How wise is the providence that makes salvation dependent upon prophets who appear only for a short time in a particular locality, and upon books written in dead languages and subject to the errors of copyists, the tampering of politicians and pious frauds, and the gnawing criticism of mice? How just is a God who condemns good-hearted people who have lived lives of virtue and charity but never became Christians, while granting salvation to lifelong scoundrels who ask for it only on their deathbeds? Swedenborg's answers are heartening, particularly to those who believe that the divine reveals

---

33. For a useful summary of these objections, see "Profession of Faith of a Vicar of Savoy" in book 4 of Jean-Jacques Rousseau's *Émile, or On Education* (Rousseau [1762] 1979, 295–310).

itself through all religious and spiritual traditions.[34] Since God is good, he wants all people to be saved. Since he wills the end, he wills the means. The only reliable means of assuring all people the opportunity of salvation is to spread both religion and moral knowledge to the farthest reaches of the earth and to open heaven to all those who honor God (in whatever guise) and lead good lives because of this.

XI. The Laws of Providence and the Laws of Nature

Under the heading "The Lord Cannot Act Contrary to the Laws of Divine Providence, Because to Do So Would Be to Act Contrary to His Own Divine Love and His Own Divine Wisdom, and Therefore Contrary to Himself" (§§331–340), Swedenborg stresses again that providence works through natural laws, not against them. The natural order is the means by which providence operates, not an impediment that must be cleared by miraculous leaps. God does not contradict the order of nature and providence, because these are expressions of his divine nature. Thus to contradict them would be to contradict himself. The rest is given to an amplification of Swedenborg's critique of the idea of instantaneous salvation.

Divine Providence then ends on an enigmatic note. His arguments completed, Swedenborg begs our pardon to fill up the remainder of his last page. He then "gives the Devil his due," inviting some spirits from hell to dictate the rest of his book. In their brief conversation with Swedenborg, the demons confirm Swedenborg's claim that evil involves a perversion of both volition and discernment, so that good things are experienced as bad and revolting, and evil things are experienced as good and pleasurable. The empty space on the page filled up, the evil spirits are taken back to hell before they can spoil matters, and *Divine Providence* stands complete.

---

34. Swedenborg's remarkably broad-minded and ecumenical view that all religions can serve as paths to salvation was observed by Ralph Waldo Emerson in a letter of November 20, 1834, to Thomas Carlyle (1795–1881) about Emerson's Swedenborgian friend Sampson Reed (1800–1880). The Swedenborgians, Emerson wrote, "are to me . . . deeply interesting, as a sect which I think must contribute more than all other sects to the new faith which must arise out of all" (Emerson 1883, 32).

Works Cited
in the Introduction

Dole, George F. 2001. *Freedom and Evil: A Pilgrim's Guide to Hell.* West Chester, Pa.: Swedenborg Foundation.

Dole, George F. and Robert H. Kirven. 1992. *A Scientist Explores Spirit: A Compact Biography of Emanuel Swedenborg with Key Concepts of Swedenborg's Theology.* West Chester, Pa.: Swedenborg Foundation.

Emerson, Ralph Waldo. 1883. *The Correspondence of Thomas Carlyle and Ralph Waldo Emerson, 1834–1872.* Vol. 1. Edited by Charles Eliot Norton. Boston: James R. Osgood.

Epicurus. 1994. *The Epicurus Reader: Selected Writings and Testimonia.* Edited and translated by Brad Inwood and L. P. Gerson. Indianapolis: Hackett.

Fox, Leonard. 2000. "*Unde Malum*—From Whence Evil?" Introduction to *Debates with Devils: What Swedenborg Heard in Hell,* edited by Donald L. Rose, with translations by Lisa Hyatt Cooper. West Chester, Pa.: Swedenborg Foundation.

Hume, David. 1992. *Writings on Religion.* Edited by Anthony Flew. La Salle, Ill.: Open Court.

James, William. [1897] 1956. "The Dilemma of Determinism." In *The Will to Believe and Other Essays on Popular Philosophy.* New York: Dover.

———. [1902] 1994. *Varieties of Religious Experience.* New York: Modern Library.

Kant, Immanuel. [1788] 1996. *Critique of Practical Reason.* In *Practical Philosophy,* edited and translated by Mary J. Gregor. Cambridge: Cambridge University Press.

———. [1791] 1996. "On the Miscarriage of All Philosophical Trials in Theodicy." Translated by George di Giovanni. In *Religion and Rational Theology,* edited and translated by Allen W. Wood and George di Giovanni. Cambridge: Cambridge University Press.

———. [1781, 1787] 1929. *Critique of Pure Reason.* Translated by Norman Kemp Smith. New York: Saint Martin's Press.

Kolakowski, Leszek. 1995. *God Owes Us Nothing: A Brief Remark on Pascal's Religion and the Spirit of Jansenism.* Chicago: University of Chicago Press.

Larrimore, Mark, ed. 2001. *The Problem of Evil: A Reader.* Oxford: Blackwell.

Leaman, Oliver. 1995. *Evil and Suffering in Jewish Philosophy.* Cambridge: Cambridge University Press.

Leibniz, Gottfried Wilhelm Freiherr von. [1710] 1985. *Theodicy: Essays on the Goodness of God, the Freedom of Man, and the Origin of Evil.* Translated by Austin Farrer. La Salle, Ill.: Open Court.

———. [1714] 1989. *The Principles of Nature and Grace, Based on Reason.* In *Philosophical Papers and Letters,* edited and translated by Leroy E. Loemker. 2nd ed. Boston: Kluwer Academic Publishers.

Lovejoy, Arthur O. 1936. *The Great Chain of Being: A Study of the History of an Idea.* Cambridge: Harvard University Press.

Malebranche, Nicholas. [1680] 1958. *Traité de la nature et de la grâce.* In volume 5 of *Oeuvres complètes de Malebranche.* Paris: Librairie Vrin.

———. [1680] 1992. *Treatise on Nature and Grace.* Translated by Patrick Riley. Oxford: Clarendon Press.

Pascal, Blaise. 1914. *Pensées.* In volume 2 of *Oeuvres de Blaise Pascal,* edited by L. Brunschvicg. Paris: Librairie Hachette.

Pope, Alexander. [1734] 1958. *Essay on Man.* Edited by Maynard Mack. London: Methuen.

Riley, Patrick. 1986. *The General Will before Rousseau: The Transformation of the Divine into the Civic.* Princeton: Princeton University Press.

Ross, W. D. 1959. *Aristotle: A Complete Exposition of His Work and Thought.* New York: World Publishing.

Rousseau, Jean-Jacques. [1762] 1979. *Émile, or On Education.* Translated by Allan Bloom. New York: Basic Books.

Sokolowski, Robert. 1995. *The God of Faith and Reason: Foundations of Christian Theology.* 2nd ed. Washington, D.C.: Catholic University of America Press.

Swedenborg, Emanuel. 1931. *A Philosopher's Note Book: Excerpts from Philosophical Writers and from the Sacred Scriptures on a Variety of Philosophical Subjects; Together with Some Reflections, and Sundry Notes and Memoranda by Emanuel Swedenborg.* Edited and translated by Alfred Acton. Philadelphia: Swedenborg Scientific Association.

Versluis, Arthur. 1992. "'Gnosticism,' Ancient and Modern." In *Alexandria* 1. Grand Rapids, Mich.: Phanes Press.

Voltaire. 1949. *The Portable Voltaire.* Edited by Ben Ray Redman. New York: Viking.

———. [1759] 1966. *Candide, or Optimism.* Translated by R. M. Adams. New York: Norton.

Short Titles and Other Conventions
Used in This Work

A S is common in Swedenborgian studies, text citations of Swedenborg's works refer not to page numbers but to Swedenborg's section numbers, which are uniform in all editions. Thus *"Secrets of Heaven 29"* refers to section 29 (§29) of Swedenborg's *Secrets of Heaven.* A reference such as "29:2" indicates subsection 2 of section 29. In the text of the section itself, this subsection would be marked [2].

Swedenborg made extensive cross-references within *Divine Providence,* but often did not cite the number of the section or sections to which he was referring. These omitted cross-reference numbers have been inserted in brackets in this edition.

In a few cases Swedenborg supplied the section numbers, but they are obviously in error. Where a plausible correction has been found, it has been inserted in square brackets. These corrections have, furthermore, been italicized as an indication that they are intended to replace the preceding entry, not augment it.

This system has also been applied to citations of the Bible and of Swedenborg's works that appear in the main text of the translation: that is, italicized brackets indicate a correction and roman brackets indicate an addition. Words not appearing in the original but necessary for the understanding of the text also appear in roman brackets; this device has been used sparingly, however, even at the risk of some inconsistency in its application.

Comments on the text are printed as endnotes, referenced by superscript numbers appearing in the main text. The initials of the writer or writers of each note are given in square brackets. Translations of material quoted in the endnotes are those of the indicated writer, except in cases in which the cited source is a translated text.

Swedenborg did not number the divisions of *Divine Providence.* His decision not to do so seems to have been deliberate, and in accord with it chapter numbers are not included in the text. However, the table of contents provides such numbers in square brackets for the convenience of readers.

References to Swedenborg's works in this volume accord with the short titles listed below, except where he gives his own version of a title in the text of the translation, or where other translations are cited by the annotators. In this list, the short title is followed by the traditional translation for the title; by the original Latin title, with its full translation; and finally by the place and date of original publication if Swedenborg published it himself, or the approximate date of writing if he did not. The list is chronological within each of the two groups shown—the published theological works, and the nontheological and posthumously published works. The titles given below as theological works published by Swedenborg are generally not further referenced in lists of works cited in the preface, introduction, and endnotes.

Theological Works Published by Swedenborg

Secrets of Heaven
Traditional title: *Arcana Coelestia*
Original title: *Arcana Coelestia, Quae in Scriptura Sacra, seu Verbo Domini Sunt, Detecta: . . . Una cum Mirabilibus Quae Visa Sunt in Mundo Spirituum, et in Coelo Angelorum* [A Disclosure of Secrets of Heaven Contained in Sacred Scripture, or the Word of the Lord, . . . Together with Amazing Things Seen in the World of Spirits and in the Heaven of Angels]. London: 1749–1756.

Heaven and Hell
Traditional title: *Heaven and Hell*
Original title: *De Coelo et Ejus Mirabilibus, et de Inferno, ex Auditis et Visis* [Heaven and Its Wonders and Hell: Drawn from Things Heard and Seen]. London: 1758.

New Jerusalem
Traditional title: *New Jerusalem and Its Heavenly Doctrine*
Original title: *De Nova Hierosolyma et Ejus Doctrina Coelesti: Ex Auditis e Coelo: Quibus Praemittitur Aliquid de Novo Coelo et Nova Terra* [The New Jerusalem and Its Heavenly Teaching: Drawn from Things Heard from Heaven: Preceded by a Discussion of the New Heaven and the New Earth]. London: 1758.

Last Judgment
Traditional title: *The Last Judgment*

Original title: *De Ultimo Judicio, et de Babylonia Destructa: Ita Quod Omnia, Quae in Apocalypsi Praedicta Sunt, Hodie Impleta Sunt: Ex Auditis et Visis* [The Last Judgment and Babylon Destroyed, Showing That at This Day All the Predictions of the Book of Revelation Have Been Fulfilled: Drawn from Things Heard and Seen]. London: 1758.

White Horse
Traditional title: *The White Horse*
Original title: *De Equo Albo, de Quo in Apocalypsi, Cap. XIX: Et Dein de Verbo et Ejus Sensu Spirituali seu Interno, ex Arcanis Coelestibus* [The White Horse in Revelation Chapter 19, and the Word and Its Spiritual or Inner Sense (from *Secrets of Heaven*)]. London: 1758.

Other Planets
Traditional title: *Earths in the Universe*
Original title: *De Telluribus in Mundo Nostro Solari, Quae Vocantur Planetae, et de Telluribus in Coelo Astrifero, deque Illarum Incolis, Tum de Spiritibus et Angelis Ibi: Ex Auditis et Visis* [Planets or Worlds in Our Solar System, and Worlds in the Starry Heavens, and Their Inhabitants, as Well as the Spirits and Angels There: Drawn from Things Heard and Seen]. London: 1758.

The Lord
Traditional title: *Doctrine of the Lord*
Original title: *Doctrina Novae Hierosolymae de Domino* [Teachings for the New Jerusalem on the Lord]. Amsterdam: 1763.

Sacred Scripture
Traditional title: *Doctrine of the Sacred Scripture*
Original title: *Doctrina Novae Hierosolymae de Scriptura Sacra* [Teachings for the New Jerusalem on Sacred Scripture]. Amsterdam: 1763.

Life
Traditional title: *Doctrine of Life*
Original title: *Doctrina Vitae pro Nova Hierosolyma ex Praeceptis Decalogi* [Teachings about Life for the New Jerusalem: Drawn from the Ten Commandments]. Amsterdam: 1763.

Faith
Traditional title: *Doctrine of Faith*
Original title: *Doctrina Novae Hierosolymae de Fide* [Teachings for the New Jerusalem on Faith]. Amsterdam: 1763.

Supplements
Traditional title: *Continuation Concerning the Last Judgment*
Original title: *Continuatio de Ultimo Judicio: Et de Mundo Spirituali* [Supplements on the Last Judgment and the Spiritual World]. Amsterdam: 1763.

Divine Love and Wisdom
Traditional title: *Divine Love and Wisdom*
Original title: *Sapientia Angelica de Divino Amore et de Divina Sapientia* [Angelic Wisdom about Divine Love and Wisdom]. Amsterdam: 1763.

Divine Providence
Traditional title: *Divine Providence*
Original title: *Sapientia Angelica de Divina Providentia* [Angelic Wisdom about Divine Providence]. Amsterdam: 1764.

Revelation Unveiled
Traditional title: *Apocalypse Revealed*
Original title: *Apocalypsis Revelata, in Qua Deteguntur Arcana Quae Ibi Praedicta Sunt, et Hactenus Recondita Latuerunt* [The Book of Revelation Unveiled, Uncovering the Secrets That Were Foretold There and Have Lain Hidden until Now]. Amsterdam: 1766.

Marriage Love
Traditional title: *Conjugial Love*
Original title: *Delitiae Sapientiae de Amore Conjugiali: Post Quas Sequuntur Voluptates Insaniae de Amore Scortatorio* [Wisdom's Delight in Marriage Love: Followed by Insanity's Pleasure in Promiscuous Love]. Amsterdam: 1768.

Survey
Traditional title: *Brief Exposition*
Original title: *Summaria Expositio Doctrinae Novae Ecclesiae, Quae per Novam Hierosolymam in Apocalypsi Intelligitur* [Survey of Teachings for the New Church Meant by the New Jerusalem in the Book of Revelation]. Amsterdam: 1769.

Soul-Body Interaction
Traditional title: *Intercourse between the Soul and Body*
Original title: *De Commercio Animae et Corporis, Quod Creditur Fieri vel per Influxum Physicum, vel per Influxum Spiritualem, vel per Harmoniam Praestabilitam* [Soul-Body Interaction, Believed to Occur Either by a Physical Inflow, or by a Spiritual Inflow, or by a Preestablished Harmony]. London: 1769.

True Christianity

Traditional title: *True Christian Religion*

Original title: *Vera Christiana Religio, Continens Universam Theologiam Novae Ecclesiae a Domino apud Danielem Cap. VII:13–14, et in Apocalypsi Cap. XXI:1, 2 Praedictae* [True Christianity: Containing the Whole Theology of the New Church Predicted by the Lord in Daniel 7:13–14 and Revelation 21:1, 2]. Amsterdam: 1771.

Nontheological and Posthumously Published Works by Swedenborg Cited in This Volume

Basic Principles of Nature

Traditional title: *Principia*

Original title: *Principia Rerum Naturalium sive Novorum Tentaminum Phaenomena Mundi Elementaris Philosophice Explicandi* [Basic Principles of Nature or of New Attempts to Explain Philosophically the Phenomena of the Elemental World]. Dresden and Leipzig: 1734.

Soul-Body Mechanism

Traditional title: *Mechanism of the Soul and Body*

Original title: *De Mechanismo Animae et Corporis* [Mechanism of the Soul and Body]. 1734.

The Soul's Fluid

Traditional title: *Animal Spirit(s)*

Original title: *De Spiritu Animali* [The Soul's Fluid]. 1741.

Ontology

Traditional title: *Ontology*

Original title: *Ontologia* [Ontology]. 1742.

The Soul's Domain

Traditional title: *The Animal Kingdom*

Original title: *Regnum Animale, Anatomice, Physice, et Philosophice Perlustratum* [The Soul's Domain Thoroughly Examined by Means of Anatomy, Physics, and Philosophy]. The Hague: 1744–1745.

Worship and Love of God

Traditional title: *Worship and Love of God*

Original title: *Pars Prima de Cultu et Amore Dei; Ubi Agitur de Telluris Ortu, Paradiso, & Vivario, Tum de Primogeniti seu Adami Nativitate, Infantia, & Amore. Pars Secunda de Cultu et Amore Dei; Ubi Agitur de Conjugio Primogeniti seu Adami, et Inibi de Anima, Mente Intellectuali, Statu Integritatis, & Imagine Dei. Pars Tertia, de Vita Conjugii Paris Primogeniti* [First Part Concerning the Worship and Love of God; in Which Is Discussed the Earth's Origin, Paradise, and the Garden, and then the Birth of the Firstborn, or Adam, His Infancy, and Love. Second Part Concerning the Worship and Love of God; in Which Is Discussed the Marriage of the Firstborn, or Adam, and Therein the Soul, the Understanding Mind, the State of Wholeness, and the Image of God. Part Three, Concerning the Life of the Firstborn Married Couple]. London: 1745.

The Old Testament Explained
Traditional title: *The Word Explained*
Original title: *Explicatio in Verbum Historicum Veteris Testamenti* [The Historical Word of the Old Testament Explained]. 1745–1747.

Spiritual Experiences
Traditional title: *The Spiritual Diary*
Original title: *Experientiae Spirituales* [Spiritual Experiences]. 1745–1765.

Revelation Explained
Traditional title: *Apocalypse Explained*
Original title: *Apocalypsis Explicata secundum Sensum Spiritualem, Ubi Revelantur Arcana, Quae Ibi Praedicta, et Hactenus Recondita Fuerunt* [The Book of Revelation Explained as to Its Spiritual Meaning, Which Reveals Secret Wonders That Were Predicted There and Have Been Hidden until Now]. 1757–1759.

Sketch for Divine Love
Traditional title: *On Divine Love*
Original title: *De Divino Amore* [Divine Love]. 1762–1763.

Biblical Titles

Swedenborg referred to the Hebrew Scriptures as the Old Testament; his terminology has been adopted in this edition. As was the custom in his day, he referred to the Pentateuch (Genesis, Exodus, Leviticus, Numbers, and Deuteronomy) as the books of Moses; to the Psalms as the book of David; and occasionally to the Book of Revelation as John.

DIVINE PROVIDENCE

ANGELIC WISDOM
ABOUT
DIVINE PROVIDENCE

◁(❀)◃✛◁(❀)◃✛◁(❀)◃✛◁(❀)◃✛◁(❀)◃✛◁(❀)◃✛◁(❀)◃✛◁(❀)◃✛◁(❀)◃

Divine Providence Is the Form of Government Exercised by the Lord's Divine Love and Wisdom

TO understand what divine providence is—that it is the way the Lord's[1] divine love and wisdom govern us—it is important to be aware of the following things, which were presented in my book on the subject.[2] In the Lord, divine love is a property of divine wisdom and divine wisdom is a property of divine love (*Divine Love and Wisdom* 34–39).[3] Divine love and wisdom cannot fail to be and to be manifested in others that it has created (§§47–51). Everything in the universe was created by divine love and wisdom (§§52, 53, 151–156). Everything in the created universe is a vessel of divine love and wisdom (§§54–60 *[55–60]*). The Lord looks like the sun to angels; its radiating warmth is love and its radiating light is wisdom (§§83–88, 89–92, 93–98, 296–301). The divine love and wisdom that emanate from the Lord constitute a single whole (§§99–102). The Lord from eternity, who is Jehovah,[4] created the universe and everything in it from himself and not from nothing

1

47

(§§282–284, 290–295). These propositions may be found in the work entitled *Angelic Wisdom about Divine Love and Wisdom*.[5]

2 Further, if we put these propositions together with what I said about creation in that work, it shows that the way the Lord's divine love and wisdom look after us is what we call divine providence. However, since that book was about creation and not about how the state of things was maintained after creation (which is the way the Lord is looking after us), I need to deal with that now. In this section, though, I will be dealing with the way the oneness of divine love and wisdom (or of what is good and true in divinity) is maintained in what has been created; and I will do so in the following sequence:[6]

1. The universe as a whole and in every detail was created out of divine love, by means of divine wisdom.

2. Divine love and wisdom radiate from the Lord as a single whole.

3. There is some image of this whole in everything that has been created.

4. It is the intent of divine providence that everything created, collectively and in every detail, should be this kind of whole, and that if it is not, it should become one.

5. The good that love does is actually good only to the extent that it is united to the truth that wisdom perceives, and the truth that wisdom perceives is actually true only to the extent that it is united to the good that love does.

6. If the good that love does is not united to the truth that wisdom perceives, it is not really good, but it may seem to be; and if the truth that wisdom perceives is not united to the good that love does, it is not really true, but it may seem to be.

7. The Lord does not let anything remain divided. This means that things must be focused either on what is both good and true or on what is both evil and false.

8. If something is focused on what is both good and true, then it is something; but if it is focused on what is both evil and false, it is not anything at all.

9. The Lord's divine providence works things out so that what is both evil and false promotes balance, evaluation, and purification, which means that it promotes the union of what is good and true in others.

1. *The universe as a whole and in every detail was created out of divine love, by means of divine wisdom.* I explained in *Divine Love and Wisdom* that the Lord from eternity, who is Jehovah, is essentially divine love and wisdom, and that he himself created the universe and everything in it out of himself [§§28–33, 52–60, 282–295]. It then follows that the universe and everything in it was created out of divine love by means of divine wisdom.

I also explained in that work that love cannot do anything apart from wisdom and that wisdom cannot do anything apart from love [§401]. Love without wisdom (or our volition apart from our discernment)[7] cannot think anything. It cannot actually see, feel, or say anything. This means that love apart from wisdom (or our volition apart from our discernment) cannot do anything. By the same token, wisdom apart from love (or our discernment apart from our volition) cannot think anything, see or sense anything, or even say anything. This means that wisdom apart from love (or our discernment apart from our volition) cannot do anything. If you take the love away, there is no longer any intention, so there is no action. If this is how things work for us when we do something, it was all the more true of the God who is love itself and wisdom itself when he created and made the universe and everything in it.

[2] Everything that meets our eyes in this world can serve to convince us that the universe and absolutely everything in it was created out of divine love by means of divine wisdom. Take any particular thing and look at it with some wisdom, and this will be clear. Look at a tree—or its seed, its fruit, its flower, or its leaf. Collect your wits and look through a good microscope and you will see incredible things; and the deeper things that you cannot see are even more incredible.[8] Look at the design of the sequence by which a tree grows from its seed all the way to a new seed, and ask yourself, "In this whole process, is there not a constant effort toward ongoing self-propagation?" The goal it is headed for is a seed that has a new power to reproduce. If you are willing to think spiritually (and you can if you want to), surely you see wisdom in this. Then too, if you are willing to press your spiritual thinking further, surely you see that this power does not come from the seed or from our world's sun, which is nothing but fire, but that it was put into the seed by a creator God who has infinite wisdom. This is not just something that happened at its creation; it is something that has been happening constantly ever since. Maintenance is constant creation, just as enduring is a constant coming

into being.[9] This is like the way labor ceases if you take the intention out of the activity, the way speech ceases if you take thinking out of it, or the way motion ceases if you take the energy out of it, and so on. In short, if you take the cause away from the effect, the effect ceases.

[3] A force is instilled into everything that has been created. However, the force does not do anything on its own; it depends on the one who instilled it. Look at some other subject on our planet. Look at a silkworm or a bee or some little creature and examine it, first physically, then rationally, and finally spiritually. If you can think deeply, you will be stunned at everything. If you listen to the inner voice of wisdom, you will exclaim in amazement, "Can anyone fail to see Divinity here? These are the marks of divine wisdom!"

Beyond this even, if you look at the functions of everything that has been created, you will see how they follow in sequence all the way to humanity and from us to our source, the Creator. You will see how the connectedness of everything depends on the Creator's union with us; and if you are willing to admit it, the preservation of everything depends on this as well.

In what follows, you will see that divine love created everything, but that it did nothing apart from divine wisdom.

4   2. *Divine love and wisdom radiate from the Lord as a single whole.* We can see this from several things that I explained in *Divine Love and Wisdom,* especially the following. In the Lord, reality and its manifestation[10] are both distinguishable and united (§§14–17 *[14–16]*). In the Lord, infinite things are distinguishably one (§§17–22). Divine love is a property of divine wisdom, and divine wisdom is a property of divine love (§§34–39). Unless it is married to wisdom, love cannot accomplish anything (§§401–403). Love or volition does not do anything without wisdom or discernment (§§409–410). As spiritual warmth and light radiate from the Lord as the sun, they make a unity the way divine love and divine wisdom make a single whole in the Lord (§§99–132 *[99–102]*).

We can see the truth of the present proposition from what is explained in these passages. However, since people do not know how two things can act in unison if they are different from each other, I should like to show at this point that no unity occurs apart from a form. Rather, the form itself is what makes the whole. Then I should like to show that a form makes a whole more perfectly as its constituents are distinguishably different and yet united.

[2] *No whole occurs apart from a form. Rather, the form itself is what makes the whole.*[11] Anyone who thinks with real mental focus will see

clearly that no whole occurs apart from a form. If a whole occurs, it is a form. Whatever comes into being derives from its form what we refer to as its quality, attributes, changes of state, relationships, and the like. So anything that is not in some form is of no effect, and anything that is of no effect is of no substance.[12] The form itself is the source of all these qualities. Further, since all the constituents of a form—if the form is complete—relate to each other like link to link in a chain, it follows that the form itself is what makes the whole and therefore is the object to which we can attribute quality, state, effect, and so on, all depending on the completeness of the form.

[3] Everything we see with our eyes in this world is this kind of whole, and so is everything we do not see with our eyes, either in the depths of nature or in the spiritual world. An individual is this kind of whole, and so is a human community. Further, the church[13] is this kind of whole, and so is the whole angelic heaven in the Lord's sight. In short, the created universe is this kind of whole not only in its entirety but also in every detail.

If the whole and every part is to be a form, it is necessary that the one who created them all should be form itself and that all the things that have been created in their particular forms should come from that essential form. That is the reason for a number of statements in *Divine Love and Wisdom;* for example, the following: Divine love and wisdom is substance and is form[14] (§§40–43). Divine love and wisdom are form in and of themselves, and are therefore wholly "itself" and unique[15] (§§44–46). Divine love and divine wisdom are a single whole in the Lord (§§14–17 *[14–16],* 18–22 *[17–22]*). They emanate from the Lord as a single whole (§§99–102 and elsewhere [§125]).

[4] *A form makes a unity more perfectly as its constituents are distinguishably different, and yet united.* It is hard for our discernment to accept this unless it is raised up, because it seems as though the only way a form can make a single whole is if its constituents have some regular similarity.

I have often talked with angels about this. They have told me that this is a mystery clearly grasped by the wise among them but dimly grasped by the less wise. Still, the truth is that a form is more perfect as its constituents are distinguishably different but still united in some particular way. In support of this, angels have cited the communities in the heavens. Taken all together, these communities make up the form of heaven. They have also cited the angels in each community, saying that the more clearly individual angels are on their own—are therefore free—

and love the other members of their community on the basis of their own affection, in apparent freedom, the more perfect is the form of the community.

They have also referred by way of illustration to the marriage of what is good and what is true. The more clearly these are two, the more perfectly they can form a unity. It is the same with love and wisdom. Anything unclear is confused, and this is what gives rise to all imperfection of form.

[5] Angels have also offered abundant evidence of the way completely different things are united so that they form a single whole. They have called attention particularly to things within a person, where all the countless parts are similarly differentiated and yet are united—differentiated by membranes and united by ligaments. They have said that it is the same with love and all its components and with wisdom and all its components, which are perceived simply as unities.

There is more on this subject in *Divine Love and Wisdom* 14–22 and in *Heaven and Hell* 56, 489 *[56, 71, 418]*.[16] I include all this because it is a matter of angelic wisdom.

5   3. *There is some image of this unity in everything that has been created.* We can tell from what is presented throughout *Divine Love and Wisdom* that in everything created there is some image of the divine love and wisdom that are a whole in the Lord and that emanate from him as a whole. See especially §§47–51, 54–60 *[55–60]*, 282–284, 290–295, 316–318 *[313–318]*, 319–326, and 349–457 *[349–357]*. I have explained in these passages that Divinity is present in everything that has been created because God the Creator, who is the Lord from eternity, brought forth the sun of the spiritual world from his actual self, and by means of that sun brought forth the whole universe. This means that that sun, which is from the Lord and is where the Lord is, is not only the first but the only substance of which everything is made. Since it is the only substance, it follows that it is present in everything that has been created, but with infinite variety depending on function.

[2] In the Lord, then, there is divine love and wisdom; in the sun that comes from him there is divine fire and divine radiance; and from that sun come spiritual warmth and spiritual light, with the two making a single whole. It follows, then, that some image of this whole is present in everything that has been created.

This is why everything in the universe is based on what is good and what is true and in fact on their union, or (which amounts to the same thing) everything in the universe is based on love and wisdom and on their union, since goodness is a matter of love and truth is a matter of wisdom. Love in fact calls everything of its own good, and wisdom calls everything of its own true.

We will see now that this union is present in everything that has been created.

6 It is widely recognized that there is only one substance that is the first and is the basis of everything, but the nature of that substance is a mystery. People think that it is so simple that nothing could be simpler, that it is like a dimensionless point, and that dimensional forms emerge from an infinite number of such points.[17] However, this is an illusion arising from spatial thinking; spatial thinking makes the smallest element look like this. The truth is, though, that the simpler and purer anything is the greater and fuller it is. This is why the more deeply we look into anything, the more amazing, perfect, and beautiful are the things we see; so in the first substance of all there must be the most amazing, perfect, and beautiful things of all.

This is because the first substance comes from the spiritual sun, which as already noted [§5] is from the Lord and is where the Lord is. That sun itself is therefore the only substance, and since it is not in space, it is totally present in everything, in the largest and the smallest components of the created universe.

[2] Since that sun is the first and only substance that gives rise to everything, it follows that it contains infinitely more things than we can see in the substances that arise from it, which we refer to as derivative substances and ultimately matter. The reason we cannot see these things is that they come down from the sun by two kinds of level, and that all aspects of their perfection decrease by these two kinds of level. This is why the more deeply we look into anything, the more amazing, perfect, and beautiful are the things we see, as just noted.

I mention this in support of the proposition that there is some image of Divinity in everything that has been created, allowing for the fact that this image is less and less apparent as we come down level by level.[18] It is even less apparent when a lower level, separated from a higher one by its closure, is clogged by earthly matter.

Still, all this cannot help but seem obscure unless you have read and comprehended what was explained in *Divine Love and Wisdom* about the spiritual sun (§§53–172 [83–172]), levels (§§173–281), and the creation of the universe (§§282–357).

7 4. *It is the intent of divine providence that everything created, collectively and in every detail, should be this kind of whole, and that if it is not,*

it should become one. This means that there should be something of divine love and something of divine wisdom together in everything that has been created, or (which amounts to the same thing) something good and something true in everything that has been created—or a union of what is good and what is true. Since what is good is a matter of love and what is true is a matter of wisdom, as I noted in §5 above, throughout the following pages I will be talking about what is good and what is true instead of about love and wisdom, and about the marriage of goodness and truth instead of the union of love and wisdom.[19]

8   We can see from the preceding section that in everything that has been created by the Lord there is a kind of image of the divine love and wisdom that are a unity in the Lord and that emanate from the Lord as a single whole. Now I need to say something more specific about the unity or union that is called the marriage of goodness and truth.

(a) This marriage is in the Lord himself, since as already noted divine love and wisdom are a unity in him.[20] (b) It is from the Lord, since love and wisdom are completely united in everything that emanates from him. They both emanate from the Lord as the sun—divine love as warmth and divine wisdom as light. (c) Angels accept them as two, but the Lord unites them within the angels; and the same holds true for people of the church. (d) It is because of the inflow of love and wisdom from the Lord as a single whole into angels of heaven and people of the church and because of their acceptance by angels and people that the Lord is called the bridegroom and husband in the Word[21] and the church is called the bride and wife. (e) To the extent, then, that heaven and the church in general, or angels of heaven and people of the church in particular, participate in this union, or in the marriage of goodness and truth, they are images and likenesses of the Lord. This is because these two realities are a single whole in the Lord and in fact are the Lord. (f) In heaven and the church in general, and in angels of heaven and people of the church in particular, love and wisdom are a single whole when volition and discernment (and therefore goodness and truth) form a single whole, or what is the same thing, when charity and faith form a single whole; or what is also the same thing, when a belief system from the Word and a life according to it form a single whole. (g) I have, however, explained how these two realities form a single whole in us and in all aspects of our being in part 5 of *Divine Love and Wisdom,* where I dealt with our creation and especially with the correspondence[22] of our volition and discernment to our heart and lungs (§§385–432 *[358–432]*).

9   As for the way love and wisdom form a unity in things beneath or outside us—in the animal kingdom and the plant kingdom—this will come up throughout the following pages. I may mention three things by way of preface. First, there was a marriage of goodness and truth in the universe and in absolutely everything in it that the Lord created. Second, this marriage was broken up in us after creation. Third, it is a goal of divine providence that what has been broken apart should become a whole and therefore that the marriage of goodness and truth should be restored.

These three propositions have been given ample support in *Divine Love and Wisdom,* so there is no need of further support. Then too, everyone can see on the basis of reason that if there was a marriage of goodness and truth in everything that was created and this marriage was later broken up, the Lord would be constantly working for its restoration. This means that its restoration and therefore the union of the created universe with the Lord by means of us must be a goal of divine providence.

5. *The good that love does is actually good only to the extent that it is united to the truth that wisdom perceives, and the truth that wisdom perceives is actually true only to the extent that it is united to the good that love does.* The reason for this lies in the origin of goodness and truth. Goodness has its origin in the Lord and so does truth, because the Lord is goodness itself and truth itself, and these two form a unity in him. This is why the goodness in heaven's angels and in us on earth is not really good except to the extent that it is united to truth, and why the truth is not really true except to the extent that it is united to goodness.

10

We know that everything good and true comes from the Lord, so because goodness forms a single whole with truth and truth with goodness, it follows that if anything good is to be really good and anything true is to be really true, they need to form a single whole in their vessels. These vessels are heaven's angels and we who are on earth.

It is generally recognized that everything in the universe involves what is good and what is true. That is, we understand "goodness" to mean that which everywhere comprehends and comprises everything that has to do with love, and we understand "truth" to mean that which everywhere comprehends and comprises everything that has to do with wisdom. It has not been generally recognized, though, that something good is nothing unless it is united to something true and that something true is nothing unless it is united to something good.

11

It does seem as though something good could be real apart from something true and that something true could be real apart from something good, but this is not the case. In fact, love (all of whose elements are called good) is the reality of anything, and wisdom (all of whose elements are called true) is the manifestation of that thing that follows from its reality, as I explained in *Divine Love and Wisdom* 14–16. Just as reality is nothing apart from manifestation, then, and manifestation is nothing apart from reality, so goodness apart from truth or truth apart from goodness is nothing. By the same token, what is something good apart from its relationship to something else? Can we really call it good? There is no effectiveness or perception involved in it.

[2] The element that has an effect when it is united to goodness, the element that makes perception and sensation possible, involves what is true because it involves what is in our discernment. Say to someone simply "goodness" without saying that some particular thing is good—is that "goodness" really anything? It is something only because of the particular thing that we identify with it. The only place this identification occurs is in our discernment, and our discernment involves what is true.

The same holds true for intending. To intend without knowing, perceiving, and considering what we intend is nothing, but together with these functions it is something. All our intending is a matter of love and involves what is good; and all our knowing, perceiving, and considering is a matter of discernment and involves what is true; so we can see that "intending" is nothing. Intending something in particular, though, is something.

[3] It is the same with all acts of service, because acts of service are good. Unless an act of service is focused on some benefit that is integral to it, it is not really an act of service, so it is nothing. It gets its focus from our discernment; and what is therefore united to or associated with the act involves what is true. This is where the act of service gets its quality.

[4] We can tell from these few examples that nothing good is really anything at all apart from something true, and that nothing true is anything at all apart from something good. We say that goodness together with truth, or truth together with goodness, is something. It follows, then, that evil together with falsity, or falsity together with evil, is nothing. This is because they are opposites to goodness and truth, and an opposite is destructive. In this case, it destroys the "something." But more on this later [§19].

12 However, there is a marriage of goodness and truth in a cause, and from that cause there is a marriage of goodness and truth in an effect. The marriage of goodness and truth in a cause is a marriage of our volition and discernment, or of our love and wisdom. This marriage is happening in everything we intend and think and therefore decide and focus on.

This marriage enters into the effect and makes it happen, but as it makes it happen the two aspects seem like different events because something that is simultaneous is working itself out by stages. For instance, when we intend and consider providing ourselves with food, clothing, or shelter, or engaging in our job or some task or in social interaction, then at first we are intending and considering it (or deciding and focusing on it), both at the same time. When we express these intentions in specific effects, though, one action follows another, even though in our intent and thought they still form a single whole.

The services that are performed in these effects are the results of love or of goodness. The means to these services are the effects of discernment or truth. Anyone can support these general observations by specific examples, provided there is a clear sense of what belongs to the good that love can do and what belongs to the truth that wisdom perceives, and provided there is a clear grasp of how they are reflected in a cause and how they are reflected in an effect.[23]

I have stated on occasion that love is what constitutes our life, but this does not mean love separated from wisdom, or what is good separated from what is true in the cause. This is because love by itself, or what is good by itself, is nothing. Consequently, the love that constitutes our deepest life, the life that comes from the Lord, is love and wisdom together. So too, the love that constitutes our life to the extent that we are open to it is not love by itself in the cause, though it is by itself in the result. Love is incomprehensible apart from its quality, and its quality is wisdom. That quality or wisdom can come only from its underlying reality, which is love. This is why they are a single whole; and the same holds true for what is good and what is true.   **13**

Now since what is true comes from what is good the way wisdom comes from love, both together are called love or good. Love in its form actually is wisdom, and what is good in its form is true. Form is the one and only source of quality.[24]

We can therefore conclude that what is good is actually good only to the extent that it is united to what is appropriately true, and that what is true is actually true only to the extent that it is united to what is appropriately good.

6. *If the good that love does is not united to the truth that wisdom perceives, it is not really good, but it may seem to be; and if the truth that wisdom perceives is not united to the good that love does, it is not really true, but it may seem to be.* The truth of the matter is that nothing good occurs that is really good unless it is united to something true that is appropriate to it, and nothing true occurs that is really true unless it is united to something good that is appropriate to it.   **14**

Still, there is such a thing as something good separated from what is true and something true separated from what is good. This happens with hypocrites and flatterers, with all kinds of evil people, and with people who are involved in good on the earthly[25] level but not at all on the spiritual level. All of these people can do things that are good for church, country, community, and fellow citizen, for the poor and needy, and for widows and orphans. They can understand truths, too, and can think about them discerningly and talk about them and teach them. However, those good and true characteristics are not particularly deep, so they are not essentially good and true for the people who display them. They are outwardly good and true, and therefore are only facades.[26] They exist solely for the sake of themselves and the world and not for the sake of goodness itself and truth itself, which means that they are not derived from what is good and true. They come simply from the mouth and the body, then, and not from the heart.

[2] We might compare them to gold or silver that has been overlaid on slag, rotten wood, or dung, and we might compare the uttered truths to our breath, which dissipates, or to a will-o'-the-wisp that vanishes. Outwardly, they may still seem genuine. While these truths have one guise for the people themselves, however, they can look very different to people who hear and accept them without knowing their source. The way we are affected outwardly depends on what lies within us. Some truth enters the hearing of others, and no matter whose mouth it has come from, the way the other minds grasp it depends on their own state and quality.

It is much the same for people who by reason of their heredity are involved in something that is good on the earthly level but not in something that is spiritually good. What lies within anything good and anything true is spiritual, and this banishes whatever is false and evil. Still, what is solely earthly sides with what is evil and false, and siding with evil is not in harmony with doing good.

15 The reason that goodness can be separated from truth and truth from goodness and that they still seem good and true even when separated is that we have an ability to act, called freedom, and an ability to discern, called rationality. It is by the misuse of these abilities that we can seem different outwardly than we actually are inwardly, so that an evil individual can do what is good and say what is true, and so that a devil can pretend to be an angel of light.[27]

On this subject, see the following propositions from *Divine Love and Wisdom*. The origin of evil is in the abuse of the abilities proper to us called rationality and freedom (§§264–270). These two abilities exist in both evil and good individuals (§425). If love is not married to wisdom (or if goodness is not married to truth), it cannot accomplish anything (§401). Love or volition does not do anything without wisdom or discernment (§409). Love or volition marries wisdom or discernment to itself and arranges things so that wisdom or discernment marries it willingly (§§410–412). Because of the power given it by love, wisdom or discernment can be raised up, can accept things in heaven's light, and can grasp them (§413). Love can be raised up in the same way and can grasp things in heaven's warmth provided it loves its spouse, wisdom, to that degree (§§414–415). Otherwise, love pulls wisdom or discernment back from its height so that they act in unison (§§416–418). If they are raised up together, love is cleansed in our discernment (§§419–421). Love that has been cleansed by wisdom in our discernment becomes spiritual and heavenly, and love that has been polluted in our discernment becomes limited to our senses and our bodies (§§422–424). It is the same for charity and faith and their union as it is for love and wisdom and their union (§§427–430). What charity in the heavens is (§431).[28]

7. *The Lord does not let anything remain divided. This means that things must be focused either on what is both good and true or on what is both evil and false.* The first of the goals toward which the Lord's divine providence works is that we should be engaged in what is good and what is true together. That is our "good" and our love and that is our truth and our wisdom, because that is what makes us human and images of the Lord. However, since while we are living in this world we can be engaged simultaneously in what is good and what is false, or in what is evil and what is true—even in what is at once evil and good, and therefore double—and since this division destroys that image and therefore our very humanity, the Lord's divine providence is trying to get rid of this division in everything it does.

Further, since it is better for us to be engaged in something evil and something false than in something good and something evil at the same time, the Lord lets the first of these pairings occur. He does so not from intent but from an inability to prevent it because of the ultimate goal, which is our salvation. It is because of these two factors—our ability to be engaged in something evil and something true at the same time, and the Lord's inability to prevent this because of the goal, which is our salvation—that our discernment can be lifted up into heaven's light and see what is true or recognize it when we hear it even while our love remains down below. This means that we can be in heaven in our discernment

16

and in hell in our love; and we cannot be denied this possibility because we cannot be deprived of the two abilities that make us human and distinguish us from the beasts, the two abilities that alone make our rebirth and salvation possible, namely, our rationality and our freedom. These two abilities, that is, are what enable us to act in keeping with wisdom or to act in keeping with a love that has no wisdom. These are what enable us to look down from wisdom on our love below and therefore see our thoughts, intentions, and feelings, to see what is evil and false and what is good and true in our life and our beliefs. If we could not recognize and admit these things in ourselves, we could not be remade. I have already discussed these abilities [§15] and will have more to say about them later [§§71–99].

This is how we can be engaged in what is good and what is true together and in what is evil and what is false together, and do this alternately.

17   It is hard for us to attain union or unity (of what is good and what is true or of what is evil and what is false) in this world, because as long as we are living here we are kept in a state of reformation or rebirth. We all attain one union or the other after death, though, because then we can no longer be remade or reborn: we keep the quality of the life we led in the world, that is, the quality of our primary love. If our life was governed by evil love, anything true we have learned in this world from teachers, sermons, or the Word is taken away. Once it is gone, we soak up the falsity that agrees with our evil the way a sponge soaks up water.

Conversely, if our life has been governed by good love, then everything false we have picked up from what we have heard and read in the world without intentionally adopting it is taken away, and in its place we are given the truth that agrees with our good.

This is the intent of these words of the Lord:

> Take the talent from this one and give it to the one who has ten talents.
> To all those who have, more will be given, in ample supply; but from those who do not have, even what they have will be taken away. (Matthew 25:28, 29; 13:12; Mark 4:25; Luke 8:18; 19:24–26)

18   The reason everyone must be engaged in what is good and what is true together after death or in what is evil and what is false is that good and evil cannot be united. Neither can good and any falsity that is prompted by evil, or evil and any truth that is prompted by anything good. Such things are opposites, and opposites battle with each other until one destroys the other.

It is people who are engaged in evil and good at the same time that are referred to in these words of the Lord to the church in Laodicea in the Book of Revelation:

> I know your works,[29] that you are neither cold nor hot. I wish that you were either cold or hot. However, since you are lukewarm and neither cold nor hot, I am about to spit you out of my mouth (Revelation 3:15, 16),

and by these words of the Lord:

> No one can serve two masters. You will either hate one and love the other or cling to one and ignore the other. (Matthew 6:24)

8. *If something is focused on what is both good and true, then it is something; but if it is focused on what is both evil and false, it is not anything at all.* Section 11 above shows that whatever is focused on what is both good and true is something, and it follows from this that anything that is both evil and false is nothing. "Being nothing" means having no power, no trace of spiritual life.

People who are focused on what is evil and false together (all of whom are in hell) do have a kind of power among themselves. An evil individual can do harm and in fact does harm in thousands of ways, though it is only from evil that an evil individual can harm evil people. Still, an evil person can do no harm whatever to good people. If that happens (which it sometimes does), it is through the evil one identifying with something evil in the good.[30] [2] This gives rise to temptations that are attacks by evil people among themselves, resulting in the struggles that enable good people to be freed from their evils.

Because evil people have no power, all hell is a virtual nothing in the Lord's sight, an absolute nothing when it comes to power. I have seen this quite convincingly time after time.

The remarkable thing is, though, that all the evil people believe they are powerful and all the good people believe they themselves are not. This is because evil people ascribe everything to their own power, their own deviousness and malice, and nothing to the Lord, while good people ascribe nothing to their own prudence and everything to the Lord, who is omnipotent.

Another reason anything both evil and false is nothing is that it has no trace of spiritual life. This is why a hellish life is called "death" rather than "life"; so since anything that exists belongs to life, nothing that exists can belong to death.

20   People who are involved in evil and in truth at the same time can be compared to eagles that soar high overhead but plunge down if they lose their wings. Something like this happens to people after death, when they become spirits, if they have understood, discussed, and taught truths but have never turned to God in their lives. Their comprehension lifts them on high; and sometimes they get into heaven and pretend to be angels of light.[31] However, when they are deprived of their truths and dismissed, they plunge into hell. Eagles mean predatory people who have intellectual vision, and wings mean spiritual truths.

I mentioned that these are people who never turn to God in their lives. "Turning to God in our lives" simply means thinking that some particular evil action is a sin against God and therefore not doing it.

21   9. *The Lord's divine providence works things out so that what is both evil and false promotes balance, comparison, and purification, which means that it promotes the union of what is good and true in others.* It follows from what has just been said that the Lord's divine providence is constantly working to unite what is true with what is good and what is good with what is true within us, because this union is the church and heaven. This union exists in the Lord and in everything that emanates from him. It is because of this union that heaven is called "a marriage," as is the church; so in the Word the kingdom of God is compared to a marriage.[32] This union is the reason the Sabbath was the holiest part of worship in the Israelite church,[33] since it means that union. This is also why there is a marriage of what is good and what is true throughout the Word and in every detail of it (see *Teachings for the New Jerusalem on Sacred Scripture* 80–90).[34]

The marriage of what is good and what is true comes from the marriage of the Lord and the church, and this in turn comes from the marriage of love and wisdom in the Lord. Goodness is actually a matter of love, and truth is a matter of wisdom. We can see from this that the constant objective of divine providence is to unite what is good to what is true and what is true to what is good within us. This is how we are united to the Lord.

22   However, many people have broken this marriage and still do. They do this especially by separating faith from thoughtful living (faith being a matter of truth and truth a matter of faith, with thoughtful living being a matter of goodness and goodness being a matter of thoughtful living). By so doing they unite what is evil and false within themselves and have become opponents, and continue to be so.[35] The Lord nevertheless provides that they may still help unite what is good and true in others through balance, comparison, and purification.

The Lord provides for the union of what is good and true in others 23 by the *balance* between heaven and hell. What is evil and what is false are continually breathing out together from hell, and what is good and what is true are continually breathing out together from heaven. Every one of us is kept in that balance as long as we are living in this world, and this is what gives us our freedom to think, intend, speak, and act, the freedom in which we can be reformed. (On this spiritual balance that gives us our freedom, see *Heaven and Hell* 589–596 and 597–603).

The Lord provides for the union of what is good and what is true by 24 *comparison*. We recognize the quality of what is good only by its relationship to something that is less good and by its opposition to what is evil. This is the source of everything in us that is perceptive and sensitive, because this is what gives perception and sensitivity their quality. That is, anything pleasing is perceived and sensed by contrast with something that is less pleasing and by what is unpleasant, anything beautiful by something less beautiful and by something ugly. By the same token, any good that love does is perceived and sensed by contrast with what is less good and by something evil, and anything true that wisdom offers is perceived and sensed by contrast with what is less true and by something false.

There need to be differences in everything, whether great or small; and when these differences create a balanced opposition between the great and the small, then there is a comparison between the levels in each direction. As a result, our perception and sensation are either enhanced or dulled.

We need to realize, that is, that the opposition may either deaden or intensify our perceptions and sensations. It deadens them when the opposites are mingled and intensifies them when they are not mingled. This is why the Lord separates goodness from evil very precisely so that they will not be mingled in us, just as he keeps heaven and hell separate.

The Lord provides for the union of what is good and true in others 25 by *purification*. This happens in two ways, by temptations and by fermenting. Spiritual temptations are simply battles against the evil and false things that breathe forth from hell and affect us. These battles purify us from things that are evil and false, so that goodness in us is united to truth and truth to goodness.

Spiritual fermenting happens in many ways both in the heavens and on earth, but people in our world do not know what these processes are or how they happen. There are things that are both evil and false that are injected into communities the way agents of fermentation are injected into flour or grape juice. These serve to separate things that do not belong together and unite things that do, so that the substance becomes pure and clear.

These are the processes referred to by the Lord's words,

> The kingdom of heaven is like yeast that a woman took and hid in three measures of flour until it was all leavened. (Matthew 13:33; Luke 13:21)

26   These useful functions are provided by the Lord through the union of what is evil and false that prevails among people in hell, since the Lord's rule (which is not only over heaven but also over hell) is a functional rule and the Lord's providence intends that there should be no one and nothing there that does not do some service or enable some service to happen.

The Lord's Divine Providence Has as Its Goal a Heaven from the Human Race

27   I have explained elsewhere that heaven did not originate in angels who were created angels at the beginning, and that hell did not originate in a devil who was created an angel of light and was cast down from heaven. Rather, both heaven and hell are from the human race. Heaven is made up of people who are involved in a love for what is good and a consequent discernment of what is true, and hell of people who are involved in a love for what is evil and a discernment of what is false. I have been given convincing evidence of this through long-term association with angels and spirits, and would refer you to *Heaven and Hell* 311–316, the booklet *Last Judgment* 14–27,[36] and the whole of *Supplements on the Last Judgment and the Spiritual World.*[37]

[2] Since heaven comes from the human race, then, and since heaven is living with the Lord forever, it follows that this was the Lord's goal for creation. Further, since this was the goal of creation, it is the goal of the Lord's divine providence.

The Lord did not create the universe for his own sake but for the sake of people he would be with in heaven. By its very nature, spiritual love wants to share what it has with others, and to the extent that it can do so, it is totally present,[38] experiencing its peace and bliss. Spiritual love gets this quality from the Lord's divine love, which is like this in infinite measure.

It then follows that divine love (and therefore divine providence) has the goal of a heaven made up of people who have become angels and are becoming angels, people with whom it can share all the bliss and joy of love and wisdom, giving them these blessings from the Lord's own presence within them. He cannot help doing this, because his image and likeness is in us from creation. His image in us is wisdom and his likeness in us is love; and the Lord within us is love united to wisdom and wisdom united to love, or goodness united to truth and truth united to goodness, which is the same thing. (See the preceding section for a description of this union.)

[3] However, people do not know what heaven is in general or in groups of people and what heaven is in particular or in an individual. They do not know what heaven is in the spiritual world and what it is in the physical world, either; and yet it is important to know about these matters. Consequently, I want to shed some light on this, in the following sequence.

1. Heaven is union with the Lord.
2. Our nature from creation enables us to be more and more closely united to the Lord.
3. The more closely we are united to the Lord, the wiser we become.
4. The more closely we are united to the Lord, the happier we become.
5. The more closely we are united to the Lord, the more clearly we seem to have our own identity, and yet the more obvious it is to us that we belong to the Lord.

1. *Heaven is union with the Lord.* Heaven is not heaven because of angels but because of the Lord. The reason for this is that the love and wisdom that angels enjoy and that make heaven do not come from them but from the Lord—love and wisdom actually are the Lord within the angels. Since love and wisdom belong to the Lord and are the Lord in heaven, and since love and wisdom make up the life of

28

angels, we can see as well that their life belongs to the Lord and that in fact their life is the Lord. The angels themselves insist that they are living from the Lord. We can therefore conclude that heaven is union with the Lord.

Since union with the Lord varies, though, and heaven is therefore not the same in one angel as it is in another, it also follows that the nature of heaven depends on the nature of the union with the Lord. The next section [§§32–33] will explain that the union may be closer and closer, or more and more distant.

[2] Now I need to say something about how that union happens and what it is like. There is a union of the Lord with angels and a union of angels with the Lord; so it is a mutual relationship. The Lord flows into the love of angels' lives, and angels accept the Lord in their wisdom, in this way uniting themselves to the Lord in return. It needs to be clearly understood, though, that although it seems to angels that they are uniting themselves to the Lord through their wisdom, in fact the Lord is uniting them to himself through that wisdom, since their wisdom also comes from the Lord.

We could just as well say that the Lord unites himself to angels through what is good and that they in turn unite themselves to the Lord through what is true, since everything good is a matter of love and everything true is a matter of wisdom. [3] However, since this mutual union is a mystery that not many people can grasp unless it is explained, I want to lay it out in a comprehensible fashion to the extent that it is possible.

I explained in *Divine Love and Wisdom* 404–405 how love unites itself to wisdom, specifically through a desire for knowing that gives rise to a desire for what is true, a desire for discerning that gives rise to a desire to grasp what is true, and a desire to see what we know and discern that gives rise to thought. The Lord flows into these desires, which are branches of the love of every individual's life; and angels accept that inflow in their perception of what is true and in their thinking. They notice the inflow in their perception, not in their desires.

[4] Since it seems to angels that their perceptions and thoughts are their own even though they arise from desires that come from the Lord, the appearance is also that angels are uniting themselves to the Lord in return when in fact the Lord is uniting them to himself. That is, the desire itself is bringing forth the perceptions and thoughts.[39] Desire, a matter of love, is actually the soul of their perceptions and thoughts.[40] No one can perceive or think anything apart from desires, and all of us perceive and think in keeping with our desires. We can see from this that the

mutual union of angels with the Lord does not come from them even though it seems to.

There is the same kind of union of the Lord with the church and of the church with the Lord, a union called a spiritual and heavenly marriage.

In the spiritual world, all union takes place by means of attentiveness. When anyone there is thinking about someone else because of a desire to talk with her or him, that other person is immediately present. They see each other face to face. The same thing happens when someone is thinking about someone else because of a loving affection, but in this case the result is a union, while in the former case it is only presence.

29

This phenomenon is unique to the spiritual world. The reason is that everyone there is spiritual. It is different in the physical world, where all of us are material. In this physical world, the same thing is happening in the feelings and thoughts of our spirits, but since there is space in this world, while in the spiritual world there only seems to be space, the things that happen in the thoughts of our spirits come out in actions there.[41]

[2] I mention this to show how the Lord's union with angels and their apparent mutual union with the Lord take place. All the angels turn their faces toward the Lord. The Lord looks at them in the forehead, while the angels look at the Lord with their eyes. This is because the forehead corresponds to love and its desires, and the eyes correspond to wisdom and its perceptions. Still, angels are not turning their faces toward the Lord on their own; the Lord is turning them toward himself, and doing so by flowing into the love of their lives. He comes through this into their perceptions and thoughts; and that is how he turns them.

[3] This circle of love to thoughts and of thoughts-from-love to love occurs in all the functions of the human mind—we can call it the circle of life. There is information about it in *Divine Love and Wisdom:* for example, angels always face the Lord as the sun (§§129–134); everything in the deeper reaches of angels' minds and bodies alike is turned toward the Lord as the sun in the same way (§§135–139); every kind of spirit turns toward his or her ruling love in the same way (§§140–145); love marries wisdom to itself and arranges things so that wisdom marries it willingly (§§410–412); angels are in the Lord and the Lord is in them; and since angels are vessels, the Lord alone is heaven (§§113–118).

The Lord's heaven in our physical world is called the church, and an angel of this heaven is a church member who is united to the Lord. After leaving this world, people like this become angels of the spiritual heaven;

30

so we can see that the sort of thing I have been saying about the angelic heaven applies also to the human heaven called the church.

The mutual union with the Lord that constitutes heaven for us was revealed by the Lord in this passage from John:

> Abide in me, and I in you. People who abide in me, and I in them, bear an abundance of fruit; for without me you cannot do anything. (John 15:4, 5, 7 [15:4, 5])

31   We can therefore tell that the Lord is heaven not only in a general way (for all who are there), but also specifically (for every individual who is there). An angel is actually a heaven in smallest form; and heaven in general is made up of as many heavens as there are angels. (On this point, see *Heaven and Hell* 51–58.)

Given this fact, no one should become attached to the mistaken notion that the Lord lives among the angels in heaven or dwells with them the way a monarch dwells in a realm—an idea that crosses many minds when they first think about the matter. Visually, the Lord is above them there like a sun; though as far as the life of their love and wisdom is concerned, he is within them.

32   2. *Our nature from creation enables us to be more and more closely united to the Lord.* Support for this may be found in the material about levels in part 3 of *Divine Love and Wisdom,* particularly on the following points. There are three distinct or vertical levels in us from creation (§§230–235). These three levels exist in each of us from birth and can be opened. As they are opened, we are in the Lord and the Lord is in us (§§236–241).[42] All processes of perfection increase and rise by and according to levels (§§199–204). We can see from this that the nature we have from creation enables us to be united to the Lord more and more closely, level by level.

[2] It is vital, however, that we know what these levels are. There are two kinds, distinct or vertical and gradual or horizontal, and it is vital to know how they differ.[43] All of us have the three distinct or vertical levels within us by creation and therefore from birth. We become involved in the first level, the one called "earthly," when we are born, and we can gradually expand this level within us until we become rational. We become involved in the second level, the one called "spiritual," if we live by the spiritual laws of the divine design, laws that are divine as to their truth; and we can also become involved in the third level, the one called "heavenly," if we live by the heavenly laws of the divine design, laws that are divine as to their goodness.

[3] The Lord opens these levels within us depending on the way we live. This is really happening in this world, but not so that we can sense or feel it until after we leave this world. As the levels are then opened and perfected, we are more and more closely united to the Lord. This union can intensify to eternity as we grow closer; for angels it actually does keep intensifying to eternity. Still, no angel can enter into the first level of the Lord's love and wisdom or reach its boundary, because the Lord is infinite and angels are finite, and there is no ratio between what is infinite and what is finite.

Since a knowledge of these levels is necessary for understanding the human condition and the way it is raised and brought closer to the Lord, I dealt with this specifically in *Divine Love and Wisdom* 173–281, to which you may refer.

I need to explain briefly how we can be more closely united to the Lord and then how that union can seem closer and closer. As to *how we can be more closely united to the Lord,* this does not happen by simply knowing or by simply understanding or even by simply being wise; it happens by a life that is one with these states.

Our life is our love, and there are many kinds of love. Broadly, there is love for what is evil and love for what is good. Love for what is evil is love for adultery, vengeance, cheating, blasphemy, and taking others' possessions. A love for evil finds delight and gratification in thinking about such things and in doing them. There are as many derivative motivations or desires of this love as there are evil deeds in which it takes specific form; and there are as many perceptions and thoughts of this love as there are distortions that nurture and justify these evil deeds. These distortions are integral to the evils themselves just as our discernment is integral to our volition. They do not part from each other, because they belong to each other.

[2] Now since the Lord flows into everyone's life and flows through our life's desires into our perceptions and thoughts (and not the reverse), as already noted [§28], it follows that the closeness of our union with the Lord depends on the extent to which our love for evil and its desires—its compulsions—is dismissed. Further, since these compulsions have their home in the level of our being that deals with this world, and since anything we do that is rooted in that level feels as though it belongs to us, we need to dismiss the evils of this love with what seems to be our own strength. To the extent that we do this, the Lord draws near and unites us to himself.

Surely anyone can see simply on the basis of reason that our compulsions and the gratifications they offer shut the door firmly in the Lord's face, and that they cannot be ousted by the Lord as long as we ourselves keep that door closed and throw our weight against it from the other side[44] to keep it from opening. The Lord's words in the Book of Revelation show that we ourselves need to open the door:

> Here I am, standing at the door and knocking. If any hear my voice and open the door, I will come in to them and dine with them, and they with me. (Revelation 3:20)

[3] We can see from this that the closeness of our union with the Lord depends on the extent to which we abstain from evils as coming from the devil[45] and as blocking the Lord's entry. We can see that the union is closest for people who loathe these evils as though they were actually foul and fiery devils, since evil and the devil are one and the same, just as malicious falsity and Satan[46] are one and the same. As a result, just as the Lord's inflow is into a love for what is good and its desires and through these into our perceptions and thoughts (which derive all their truth from the fact that they stem from goodness we are engaged in), so the inflow of the devil or hell is into a love for what is evil and its desires—its compulsions—and through these into our perceptions and thoughts, which derive all their falsity from the fact that they stem from what is evil.

[4] As to *how that union can seem closer and closer,* the more completely the evils in our earthly self are dismissed by our abstaining from and rejecting them, the more closely we are united to the Lord. Further, since the love and wisdom that are the Lord himself are not in space, and since a desire of love and a thought of wisdom have nothing in common with space, the Lord seems to be closer in proportion to the union occasioned by love and wisdom. By the same token, he seems more distant as we spurn love and wisdom.

Space does not exist in the spiritual world. Instead, distance and presence there are appearances that depend on likeness or dissimilarity of desire. This is because, as just noted, desires (or properties of love) and thoughts (or properties of wisdom) are intrinsically spiritual. They are not in space, as explained in *Divine Love and Wisdom* 7–10, 69–72, and elsewhere.[47]

[5] Our union with the Lord once our evils have been dismissed is what is referred to in the Lord's words, "The pure in heart will see God" (Matthew 5:8) and "I will make my dwelling with everyone who has my precepts and keeps them" (John 14:21, 23). "Having the precepts" is knowing, and "keeping the precepts" is loving, since it also says in the same passage that "whoever keeps my precepts is one who loves me."

3. *The more closely we are united to the Lord, the wiser we become.* Since there are three levels of life in us from creation and therefore from birth (see §32 above), there are quite specifically three levels of wisdom in us as well. It is these levels that are opened for us in proportion to our union; they are opened in proportion to our love, that is, since love is union itself.

However, we sense this level-by-level ascent of love only dimly, while we sense an ascent of wisdom clearly if we know and see what wisdom is. The reason we are aware of levels of wisdom is that love enters our perceptions and thoughts through its desires, and our perceptions and thoughts stand out in the inner sight of our minds, the sight that answers to our outer, physical sight. This is why we can be conscious of our wisdom, but not so conscious of the desire of love that is giving rise to it. It is much the same as it is with the things that we do behaviorally. We notice how our bodies are doing things, but not how our souls are behaving. So too, we are aware of how we contemplate, perceive, and think, but not of the way the soul of these activities, the desire for what is good and true, is giving rise to them.

[2] There are, though, three levels of wisdom: earthly, spiritual, and heavenly. We are on the earthly level of wisdom while we are living in this world. This level can be brought to its height of perfection within us and still not cross the border to the spiritual level, because this level is not just an incremental extension of the earthly level. These two levels are united by their correspondence to each other. We arrive in the spiritual level of wisdom after death. This level too can be brought to the height of its perfection but still not cross the border to the heavenly level of wisdom. This latter level, again, is not just an incremental extension of the spiritual level, but is united to it by their mutual correspondence.

We may therefore conclude that wisdom can be raised up threefold, and that on each level it can be brought to a height of perfection by simple increment.

[3] Once we understand the ascent and perfection of these levels, we can to some extent understand what people say about angelic wisdom, namely, that it is inexpressible. It is so far beyond description that a thousand images of angels' thought, arising from their wisdom, can present only a single image to our thought, arising from our wisdom. The other nine hundred and ninety-nine images of angels' thought cannot find entrance because they transcend the material world.[48] I have often been taught this by vivid experience.

34

However, as already noted [§33], the only way to arrive at this indescribable angelic wisdom is through union with the Lord and in proportion to that union, since only the Lord opens the spiritual level and the heavenly level. This step is limited to people who are wise because of him, and we are wise because of the Lord when we cast the devil, or evil, away from ourselves.

35   No one, though, should believe that we have wisdom if we know a lot, grasp what we know fairly clearly, and can talk about things intelligently. We are wise only if these abilities are united to love. Love is what produces wisdom, through its desires. If wisdom is not united to love it is like a meteor in the sky that vanishes, like a falling star.[49] Wisdom united to love is like the constant light of the sun and like a fixed star. We have a love for wisdom to the extent that we fight off the demonic horde—our cravings for whatever is evil and false.

36   The wisdom that comes to our consciousness is a sense of what is true prompted by a desire for it. This is the case particularly for spiritual truth: for there is civic truth, there is moral truth, and there is spiritual truth. When we are conscious of spiritual truth because we are drawn to it we are conscious of moral and civic truth as well, because a desire for spiritual truth is their soul.

I have talked with angels about wisdom on occasion, and they have told me that wisdom is union with the Lord because the Lord is wisdom itself. They have told me that they attain this union when they banish hell from themselves, and that the union is in direct proportion to the banishment.

They picture wisdom, they said, as a wonderfully elegant palace with twelve steps leading up to it.[50] No one gets to the first step except with the Lord's help and by union with him, and for all of us, the ascent depends on that union. The higher we climb, the more clearly we realize that no one is wise on her or his own, but only from the Lord. We also realize that relative to what we do not know, what we do know is like a droplet compared to a vast lake. The twelve steps to the palace of wisdom mean whatever is good united to what is true and whatever is true united to what is good.

37   4. *The more closely we are united to the Lord, the happier we become.* We can say much the same about levels of happiness as was said above (§§32 and 34) about levels of life and wisdom[51] that depend on our union with the Lord. These times of happiness, bliss, and sheer delight intensify as the higher levels of our minds are opened within us, the levels we call spiritual and heavenly. Once our life on earth is over, these levels keep rising forever.

No one who is caught up in the pleasures of cravings for evil can know anything about the pleasures of desires for what is good, the delight that fills the angelic heaven. This is because these two kinds of pleasure are absolute opposites inwardly and therefore just under the surface, even though they differ very little on the surface itself.

Every love has its own pleasures. A love for what is evil gives us pleasure when we are caught up in its compulsions. This holds, for example, for loving adultery, vengeance, cheating, theft, or cruelty, and among the worst of us, for loving blasphemy against the holy values of the church and spouting venomous nonsense about God. The wellspring of these pleasures is a love for being in control prompted by a love for ourselves.

These pleasures come from compulsions that obsess the deeper levels of our minds and flow down from there into our bodies, where they stimulate filthy reactions that excite our very fibers. The result is a physical pleasure prompted by mental pleasure in proportion to our compulsions.

[2] After death, in the spiritual world, we can all discover the identity and nature of the filthy things that excite our physical fibers. In general, they are like corpses, excrement, manure, sickening odors, and urine. The hells are overflowing with filth like this. (On their correspondence, see material in *Divine Love and Wisdom* 422–424.) Once we enter hell, though, these filthy pleasures turn into dreadful things.

I mention all this to aid in understanding the nature and quality of heavenly happiness in what follows. We recognize things by their opposites.

Words cannot describe the varieties of heaven's bliss, rapture, pleasure, and delight—the joys of heaven—though these joys give us perceptible feelings in heaven. Anything we perceive only as a feeling is beyond description, because it does not fit neatly into mental concepts and therefore into words. Our discernment simply sees, and it sees things that have to do with wisdom or truth but not things that have to do with love or what is good. The result is that heaven's joys are inexpressible even though they are on the same rising scale as wisdom. They come in infinite variations, each one indescribable. I have both heard and felt this.

[2] However, these joys enter us only as we distance ourselves from compulsions to love what is evil and false, which distancing we do apparently with our own strength, but in fact from the Lord's strength. These joys are actually joys of loving desires for what is good and true, and they are directly opposed to the compulsions to love what is evil and false.

The joys proper to desires for what is good and true have their source in the Lord, so they come from the center of our being. From there they spread into our lower reaches, all the way to the lowest. So they fill angels and make them virtually nothing but delight. These joys, with all their infinite variations, are found in every desire for what is good and true, especially in the desire for wisdom.

40   There is no comparison between the pleasures of cravings for evil and the pleasures of desires for what is good, because within the pleasures of cravings for evil lies the devil[52] and within the pleasures of desires for what is good dwells the Lord. If comparison is needed, we could compare the pleasures of cravings for evil to the pleasures of frogs copulating in a swamp or of snakes in a garbage dump.[53] The pleasures of desires for what is good, though, can be compared to the pleasures that lift our spirits in flower gardens. In fact, the same kinds of things that appeal to frogs and snakes also appeal to people in the hells who are caught up in their cravings for evil, and the kinds of things that appeal to our spirits in flower gardens also appeal to people in the heavens who are caught up in desires for what is good. As already noted [§§38–39], things that answer to filth appeal to evil people and things that answer to what is clean appeal to good people.

41   We may conclude from this that the more closely we are united to the Lord, the happier we become. This happiness is rarely evident in the world, though, because in this world we are in an earthly state, and things on the earthly level do not communicate directly with things on the spiritual level; they communicate only by correspondence. This kind of communication is felt only as a kind of quiet peace of spirit, especially after struggles against our evils.

However, once we leave this earthly state and come into a spiritual state, which happens when we depart from this world, a happiness gradually emerges that is beyond description.

42   *5. The more closely we are united to the Lord, the more clearly we seem to have our own identity, and yet the more obvious it is to us that we belong to the Lord.* It seems as though the more closely we are united to the Lord the less sense of identity we have. This is indeed how it seems to all evil people and to people who believe on religious grounds that they are not subject to the yoke of the law[54] and that none of us can do anything good on our own. These two kinds of people cannot help seeing that if they are not allowed to think and intend what is evil, but only what is good, they have lost their identity. Since people who are united to the Lord are neither willing nor able to think and intend what is evil, the outward appearance leads others to believe that this amounts to a loss of identity; yet it is the exact opposite.

There is hellish freedom, and there is heavenly freedom. Our ability 43 to think and intend what is evil, and to say and do it to the extent that civil and moral laws do not restrain us, comes from hellish freedom. Our ability to think and intend what is good, and to say and do it when circumstances permit, comes from heavenly freedom. Whatever we think, intend, say, and do freely we feel is truly ours because all the freedom we have comes from our love. This means that if we are caught up in loving what is evil, we cannot help feeling that hellish freedom is freedom itself; while if we are caught up in loving what is good, we feel that heavenly freedom is freedom itself. As a result, each freedom regards the other as slavery.

No one, though, can deny that one or the other must be real freedom. Two kinds of freedom that are opposite to each other cannot both be true freedoms. Further, we cannot deny that being led by what is good is freedom and being led by what is evil is slavery, since being led by what is good is being led by the Lord and being led by what is evil is being led by the devil.

Now since anything we do freely seems to be our own because it comes from our love (acting from our love is acting freely, as already noted), it follows that union with the Lord makes us feel that we have freedom and therefore identity; and the closer our union with the Lord, the greater our freedom and our identity. The reason our identity seems clearer is that divine love by its very nature wants to give what it has to others, which means to us on earth and to angels. All spiritual love is like this; divine love most of all. Further, the Lord never forces anyone, because anything we are forced to do does not seem to be ours and anything that does not seem to be ours cannot become part of our love and so be accepted as our own. This is why the Lord is always leading us in freedom, and reforming and regenerating us in freedom.

There will be more on this later,[55] and you may also refer to §4 above.

The reason we are more clearly aware that we belong to the Lord as 44 our sense of identity becomes clearer is that the more closely we are united to the Lord the wiser we become (see §§34–36 above); and wisdom both teaches this and is conscious of it. Because angels of the third heaven are the wisest of angels, they even sense it and actually call it freedom itself. They refer to being led by themselves, though, as slavery.

The reason, they say, is that the Lord does not flow directly into the things that their wisdom enables them to sense and think but into the desires of their love for what is good, and through these desires into the effects of their wisdom. They sense the flow into the desire that prompts their wisdom. Then everything they think because of their wisdom feels as though it is coming from themselves and is therefore their own. This is what makes the union mutual.

45   Since the goal of the Lord's divine providence is a heaven from the human race, it follows that the goal is the union of the human race with the Lord (see §§28–31). It follows also that the goal is that we should be more closely united to him (§§32–33) and thereby be granted a more inward heaven. It also follows that the goal is for us to become wiser (§§34–36) and happier (§§37–41) because of this union, because we are given heaven through our wisdom and in proportion to it, and this is what gives us happiness. Lastly, it follows that the goal is for us to have a clearer sense of our identity and yet to be more clearly aware that we belong to the Lord (§§42–44).

All of these are part of the Lord's divine providence, because all of them are heaven, which is the goal.

In Everything That It Does, the Lord's Divine Providence Is Focusing on What Is Infinite and Eternal

46   IT is widely recognized in Christian circles that God is infinite and eternal. In fact, it says in the doctrine of the Trinity named after Athanasius that God the Father is infinite, eternal, and omnipotent, as are God the Son and God the Holy Spirit, but that there are not three infinite, eternal, and omnipotent beings, but only one. It follows from this that since God is infinite and eternal, only what is infinite and eternal can be attributed to him.

However, we finite beings cannot grasp what anything infinite and eternal is—and yet at the same time we can. We cannot grasp it because the finite cannot contain the infinite; and we can grasp it because there are abstract notions that enable us to see that certain things do exist even though we cannot see what their nature is.

There are such notions about the infinite—for example, that because God is infinite, or Divinity is infinite, God is reality itself or essence[56] itself and substance itself, love itself and wisdom itself, what is good itself and what is true itself, the Only—in fact, the essential Human. Then too, if we say that the infinite is the all, then infinite wisdom is omniscience and infinite power is omnipotence.

[2] These concepts, though, will get lost in the dim depths of our thought and perhaps even fall from incomprehension into denial unless we can rid them of elements that our thought gets from the material world, particularly those two essential features of the material world called space and time. These can only limit our concepts and make abstract concepts seem like nothing at all. However, if we can rid ourselves of them the way angels do, then the infinite can be grasped by means of the things I have just listed. This leads to a grasp of the fact that we ourselves are real because we have been created by the infinite God who is the All, that we are finite substances because we have been created by the infinite God who is substance itself, that we are wisdom because we have been created by the infinite God who is wisdom itself, and so on. For if the infinite God were not the All, substance itself, and wisdom itself, we would not be real, or would simply be nothing, or would be only ideas of existence, according to those dreamers called idealists.[57]

[3] Material presented in the work *Divine Love and Wisdom* may serve to show that the divine essence is love and wisdom (§§28–39), that divine love and wisdom are substance itself, and form itself and that divine love and wisdom are substance and form in and of themselves, and are therefore wholly "itself" and unique (§§40–46), and that God created the universe and everything in it not from nothing but from himself (§§282–284). It follows from this that everything that has been created, especially ourselves and the love and wisdom within us, is real, and is not just an image of reality.[58]

If God were not infinite, then, nothing finite would exist; if the Infinite were not the All, there would not be anything; and if God had not created everything from himself, there would be nothing real, nothing at all. In short, *we are because God is.*

Now, since we are dealing with divine providence, and are dealing at this point with the fact that it focuses on what is infinite and eternal in

47

everything it does, and since this can be conveyed clearly only if it is put in a particular sequence, that sequence will be as follows:

1. What is intrinsically infinite and intrinsically eternal is the same as Divinity.
2. What is intrinsically infinite and eternal can only focus on what is infinite from itself in what is finite.
3. In everything it does, divine providence focuses on what is infinite and eternal from itself, especially in the intent to save the human race.
4. There is an image of what is infinite and eternal in the angelic heaven made up of members of the human race who have been saved.
5. The very core of divine providence is its focus on what is infinite and eternal in the forming of the angelic heaven so that it can be a single person in the Lord's sight, a person who is his image.

48　　1. *What is intrinsically infinite and intrinsically eternal is the same as Divinity.* This is supported by material presented in a number of places in *Divine Love and Wisdom.* The principle that what is intrinsically infinite and intrinsically eternal is Divinity comes from an angelic concept. By "what is infinite," angels understand simply the divine reality; and by "what is eternal" the divine manifestation. We on earth, though, both *can* see and *cannot* see that what is intrinsically infinite and intrinsically eternal is Divinity. We can see it if we think of what is infinite nonspatially and of what is eternal nontemporally. We cannot see it if we think about what is infinite and eternal on the basis of space and time. This means that we can see it if we think on a higher level, that is, with a deeper kind of rationality; but we cannot see it if we think on a lower level, that is, more superficially.

[2] People who see it think that there cannot be an infinite amount of space or an infinite amount of time, so there can be no infinite amount of time as the eternity from which all things arise. This is because what is infinite has no first or last limit, no boundaries. They also think that there can be no derivative infinite being, because this presupposes a boundary and a beginning, something prior as source. This makes it meaningless to talk about a derivative infinite and eternal being, because that would be like talking about a derivative reality, which is a contradiction in terms. A derivative infinite being would be an infinite being derived from infinite being, and a derivative

reality would be a reality derived from reality, so that infinite being or reality would either be the same as the original infinite being or would actually be finite.

We can see from things like this that are evident to our deeper rationality that there is something intrinsically infinite and intrinsically eternal, and that these are Divinity, the source of everything.

I realize that many people will be saying to themselves, "How can anyone grasp something on a deeper level of rationality, something that has nothing to do with space and time? How can anyone grasp the notion that this not only exists but is the All, the very source of everything?" Think more deeply, though. Think whether love or any of its desires, whether wisdom or any of its perceptions, whether even your thought itself is in space and time, and you will discover that they are not. Given the fact that Divinity is love itself and wisdom itself, then, it follows that Divinity cannot be conceived of in space and time, so neither can the Infinite.

To understand this more clearly, consider whether your thought is in time and space. Take the course of your thinking over ten or twelve hours—is it not true that this span of time can seem like one or two hours and can also seem like one or two days? It depends on the emotional state that underlies the thinking. If you are feeling happy with no awareness of the passage of time, the thoughts of ten or twelve hours can seem to take one or two hours, and if you are feeling distress and are conscious of the passage of time, it is just the reverse.

We can see from this that time is simply an appearance that depends on the emotional state that gives rise to our thoughts. The same is true of spatial distances in thought, whether on a walk or on a journey.[59]

Since angels and spirits are feelings derived from love and their consequent thoughts, they are not in space and time; they are simply in what seems to be space and time. The kind of apparent space and time they are in depends on the state of their feelings and consequent thoughts. As a result, when anyone thinks affectionately about someone else, with the focused intent of seeing or talking with that other individual, there is an instantaneous presence.

[2] This is why we all have spirits present with us who are feeling the way we are. There are evil spirits with us when we feel drawn toward something that is evil the way evil spirits are, and good spirits with us when we feel drawn toward something that is good the way good spirits are. They are just as present as though we were accepted members of their community. Space and time have nothing to do with

this presence, because a feeling and its consequent thought are not in space and time, and spirits and angels are feelings and their consequent thoughts.

[3] Firsthand experience over many years has taught me that this is so. I have also learned it from talking with any number of people after their death, both people from the various nations of Europe and people from various nations in Asia and Africa, and all of them were near at hand. If they had been in space and time, it would have taken a journey and the time that a journey requires.

[4] Actually, we all know this instinctively, or in our own minds. This has been brought home to me by the fact that no one has started thinking in terms of spatial distances when I have described conversations with deceased people in Asia, Africa, or Europe; with Calvin, Luther, or Melanchthon,[60] for example; or with some monarch, official, or priest in a faraway land. It has not occurred to people to ask, "How could anyone talk with people who lived there, and how could they get here when there are so many lands and seas in between?" This also showed me that people are not thinking on the basis of space and time when they think about people who are in the spiritual world.

See *Heaven and Hell* 62–169 *[162–169]* and 191–199, though, on the fact that people in the spiritual world do have what seem to be space and time.

51   This leads us to the conclusion that we should think about what is infinite and eternal and therefore about the Lord nontemporally and nonspatially, and that we can do so. Further, it shows that this is how we think on the deeper level of our rationality, and that what is infinite and eternal is the same as the Lord. That is how angels and spirits think. Thought withdrawn from space and time enables us to understand divine omnipresence and omniscience and Divinity from eternity; while this is absolutely impossible for thought that has spatial and temporal concepts in it.

We can see from this that it is possible to think about God from eternity but definitely not about the material world from eternity. We can therefore think about the creation of the universe by God but definitely not at all about a creation by the material world, since space and time are properties of the material world, while Divinity is devoid of them. On Divinity being devoid of space and time, see *Divine Love and Wisdom* 7–10, 69–72, 73–76, and elsewhere [§§130, 156, 285].

52   2. *What is intrinsically infinite and eternal can only focus on what is infinite from itself in what is finite.* By "what is intrinsically infinite and eternal," I mean Divinity itself, as explained in the previous section

[§§48–51]. By "what is finite," I mean everything created by Divinity, especially people, spirits, and angels. By "focusing on what is infinite and eternal from itself," I mean focusing on what is divine in them—on it-self, that is—the way we look at ourselves in a mirror. The truth of this has been amply demonstrated in *Divine Love and Wisdom,* especially where I explained that there is a human image in the created universe and that this is an image of what is infinite and eternal (§§317–318) and therefore an image of God the Creator or the Lord from eternity.

We still need to realize that intrinsic divinity is in the Lord, while de-rivative divinity is divinity from the Lord in his creatures.

Examples are needed, though, if this is to be more clearly under-stood.

53

Divinity cannot focus on anything but Divinity, and it cannot focus on that anywhere except in what it has created. This is evidenced by the fact that none of us can focus on others except on the basis of what is inwardly our own. If we love others, we look at them from our own love within us. If we are wise, we look at others from our own wisdom within us.

It may seem as though others either love us or do not love us, that they are either wise or not, but we see this on the basis of the love and wisdom that is within ourselves. This means that we unite ourselves to them to the extent that they love us the way we love them, or to the ex-tent that their wisdom is like ours. That is how we unite.

[2] It is the same with Divinity in itself. The inner Divinity cannot look at itself from some other, from any person, spirit, or angel, because they have nothing within themselves of the Divinity that is their source. To look at divinity from some other individual in whom there is no trace of divinity would be to look at divinity from no divinity, which is impos-sible. This is why the Lord is united to people, spirits, and angels in such a way that everything that has to do with divinity is not from them but from the Lord. It is common knowledge, that is, that everything good and everything true that anyone has is not from us but from the Lord. We cannot even name the Lord or say the names "Jesus" or "Christ" ex-cept from him.[61]

[3] It follows, then, that what is infinite and eternal (which is the same as Divinity) has an infinite regard for everything in finite beings and unites itself to them in proportion to their inner acceptance of wis-dom and love. In short, the Lord cannot make his home and dwell with us or with angels in anything but what is his own. He cannot dwell in what belongs to us or to angels, because that is evil. Even if it were good it would still be finite, and that cannot contain what is infinite within it-self or in anything it produces.

We can see from this that there is no way for any finite being to look at what is infinite, but that it is possible for the infinite One to look at what is infinite from himself in finite beings.

54 It seems as though what is infinite cannot be united to what is finite because there is no ratio between the infinite and the finite and because the finite cannot contain the infinite. There are two reasons, though, why there can be a union. The first is that the Infinite One created everything from himself (as explained in *Divine Love and Wisdom* 282–284); and the second is that the Infinite One cannot focus on anything in finite beings except what is infinite from him. This can seem to finite beings as though it were within them; and this provides a ratio between what is finite and what is infinite. The ratio does not come from anything finite but from the Infinite One within it. In this way, too, the finite can contain the infinite. What does this is not the finite being in and of itself, but the finite being in its apparent autonomy, derived from the One who is intrinsically infinite. (There will be more on this subject later [§§55, 64, 202, 219, 294].)

55 3. *In everything it does, divine providence focuses on what is infinite and eternal from itself, especially in the intent to save the human race.* What is intrinsically infinite and eternal is Divinity itself or the essential Lord. What is secondarily infinite and eternal, though, is divinity emanating, or the Lord in others created from himself—in us and in angels, that is. This divinity is the same as divine providence because the Lord provides by means of that derivative divinity that everything be kept in the design in which and into which it was created. Since it is emanating divinity that is accomplishing this, it follows that all of it is divine providence.

56 We may be assured that divine providence focuses on what is infinite and eternal in everything it does by the fact that everything that has been created by a First Being who is infinite and eternal goes to its limits, and then from those limits goes back to the First Being who is its source (see the section of *Divine Love and Wisdom* that deals with the creation of the universe).[62] Further, since the First, the source, is present at the heart of every sequence, it follows that the emanating divinity or divine providence focuses on some image of what is infinite and eternal in everything it does. It does so in all cases, though in some instances it is clearly noticeable and in others it is not.

Divinity shows us this image clearly in the variety of everything and in the way everything bears fruit and multiplies.

[2] We can see *an image of what is infinite and eternal in the variety of everything* in the fact that nothing is exactly like anything else and

nothing can be to eternity. We can see this in the faces of all the people there have been since the beginning of creation, and from their characters as well, which are reflected in their faces. We can see it from their feelings, perceptions, and thoughts, too, since these are elements of their character. This is why there are no two identical angels or spirits in all of heaven and never will be to eternity. It is the same for everything we can see in both worlds, the physical and the spiritual. This shows that the variety is infinite and eternal.

[3] There is evidence of *an image of what is infinite and eternal in the way everything bears fruit and multiplies* in the [reproductive] ability of seeds in the plant kingdom and in the process of reproduction in the animal kingdom,[63] especially in the genus of fish. If they were to be fruitful and multiply to the full extent of their ability, they would fill all the space in the world, even in the universe, within a century. We can see from this that within this ability there lies an impulse to reproduce to infinity. Then too, since this fruitfulness and multiplication have not failed since the beginning of creation and will never fail, not to eternity, it follows that there is also within this ability an impulse to reproduce to eternity.

It is the same for us in regard to the desires of our love and the perceptions of our wisdom. For both, the variety is infinite and eternal; and the same holds true for the ways they bear fruit and multiply, which are spiritual. No individual enjoys any desire or perception so much like someone else's as to be identical, and no one can to eternity. Further, desires can bear fruit endlessly and perceptions can multiply endlessly: It is widely understood that we can never exhaust the store of knowledge.

This ability to bear fruit and multiply endlessly, or to infinity and eternity, applies to earthly matters for us, to spiritual matters for spiritual angels, and to heavenly matters for heavenly angels.[64] Nor does it apply only to desires, perceptions, and information in general, it applies specifically to every element of them, even the slightest. These elements have this nature because they arise from the One who is intrinsically infinite and eternal, coming about by means of what is secondarily infinite and eternal.

However, since what is finite cannot contain anything of Divinity, there is no such thing in any person or angel as a possession, not in the least. We and angels are finite. We are only vessels, essentially dead. Whatever is alive in us comes from the emanating divinity united to us by proximity so that it seems to be ours. This will become clear in what follows [§§174, 191–213].

58 The reason divine providence focuses on what is infinite and eternal particularly in its intent to save the human race is that the goal of divine providence is a heaven from the human race (see §§37–45 *[27–45]* above). Since this is the goal, it follows that the main focus of divine providence is reforming and regenerating us, that is, saving us, since heaven is made up of people who have been reformed and regenerated.

Since regenerating us is a matter of uniting what is good and what is true, or love and wisdom, within us the way they are united in divinity that emanates from the Lord, divine providence focuses primarily on this in its intent to save the human race. The image of the Infinite and Eternal One can be found in us only in the marriage of what is good and what is true. We know that emanating divinity accomplishes this for the human race because of individuals described in the Word, individuals who have prophesied after being filled with that emanating divinity called the Holy Spirit, as well as because of enlightened people who see divine truths in the light of heaven. We see this particularly in angels, who have a sensory awareness of the presence, inflow, and union. Angels are also aware, though, that the true nature of this union could be called a direct contact.[65]

59 It has not yet been realized that divine providence focuses on our eternal state at every step of our journey. It cannot focus on anything else because Divinity is infinite and eternal, and what is infinite or eternal or divine is not in time. It therefore sees the whole future as present. Since this is the nature of Divinity, it follows that there is something eternal in everything it does, overall and in detail.

People who think in terms of time and space find this hard to grasp, though, not only because they love temporal matters but also because they think in terms of what is present to people in the world and not what is present to people in heaven. This latter is as remote from them as the ends of the earth. However, people who are engaged with divinity[66] base their thinking on the Lord and are thinking in eternal terms even while they think about what is present to them; so they say to themselves, "What is anything that is not eternal? Aren't temporal things nothing at all by comparison, and don't they become nothing when they end?" What is eternal is different. It simply *is* because there is no limit to its being.

Thinking like this is thinking in terms of eternity even while we are thinking about what is present; and when we both think and live this way, then emanating divinity with us, or divine providence, focuses on the state of our eternal life in heaven at every step of our journey, and is leading us to it.

We will see in what follows that Divinity focuses on what is eternal in everyone, whether evil or good.

4. *There is a clear image of what is infinite and eternal in the angelic heaven.* The angelic heaven is also one of the things we need to know about. Every religious person thinks about it and wants to go there. Heaven, though, is granted only to people who know the path to it and follow that path. We can know the path to heaven to some extent simply by considering what the people who make up heaven are like, realizing that no one can become an angel or get to heaven unless he or she arrives bringing along some angelic quality from the world. Inherent in that angelic quality is a knowing of the path from having walked it and a walking in the path from the knowing of it.

There really are paths in the spiritual world, paths that lead to each community of heaven and to each community of hell. We all see our own paths, spontaneously, it seems. We see them because the paths there are for the loves of each individual. Love opens the paths and leads us to our kindred spirits. No one sees any paths except those of her or his love.

We can see from this that angels are simply heavenly loves, since otherwise they would not have seen the paths that lead to heaven. However, this is better supported by a description of heaven.

Our whole spirit is desire and its consequent thought; and since all desire is a matter of love and all thought a matter of discernment, our whole spirit is its love and its consequent discernment. This is why our thinking flows from the desires of our love when we are thinking solely from our own spirit, as we do when we are in reflective moods at home.

We may conclude, then, that when we become spirits (which happens after death), we are the desire of our love, and not our thought except to the extent that it comes from that desire. We are drawn to what is evil (which amounts to a compulsion) if our love has been a love for what is evil, and we are drawn to what is good if our love has been a love for what is good. We are drawn to what is good to the extent that we have abstained from evils as sins; and we are drawn to what is evil to the extent that we have not abstained from evils.

Since all spirits and angels are desires, then, we can see that the whole angelic heaven is nothing but a love that embraces all desires for what is good and therefore a wisdom that embraces all perceptions of what is true. Further, since everything good and true comes from the Lord and the Lord is love itself and wisdom itself, it follows that the angelic heaven is an image of him; and since divine love and wisdom are human in

60

61

form, it also follows that this is the only possible form the angelic heaven can have. But I will have more to say about this in the next section.

62   The reason the angelic heaven is an image of what is infinite and eternal is that it is an image of the Lord, who is the Infinite and Eternal One. We can see an image of his infinite and eternal nature in the fact that there are millions[67] of angels who make up heaven, and that they make up as many communities as there are general desires of heavenly love, with each individual angel in each community being quite clearly his or her own desire. The form of heaven is made up of all these general and specific desires, a form that is like a single being in the Lord's sight just the way a person is a single being. This form is becoming more perfect to eternity as its numbers increase, because the more people there are who are participating in the form of divine love, which is the form of forms, the more perfect is the union.[68]

We can see quite plainly from this that there is an image of what is infinite and eternal in the angelic heaven.

63   The view of heaven provided by this brief description enables us to see that what makes heaven in us is the desire that comes from a love for what is good. But who knows this nowadays? Who actually realizes what "a desire that comes from a love for what is good" is, or realizes that the desires that come from a love for what is good are beyond number, infinite? For as already noted [§61], every angel is quite clearly her or his desire, and heaven in form is the form of all the desires of divine love there.

No one can unite all these desires into this form except the One who is both love itself and wisdom itself and is at the same time infinite and eternal, since there is something infinite and eternal in every form—something infinite in its union and something eternal in its perpetuity. If that infinite and eternal element were taken away, there would be an instantaneous collapse.

Who else can unite desires into a form?[69] Really, who else can unite one part of it? No part of it can be united except on the basis of an all-embracing concept of all the parts, and the all-embracing whole depends on a concept of each particular component of it. There are millions of components of [heaven's] form, there are thousands entering every year, and there will be thousands entering forever. All little children go there, as do all the adults who are desires that come from a love for what is good.

This again shows that there is an image of what is infinite and eternal in the angelic heaven.

64   5. *The very core of divine providence is its focus on what is infinite and eternal in the forming of the angelic heaven so that it can be a single person*

in the Lord's sight, a person who is his image. I explained in *Heaven and Hell* 59–86 that heaven as a whole is like a single person in the Lord's sight, that the same holds true for each community of heaven, that this is why every angel is a perfectly formed person, and that this is because God the Creator, who is the Lord from eternity, is a person. I also explained that there is therefore a correspondence of everything in heaven with everything in the human being (*Heaven and Hell* 87–102). I myself have not seen that the whole heaven is like a single person, because no one can see the whole heaven but the Lord alone. However, I have at times seen that entire communities of heaven, large and small, have looked like a single individual. I have been told at such times that the largest community, heaven in its entirety, looks the same, but only in the Lord's sight, and that this is why every angel is a person in complete form.

Since the whole heaven is like a single person in the Lord's sight, **65** heaven is divided into as many inclusive bodies as there are organs, viscera, and members in us; and each larger community is divided into as many less inclusive or specific communities as there are major parts of our viscera and organs. We can see from this what heaven is like.

Now, since the Lord is the essential Person and heaven is an image of him, we refer to being in heaven as "being in the Lord." On the Lord as the essential person, see *Divine Love and Wisdom* 11–13 and 285–289.

This enables us to understand to some extent a mystery we can call **66** angelic, namely, that every desire for what is both good and true is human as to its form. That is, whatever emanates from the Lord is a desire for what is good because it comes from his divine love and is a desire for what is true because it comes from his divine wisdom. In angels and in us, the desire for what is true that emanates from the Lord seems like a perception of what is true and like thought about it because we are attentive to perception and thought and not particularly attentive to the desire that they come from, even though [the perception and thought] emanate from the Lord as integral to the desire for what is true.

Next, since we are by creation heavens in smallest form and therefore **67** images of the Lord, and since heaven is made up of as many desires as there are angels, each of which is a person as to its form, it follows that the constant effort in divine providence is for each of us to become a heaven in form and therefore an image of the Lord. Further, since this is accomplished by means of the desire for what is good and true, it is for us to become that desire. This, then, is the constant effort in divine providence.

The very heart of providence, though, is that we should be in some particular place in heaven or in some particular place in the divine heavenly person and therefore in the Lord. This is what happens for people whom the Lord can lead to heaven. Since the Lord foresees this, he also constantly provides for it, with the result that all of us who are allowing ourselves to be led to heaven are being prepared for our own places in heaven.

68   As already noted [§65], heaven is divided into as many communities as there are organs, viscera, and members in us, and no part of these can be anywhere except where it belongs. Since angels are parts like this in the divine heavenly person, then, and only people who have lived on earth become angels, it follows that people who allow themselves to be led to heaven are constantly being prepared by the Lord for their places. This happens by means of the kind of desire for what is good and true that corresponds,[70] and every angel-person is enrolled in this place after leaving our world. This is the very core of divine providence in respect to heaven.

69   In contrast, people who do not allow themselves to be led to heaven and enrolled there are prepared for their places in hell. Left to ourselves, we constantly gravitate toward the very depths of hell, while the Lord is constantly drawing us back. If we do not let ourselves be drawn back, we are prepared for particular places in hell, where we are enrolled immediately after our departure from this world. Each such place is opposite to a particular place in heaven because hell is directly opposed to heaven. So just as angel-people are assigned their places in heaven according to their desires for what is good and true, devil-people are assigned their places in hell according to their desires for what is evil and false. Two opposing entities set against each other in parallel arrangement are kept in connection.

This is the very heart of divine providence in respect to hell.

There Are Laws of Divine Providence That People Do Not Know

THE existence of divine providence is generally recognized, but people do not know its nature. The reason the nature of divine providence is a mystery is that its laws have been hidden up to now, stored up in the wisdom of angels; but now they are to be revealed so that the Lord may receive the credit he deserves and we may stop claiming credit for what is not ours. Many people in this world attribute everything to themselves and to their own prudence, and anything they cannot claim in this way they attribute to chance or coincidence. They do not realize that human prudence is nothing and that "chance" and "coincidence" are empty words.

[2] I have stated that the laws of divine providence are hidden and have been stored up in the wisdom of angels until now. This is because discernment in divine matters has been closed in the Christian world because of our religion. This has made our discernment so dull and stubborn that we cannot understand anything about divine providence except that it exists, because we do not want to—or we do not want to understand because we cannot. All we can do is argue about whether it is real or not and whether it is only general or whether it deals with details. That is as far as a mind can go once it has been closed in divine matters because of its religion.

[3] However, since it is acknowledged in the church that on our own we cannot do anything that is really good or think anything that is really true, and since these facts are integral to divine providence, believing in the one depends on believing in the other. To prevent one of these principles being affirmed and the other denied, which leads to the collapse of both, it is absolutely necessary, then, that the nature of divine providence be revealed.

This cannot be revealed unless the laws are unveiled by which the Lord provides and oversees our emotional and mental processes. These laws enable us to know the nature of providence, and people who know its nature cannot help but acknowledge it, because they actually see it. This is why it is now time for the laws of divine providence to be revealed that have been stored away in the wisdom of angels until the present.

It Is a Law of Divine Providence That We Should Act in Freedom and in Accord with Reason

71 IT is generally recognized that we have a freedom to think and intend whatever we wish but not a freedom to say whatever we think or to do whatever we wish. The freedom under discussion here, then, is freedom on the spiritual level and not freedom on the earthly level, except to the extent that the two coincide. Thinking and intending are spiritual, while speaking and acting are earthly.

There is a clear distinction between these kinds of freedom in us, since we can think things that we do not express and intend things that we do not act out; so we can see that the spiritual and the earthly in us are differentiated. As a result, we cannot cross the line from one to the other except by making a decision, a decision that can be compared to a door that has first to be unlocked and opened.

This door stands open, though, in people who think and intend rationally, in accord with the civil laws of the state and the moral laws of society. People like this say what they think and do what they wish. In contrast, the door is closed, so to speak, for people who think and intend things that are contrary to those laws. If we pay close attention to our intentions and the deeds they prompt, we will notice that there is this kind of decision between them, sometimes several times in a single conversation or a single undertaking.

I mention this at the outset so that the reader may know that "acting from freedom and in accord with reason" means thinking and intending freely, and then freely saying and doing what is in accord with reason.

72 However, since not many people know that this law can be a law of divine providence (primarily because in spite of the fact that divine providence is constantly leading us to think and intend what is good and true, we have a freedom to consider what is evil and false), I need to proceed clearly, step by step, so that this will be grasped. The sequence will be as follows:

1. We have a capacity for disciplined thought and a certain latitude, or rationality and freedom, and these two abilities are in us as gifts from the Lord.

2. Whatever we do from our freedom, whether we have thought it through rationally or not, seems to be ours as long as it is in accord with our reason.

3. Whatever we have done from our freedom in accord with our thinking becomes a permanent part of us.

4. It is by means of these two abilities that the Lord reforms and regenerates us; without them we could not be reformed and regenerated.

5. We can be reformed and regenerated by means of these two abilities to the extent that we are brought to a realization that anything good and true that we think and do comes from the Lord and not from us.

6. The Lord's union with us and our responsive union with the Lord comes about by means of these two abilities.

7. Through the whole course of his divine providence, the Lord protects these two abilities untouched within us, as though they were sacred.

8. This is why it is integral to divine providence that we act from freedom, and in accord with reason.

1. *We have a capacity for disciplined thought and a certain latitude, or rationality and freedom, and these two abilities are in us as gifts from the Lord.* In *Divine Love and Wisdom* 264–270 and 425 and also in §§43–44 above, I discussed the fact that we have an ability to discern, which is rationality, and an ability to think, intend, speak, and do what we understand, which is freedom. I also discussed the fact that these two abilities are the Lord's gifts within us. However, since any number of doubts may arise about both of these abilities when we think about them, at this juncture I want simply to convey something about the freedom we have to act in accord with reason.

[2] First, though, it needs to be clear that all freedom is a matter of love, even to the point that love and freedom are the same thing. Since love is our life, freedom is also essential to our life. Every pleasure we experience comes from our love; there is no other source of pleasure. Acting for the sake of the pleasure of our love is acting in freedom, because pleasure leads us along, the way a river bears its burdens quite naturally along its current.

Since we have many loves, some of which agree with each other and some of which disagree, it follows that we likewise have many kinds of freedom. In general, though, there are three kinds: earthly, rational, and spiritual.

73

[3] All of us have earthly freedom by heredity. It is what makes us love nothing but ourselves and the world, and it is all there is to our life at first. Further, since all evils stem from these two loves and evils therefore become objects of our love, it follows that thinking and intending evil is our earthly freedom. It also follows that when we support these intentions with reasons, we are acting in our freedom and in accord with our reason. Acting in this way is acting from the ability we call "freedom," and supporting the actions is from the ability we call "rationality."

[4] For example, it is from the love we are born into that we want to commit adultery, cheat, blaspheme, and get even; and when we rationalize these evils inwardly and thereby make them legal, then we are thinking and intending them because of the pleasure of the love we have for them and in accord with a kind of reason; and to the extent that civil laws do not prevent it, we speak out and act out. We can behave like this because of divine providence, since we do have that latitude or freedom. We enjoy the latitude naturally because we get it through heredity, and we actively enjoy this latitude whenever we rationalize it because of the pleasure inherent in our love for ourselves and for the world.

[5] Rational freedom comes from a love for our own reputation, either for the sake of respect or for the sake of profit. This love finds its pleasure in putting on the outward appearance of moral character; and because we love this kind of reputation, we do not cheat, commit adultery, take vengeance, or blaspheme. Since this is the substance of our reasoning, we are also doing what is honest, fair, chaste, and cordial in freedom and according to reason. In fact, we can even talk rationally in favor of these virtues.

However, if our rational activity is only earthly and not spiritual, this is only an external freedom and not an internal one. We still do not love these virtues inwardly, only outwardly, for the sake of our reputation, as just noted. This means that the good things we do are not really good. We might be saying that they are to be done for the sake of the public good, but we are not saying this because of any love for the public good, only because of our love for our own reputation or for profit. Consequently, this freedom of ours has nothing of love for the public good in it, and neither does our reasoning, since this simply agrees with our love. As a result, this "rational freedom" is inwardly an earthly freedom. It too is left to us by divine providence.

[6] Spiritual freedom comes from a love for eternal life. The only people who arrive at this love and its pleasure are people who think that evils are sins and therefore do not want to do them, and who at the same

time turn toward the Lord. The moment we do this, we are in spiritual freedom, because it is only from an inner or higher freedom that we can stop intending evils because they are sins and therefore not do them. This kind of freedom comes from an inner or higher love.

At first, it does not seem like freedom, but it is, nevertheless. Later it does seem that way, and then we act from real freedom and in accord with real rationality by thinking and intending and saying and doing what is good and true.

This freedom grows stronger as our earthly freedom wanes and becomes subservient; it unites itself with rational freedom and purifies it.

[7] We can all arrive at this kind of freedom if we are just willing to think that there is an eternal life and that the temporary pleasure and bliss of life in time is like a passing shadow compared to the eternal pleasure and bliss of life in eternity. We can think this way if we want to, because we do have rationality and liberty, and because the Lord, who is the source of these two abilities, constantly gives us the power to do so.

2. *Whatever we do from our freedom, whether we have thought it through rationally or not, seems to be ours as long as it is in accord with our reason.* The clearest way to show what the rationality and freedom are that are proper to humans is to compare us with animals.[71] They have no rationality or ability to comprehend and no freedom or ability to intend freely. Instead of discernment they have knowledge, and instead of intention they have desire, both on the physical level.

Since they lack these two abilities, they also lack thinking. Instead of thinking, they have an inner sight that is merged with their outer sight because it answers to it.

[2] Every impulse or desire has its own partner or spouse. A desire of physical love has knowledge, a desire of spiritual love has intelligence, and a desire of heavenly love has wisdom. This is because a desire without its partner—its spouse, so to speak—is nothing. It is like a reality with no manifestation or a substance with no form, neither of which can have any attributes. This is why there is something in everything that has been created that we can trace back to the marriage of what is good and what is true, as I have often explained before [§§5–9, 11].

In animals, there is a marriage of desire and knowledge. The desire involved comes from what is good on the physical level, and the knowledge comes from what is true on the physical level.

[3] Now, their desires and their knowledge act in absolute unison, and their desires cannot rise above the level of their knowledge or their knowledge above the level of their desires: if they do rise, they both rise

together. Further, they have no spiritual mind into which—or into whose light and warmth—they can rise. Consequently, they do not have an ability to discern, or rationality, and do not have an ability to intend freely, or freedom. Instead they have simply physical desires and the knowledge that goes with them. Their physical desires are desires to find food and shelter, to procreate, and to avoid being hurt, with all the knowledge these impulses need.

Since this is the nature of their life, they cannot think, "I want this," or "I do not want this," or "I know this," or "I do not know this," let alone "I understand this" or "I love this." They are simply carried along by their desires according to their knowledge without reasoning or freedom.

This "carrying" comes not from the physical world but from the spiritual world, since there is nothing in the physical world that is not connected to the spiritual world. That is the source of every cause that makes something happen. There will be more on this below (see §96).

75   It is different for us, since we have not only desires of earthly love but desires of spiritual love and desires of heavenly love as well. Our human mind has three levels, as I explained in part 3 of *Divine Love and Wisdom*.⁷² This means that we can rise from earthly knowledge to spiritual intelligence and from there to heavenly wisdom; and because of these latter two, the intelligence and the wisdom, we can turn to the Lord, be united to him, and therefore live forever. This raising of our desires would not be possible, though, if we did not have the ability to raise our discernment because we are rational and to do so intentionally because we are free.

[2] It is by means of these two abilities that we can think inwardly about what we are perceiving outwardly with our physical senses and can think on a higher level about what we are thinking on a lower level. Any one of us can say, "I was thinking about this," or "I am thinking about this," or "I intended this," or "I intend this," or "I understand that this is true," or "I love this because of its quality," and so on. We can see from this that we are able to think about our thinking from a higher perspective and apparently see it down below. This ability of ours comes from our rationality and our freedom. Rationality enables us to think on a higher level, and freedom enables us to think that way from desire, intentionally. If we did not have the freedom to think that way, that is, we would not have the intention and therefore would not have the thought.

[3] The result is that if we do not want to understand anything except what has to do with this world and its nature, if we do not want to

understand what is good and true on moral and spiritual levels, we cannot rise from knowledge into intelligence, let alone from intelligence into wisdom, because we have blocked off these abilities. We have then made ourselves human only in the limited sense that we could understand if we wanted to, because of our inborn rationality and freedom and because we are able to want to.

It is these two abilities that enable us to think and to express our thoughts by talking. In other respects, we are not people but animals, and actually worse than animals because of our misuse of these abilities.

Anyone whose rationality has not been beclouded can see or grasp the fact that if we did not seem to be in possession of ourselves, we would not experience any wish to know anything or any wish to understand anything, since all pleasure and satisfaction and therefore all volition comes from feelings that derive from love. Who could set out to know or understand something unless there were some feeling of satisfaction involved? Could we have any such feeling of satisfaction unless what moved us seemed to be really ours? If it were not ours at all, but came from someone else—that is, if one person were instilling some of his or her feelings into the mind of someone who really had no inclinations to know or to understand—would that second person accept the feelings? *Could* that second person accept them? Could we call that second person anything but a dumb animal or a passive lump?

Clearly, then, it stands to reason that even though everything is flowing in, everything we perceive and therefore think and know, everything we intend and do in response to our perceptions, still it is by divine providence that it all seems to be ours. Otherwise, as just noted, we would not accept anything and could not be given any intelligence or wisdom.

It is acknowledged that everything good and true belongs not to us but to the Lord, even though it does seem to us to be ours. Since everything good and true does seem to be ours, so does everything that has to do with the church and heaven, with love and wisdom, and with charity and faith, even though no element of them really belongs to us. None of us could accept them from the Lord if we did not seem to perceive them as our own.

This supports the truth of the matter, namely, that whatever we do freely, whether or not it is guided by reason, seems to be ours as long as it is in accord with our reason.

Is there anyone who cannot see from that inherent ability called rationality that one particular thing is good and useful to society while another thing is bad and harmful? Justice, for example, and honesty and marital fidelity are useful to society, while injustice, dishonesty, and sex with other people's spouses are harmful to society. This means that evil acts are intrinsically damaging, while good acts are intrinsically beneficial. Is there anyone, then, who cannot incorporate this into rational thought, given the will to do so?

We do have rationality, and we do have freedom. Our rationality and freedom are uncovered, brought to light, and used judiciously, and they enable us to perceive and to act, to the extent that we abstain from our inner evils with these goals in mind. To the extent that we do, we turn toward those good acts the way one friend turns to another.

[2] This enables us—again using that ability of ours called rationality—to make decisions about the good qualities that are useful to society in the spiritual world and the evil qualities that are harmful there. All we have to do is to see sins as the evil ones and good, thoughtful acts as the good ones. Again, we can incorporate this into our rational thought if we want to, because we do have rationality and freedom. Our rationality and freedom are uncovered, brought to light, and used judiciously, and they enable us to perceive and to act, to the extent that we abstain from these evils as sins. To the extent that we do, we turn toward good, thoughtful deeds the way one neighbor turns lovingly toward another.

[3] Now, since the Lord wants whatever we do freely and rationally to seem to be ours, for the sake of our acceptance and union, it follows that we can intend things rationally because they involve our eternal happiness and that with a strength we have asked for from the Lord, we can do them.

78 3. *Whatever we have done from our freedom in accord with our thinking becomes a permanent part of us.* This is because our sense of who we are[73] and our freedom are integral to each other. Our sense of who we are is part of our life, and whatever we do from our life we do freely. Then again, our sense of who we are includes everything that comes from our love, because our love is our life; and whatever we do because of our life's love, we do freely.

We act freely and in keeping with our thought because we do think about whatever arises from our life or our love. We validate it in our thought; and once it is validated, we do it freely and in keeping with our thought. [2] This is because everything we do, we do from our volition by means of our discernment, and freedom is a matter of volition and thought a matter of discernment.

We can also act freely and irrationally, and rationally but not freely. These actions do not become a permanent part of us, though. They come only from our mouths and our bodies, not from our spirits and our hearts. The things that come from our spirits and our hearts become part of us when they are owned by our mouths and our bodies. I could provide any number of examples, but this is not the place for it.

[3] "Becoming part of us" means entering our life and becoming a matter of life and therefore becoming part of our sense of who we are.[74] However, I will be explaining later[75] that there is really no "who we are," even though there does seem to be. At this point I will say only that everything good that we do freely, in keeping with reason, is incorporated into us as though it were ours, because it seems to us that it is ours when we think and intend and speak and act. Still, the goodness is not ours but the Lord's within us (see §76 above). There will be a separate section on how this incorporation takes place.[76]

We say that whatever we do freely and in keeping with our thought is permanent because nothing we make part of ourselves can be eliminated. It has become part of both our love and our reasoning, part of our volition and our discernment, that is, and therefore part of our life. Actually, it can be displaced, but it still cannot be ousted. When it is displaced, it is moved from the center to the periphery, and there it dwells. This is what "being permanent" means.

[2] For example, suppose that in youth and early maturity we have taken into ourselves a pattern of doing something wrong because of the pleasure it gives to our love—cheating, perhaps, or blasphemy, or revenge, or promiscuity. Since we have done so freely, in keeping with our thought, we have made this part of ourselves. Later, though, if we repent, turn away from this behavior, and regard it as sin that is to be rejected, and therefore refrain from it freely and rationally, then we make part of ourselves the good behavior that is opposite to the evil. This good behavior then takes its place in the center and moves the evil toward the periphery, farther and farther out depending on our distaste for and rejection of it. The evil still cannot be ousted to the point of being uprooted, even though it may seem to be so. What is happening is that the Lord is restraining us from the evil behavior and keeping us in the good. This is what happens with all the evil we inherit and with all the evil we act out.

[3] I have seen things that bore witness to this in some people in heaven, people who thought they were free of evils because the Lord was keeping them involved in what is good. To prevent them from thinking that they actually owned the good qualities they were enjoying, they were let down from heaven and back into their evils until finally they recognized that on their own, they were immersed in evils, but were being held in what is good by the Lord. Once they recognized this, they were brought back into heaven.

[4] It is important to know also that these good qualities are made part of us only as long as they are the Lord's within us. To the extent that we recognize this, the Lord allows us to experience the goodness as our own, so that it seems to us as though we ourselves love our neighbor or are truly considerate, as though we ourselves have faith, and do what is good and understand what is true, as though we ourselves are therefore wise. Such examples help us see the nature and the strength of the appearance the Lord wants us to enjoy for the sake of our salvation; for without this appearance, none of us could be saved.

On this subject, see also §§42–45 above.

80 Nothing that we simply think about becomes part of us, even though we think we intend to do it, unless we intend it to the point that we would actually do it if the opportunity arose. This is because when we do things for this reason, from intent with the aid of discernment or from a desire of intent with the aid of thought from discernment, then we really do them. As long as it is a matter of thought alone it cannot be made part of us, because our discernment does not unite itself to our volition, or the thinking of our discernment to the desire of our intent. Our intent and its desire, though, do unite themselves to our discernment and its thinking, as has been amply explained in part 5 of *Divine Love and Wisdom*.[77]

This is the intent of the Lord's words, "It is not what goes into peoples' mouths that makes them unclean; rather, what comes out through the mouth from the heart makes them unclean" (Matthew 15:11, 17, 18, 19). Spiritually understood, "the mouth" means our thought, because thought is expressed through the mouth, and "the heart," spiritually, means the desire that comes from love. If this is the source of what we think and say, then it makes us unclean. In Luke 6:45 as well, "the heart" means the desire that comes from love or volition and "the mouth" means the thought of our discernment.[78]

81 If we believe that particular evils are permissible, then they do become part of us even though we do not do them, since the permission we grant them in our thought comes from our intent, and there is an agreement. As a result, when we believe that some particular evil is permissible, we have relaxed the inner restraint against it and are kept from doing it only by outward restraints, which are fears.[79]

Since our spirit is cherishing this evil, once the outward restraints are removed we feel free to do it. In the meanwhile, we are constantly doing it in our spirits. On this subject, though, see *Teachings about Life for the New Jerusalem* 108–113.[80]

4. *It is by means of these two abilities that the Lord reforms and regener-* **82** *ates us; without them we could not be reformed and regenerated.* The Lord teaches us that "No one can see the kingdom of God except by being born again" (John 3:3, 5, 7). However, not many people know what "being born again" or "being regenerated" actually is.[81] This is because people do not know what love and thoughtful living are; so they do not know what faith is, either, because anyone who does not know what love and thoughtful living are cannot know what faith is. Thoughtful living and faith are integral to each other the way what is good and what is true are, the way desires of our volition and thoughts of our discernment are. On this union see *Divine Love and Wisdom* 427–431; *Teachings for the New Jerusalem [on Faith]* 13–24;[82] and §§3–20 above.

The reason no one can enter heaven without being born again is **83** that we are involved in all kinds of evil through what we inherit from our parents; we also inherit an ability to become spiritual by the removal of those evils. Unless we do become spiritual, we cannot enter heaven; and changing from being earthly to being spiritual is being reborn or regenerated.

If we are to understand how we are regenerated, though, we need to keep three things in mind, namely, the nature of our first state, a state of damnation; the nature of our second state, a state of reformation; and the nature of our third state, a state of regeneration.

[2] Our first state, the state of damnation, is the one we get from our parents by heredity. Each of us is born with a predilection to love ourselves and the world, and subject to all kinds of evil that have these forms of love as their wellspring. It is the pleasures of these loves that guide us; and they render us unaware of our involvement in evils. This is because every pleasure that stems from love simply feels good to us. Unless we are regenerated, then, all we know is that loving ourselves and the world more than anything else is goodness itself, and dominating others and possessing all their wealth is the greatest good there is.[83]

This, too, is where all evil comes from, since we do not focus on anyone but ourselves out of love. If we do focus on someone else out of love, it is the way one demon focuses on another or one thief on another when they are cooperating.

[3] If we justify these loves within ourselves and the evils that spring from them because of the pleasure they give us, then we remain bound by the material world and become imprisoned in our physical senses. In our own thinking, the thinking of our spirits, we are insane. As long as we are in this world, though, we can talk and act rationally and wisely,

because we are human and therefore have rationality and freedom. However, we are doing all this out of our love for ourselves and the world.

After death, when we become spirits, we are capable of no pleasure except that which we felt in our spirits in this world. This is the pleasure of hellish love, which turns into the profound and agonizing pain that the Word refers to as the torment and fire of hell. We can see from this that our first state is one of damnation, and that we are in this state if we do not let ourselves be regenerated.

[4] Our second state, the state of reformation, starts when we begin to think about heaven in terms of its joy and therefore to think about God as the one who gives us heavenly joy. At first our thinking is prompted by the pleasure we find in self-love, and heavenly joy is that kind of pleasure for us. As long as the pleasure from that love and the pleasure we find in the evils that arise from it are in control, though, we can only think that we get to heaven by pouring out prayers, listening to sermons, taking communion, giving to the poor and helping the needy, contributing to churches, supporting hospices, and the like. In this state, all we know is that salvation comes by thinking about what our religion teaches us, whether that is what we call faith or whether it is what we call faith and charity.

The reason we are totally convinced that thinking about these things saves us is that we are not thinking about the evils that give us pleasure, and as long as these pleasures are with us, so are the evils themselves. Their pleasures come from our impulses toward them, impulses that constantly crave them and make them happen whenever some fear does not prevent it.

[5] As long as these evils stay in the compulsions of our love and their pleasures, the only faith or charity or devotion or worship we have is on the surface. They seem to the world to be real, but they are not. We might compare them to waters from a polluted spring, waters that are undrinkable.

As long as our nature leads us to think about heaven and God as matters of religion and not to think at all about evils as sins, we are still in the first state. We reach the second state, the state of reformation, when we begin to think that there is such a thing as a sin, and especially when we identify some particular thing as a sin, and when we look into it in ourselves, even briefly, and do not want to do it.

[6] Our third state, the state of reformation, picks up on this prior state and carries the process further. It begins when we stop doing wrong things because they are sins, advances as we abstain from them, and

becomes complete as we fight against them. Then, as we overcome in the Lord's strength, we are regenerated.

When we are regenerated, the whole pattern of our life is inverted. We become spiritual instead of earthly, since what is earthly is contrary to the divine design when it is separated from what is spiritual, and what is spiritual is in keeping with the divine design. The result is that when we have been regenerated, we act out of thoughtfulness and make the elements of that thoughtfulness part of our faith.

Still, we are spiritual only to the extent that we are attentive to what is true, since everyone is regenerated by means of truths and through living by them. It is truths that enable us to know what life is, and life that enables us to practice truths. This is how goodness and truth are united in the spiritual marriage where we find heaven.

The reason we are reformed and regenerated by means of the two abilities known as rationality and freedom, the reason that in fact we cannot be reformed and regenerated without them, is that it is through our rationality that we can discern and know what is evil and what is good and therefore what is false and what is true. Then through our freedom we can intend what we discern and know. As long as the pleasure of a love for evil is in control, though, we are not free to intend things that are good and true and make them a matter of our rationality, so we cannot make them part of ourselves. This is because the things that we do freely and in accord with reason, as already explained [§§78–81], become virtually part of us, and unless they do become part of us, we cannot be reformed and regenerated. We do not act because of the pleasure that comes from a love for what is good and true until the pleasure of a love for what is evil and false has been displaced, since the pleasures of two opposite loves cannot coexist.

Acting from the pleasure that comes from love is acting freely, and since our reason seconds our love, it is also acting rationally.

Since both evil and good people have rationality and freedom, both evil and good people can discern what is true and do what is good. However, evil people cannot do this freely and rationally, while good people can, because evil people are caught up in the pleasures of a love for evil while good people are caught up in a love for what is good.

The result is that any truth that evil people discern and any good that they do does not become part of them, though it does for good people; and if it does not become virtually part of them, there is no reformation and regeneration. For evil people, the evil intentions and their distortions are in the center and the good intentions and their truths are on the periphery, while for good people the good intentions and their truths are in the center and the evil intentions and their distortions are on the periphery. In each case, the qualities that are central spread all the way out to the periphery the way warmth spreads from a central fire or chill spreads from a central source of coldness. So for evil people, the peripheral good is corrupted by the central evils, and for good people the peripheral evil is mitigated by the central goodness. This is why evil deeds do not damn people who have been regenerated and good deeds do not save people who have not.

87   5. *We can be reformed and regenerated by means of these two abilities to the extent that we are brought to a realization that anything good and true that we think and do comes from the Lord and not from us.* I have already explained [§83] what reformation and regeneration are, and have also explained [§§82–86] that we are reformed and regenerated by means of these two abilities, rationality and freedom. Since the change is accomplished by means of the abilities, I need to say a little more about them.

It is our rationality that enables us to discern and our freedom that enables us to intend, in each case apparently on our own. However, the only people who can intend what is good and do good in a rational manner are people who have been regenerated. Evil people can only intend evil freely, and do it in keeping with their thought, by rationalizations that seem to be reasonable. Evil can be justified just the way good can, but only by the use of deceptive appearances. Once these appearances are taken as certainties, they become falsities; and anything that is taken as a certainty seems to be reasonable.

88   Anyone capable of thinking with deeper discernment can see that our ability to intend and our ability to act do not come from ourselves but from the one who is Ability itself, that is, who has the very essence of ability. Simply consider where ability comes from. Does it not come from the One who possesses it at its fullest strength, that is, who has it in its own essence and therefore from its own essence? This means that ability is essentially divine.

Every ability needs resources that must be provided, so there must be some directive from within or above. The eye cannot see on its own, the ear cannot hear on its own, the mouth cannot speak on its own, the hand cannot act on its own—there must be some resource and therefore some directive from the mind. The mind, too, cannot think and intend anything in particular on its own unless something inner or higher directs it to do so. It is the same with our abilities to discern and to intend. These can come only from One who is intrinsically able to intend and able to discern.

[2] We can see from this that the two abilities called rationality and freedom come from the Lord and not from us. Since they do come from the Lord, it follows that we cannot intend anything on our own or discern anything on our own: it only seems that way. Anyone can become assured of this who knows and believes that the intending of everything good and the discernment of everything true comes from the Lord and not from us. The Word teaches in John 3:27 and 15:5 that we cannot receive anything on our own or do anything on our own.

Now, since all our intending stems from love and all our discerning stems from wisdom, it follows that our ability to intend stems from divine love and our ability to discern stems from divine wisdom. This means that both come from the Lord, who is divine love itself and divine wisdom itself. Naturally, then, this is the only source of our acting freely and rationally. We all act [freely and] rationally because our freedom, like our love, is inseparable from our intentions.[85]

However, we have more inward and more outward intentions, and we can act on the more outward ones and not at the same time on the more inward ones. This is what hypocrites and flatterers do. Their outer intentions are free because they come from a desire to appear other than they really are[86] or because of a love for something evil, a love that is an extension of the love of their deeper intentions. But as already noted [§86], evil people cannot freely and rationally do anything but evil; they cannot freely and rationally do anything good. They can do good, but not from their inner freedom, the freedom that is really theirs. The result is that there is nothing good about their outer freedom.

I am saying that we can be reformed and regenerated only to the extent that, through these two abilities, we can be brought to a recognition that everything good and everything true that we think and do comes from the Lord and not from us. The reason we cannot recognize this except through these two abilities is that these two abilities themselves come from the Lord. They are the Lord's within us, as you can see from what has already been presented [§§73, 88].

It then follows that we cannot have this recognition on our own, but only from the Lord, though we still seem to be having it independently. This is the Lord's gift to every one of us. Let us then believe that we are independent but know and acknowledge that we are not. Otherwise any true thoughts that we think and any good things that we do are not really true and good. We are present in them and the Lord is not present in them. If we are present in anything good, if we are doing it for the sake of our salvation, then it is good done for credit; while if the Lord is present in the good that we do, it is not for credit.

91 The fact is that recognition of the Lord and recognition that everything good and true comes from him are what make our reformation and regeneration possible; but not many people can see this intelligently. That is, people can wonder, "What is the use of this recognition, when the Lord is omnipotent and wants to save everyone? Surely, then, he can and he wants to, provided only that he is moved to pity."

This kind of thinking does not come from the Lord, though, so it is not based on any deeper intellectual sight, that is, on any enlightenment. I need therefore to say briefly what that acknowledgment accomplishes.

[2] In the spiritual world, where space is only apparent, wisdom causes presence and love causes union, and the reverse. There is an acknowledgment of the Lord from wisdom and there is an acknowledgment of the Lord from love. Acknowledgment of the Lord from wisdom, which in its own right is only a kind of knowing, comes from a belief system. Acknowledgment of the Lord from love comes from living by what that belief system teaches. This latter brings about union, the other brings about presence. This is why people who reject beliefs about the Lord move away from him; and if they also reject the life, they cut themselves off from him. If they reject only the life but not the beliefs, they are present but still cut off. They are like acquaintances who talk with each other but have no love for each other, or like two people when one talks cordially with the other but is still an enemy, full of hatred.

[3] The truth of this is recognized in the widely accepted notion that people who teach the truth and live well are saved but not people who teach the truth and live evil lives, as well as in the notion that people who do not acknowledge God cannot be saved. We can see from this what kind of religion is involved in thinking about God from what we call faith but not doing anything out of caring. This is why the Lord said,

> Why do you call me "Lord, Lord," and do not do what I say? Whoever comes to me and hears my words and does them I will compare to someone who built a house and laid its foundation on a rock; but whoever hears my words and does not do them is like someone who builds a house on the ground without any foundation. (Luke 6:46–49)

6. *The Lord's union with us and our responsive union with the Lord* **92** *come about by means of these two abilities.* Union with the Lord and regeneration are the same thing, because we are regenerated to the extent that we are united to the Lord. So everything I have already said about regeneration can be said about union, and what I am about to say about union can be said about regeneration.

The Lord teaches in John that there is a mutual union of the Lord with us and of us with the Lord:

> Abide in me, and I in you. If people abide in me and I in them, they bear abundant fruit. (John 15:4, 5)

> In that day you will realize that you are in me and I am in you. (John 14:20)

[2] On the basis of reason alone, anyone can see that there is no union of spirits unless it is mutual and that mutuality is what unites. If one person loves another and is not loved in return, then as the one draws near the other backs off; while if there is love in response, as the one draws near so does the other, and this brings about union. Love wants to be loved. This is its inner instinct. To the extent that it is loved in return, it is filled with pleasure.

We can see from this that if the Lord loves us and we do not love the Lord in return, the Lord draws near us and we back off. So the Lord is constantly trying to come to us and enter us, and we are turning away and moving off. That is how it is with people in hell, though for people in heaven there is a mutual union.

[3] Since the Lord does want to be united to us for the sake of our salvation, he has provided a means of mutuality. For us, that means is the appearance that the good we intend and do freely and the truth that we think and speak rationally from these intentions originate in us. It is the appearance that the goodness in our intentions and the truth in our minds seem to be our own. In fact the appearance that they come from us as though they belonged to us is so complete that they do seem to be ours. There is no way to tell that they are not. Check to see whether anyone has any sense at all to the contrary.

On our apparent independence, see §§74–77 above, and on our incorporation of it as our own, see §§78–81. The only difference is that we are to recognize that we are not doing what is good and thinking what is true on our own, but from the Lord, so that the good that we do and the truth that we think are not ours. Thinking like this out of a loving intent, simply because it is true, brings about union, because this is how we turn toward the Lord and the Lord turns toward us.

93   In the spiritual world you can hear and see what the difference is like between people who believe that everything good comes from the Lord and people who believe that goodness comes from themselves. People who believe that goodness comes from the Lord turn their faces toward him and find a pleasure and a bliss in what is good. In contrast, people who believe that goodness comes from themselves focus on themselves, thinking inwardly that they have earned it. Since they are focused on themselves, all they can feel is a pleasure in their own goodness, and this is not a pleasure in goodness but a pleasure in evil—because what really belongs to us is evil. When pleasure in evil is felt as good, that is hell.

After death, people who have done good in the belief that it came from them cannot accept the fact that everything good comes from the Lord. They mingle with hellish demons and eventually unite with them. However, people who accept this truth are reformed, though the only people who do accept it are the ones who have turned to God during their lives. Turning to God during our lives is nothing but abstaining from evils as sins.

94   The Lord's union with us and our mutual union with the Lord are accomplished through our loving our neighbor as ourselves and loving the Lord above all.

Loving our neighbor as ourselves is simply not dealing dishonestly or unfairly with people, not harboring hatred or burning with revenge against them, not speaking ill of them or slandering them, not committing adultery with their spouses, and not doing anything of that nature to them. Can anyone fail to see that people who *do* do things like this are not loving their neighbor as themselves? However, people who do not do such things because they are both bad for their neighbor and sins against God treat their neighbor honestly, fairly, cordially, and faithfully. Since the Lord acts in the same way, a mutual union results.

When there is a mutual union, then whatever we do for our neighbor we do from the Lord, and whatever we do from the Lord is good. Then our neighbor is not the visible individual[87] but the goodness within that individual.

Loving the Lord above all is simply not doing violence to the Word because the Lord is in the Word, not doing violence to the holy practices of the church because the Lord is in the holy practices of the church, and not doing violence to any soul whatever, because everyone's soul is in the hand of the Lord. When we abstain from these evils as appalling sins, we are loving the Lord above all; but only people who love their neighbor as themselves can do so, because the two kinds of love are essentially one.

Since there is a union of the Lord with us and of us with the Lord, there are two tablets of the law—one for the Lord and the second for us.[88] To the extent that we keep the laws of our tablet, apparently on our own, the Lord enables us to keep the laws of his tablet. However, if we do not keep the laws of our tablet, all of which have to do with loving our neighbor, we cannot keep the laws of the Lord's tablet, all of which have to do with loving the Lord. How can a murderer, a thief, an adulterer, or a perjurer love the Lord? Surely reason tells us that being like this and loving the Lord is a contradiction. Is this not what the devil is like? Can people like this harbor anything but hatred for God?

When we do turn back from murder, adultery, theft, and perjury as hellish, though, then we can [harbor other feelings than hatred for God]. That is, we then turn our faces away from the devil and toward the Lord; and when we turn our faces toward the Lord, he gives us love and wisdom. These come into us through our faces, not through the backs of our necks. Because this is the only way union with the Lord is brought about, the two tablets were called a covenant. There are two parties to a covenant.

7. *The Lord protects these two abilities untouched within us and as things that are sacred through the whole course of his divine providence.* There are several reasons for this. One is that without these two abilities there, we would have no discernment or volition and would therefore not be human. Another is that without these two abilities we could not be united to the Lord and therefore could not be reformed and regenerated. Then too, without these two abilities we would not have immortality or eternal life. We can see this to some extent from the view already given [§§71–95] of what freedom and rationality are (these are the two abilities). We cannot see this clearly, though, unless the propositions are presented to view as inferences, so I need to shed some light on them.

[2] *Without these two abilities there we would have no discernment or volition and would therefore not be human.* The only basis of our volition is our ability to intend as though we were doing so ourselves. Intending freely, with this apparent autonomy, comes from the ability the Lord is constantly giving us, the ability called freedom. For another thing, the only basis of our discernment is our ability to discern whether something

is reasonable or not, again as though we were doing so ourselves. Discerning whether something is reasonable or not comes from the second ability that the Lord is constantly giving us, the ability called rationality.

These two abilities unite within us the way volition and discernment do, because there is no intent without discernment. Discerning is the mate or match of intending, necessary to its existence; so along with the ability called freedom we are given the ability called rationality.

[3] Then too, if you take away intending from discerning, you will not discern anything at all. You can understand to the extent that you try to, provided you have or have access to the resources called perceptions,[89] since these are like an artisan's tools. When I say that you can discern to the extent that you try, it means to the extent that you love to discern, since volition and love are the same thing.

This may seem like a paradox, but that is only how it seems to people who do not love to discern and therefore do not try to; and people who do not try to discern claim that they cannot. I will, however, be explaining later [§98] which people really cannot discern and which ones find it hard.

[4] We need no further support for the statement that if we did not have volition based on the ability called freedom and discernment based on the ability called rationality, we would not be human. Animals do not have these abilities. It may seem as though animals, too, can intend and can discern, but they cannot. There is an earthly desire, basically an impulse, with matching knowledge, that guides and impels them to do what they do. There is a social and moral component to this knowledge, but it does not transcend their knowledge, because animals have no spiritual level that would enable them to perceive what is moral and therefore think about it. They can be taught to do particular things, but this is strictly on the physical level. What they learn is added to their knowledge and to their impulses and is called forth either by sight or by hearing. However, it never becomes something that they think about, let alone something that they reason about. There is more on this subject above (see §74).

[5] *Without these two abilities we could not be united to the Lord and therefore could not be reformed and regenerated.* This has already been explained [§§82–86]. The Lord dwells within us in these two abilities whether we are evil or good, and uses them to unite everyone to himself. This is why evil people are as capable of discernment as good people, why potentially they intend what is good and discern what is true. If they

do not have these characteristics in act, that is because of their misuse of the abilities.

The reason the Lord dwells in these abilities in each of us is found in the inflow of the Lord's intent, an intent that wants to be accepted by us, to make its dwelling within us, and to give us the happiness of eternal life. This is the Lord's intent because it comes from his divine love. It is this intent of the Lord that makes whatever we think and say and intend and do seem to be our own.

[6] There is ample evidence in the spiritual world that the inflow of the Lord's intent makes this happen. Sometimes the Lord fills an angel with his divine nature so completely that the angel's whole consciousness is of being the Lord. That is how the angels were filled whom Abraham, Hagar, and Gideon[90] saw, angels who therefore called themselves Jehovah, as we read in the Word. In the same way, one spirit can be filled by another to the point of not realizing that she or he is not that other. I have seen this happen often. It is also common knowledge in heaven that the Lord always works through intention and that what happens is what he intends.

We can see from this that it is through these two abilities that the Lord unites himself to us and works things out so that we are united to him in return. I have already explained how we are united mutually through these abilities and how we are therefore reformed and regenerated, and will have much more to say about this below.[91]

[7] *Without these two abilities we would not have immortality or eternal life.* This follows from what has already been presented, namely, that these abilities are the means to our union with the Lord and to our reformation and regeneration. It is through them that we have immortality and through reformation and regeneration that we have eternal life. Since we are all united to the Lord through these two abilities whether we are evil or good, as just noted, we all have immortality. However, we have eternal life, heaven's life, only if that union is mutual, from the core of our being to its outer limits.[92] This enables us to see why the Lord protects these two abilities untouched within us and as things that are sacred through the whole course of his divine providence.

8. *This is why it is integral to divine providence that we act from freedom and in accord with reason.* Acting freely and rationally and acting on the basis of our freedom and our rationality are the same thing, as is acting on the basis of our intent and discernment. There is a difference, though, between acting freely and rationally or on the basis of our freedom and our rationality on the one hand, and acting in ways that are truly free and rational or on the basis of genuine freedom and

97

genuine rationality. This is because people who do evil out of a love for doing evil and who justify it are, in a way, acting freely and rationally. However, their freedom is not freedom in essence or real freedom. It is actually a hellish freedom that in essence is slavery. Their reason is not reason in essence, either. It is an imitation of reason, or distorted reason, or a facade made up of rationalizations.

Still, both ways of acting are under divine providence, for if we on the earthly level were deprived of the freedom to intend evil and to make it seem reasonable by rationalizations, that would be the end of our freedom and rationality and of our volition and discernment. We could not be led away from our evils and reformed, so we could not be united with the Lord and live forever. That is why the Lord protects our freedom the way we protect the pupil of our eye. The Lord, though, is constantly using our freedom to lead us away from our evils, and to the extent that he can do so through our freedom, he uses that freedom to plant good things within us. In this way, step by step he gives us heavenly freedom in place of hellish freedom.

98 I have stated [§73] that everyone has the ability to intend called freedom and the ability to discern called rationality, but it needs to be clearly understood that these abilities are virtually instinctive in us. They are what make us human.

As I have already explained [§97], it is one thing to act freely and rationally and another thing to act in true freedom and with true rationality. Only people who have allowed themselves to be regenerated by the Lord can act in true freedom and with true rationality. Others act freely and in keeping with a kind of thinking that they shape into an image of rationality. Still, everyone can attain to true rationality, and through that rationality to true freedom, except people who are born feebleminded or terribly dense. There are many reasons why people do not do so, reasons I will be disclosing later.[93] For now, let me simply mention the kinds of people who cannot be given true latitude or true freedom, and true reason or true rationality, and the kinds of people who have great difficulty.

[2] Real freedom and real rationality are impossible for people who are born feebleminded or who have become so, as long as they remain feebleminded. Real freedom and real rationality are impossible for people who are born dense and dull or who have become so through idleness or some sickness that distorts or shuts down the deeper levels of the mind, or else through a love for bestial living.

[3] Real freedom and real rationality are impossible for people in the Christian world who resolutely deny the Lord's divine nature and the

holiness of the Word and who maintain this denial decisively all the way to the end of their lives. This is what "the sin against the Holy Spirit" means, the sin that is not forgiven in this age or in the age to come (Matthew 12:31, 32). [4] Real freedom and real rationality are also impossible for people who attribute everything to the material world and nothing to Divinity and who make this a part of their faith by arguments based on visual evidence, because they are atheists.

[5] Real freedom and real rationality are difficult for people who have to a large extent convinced themselves of false religious principles, because people who convince themselves of false principles are denying true ones. If they have not convinced themselves, though, they can [have true freedom and rationality] no matter what their religion is. On this point, see the material collected in *Teachings for the New Jerusalem on Sacred Scripture* 91–97.

[6] Little children and youths cannot attain to true freedom and rationality until they reach the age of maturity, because the deeper levels of our minds are opened only gradually. In the meanwhile they are like seeds in unripe fruit that cannot sprout when they are planted.

I have mentioned [§98] that real freedom and real rationality are impossible for people who deny the Lord's divine nature and the holiness of the Word and for people who opt decisively for the material world and against Divinity, and also that they are difficult for people who have to a large extent convinced themselves of false religious principles. Still, none of these people actually loses these abilities. I have heard atheists who had become demons and satans[94] understand mysteries of wisdom just as well as angels do, but only when they heard someone else saying them. As soon as they turned back to their own thoughts, they stopped understanding. This was because they did not want to understand.

Still, they were shown that they would want to understand if they had not been led astray by their love for evil and the pleasure that it brought them. They understood this, too, when they heard it. They even agreed that they could want to, but said that they did not want to be able to, because then they would not be able to want what they really wanted, namely, the evil that followed from the pleasure of their compulsions.

I have often heard remarkable things like this in the spiritual world, and am completely convinced that everyone does have freedom and rationality. I am convinced that everyone can attain to real freedom and real rationality simply by abstaining from evils as sins. However, any adult who does not attain to real freedom and real rationality in this world will never do so after death, since then the state of life[95] we had while we were in the world lasts forever.

It Is a Law of Divine Providence That We Should Put Aside Evils in Our Outer Nature, Regarding Them as Sins and Doing So in Apparent Autonomy, and That This Is the Only Way the Lord Can Put Aside the Evils in Our Inner Nature and in Our Outer Nature Alike

100 ON the basis of reason alone everyone can see that the Lord, who is goodness itself and truth itself, cannot enter us unless what is evil and false in us has been banished. What is evil is the opposite of what is good and what is false is the opposite of what is true, and there is no way that opposites can mingle. No, when one approaches the other, there is a battle that lasts until one gives way to the other. Then the one that gives way moves off and the other takes its place. There is this kind of opposition between heaven and hell, or between the Lord and the devil.

Is it reasonable for anyone to think that the Lord can enter where the devil is in control, or that heaven can be in the same place as hell? With the rationality given to everyone who is sane, can we not see that the devil must be expelled for the Lord to enter, that hell must be banished for heaven to come in?

[2] This opposition is meant by what Abraham said from heaven to the rich man in hell:

> There is a huge, fixed chasm between you and us, so that people who want to cross to you from our side cannot, nor can you cross over to us. (Luke 16:26)

Real evil is hell and real goodness is heaven, or in other words, real evil is the devil and real goodness is the Lord. Anyone controlled by what is evil is a miniature hell, and anyone controlled by what is good is a miniature heaven. How, then, can heaven enter hell when there is such a huge, fixed chasm between them that you cannot get from one to the other? It follows from this that hell must at all costs be banished so that the Lord can enter in with heaven.

101 However, many people—especially people who have convinced themselves of a faith that is devoid of caring—do not know that they are in hell when they are engaged in evil pursuits. They have no idea what evils really are, because they give no thought to them. They say that they are not under the yoke of the law,[96] which means that the law does not condemn them. They also say that since they cannot contribute anything to their own salvation they cannot rid themselves of anything evil, let alone do anything good on their own.

They are people who give no thought to the evil within themselves and who are constantly engaged in it because of this neglect. I explained in *Teachings for the New Jerusalem on Faith* 61–68 that they are the ones the Lord referred to as "goats" in Matthew 41–46 *[25:32–33, 41–46]*, telling them to "Go away from me, cursed ones, into the eternal fire prepared for the devil and his angels" (Matthew 25:41).

[2] If we give no thought to the evils within us, that is, if we do not examine ourselves and then refrain from doing them, we wind up inevitably not knowing what evil is and then loving it because of the pleasure it offers us. This is because anyone who does not know about evil loves it, and anyone who neglects thinking about evil is constantly involved in it. People like this are like blind people, people who cannot see, since thought sees what is good and what is evil the way the eye sees what is beautiful and what is ugly. We are caught up in evil if we consider and intend it and if we think it is hidden from God and would be forgiven if it came to light. This is actually thinking that we are free of evil.

If we do then refrain from evil deeds, we do so not because they are sins against God but because we are afraid of the laws and afraid for our reputation. We are still doing them in spirit, though, because it is our spirit that thinks and intends. As a result, whatever we think in our spirit in this world we do after we leave this world when we become spirits.

[3] In the spiritual world where we all arrive after death, no one asks what our faith has been or what our beliefs have been, only what our life has been, whether we are one kind of person or another. They know that the quality of our faith and the quality of our beliefs depend on the quality of our life, because life constructs a belief system for itself and constructs a faith for itself.

All this leads to the conclusion that it is a law of divine providence **102** that we should rid ourselves of our evils. If we do not, then the Lord cannot be united to us and bring us to himself in heaven. However, it is not generally known that we need to rid ourselves of evils in our outer nature, and do this in apparent autonomy, or that the Lord cannot rid us of the evils in our inner nature unless we do this, apparently on our own.

Several principles, then, need to be presented in the light for rational consideration in the following sequence.

1. Everyone has an inner and an outer level of thinking.
2. The essential quality of our outer thinking is determined by the quality of our inner thinking.
3. Our inner nature cannot be cleansed from compulsions to evil as long as the evils in our outer nature are not banished, because these outer evils stand in the way.
4. The Lord cannot rid us of the evils in our outer nature without our help.
5. Therefore we need to banish the evils from our outer nature in apparent autonomy.
6. Then the Lord cleanses us from the compulsions to evil in our inner nature and from the evil practices themselves in our outer nature.
7. It is the unceasing effort of the Lord's divine providence to unite us to himself and himself to us in order to give us the joys of eternal life; and this can happen only to the extent that our evils and their compulsions are banished.

103   1. *Everyone has an inner and an outer level of thinking.* Our outer and inner levels of thinking mean much the same as our outer and inner selves, which is the same as our outer and inner volition and discernment, because volition and discernment are what make us human. Further, since volition and discernment come to our consciousness in thoughts, we can speak of outer and inner levels of thinking.

Since it is not our bodies but our spirits that intend and discern and therefore think, it follows that this outer level and inner level are outer and inner levels of our spirit. Our physical behavior, whether in speech or in action, is nothing but an effect of the inner and outer levels of our spirits, since the body is simply obedience.

104   To see that everyone who is old enough has an outer and an inner thinking, an outer [and an inner] volition and discernment, or outer and inner levels of spirit that amount to outer and inner levels of self, we need only look closely at the thoughts and intentions of other people on the basis of what they say and do. We may also look at our own thoughts and intentions when we are in company and when we are by ourselves.

People can talk cordially with others on the basis of their outer thinking and yet be hostile to them in their inner thinking. They can talk about love for their neighbor and love for God on the basis of their outer thinking, and do so with feeling, when in their inner thinking they are trivializing their neighbor and have no fear of God. People can talk thoughtfully and with feeling about the justice of our civil laws, the virtues of moral living, and the theological issues of spiritual life, and yet when they are by themselves, moved by their inner thinking and its feeling, they can argue against our civil laws, against the virtues of moral living, and against the theological issues of spiritual life. We do this when we are driven by our compulsions to evil but want it to seem to the world that we are not.

[2] When they are listening to what others say, many people are thinking, "Are their private thoughts the same as the thoughts they are expressing? Should I believe them or not? What are their intentions?" Everyone knows that flatterers and hypocrites have two levels of thought. They can control themselves and prevent their inner thinking from being seen, hiding it deeper and deeper within and virtually locking the doors to keep it hidden. We can also see quite clearly that we have inner and outer levels of thinking from the fact that we can see our own outer thought from the vantage point of our inner thought. We can reflect on it as well, and decide whether it is evil or not.

We may attribute this characteristic of the human mind to the two abilities we are given by the Lord, namely, freedom and rationality. If we did not have outer and inner levels of thought, these abilities would not enable us to sense and see anything evil in ourselves and be reformed. In fact, we would not even be able to talk; we would only be able to make noises like animals.

The inner level of our thinking comes from our life's love[97] and from the feelings and consequent perceptions that this love prompts. The outer level of our thinking comes from items we have in our memory that are useful to our life's love as supports and as means to its ends. From early childhood to young adulthood we are absorbed in the outer level of our thinking because of our impulses to learn, which at this point constitute our inner level. Some elements of desire and resulting tendencies [to action] seep through from the life's love we have inherited from our parents as well.

Later, though, the way we live shapes our life's love, whose feelings and consequent perceptions make up the inner level of our thinking. Then our life's love gives rise to a love of means;[98] and the pleasures and the information those means elicit from our memory make up the outer level of our thinking.

105

106   2. *The quality of our outer thinking is determined by the quality of our inner thinking.* I have already explained[99] that our quality from head to toe is determined by the quality of our life's love. I need to begin at this point, then, by saying something about our life's love, since until that is done I cannot say anything about the desires that, together with our perceptions, make up our inner human nature, or about the pleasures of our desires that, together with our thoughts, make up our outer human nature.

There are many loves, but there are two that are like lords or rulers: heavenly love and hellish love. Heavenly love is love for the Lord and for our neighbor, and hellish love is love for ourselves and for the world. The two kinds of love are as opposite to each other as heaven and hell, because when we are caught up in love for ourselves and for the world we intend good to no one but ourselves, while when we are caught up in love for the Lord and our neighbor we intend good to everyone. These two loves are our life's love, but they come in many different forms. Heavenly love is the life's love of people whom the Lord is leading, and hellish love is the life's love of people whom the devil is leading.

[2] No one can have a life's love, though, without the derivatives we refer to as desires. The derivatives of hellish love are attractions to what is evil and false—strictly speaking, compulsions; while the derivatives of heavenly love are attractions to what is good and true—strictly speaking, predilections. There are as many feelings of hellish love (strictly speaking, compulsions) as there are varieties of evil; and there are as many feelings of heavenly love (strictly speaking, predilections) as there are varieties of goodness.

Love dwells in its desires like a lord in a manor or a ruler in a realm. Their lordship and rule is over the elements of our minds, that is, of our volition and discernment, and through these over our bodies. Through its desires and consequent perceptions, and through its pleasures and consequent thoughts, our life's love rules over the whole person. It rules over the inner level of our minds through our desires and their perceptions and over the outer level of our minds through the pleasures of those desires and the thoughts that result from them.

107   We can see what this governmental structure is like to some extent from comparisons.

As for heavenly love with its desires for what is good and true and the perceptions they prompt—the pleasures of those desires and the thoughts that the pleasures prompt—these can be compared to a tree with all its branches, leaves, and fruit. The life's love is the tree; the branches and leaves are the desires for what is good and true and their perceptions; and the fruit is the pleasures of those desires and their thoughts.

As for hellish love, though, with its desires for what is evil and false, its compulsions, and the pleasures of those compulsions and the thoughts that they prompt, they can be compared to a spider in the middle of its web. The love itself is the spider; the cravings for what is evil and false and their deeper deceptions are the web of threads right where the spider sits; and the pleasures of those compulsions with their vicious schemes are the outer threads where flying insects are caught, wrapped up, and eaten.

These comparisons enable us to see how everything in our volition ⟨108⟩ and discernment, everything in our mind, is united to our life's love, but they do not enable us to see this rationally. We can see the union rationally as follows. There are always three things that make up a unity, namely, purpose, means, and result.[100] The life's love is the purpose; the desires and their perceptions are the means; and the pleasures of those desires and their thoughts are the results. This is because just as a purpose attains its result through means, love attains its pleasures through desires and reaches into thoughts through perceptions.

The actual effects occur in the mind's pleasures and their thoughts when the pleasures come from our volition and the thoughts come from the resulting discernment; that is, when there is complete agreement between them. The results are then part of our spirit; and even if they do not come out in physical action, they are virtually in action when this agreement is reached. They are in our bodies as well and are dwelling there with our life's love, eager to act; and they act whenever nothing prevents it. This is what cravings for evil and actual evils are like for people who in their spirit regard them as permissible.

[2] Just as a purpose unites with its means and through its means with a result, then, our life's love unites with the inner processes of our thought and through them with its outer processes. We can therefore see that the quality of the outer processes of our thinking is essentially the same as the quality of the inner ones, since a purpose instills itself completely into its means and through its means into its result. Nothing essential happens in the result except what is in the means and what lies behind the means in the purpose; and since the purpose is therefore the very essence that fills the means and the result, we refer to the means and the result as the intermediate purpose and the final purpose.

It does sometimes seem as though the outer processes of our thinking ⟨109⟩ were not really of the same nature as the inner ones. This happens, though, because the life's love, with the inner things that surround it, appoints a subsidiary agent called "the love of means" and commissions it to make very sure that nothing of its compulsions comes to light. Consequently, this agent speaks and acts in accord with the civic principles of the country, the moral principles of reason, and the spiritual principles of the church, all because of the deviousness of its ruler, the life's love. It does this so deviously and cleverly that no one even sees that such people are not really like what they are saying and doing. Eventually, they cover up so completely that they themselves can hardly tell. All hypocrites are like this, as are priests who at heart trivialize the neighbor and have no fear of God, although they are preaching about love for our neighbor and love for God. Judges are like this who make decisions on the basis of bribes and friendships while pretending to be passionate advocates of justice and making reasonable statements about judicial matters. Business people are like this who are dishonest and deceptive at heart while they are acting honestly for the sake of their profits. Adulterers are like this when they use the rationality we all have to talk about the chastity of marriage. The list could go on.

[2] If these same people take off the robes of purple and linen with which they have clothed their love of means, the agent of their life's love, and dress it in its everyday clothes, then they think the exact opposite and express these thoughts in words when they are with their intimates, with people whose life's loves are of the same nature.

Some might believe that when these people are talking so fairly, honestly, and devoutly because of their love of means, the quality of their inner thought processes was not present in their outer thinking; but it is. There is a hypocrisy in them, a self-centeredness and love for the world, whose wiles aim at getting a reputation for decency, with profits in mind; and this is present in the smallest details of their facade. This quality of their inner thinking is present in the processes of their outer thought whenever they are thinking and acting like this.

110 In people who are being led by heavenly love, the inner and outer processes of their thinking, their inner and outer selves, are acting in unison when they talk. There is no awareness of any distinction between them. Their life's love, together with its desires for what is good and their perceptions of what is true, is like the soul within the things they are thinking and the things they say and do as a result. If they are priests, then they preach out of their love for their neighbor and their love for the Lord. If they are judges, then they make decisions on the basis of true justice. If they are merchants, then they act out of real honesty. If they are married, then they love their spouses with real chastity; and the list could go on.

Their life's love also has a love of means as its agent, an agent whom it teaches and guides to act thoughtfully, clothing it with robes of a passion for both theological truth and good deeds of daily life.

3. *Our inner nature cannot be cleansed from compulsions to evil as long as the evils in our outer nature are not banished, because these outer evils stand in the way.* This follows from what I have already said [§§106–110] about the essential nature of our outer thought processes being determined by the nature of our inner thought processes and about their being consistent with each other, the way things are when one is not only within the other but also derives from it, so that one cannot be removed unless the other is as well. That is the way it is with any outward thing that comes from an inner cause, any consequence from some precedent, and any result from some means.

[2] Now, since compulsions combine with their deviousness to make up the inner thought processes of evil people, and since the pleasures of those compulsions combine with their intrigues to make up their outer thought processes, and since these two processes are so united that they function in unison, it follows that our inner nature cannot be cleansed from its compulsions as long as the evil deeds in our outer character are not banished. We need to realize that what lies within our compulsions is our volition, and what lies within our deviousness is the discernment of our inner self; while what lies within the pleasures of our compulsions is our outer volition, and what lies within the intrigues of our deviousness is our outer discernment.

We can all see that our compulsions and their pleasures form a single whole, and that our deviousness and its intrigues form a single whole, and that these four occur in a single sequence and come together in a kind of sheaf. Then we can also see that the only way to get rid of an inner nature that is made up of compulsions is by getting rid of an outer nature that is made up of evil deeds. It is our compulsions that bring forth the evil deeds through their pleasures; but once the evil deeds are considered permissible (which happens when our volition and discernment agree), then the pleasures and the evil deeds make a single whole. We know that consent is the same as action—this is what the Lord says in Matthew 5:28: "If anyone has looked at someone else's wife so as to lust for her, he has already committed adultery with her in his heart." It is the same with our other evils.

All this shows that if we are to be cleansed from our compulsions to do evil, it is absolutely necessary that the evils be banished from our outer self. Until that happens, there is no vent for our compulsions, and if there is no vent, then they remain pent up inside, breathing out their pleasures and urging us to consent and then to act. Our inner compulsions enter our bodies through our outer thought processes; so the moment there is consent in our outer thought processes, the compulsions are present in our bodies. That is the locus of the pleasure that we feel. (On the quality of the mind determining that of the body and therefore the whole person, see *Divine Love and Wisdom* 362–370.)

I may illustrate this by comparisons and by examples. [2] As for comparisons, we can compare our compulsions and their pleasures to a fire that burns more intensely the more it is fed and that spreads wider the more room it is given, until it destroys the houses in a city or the trees in a forest. In fact, our compulsions for what is evil are compared to fire in the Word, and the evils they cause are compared to destruction by fire. Then too, in the spiritual world our cravings for evil and their pleasures look like fires. That is exactly what hellfire is.

We can also compare them to the deluges and floods that happen when dikes or levees are breached, or to cases of gangrene or abscesses that cause physical death if they spread or are not healed.

[3] As for examples, it is obvious that if evils are not banished from our outer self, the compulsions and their pleasures will increase dramatically. The more thieves steal, the more obsessed they are with stealing until eventually they cannot help themselves. It is the same with the cheating of cheaters, with hatred and vengefulness, with hedonism and gluttony, with promiscuity, blasphemy, and the like. Everyone knows that a love of power for self-aggrandizement grows to the extent that restraints are relaxed,[101] and the same holds for a love of possessions for worldly reasons. It seems as though there were no limit to them, no end.

We can see from all this that to the extent that evils are not banished from our outer self, their compulsions flourish, and that as restraints on evil behavior are relaxed, the compulsions intensify.

113   We cannot sense the compulsions that underlie our own evils. We are aware of their pleasures, but we give them little conscious thought because the pleasures seduce our thinking and distract our reflections. As a result, unless we discover from some other source that they are evil, we call them good and commit them freely, in accord with the reasoning of our thoughts. When we do this, we incorporate them into ourselves.

To the extent that we rationalize them as permissible, we enlarge the court of our ruling love, our life's love. Its "court" is made up of our compulsions, since they are like its servants and courtiers through which it governs the more outward activities that are its realm. The nature of the ruler determines the nature of the servants and courtiers, and the nature of the whole realm as well. If the ruler is a devil, the ruler's servants and courtiers will be forms of madness and the general populace will be all kinds of distortion. The servants (who are called "wise" even though they are insane) use imaginary constructs and arguments based on illusions to make the distortions seem true and to be accepted as true.

Is there any way to change the state of people like this except by banishing the evils from their outer self? This is how the compulsions that are inherent in our evils are banished. Otherwise, no exit is offered to the compulsions and they remain pent up like a city under siege or a sealed abscess.

4. *The Lord cannot rid us of the evils in our outer nature without our help.* In all Christian churches the accepted teaching is that before we come to take Holy Communion we should examine ourselves, see and admit our sins, and repent by refraining from them and rejecting them because they come from the devil. Otherwise our sins are not forgiven, and we are damned.

Even though the English accept a theology of faith alone, in the prayer before Holy Communion they explicitly enjoin self-examination, acknowledgment, confession of sins, repentance, and taking up a new life. They threaten people who do not do so by saying that the devil will enter into them as he entered into Judas and fill them with all iniquity, destroying both body and soul. The Germans, Swedes, and Danes, who also accept a theology of faith alone, teach much the same in their prayer before Holy Communion, adding the threat that otherwise we will render ourselves liable to the punishments of hell and eternal damnation because of this mixture of the sacred and the profane. The priest reads these words with a loud voice to the people who come to Holy Communion, and the people hear them with a full recognition of their truth.

[2] However, when these same people hear a sermon about faith alone on the very same day, when they hear that the law does not condemn them because the Lord has fulfilled it for them, that on their own they cannot do anything good without claiming credit for it, and that therefore their deeds contribute nothing whatever to their salvation and only their faith does, then they go home totally oblivious to their earlier confession. In fact, they dismiss it to the extent that they are thinking about this sermon on faith alone.

So which is true, the first or the second? Two mutually contradictory statements cannot both be true. For example, one option is that there is no forgiveness of sins and therefore no salvation, only eternal damnation, unless we examine and identify and recognize and confess and reject our sins—unless we repent. The other option is that things like this contribute nothing to our salvation, because by suffering on the cross the Lord has made full satisfaction for people who have faith; and if we only have faith—a trust that this is true—and are sure that the Lord's merit has been credited to our accounts, then we are sinless and appear before God with faces washed gleaming-clean. We can see, then, that all Christian churches share the basic conviction that we need to examine ourselves, see and admit our sins, and then refrain from them; and that otherwise we face not salvation but damnation.

We can see that this is also divine truth itself in passages in the Word where we are commanded to repent, passages like these:

> John[102] said, "Bring forth fruits worthy of repentance. Right now, the axe is lying at the root of the tree. Every tree that does not bring forth good fruit will be cut down and thrown into the fire." (Luke 3:8–9)

> Jesus said, "Unless you repent, you will all be destroyed." (Luke 13:3, 5)

> Jesus proclaimed the good news of the kingdom of God: "Repent, and believe the good news." (Mark 1:14–15)

> Jesus sent out his disciples who preached repentance as they went forth. (Mark 6:12)

> Jesus told the apostles that they were to preach repentance and the forgiveness of sins to all nations. (Luke 24:47)

> John preached the baptism of repentance for the forgiveness of sins. (Mark 1:4; Luke 3:3)

Think about this, then, with some clarity of mind and if you are religious you will see that repentance from sins is the pathway to heaven. You will see that faith apart from repentance is not really faith and that people who are without faith because they are without repentance are on the road to hell.

115   There are people who accept a faith separate from charity and who justify themselves by what Paul says to the Romans: "We are justified by faith apart from works of the Law" (Romans 3:28). They worship this statement like people who worship the sun; and they become like people who stare so constantly at the sun that their eyesight becomes dull and incapable of seeing things in normal light. They do not see what "works of the Law" means here—not the Ten Commandments, but the rituals described by Moses in his books, everywhere referred to as "the Law."[103]

To keep us from thinking that it means the Ten Commandments, Paul goes on to explain, "Then do we abolish the Law by faith? Far from it, we strengthen the Law" (Romans 3:31).

If we convince ourselves of faith alone on the basis of this statement, then by staring at this passage like the sun we blind ourselves to places where Paul lists the laws of faith and says that they are in fact deeds of charity.[104] After all, what is faith apart from its laws? We blind ourselves to the places where he lists evil deeds, saying that people who do them cannot enter heaven.[105]

We can see from this what blindness comes from a misunderstanding of this one passage.

The reason the evils in our outer self cannot be expelled without our   **116**
cooperation is this. One of the principles of the Lord's divine providence is that whatever we hear, see, think, intend, say, and do seems to belong to us completely. I have already explained (§§71–95 and following above) that if it did not seem like this, we would not be able to accept divine truth, decide to do good, or internalize love and wisdom. We would have no charity and faith and therefore no union with the Lord, no reformation and regeneration, and no salvation.

It is obvious that if it did not seem like this there would be no possibility of repentance from our sins and in fact no faith whatever, and that if it did not seem like this we would not be human but would be devoid of any rational life, like animals. Submit the matter to reason, if you will. Does it not seem exactly as though we ourselves think about what is good and true in spiritual, civic, and moral matters? Then accept the theological principle that everything good and true comes from the Lord and nothing from us. Can we not recognize the conclusion that we should do what is good and think what is true as though we were autonomous, but that we should still admit that these actions are being done by the Lord? Particularly, can you not see that we are to expel evils in apparent autonomy but still admit that the source of our doing this is the Lord?

There are a great many people who do not know that they are in-   **117**
volved in evil because they do not do evil things outwardly. They are afraid of civil laws and of losing their reputations, so by habitual practice they have trained themselves to avoid evil deeds as harmful both to their reputations and to their purses. However, if they do not avoid evil deeds on religious grounds, because they are sins and are in conflict with God, then the cravings for evils and their pleasures are still there within them like foul water that is dammed up and stagnant. They might examine

their thoughts and intentions and discover these compulsions if they only knew what sins were.

[2] A great many people who have settled on faith divorced from charity are like this. Since they believe that the law does not condemn them, they pay no attention to sins. They even doubt whether there are such things as sins. If there are, they are not sins in God's sight, because they have been pardoned.

Natural moralists[106] are like this as well, people who believe that everything depends on our civic and moral life and its vigilance and nothing on divine providence. People are like this too who take great care to cultivate a reputation and a name for decency and honesty for the sake of position or profit. After death, though, people like this who have had no use for religion become spirits that embody their compulsions. They look absolutely human to themselves, but from a distance they look like images of Priapus to others.[107] They see everything in darkness and nothing in light, like owls.

118 This provides solid support for the fifth proposition, namely, that *therefore we need to banish the evils from our outer nature in apparent autonomy,* a proposition also explained in three chapters in *Teachings about Life for the New Jerusalem*. First, there is no way we can abstain from evils as sins so as to turn against them inwardly unless we engage in struggles against them (§§92–100). Second, we are to abstain from evils as sins and struggle against them in apparent autonomy (§§101–107). Third, if we abstain from evils for any other reason than that they are sins, we are not really abstaining from them. We are only preventing them from being visible in the world (§§108–113).[108]

119 6. *Then the Lord cleanses us from the compulsions in our inner nature and from the evil practices themselves in our outer nature.* The reason the Lord cleanses us from our compulsions to evil when we expel evils in apparent autonomy is that the Lord cannot cleanse us until we have done our part. The evils are in our outer self and the compulsions to evil in our inner self, as closely connected as roots and trunk. Unless the evils are expelled, then, there is no opening. The evils block the way and close the door, a door that the Lord cannot open unless we cooperate, as I have already explained [§§114–118]. So when we, apparently on our own, open the door, the Lord uproots our compulsions at the same time.

Another reason is that the Lord is at work in the center of our being, and works from that center into everything that depends on it all the way to our boundaries, and we are living at these boundaries while this is happening. As long as we ourselves are keeping these boundaries closed, then, no cleansing can take place. There can be only the kind of work within us by the Lord that the Lord does in hell—we are forms of hell when we are in the grip of our compulsions and the evils they cause. This work is simply arranging it so that one thing does not destroy another, and so that what is good and true is not harmed.

The Lord's words in the Book of Revelation show that the Lord is constantly pressing us, urging us, to open the door: "Look, I am standing at the door and knocking. To all who hear my voice and open the door I will enter, and I will dine with them, and they with me" (Revelation 3:20).

We know absolutely nothing about the inner state of our minds; yet there are infinite things there, none of which comes to our awareness.[109] The inner working of our thought or our inner self is our actual spirit, and there are infinite elements there, innumerable elements, just as there are in our physical bodies. In fact, there are even more, since our spirit is human as to its form, and there are elements in it to answer to everything in our bodies.

Now, since our senses tell us nothing about the way our minds or souls are at work, both together and separately, in all the elements of our bodies,[110] we do not know how the Lord is at work in all the elements of our minds or souls, that is, in all the elements of our spirits. This activity is constant. We have no part in it; but still the Lord cannot cleanse us from any compulsion to evil in our spirits or inner selves as long as we keep the outer self closed. Each of the evils that we use to keep our outer selves closed seems to be a single item, but there are infinite elements within it. When we dismiss it as a single item, then the Lord dismisses the infinite elements that it contains.

This is what it means to say that the Lord then cleanses us from the compulsions to evil in our inner nature and from the evil practices themselves in our outer nature.

Many people believe that simply believing what the church teaches cleanses us from our evils; some believe that this is achieved by doing good, some that what is needed is knowing, discussing, and teaching about churchly matters; some opt for reading the Word and devotional literature, some for going to church and listening to sermons and especially taking Communion, some for renouncing the world and being resolutely devout, some for confessing themselves guilty of all sins—the list goes on and on. However, none of these activities cleanses us unless we examine ourselves, see our sins, admit them, accept responsibility for them, and repent by not committing them any more, doing all this

120

121

apparently on our own but at heart acknowledging that it comes from the Lord.

[2] Until this happens, none of the things I just listed helps. They are being done either for credit or hypocritically. To angels in heaven, people of this sort look either like beautiful harlots with the rank smell of disease, or like misshapen women made up to look attractive. Or again, they may look like actors playing their roles, like mimes on stage, or like apes dressed up in human clothes.

Once the evils have been banished, though, then the behaviors I have listed become filled with love, and these individuals look beautifully human to angels in heaven, like their own friends and companions.

122 We need to be fully aware, however, that when we are about to repent we need to turn to the Lord alone. If we turn only to God the Father we cannot be cleansed, nor if we turn to the Father for the sake of the Son or to the Son as merely human. There is only one God, and the Lord is that God because his divine and his human natures are one person, as I have explained in *Teachings for the New Jerusalem on the Lord*.[111] To enable us to turn to the Lord alone when we are about to repent, the Lord instituted the Holy Supper, assuring forgiveness of sins to those who repent. The sacrament offers that assurance because during that Supper or Communion, each participant is kept focused on the Lord alone.

123 7. *It is the unceasing effort of the Lord's divine providence to unite us to himself and himself to us in order to give us the joys of eternal life; and this can happen only to the extent that our evils and their compulsions are banished.* I explained in §§27–45 that it is the constant effort of the Lord's divine providence to unite us to himself and himself to us, and that this union is what we call reformation and regeneration. I explained also that this is the source of our salvation. Can anyone fail to see that union with the Lord is eternal life and salvation? Everyone can see this who believes that we were originally created in the image and likeness of God (see Genesis 1:26, 27) and who knows what the image and likeness of God are.

[2] If we are truly rational and use our rationality when we think and use our freedom when we try to think, can any of us believe that there are three gods equal in essence and that the divine Being[112] or divine Essence can be divided? As for a threefold nature in one God, that is something we can conceive and understand, just as we understand the soul and the body of an angel or a person and the life that they bring forth. Further, since this threefold nature in a single Being exists only in the Lord, it follows that any union must be a union with him.

Use your rationality and think freely, and you will see this truth in its own light. First, though, admit that the Lord, heaven, and eternal life are real.

[3] Now, since God is one and since by creation we have been made in his image and likeness, and since we have come into a love for all our evils through our hellish love, its compulsions, and their pleasures, thereby destroying the image and likeness of God within us, it follows that it is the constant effort of the Lord's divine providence to unite us with himself and himself with us and thereby to make us his images. It also follows that the Lord is doing this so that he may give us the bliss of eternal life, since this is the nature of divine love.

[4] The reason he cannot make this gift, cannot make us images of himself, unless we banish sins from our outer self in apparent autonomy is that the Lord is not just divine love but divine wisdom as well; and divine love does nothing unless it stems from divine wisdom and is in accord with it. It is in accord with divine wisdom that we cannot be united to the Lord and thus reformed, regenerated, and saved unless we are allowed to act freely and rationally. This is what makes us human. Anything that is in accord with the Lord's divine wisdom is also in accord with his divine providence.

At this point, I may add two secrets of angelic wisdom that will enable us to see what divine providence is like. The first is that the Lord never acts in any detail of our being by itself unless he acts in all the details at once. The second is that the Lord acts from the center and the boundaries at the same time.

124

The reason *the Lord never acts in any detail of our being by itself unless he acts in all the details at once* is that everything in us is so knit together and therefore so united in a single form that it does not act as a plurality but as a single whole. We know that we are knit together and therefore formed in this way as far as our bodies are concerned. The human mind is also in the same kind of form and has the same kind of all-inclusive connectedness, because the human mind is a spiritual person and in fact acts as a single person. This is why our spirit, the mind that is in our body, has a complete human form, so that after death we are people just as much as we are in this world. The only difference is that we have cast off the skin that made up our body in this world.

[2] Since it is the nature of the human form that all its parts make an inclusive entity that acts as a single whole, it follows that one element cannot be shifted from its place and changed with respect to state except

with the consent of the others; for if one element were moved out of place and changed in state, there would be a gap in the form that was intended to act as a single whole. We can see from this that the Lord never acts on any detail without acting on all of them at the same time.

This is how the Lord works in the whole angelic heaven, because the whole angelic heaven is like a single person in his sight.[113] This is also how the Lord acts on every individual angel, because every angel is a miniature heaven. This is also how he acts on each of us, most directly on our minds, and through them on everything in our bodies. This is because our mind is our spirit—an angel to the extent that it is united to the Lord—and our body is obedience.

[3] However, we need to be acutely aware that the Lord acts precisely, most precisely in fact, on every detail of our being while working through everything in our form. He does not, though, change the state of any part or any element in specific unless all the elements of the form concur. There will be more on this later,[114] when I explain that the Lord's divine providence is all-inclusive because it deals with details and that it deals with details because it is all-inclusive.

[4] The reason *the Lord acts from the center and the boundaries at the same time* is that this is the only way the whole and all its elements can be kept connected. The things in between depend in sequence on the central ones, all the way to the boundaries, and they are all gathered together at the boundaries; for as explained in part 3 of *Divine Love and Wisdom*,[115] there is a gathering at the boundaries of everything that comes from the First. This is why the Lord from eternity or Jehovah came into the world and put on the clothing of a human nature there in outermost form in order to be present in first and last things at the same time, and therefore from the first things to govern the whole world through the last things.[116] This enabled him to save those people whom he could save under the laws of his divine providence, which are also the laws of his divine wisdom. This involves the fact acknowledged in the Christian world that no one could have been saved unless the Lord had come into the world (see *Teachings for the New Jerusalem on Faith* 35). This is why the Lord is called the First and the Last.[117]

125   These angelic secrets have been presented first to make possible an understanding of the way the Lord's divine providence works to unite us to him and him to us. This does not happen in any detail by itself unless it is happening in everything else at the same time; and it happens from our center and from our boundaries at the same time. Our center is our life's love, and our boundaries are the contents of our outward thinking.

In between are the contents of our deeper thinking; and I have already explained [§§104–109] what these are like in evil people. Again, then, we can see that the Lord cannot work from our center and our boundaries at the same time unless he works with us (we are actually with the Lord in our most external activities).

This means that in those matters where we make choices because they are within the limits of our freedom, when we do something outwardly, the Lord is working from our center and in successive stages all the way to our boundaries.

We have no knowledge whatever of what is at our center or what is in those successive stages from the center to our boundaries, so we have no knowledge whatever of how the Lord is at work or what he is doing there. However, since all of these events constitute one coherent process all the way to the boundaries, all we need to know is that we should abstain from evils as sins and turn to the Lord. This is the only way the Lord can set aside our life's love, which is hellish from our birth, and transplant a love for heavenly life in its place.

Once the Lord has transplanted a love for heavenly life in place of a love for hellish life, then he transplants desires for what is good and true in place of cravings for what is evil and false, the pleasures of impulses to do good in place of the pleasures of impulses toward what is evil and false, and the good actions of heavenly love in place of the evil actions of hellish love—eventually genuine care in place of cleverness, and wise thought processes in place of malicious ones. In this way we are begotten anew and become new people.

Teachings about Life for the New Jerusalem 67–73, 74–79, 80–86, and 87–91 tells which good qualities take the place of evil ones. In §§32–41, it explains that we come to love truths of wisdom to the extent that we abstain from evils as sins and dislike them; and in §§42–52 that we have faith and become spiritual to the same extent.

By citing the prayers that are said before Holy Communion in all Christian churches, I have already shown [§114] that the basic theology throughout Christendom enjoins us to explore ourselves, see our sins, admit them, confess them to God, and stop committing them; and that this is repentance, the forgiveness of sins, and consequently salvation.

The faith named after Athanasius leads us to the same conclusion. This too is accepted throughout the Christian world; and it says at the end, "The Lord will come to judge the living and the dead; and when he comes, those who have done what is good will enter eternal life and those who have done what is evil will enter eternal fire."

128   Is there anyone who does not know from the Word that our fate after death depends on what we have done? Open the Word and read it and you will see this clearly: but set aside any thoughts based on faith and on our justification by faith alone. Here are a few passages to witness to the fact that the Lord teaches this throughout his Word.

> Every tree that does not *bear good fruit* is cut down and thrown into the fire; so you will know them by their *fruits*. (Matthew 7:19, 20)

> Many people will say to me on that day, "Lord, have we not prophesied in your name and done many good deeds in your name?" But I will profess to them, "I do not recognize you. Depart from me, you who do *injustice.*" (Matthew 7:22, 23)

> I will compare anyone who hears my words and *does them* to a wise man who built his house on a rock; but I will compare anyone who hears my words and *does not do them* to a senseless man who built his house on the ground without a foundation. (Matthew 7:24, 26; Luke 6:46–49)

> [2] The Human-born One will come in the glory of his Father, and then *he will reward all according to their deeds.* (Matthew 16:27)

> The kingdom of God will be taken away from you and *will be given to a nation that brings forth its fruits.* (Matthew 21:53 *[21:43]*)

> Jesus said, "My mother and my brothers are the people who hear the word of God and *do it.*" (Luke 8:21)

> Then you will come and stand there and knock on the door and say, "Open the door for us, Lord"; but he will answer, "I do not know where you come from. Go away from me, *all you who do* injustice." (Luke 13:25–27)

> Those who have done what is good will go forth to a resurrection of life, but those who *have done what is evil* to a resurrection of judgment. (John 5:29)

> [3] We know that God does not listen to *sinners,* but that he listens to anyone who worships God and *does his will.* (John 9:31)

> If you know these things, you are blessed if you do them. (John 13:17)

> Those who know my precepts and *do them* are the ones who love me; and I will love them and come to them and make my dwelling with them. (John 14:15, 21–24)

You are my friends *if you do* whatever I tell you to. I have chosen you so that *you would bear* fruit and so that your *fruit* would last. (John 15:14, 16)

[4] The Lord said to John, "Write to the angel of the church in Ephesus, '*I know your works*.[118] My complaint against you is that you have left your first *charity. Repent and do the earlier works.* If you do not, I will remove your lampstand from its place.'" (Revelation 2:1, 2, 4, 5)

Write to the angel of the church in Smyrna, "I know *your works.*"(Revelation 2:8 *[2:8, 9]*)

Write to the angel of the church in Pergamos, *"I know your works,"* "*Repent."*(Revelation 2:13, 16 *[2:12, 13, 16]*)

Write to the angel of the church in Thyatira, "*I know your works and your charity,* and *your* later *works* are more than the first ones." (Revelation 2:26 *[2:18, 19]*)

Write to the angel of the church in Sardis, "*I know your works,* that you have a reputation of being alive, but you are dead. *I have not found your works perfect in God's sight. Repent."* (Revelation 3:1, 2, 3)

To the angel of the church in Philadelphia write, "*I know your works.*" (Revelation 3:7, 8)

To the angel of the church in Laodicea write, "*I know your works. Repent."* (Revelation 3:14, 15, 19)

I heard a voice from heaven saying, "Write, 'Blessed are the dead who die in the Lord from now onward; *their works follow them.*'"(Revelation 5:13 *[14:13]*)

A book was opened that was the book of life, and the dead were judged, *all of them according to their works.* (Revelation 20:12, 13)

Look, I am coming quickly, and my reward is with me, *that I might give to all according to their works.* (Revelation 22:12)

These come from the New Testament. [5] There are still more in the Old, and I may cite just this one.

Stand in the gate of Jehovah and proclaim this word there. Thus says the Lord of Hosts, the God of Israel, "Make your ways and your deeds good. Do not put your trust in deceitful words, saying 'The temple of

Jehovah, the temple of Jehovah, the temple of Jehovah!' Will you be stealing and murdering and committing adultery and perjuring yourselves and then come and stand in my presence in this house that bears my name and say, 'We are exempt when we do these disgusting things'? Will you make this house a robbers' cave? I myself have seen it," says Jehovah. (Jeremiah 7:1, 3, 4, 9, 10, 11 *[7:2, 3, 4, 9, 10, 11]*)

It Is a Law of Divine Providence That We Should Not Be Compelled by Outside Forces to Think and Intend and So to Believe and Love in Matters of Our Religion, but That We Should Guide Ourselves and Sometimes Compel Ourselves

129 THIS law of divine providence follows from the two preceding ones, namely, that we should act in freedom and in accord with reason (§§71–99), and that we should do this for ourselves, even though it is being done by the Lord—that is, in apparent autonomy (§§100–128). Since it is not from freedom and according to reason and not in autonomy to be compelled but comes from the absence of freedom and from someone else, this law of divine providence follows directly from the two earlier ones. Everyone recognizes that none of us can be compelled to think what we do not want to think or to intend what we think we do not want to intend. So we cannot be compelled to believe what we do not believe, and certainly not anything that we do not want to believe; or to love what we do not love, and certainly not anything that we do not want to love. Our spirit or mind has complete freedom to think, intend, believe, and love. This freedom comes to us by an inflow from the spiritual world, which does not compel us. Our spirit or mind is actually in that world. The freedom does not flow in from the physical world, which accepts the inflow only when the two worlds are in unison.

[2] We can be compelled to say that we think and intend some-thing or that we believe and love something, but unless this is or be-comes a matter of our own desire and our consequent reasoning, it is not something that we really think, intend, believe, and love. We can also be compelled to speak in favor of religion and to act according to religion, but we cannot be compelled to think in its favor as a matter of our own faith and to intend it as a matter of our own love. In coun-tries where justice and judgment are cherished, everyone is obliged not to speak against religion or to violate it in action, but still no one can be compelled to think and intend in its favor. This is because each of us has a freedom to think in sympathy with hell and to intend in its favor, or to think in sympathy with heaven and to intend in its favor. Still, our reason tells us what the quality is of the one and of the other and what lot awaits the one and what lot awaits the other. Our ability to intend on the basis of reason is our capacity to choose and to decide.

[3] This may serve to show that what is outside cannot compel what is inside. However, it does happen sometimes,[119] and I need to show that it is harmful in the following sequence.

1. No one is reformed by miracles and signs, because they com-pel.
2. No one is reformed by visions or by conversations with the dead, because they compel.
3. No one is reformed by threats or by punishment, because they compel.
4. No one is reformed in states where freedom and rationality are absent.
5. Self-compulsion is not inconsistent with rationality and free-dom.
6. Our outer self has to be reformed by means of our inner self, and not the reverse.

1. *No one is reformed by miracles and signs, because they compel.* I have already explained [§§103, 119] that we have inner and outer processes of thought and that the Lord flows through our inner thought processes into the outer, this being the way he teaches and guides us. I have also ex-plained [§§71–99] that it is the intent of the Lord's divine providence that we act in freedom and in accord with reason. Both of these abilities in us would be destroyed if miracles happened and we were forced into belief by them.

130

We can see the truth of this rationally as follows. We cannot deny that miracles induce faith and that they persuade us convincingly that what the miracle-worker says and teaches is true. To begin with, this conviction takes over the outer processes of our thought so completely that it virtually constrains and bewitches them. However, this deprives us of the two abilities called freedom and rationality and therefore of our ability to act in freedom and in accord with reason. Then the Lord cannot flow in through our inner thought processes into the outer ones; all he can do is leave us to convince ourselves by rational means of the truth of anything that has become a matter of faith for us because of the miracle.

[2] The basic state of our thought is that we look from our inner thinking and see things in our outer thinking in a kind of mirror, because as already noted [§104] we can look at our own thinking, which can be done only by a deeper level of thinking. When we look at something in this mirrorlike way, we can turn it this way and that and shape it so that it seems attractive to us. If what we are looking at is something true, we could compare it to a good-looking, vibrant young woman or young man. However, if we cannot turn it this way and that and shape it but only believe it at second hand, influenced by a miracle, then even if it is true it is like a young woman or young man carved of stone or wood, with no life in it. We might also compare it to something that is constantly before our eyes, something that is all we look at, hiding whatever is on either side of it and behind it. Or we could compare it to a sound that is constantly in our ears, robbing us of any perception of the harmony of multiple sounds. This kind of blindness and deafness is imposed on our minds by miracles.

The same holds true for any conviction that is not looked at rationally before it becomes a conviction.

131 This shows us that a faith caused by miracles is not real faith but only second-hand belief.[120] It has no rational content, let alone spiritual content. It is actually an outer shell with nothing inside it. The same holds true of everything we do on the basis of this kind of second-hand faith, whether it is acknowledging God, worshiping him at home or in church, or benefiting others. When the only thing that prompts the acknowledgment, the worship, and the devotion is some miracle, then we are acting from the earthly level of our human nature and not from the spiritual level, because the miracle instills faith from the outside and not from the inside—from the world, then, and not from heaven. The Lord enters us only from the inside, that is, by means of the Word and by lessons and sermons based on the Word.[121] Since miracles close this inner route, miracles do not happen nowadays.[122]

We can see this characteristic of miracles very clearly in the miracles   132
that were witnessed by the Jews and Israelites. Even though they saw so
many miracles in the land of Egypt and then at the Reed Sea,[123] and even
more in the wilderness, and especially at Mount Sinai when the Law was
given—all the same, after that month when Moses stayed on the mountain, they made themselves a golden calf and acknowledged it instead of
Jehovah, who had brought them out of the land of Egypt (Exodus 32:4, 5,
6). We can see this also from the miracles that were done later in the land
of Canaan, when the Israelites still fell away from their required worship
so often. The same holds for the miracles that the Lord did in their presence when he was in the world: even so, they crucified him.

[2] The reason these miracles were done is that the Jews and Israelites
were totally focused on earthly concerns. They were brought into the
land of Canaan simply to portray the church and its deeper values by
means of their outward worship; and evil people[124] can portray this just
as well as good ones because these outward activities are rituals, all pointing to spiritual and heavenly realities for them. So even though Aaron
had made the golden calf and commanded the people to worship it (Exodus 32:2, 3, 4, 5, 35), he could still portray the Lord and his work of salvation. Further, since they could not be led to portray these things
through inner worship, they were led by miracles, actually constrained
and compelled.

[3] The reason they could not be led through internal worship is that
they consistently failed to acknowledge the Lord, even though the whole
Word that was present with them is about him and no one else.[125] People
who do not acknowledge the Lord are not open to any inner worship.
After the Lord had made himself known, though, and had been accepted
and recognized in the church as the eternal God, miracles stopped
happening.

However, the effect of miracles on good people is different from their   133
effect on evil people. Good people have no desire for miracles, but they
believe the miracles in the Word. If they do hear anything about a miracle, they think of it only as a minor argument that strengthens their faith,
because they base their thinking on the Word and therefore on the Lord
and not on the miracle.

It is different for evil people. They can actually be constrained and
compelled to faith and even to worship and devotion by miracles. This
lasts only a short while, though, because their evils are pent up inside,
and the compulsions and gratifications of those evils are constantly
working away inside their outward worship and devotion. In the effort

to let them break free of this confinement, these people think about the miracle and wind up calling it a sham, a trick, or a natural event, which enables them to return to their evil ways. People who go back to their evil ways after being worshipful profane what is good and true in worship, and the fate after death of people who profane what is holy is the worst of all. These are the people referred to in the Lord's discourse in Matthew 12:43, 44, 45, the people whose last state is worse than the first.[126]

Besides, if miracles did happen for people who do not believe in the miracles in the Word, they would be happening constantly where everyone like this could see them. This shows why miracles do not happen nowadays.

134a [127]   2. *No one is reformed by visions or by conversations with the dead, because they compel.* There are two kinds of visions, divine and demonic. Divine visions are given by means of portrayals in heaven, while demonic visions are effected though magical events in hell. There are imaginary visions as well, visions that are the illusions of a mind that has lost its bearings.

Divine visions (which as just noted are given by means of portrayals in heaven) are the kind that happened to the prophets. When they were having these visions they were not in the body but in the spirit, because visions cannot happen to us while we are physically awake. So when the prophets saw visions, it says that they were in the spirit, as the following passages show.

Ezekiel said, "The spirit lifted me up and took me back to Chaldea to the captivity in *a vision of God,* in *the spirit of God;* so the vision that I saw came over me" (Ezekiel 11:1, 24). Then too, spirits held him up between earth and heaven and brought him to Jerusalem in *visions of God* (Ezekiel 8:3 and following). The same thing happened in a vision of God or in the spirit when he saw the four animals that were cherubim (Ezekiel chapters 1 and 10) and when he saw the new temple, the new earth, and the angel measuring them (Ezekiel chapters 40–48). It says in chapter 40:2, 26 that he was in visions of God at the time, and in chapter 43:5 that he was in the spirit.

[2] Zechariah was in the same kind of state when he saw the man on horseback among the myrtle trees (Zechariah 1:8 and following), when he saw the four horns and the man with a measuring line in his hand (Zechariah 1:18, 20, 21; 2:1 and following),[128] when he saw the lampstand and the two olive trees (Zechariah 4:1 and following), when he saw the flying scroll and the ephah (Zechariah 5:1, 6), and when he saw the four

chariots coming out from the four mountains, and the horses (Zechariah 6:1 and following).

Daniel was in the same kind of state when he saw the four beasts rising from the sea (Daniel 6:1 *[7:1]* and following), and when he saw the battles of the ram and the goat (Daniel 8:1 and following). It says in 7:1, 2, 7, and 13; in 8:2; and in 10:1, 7, and 8 that he saw these things in the vision of his spirit, and it says in 9:21 that he saw the angel Gabriel in a vision.

[3] John was in the vision of the spirit when he saw the things he describes in the Book of Revelation—for example, when he saw the seven lampstands with the Human-born One in their midst (Revelation 1:12–16), when he saw the throne in heaven with someone sitting on it, surrounded by the four animals that were cherubim (Revelation 4), when he saw the book of life taken by the Lamb (Revelation 5), when he saw the horses come out of the book (Revelation 6), when he saw the seven angels with their trumpets (Revelation 8), when he saw the pit of the abyss opened with the locusts coming out of it (Revelation 9), when he saw the dragon and its battle with Michael (Revelation 12), when he saw the two beasts rise up, one from the sea and one from the land (Revelation 13), when he saw the woman sitting on the scarlet beast (Revelation 17) and the destruction of Babylon (Revelation 18), when he saw the white horse with someone riding it (Revelation 18 *[19]*), when he saw the new heaven and the new earth and the holy Jerusalem coming down from heaven (Revelation 21), and when he saw the river of water of life (Revelation 22). It says that he saw these things in the vision of his spirit in 1:11 *[1:10]*; 4:2; 5:1; 6:1; and 21:12 *[21:10]*.

These were the kinds of visions that were visible from heaven to the sight of their spirits and not to their physical sight.

Things like this do not happen nowadays, because if they did they would not be understood, since they happen by means of images whose details are pointing to inner features of the church and secrets of heaven. It was foretold in Daniel 9:24 that they would stop when the Lord came into the world.

However, *demonic visions* have sometimes occurred. They are brought about by spirits who inspire deceptive passions and visions[129] and who call themselves the Holy Spirit because of a mental confusion that engulfs them. Now, however, these spirits have been gathered in by the Lord and consigned to a hell separate from the other hells.[130]

We can see from all this that no one can be reformed by any visions except the ones that are in the Word. There are *imaginary visions* as well, but these are nothing but the illusions of a mind that has lost its bearings.

134b   The story that the Lord told about the rich man in hell and Lazarus in Abraham's lap shows that no one is reformed by conversations with the dead. The rich man said, "Father Abraham, I beg you to send Lazarus to my father's house where I have five brothers, to bear witness to them so that they do not come to this place of torment." Abraham said to him, "They have Moses and the prophets: let them heed them." But he said, "No, father Abraham, but if someone came to them from the dead, they would repent." He answered him, "If they do not heed Moses and the prophets, they would not be convinced if someone rose from the dead" (Luke 16:27–31).

Conversations with the dead may lead to the same results as miracles that I have just described. That is, we may be convinced and be constrained to worship for a short while. However, since this deprives us of rational functioning at the same time that it hems in our evils, as already noted [§§130–131, 133], this spell or inner restraint is released and the pent-up evils erupt in blasphemy and profanation. Still, this happens only when spirits have imposed some religious dogma. No good spirit—let alone any angel of heaven—would ever do this.

135   We are allowed to talk with spirits (though rarely with angels of heaven), and many people have been allowed to for centuries. When it happens, though, they talk with us in our own everyday language and use only a few words. Further, the ones who have the Lord's permission to talk with us never say anything that would take away our freedom to think rationally; and they do not teach, either. Only the Lord teaches us, indirectly, through the Word, when we are enlightened (there will be more on this later [§§171–174]). I have been granted knowledge of this by personal experience. I have been talking with spirits and angels now for many years,[131] and no spirit has dared, and no angel has wanted, to tell me anything, let alone teach me, about things in the Word or any aspect of theology based on the Word.[132] Only the Lord has taught me, the Lord who was revealed to me and who since then has been and is constantly before my eyes as the sun in which he dwells, just as he is for angels. He has enlightened me.

136   *3. No one is reformed by threats or by punishment, because they compel.* It is generally recognized that what is outside us cannot control what is inside us, but that what is inside can control what is outside. It is also recognized that what is inside us resists compulsion from the outside so definitely that it turns the other way; and it is recognized that outward pleasures attract what is inside toward assent and toward love. We might also realize that there is inner compulsion and inner freedom.

Even though these facts are generally recognized, we still need examples, because there are a great many things that we sense to be true as soon as we hear them, simply because they are true; so we affirm them. If they are not supported by rational considerations, though, they can be undermined by arguments based on deceptive appearances and eventually denied. So I need to go back to the principles I have just described as "recognized" and give them rational support.

[2] First, *what is outside us cannot control what is inside us, but what is inside can control what is outside.* Can anyone be forced to believe and to love? We can no more be forced to believe than we can be forced to think what we do not think. We can no more be compelled to love than we can be compelled to intend what we do not intend. Faith, too, is a matter of thought, and love is a matter of volition. However, what is inside can be compelled from the outside not to speak maliciously against the laws of the realm, the customs of everyday living, and the holy values of the church. What is inside can be compelled in this regard by threats and by punishments. It is so compelled, and it needs to be. However, this internal part of us is not truly human. It is an inner nature that we have in common with animals who can also be controlled. Our human inner nature dwells on a higher level than this animal inner nature. This is what I mean by the inner human nature that cannot be compelled.

[3] Second, *what is inside us resists compulsion from the outside so definitely that it turns the other way.* This is because our inner nature wants to be in freedom and loves its freedom. As I have already explained [§73], freedom is a matter of our love or our life; so when something free feels that it is being controlled, it withdraws into itself, so to speak, and turns in the opposite direction. It looks at the compulsion as an enemy. The love that is the substance of our life is irritated, which makes us think that we are not in control of ourselves and that we are therefore not living our own life.

The reason our inner nature is like this is found in the law of the Lord's divine providence that says we should act in freedom and in accord with reason.

[4] We can see from this that it is harmful to compel people to worship God by threats and punishments.

Still, there are people who are willing to be compelled to religious observance and people who are not. Most of the ones who are willing to be compelled to religious observance are Roman Catholics, but this applies to the ones whose worship has no inner substance but is all on the surface. Most of the ones who are not willing to be compelled are Anglicans; and the result is that there is an inner substance to their worship so that what they do outwardly comes from an inner source. In a spiritual light, the religious aspects of their inner natures look like bright clouds, while in heaven's light the religious aspects of the inner natures of the others look like dark clouds. I have been allowed to see both of them in the spiritual world; and anyone who wants to do so will see the same on arrival in that world after death.

Further, compulsory worship pens in our evils, so that they lie hidden like fire in bits of wood buried in ashes that keep smoldering and spreading until they break out in flame. Worship that is not compulsory but completely voluntary does not pen in our evils, so they are like flames that flare up quickly and then go out. We can see from this that our inner nature resists compulsion so definitely that it turns in the opposite direction.

The reason what is inside us can control what is outside is that what is inside is like a master and what is outside is like a servant.

[5] Third, *outward pleasures attract what is inside toward assent and toward love.* There are two kinds of pleasure, mental and volitional. Mental pleasures are also the pleasures of wisdom, and volitional pleasures are the pleasures of love, because wisdom is a matter of discernment and love is a matter of volition. Next, since the pleasures of our bodies and their senses (which are outward pleasures) work in unison with our inner pleasures—pleasures of mind and feeling—it follows that just as our inner nature resists compulsion from the outside so definitely that it turns in the opposite direction, so our inner nature turns spontaneously toward pleasure in our outer being until it is actually facing it. This brings about agreement on the part of our discernment, and brings about love on the part of our volition.

[6] In the spiritual world, all little children are led by the Lord into angelic wisdom, and through angelic wisdom into heavenly love, by means of things that are delightful and charming: at first by beautiful objects indoors and charming things in their gardens, then by portrayals of spiritual things that touch the inner levels of their minds with delight, and ultimately by truths of wisdom and virtues of love. So the children are led throughout by pleasures in their proper sequence: first by the pleasures of a love for discernment and its wisdom, and finally by the pleasures of a willing love that becomes their life's love. Then whatever

they have internalized through the earlier pleasures is kept in order under this love. [7] It happens like this because everything that has to do with our discernment and volition is given form by outward means before it is given form by inward means. In fact, everything that makes up our discernment and volition is first given form by things that come in through our physical senses, especially sight and hearing. Then, once our first discernment and first volition have taken shape, our inner thinking regards them as the outside of its own thought processes and either unites with them or distances itself from them. It unites with them if they are pleasing and distances itself from them if they are not.

[8] We need to realize quite clearly, though, that the inside of our discernment does not unite with the inside of our volition. No, the inside of our volition unites with the inside of our discernment and arranges things so that the union is mutual. But all of this is accomplished by the inside of our volition, and none of it by the inside of our discernment.[133] This is why we cannot be reformed by faith alone.[134] It takes our volition's love, which constructs a faith for itself.

[9] Fourth, *there is inner compulsion and inner freedom.* Inner compulsion is found in people who are busy with outward worship alone and not with inner worship. Their inner process is to think and intend whatever is demanded of their outward nature. These are people who are caught up in worship of living or dead individuals and are therefore involved in the worship of idols and in belief in miracles. The only inner nature they have is one that is superficial at the same time.

For people involved in inner worship, though, there are two kinds of inner compulsion, one based on fear and the other based on love. The inner compulsion that is based on fear is characteristic of people who engage in worship out of fear of the torment of hell and its flames. However, this inner compulsion is not the inner thought process mentioned above [§§103–105, 110, 111, 120, 130] but an outer thought process, one that we call "inner" at this point simply because it has to do with thinking. The inner thought process discussed earlier cannot be controlled by any kind of fear. It can be compelled, though, by love and by a fear of losing love. This is precisely what is meant by a real "fear of God." Being controlled by love and by a fear of losing it is self-compulsion. It will become clear later [§§145–149] that self-compulsion is not contrary to our freedom and rationality.

This shows the nature of compulsory worship and of voluntary worship. Compulsory worship is physical, lifeless, dark, and depressing. It is physical because it engages the body but not the mind; it is lifeless

137

because our life is not in it; it is dark because our discernment is not in it; and it is depressing because the joy of heaven is not in it. On the other hand, when voluntary worship is sincere it is spiritual, living, bright, and joyful. It is spiritual because there is a spirit from the Lord in it; it is living because there is life from the Lord in it; it is bright because there is wisdom from the Lord in it; and it is joyful because there is heaven from the Lord in it.

138   4. *No one is reformed in states where freedom and rationality are absent.* I have already explained [§§78–81] that nothing becomes part of us except what we do in freedom and in accord with reason. This is because freedom is a matter of our volition and reason is a matter of our discernment. When we do something in freedom and in accord with reason, then we do it of our own volition by means of our own discernment, and whatever is done by these two united becomes part of us.

Since the Lord wants us to be reformed and reborn in order to have eternal life, or the life of heaven, and since we cannot be reformed and regenerated unless goodness is taken into our volition as part of it and truth is taken into our discernment as part of it, and since nothing can become part of us except what is done of our own free volition and in accord with our own rational discernment, it follows that no one is reformed in states that lack freedom and rationality.

There are many states that lack freedom and rationality, but in general they can be assigned to the following categories: states of fear, emergency, mental illness, serious physical illness, ignorance, and intellectual blindness. I need to say something specific about each of these states.

139   The reason no one is reformed in a state of fear is that fear takes away our freedom and rationality, or our "freeness" and our "reasonableness." Love opens the inner reaches of the mind, but fear closes them; and when they are closed, we do very little actual thinking, being conscious then only of what is impinging on our feelings or our senses. All the fears that beset our minds are like this.

[2] I have already explained [§104] that we have inner and outer processes of thought. Fear can never occupy our inner thought processes. These are always in freedom because they are in our life's love. Fear can occupy our outer thought processes, though, and when it does, it closes off the inner thought processes. Once they are closed, we are no longer able to act freely and rationally, so we cannot be reformed.

[3] The fear that occupies our outer thought processes and closes in the deeper ones is primarily a fear of losing rank and losing wealth. The fear of outward civil and ecclesiastical penalties does not close them in,

because these laws prescribe penalties only for people who speak and act contrary to the civil principles of the state and the spiritual principles of the church, not for people who think contrary to those principles. [4] A fear of punishments in hell actually does occupy our outer thought processes, but only for a moment or a few hours or days. Before long, our thinking is released back into its own freedom because of our inner thinking, the thinking proper to our spirit and our life's love, the thinking we call the thought of the heart.

[5] However, a fear of the loss of position and profit does occupy our outer thought processes, and when it does it closes off our inner thinking from above, from any inflow from heaven. This makes it impossible for us to be reformed. The reason is that from birth, our life's love is a love for ourselves and for the world. Love for ourselves and love of rank are a unity, and love for the world and love of wealth are a unity. So when we have rank or wealth, we justify for ourselves whatever means promote our rank and our wealth, because of our fear of losing them. These means may be both civil and ecclesiastical, from either domain. We do the same if we do not yet have rank and wealth but covet them, though in this case it is from a fear of losing reputation on their account. [6] I have just mentioned that the fear occupies our outer thought processes and closes off the inner ones from above, from any inflow from heaven. We say that the inner thinking is closed when it is wholly identified with the outer thinking, because then it is not functioning on its own, but is governed by the outer.

Since love for ourselves and love for the world are hellish loves and are the wellsprings of everything evil, we can see the intrinsic quality of the inner thinking of people for whom those are their life's loves, people in whom those loves are in control. It is full of compulsions to all kinds of evil.

People are unaware of this if they are fanatically convinced of their own religion because they are afraid of losing their own eminence and splendor, especially if their religion involves their being revered as demigods—and as rulers[135] in hell at the same time. They can be on fire for the salvation of souls even though the fire is a hellish one. Since this fear especially robs us of our essential freedom and our essential rationality, which are heavenly in origin, we can see that it blocks us from any possibility of reformation.

The reason no one is reformed by thinking of God and pleading for help in a state of emergency is that this is a state of compulsion, so as soon as we return to a state of freedom we return to our former state

140

when we rarely if ever thought about God. It is different for people who feared God in their former, free state.

"Fearing God" means fearing to offend him, and sinning is offending him. This really comes from love rather than from fear. If we love others, are we not afraid of hurting them? The more we love them, the greater the fear. Without this fear our love is insipid, only skin deep. It occupies our thoughts only, and not our intentions.

"States of emergency" mean states when hope is threatened by danger, as happens in battles, duels, shipwrecks, falls, and fires; the sudden, threatened loss of wealth or of employment and its prestige; and the like. Thinking about God in these circumstances comes from ourselves, not from God. Our minds are then virtually imprisoned in our bodies and therefore are not in freedom, which means they lack rationality as well; and without these there is no possibility of reformation.

141 The reason no one is reformed in a state of mental illness is that mental illness deprives us of rationality and therefore of the freedom to act rationally. The mind is sick and not healthy, and while a healthy mind is rational, a sick one is not. The illnesses are things like depression, imagined or illusory guilt,[136] various kinds of hallucinations, mental anguish brought on by misfortunes, and mental anxiety and pain brought on by physical disorders. These are sometimes thought of as temptations, but they are not. Real temptations focus on spiritual issues, and during them the mind is in possession of its skills. The states I am talking about focus on earthly issues, and during them the mind goes mad.

142 The reason no one is reformed in a state of serious physical illness is that at such times our reason is not in a state of freedom. The state of the mind depends on that of the body. When the body is afflicted, the mind is as well, if only by being out of touch with the world. A mind that is out of touch with the world may think about God, but not with God, because its reasoning is not free. Our rational freedom comes from our being midway between heaven and the world. This enables us to think in terms of heaven or in terms of the world, so we can think in heavenly terms about the world or in worldly terms about heaven. When we are seriously ill and are thinking about death and the state of our souls after death, then we are not in touch with the world. We are withdrawn in spirit, and when we are completely withdrawn we cannot be reformed. It can strengthen us, though, if we had been reformed before we fell sick.

[2] The same holds true for people who renounce the world and all its dealings and devote themselves totally to thoughts of God and heaven and salvation; but there is more on this elsewhere.[137]

The result is that if people like this have not been reformed before their illness, then afterwards, if they do die, they are the same kind of people they were before the illness. This means that it is pointless to think that we can repent or accept any faith while we are seriously ill, because there is no trace of action involved in our repentance, no trace of caring in our faith. Thus both our repentance and our faith are all talk and no heart.

The reason no one is reformed in a state of ignorance is that our reformation takes place by means of truths and by means of our living by them, so if people do not know what is true, they cannot be reformed. However, if they long for truths because they are drawn to them, then they are reformed in the spiritual world after death.[138] **143**

No one is reformed in a state of intellectual blindness, either. These individuals, too, are not aware of truths and do not know about life, because it is our discernment that must instruct us in these matters and our volition that must act them out. When our volition is doing what our discernment tells it to, then we have a life in accord with truths; but when our discernment is blind, our volition is blocked as well. All it can do freely in accord with its own reasoning is the evil that it has justified in its discernment, which is false. **144**

If religion teaches a blind faith, it blinds our discernment just the way ignorance does. It is then teaching a false theology; for just as truths open our discernment, falsities close it. They close it from above but open it downward; and discernment that is open only downward cannot see truths. All it can do is justify whatever it wants to, especially anything false.

Our discernment is also blinded by compulsions to evil. As long as our intentions are caught up in these compulsions, they prompt our discernment to justify them; and to the extent that we justify our compulsions to evil, our volition cannot enjoy good desires, see truths on that basis, and so be reformed.

[2] For example, if people are compulsive adulterers, their intentions, being caught up in the pleasures of that love, prompt their discernment to justify it. They say, "What is adultery? Is there anything wrong about it? Isn't it just like what happens between a husband and a wife? Can't children just as well be born from adultery? Can't a woman accept more than one man without being harmed? What does sex have to do with spirituality, anyway?" This is how a discernment that has become prostituted by its volition thinks. It becomes so stupid because of its debauchery with volition that it cannot see that marriage love is the essence

of spiritual heavenly love, the image of the love between the Lord and the church from which it flows; that it is inherently holy, the essence of chastity and purity and innocence; that it makes us forms expressive of love itself, because married partners can love each other from the center of their being and so make themselves loves; that adultery destroys this form together with the image of the Lord; and that it is horrendous for an adulterer to mingle his life with the life of the husband in his wife, since there is human life in semen. [3] Because this is a profanation, hell is called "adultery" and heaven is called "marriage."[139] A love for adultery is in direct touch with the deepest hell, and a true love for marriage with the highest heaven. The reproductive organs of both sexes correspond to communities of the highest heaven.

I mention all this to show how blind our discernment is when our volition is caught up in compulsions to evil, and to show that no one can be reformed in this state of intellectual blindness.

145 5. *Self-compulsion is not inconsistent with rationality and freedom.* I have already explained [§§103–104] that we have inner and outer thought processes and that these are as distinct from each other as prologue and consequence, or as height and depth. I have explained that because they are so distinct, they can act separately as well as together. They act separately when we talk and act on the basis of our outer thought in ways that differ from our deeper thought and intent; and they act together when we say and do what we think and intend inwardly. This latter state is characteristic of honest people, while the former is characteristic of dishonest people.

[2] Since the inner and outer processes of our minds are distinct, then, the inner can even fight against the outer and forcibly make it consent. The struggle starts when we think of evils as sins and therefore try to refrain from them; since to the extent that we do refrain a door is opened for us. Once this door has been opened, the Lord expels the compulsions to evil that have kept our inner thought processes penned in. In their place, he plants desires for what is good, again in the inner levels of our thought. However, since the pleasures of our compulsions to evil that have been besieging our outer thought processes cannot be expelled at the same time, a fight starts between our inner and outer thinking. The inner thinking wants to expel those pleasures because they are pleasures in evil deeds and are incompatible with the desires for goodness that the inner thinking now enjoys. It wants to replace the pleasures of evil with pleasures in goodness because they are in harmony with it. The

"pleasures in what is good" are what we refer to as the benefits that arise from our caring.

The struggle begins with this disagreement; and if it becomes more severe, it is called a temptation.

[3] Since we are human because of our inner thought, which is actually the human spirit, it follows that we are compelling ourselves when we force our outer thought processes to consent, or to accept the pleasures of our inner desires, the benefits that arise from our caring.

We can see that this is not inconsistent but in accord with our rationality and freedom, since it is our rationality that starts this struggle and our freedom that pursues it. Our essential freedom, together with our rationality, dwells in our inner self, and comes into our outer self from there. [4] So when the inner conquers (which happens when the inner self has brought the outer self into agreement and compliance) then we are given true freedom and true rationality by the Lord. Then, that is, the Lord brings us out of that hellish freedom that is really slavery and into the heavenly freedom that is truly, inherently free.

The Lord teaches us in John that we are slaves when we are in our sins and that the Lord liberates us when we accept truth from him through the Word (John 8:31–36).

An example may help. Suppose we have felt pleasure in cheating and in undetected theft, but we see and inwardly admit that these are sins and therefore want to refrain from them. When we refrain, a battle between the inner self and the outer self begins. The inner self is full of desire for honesty, while the outer self still enjoys cheating. Because this pleasure is diametrically opposed to the pleasure of honesty, it does not go away unless it is forced to; and the only way it can be forced is through fighting against it. Once the battle is won, the outer self comes into that love-filled delight in honesty that is true caring. Gradually thereafter our pleasure in cheating becomes distasteful to us. **146**

It is much the same with other sins—with adultery and promiscuity, with vengefulness and hatred, with blasphemy and deceit. The hardest battle of all, though, is with our love of being in control because of our sense of self-importance. If we overcome this, we have no trouble overcoming our other evil loves, because this is the head of them all.

Let me briefly mention how the Lord expels the compulsions to evil that besiege our inner self right from our birth, and how he provides desires for what is good in their place when we use our apparent autonomy to put away evils as sins. **147**

I have already explained [§§75, 139] that we have an earthly mind, a spiritual mind, and a heavenly mind, and that we are wholly locked into our earthly mind as long as we are caught up in our compulsions to evil and their pleasures. During all this our spiritual mind is closed. However, as soon as we look into ourselves and realize that our evils are sins against God because they are against divine laws, and therefore try to refrain from them, the Lord opens our spiritual mind and comes into our earthly mind by way of its desires for what is true and good. He comes also into our rational processes and from there rearranges the things in our lower, earthly mind that have been in disorder. This is what feels to us like a battle, or like a temptation if we have indulged in these evil pleasures a great deal. There is actually a psychological pain when the pattern of our thoughts is being inverted.

This is a battle against things that are actually within us, things that we feel are part of us; and we cannot fight against ourselves except from a deeper self, and only because of a freedom there. It then follows that the inner self is fighting against the outer self at such times, is doing so in freedom, and is forcing the outer self to obey. This is self-compulsion; and we can see that it is not inconsistent with our freedom and rationality, but quite in accord with them.

148 Beyond this, we all want to be free. We want to get rid of nonfreedom or servitude. As children subject to teachers, we want to be on our own and therefore free. The same holds true for every servant subject to a master and every maid subject to a mistress. Every young woman wants to leave her parents' house and marry so that she can function freely in her own household. Every young man who is intending to have a job, go into business, or hold some office wants to be set free throughout his apprenticeship so that he can make his own decisions. All the people who decide to go into service in order to gain their freedom are compelling themselves; and when they compel themselves they are acting freely and rationally. This comes from an inner freedom though, and from its point of view the outer freedom looks like servitude.

This needs to be included to reinforce the point that self-compulsion is not inconsistent with rationality and freedom.

149 One reason people do not make a similar effort to move from spiritual slavery to spiritual freedom is that they do not know what spiritual slavery and spiritual freedom are. They do not have the truths that would teach them, and in the absence of truths, they think that spiritual slavery is freedom and spiritual freedom is slavery.

A second reason is that the Christian religion has closed the door on intelligence, and the theology of faith alone has sealed it shut. Each of these erects an iron wall around itself, the wall being the dogma that theological matters are beyond our grasp and that we should therefore not use our rationality in our approach to them, that they are for the blind, not for the sighted. This hides from view the truths that teach what spiritual freedom is.

A third reason is that not many people look into themselves and see their sins; and if they do not see them and refrain from them, they are in the freedom of their sins, a hellish freedom that is essentially slavery. Looking at heavenly freedom (which is freedom in its essence) from this perspective is like seeing daylight in darkness, like looking under a black cloud at what comes from the sun overhead. This is why they do not know what heavenly freedom is, or know that the difference between it and hellish freedom is like the difference between life and death.

6. *Our outer self has to be reformed by means of our inner self, and not the reverse.* "The inner and outer self" means the same thing as "our inner and outer thought processes," already discussed in a number of places [§§103–111, 120, 130, 139, 145]. The reason the outer has to be reformed by means of the inner is that the inner flows into the outer, and not the reverse. The scholarly world recognizes that there is a flow of spirit into matter, and not the reverse; and the church recognizes that the inner self needs to be cleansed and renewed first, and then the outer. This is recognized because the Lord and reason both say so. The Lord says it this way:

150

> Woe to you hypocrites, because you cleanse the outside of the cup and the platter while the insides are full of plunder and excess. Blind Pharisee, first cleanse the inside of the cup and the platter, and then the outside will be clean as well. (Matthew 23:25, 26)

[2] In *Divine Love and Wisdom* I have presented ample evidence that reason teaches this.[140] In fact, whatever the Lord teaches, he enables us to perceive rationally. This happens in two ways. One is by our seeing its truth within ourselves as soon as we hear it; the second is understanding it through rational analysis. Seeing it in ourselves happens in our inner self, and seeing it rationally happens in our outer self. Can anyone fail to see within, on first hearing, that the inner self needs to be cleansed first and the outer self cleansed by means of it? However, if we have not accepted some general image of this from the inflow from heaven, we can go wildly astray when we rely on our outer thought processes. They show

us simply that outward actions, deeds of charity and piety, bring us salvation apart from deeper values. In the same vein, they tell us that sight and hearing flow into our thought, that smell and taste flow into our perception—that is, that the outside flows into the inside—when the opposite is true. It is an illusion that sight and hearing are flowing into our thought, because it is our intelligence that is seeing through our eyes and hearing through our ears, not the reverse. The same holds true for the other senses.

151 At this point, though, I need to explain how the inner self is reformed and how this leads to the reformation of the outer self.

The inner self is not reformed simply by gaining knowledge, understanding, and wisdom, not, that is, simply by thinking. We are reformed inwardly by intending to do what our knowledge, intelligence, and wisdom tell us. When our knowledge, intelligence, and wisdom tell us that there is a heaven and a hell, that everything evil comes from hell, and that everything good comes from heaven, then if we do not intend evil, on the grounds that it is from hell, and instead intend good, on the grounds that it is from heaven, we are on the first step of reformation. We are on the threshold of hell, facing heaven. When we take the next step and intend to stop doing wrong, we are on the second step of reformation. We are outside of hell, but not yet in heaven. We see heaven as above us, and it has to be within us if we are to be completely reformed. Still, we are not reformed until both the outer and the inner self are reformed. The outer self is reformed by means of the inner self when the outer self refrains from the evils that the inner self intends not to do because they are from hell. We are more completely reformed when for that reason we abstain from them and fight against them. In this way, what is within is intending and what is outside is acting; for unless we do what we intend, there is a lack of real intention inside that eventually becomes unwillingness.

[2] These few observations show how our outer self is reformed by means of our inner self. This is what the Lord's words to Peter mean as well:

> Jesus said, "If I do not wash you, you have no part in me." Peter said to him, "Lord, don't wash just my feet; wash my hands and head as well." Jesus said to him, "Those who have been washed need only to have their feet washed, and they are wholly clean." (John 13:8, 9, 10)

Washing means spiritual washing, which is cleansing from evils. Washing head and hands means cleansing the inner self, and washing feet means cleansing the outer self. When the inner self has been cleansed, the outer self needs to be cleansed, which is what is meant by saying that those who are washed need only to have their feet washed. It means that all cleansing from evils is done by the Lord when it says that "If I do not wash you, you have no part in me."

There is ample evidence in *Secrets of Heaven*[141] that for the Jews washing meant cleansing from evils, that this is what washing means in the Word, and that washing feet means cleansing the earthly or outer self.[142]

Since we do have an inside and an outside, since both of them need to be reformed if we ourselves are to be reformed, and since we cannot be reformed unless we look into ourselves, see and admit what is wrong with us, and then refrain from doing it, it follows that it is not just the outside that needs to be looked into but the inside as well. If only the outside is looked into, then all we see is what we have actually done— we have not killed anyone or committed adultery or stolen anything or perjured ourselves, and so on. That is, we look into our physical evils but not into our spiritual ones. However, we do need to look into the evils of our spirit in order to be reformed, since we live as spirits after death and all the evils in our spirits are still there. The only way to look into our spirits is to pay attention to what we are thinking and especially to what we are striving for, since what we are striving for is what we have in mind because of our intentions. That is where our evils have their origin and their roots, in their compulsions and pleasures; and unless we see and acknowledge them we are still caught up in them even though we may not act on them outwardly. We can see from the following words of the Lord that thinking on the basis of our intentions is both intending and doing:

> If anyone has looked at someone else's wife so as to lust for her, he has already committed adultery with her in his heart. (Matthew 5:28)

This kind of examination is proper to the inner self and in essence leads to the examination of the outer self.

I have often been struck by the fact that even though the whole Christian world recognizes that evils are to be avoided as sins and that otherwise they are not forgiven, even though Christians recognize that if sins are not forgiven there is no salvation, still there is scarcely one in a thousand who actually knows this for a fact. I have made inquiries in the spiritual world and found that this is true. Everyone in the Christian world is aware of it because of the prayers that are read to people who come to the Holy Supper, because these things are very clearly stated then; yet when you ask whether people know this for a fact, they say that they do not now and did not in the past. This is because they have not thought about it, most of them thinking only about faith and about salvation because of their faith alone.

I have also been struck by the fact that faith alone closes the eyes so completely that when people who are convinced of it read the Word, they do not see anything that it says about love, caring, and doing. It is as though they painted a coating of faith over the whole Word like someone who paints a manuscript over with crimson so that nothing shows through from underneath; and if anything does show through, it is swallowed up by faith and becomes identified with it.

It Is a Law of Divine Providence That We Should Be Led and Taught by the Lord, from Heaven, by Means of the Word, and Teaching and Preaching from the Word, and That This Should Happen While to All Appearances We Are Acting Independently

154 TO all appearances, we are leading and teaching ourselves, while the truth is that we are being led and taught by the Lord alone. If we convince ourselves only of the appearance and not of the truth along with it, we cannot get rid of our evils as sins. On the other hand, if we convince ourselves of both the appearance and the truth, we can get rid of them, because getting rid of evils as sins is accomplished apparently by our own efforts, but actually by the Lord. In the latter case we can be reformed; in the former case we cannot.

[2] People who convince themselves of the appearance alone and not of the truth along with it are all idolaters on a deeper level. They actually worship themselves and the world. If they have no religion, they worship the material world and are therefore atheists.[143] If they have any religion, then they worship individuals and images alike. These are the people in

our own times who are intended in the first of the Ten Commandments, the ones who worship other gods. However, people who convince themselves of both the appearance and the truth worship the Lord because the Lord is raising them above that sense of self-importance that is caught up in the illusion; the Lord leads them into the light that surrounds truth and that is truth. This gives them a profound sense that they are being led and taught not by themselves but by the Lord.

[3] The rational processes of these two kinds of individual look alike to most people, but they are not. The rational processes of individuals who entertain both the appearance and the truth are spiritual, while the rational processes of people who entertain the appearance but not the truth are bound by the material world. These latter processes could be compared to a garden as we see it in the light of winter, while the former could be compared to a garden as we see it in the light of springtime.

There is more to be said about this next, in the following sequence.

1. We are led and taught by the Lord alone.
2. We are led and taught by the Lord alone through and from the angelic heaven.
3. We are led by the Lord through an inflow and taught by being enlightened.
4. We are taught by the Lord through the Word, and teaching and preaching from the Word, and therefore directly by the Lord alone.
5. Outwardly, we are led and taught by the Lord to all appearances as though we were leading and teaching ourselves.

1. *We are led and taught by the Lord alone.* This flows naturally and inevitably from everything that was presented in the material about *Divine Love and Wisdom*—what was said there about the Lord's divine love and wisdom in part 1, about the sun of the spiritual world and the sun of the physical world in part 2, about levels in part 3, about the creation of the universe in part 4, and about our own creation in part 5.

155

To say that we are led and taught by the Lord alone is to say that the Lord is the only source of our life, since it is the intentions of our life that are led and the intelligence of our life that is taught. This is not the way it seems, though. It seems to us as though we live on our own, when the truth is that the Lord is the source of our life and we are not. As long as we are living in this world, we cannot be given a palpable sense that our life is coming from the Lord alone. We are not deprived of our sense of

156

living on our own, because that is what makes us human. This is why I need to prove the matter with rational arguments that can then be tested against experience and finally tested against the Word.

157   The following rational propositions will prove that our life comes from the Lord alone and not from us. (a) There is only one essence, only one substance, and only one form from which have come all the essences, substances, and forms that have been created.[144] (b) The only essence, substance, and form is divine love and divine wisdom, and everything in us that has to do with love and wisdom comes from that source. (c) This is also the goodness itself and the truth itself that underlie everything. (d) These are the life that is the source of the life of everything and of every aspect of life. (e) This single, essential reality is omnipresent, omniscient, and omnipotent. (f) This single, essential reality is the Lord from eternity, or Jehovah.

[2] (a) *There is only one essence, only one substance, and only one form from which have come all the essences, substances, and forms that have been created.* I explained in *Divine Love and Wisdom* 44–46 and in its part 2 that the sun of the angelic heaven, which comes from the Lord and in which the Lord is present, is the single substance and form that is the source of everything that has been created, and that there neither is nor can be anything that does not come from that source. I explained in part 3 of that work that everything comes from that source by development according to different levels. [3] Can anyone fail to see and admit on rational grounds that there is only one essence that is the source of all essence, one reality that is the source of all reality? What could become manifest except from some reality, and what is the reality behind all reality except reality itself? And whatever is reality itself is also the only reality, reality in its own right. Since this is the case—and everyone sees and admits it on rational grounds and could see and recognize it if it were not the case—what other conclusion is there than that this reality that is Deity itself, that is Jehovah, is all there is to everything that exists and happens?

[4] This is the same as saying that there is only one substance that underlies everything; and since substance is nothing apart from form, it follows that there is only one form that underlies everything. I have explained in the book just mentioned that the sun of the angelic heaven is that one substance and form, and have explained how that essence, substance, and form come out variously in things created.[145]

[5] (b) *The only essence, substance, and form is divine love and divine wisdom, and everything in us that has to do with love and wisdom comes*

from that source. I have given ample evidence of this in *Divine Love and Wisdom* as well. Everything about us that seems to be alive involves our volition and our discernment, and everyone sees and admits on rational grounds that these two abilities constitute our life. This is simply saying, "This is what I intend," "This is what I discern," "This is what I love," or "This is what I think"; and since we intend what we love and think about what we discern, all our volition has to do with love and all our discernment has to do with wisdom. Further, since these two abilities cannot occur in any of us from ourselves, only from the one who is love itself and wisdom itself, it follows that this comes from the Lord from eternity or Jehovah. Otherwise, we would be love itself and wisdom itself, we would be God from eternity, and human reason itself recoils from this thought in horror.

Can anything exist except from some prior source, and can this prior source exist except from some source still prior, and so on finally back to a First that simply exists in its own right?

[6] (c) *By the same token, this is also the goodness itself and the truth itself that underlie everything.* Everyone possessed of reason accepts and admits the fact that God is goodness itself and truth itself and that everything good and true comes from him. In fact, nothing that is good and true can come from any other source than from the one who is goodness itself and truth itself. Every rational individual admits this on first hearing it. If we go on to say that when we are being led by the Lord everything that has to do with our volition and discernment, with our love and wisdom, with our feelings and thoughts, rests in what is good and true, it follows that everything we then intend and think, every exercise of our love and wisdom, everything that moves us or occupies our thoughts, comes from the Lord. This is why everyone in the church knows that everything good and true within us that originates in us is not really good or true, only what comes from the Lord.

Since this is the case, everything that we intend and think under this leading comes from the Lord. We will see later [§§285–294] that even evil people cannot intend and think from any other source.

[7] (d) *These are the life that is the source of the life of everything and of every aspect of life.* I have given ample evidence of this in *Divine Love and Wisdom.*146 On first hearing, human reason accepts and admits the fact that our whole life is a matter of our intending and its discerning, because if we were deprived of our ability to intend and discern, we would not be alive. This is the same as saying that our whole life is a matter of our love and its thinking, because if we were deprived of our ability to love and

to think we would not be alive. Since the Lord is the only source of everything in us that has to do with intent and discernment, or with love and thought, as just noted, it follows that all our life comes from him.

[8] (e) *This single, essential reality is omnipresent, omniscient, and omnipotent.* All Christians know this on the basis of their theology and all non-Christians on the basis of their religions. This is also why all of us think that God is present wherever we happen to be, why we pray to God as present with us; and since we all do think this way while we are praying, it follows that the only way we can think is that God is everywhere, that God is therefore omnipresent. The same holds true for God's omniscience and omnipotence. This is why everyone who prays to God is asking at heart for guidance—because God is able to guide; and this means that we all recognize divine omnipresence, omniscience, and omnipotence. We recognize it because then we are turning our faces toward the Lord, and this truth flows into us from him.

[9] (f) *This single, essential reality is the Lord from eternity, or Jehovah.* In *Teachings for the New Jerusalem on the Lord,* I explained that God is one in essence and in person and that this God is the Lord. I also explained[147] that the essential Deity called Jehovah the Father is the Lord from eternity, that the Son conceived by Deity from eternity and born into the world is the Divine-Human One, and that the Holy Spirit is the Deity emanating.

This reality is called "single" and "essential" because it has already been stated that the Lord from eternity or Jehovah is life itself because he is love itself and wisdom itself, or goodness itself and truth itself, the source of everything. I have shown in *Divine Love and Wisdom* 282–284 and 349–357 that the Lord created everything from his own self and not from nothing.

These propositions may serve as rational evidence of the truth that we are led and taught by the Lord alone.

158   The same truth is demonstrated to angels not only by rational propositions but also by direct perception, especially for angels of the third heaven. They feel the inflow of divine love and wisdom from the Lord, and since they feel it and in their wisdom realize that these constitute their life, they say that their life comes from the Lord and not from themselves. They not only say this, they love to have it that way and want it to be that way. All the same, it seems to them completely as though they lived on their own. In fact, this appearance is stronger for them than it is for other angels, for as noted in §§42–45 above, *the more closely we are united to the Lord, the more clearly we seem to have our own identity, and yet the more obvious it is to us that we belong to the Lord.*

For some years now, I have been granted the same kind of sense and the same appearance; and as a result I am wholly convinced that I do not intend and think anything on my own, though it seems as though I do; and I am blessed with the desire and the love of having it so. I could support this with any number of other instances from the spiritual world, but for now these two will do.

The following passages from the Word show that only the Lord possesses life.   159

> I am the resurrection and the life. All who believe in me will live even though they die. (John 11:25)

> I am the way, the truth, and the life. (John 14:6)

> God was the Word: in him was life, and the life was our light. (John 1:1, 4)

The Word here is the Lord.

> As the Father has life in himself, so he has granted the Son to have life in himself. (John 5:26)

The following passages show that we are led and taught by the Lord alone.

> Without me you cannot do anything. (John 15:5)

> No one can undertake anything unless it is granted from heaven. (John 3:27)

> You cannot make a single hair white or black. (Matthew 5:36)

In the Word, a hair means the slightest thing of all.

I will explain in its own section [§§285–294] that the life of evil people comes from the same source. For now, I need only to illustrate the   160 point by comparison. Both warmth and light flow from the sun of our world, and they flow into trees that yield harmful fruit just the way they do into trees that yield good fruit. The two kinds of tree sprout and grow in the same way. The forms into which the warmth flows make the difference, not the warmth itself.

It is the same with the light. This is diversified into colors depending on the forms into which it flows. There are beautiful and cheerful colors, and ugly and depressing ones, yet the light is the same in either case.

The same holds true for the inflow from the spiritual world's sun of the spiritual warmth that is essentially love and the spiritual light that is essentially wisdom. The forms into which they flow make the difference, not the warmth that is love or the light that is wisdom in their own right. The forms into which they flow are our minds.

We can see from this, then, that we are led and taught by the Lord.

161 I have already explained [§§16, 96] what animal life is, a life of merely physical impulses accompanied by knowledge that matches them; and I have noted that this life comes to animals indirectly and is analogous to the life of people in the spiritual world.

162 2. *We are led and taught by the Lord alone through and from the angelic heaven.* The statement is that we are led by the Lord through and from the angelic heaven. However, it is an appearance only that we are led through the angelic heaven, the truth being that we are led from it. The reason for the appearance that it is through the angelic heaven is that the Lord is seen as a sun above that heaven. The truth that it is from heaven is because the Lord is in heaven the way our soul is in us. The Lord is omnipresent and not in space, as already noted,[148] so distance is an appearance that depends on union with him, and union depends on acceptance of love and wisdom from him. Further, since no one can be united to the Lord as he is in himself, he appears like the sun to angels at a distance. Still, he is in the whole angelic heaven the way our soul is in us, in every community of heaven in the same way, and likewise in every individual angel there. Our soul is not just the soul of our whole being but the soul of every part of us.

[2] However, since it does seem as though the Lord were governing the whole heaven, and through it, the world, from the sun that comes from him and surrounds him (on this sun, see part 2 of *Divine Love and Wisdom*), and since there is nothing wrong with talking in terms of appearances (that is actually the only way we can talk), there is nothing wrong for anyone who does not have actual wisdom in thinking that the Lord is governing all this from his sun and that he is governing our world through the angelic heaven. Angels of the lower heavens think in terms of this appearance, while angels of the higher heavens talk in the same terms but think in terms of the truth, namely, that the Lord governs the universe from the angelic heaven that comes from his very self.

[3] The sun of our own world may serve to illustrate how simple and wise individuals talk similarly but do not think similarly. Both talk as though the sun rose and set; but even though wise people talk that way, they are aware in their thought that it stands immobile. This is the truth; the other is the appearance.

We might illustrate the same point with the way things seem in the spiritual world. There seem to be space and distance there just as there are in our physical world, but these are actually appearances that reflect differences in feelings and therefore in thoughts. This is like the Lord seeming to be in his sun.

I need to describe briefly, though, how the Lord guides and teaches 163 each of us from the angelic heaven. In the work on *Divine Love and Wisdom,* earlier in this work on *Divine Providence,* and in the work on *Heaven and Hell* (published in London in 1758), I let it be known on the basis of things I have heard and seen that in the Lord's view the whole angelic heaven looks like a single person and that the same holds true for each heavenly community. This is why each individual spirit and angel is a perfectly formed person.[149] In these works I have also explained that heaven is not heaven because of anything that belongs to angels but because of their acceptance of divine love and wisdom from the Lord.[150]

This shows that the Lord governs the whole angelic heaven as though it were a single individual and that this heaven is the very image and likeness of the Lord because it is essentially a person. It shows also that the Lord himself governs that heaven the way a soul governs its body.

Since the whole human race is governed by the Lord, then, it shows that it is not governed by the Lord through heaven but from heaven, from himself, because as already noted,[151] he is heaven.

However, since this is a secret of angelic wisdom, people cannot un- 164 derstand it unless their spiritual minds have been opened. Such people are angels by virtue of their union with the Lord and will be able to understand what follows on the basis of what has already been said. (a) Both we and angels are in the Lord, and the Lord is in both us and angels, to the extent that we are united with him—that is, to the extent that we accept love and wisdom from him. [2] (b) Each of us is assigned a place in the Lord—that is, in heaven—according to the quality of that union or acceptance of him. [3] (c) Each of us has a specific state in that place, a state different from that of anyone else, and from the commonwealth we are granted a livelihood appropriate to our place, our responsibilities, and our needs, just the way it happens in the human body. [4] (d) Each of us is led into our place by the Lord, in keeping with our lives. [5] (e) Each of us is introduced at infancy into that divine-human being whose soul and life is the Lord; and we are led and taught out of divine love itself according to divine wisdom itself, within the Lord and not outside him. However, since we are not deprived of our freedom, the only way we can be led and taught is within the limits of our apparently autonomous acceptance. [6] (f) People who do accept [divine love and wisdom] are brought to their places by countless winding and roundabout ways, almost like the way the chyle is brought through the mesentery and the lacteals into its reservoir, and from there through the thoracic duct into the blood and therefore to its proper place.¹⁵² [7] (g) People who do not accept [divine love and wisdom] are separated from those who are inside the divine person the way feces and urine are excreted from us.

These are secrets of angelic wisdom that people can understand to some extent; but there are many other secrets that they cannot understand.

165   3. *We are led by the Lord through an inflow and taught by being enlightened.* The reason we are led by the Lord through an inflow is that both the being led and the flowing in are connected to our love and volition. The reason we are taught by the Lord by being enlightened is that being taught and being enlightened are properly connected with our wisdom and discernment. It is common knowledge that we lead ourselves on the basis of our love, and are led by others within the limits of that love, rather than being led by our discernment. We are led by and according to our discernment only as the love of our volition makes it happen; and when this is the case, we might describe our discernment as being led, though in fact it is not really our discernment that is being led but the volition that underlies it.

We use the word "inflow" because the standard practice is to say that the soul flows into the body and that the inflow is spiritual and not physical. Our soul or life is our love or volition, as already noted.¹⁵³ We use the word also because the inflow is much like the flow of blood into the heart and from the heart into the lungs. I have explained in *Divine Love and Wisdom* 371–432 that there is a correspondence of the heart with our volition and of the lungs with our discernment, and that the union of volition and discernment is like the flow of blood from the heart into the lungs.

166   The reason we are taught by being enlightened is that enlightenment is an attribute of both our learning and our discernment, since our discernment, the sight of our inner self, is enlightened by spiritual light exactly the way our eyes, the sight of our outer self, are enlightened by physical light. There is the same kind of teaching in each case, but our inner sight, the sight of our discernment, is taught by spiritual objects, while our outer sight, that of our eyes, is taught by physical objects.

There is spiritual light and there is physical light. Outwardly, they seem to be alike, but inwardly they are different. Physical light comes from the sun of the physical world and is essentially dead, while spiritual light comes from the sun of the spiritual world and is essentially alive. This latter light enlightens our discernment, but physical light does not. Our earthly and rational illumination comes from spiritual and not from physical light. We speak of it as earthly and rational because it is "spiritual-earthly."[154]

[2] There are three levels of light in the spiritual world: heavenly light, spiritual light, and spiritual-earthly light. Heavenly light, the light of people in the third heaven, is rich and flamelike; spiritual light, the light of people in the middle heaven, is brilliantly clear; and spiritual-earthly light is like daylight in our world. It is the light of people in the lowest heaven and in the world of spirits[155] that is halfway between heaven and hell. In that world, though, it is like our summer light for good people and like winter light for evil ones.

[3] Still, we need to be aware that the light of the spiritual world has nothing in common with that of our physical world. They are as different as life and death. We can therefore see that the physical light we see with our eyes does not enlighten our discernment; only spiritual light does. People are unaware of this because they have not known anything about spiritual light before. I explained in *Heaven and Hell* 126–140 that in its origin spiritual light is divine wisdom or divine truth.

Since heaven's light has been discussed [§166], something needs to be said about hell's light as well. There are three levels of light in hell, too. The light in the deepest hell is like that of glowing coals; the light in the middle hell is like that of a fireplace; and the light of the uppermost hell is like that of candles, and for some people like moonlight at night. These lights are not physical but spiritual, since all physical light is dead and snuffs out discernment. People in hell do have that ability to discern that is called rationality, as already noted.[156] True rationality comes from spiritual light; not a trace of it comes from physical light. The spiritual light that gives people in hell their rationality is turned into hellish light the way daylight turns to the gloom of night.

All the people in the spiritual world, though, whether in the heavens or in the hells, see just as clearly in their own light as we do in our own daylight. This is because for all of us, our eyes are adapted to receive the light we live in. So the eyesight of heaven's angels is adapted to receive the light that surrounds it and the eyesight of hell's spirits is adapted to receive its own light. This eyesight is like the sight of owls and bats, who see things at night or in the twilight just as clearly as other winged creatures see them in daytime. Their eyes are adapted to receive their own light.

167

However, the difference between the lights is obvious to people who look from one light into another. For example, when angels of heaven look into hell, they see nothing but pure darkness there, and when spirits of hell look into heaven, they see nothing but darkness there. This is because heavenly wisdom is like darkness to people in hell; and conversely, hellish insanity is like darkness to people in heaven.

This shows that the nature of our understanding determines the nature of our light, and that each one of us will come into his or her own light after death. We have no sight in any other. In the spiritual world, where we are all spiritual even in respect to our bodies, our eyes are adapted to see in their own light. The love of our life makes an intelligence for itself and therefore a light as well. Love is actually like the fire of life that gives off the light of life.

168   Since there are not many people who know anything about the enlightenment that envelops the discernment of people who are being led by the Lord, I need to say something about that.

There is inner and outer enlightenment from the Lord and inner and outer enlightenment from ourselves. The inner enlightenment from the Lord is our sensing on first hearing whether what someone is telling us is true or not. The outer enlightenment occurs in the thinking we do on that basis. The inner enlightenment from ourselves comes strictly from our own convictions, and the outer enlightenment from ourselves comes simply from the information we possess. But let me offer some detail.

[2] *People who are rational because of an inner enlightenment from the Lord* sense instantly, the moment they hear, whether most things are true or not. They know, for example, that love is the life of faith or that faith gets its life from love. It is from inner enlightenment that people sense that we intend what we love, and do what we intend, which means that loving is doing. They sense that what we believe because of our love we also intend and do, which means that having faith is also doing. They sense that irreverent people cannot have a love for God or faith in God.

People who are rational because of their inner enlightenment also sense certain things the moment they hear that God is one—they sense that God is omnipresent, that everything good comes from him, that everything goes back to what is good and what is true, and that everything good comes from goodness itself and everything true from truth itself. We sense these things, and others like them, deep within ourselves when we hear them; and we have this sensitivity because we have rationality, and because it is in a light of heaven that enlightens it.

[3] *Outer enlightenment* is enlightenment of our thinking because of that inner enlightenment, and our thinking enjoys this enlightenment to the extent that it retains the sense granted by that inner enlightenment and also knows from experience what is true and good. It picks up from these the reasons that support it. Thinking from this kind of outer enlightenment sees things from both sides. On the one side such thinking sees the reasons that support it, and on the other side it sees the illusions that undermine it. It dismisses the latter and gathers in the former.

[4] *Inner enlightenment from ourselves,* though, is totally different. In this light, we see things from one side and not from the other, and once we have made up our minds, we see things in a light that looks like the light we have been talking about, but it is a wintry light. Take, for example, judges who make unjust decisions for bribes or for profit. Once they have rationalized their decisions by laws and arguments, it looks to them as though they have been fair in their decisions. They may actually see some unfairness, but since they do not want to see it, they veil it over and blind themselves so completely that they no longer see it. It is the same with judges who make decisions on the basis of friendship, to curry favor, or because of family relationships.

Much the same holds for anything that such people accept on the word of someone in authority or someone famous, or for anything they construct out of their own intellects. These are blind reasons because the distortions that convince them are the basis of their sight, and distortion closes sight, while truth opens it.

[5] People like this see nothing true in the light of truth and nothing fair from a love of fairness. They see from the light of their own convictions, which is a feeble light. In the spiritual world they look like faces without a head or like humanoid faces on heads of wood; and they are called rational sheep because potentially they do have rationality.

Outer enlightenment from ourselves, though, is characteristic of people who do their thinking and talking solely on the basis of information stamped on their memories. They are scarcely capable of coming to any conclusions on their own.

These are varieties of enlightenment and of the sensitivity and thought that it produces. There is an effective enlightenment by spiritual light, but the actual enlightenment that comes from this light is not perceptible to anyone in the physical world, because physical light has

169

nothing in common with spiritual light. I have seen this enlightenment several times in the spiritual world, though. It was visible with people who were being enlightened by the Lord as a radiance around their heads, the ruddy color of some human faces. A kind of radiance also appeared with people who were self-enlightened, but around their mouths and chins rather than their heads.

170   There is another kind of enlightenment besides these, one by which it is revealed to people what kind of faith and what kind of intelligence and wisdom they have. It works by enabling them to see this within themselves. They are brought into a community where there is real faith and real intelligence and wisdom and then the deeper levels of their rationality are opened. This enables them to see their own faith and their own intelligence and wisdom, to see convincingly what kind of people they are. I have seen some [spirits] coming back from these visits and heard them admit that they really did not have any faith, though in the world they had thought they had great faith—outstanding, exemplary faith—admitting the same about their intelligence and wisdom as well. They were people who had lived in faith alone and not in charity and had been impressed with their own intelligence.

171   4. *We are taught by the Lord through the Word, and teaching and preaching from the Word, and therefore directly by the Lord alone.* It has already been clearly explained [§§155–164] that we are led and taught by the Lord alone and that this happens from heaven, not through heaven or through any angel there. Since it is only the Lord who leads us, it follows that we are led directly, not indirectly. Now an explanation of how this happens is needed.

172   I explained in *Teachings for the New Jerusalem on Sacred Scripture* that the Lord is the Word and that all the teaching of the church should be based on the Word.[157] Since the Lord is the Word, then, it follows that when we are being taught by the Word we are being taught by the Lord alone. However, since this is hard to grasp, I need to make it clear in the following sequence. (a) The Lord is the Word because it comes from him and is about him. (b) [The Lord is the Word] also because it is divine truth coming from divine good. (c) Being taught from the Word is therefore being taught from him. (d) It does not reduce the immediacy that this happens indirectly, through sermons.[158]

[2] (a) *The Lord is the Word because it comes from him and is about him.* No one in the church denies that the Word comes from the Lord, but even though no one denies that the Word is about no one but the Lord, no one really knows this. I have, however, explained it in *Teachings for the New Jerusalem on the Lord* 1–7, 37–44; and *Teachings for the*

New Jerusalem on Sacred Scripture 62–69, 80–90, and 98–100. Since the Word comes from the Lord alone and is about the Lord alone, it follows that when we are being taught from the Word we are being taught from the Lord. The Word is actually divine. Who is able to communicate something divine and instill it into our hearts except Divinity itself, the source and the subject? This is why when the Lord talks with his disciples about their union with him he talks about their abiding in him and his words abiding in them (John 15:7), about his words being spirit and life (John 6:63), and about making his dwelling with people who keep his words (John 14:20–24). This means that thinking from the Lord is thinking from the Word, to all appearances thinking by means of the Word.

I have explained throughout *Teachings for the New Jerusalem on Sacred Scripture,* from beginning to end, that everything in the Word is in touch with heaven; and since the Lord is heaven, this means that everything in the Word is in touch with the Lord himself. Heaven's angels do have access to heaven, but this too is from the Lord.

[3] (b) *The Lord is the Word also because it is divine truth coming from divine good.* The Lord teaches that he is the Word in John by saying, "In the beginning was the Word, and the Word was with God, and God was the Word, and the Word was made flesh and dwelt among us" (John 1:1, 14). Because until now this has been understood only as saying that the Lord teaches us through the Word, it has been taken as hyperbole with the implication that the Lord is not really the Word. This is because people have not realized that "the Word" means what is divine and true coming from what is divine and good, or in other words, divine wisdom from divine love. I explained that these are the Lord himself in part 1 of *Divine Love and Wisdom,* and explained that they are the Word in *Teachings for the New Jerusalem on Sacred Scripture* 1–86 *[1–26].*

[4] Now I need to explain briefly how the Lord is what is divine and true from what is divine and good. We are not human because of our faces and bodies but because of the goodness of our love and the truths of our wisdom; and since this is what makes us human, we are also whatever is true and good about us, our own love and our own wisdom. Apart from these, we are not human. The Lord, though, is what is essentially true and essentially good, or love itself and wisdom itself; and these are the Word that was in the beginning with God, that was God, and that was made flesh.

[5] (c) *Being taught from the Word is therefore being taught by the Lord himself* because it is being taught from what is essentially good and essentially true, or from the love itself and wisdom itself that are the Word, as

just stated. Still, we all learn within the limits of the comprehension of our love. Anything beyond that is transient.

People who are taught by the Lord in the Word learn a few truths in this world, but they learn a great many when they become angels. The deeper levels of the Word, the divine spiritual and divine heavenly contents, are being instilled at the same time. However, these are not opened up until after our death, in heaven, where we come into an angelic wisdom that in comparison to our earlier human wisdom is simply indescribable. You may see in *Teachings for the New Jerusalem on Sacred Scripture* 5–26 that the divine spiritual and divine heavenly contents that constitute the wisdom of angels are present throughout the Word, in its every detail.

[6] (d) *It does not reduce the immediacy that this happens indirectly, through sermons.* The only way the Word can be taught is indirectly, through our parents, teachers, preachers, and books, and especially by our reading it. Still, these are not our teachers: the Lord is, using them as means. This is derived from what preachers know, too. They say that they are not talking from their own resources but from the spirit of God and that everything true, like everything good, comes from God. They can talk and can convey things to the minds of many, but not to anyone's heart; and anything that does not enter the heart dies in the mind. "The heart" means our love.

We can see from this that we are led and taught by the Lord alone and that this happens directly from him when it happens from the Word. This is a most treasured secret of angelic wisdom.

173   I explained in *Teachings for the New Jerusalem on Sacred Scripture* 104–113 that people who are outside the church and do not have the Word also receive light by means of the Word. Since light comes to us through the Word, and since we derive from that light a discernment (which both evil and good people possess), it follows that from its source light comes into those derivative forms that are our sensations and thoughts about whatever concerns us. The Lord said that we can do nothing apart from him (John 15:5), that we can acquire nothing unless it is given us from heaven (John 3:27), and that the Father in heaven makes his sun rise on the evil and the good and sends rain on the just and the unjust (Matthew 5:45). Here as elsewhere in the Word, the sun in its spiritual sense means the divine good of divine love, and the rain means the divine truth of divine wisdom. These are given to evil people and good people, to just people and unjust people, because otherwise no one would have either sensation or thought.

I have already explained [§157] that there is only one life that is the source of life for us all; and sensation and thought are functions of life, so we get sensation and thought from the same source as life. I have also presented ample evidence that all the light that constitutes our discernment comes from the sun of the spiritual world, which is the Lord.[159]

5. *Outwardly, we are led and taught by the Lord to all appearances as though we were leading and teaching ourselves.* This happens outwardly but not inwardly. No one knows how the Lord is leading and teaching us inwardly, just as no one knows how the soul is working so that the eye can see and the ear can hear, the tongue and mouth can speak, the heart can impel the blood, the lungs can breathe, the stomach can digest, the liver and pancreas can organize, the kidneys can make separations, and countless other processes. These do not reach our notice and sensation. The same holds for the things that the Lord is doing in the inner substances and forms of our minds, which are infinitely more numerous. The Lord's workings in this realm are imperceptible to us, but their many very real effects are perceptible and so are some of the causes of those effects. These are the outward events where we are present with the Lord; and since outward things are united to inner ones, being connected in a single sequence, we cannot be inwardly organized by the Lord except to the extent that outward matters are set in order through our own efforts.

174

[2] Everyone knows that we think, intend, speak, and act with every appearance of autonomy, and everyone can see that if it were not for this appearance we would have no volition and discernment. We would therefore have no motivation and thought and no acceptance of anything good and true from the Lord. This means that without this appearance we would have no acknowledgment of God, no charity and faith, no consequent reformation and regeneration, and therefore no salvation.

We can see from this that this appearance is granted us by the Lord for all these functions, especially so that there may be something receptive and responsive within us through which the Lord can be united to us and we can be united to the Lord, and that by virtue of this union we can live forever. That is the appearance that is meant here.

It Is a Law of Divine Providence That We Should Not Sense or Feel Anything of the Working of Divine Providence, but That We Should Still Know about It and Acknowledge It

175 MATERIALISTS who do not believe in divine providence think privately, "What is divine providence when evil people are promoted to high office, when their efforts are rewarded more than those of good people, when so many things go better for people who do not believe in divine providence than for people who do? Not only that, faithless and irreverent people can wreak harm, do damage, and cause misfortune to faithful and reverent people, and sometimes even murder them with their vicious schemes." So they wind up thinking, "Can't I see as clear as day from my own experience that as long as we use our subtle skills to make our devious plots seem honest and fair, they will defeat honesty and fairness? What is left but necessity, consequences, and chance, with no visible trace of divine providence? Is necessity anything but a characteristic of the material world? Are consequences anything more than causal chains that flow from physical or civil order?[160] Is chance anything more than unknown causes or no cause at all?" This is how materialists think, people who attribute everything to the material world and nothing to God; because people who ignore God ignore divine providence as well. After all, God and divine providence are inseparable.

[2] Spiritual people think and speak differently, though, within themselves. Even though they do not sense the ongoing workings of divine providence in their thoughts or see it with their eyes, they still know and acknowledge it.

The superficial views and consequent illusions I have just mentioned blind our discernment, and our discernment cannot gain any sight unless the illusions that blind it and the distortions that becloud it are dispelled. This cannot be accomplished except by means of truths that have the inherent power to dispel distortions. For these reasons, I need to disclose these truths now, and to do so in the following sequence if they are to be clear.

1. If we sensed and felt the working of divine providence, we would not act freely and rationally, and nothing would seem to be really ours. The same would hold true if we knew what was going to happen.
2. If we saw divine providence clearly, we would interfere with the orderly sequence of its processes and corrupt and destroy it.
3. If we saw divine providence clearly, we would either deny God or make ourselves God.
4. We are allowed to see divine providence from behind but not face to face, and when we are in a spiritual state, not in a materialistic state.

1. *If we sensed and felt the working of divine providence, we would not act freely and rationally, and nothing would seem to be really ours. The same would hold true if we knew what was going to happen.* In the appropriate sections above,[161] I have explained a number of things to the discerning mind: that it is a law of divine providence that we should act freely and rationally; that everything we intend, think, say, and do seems to be on our own; that if it did not seem so, nothing would be ours, not even our selves, so we would have no sense of self and therefore no sense of worth, and without this it would make no difference whether we did evil or good, whether we had faith in God or accepted the principles of hell—in short, we would not be human.

[2] Now I need to show that we would have no freedom to act rationally and no appearance of independence if we sensed and felt the working of divine providence. This is because if we did sense and feel it we would also be led by it, since the Lord is leading us all by his divine providence and it is only an appearance that we are leading ourselves, as already explained.[162] So if our immediate feelings and sensations told us that we were being led, we would not be aware of our own life. We would then be impelled to make sounds and motions almost like some statue. If we were aware of our life, the only way we could be led would be like someone in handcuffs and shackles or like a cart horse. Can anyone fail to see that in this case we would have no freedom, and that if we had no freedom we would have no rationality? That is, we all think because we are free and we all think freely; and anything we think apart from this freedom or in any other way does not seem to be ours but to come from someone else. No, if you look into this more deeply, you will find that we would have no thought, let alone rationality, and that therefore we would not be human.

176

177   The unceasing effort of the Lord's divine providence is to deliver us from our evils. If we were to sense and feel that constant effort and still not be led like prisoners, how could we help constantly resisting and either arguing with God or becoming involved in divine providence? To do the latter is to make ourselves God; to do the former is to cast off the chains and deny God. It is quite clear that there are two forces constantly acting against each other, a force of evil from us and a force of good from the Lord. When two opposing forces act against each other, then one or the other wins, or they are both destroyed. In this case, though, if one wins then both of them lose. The evil that is ours does not instantly accept the goodness that the Lord is giving, and the goodness from the Lord does not rid us of our evil instantly. If either of these things did happen instantly, we would have no life left.

This is just some of the damage that would be done if we sensed or felt the working of divine providence vividly. I will illustrate this clearly by examples in what follows.

178   The need to preserve our ability to act in freedom and to act rationally is also the reason we are not granted foreknowledge of events. That is, it is common knowledge that if we love something, we want it to happen and we use our reason to move in that direction. Further, whenever we are considering something rationally, it is from a love of having it become a reality by means of our thought. So if we knew the result or the outcome because of some divine prediction, our reason would yield, and our love would yield along with it. Love and reason together find closure in results, and a new love takes over from there.

The very delight of our reason is to see a result that comes from love by thought, not as it happens but beforehand, or not in the present but in the future. This is what gives us what we call *hope,* waxing and waning in our rationality as we see or await a result. This delight finds its fulfillment in the outcome, but then both it and thought about it are cancelled. [2] The same thing would happen if an outcome were foreknown.

The human mind is constantly engaged with three matters called purposes, means, and results. If any of these is lacking, our mind is not engaged in its own life. The impulse of our volition is the originating purpose; the thinking of our discernment is the effectual means; and the action of the body, the speech of the mouth, or our physical sensation, is the result of the purpose that is achieved through thought. Anyone can see that the human mind is not engaged in its life when it is occupied only with the impulse of its volition and nothing more, and that the same is true if it is occupied only with the result. This means that our minds do not have their life from any one of these elements by itself, but from the three of them together. This life of our minds wanes and ebbs when an outcome is foretold.

Since foreknowledge of what will happen destroys our essential human nature, our ability to act in freedom and rationally, no one is allowed to know the future. We can, though, draw conclusions about the future on the basis of reason. This is what brings reason and all its powers to life. This is why we do not know what our lot will be after death or know anything that is happening before we are involved in it, because if we did know we would no longer think in our deeper self about what we should do or how we should live in order to reach some particular goal. We would only think with our outer self that this was coming; and this state closes the deeper levels of the mind where, principally, those two abilities of our life dwell, freedom and rationality.

179

A desire to know the future is innate in many people, but since this desire originates in a love for what is evil, it is taken away from people who believe in divine providence, and they are given a trust that the Lord will take care of their fate. So they do not want to know it in advance, fearing that they might in some way interfere with the divine providence. The Lord teaches us this in several ways in Luke 12:14–48.[163]

[2] There is ample proof in the spiritual world that this is a law of divine providence. Most people who arrive there after death want to know what their lot will be; but they are told that if they have lived well their lot will be in heaven and if they have lived badly it will be in hell. However, since all are afraid of hell, even evil people, they ask what they need to do and what they need to believe in order to get into heaven. They are told that they should do and believe whatever they like; but they should realize that in hell people do not do anything that is good or believe anything that is true, only in heaven: "Ask what is good and what is true and think about it and do it if you can." So we are all left to act in freedom and to act rationally in the spiritual world just the way we are in this world. However, in that world we will behave the way we have behaved here, since in every case our own life stays with us. So does our lot, then, because our life determines our lot.

2. *If we saw divine providence clearly, we would interfere with the orderly sequence of its processes and distort and destroy it.* If these matters are to get through clearly to rational comprehension and to materialistic people, I need to illustrate them with examples in the following sequence. (a) Outward things are so closely connected to inward things that they act as a single entity in everything they do. (b) We cooperate

180

with the Lord only in some outward matters. If we did so in inner ones at the same time, we would corrupt and destroy the whole orderly sequence of divine providence.

However, as already stated, I need to illustrate this with examples.

[2] (a) *Outward things are so closely connected to inward things that they act as a single entity in everything they do.* This can be illustrated here by some features of the human body. There are inner and outer components of the whole body and of every part of it. The outer components are called skins and membranes and envelopes, while the inner are the forms that are variously composed and woven of nerve fibers and blood vessels. The envelope that surrounds them penetrates throughout the inner forms to their very center through extensions from itself; so the outer component, which is the envelope, unites itself to everything inside it, which comprises the forms organized from fibers and vessels. It follows from this that as the outer component acts or is acted upon, the inner ones act or are acted upon as well. There is a constant binding together of all the elements.

[3] Take just one of the body's general envelopes as an example, say the *pleura,* the general envelope of the chest cavity or of the heart and lungs, and look at it with the anatomist's eye—or if that is not your field, check with anatomists, and you will be told that by various circlings and extensions from itself, more and more delicate, this general envelope reaches deep into the lungs, even to the smallest bronchial passages and the tiny sacs that are the beginnings of the lungs, not to mention their further extension into the trachea and the larynx toward the tongue. We can see from this that there is a constant connection between the outermost and the innermost things; so if the outermost things act or are acted upon, the deeper things act or are acted upon from the very center. This is why the lungs labor from their very center when their outermost covering, the pleura, is flooded, inflamed, or afflicted with sores; and if the problems get too serious, all the action of the lungs ceases and the individual dies.

[4] It is much the same everywhere throughout the body, with the peritoneum, for example, the general envelope of all the inner organs of the abdominal cavity, and with the envelopes around each organ—the stomach, liver, pancreas, spleen, intestines, mesentery, kidneys, and reproductive organs of both sexes. Take any one of these and either examine it yourself and you will see this, or check with someone skilled in the field and you will be told this. Take the liver, for example, and you will find that there is a connection of the peritoneum with the envelope of

that organ, and a connection through that envelope with its innermost regions. There are actually constant extensions from it that reach inward toward the depths, causing continuations to the very center. This results in everything being bound together in such a way that when the envelope either acts or is acted upon, the whole form either acts or is acted upon in the same way.

It is the same with the other organs. This is because in every form, what is general and what is specific, or what is inclusive and what is individual, act as a single entity by virtue of their wonderful interconnection.

[5] We will see later [§181] that what holds true for physical forms and their workings, which have to do with motion and action, holds true also for spiritual forms, and applies to their changes and variations of state, which have to do with the workings of our volition and discernment.

Since we are cooperating with the Lord in certain outward workings, and since we are not deprived of the freedom to act rationally, it follows that the Lord can act within us only in keeping with what we are doing outwardly. So if we do not abstain and turn from evils as sins, the outer component of our thought and volition is corrupted and weakened, together with their inner components, much the way the pleura suffers from the disease called pleuritis, which leads to the death of the body.

[6] (b) *If we were conscious of inner processes at the same time, we would corrupt and destroy the whole orderly sequence of divine providence.* This too can be illustrated by examples from the human body. If we knew all the ways the two hemispheres of our brains act through our nerve fibers, how these fibers affect our muscles, and how our muscles produce actions, and used this knowledge to control these processes the way we control our actions, would we not corrupt and destroy them all? [7] If we knew how our stomachs digest, how the organs around it draw out what they need, make up our blood, and send it out for all the tasks of our lives—if we knew all this, and in our management of it behaved the way we do in outward matters like eating and drinking, would we not corrupt and destroy them all? If we cannot manage the outward realm, which seems so simple, without destroying it by our self-indulgence and excess, what would happen if we had control of inner matters, which are infinite? So to prevent us from intruding our will into these inner matters and taking control of them, they are completely exempt from our volition, except for the muscles that enclose them. We do not even know how they work; we know only that they do.

[8] It is the same with other processes. If we controlled the inner workings of our eyes for seeing, the inner workings of our ears for hearing, those of our tongues for tasting, of our skin for feeling, of our hearts for contracting, of our lungs for breathing, of our mesentery for the distribution of chyle, of our kidneys for separating elements, of our reproductive organs for generation, of our wombs for perfecting the embryo, and so on, would we not find countless ways to corrupt and destroy the orderly processes of divine providence in them? We know that we do outward things consciously—we see with our eyes, hear with our ears, taste with our tongues, feel with our skin, breathe with our lungs, impregnate our wives, and so on.[164] It is enough that we are conscious of these external processes and manage them for the health of body and mind. If we cannot do this, what would happen if we had control of the inner processes as well?

This shows that if we saw divine providence clearly, we would interfere with the orderly sequence of its processes and corrupt and destroy it.

181   The reason for the parallelism between the spiritual events of the mind and the physical events of the body is that there is a correspondential relationship between everything mental and everything physical. So too, the mind activates the body in its outward functions, generally doing so at will. It activates the eyes to see, the ears to hear, the mouth and tongue to eat and drink and also to talk, the hands to work, the feet to walk, and the reproductive organs to propagate. The mind not only activates our outer organs to do all this, it activates the inner ones at every step, affecting the outermost ones from the innermost, and the innermost from the outermost. So when it is activating the mouth to speak, it is activating the lungs, the larynx, the glottis, the tongue, and the lips, each one individually for its particular function, and all at once. It also makes the face adapt.

[2] We can therefore see that the kind of thing we say about the physical forms of the body must also be said about the spiritual forms of the mind, and that whatever we say about the physical workings of the body must also be said about the spiritual workings of the mind. Specifically, the Lord arranges the inner forms and workings the way we arrange the outer ones. He does this differently, then, depending on whether we arrange the outer ones on our own, or whether we do so both from him and in apparent autonomy.

The human mind is a person in every element of its form. It is our spirit, which after death looks just as human as it does in this world. So there are similarities between the two, and what we have said about the union of outer and inner events in the body must be applied also to the union of outer and inner events in the mind. The only difference is that the one realm is physical and the other spiritual.

3. *If we saw divine providence clearly, we would either deny God or make ourselves God.* People who are completely materialistic say to themselves, "What is divine providence? Is it anything but a word that the masses hear from the clergy? Has anyone ever seen a trace of it? Aren't our planning and wisdom and deceit and malice the real causes of everything that happens in this world? Is the rest anything but needs and deductions and a lot of accidents? Is divine providence hidden away somewhere in all this? How can it be present in trickery and deceit? Yet these people say that divine providence is in control of everything. Show it to me, and I'll believe it. Can anyone believe in it otherwise?"

[2] This is the voice of the strict materialist, but spiritually-minded people speak differently. Since they acknowledge God, they acknowledge divine providence too. They see it as well, but they cannot show it to anyone who thinks only in physical terms, on the basis of physical events. These people cannot raise their minds above the material world and see the signs of divine providence in its outward appearances. They cannot figure out anything about it on the basis of its laws, which are laws of divine wisdom. So if they were to see it with any clarity, they would make it material and thereby not only becloud it with distortions but also profane it. Instead of recognizing it, they would deny it; and anyone who at heart denies divine providence is denying the Lord as well.

[3] We either think that God is governing everything or that the material world is governing everything. If we think that God is governing everything, then we think that this is love itself and wisdom itself and therefore life itself. If we think that the material world is governing everything, though, we think of physical warmth and physical light, which in and of themselves are dead because they come from a lifeless sun. Does what is essentially living not govern what is dead? Can what is dead govern anything? If you think that what is dead can give you life, you are out of your mind. Life must come from life.

It may seem unlikely that we would deny God if we were to see divine providence and its workings clearly, because it would seem that if we were to see it clearly we could not help but acknowledge it and thereby acknowledge God. However, the opposite is the case.

Divine providence is never acting in the same direction as our deliberate love. It is always acting against it. This is because from our own inherited evil we are constantly hungering for the deepest hell, while the

Lord, through his divine providence, is constantly leading us away from it and drawing us out of it, first to some milder hell, then out of hell, and eventually to himself in heaven. This effort of divine providence is going on all the time; so if we were to see or feel vividly this carrying off and pulling away, we would be outraged. God would become our enemy, and in the evil of our self-centeredness we would deny him. So to prevent us from knowing about this, we are kept in a free state where all we can know is that *we* are leading ourselves.

[2] Let some examples serve to illustrate this. By heredity, we want to become powerful and rich, and to the extent that these loves are not held in check, we want to become more powerful and more rich until we are the most powerful and most rich of all. Even then we are not satisfied, but want to be more powerful than God and to possess heaven itself. This obsession lies hidden deep within our inherited evil and is therefore within our life and in the very nature of that life.

Divine providence does not take this evil away instantly, because if it did we would not be alive. It takes it away quietly and gradually without our knowing anything about it. It does so by letting us act according to thoughts that we fashion rationally, and then it uses various rational, civil, and moral means to lead us away. So we are led away to the extent that we can be led in freedom. Further, no evil can be taken from us unless it surfaces and is seen and recognized. It is like a wound that is not healed until it has been opened.

[3] This means that if we were to know and see that with his divine providence the Lord is acting against the love of our life, the love that gives us the greatest pleasure, all we could do would be to go in the opposite direction, to be outraged, to fight back, and to scold, ultimately distancing the working of divine providence from our own evil by denying providence, which means denying God. We would do this particularly if we saw ourselves being blocked from success, lowered in rank, or deprived of wealth.

[4] We should realize, though, that the Lord never leads us away from striving for high positions or from gaining wealth, only from an obsession with striving for high position simply for the sake of eminence, or for self-seeking reasons, and similarly from gathering wealth solely for display or for its own sake. As he leads us away from these obsessions, he brings us into a love of service so that we look at eminence not for our own sake but for the sake of service. So it becomes something we seek for service primarily and for ourselves secondarily, and not for ourselves primarily and for service secondarily. The same applies to wealth.

The Lord tells us in many places in the Word that he always humbles the proud and raises up the humble; and what it says in the Word is characteristic of his divine providence.

It is the same with any other of the evils we have by heredity—with adultery, for example, and with fraud, vengeance, blasphemy, and the like. None of these can be expelled unless our freedom to consider and intend them is preserved and we use what seems to be our own autonomy to expel them from ourselves in this way. We cannot do this unless we acknowledge divine providence and pray that the evils be expelled through providence. If it were not for this freedom and for divine providence, the evils would be like poison closed in and not excreted, which soon spreads and brings death everywhere, or like a disease of the heart itself that soon proves fatal to the whole body.

184

There is no better way to learn the truth of this than from people in the spiritual world after death. Many of them who had become powerful and wealthy in the physical world but had focused solely on themselves in their power and their wealth talk about God and divine providence at first as though they had sincerely believed in them. However, since they come to see divine providence clearly and therefore see their eventual lot, which is that they are headed for hell, they make common cause with demons there and then not only deny God but even blaspheme. They lose touch with reality so completely that they recognize the more powerful of these demons as their gods; and their most burning passion is to become gods themselves as well.

185

The reason we would go counter to God and deny him if we were to see clearly what divine providence itself is doing is that we are caught up in the pleasure of our love, and this pleasure is integral to our very life. This means that when we are kept in the pleasure of our love we are in our own freedom, our freedom and this pleasure being inseparable from each other. If we were to sense, then, that we were constantly being led away from our pleasure, we would be as angry as though someone were trying to destroy our life and would regard that person as our enemy. To prevent this from happening, the Lord does not show himself clearly in his divine providence. Rather, he uses it to lead us subtly, the way a hidden stream or favorable current carries a boat. Consequently, all we know is that we are always on our own, since this freedom is united to our sense of self. We can see from this that our freedom incorporates into us what divine providence offers, which would not happen if providence made itself known. To become incorporated is to become part of our life.

186

187   4. *We are allowed to see divine providence from behind but not face to face, and when we are in a spiritual state, not in a materialistic state.* Seeing divine providence from behind but not face to face is seeing it after the fact but not before; and seeing it when we are in a spiritual state and not in a materialistic state is seeing it from heaven and not from this world. Everyone who accepts inflow from heaven and recognizes divine providence (and especially people who have become spiritual by virtue of their reformation), on seeing events in their amazing kind of sequence, virtually sees providence from a deep recognition and confesses it. Such people do not want to see it face to face, that is, before things happen, because they are afraid their own volition would interfere with some element of its orderly sequence.

[2] It is different for people who do not let any inflow in from heaven but only from this world, especially people who have become complete materialists by accepting outward appearances as absolute truth. They see no trace of divine providence from behind, or after the fact, but they do want to see it face to face, or before things happen. Since divine providence works through means, and since these means include us and this world, if people like this were to see it either face to face or behind, they would ascribe it either to themselves or to the material world and so become even more certain in their denial.

The reason they would come to this conclusion is that their discernment is closed upward and open only downward, closed toward heaven and open toward this world, and we cannot see divine providence from this world, only from heaven.

I have sometimes asked myself whether these people would acknowledge divine providence if their minds were opened upward and they were to see in broad daylight that the material world is essentially dead and human intelligence essentially nothing, and that the contrary appearance in each case is the result of inflow. I have realized that people who have convinced themselves of the supreme value of the physical world and human prudence would not acknowledge providence, because the earthly light that flows up from below snuffs out the spiritual light that flows down from above.

189 [165]   People who have become spiritual by virtue of their recognition of God and have become wise by casting off their sense of self-importance see divine providence in the whole world and in every least part of it. They see it if they look at natural events, they see it if they look at civic events, they see it if they look at spiritual events, in the way things coincide and the way they follow in sequence, in purposes and means and results, in useful events, in forms, in things great and things small. They see it especially in our salvation, in the fact that Jehovah gave us the Word that tells us about God, heaven, hell, and eternal life, and that he himself came into the world to redeem and save us. All this and much more, and the divine providence within it all, people see from spiritual light within earthly light.

The strict materialist, though, sees none of this. [2] The materialist is like someone who goes to a beautiful cathedral and hears an enlightened minister preach about divine matters and then goes home and says, "All I saw was a stone building, and all I heard was some complicated noise." Or the materialist is like someone with poor eyesight who goes into an orchard gleaming with all kinds of fruit and then goes home and says, "All I saw was some forest and some trees." When people like this become spirits after death and are raised up into an angelic heaven where everything is in forms that portray love and wisdom, they do not see any of it. They do not even see that there is anything there. I have seen this happen with any number of people who have denied the Lord's divine providence.

There are many constants that have been created so that varying things can happen. The fixed regularities of the rising and setting of sun, moon, and stars are constants. There are the times called eclipses when they obscure and block out each other. There are the warmth and light they provide. There are the times of the year that we call spring, summer, fall, and winter and the times of the day called morning, noon, evening, and night. There are also atmospheres, liquids, and solids in their own right; there is the power of germination in the plant kingdom; there is this power as well as the power of reproduction in the animal kingdom; and there are all the events that consistently result from these powers when they are put into action according to the principles of the design. **190**

These and many other constants have been provided from creation itself in order that an infinite variety of events may happen. These various events could not happen except in the context of things that are constant, fixed, and reliable.

[2] Some examples may serve to illustrate. The various kinds of vegetation could not exist if it were not for the constant rising and setting of the sun and the constancy of heat and light. There is an infinite variety of harmony, but this would be impossible if the atmosphere were not constant in its principles and the ears were not constant in their form. The things we see are of infinite variety as well, which would not happen unless the ether were constant in its laws and the eye in its form. Colors

would not be possible if light were not constant. The same holds true for our thoughts, our words, and our actions. These are of infinite variety, which would not happen unless the organization of our bodies were constant. Does not a house have to be constant so that people can do different things in it; a church, too, so that various acts of worship, sermons, teaching, and devout thoughts can happen in it? The same holds true in other matters.

[3] As for the variations themselves that happen in the context of things that are constant, fixed, and reliable, they extend to infinity and have no limit, yet there will never be one exactly like another in all the universe or any of its smallest parts. There cannot be in the march of time to eternity. Given these variations marching on to infinity and eternity, who is arranging them so that they are orderly except the one who has created the constants so that these changes can take place within them? And who is able to manage the infinite varieties of life in humans except one who is life itself, that is, love itself and wisdom itself? If it were not for his divine providence, which is like a constant creation, could the infinitely varied desires and consequent thoughts of humanity, and therefore the individual people themselves, be so arranged that they form a single whole,[166] with the evil desires and their thoughts forming a single demon who is hell and the good desires and thoughts a single Lord in heaven? (I have already explained a number of times that in the Lord's sight, the whole angelic heaven looks like a single person who is his image and likeness, while the whole hell, conversely, looks like one grotesque person.)[167]

I present this because some materialistic people have used the existence of constant and reliable laws, which are essential as the context for the variety of events, as a basis for senseless arguments in favor of the material world and human prudence.[168]

Our Own Prudence Is Nothing—It Only Seems to Be Something, As It Should. Rather, Divine Providence Is All-Inclusive Because It Extends to the Smallest Details

THE idea that our own prudence is nothing runs directly counter to the way things seem, and therefore directly counter to most people's belief. Since this is the case, if people believe on the basis of appearances that human prudence accounts for everything, the only way to convince them is with reasoning based on deeper investigation, reasoning that must be drawn from the realm of causes. The outward appearance is an effect, and causes show where this effect comes from. **191**

In this prologue, I need to say something about common belief on the subject. What the church teaches is contrary to the appearance; namely, it teaches that love and faith do not come from us but from God, as do wisdom and intelligence, prudence, and in general everything that is good and true. When these principles are accepted, we must also accept the fact that our own prudence is nothing but only seems to be something. The only basis of prudence is intelligence and wisdom, and these two qualities come only from our discernment and consequent thought about what is true and good.

What I have just said is accepted and believed by people who acknowledge divine providence and not by people who acknowledge only human prudence. [2] One thing or the other must be true—either what the church teaches, that all wisdom and prudence come from God, or what the world teaches, that all wisdom and prudence come from us. Is there any other way to resolve the contradiction than to accept the church's teaching as true and to see what the world teaches as the appearance? The church finds support for its belief in the Word, while the world finds support for its belief in our self-importance. The Word comes from God, and self-importance comes from us.

Because prudence is from God and not from us, when Christians are at worship they pray that God may guide their thoughts, plans, and deeds, adding that this is because they cannot do so on their own. Then too, when they see people doing good, they say that God has led them to do this, and so on. Could we say this if we did not believe it at some deeper level? That deeper level of belief comes from heaven. But when we think privately and gather arguments in favor of human prudence, we can believe the opposite, which comes from this world. However, the inner belief wins out for people who at heart acknowledge God, while the outer belief wins for people who do not acknowledge God at heart, no matter what they may say.

192 I have stated that if people believe on the basis of appearances that human prudence accounts for everything, the only way to convince them is with reasoning based on deeper investigation, reasoning that must be drawn from the realm of causes. So to make these points of reasoning drawn from the realm of causes clear to the discerning mind, I need to present them in their proper sequence, which will be as follows.

1. All our thoughts arise from impulses of our life's love; there are no thoughts whatever that arise from any other source.
2. Only the Lord knows the impulses of our life's love.
3. The Lord guides the impulses of our life's love by his divine providence, and with them guides the thoughts that give rise to our prudence.
4. By his divine providence the Lord gathers these impulses of the whole human race into a single form, which is a human form.
5. Heaven and hell, which come from the human race, are therefore in this kind of form.
6. People who acknowledge only the physical world and human prudence constitute hell, while people who acknowledge God and his divine providence constitute heaven.
7. None of this could happen if it did not seem to us that we think autonomously and manage our lives autonomously.

193 1. *All our thoughts arise from impulses of our life's love, and there are no thoughts whatever that arise from any other source.* Earlier in this work, and also in the work titled *Angelic Wisdom about Divine Love and Wisdom* (especially in parts 1 and 5), I have explained[169] the essential nature of our life's love, of our desires and consequent thoughts, and of the resulting sensations and actions that occur in our bodies. Since these are the source of the causes from which our prudence flows as an effect, I need to include something about them at this point. What has been written earlier cannot be connected all that closely with things that are written later without being recalled and brought into view.

[2] Earlier in this work and in the aforementioned *Divine Love and Wisdom*,¹⁷⁰ I explained that there is divine love and wisdom in the Lord, that these two are life itself, and that it is from these two that we get our volition and discernment, volition from divine love and discernment from divine wisdom. I have explained that in the body, these two have their analogues in our heart and lungs, and that this enables us to conclude that just as our heartbeat, united to the breathing of our lungs, governs the whole person physically, so our volition united to our discernment governs the whole person mentally. I have explained that these two fundamentals of life, the one physical and the other spiritual, are in each one of us, and that the physical basis of our life is the beating of the heart and the spiritual basis of our life is the volition of the mind. I have explained that each of these attaches to itself a partner with which it lives and carries on the business of life, the heart uniting the lungs to itself and volition uniting discernment to itself.¹⁷¹

[3] Since the soul of our volition is love, then, and the soul of our discernment is wisdom, each coming from the Lord, it follows that love is the life of each one of us and that the quality of that life depends on the quality of our love's union with wisdom. In other words, volition is the life of each one of us, and the quality of that life depends on the quality of our volition's union with discernment. However, there is more on this subject above and especially in *Angelic Wisdom about Divine Love and Wisdom* in parts 1 and 5.

I have also explained in the aforementioned book that the life's love brings forth from itself subsidiary loves called impulses, that these may be more outward or more inward, and that all together they constitute a kind of single domain or realm in which the life's love is the lord or monarch.¹⁷² I have also explained that these subsidiary loves or impulses attach partners to themselves, each individually, the deeper impulses choosing partners called perceptions and the more outward impulses choosing partners called thoughts, and that each lives with its partner and meets the responsibilities of its own life. The union of each pair is like the union of the reality of life with its manifestation, namely, that neither one is anything apart from the other. After all, what is the reality of life unless it becomes manifest, and what is a manifestation of life if it does not come from the reality of life? The union of life is like the union of sound and harmony or sound and speech or, broadly, like the union of the heart's beating and the lungs' breathing, the kind of union in which neither partner is anything apart from the other but in which each

194

becomes something through its union with the other. These unions must happen either in or through their components. Take sound, for example. Anyone who thinks that sound is something unless there is something distinctive about it is in error. Sound corresponds to feelings in us; and since there is always something distinctive in it, we can tell the feelings of people's loves from the sound of their voices, and we can tell what they are thinking from the variations that constitute language. This why the wiser angels can sense the life's loves of people simply from the sounds of their voices, and can distinguish the subsidiary feelings as well.

I mention this to let it be known that there is no feeling without its own thought and no thought without its own feeling. There is more on this subject earlier in the present work [§106], and in *Angelic Wisdom about Divine Love and Wisdom*.

195 Since our life's love has its own pleasure and its wisdom has its own appeal, so too does every impulse or feeling, which is essentially a subsidiary love derived from the life's love like a stream from a spring, a branch from a tree, or an artery from the heart. This means that each impulse has its own distinctive pleasure and each consequent perception and thought its own distinctive appeal. It follows, then, that this pleasure and appeal constitute our life. What is life without pleasure and appeal? There is nothing lively about it, only lifelessness. Reduce the pleasure and appeal and you grow cold and sluggish, take them away and you breathe your last and die. [2] Our very vital warmth comes from the pleasures of our feelings and the appeal of our perceptions and thoughts.

Since every feeling has its own pleasure and every thought therefore has its own appeal, we can tell where goodness and truth come from or what goodness and truth are in their essence. Goodness is what pleases our feelings and truth is what therefore appeals to our thinking. We call "good" whatever we feel as pleasant because of the love of our volition, and we call "true" whatever we therefore sense as appealing because of the wisdom of our discernment. In each case, this flows from our life's love like water from a spring or blood from a heart. Together they are like an atmosphere or a wave that surrounds the whole human mind.

[3] These two (the pleasure and the appeal) are spiritual in our minds and physical in our bodies. They constitute our life.

We can see from this what it is in ourselves that we call good and what it is that we call true; and we can see what it is in ourselves that we call evil and what it is that we call false. Specifically, we call something evil if it ruins the pleasure of our feeling and we call something false if it ruins the appeal of our consequent thoughts. Because of the pleasure of evil and the appeal of falsity, we are quite capable of calling them good and true, and of believing it.

In fact, goodness and truth are shifts and variations of the state of our minds' forms, but they are sensed and come to life only through the pleasure and appeal they present. I include all this to make it clear what feeling and thought really are in their own life.

Since it is our mind, not our body, that thinks, and since its thinking is prompted by the pleasure of its feelings, and since our mind is our spirit that lives after death, it follows that our spirit is nothing but our feelings and consequent thinking. **196**

It is obvious from spirits and angels in the spiritual world that there can be no thinking apart from feeling. All the people there think on the basis of the feelings of their life's loves, and the pleasure of these feelings surrounds everyone like his or her own atmosphere. All the people there are united according to these auras that are breathing out from their feelings through their thoughts, and the nature of everyone there is recognized by the aura of her or his life.

We can tell from this that every thought arises from some feeling and is the form of its feeling. It is the same with our volition and discernment, and the same with what is good and what is true, and with caring and faith.

2. *Only the Lord knows the impulses of our life's love.* We know our thoughts and the intentions that arise from them, because we see them within ourselves; and since they are the source of all our prudence, we see that in ourselves as well. If our life's love is a love for ourselves, then we find ourselves taking pride in our own intelligence and giving it credit for our prudence. We gather arguments in favor of it and drift away from any acknowledgment of divine providence. Much the same thing happens if our life's love is a love for the world, though in this case the drift is not so pronounced. We can see from this that these two loves attribute everything to ourselves and to our own prudence. If we probe deeper, we find that they attribute nothing to God and his providence. As a result, if we happen to hear someone say that human prudence is nothing, but that divine providence by itself is what controls everything, which is the truth, then if we are complete atheists we laugh at it. If we have some remnant of religion in our memory, though, and someone tells us that all wisdom comes from God, then we agree on first hearing, though inwardly, in our spirits, we are denying it. **197**

This applies particularly to ministers who love themselves more than God and the world more than heaven—in other words, ministers who worship God for the sake of high position and money—but still preach that charity and faith, everything good and true, all wisdom and in fact all prudence come from God, and nothing from us.

[2] In the spiritual world I once heard two ministers arguing with a royal envoy about whether our prudence comes from God or from ourselves. It was a lively argument. At heart, the three believed much the same thing, namely, that our own prudence accounts for everything and divine providence for nothing. However, at that point the priests, carried away by their theological zeal, kept saying that no element of wisdom or prudence comes from us; and when the envoy retorted that this meant no element of thought came from us, they said, "Not a bit."

Since the angels noticed that the three actually shared the same belief, they said to the envoy, "Put on some priestly robes and believe that you are a priest, and then start talking." He put on the robes and the belief, and proclaimed emphatically that there could be no possible trace of wisdom or prudence in us unless it came from God, defending this position with characteristic eloquence abundantly furnished with rational arguments. The angels then said to the two ministers, "Take off your robes and put on politicians' robes and believe that you are politicians." They did so, and as they did, they thought from their deeper selves and based their speech on arguments they had previously treasured up inside, arguments in favor of human prudence and against divine providence. After this, since the three of them shared the same belief, they became cordial friends and started off together down the path of human prudence, which leads to hell.

198   I have already explained [§196] that we do not have any thoughts that do not come from some feeling of our life's love, and that thought is simply a form of feeling. This means that when we see our thoughts but cannot see our feelings (we only sense them), then on the basis of what we can see, on the basis of the way things seem, we presume that our own prudence accounts for everything. We attribute nothing to our feelings, because they do not come into our view, but are only sensed. Our feelings make themselves known only through a kind of pleasure in thinking and a sense of gratification when we reason about something. This pleasure and gratification then make common cause with the thinking in people who believe in their own prudence because they love themselves or love the world. Their thought drifts along in its pleasure like a boat in the current of a river, a current that the skipper does not notice because all attention is on the billowing sail.

199   We are actually able to reflect on the pleasure of our outward feelings when these are acting in consort with the pleasure of some physical sense.

However, we do not reflect on the fact that this pleasure comes from the pleasure of a feeling within our thinking. For example, take someone looking for sex who sees a prostitute. His eye glows with the fire of his lust, and this calls up a sensation of physical pleasure. Still, he does not feel the pleasure of the feeling or desire in his thinking except as a kind of virtually physical urge. The same holds true of a robber in a forest when he sees travelers, and for a pirate at sea when he sees ships.[173] I could give other examples as well. Clearly, the pleasures are governing their thoughts, and their thoughts would not even exist apart from the pleasures; yet they think that only the thoughts are real. In fact, the thoughts are nothing but feelings gathered into forms by their life's love so that they can be seen in the light, since all feeling is in warmth and all thought is in light. [2] We are talking here about feelings of our outer thinking that sometimes make themselves known in physical sensations but rarely in the thinking of our minds.

In contrast, the feelings of our inner thinking that give rise to the outer ones never to come to our notice. We are no more aware of them than a sleeping passenger in a carriage is aware of the road, or than we are aware of the earth's rotation. Given the fact that we know nothing about the events that are happening in the depths of our minds, which are so infinite that there are no numbers to count them, and yet the few outward events that do reach our conscious thought are all brought forth by these inner ones, and the depths are governed by the Lord alone through his divine providence, and we cooperate only in the few outer ones—given all this, how can anyone say that our own prudence accounts for everything?

If you were to see only one concept of our thought fully opened up, you would see more astounding things than language can express.

[3] To see that in the depths of our minds there are so infinitely many things that there are no numbers to count them, we need only look at the infinitely many components of our bodies, none of which comes to our sight or our consciousness. All we are aware of is a single action in its utter simplicity, an action, though, that represents the concurrence of thousands of motor fibers or muscles, thousands of nerve fibers, thousands of blood vessels, thousands of lung passages all working together in this action, thousands of things in our brains and spinal column, and far more in our spiritual selves, our human minds, all of which are forms of feelings and their consequent perceptions and thoughts.

Is it not the same soul that is arranging the inner events that is arranging the actions that derive from them as well? Our soul is simply the love of our volition and the consequent love of our discernment. The nature of this love determines the nature of the whole person. We acquire this nature by the way we manage things outwardly, where we are at work with the Lord; so if we ascribe everything to ourselves and the material world, our soul is a love for ourselves, while if we ascribe everything to the Lord, our soul is a love for the Lord. This latter love is heavenly; the other is hellish.

200   Since it is the pleasures of our feelings, working from the center through our depths out into the more outward elements and eventually into those outermost elements that are in our bodies, that carry us along the way wave and wind carry a boat, and since nothing of this comes to our awareness except what is happening in the outermost functions of our minds and the outermost functions of our bodies, how can we claim anything divine for ourselves simply because a few superficial matters seem to be under our control? How much less warrant do we have for claiming divinity for ourselves when we know from the *Word* that we can acquire nothing unless it is given is from heaven[174] and from *reason* that this appearance is granted us so that we can live human lives, see what is good and what is evil, choose one or the other, incorporate what we have chosen, and in this way be mutually united to the Lord, reformed, regenerated, and saved, and live forever?

I have already explained that we are granted this appearance so that we may act freely and rationally and therefore in apparent autonomy, and not slacken our hands and wait for inflow.[175] This provides support for principle 3 proposed above, namely, that *the Lord guides the impulses of our life's love by his divine providence, and with them guides the thoughts that give rise to our prudence.*

201   4. *By his divine providence the Lord gathers the impulses of the whole human race into a single form, which is a human form.* We will see in the next section that this is a pervasive feature of the Lord's providence. People who credit everything to the material world also credit everything to human prudence. This is because people who credit everything to the material world are at heart denying God, and people who credit everything to human prudence are at heart denying divine providence: the two are inseparable.

Still, for the sake of their good name and out of a fear of losing it, both kinds of person will claim verbally that divine providence is universal and that we are responsible for the details, the aggregate of these details being what we mean by our prudence.[176] [2] But think seriously: what is "universal providence" when the details are taken away? Is it anything but a mere word? By "universal" we mean something that comes from details taken together, as a generality arises from specific instances.

If you take the details away, then, what is the "universal" but something with a vacuum inside, like a surface with nothing inside it, or like a compound with no components?

If we say that divine providence is a universal government and that things are not governed but just kept connected and that the activities of government are managed by others, could this be called a universal government? No king has this kind of government, because if some king were to give his subjects control over everything in his kingdom he would no longer be a king, he would simply be called a king. He would have only the honor of the name, and no honor of real substance. We could not credit such a king with any government at all, let alone a universal government.

[3] Providence on God's part is called prudence on our level. If we cannot speak of universal prudence in the case of a king who has not kept anything for himself but the name, so that the kingdom can be called a kingdom and thereby held together, by the same token we cannot speak of a universal providence if we are taking care of everything with our own prudence.

Much the same holds for the terms "universal providence" and "universal government" when we talk about the material world, if we assert that God created the universe and then provided the material world with the ability to manage everything on its own. What is "universal providence" in this case but a metaphysical term that apart from being a term has no reality whatever?

Many of the people who give the material world credit for everything that is brought forth and give our own prudence credit for everything that happens, but who still say that God created the material world, think of divine providence only as an empty phrase. As things really are, though, divine providence includes the smallest details of the material world and the smallest details of our prudence, which is why it is universal.

The Lord's divine providence is universal by virtue of its attention to the smallest details, specifically through his having created the universe in such a way that an infinite and eternal process of creation by him could occur in it. This creation takes place by the Lord's forming a heaven from humans, a heaven that in his sight is like a single individual that is his own image and likeness. I have explained in §§27–45 above that the heaven formed from humanity looks like this in the Lord's sight, and that this was the purpose of creation. I have also explained that Divinity focuses on what is infinite and eternal in everything it does

202

(§§56–69 *[46–69]*). The infinite and eternal goal that the Lord focuses on in forming his heaven from humanity is that this heaven should keep growing without limit and forever, so that in this way he might constantly dwell in the purpose of his creation.

It is this infinite and eternal creation that the Lord provided for in creating the universe, and he is constantly present in that creation through his divine providence.

[2] *It is common to the teaching of all the churches in the Christian world that God the Father, God the Son, and God the Holy Spirit is infinite, eternal, uncreated, and omnipotent (see the Athanasian Creed).* Can people who know and believe, on this basis, that God is infinite and eternal be so completely devoid of rationality that they will not agree on first hearing that Divinity must focus on what is infinite and eternal in the masterwork of its creation? What else can it do when it acts from itself? Must we not also agree that it focuses on this in the human race from which it is forming its heaven?

What other goal can divine providence have, then, than the reformation of the human race and its salvation? No one can be reformed by his or her own efforts and prudence, only by the Lord, through his divine providence. It follows that unless the Lord led us at every moment, even the very smallest, we would wander from the way of reformation and die. [3] Every shift and change in the state of our minds shifts and changes a whole series of present and therefore of subsequent events— why not on and on to eternity? It is like an arrow shot from a bow. If the arrow were deflected the least bit from its aim at the target, the deflection would be huge at a distance of a mile or more. That is how it would be if the Lord were not guiding the states of our minds at every least moment.

The Lord does this in keeping with the laws of his divine providence, including the law that says it seems as though we are leading ourselves. However, the Lord foresees how we will lead ourselves and constantly makes adjustments.

We will see below [§§234–274, 322–330] that the laws of permission[177] are also laws of divine providence, that everyone can be reformed and regenerated, and that there is no predestination.

203 Since we all live forever after death, then, and are assigned places either in heaven or in hell depending on how we have lived, and since both heaven and hell are necessarily in a form that causes them to act as unities (as already noted [§124]), and since none of us can be assigned to any place in that form except our own, it follows that the human race throughout the whole world is under the Lord's supervision, and that each one of us is being led by him in the slightest details, from infancy to the end of life, with a particular place foreseen and provided for.

[2] We can see from this that divine providence is universal because it attends to the slightest details, and that it is an infinite and eternal creation that the Lord has provided for himself by creating the universe.

We see nothing of this universal providence, and if we did see it, it would look to our sight like the scattered piles and random heaps that passers-by see when a house is being built. The Lord, though, sees a magnificent palace constantly under construction and constantly being enlarged.

5. *Heaven and hell are in this kind of form.* I have noted in *Heaven and Hell* 59–102 (published in London in 1758) that heaven is in the human form and have mentioned the same in *Divine Love and Wisdom* and occasionally in the present work,[178] so I refrain from presenting further support.

204

I have said that hell is also in a human form, but it is in a grotesque human form, the kind of form the devil has, the devil meaning hell taken as a whole. Hell has a human form because the people there were born human and have those two human capacities called freedom and rationality even though they have misused their freedom for intending and doing evil and their rationality for thinking and justifying it.

6. *People who have acknowledged only the physical world and human prudence constitute hell, while people who have acknowledged God and divine providence constitute heaven.* All the people who lead evil lives inwardly recognize the material world and human prudence alone. This attitude is latent in all evil, no matter how well it is veiled by things that are good and true. These veils are nothing but clothes borrowed from a friend or garlands of flowers that fade, put on to hide evil in all its nakedness.

205

Because this common practice of concealment distracts our sight, people do not realize that everyone who is leading an evil life is inwardly recognizing the material world alone and human prudence alone. We can tell that this is what such people recognize if we know the source of this recognition and its reason. To uncover this, I need to explain where our own prudence comes from and what it is, then where divine providence comes from and what it is, then who the two kinds of people are and what they are like, and finally that people who acknowledge divine providence are in heaven and people who acknowledge human prudence are in hell.

206   *Where our own prudence comes from and what it is.* It comes from what we regard as our own. This is natural to us and is called the soul we get from our parent. This possession of ours is a love for ourselves and a consequent love for the world, or a love for the world and a consequent love for ourselves. By its nature, love for ourselves focuses solely on ourselves and regards others either as worthless or as nothing. If it attaches any importance to them, it lasts only as long as they respect and worship it. At the heart of this love, like the effort to bear fruit and propagate in a seed, is a latent desire to become great—if possible, to become monarch, and then if possible to become God. The devil is like this because the devil is pure love for oneself, a love that inherently worships only itself and favors only those who also worship it. It hates any other devil who is like itself, because it wants to be the only object of worship.

Since no love can exist without its partner, and since the partner of love or volition in humans is called discernment, when love for oneself breathes its love into its consorting discernment, that love becomes a pride that is pride in our own intelligence. That pride is the source of our own prudence.

[2] Further, since love for ourselves wants to be the only master of the world and wants to be God as well, the cravings of evil that descend from it derive their life from it, and so do the perceptions of those cravings, which are schemes. The same holds true for the pleasures of those cravings, which are evil, and for their thoughts, which are distortions. All of them are like servants and employees of their lord, and they all obey every command of their lord without realizing that they are not really acting but are being impelled, impelled by love for ourselves through the means of pride in our own intelligence. This is why our own prudence is latent in every evil from its very beginning.

[3] The reason a recognition of the material world alone is latent in it as well is that it closes the skylights through which we can see heaven and the windows in the walls as well, to prevent us from seeing or hearing that the Lord alone is in control of everything and that the material world is essentially dead, that everything that belongs to us is hell, and that love for what is our own is therefore a devil. With these windows closed, we are in darkness, so we build a hearth in the darkness and sit there with our partners, chatting cordially about the material world as opposed to God and our own prudence as opposed to divine providence.

207   *Where divine providence comes from and what it is.* It is Divinity working among us, banishing our love for ourselves. As already noted [§206], love for ourselves is the devil, and its cravings and their pleasures are the evils of its kingdom, hell. Once this has been banished, the Lord comes in with impulses of love for our neighbor. He opens the skylights and then the windows in our walls and enables us to see that heaven is real, that there is a life after death, and that there is eternal happiness. By the spiritual light and the spiritual love that then flow in together, he enables us to recognize that through his divine providence, God is taking care of everything.

Who the two kinds of people are and what they are like. People who acknowledge God and divine providence are like angels of heaven, angels who hate to lead themselves and love to be led by the Lord. The sign that the Lord is leading them is that they love their neighbor.

On the other hand, people who acknowledge [only] the material world and their own prudence are like spirits of hell, spirits who hate to be led by the Lord and love to lead themselves. If they had been prominent in government, they want to control everything, as they do if they had been prominent in the church. If they had been judges, they warp their judicial decisions and manipulate the laws. If they had been academics, they use their scholarship to bolster human self-importance and the material world. If they had been in business, they are robbers, and if they had been farmers, they are thieves. They are all enemies of God and mockers of divine providence.

The striking fact is that when heaven is opened to people like this and they are told that they are out of their minds and even shown this with utter clarity (which is done by inflow and enlightenment), they feel insulted, close heaven to themselves, and look at the ground under which hell lies. This happens to people in the spiritual world who are still outside of hell but who are of this nature. It shows the error of people who think, "If I see heaven and hear angels talking with me, then I will believe." However, while their discernment might believe, if their volition does not concur, then they themselves do not believe. This is because our volition's love breathes into discernment whatever it wants to, not the other way around. In fact, our love erases anything in our discernment that it has not put there.

7. *None of this could happen if it did not seem to us that we think autonomously and manage our lives autonomously.* I have already given ample evidence that we would not be human if it did not seem to us that we lived on our own and that we therefore thought, intended, spoke, and acted on our own [§§71–99, 174, 176]. It follows from this that unless we seemed to be managing everything that has to do with our occupations and our lives by our own prudence, we could not be led and managed by

divine providence. It would be as though we stood there with our hands hanging limp, mouths open, eyes closed, holding our breath and waiting for something to flow into us. In this way we would divest ourselves of everything human, which we get from the sense and feeling that we live, think, intend, speak, and act on our own; and as we did so, we would also divest ourselves of those two abilities called freedom and rationality by which we are differentiated from animals. Earlier in this work and also in *Divine Love and Wisdom*[179] I have explained that if it were not for this appearance we would be incapable of receptivity and reciprocity, and therefore of immortality.

[2] So if you want to be led by divine providence, use your prudence as a servant and employee who faithfully manages the employer's assets. Prudence is the "talent" that was given to servants for business purposes, with an accounting required (Luke 19:13–25 [19:12–25]; Matthew 25:14–31).

Prudence itself seems to be something we possess, and we believe that it is, as long as we keep that deadliest enemy of God and divine providence, love for ourselves, shut in. It lives in the depths of each one of us from birth. If we do not recognize it—and it does not want to be recognized—then it lives in perfect safety and guards the door to prevent us from opening it so the Lord can evict it.

We open the door by abstaining from evils as sins, apparently on our own, but admitting that it is being done by the Lord. This is the kind of prudence with which the divine providence can cooperate.

211 There is a reason why divine providence works so subtly that hardly anyone knows it is there—to keep us from dying. That is, our own self-importance, which is what motivates us, never cooperates with divine providence. Our self-importance has an inborn hatred of divine providence. It is actually the serpent that misled our first parents, the serpent of whom it is said, "I will set enmity between you and the woman and between your seed and her seed, and it will trample your head" (Genesis 3:15). "The serpent" is any kind of evil, and "its head" is love for ourselves. "The woman's seed" is the Lord, and "the enmity that is set" is between our love of self-importance and the Lord, and therefore also between our own prudence and the Lord's divine providence. This is because our prudence is constantly trying to raise its head and divine providence is constantly trying to push it down.

[2] If we sensed this, we would be outraged and enraged against God, and we would die. When we do not sense it, though, we get outraged and enraged against others, against ourselves, and against chance, which is not fatal.

This is why the Lord in his divine providence is constantly leading us in our freedom, and to us it seems as though this freedom were our own. Leading us against ourselves in freedom is like lifting a massive and stubborn weight from the ground with jacks and not being able to feel the weight and the resistance because of their strength. Or it is like people surrounded by enemies intent on murder, unaware that a friend is leading them out by unknown paths and will later disclose the plan of their enemies.

Is there anyone who does not talk about luck, anyone who does not acknowledge it? After all, we do talk about it and we know something about it from experience—but does anyone know what it is? No one can deny that it is something, because it does exist and it does happen, and nothing can be something or happen without some cause. However, we do not know what causes one thing and another or what causes luck. To prevent denial simply because of ignorance of a cause, think of dice or cards, and either play or talk with players. Do any of them deny luck? They play with it, and it plays with them, in quite wonderful ways. Can any succeed against it if it is against them? It laughs at prudence and wisdom then. When you roll the dice or deal the cards, does it not seem as though luck knew and managed the rolls and the deals of your wrists and for some reason favored one player more than another? Can the reason be found anywhere but in divine providence in outermost matters, where in constancy and in change alike it is working with our prudence in marvelous ways, all the while remaining hidden?

212

[2] It is common knowledge that non-Christians once recognized Luck and built a temple to her, as the Romans did. There is a great deal to know about this Luck (which as mentioned is divine providence in outermost matters) that I am not free to disclose. This has showed me that it is not a figment of our imagination or a trick of the material world or something with no reason: that would actually be nothing at all. Rather, it is a visible witness that divine providence is present in the slightest details of our thoughts and actions. If divine providence is at work in the slightest details of such trivial and inconsequential matters, what else can we expect in the details of matters that are not trivial and inconsequential, in matters of peace and war in this world, and in matters of salvation and life in heaven?

I do know, though, that our prudence is more persuasive to our reasoning than divine providence, because we can see prudence but not providence. It is actually easier for us to accept the notion that there is only one life, which is God, and that we are all life-receivers from him, as

213

I have already often explained;[180] and yet this amounts to the same thing, because prudence is a property of life.

Do we not all speak in favor of our own prudence and of the material world when we are arguing from our earthly or outward selves, and speak in favor of divine providence and God when we are arguing from our spiritual or inner selves?

But I have a request, a message to the materialist: Write some books and fill them with plausible, probable, credible arguments, arguments that in your judgment are solid. Write one in favor of our own prudence and one in favor of the material world, and then hand them to an angel. I know the few words the angel will inscribe on your pages: "These are all illusions and distortions."

Divine Providence Focuses on Eternal Matters, and Focuses on Temporal Matters Only As They Coincide with Eternal Ones

214 I need to show that divine providence focuses on eternal matters and focuses on temporal matters only as they coincide with eternal ones, in the following sequence.

1. Temporal matters involve position and wealth, and therefore rank and money, in this world.
2. Eternal matters involve spiritual rank and wealth, which have to do with love and wisdom, in heaven.
3. We keep temporal and eternal matters separate, but the Lord unites them.
4. The union of temporal and eternal matters is the Lord's divine providence.

215 1. *Temporal matters involve eminence and wealth, and therefore rank and money, in this world.* There are a great many temporal matters, but they all boil down to eminence and wealth. By "temporal matters" I mean things that either die off in time or simply cease when our life on earth is over. By "eternal matters" I mean things that do not die off and stop either in time or at the end of our life on earth.

Since all these temporal matters boil down to eminence and wealth, as just noted, it is important to know the following things: what eminence and wealth are and where they come from; the nature of a love of them for their own sake and the nature of a love of them for the sake of service; and that the difference between them is like the difference between heaven and hell, a distinction of loves that most people find difficult to recognize. But let me discuss these one at a time.

[2] (a) *What eminence and wealth are and where they come from.* Eminence and wealth were very different in the earliest times from what they gradually became later. In the earliest times, eminence involved simply the relationships between parents and children. It was an eminence of love, full of profound respect, not for parents as the source of birth but for parents as the source of teaching and wisdom, which constitute a second birth, essentially a spiritual one, because it is a birth of their spirit. This was the only kind of eminence in the earliest times, because people were living separately in tribes, families, and households then and not under governments the way we are today. The head of the clan was the one with the eminence. The ancients called this period the Golden Age.[181]

[3] Later, though, a love of being in power simply for the pleasures of power gradually took over; and since it brought with it belligerence and enmity against anyone who was not willing to submit, people necessarily gathered their tribes, families, and households into alliances and appointed someone who was at first called a judge, then a chief, and eventually a monarch and an emperor. They also began fortifications—towers, earthworks, and walls. From these judges, chiefs, monarchs, and emperors, as from a head into the body, the craving for power spread like a contagious disease to the many. This was the beginning of grades of eminence and of corresponding grades of respect. Love for themselves accompanied all this, and pride in human prudence.

[4] Much the same happened with the love for wealth. In the earliest times, when tribes and families lived separately from each other, a love for wealth meant nothing more than having the necessities of life. People acquired these in the form of flocks and herds and in the form of the fields, pastures, and gardens that provided them with food. Their necessities of life also included attractive homes furnished with all kinds of

utensils and clothing. The parents, children, servants, and maids in a home were busily engaged with all this.

[5] After a love for being in power took over and destroyed this commonwealth, though, a love for possessing wealth beyond the limits of need took over, culminating in a desire to possess the wealth of everyone else.

These two loves are close relatives. People who want to control others also want to own everything, because this makes others their servants and makes themselves the sole masters. We can see this clearly in those individuals in Catholicism who have exalted their lordship all the way into heaven, to the very throne of the Lord, and have placed themselves upon it. We can see it also in their acquisition of all the wealth in the world and filling their treasuries without limit.

[6] (b) *The nature of a love of eminence and wealth for their own sake and the nature of a love of them for the sake of service.* A love of eminence and wealth for their own sake is a love for ourselves—strictly speaking, a love of being in control that arises from self-love; and a love of wealth and money for their own sake is a love for this world—strictly speaking, a love of gaining ownership of what belongs to others by fair means or foul. However, a love of eminence and wealth for the sake of service is a love of service. This is the same as a love for our neighbor, since the purpose of our actions is the goal that prompts them. It is the first and primary element, and everything else is intermediate and secondary.

[7] As for a love of eminence and wealth for their own sake (which is identical to love for ourselves, or strictly speaking, to a love of being in control that arises from self-love), it is a love for our own self-importance, and our sense of self-importance is wholly evil. That is why we say that we are born into utter evil and that what we inherit is nothing but evil. What we inherit is the sense of self that encompasses us and that we participate in by virtue of our self-love—especially by our love of being in control because of our self-love. This is because when we are wrapped up in this love we are totally focused on ourselves and therefore immerse our thoughts and feelings in our own sense of self-importance. As a result, within our self-love there is a love of doing harm because we have no love for our neighbor, only for ourselves. When we love only ourselves, we see others only as outside ourselves, either as completely worthless or as simply nothing. We regard them as inferior to ourselves and think nothing of doing them harm. [8] This is why people who are possessed by a love of being in control because of their self-love think nothing of cheating their neighbors, committing adultery with their neighbor's

spouses, slandering their neighbors, plotting vengeance and even murder, torturing their neighbors, and the like. We get these attitudes from the fact that the devil itself is nothing but a love of being in control because of self-love, and we are united to and being led by the devil. When we are being led by the devil, by hell, that is, we are being led into all these evils. We are constantly being led by the pleasures of these evils, which is why all the people who are in hell want to harm everyone, while the people who are in heaven want to help everyone.

From this opposition there arises an intermediate space where we are. We are in a kind of balance in this space so that we can turn either toward hell or toward heaven. As we approve of the evils of self-love we turn toward hell; as we banish them from ourselves we turn toward heaven.

[9] I have been allowed to feel the nature and strength of the pleasure of a love of being in control because of self-love. I was plunged into it in order to know it from experience, and it was so intense that it transcended all the pleasures in the world. It took over my whole mind from center to surface, while in my body it felt congenial and gratifying, a free expansion of my chest. I was also allowed to feel that the pleasures of all kinds of evil deeds bubbled up from it like water from a spring, pleasures in adultery, vengeance, fraud, and slander—in general, pleasures in doing harm.

There is a similar pleasure in the love of possessing what belongs to others by fair means or foul, and this pleasure gives rise to various compulsions that branch off from it. However, it is not so intense unless it is united to self-love.

As for eminence and wealth not for their own sake but for the sake of service, though, this is not a love of eminence and wealth but a love of service, with the eminence and wealth functioning as means. This is a heavenly love, which will be more fully discussed later [§217].

[10] (c) *The difference between these two loves is like the difference between heaven and hell.* This should be clear from what has already been said, to which I may add the following. In spirit, all the people who are caught up in a love of being in control because of their self-love are in hell. It does not matter who they are, whether they are prominent people or ordinary folk. All the people who are caught up in this love are caught up also in a love for all kinds of evil deeds. If they do not actually commit them, they still believe in their spirits that there is nothing wrong with them and therefore do them physically whenever their own eminence and respect, or a fear of the law, does not get in the way.

Beyond this, though, at the center of a love of being in control because of self-love lies a hidden hatred of God and therefore a hatred of the divine values of the church, especially a hatred of the Lord. If they do acknowledge God, it is nothing but words; and if they acknowledge the divine values of the church, it is simply from a fear of losing respect. The reason this hatred of God lies hidden deeply within is that at the center of this love there is a desire to be God, a worship and reverence of no one but themselves. This is why there is a heartfelt love for anyone who respects them to the point of saying that they have divine wisdom and are worldly demigods.

[11] It is different with a love of eminence and wealth for the sake of service. This is a heavenly love because it is the same as a love for our neighbor, as just noted.

"Service" means good actions, so performing services means doing good things; and performing services or doing good things means helping others and serving them. Even though the people who are doing this are eminent and wealthy, they still do not regard their eminence and wealth as anything but means to being helpful and therefore means to service and ministry. These are the people meant by the Lord's statement, "Whoever of you wants to be great, must be your servant; whoever of you wants to be first must be your slave" (Matthew 20:26, 27). These are also the people whom the Lord entrusts with authority in heaven. For them, authority is a means of helping or doing good, that is, of serving; and when services or good actions are the goals or the loves, then it is not they who are in authority but the Lord, because everything good comes from him.

[12] (d) *This is a distinction of loves that most people find difficult to recognize.* This is because most people of eminence and wealth also do helpful things, but without realizing whether they are doing them for the sake of themselves or for the sake of service. It is particularly hard to tell because there is more fire and passion for service in people who love themselves and the world than there is in people who are not caught up in love for themselves and the world. Yet the first are doing helpful things for the sake of their reputation or for profit and therefore for selfish reasons. In contrast, people who are being of service for the sake of service, or doing good for the sake of the goodness itself, are not acting on their own but from the Lord.

[13] It is hard for us to tell the difference because we do not know whether we are being led by the devil or by the Lord. When we are being led by the devil, we are helpful for the sake of ourselves and the world,

but when we are being led by the Lord, we are being helpful for the sake of the Lord and heaven. All the people whose helpfulness comes from the Lord are people who are abstaining from evils as sins, while all the people whose helpfulness comes from the devil are people who are not abstaining from evils as sins. Evil comes from the devil, but service, or doing good, comes from the Lord. This is the only way to tell the difference. They look alike outwardly, but their inward form is completely different. One is like a golden object that has slag inside, while the other is like a golden object that is pure gold all the way through. One is like a piece of artificial fruit that looks outwardly like fruit from a tree but actually is colored wax with powder or tar inside, while the other is like fine fruit, appealingly delicious and fragrant, with its seeds within.

2. *Eternal matters involve spiritual rank and money, which have to do with love and wisdom, in heaven.* Since materialists call the pleasures of self-love good (these pleasures are also the pleasures of compulsions to evil) and convince themselves that they are good, they call rank and money divine blessings. However, when materialists see that just as many evil as good people are raised to high rank and advanced in wealth, and even more when they see good people living in disgrace and poverty and evil people living in splendor and wealth, they think to themselves, "What is going on here? This cannot be the work of divine providence, because if it were managing everything, it would supply the good with high rank and money and humble the evil with poverty and disgrace. This would make the evil admit that God and divine providence are real."

[2] However, unless materialists are enlightened by their spiritual selves—that is, unless they are spiritual as well as materialistic—they do not see that rank and money may be either blessings or curses and that they are blessings when they come from the Lord and curses when they come from the devil. We know that the devil can give us rank and money because the devil is called "the Prince of This World."[182]

Since people do not know under what circumstances rank and money are blessings and under what circumstances they are curses, I need to explain it, but in the following sequence. (a) Rank and money may be either blessings or curses. (b) When rank and money are blessings, they are spiritual and eternal, but when they are curses, they are temporal and transient. (c) The relationship between the rank and money that are curses and the rank and money that are blessings is like a relationship of nothing to everything, or of something unreal to something real.

216

217 Now I need to illustrate these three items individually.

(a) *Rank and money may be either blessings or curses.* Everyday experience bears witness to the fact that reverent and irreverent people, just and unjust people—good and evil people, that is—may have eminence and wealth. Yet no one can deny that irreverent and unjust people, evil people, go to hell while reverent and just people, good people, go to heaven. Since this is so, it follows that eminence and wealth, or rank and money, may be either blessings or curses, and that they are blessings for the good and curses for the evil.

I explained in *Heaven and Hell* 357–365 (published in London in 1758) that both rich people and poor, both the prominent and the ordinary, may be found in heaven and in hell. This shows that for people in heaven, eminence and wealth were blessings in this world, while for people in hell, they were curses in this world.

[2] If we give the matter only a little rational thought, we can see what makes eminence and wealth blessings and what makes them curses. Specifically, they are blessings for people who do not set their heart on them and curses for people who do. To set one's heart on them is to love oneself in them, and not to set one's heart on them is to love the service they can perform and not oneself in them. I have noted in §215 above what the difference between these two loves is like; and I need to add that eminence and wealth seduce some people but not others. They are seductive when they arouse the loves of our sense of self, which is self-love.[183] (I have already noted [§§206, 207] that this is the love of hell that is called "the devil.") They are not seductive, though, when they do not arouse that love.

[3] The reason both evil and good people are elevated to high rank and advanced in wealth is that both evil and good people do worthwhile things, though the evil are doing them for the sake of their personal worth and for the benefit of their image, while the good are doing them for the sake of the worth and benefit of the actions themselves. These latter regard the worth and benefit of the actions as the principal cause and any personal worth or benefit to their image as instrumental causes, while the evil regard their personal worth and the benefit to their image as the principal cause and the worth and benefit of the actions as instrumental causes.[184] Can anyone fail to see, though, that the image, our position and rank, is for the sake of our responsibilities and not the other way around? Can anyone fail to see that judges are for the sake of justice, officials for the sake of public affairs, and the monarch for the sake of the realm, and not the other way around?[185] So the laws of the realm provide

that we should be given the eminence and rank appropriate to the importance of the tasks of our offices. The difference is like the difference between what is primary and what is instrumental.

If people attach importance to themselves or their image, when this is portrayed in the spiritual world they seem to be upside down, feet up and head down.[186]

[4] (b) *When rank and money are blessings, they are spiritual and eternal, but when they are curses, they are temporal and transient.* There are eminence and wealth in heaven just as in this world, because heaven has governments and therefore areas of responsibility and offices. There is also business and consequently wealth, because heaven has communities and associations.

Overall, heaven is divided into two kingdoms, one called the heavenly kingdom and the other called the spiritual kingdom. Each kingdom comprises countless larger and smaller communities, all organized according to differences in love and wisdom, as are their individual members. In the heavenly kingdom there are differences in heavenly love, which is love for the Lord; and in the spiritual kingdom there are differences in spiritual love, which is love for our neighbor.

That is what the communities are like; and all their members were once people on earth. This means that they keep the loves they had in this world, the difference being that now they are spiritual and that their actual eminence and wealth are spiritual in the spiritual kingdom and heavenly in the heavenly kingdom. Because of all this, the people who have the most eminence and wealth are the people who have the most love and wisdom. They are the ones for whom eminence and wealth were blessings in this world.

[5] This shows us what spiritual eminence and wealth are like. They are attributes of the task and not of the individual. True, individuals who have eminence live in striking splendor there, like some earthly monarch, but they attach no importance at all to the eminence itself, only to the services that belong to their area of responsibility and office. They accept the rank appropriate to their individual levels of eminence but attribute it to their services and not to themselves; and since all forms of service come from the Lord, they attribute them to the Lord as their source. This, then, is the nature of the spiritual eminence and wealth that are eternal.

[6] However, it is different for people for whom eminence and wealth were curses in this world. Because they attributed them to themselves and not to their forms of service, and because they did not want

service to be more important than they themselves were but wanted to be more important than their service (which they regarded as useful only to the extent that it furthered their own rank and fame), they are in hell. They are wretched slaves there, living in disgrace and misery. It is because this eminence and wealth perish that they are called temporal and transient.

This is what the Lord tells us about these two kinds of people: "Do not store up treasures for yourself on earth where rust and maggot corrupt and where thieves break in and steal. Rather, lay up for yourselves treasures in heaven, where neither rust nor maggot corrupts and where thieves do not break in and steal; for where your treasure is, there your heart will be as well" (Matthew 6:19, 20, 21).

[7] (c) *The relationship between the rank and money that are curses and the rank and money that are blessings is like a relationship of nothing to everything, or of something unreal to something real.* Everything that perishes and becomes nothing is essentially, inwardly, nothing. It is something outwardly and can seem rich, can seem to some like everything, as long as it lasts, but it is not like that essentially and inwardly. It is like a surface with nothing inside it, like an actor on the stage wearing royal robes when the play is ended. What lasts forever, though, has something lasting within it and is therefore everything. It truly exists because its reality has no end.

218   3. *We keep temporal and eternal matters separate, but the Lord unites them.* This is because everything about us is time-bound, so that we ourselves may be called time-bound, while everything about the Lord is eternal, so that the Lord is called the Eternal One. Time-bound things are the ones that have a limit and that perish, while eternal things are the ones that have no limit and do not perish.

Everyone can see that these two cannot be united except by the Lord's infinite wisdom, which means that they can be united by the Lord but not by us. To show that we separate the two but the Lord unites them, I need to present an explanation in the following sequence. (a) What "time-bound" and "eternal" things are. (b) We are essentially time-bound, and the Lord is essentially eternal. Therefore, nothing comes from us that is not time-bound, and nothing comes from the Lord that is not eternal. (c) The time-bound separates the eternal from itself, while the eternal unites the time-bound to itself. (d) The Lord unites us to himself by means of appearances, (e) and by means of correspondences.

These items need to be brought to light and defended one at a time.

219

(a) *What "time-bound" and "eternal" things are.* Time-bound things are all the properties of the physical world and therefore all of our own properties. The primary properties of the physical world are space and time, both of which have limits and boundaries. Our own properties, derived from them, involve the properties of our volition and of our discernment, and of the feelings and thoughts that they generate, and especially of our prudence. It is widely recognized that these are finite and limited.

In contrast, eternal things are all the properties of the Lord and the things from the Lord that seem to be ours. The properties of the Lord are all infinite and eternal, beyond time therefore, and consequently without limit and without end. Their derivatives that seem to be ours are likewise infinite and eternal, but nothing of them really belongs to us. They simply belong to the Lord, within us.

[2] (b) *We are essentially time-bound, and the Lord is essentially eternal. Therefore, nothing comes from us that is not time-bound and nothing comes from the Lord that is not eternal.* I have just stated that we are essentially time-bound and that the Lord is essentially eternal. Since nothing can come from anything that is not within it, it follows that nothing that is not time-bound can come from us and nothing that is not eternal can come from the Lord. The infinite cannot come from the finite: that would be a contradiction. Actually, something infinite can come from something finite, but it is not from the finite entity but through it, from the infinite. Conversely, too, the finite cannot come from the infinite: that too would be a contradiction. The finite can be produced by the infinite, but that is not "coming from," it is creating. On this subject see *Angelic Wisdom about Divine Love and Wisdom* from beginning to end.[187]

If something finite does come from the Lord (as happens with us in many respects), then it does not come from the Lord but from us. We can still say that it comes from the Lord through us, because that is how it seems.

[3] We can illustrate this by the Lord's words, "Let your speech be 'Yes, yes; no, no.' Anything beyond this comes from evil" (Matthew 5:37). This is how everyone talks in the third heaven. The people there never try to figure out whether divine things are true or not; they see within themselves, from the Lord, whether they are true or not.[188] This means that the reason people try to figure out whether divine things are true or not is that such thinkers are not seeing them from the Lord. They

are trying to see them on their own, and whatever we see on our own is evil.

All the same, the Lord wants us not only to think and talk about divine matters but also to try to figure them out so that we ourselves come to see whether they are true or not. As long as the purpose of this thought, speech, and reasoning is to see the truth, we can say that it is from the Lord within us. Still, it is from us as long as we are seeing the truth and acknowledging it. All the while, our ability to think, talk, and reason is from the Lord alone. We can do all this because of the two abilities called freedom and rationality; and we have these abilities solely from the Lord.

[4] (c) *The time-bound separates the eternal from itself, while the eternal unites the time-bound to itself.* "The time-bound separates the eternal from itself" refers to what we (who are time-bound) do because of all that is time-bound within us. "The eternal unites the time-bound to itself" refers to what the Lord (who is eternal) does because of all that is eternal within him, as already noted [§218].

I explained earlier [§92] that there is a union of the Lord with us and a mutual union of us with the Lord, but that our mutual union with the Lord is not from us but from the Lord. I noted also [§183] that our own volition is at odds with the Lord's volition, or in other words, that our prudence is at odds with the Lord's divine providence. It then follows that because of all that is time-bound within us, we separate the Lord's eternal things from ourselves, while the Lord unites his eternal things with our time-bound ones—that is, himself with us and us with him. Since I have already said so much about this, there is no need for further support.

[5] (d) *The Lord unites us to himself by means of appearances.* It does seem as though we ourselves loved our neighbor and did good and spoke the truth; and if it did not seem as though we were doing these things on our own, we would not love our neighbor, do good, or speak the truth, so we would not be united to the Lord. However, since love, goodness, and truth come from the Lord, we can see that it is through appearances that the Lord is uniting us to himself. There has been a great deal of material already [§§100–128] about this appearance and about the Lord's union with us and our responding union with the Lord by means of it.

[6] (e) *The Lord unites us to himself by means of correspondences.* This happens through the Word, whose literal meaning is made up entirely of correspondences. In *Teachings for the New Jerusalem on Sacred Scripture,*

from beginning to end, I have explained that there is a union of the Lord with us and a responding union of us with the Lord through this meaning.

4. *The union of temporal and eternal matters in us is the Lord's divine providence.* This will elude even the first grasp of discernment, though, unless it is broken down into a sequence and explained clearly step by step. The following is the necessary sequence. (a) It is by divine providence that we divest ourselves of what is physical and time-bound by dying, and put on what is spiritual and eternal. (b) Through his divine providence, the Lord unites himself to what is physical through what is spiritual, and to what is time-bound through what is eternal, doing so according to acts of service. (c) The Lord unites himself to acts of service by means of their correspondence, which means that he does so by means of appearances, depending on the extent to which we take them as fact. (d) This kind of union of temporal and eternal things is divine providence.

These propositions need to be brought into clearer light by explanations, though.

[2] (a) *It is by divine providence that we divest ourselves of what is physical and time-bound by dying, and put on what is spiritual and eternal.* The physical and time-bound things are the outermost and final substances that we first enter when we are born, in order eventually to be brought into deeper and higher things. The outermost and final things are what hold us together, and they are found in this physical world. This is why no angel or spirit has been created as such directly. Rather, all of them first came about by being born human. As a result, they all have outermost and final substances, essentially stable and constant, within which and by which their more inward substances can be held together.

[3] We ourselves, however, are clothed with even cruder elements of the material world at first. That is what our bodies are made of. We divest ourselves of them at death, though, and keep the purer elements of the material world that are closest to spiritual elements. These are what then hold us together.

Further, all the deeper and higher parts of us are present at once in these outermost or final elements, as was noted in the appropriate place above [§§108, 119]. As a result, everything the Lord does he does from beginnings and endings at once, and therefore completely.

However, the outermost and final substances of the material world cannot accept the spiritual and eternal things for which the human mind is formed, not as they are in essence, even though we are born to become spiritual and to live to eternity. We therefore divest ourselves of them and keep only the inner substances of the material world that are adapted and congenial to what is spiritual and heavenly. These serve to hold us together. We do this by casting off the limiting time-bound, physical substances, a process that we call physical death.

[4] (b) *Through his divine providence, the Lord unites himself to what is physical through what is spiritual and to what is time-bound through what is eternal, doing so according to acts of service.* The physical and time-bound things we are talking about are not just those that are proper to the physical world but those that are proper to us in this physical world as well. We divest ourselves of both when we die and put on corresponding spiritual and eternal things. We put them on according to our acts of service, as I have already explained a number of times.[189]

In general, the natural elements that are proper to the physical world involve time and space. More specifically, they are the things we see on earth. We leave them behind when we die and receive spiritual things in their stead, things that are much the same in their outer guise or appearance but not in their inner guise or actual essence. I have already spoken of this as well [§§102–110].

[5] The time-bound things that are proper to us in this physical world are, broadly speaking, matters of eminence and wealth, and more specifically, the basic necessities of life: food, clothing, and shelter. These too we shed and leave behind at death, putting on and receiving things that are similar in their outward guise and appearance but not in their inward guise and in their essence. They all get their inward guise and essence from acts of service in temporal matters in this world. These acts of service are good actions, the good effects of our caring.

This may serve to show that through his divine providence, the Lord unites spiritual and eternal things to physical and time-bound things, doing so according to acts of service.

[6] (c) *The Lord unites himself to acts of service by means of their correspondence, which means that he does so by means of appearances, depending on the extent to which we take them as fact.* Since these thoughts cannot help but seem obscure to people who have no clear notion of what correspondences and appearances are, I need to illustrate and thereby explain them with an example. All the things we read in the Word are simply images that correspond to spiritual and heavenly realities; and since they correspond, they are appearances. That is, everything in the Word is divine good coming from divine love and divine truth coming from divine wisdom. In their own right, these things are naked, but in the Word they

are clothed with a literal meaning, so they look like a fully dressed person. This means that to us, they look as though they were dressed in clothes that correspond to our own states of love and wisdom. We can see, then, that if we take these appearances as fact, it is like believing that the clothes are the person. The appearances become illusions. It is different if we are looking for truths and see them within the appearances.

[7] Now since all the acts of service, all the true and good deeds of caring that we do for our neighbor, we do either in keeping with appearances or in keeping with actual truths from the Word, therefore if we do them in keeping with the appearances we have taken as fact, we are mired in illusions, while if we do them in keeping with the truths, we do them as we should. We can tell from this what it means to say that the Lord unites himself to acts of service by means of their correspondence, which means that he does so by means of appearances, depending on the extent to which we take them as fact.

[8] (d) *This kind of union of temporal and eternal things is divine providence.* To bring this into some mental light, I need to illustrate it with two examples, one having to do with eminence and rank and the other with wealth and resources. Both of these are physical and time-bound in their outward form and spiritual and eternal in their inward form.

Both eminence and the rank it offers are physical and time-bound when we focus on ourselves and our role in them and not on the state and service. Then we cannot help but think to ourselves that the state exists for our sake and not that we exist for the sake of the state. It is like monarchs who think that the realm and all its citizens exist for their sake and not that they are monarchs for the sake of the realm and its citizens.

[9] The very same eminence and rank are spiritual and eternal, though, when we see ourselves and our role as existing for the sake of the state and service, and not the state and service for our own sake. If we do this, then we have the truth and the essence of our eminence and rank. Otherwise, we have the image and appearance; and if we take them as fact, then we are mired in illusions, and are no more united with the Lord than people who are bent on distortion and its consequent evil. After all, illusions are the distortions that evils seek out as consorts. We may actually do some good and useful things, but we do them from ourselves and not from the Lord; so we put ourselves in place of the Lord.

[10] It is much the same with wealth and resources. These are also both earthly and time-bound on the one hand and spiritual and eternal on the other. Wealth and resources are earthly and time-bound if we focus on them alone and on ourselves in them and look only for our own

comfort and pleasure in both. They are spiritual and eternal if we focus on the good we can do with them and look for a deeper comfort and pleasure in that good. In that case, even the outer comfort and pleasure is spiritual, and the time-bound is eternal. This means also that after death, people of the latter sort are in heaven, living in mansions whose useful furnishings gleam with gold and jewels. Yet all they see is an outer beauty and translucence shining through from what lies within, which is the usefulness that is the basis of their real comfort and pleasure, the essential blessedness and happiness of heaven.

The opposite lot falls to people who focused[190] on their wealth and resources solely for the sake of the wealth and resources and for themselves. This means that they valued them for their outward worth and not for their inward worth as well, guided by their appearance and not by their essence. When they are divested of them, which happens when they die, they put on what was within them; and since this was not spiritual it can only be hellish. The contents of wealth and resources must be either one or the other; they cannot coexist. So instead of wealth they have poverty, and instead of resources they have misery.

[11] Useful things include not only the necessities of life—food, clothing, and shelter for oneself and one's own—but also the good of the country, community, and fellow citizen. Business is useful when it is the real love and money is a subservient, supporting love, provided the merchant avoids and recoils from fraud and deceptive practices as sins. It is different when money is the real love and business is the subservient, supporting love. This is greed, the root of evils. See Luke 12:15 and the parable about greed in verses 16–21.[191]

We Are Not Granted Inner Access to the Truths That Our Faith Discloses and the Good Effects of Our Caring Except As We Can Be Kept in Them to the End of Our Life

IN the Christian world, people know that the Lord wants everyone to be saved. They also know that the Lord is omnipotent. As a result, many of them conclude that he can save everyone and does save those who beg for his mercy—especially if they do so with the formula of the standard faith, namely, that God the Father may have mercy for the sake of the Son, and especially if they also ask to be granted this faith. However, in the closing section of the present work [§§331–340] we shall see that the actual situation is very different indeed. There I will explain that the Lord cannot violate the laws of his divine providence, because violating them would be violating his own divine love and his own divine wisdom, actually violating himself. We shall see there that this kind of instant mercy is impossible because our salvation is accomplished by specific means. No one can lead us by these means except one who both intends the salvation of everyone and is omnipotent, namely, the Lord.

221

The means by which the Lord leads us are what we are calling "the laws of divine providence." One of them is this: that we are not granted inner access to the truths that wisdom discloses and the good that love does except as we can be kept in them to the end of our life. To demonstrate this rationally, though, I need to lay it out in the following equence.

1. It is possible for us to be granted wisdom about spiritual matters and even a love for them and still not be reformed.
2. If we then backslide from them and go against them, we profane what is holy.
3. There are many kinds of profanation, but this is the worst of all.
4. This is why the Lord does not grant us inner access to the truths that wisdom discloses and the good that love does except as we can be kept in them to the end of our life.

222   1. *It is possible for us to be granted wisdom about spiritual matters and even a love for them and still not be reformed.* This is because we have rationality and freedom. Our rationality enables us to be lifted up into a wisdom that is almost angelic; and our freedom enables us to be lifted up into a love that is not wholly unlike angelic love. However, the nature of our love determines the nature of our wisdom. If our love is heavenly and spiritual, then our wisdom is heavenly and spiritual too; but if our love is demonic and hellish, then our wisdom is demonic and hellish too. It may look heavenly and spiritual in its outward form, to others, but in its inward form or actual essence it is demonic and hellish, not outside us but within us.

People do not notice this, because they live on the earthly level and see and hear on that level, and the outward form is earthly. The inner nature is clear to angels, though, because angels are spiritual and see and hear on the spiritual level, and the inner form is spiritual.

[2] We can see from this that we can be granted wisdom about spiritual matters and a love for them as well and still not be reformed. In this case, though, we are being granted only an earthly love for these matters, not a spiritual love for them. This is because we can give ourselves earthly love, but only the Lord can give us spiritual love. If we are given this latter love, we are reformed; while if all we receive is the former love, we are not. Most hypocrites are like this, and many Jesuits,[192] people who do not believe in anything divine inwardly but outwardly go through their religious motions like actors in a play.

223   I have learned from an abundance of experience in the spiritual world that we have within us the ability to understand mysteries of wisdom just as real angels do, since I have seen fiery demons who not only understood mysteries of wisdom when they heard them but even stated them quite rationally. However, the moment they went back to their demonic love they did not understand them. They replaced them with their opposites, with insanity, and called that wisdom. I have even been allowed to hear them ridiculing their insanity when they were in their wise state and ridiculing their wisdom when they were in their insane state.

People who have been like this in the world are often led to experience alternate states of wisdom and insanity after death, when they become spirits, so that they can see each from the perspective of the other. However, even though they do see themselves as insane from the perspective of wisdom, when they are given the choice (as we all are), they commit themselves to insanity. This is what they love, and they then have nothing but hatred for wisdom. This is because their inner natures are demonic, while their outer natures seem divine. These are the people meant by devils who make themselves angels of light,[193] and by the guest at the marriage feast who was not wearing a wedding garment and was cast into outer darkness (Matthew 22:11, 12, 13).

Can anyone fail to see that it is the inner level from which the outer level arises and that the outer level therefore derives its essence from the inner level? Surely everyone knows from experience that the outer level can appear in a guise that differs from the essence that it derives from what lies within. This is obvious in the case of hypocrites, flatterers, and con artists. Then too, we can imitate the characteristics of other people outwardly, as is obvious in the case of comics and mimes. They know how to portray monarchs, emperors, and even angels with their tone of voice, language, expression, and gesture as though they really were what they seem, even though they are only actors. I mention this because we too can put on pretenses in our civic and moral dealings as well as in our spiritual ones. We know that many people do.

[2] When our inner nature is essentially hellish, then, and our outer nature seems spiritual in its form, though (as just noted) the outer derives its essence from the inner, you may ask where that essence is hiding in the outer. It is not in our gestures, our tone of voice, our language, or our expression. However, it is still hidden in all four of these. What is hidden shows through them very clearly in the spiritual world, because when we move from this physical world into the spiritual world, which happens when we die, then we leave behind those outward appearances along with our bodies, but keep the inner qualities that were hidden away in our spirits. Then if that inner nature was hellish, we look like demons just as we were in spirit while we were living in this world. Surely everyone realizes that we all leave those outward things behind along with our bodies and become engaged with deeper things when we become spirits.

[3] Let me also add that in the spiritual world there is a sharing of feelings and consequent thoughts, which means that none of us can say anything except what we are actually thinking. Also, our faces change there and become images of our feelings, so others can see from our faces what we are really like. Hypocrites are sometimes allowed to say what they are not thinking, but their tone of voice sounds discordant because of their deeper thoughts, and they can be recognized by this discord. So we can tell that the inner nature is hidden within the tone, the language, the expression, and the gestures of the outer, and that while people in the

224

physical world are not sensitive to this, it is obvious to angels in the spiritual world.

225   We can see from this that as long as we are living in this physical world, we can be let into wisdom about spiritual matters and even into a love for them, and that this does and can happen both to people who are completely earthly-minded as well as to people who are spiritual. The difference is, though, that the latter are reformed when this happens, while the former are not. It may seem as though they love wisdom, but they love it only the way an adulterer loves a fine woman—like a prostitute. He talks soothingly to her and gives her beautiful clothes, but privately he is thinking, "She is nothing but a worthless whore. I will get her to believe that I love her, because she takes my fancy, but if she does not take to me, then I will discard her." The inner self is the adulterer, and the outer self is the woman.

226   2. *If we then backslide from wisdom and love and go against them, we profane what is holy.* There are many kinds of profanation of what is holy, which will be discussed in the next section. This is the worst of all, though, because people who commit this kind of profanation are no longer human after death. They are alive, but they are trapped in their wild hallucinations. They seem to themselves to be flying around in the air; and when they come to rest they toy with their illusions, which they see as real. Since they are no longer human, they are not referred to as "he" or "she," but as "it." In fact, when they are exposed to view in heaven's light they look like skeletons, sometimes the color of bones, sometimes fiery, and sometimes charred.

In this world, people do not know that this is what happens after death to individuals who commit profanation; and they do not know this because they do not understand the reason for it. The real reason is that if we acknowledge divine things and believe them at first and then backslide and deny them, we mix what is holy with what is profane; and once they have been mixed together, the only way they can be separated results in complete destruction.

To clarify this, several things need to be set forth, as follows. (a) Everything we willingly think and say and do becomes part of us and remains so, whether it is good or evil. (b) The Lord is constantly using his divine providence to make provisions and arrangements so that what is evil will be by itself and what is good by itself, and so that they can be kept separate. (c) However, this cannot be accomplished if we first acknowledge the truths that faith discloses and live by them and afterwards backslide and deny them. (d) Then we mingle what is good and what is evil so completely that they cannot be separated. (e) Since what is good and what is evil need to be separated in each one of us, and since they cannot be separated in people like this, everything truly human about them is destroyed.

These are the reasons such disasters happen, but because of the darkness of ignorance, they need further explanation if they are to reach the light of comprehension.

227

(a) *Everything we willingly think and say and do becomes part of us and remains so, whether it is good or evil.* This has already been presented in §§78–81. We have an outer or earthly memory and an inner or spiritual memory. In this latter memory is recorded everything we have willingly thought, said, and done in this world so inclusively and in such detail that nothing whatever is left out. This memory is our "book of life" that is opened after death and by which we are judged.[194] (There is more about this memory in *Heaven and Hell* 461–465 *[461–469]*, drawn from personal experience.)

[2] (b) *The Lord is constantly using his divine providence to make provisions and arrangements so that what is evil will be by itself and what is good by itself, and so that they can be kept separate.* Each of us has both good and evil qualities. The evil ones come from us and the good ones from the Lord; and we could not be alive if we did not have both. If we were totally wrapped up in ourselves and therefore in our evil natures we would not have any trace of life; and if we were totally wrapped up in the Lord and therefore in our good natures we would not have any trace of life either. In the latter case, that is, we would be like people who are suffocating and constantly gasping for breath, or like people in the last throes of dying. In the former case life would have been snuffed out because evil totally devoid of anything good is intrinsically dead. So each of us has both. The difference is that for some the inner self is devoted to the Lord while the outer is apparently concerned with self, while in others the inner self is wrapped up in self and the outer is apparently devoted to the Lord. The one is focused on evil and the other on good, though both are present in each.

The reason evil people have both sides is that they are involved in the constructive activities of civic and moral living, and outwardly, too, in a kind of constructive spiritual life. Further, the Lord keeps them in enough rationality and freedom that they can engage in something good. It is this good through which all of us, even the evil ones, are being led by the Lord.

So we can see that the Lord keeps the evil and the goodness separate so that one is inside and the other outside, thus providing that they do not become mingled.

[3] (c) *This cannot be accomplished, however, if we first acknowledge the truths that faith discloses and live by them and afterwards backslide and deny them.* This can be seen from what has just been presented: first of all that everything we have willingly thought, said, and done becomes part of us and stays with us; and second, that the Lord is constantly using his divine providence to make provisions and arrangements that what is evil will be by itself and what is good by itself so that they can be kept separate. The Lord does separate them after our death. If we have been inwardly evil and outwardly good, then the goodness is taken away and we are left to our evil. In contrast, if we have been inwardly good, but—like everyone else—have outwardly struggled for wealth, vied for eminence, relished various worldly pleasures, and given in to some of our compulsions, then still the goodness and the evil in us have not been mingled but kept separate, one inside and the other outside. Outwardly, then, we have been very much like evil people, but not inwardly. Conversely, for evil people who have outwardly looked like good ones as far as their piety, worship, speech, and behavior are concerned, but who have still been evil inwardly, the evil is separated from the goodness in them as well.

However, if people have at first acknowledged the truths that faith discloses and have lived by them but later have turned in the opposite direction and rejected them (and especially if they have denied them), then their good and evil qualities are no longer separated but are mingled. That is, such people internalize good and also internalize evil, which unites and mingles them.

[4] (d) *We then mingle what is good and what is evil so completely that they cannot be separated.* This follows from what has just been said. If the evil in us cannot be separated from the goodness and the goodness from the evil, then we cannot be either in heaven or in hell. Each of us must be in one or the other, and we cannot be in both, now in heaven and now in hell. When we were in heaven we would be working for hell, and when we were in hell we would be working for heaven; so we would destroy the life of everyone around us, the heavenly life for angels and the hellish life for demons. This would be the end of life for both, since we all need our own life and cannot live in someone else's life, let alone in an opposite life.

This is why when we become spirits or spiritual people after our death, the Lord separates what is good from what is evil and what is evil from what is good in each one of us. The goodness is separated from the evil if we have been inwardly evil and the evil from the goodness if we have been inwardly good. This is the intent of the Lord's saying, "To all those who have, more will be given in abundance, and from those who do [not]¹⁹⁵ have, even what they have will be taken away" (Matthew 13:12; 25:29; Mark 4:25; Luke 8:18; 19:26).

[5] (e) *Since what is good and what is evil need to be separated in each one of us, and since they cannot be separated in people like this, everything truly human about them is destroyed.* What is truly human about us is our rationality, our ability to see and know, if we try, what is true and what is good, and also our ability freely to intend, think, say, and do it, as already explained [§§96–97]. However, both this freedom and its rationality are destroyed in people who have mingled good and evil in themselves. They cannot see what is evil from the perspective of what is good or recognize what is good from the perspective of what is evil because they have identified them with each other. This means that they no longer have either the actual or the potential ability to function rationally, so they no longer have any freedom. This is why they are simply like wild hallucinations, as already noted [§226], and no longer look like people but like bones with some skin on them. It is why they are not called "he" or "she" when they are named, but "it." This is what finally becomes of people who mingle sacred things with profane ones in this fashion. There are, though, other kinds of profanation that are not so dire. These will be discussed in the next section.

No one profanes holy things who does not know about them, since if we do not know about them we cannot first acknowledge and then deny them. This means that people who live outside the Christian world and know nothing about the Lord or about the redemption and salvation he offers do not profane this holy faith even when they argue against it because they do not accept it. **228**

Even Jews do not profane this holy matter either, since from infancy they have been reluctant to accept and acknowledge it. It is different if they do accept and acknowledge it, and then deny it, but this rarely happens. Many of them acknowledge it outwardly but deny it inwardly, in which case they are like hypocrites.

The people who profane holy things by mingling them with the profane, though, are the ones who accept and acknowledge at first but then backslide and deny. [2] The acceptance and belief of early childhood and youth is not at issue. That is common to all Christians. This is not profanation, because they are not accepting and acknowledging sacred things of faith and caring at all rationally and freely, that is, in their own discernment and of their own volition, but simply as a matter of memory and out of trust in their teachers. If they live by these principles, it is in blind obedience. However, when they come into their own rationality and freedom as they gradually mature and grow up, then if they acknowledge truths and live by them but later deny them, they mingle the holy with the profane and change from humans into the kind of monster I have just described.

In contrast, if people have been engaged in evil from the beginning of their rationality and freedom, the beginning of their independence, until their maturity, but later acknowledge the truths that faith discloses and live by them, they do not mingle them. The Lord then separates the evils of their former life from the good qualities of their later life. This is what happens to everyone who repents. There will be more on this later, though [§§279–280].

229   3. *There are many kinds of profanation of what is holy, but this is the worst of all.* In everyday language, profanation is understood to mean all kinds of irreverence, so the category of profane people includes everyone who at heart denies God and the holiness of the Word and therefore the spiritual gifts of the church. These are the very holy things that even irreverent people talk about.

I am not talking about these people, though, but about people who confess God, insist on the holiness of the Word, and acknowledge the spiritual gifts of the church, most of whom do so only verbally. The reason they are committing profanation is that there is something holy from the Word within and among them. It is this something within them, something that is part of their own discernment and volition, that they are profaning. In irreverent people, people who deny the Divinity and divine matters, there is nothing holy for them to profane. It is the former who commit profanation, then, even though they are not irreverent.

230   The profanation of what is holy is referred to in the second of the Ten Commandments in the words, "You shall not profane the name of your God" [Exodus 20:7; Deuteronomy 5:11]; and the Lord's prayer is telling us that we must not profane what is holy when it says, "Hallowed be your name" [Matthew 6:9; Luke 11:2]. Hardly anyone in all Christendom knows what "the name of God" means. This is because people do not know that people in the spiritual world do not have names the way we do in this physical world. Rather, each individual is named for her or his own love and wisdom. As soon as we enter a community or a gathering of people, we are immediately given a name that expresses our nature. We are named in a spiritual language that is essentially able to give a distinctive name to every individual thing, because every letter in its alphabet means something definite; and when many letters are combined into a single word, as happens with an individual's name, they include the whole state of that object. This is just one of the marvels of the spiritual world.

[2] We can see from this that in the Word, "the name of God" means both God and everything divine that is in him and that emanates from him. Since the Word is a divine emanation, it is a name of God; and since all the divine gifts that we refer to as the spiritual gifts of the church come from the Word, they too are a name of God.

This enables us to see what "You shall not profane the name of your God" means in the second of the Ten Commandments, and what "Hallowed be your name" means in the Lord's Prayer.

"The name of God" and "the name of the Lord" mean much the same in many passages in the Word in both Testaments. See, for example, Matthew 7:22; 10:22; 18:5, 20; 19:29; 21:9; 24:9, 10; John 1:12; 2:23; 3:17, 18; 12:13, 28; 14:14, 15, 16; 16:23, 24, 26, 27; 17:6; and 20:31, among others, as well as a great many in the Old Testament.[196]

[3] If you know the meaning of this "name," then you can know the meaning of the Lord's words, "Whoever accepts a prophet in the name of a prophet will receive a prophet's reward. Whoever receives a righteous person in the name of a righteous person will receive a righteous person's reward; and whoever gives one of these little ones something cold to drink in the name of a disciple will not lose the reward" (Matthew 10:21 [10:41, 42]). If you understand the name of a prophet or a righteous person or a disciple to mean nothing but the prophet or the righteous person or the disciple, then the only meaning you get will be a literal one. You will not know, either, what is meant by the reward of the prophet or the reward of the righteous person or the reward for the cold drink given on behalf of the disciple. Yet the name and the reward of the prophet mean the blessed state of people who enjoy divine gifts of truth, and the name and the reward of the righteous person mean the blessed state of people who enjoy divine gifts of what is good, while the disciple means the state of people who have some of the spiritual gifts of the church, and the cold drink is any element of truth.

[4] We can also tell that the name means the nature of the state of love and wisdom, or of what is good and true, from these words of the Lord: "The one who comes in by the door is the shepherd of the sheep. The doorkeeper opens to him and the sheep hear his voice, and he calls his own sheep by name and leads them out" (Matthew 10:2, 3 [John 10:2, 3]). "Calling sheep by name" is teaching and leading every individual

whose deeds are prompted by caring, and doing so in keeping with that individual's state of love and wisdom. "The door" means the Lord, as we can tell from verse 9: "I am the door. Anyone who enters in by me will be saved" [John 10:9]. This shows that we need to turn to the Lord himself if we are to be saved, and that the one who does turn to him is a shepherd of his sheep. Anyone who does not turn to him is a thief and a robber, as it says in the first verse of the same chapter.

231   "Profanation of what is holy" means profanation by people who know the truths that their faith discloses and the good effects of caring taught by the Word, and who in one way or another acknowledge them. It does not mean people who have no knowledge of such things or who simply reject them out of irreverence. What follows, then, is about the former people, not the latter.

There are many kinds of profanation, some less serious and some more, but they boil down to the following seven kinds.

The first kind of profanation is committed by people who make light of the Word or use it lightly, or who do the same with the divine gifts of the church. Some people do this because of habitual immorality, pulling words and phrases out of the Word and including them in conversations of questionable quality, sometimes indecent ones. This necessarily involves some disrespect for the Word, when in fact the Word is divine and holy throughout and in every detail. At the heart of everything it says, there is something divine lying hidden; and it is through this that it is in touch with heaven. This kind of profanation is more or less serious, though, depending on the recognition of the Word's holiness and on the indecency of the conversation into which the supposed humorists inject it.

[2] *A second kind of profanation is committed by people who understand and acknowledge divine truths but who violate them in their lives.* This is less serious, though, if they simply understand the truths and more serious if they actually acknowledge them. All our discernment does is teach, much the way a preacher does. It does not automatically unite the teaching with our volition. Acknowledgment, on the other hand, does unite itself. There can be no acknowledgment unless our volition agrees. Still, this union may vary, and the severity of the profanation depends on the closeness of the union when our lives violate the truths that we acknowledge. For example, if we acknowledge that vengefulness and hatred, adultery and promiscuity, fraud and deceit, slander and lying, are sins against God and still commit them, we are guilty of this more serious kind of profanation. The Lord says, "The slave who knows the Lord's will and does not do it will be beaten severely" (Luke 12:48 *[12:47]*). Elsewhere, "If

you were blind you would not have sin, but now you say that you can see, so your sin remains" (John 9:41).

Acknowledging things that are apparently true, though, is different from acknowledging things that are really true. If we acknowledge things that are really true and violate them with our lives, then in the spiritual world we seem to have no light or warmth in our voice and speech, as though we were completely listless.

[3] *A third kind of profanation is committed by people who use the literal meaning of the Word to justify their evil loves and false principles.* This is because the justification of falsity is the denial of truth and the justification of evil is the rejection of goodness; and at heart the Word is pure divine truth and divine goodness. In its outermost meaning, its literal meaning, this does not come out as real truth except where it tells about the Lord and the actual path of salvation. Rather, it comes out in those outer garments of truth that we may call "appearances of truth." As a result, this level of meaning can be persuaded to support all kinds of heresy; and if we justify our evil loves we do violence to things that are divinely good, while if we justify our false principles we do violence to things that are divinely true. This latter violence is called "the falsification of what is true," while the former is called "the adulteration of what is good." Both are meant by "blood" in the Word.

There is something spiritual and holy in the details of the literal meaning of the Word—the spirit of truth that emanates from the Lord. This holy content is damaged when the Word is falsified and adulterated. Clearly, this amounts to profanation.

[4] *A fourth kind of profanation is committed by people who utter devout and holy words and whose voice and body language seem to express loving feelings, but who at heart neither believe nor love what they are pretending.* Most of these are hypocrites and Pharisees.[197] Everything true and good is taken from them after death, and they are dismissed into outer darkness. People of this sort who have also become fixed in their rejection of Divinity, the Word, and the holy gifts of the church sit in silence in the darkness, incapable of speech. They want to utter devout and holy words the way they did in this world, but they cannot, because in the spiritual world speech must be in accord with thought. Hypocrites, though, want to say what they do not really think. This gives rise to a resistance in the mouth, and the result is that they can only be silent.

However, there are less and more serious forms of hypocrisy depending on how resolute the opposition to God is, and on the outward arguments in favor of God.

[5] *A fifth kind of profanation is committed by people who claim divine qualities for themselves.* These are the people meant by Lucifer in Isaiah 14.[198] "Lucifer" there means Babylon, as we can tell from verses 4 and 22 of the same chapter, which also tell of their fate.[199] These are the same people who are described as a harlot sitting on a scarlet beast in Revelation 17[:3].

There are many mentions of Babylon and Chaldea in the Word. "Babylon" means the profanation of what is good and "Chaldea" the profanation of what is true. In each case, it applies to people who claim divine qualities for themselves.

[6] *A sixth kind of profanation is committed by people who accept the Word but still deny the divine nature of the Lord.* These are the people known as Socinians and Arians in the world.[200] Both kinds of person ultimately find themselves praying to the Father, not to the Lord. They pray constantly to the Father for admission to heaven (some also praying for the sake of the Son), but their prayers are in vain. Eventually, they lose all hope of salvation and are sent down into hell with people who deny God. These are the people meant by those who blaspheme the Holy Spirit, who are not forgiven in this world or the next (Matthew 12:32).

The reason is that God is one in both person and essence, comprising a Trinity; and this God is the Lord. Since the Lord is heaven as well, and since this means that the people who are in heaven are in the Lord, people who deny the Lord's divine nature cannot be granted admission to heaven and be in the Lord. I have already explained [§§28, 60–67] that the Lord is heaven and that therefore people who are in heaven are in the Lord.

[7] *A seventh kind of profanation is committed by people who at first accept divine truths and live by them but later backslide from them and deny them.* The reason this is the worst kind of profanation is that these people are mixing what is holy with what is profane to the point that they cannot be separated, and yet they need to be separated for people to be either in heaven or in hell. Since this is impossible for such individuals, their whole human volition and discernment is torn away from them and they become no longer human, as already noted [§§226, 227].

Almost the same thing happens to people who at heart acknowledge the divine contents of the Word and the church but submerge them completely in their own sense of self-importance. This is the love of being in control of everything that has been mentioned several times before [§§38, 112, 146, 215]. When they become spirits after death, they are absolutely unwilling to be led by the Lord, only by themselves; and when the reins of their love are loosened, they try to control not only heaven but even the Lord. Since they cannot do this, they deny the Lord and become demons.

It is important to realize that for all of us, our life's love, our predominant love, stays the same after death and cannot be taken away.

[8] This kind of profanation is meant by the lukewarm church described in the Book of Revelation: "I know your works, that you are neither cold nor hot. If only you were cold or hot! Since you are lukewarm and neither cold nor hot, I am about to spit you out of my mouth" (Revelation 3:14, 15 [3:15, 16]). This is how the Lord describes this kind of profanation in Matthew: "When an unclean spirit leaves someone, it wanders in dry places seeking rest, but finds none. Then it says, 'I will go back to the home I left.' Then it does go back and finds it empty, swept clean and furnished for itself. It goes off and allies itself with seven other spirits worse than itself, and they come in and live there; and the latter times of that individual are worse than the earlier ones" (Matthew 12:43, 45 [12:43, 44, 45]). The departure of the unclean spirit describes our turning;[201] and the return of the unclean spirit with seven worse spirits to the house made ready for them describes our turning back to our former evils once our true and good qualities have been banished. The profanation of what is holy is described by the profanation that makes our later times worse than our former ones.

The following passage from John means much the same: "Jesus said to the man who had been healed at the Pool of Bethesda, 'Do not sin any more, or something worse will happen to you'" (John 5:14).

[9] The following passage tells of the Lord's provision that we do not inwardly acknowledge truths and then backslide and become profane: "He has closed their eyes and blinded their hearts so that they do not see with their eyes or understand with their hearts and turn themselves, and I heal them" (John 12:4 [12:40]). "So that they do not turn themselves and I heal them" means so that they do not acknowledge truths and then backslide and so become profane. This is also why the Lord spoke in parables, as he himself explained—see Matthew 13:13.[202] The Jewish prohibition against eating fat and blood (Leviticus 3:17; 7:23, 25 [7:23, 26]) meant that they should not profane holy things. The fat meant what is divinely good and the blood what is divinely true. Once we have turned to what is good and true, we should remain turned to the end of our life, as the Lord tells us in Matthew: "Jesus said, 'Whoever will have remained faithful to the end will be saved'" (Matthew 10:22; likewise Mark 13:13).

232   4. *This is why the Lord does not grant us inner access to the truths that wisdom discloses and the good that love does except as we can be kept in them to the end of our life.* I need to proceed with particular care in explaining this for two reasons: first because it is vital to our salvation, and second because an appreciation of this principle is key to appreciating the laws of permission that will be dealt with in the next section [§§234–274]. It is vital to our salvation because, as already noted [§§226–227], if we first accept the divine contents of the Word and therefore of the church but then backslide from them, we profane what is holy in the most harmful way. To uncover this secret of divine providence so that rational people can see it in their own light, then, it will be laid out in the following sequence. (a) At our deeper levels, good and evil cannot coexist within us, so neither can malicious distortion and beneficent truth. (b) The Lord can bring into our deeper levels what is good and the truth that comes from it only to the extent that evil and its distortions have been banished. (c) If what is good and its truth were brought in before evil and its distortions were removed, or to a greater extent than they were removed, then we would backslide from the goodness and return to our evil. (d) When we are absorbed in evil, much that is true can be introduced into our minds and stored in our memory without being profaned. (e) The Lord in his divine providence, however, takes the greatest care that we do not accept it into our volition before we have, in our apparent autonomy, banished evils from our outer self, or do not accept it to a greater extent than we have banished our outer evils. (f) If this were done too early or too fully, then our volition would adulterate the goodness and our discernment would falsify the truth by mingling them with what is evil and with what is false. (g) This is why the Lord does not grant us the truths that wisdom discloses and the good that love does except as we can be enabled to keep them to the end of our life.

233   To uncover this secret of divine providence so that rational people can see it in its own light, I need to explain the points just listed one at a time.

(a) *At our deeper levels, good and evil cannot coexist within us, so neither can malicious distortion and beneficent truth.* These "deeper levels" mean our inner thought processes, processes of which we are quite unaware until we come into the spiritual world and its light, which happens after death. The only way we can recognize them in this earthly world is by a pleasure of love in our outer thought processes, as well as by recognizing the evils themselves when we practice self-examination. This is because our inner and outer thought processes are so closely connected that they cannot be separated, as already noted—there is a good deal about this above.[203]

I speak of goodness and its truth and of evil and its distortions because goodness cannot exist without its truth or evil without its distortions. They are lovers or spouses, since the life of what is good comes from its truth, and the life of what is true comes from goodness. The same holds true for evil and its distortions.

[2] Rational people need no explanation to see that evil and its distortion cannot coexist with goodness and its truth at our deeper levels. Evil is the opposite of good, and good is the opposite of evil; and two opposites cannot coexist. Every evil harbors an intrinsic hatred for everything good, and everything good has an infinite love for keeping itself safe from evil and banishing it from itself. It then follows that neither can coexist with the other. If they were together, there would be at first a violent battle and eventually destruction. This is what the Lord is telling us when he says, "Every kingdom divided against itself is laid waste, and every city or home divided against itself will not stand. Anyone who is not with me is against me, and anyone who does not gather with me, scatters" (Matthew 25:30 *[12:25, 30]*). And again, "No one can serve two masters at the same time, for one or the other will be hated or loved" (Matthew 6:24).

Two opposite elements cannot coexist in one substance or form without tearing it apart and destroying it. If one comes too close to the other, they separate at all costs like two enemy forces, one withdrawing within its camp or fortifications and the other withdrawing outside. That is what happens with evil and good qualities in hypocrites. Both qualities are present, but the evil is inside and the goodness is outside so that the two are separated and not mingled.

This enables us to see that evil and its distortions and goodness and its truth cannot coexist.

[3] (b) *The Lord can bring into our deeper levels what is good and the truth that comes from it only to the extent that evil and its distortions have been banished.* This is simply a corollary of what has just been said, since if evil and good cannot coexist, goodness cannot be brought in until the evil has been moved out.

"Our deeper levels" means our inner thought processes. They are what we are dealing with. This is where either the Lord or the devil must be present. The Lord is there after our reformation and the devil is there before it. To the extent that we let ourselves be reformed, then, the devil is evicted; while to the extent that we do not let ourselves be reformed, the devil stays in residence. Can anyone fail to see that the Lord cannot enter us as long as the devil is there? And the devil is there as long as we keep the door closed where we are together with the Lord. The Lord tells us in the Book of Revelation that he will come in when that door is opened by our efforts: "I am standing at the door and knocking. If any hear my voice and open the door, I will come in to them and dine with them, and they with me" (Revelation 3:20).

The door is opened when we banish evil by abstaining and turning from it as hellish and demonic—it is one and the same thing if you say "evil" or "the devil." By the same token, it is one and the same thing if you say "goodness" or "the Lord"; because within everything good there is the Lord, and within everything evil there is the devil. This illustrates the truth of the matter.

[4] (c) *If what is good and its truth were brought in before evil and its distortions were removed, or to a greater extent than they were removed, then we would backslide from the goodness and return to our evil.* This is because the evil would be stronger, and whatever is stronger wins, eventually if not immediately. Once evil has won, the goodness cannot gain entrance to the inner suite but only to the vestibule, because evil and good cannot coexist, as just noted. Anything that is restricted to the vestibule will be evicted by its enemy who lives in the suite, which means that there will be a departure from goodness and a return to evil, which is the worst kind of profanation.

[5] Further, the essential pleasure of our life is to love ourselves and the world more than anything else. This pleasure cannot be taken away instantly, only gradually; and to the extent that any of this pleasure stays with us, evil is stronger. The only way this evil can be taken away is for our love for ourselves to become a love of service, or for our love of power for our own sake to become a love of power for the sake of service. This makes service the head and for the first time makes love for our-selves, or for power, the body beneath the head, and eventually the feet we walk on. Can anyone fail to see that goodness should be the head, and that when it is, the Lord is present? Goodness and service are the same thing. Can anyone fail to see that if evil is the head, the devil is present, and that since we still need to accept some civic and moral good and even some outward form of spiritual good, these are our feet and their soles, and are trodden down?

[6] Our state of life has to be inverted, then, so that what is on top is on the bottom, and this inversion cannot be accomplished instantly. What gives us the most pleasure of all is what comes from our love for

ourselves and therefore for power; and this fades and turns into a love of service only gradually. So the Lord cannot introduce goodness before this evil is removed, or to a greater extent than it is removed. If he did, then we would backslide from the goodness and return to our evil.

[7] (d) *When we are absorbed in evil, much that is true can be introduced into our minds and stored in our memory without being profaned.* This is because our discernment does not flow into our volition but our volition does flow into our discernment; and since our discernment does not flow into our volition, all kinds of truths can be accepted into our minds and stored in our memories without becoming mixed in with the evils in our volition; so sacred things are not profaned. It is up to us to learn truths from the Word or from sermons, to store them in memory, and to think about them. Our discernment then draws on these truths in our memory, truths we have thought about, to teach our volition, that is, to tell us what we should do. This is our primary means of reformation. As long as these truths are only in our discernment and therefore in our memory, they are not really in us but are outside of us.

[8] We might compare our memory to the ruminatory stomach that some animals have. What they eat goes there; and as long as it is there, it is not really in their body but is outside it. Only as they take it out and ingest it does it become part of their life and nourish their body. The contents of our memory are not physical foods, of course, but spiritual ones. This means that they are truths, essentially thoughts. To the extent to which we have taken them out by thinking, by ruminating, so to speak, our spiritual mind is nourished. It is our volition's love that wants this, that is in its own way hungry, and impels us to draw truths out for our nourishment. If that love is evil, then it has a longing and a kind of hunger for unclean thoughts. On the other hand, if it is good it has a longing and a kind of hunger for clean thoughts; and if thoughts are unsuitable it sets them aside, dismisses them, and evicts them by various means.

[9] (e) *The Lord in his divine providence, however, takes the greatest care that we do not accept it into our volition before we have, in our apparent autonomy, banished evils from our outer self, or do not accept it to a greater extent than we have banished our outer evils.* That is, whatever we take into ourselves willingly becomes part of us, part of our life; and in our actual life, the life we derive from our volition, evil and good cannot coexist. That would destroy us. However, we can have both in our discernment. We can have there what we call malicious distortions and beneficent truths, but not at the same time. Otherwise, we would not be

able to see what is evil from the perspective of goodness or to recognize what is good from the perspective of evil. However, they are marked off and separated there like the inside and the outside of a house. When evil people think and say good things, they are thinking and speaking outwardly, but when they think and say evil things, then they are thinking and speaking inwardly. If they say something good, then, it is like talking from the wall. They are like fruit that is superficially attractive but wormy and rotten inside, or like the shell of a dragon's egg.

[10] (f) *If this were done too early or too fully, then our volition would adulterate the goodness and our discernment would falsify the truth by mingling them with what is evil and with what is false.* When our volition is focused on something evil, it adulterates whatever is good in our discernment, and this adulterated good in our discernment is evil in our volition. It convinces us that evil is good and the reverse. Evil does this to everything good that opposes it. Evil also distorts anything that is true, because the truth that is inspired by goodness opposes the distortion that comes from evil. Our volition does this in our discernment as well: our discernment does not do so on its own.

The Word describes adulteration of what is good as adultery and the distortions of truth as promiscuity. This adulteration and distortion are accomplished through specious reasoning by that earthly self that is bent on evil as well as through finding support in the way things seem to be described in the literal sense of the Word.

[11] Our love for ourselves, the head of all our evils, is more adept than any other love at adulterating what is good and distorting what is true. It does this by misusing the rationality that the Lord gives to the worst and the best of us alike. It can actually rationalize things so that something evil seems perfectly good and something false seems perfectly true. What is beyond its power, when it can marshal a thousand arguments to prove that Nature created itself and then created humanity, animals, and plants of all kinds, and that Nature then infused something from within itself to enable us to live, think analytically, and discern wisely?

The reason our love for ourselves is so good at proving whatever it wants to is that it endows its outer surface with a kind of bright, multicolored radiance. This radiance is the love's reveling in wisdom and therefore in rank and power.

[12] However, once this love has become convinced of all this, it is so blind that all it can see is that people are animals and think like animals. It even believes that if animals could only talk, they would be humans in

a different form. If for some secondary reason this love has been led to believe that some aspect of us goes on living after death, it is so blind that it also believes that this is true of animals as well, and that what goes on living after death is nothing but some tenuous breath of life, like a mist that eventually returns to its corpse. Either that, or it is something alive with no sight, hearing, or voice—blind, then, and deaf and mute, just flying around and thinking. There are many other crazy notions as well that the material world itself, which is essentially dead, breathes into our hallucinations.

This is what our love for ourselves does, a love that in and of itself is our love for self-importance; and as far as its desires are concerned, which are all centered on this physical world, our sense of self-importance is very much like animal life. In respect to the perceptions that are prompted by these desires, our love for ourselves is very much like an owl. If we constantly immerse our thinking in our sense of self-importance, then, we cannot be raised from earthly light into spiritual light to see anything of God, heaven, or eternal life.

Since this is the nature of this love, and since it is so ingenious at proving whatever it wants to, it is just as ingenious at adulterating whatever is good in the Word and falsifying whatever is true in the Word if by some necessity it is constrained to confess them.

[13] (g) *This is why the Lord does not grant us inner access to the truths that wisdom discloses and the good that love does except as we can be kept in them to the end of our life.* The Lord does this to prevent us from falling into the worst kind of profanation of what is holy, the kind I have been discussing in this section. It is because of this danger that the Lord allows evil kinds of living and many heretical kinds of religion. The next sections will deal with the Lord's tolerance of such things.

Laws of Permission Are Also Laws
of Divine Providence

234 THERE are no "laws of permission"[204] that are simply that, or that are separate from the laws of divine providence. They are the same thing; so saying that God allows something to happen does not mean that he wants it to happen but that he cannot prevent it because of his goal, which is our salvation. Whatever happens for the sake of this goal, our salvation, is in accord with the laws of divine providence, since as already noted [§§183, 211], divine providence is always moving away from and contrary to our own intentions. It is constantly focused on its goal; so at every moment of its work, at every single step of its course, when it notices that we are straying from that goal it leads and turns and adapts us in accord with its laws, leading us away from evil and toward good. We will see shortly that this cannot be accomplished without allowing bad things to happen.

Further, nothing can be allowed to happen without some cause, and causes are to be found only in some law of divine providence, a law that tells us why something is allowed to happen.

235 At heart, people who have no belief whatever in divine providence do not believe in God either. They believe in the material world instead of God, and in their own prudence instead of divine providence. This may not be obvious, because we can think either way and talk either way. We can think and talk one way from our inner self and the other way from our outer self. It is like a hinge that enables a door to open in either direction, one way when we come in and the other way when we go out; or it is like a sail that can turn a ship one way or another depending on how the skipper sets it.

If we convince ourselves of human prudence to the point of denying divine providence, then even if we do happen to see, hear, or read something when we are thinking about it, we do not really notice it. In fact, we cannot, because we are not open to anything from heaven, only to what comes from ourselves. Since we are basing our conclusions on nothing but deceptive appearances and not actually seeing anything, we can swear that we are right. Then if we also believe in nothing but the material world, we get angry at people who stand up for divine providence—

unless they are ministers, because we think that this is a matter of their theology or their profession.

Let me list some instances of permission that are still in accord with divine providence, instances that strict materialists use to justify their preference for the material world over God and human prudence over divine providence.[205] When they read the Word, for example, they find that the wisest people[206] of all, Adam and his wife, let themselves be led astray by the serpent and that God did not use his divine providence to prevent it [Genesis 3:1–5]. Their first son, Cain, killed his brother Abel, and God did not dissuade him by talking with him beforehand, but simply cursed him after the fact [Genesis 4:1–16]. The Israelites worshiped a golden calf in the wilderness and acknowledged it as the God who had led them out of the land of Egypt, while Jehovah was watching from nearby Mount Sinai and doing nothing to prevent it [Exodus 32:1–6]. Because David had taken a census of the people a plague was sent and thousands of people died; and God did not send Gad the prophet to announce the punishment beforehand but only after the fact [2 Samuel 24:10–25]. Solomon was allowed to revive idolatrous worship, and many of the later kings were allowed to profane the temple and the holy practices of the church.[207] Finally, that nation was allowed to crucify the Lord.[208]

Worshipers of the material world and human prudence see in these instances and in many others in the Word nothing but contradictions of divine providence, so they can use them as arguments for denying providence. If they do not do so in their outward thinking, the thinking that is closest to speech, they still do it in their deeper thinking, which is distanced from their speech.

Everyone who worships self and the material world instead of divine providence feels justified in this on seeing so many irreverent people acting out their irreverence in so many ways and even boasting about it, and still not seeing any kind of punishment from God because of this. Such people feel even more justified in their rejection of divine providence when they see the success of manipulation, plots, and deceit, especially against people who are devout, fair-minded, and honest, and when they see injustice defeating justice in legal and business affairs.

Above all, they feel justified when they see irreligious people raised to high rank, getting positions of power in government and the church,[209] amply supplied with wealth, and living in ostentatious luxury, while people who worship God are living in disgrace and poverty.

People who worship themselves and the material world justify their rejection of divine providence as well when they think that wars are permitted, in which so many people are killed and so many cities, nations, and families plundered.[210] Further, victories come to the prudent side and sometimes not to the just side. It does not matter, either, whether the commander is a person of integrity or not, and so on. All these matters are instances of permission under the laws of divine providence.

238 These same materialists justify their rejection of divine providence when they look at the religious practices of various peoples. There are some with no knowledge of God at all, some who worship the sun and the moon, some who worship images and grotesque statues, and some who worship the dead. Particularly, they see that Islam[211] has been accepted by so many empires and nations while Christianity is restricted to that smallest part of the inhabited world that we call Europe, and even there is divided. There are people in the Christian world who claim divine power for themselves and want to be worshiped as gods and who call upon the dead. There are some who place salvation in particular words that they think about and say, and who attach no value to the good things that they do. In fact, there are few who actually live out their religion. Not only that, there are all the heresies of the past and some in existence today, those of the Quakers, for example, and the Moravians and the Anabaptists;[212] and there is the fact of the continued survival of Judaism.

Seeing this, people who deny divine providence draw the conclusion that religion is really nothing in its own right, but that it is still needed as a kind of restraint.

239 Nowadays, too, people whose inner thoughts favor the material world and human prudence alone could add more to the arguments they use to justify their position. There is the fact, for example, that all Christendom worships three gods, not realizing that God is one in person and in essence and that he is the Lord. There is also the fact that until now people have not known that there is spiritual meaning in the details of the Word and that this is the basis of its holiness. There is also ignorance of the fact that the essence of the Christian religion is to abstain from evils as sins and ignorance of the fact that we go on living as people after death. Skeptics can say privately and to each other, "If there is a divine providence, why is it only now revealing things like this?"

240 All the examples listed in §§237, 238, and 239 *[236, 237, 238, and 239]* have been cited to show that every least thing that happens in the world, whether to evil people or to good people, is under divine providence, and particularly that divine providence is active in the smallest details of our own thoughts and actions and is therefore universal.

However, since these examples will not make it clear without a presentation of the details of each one individually, I need to expand briefly on the items cited in the order of their listing, beginning at §236.

1. *The wisest people of all, Adam and his wife, let themselves be led astray by the serpent, and God did not use his divine providence to prevent it.* The reason for this is that Adam and his wife do not mean the first people created on earth but the people of the earliest church. It is their new creation or regeneration that is being described in this way, the actual new creation or regeneration by the creation of heaven and earth in the first chapter, their wisdom and intelligence by the Garden of Eden, and the end of that church by their eating of the tree of knowledge.

At heart, the Word is spiritual, containing secrets of divine wisdom; and in order to contain them it has been written entirely in symbolic and figurative language. We can therefore see that the people of that church—who were supremely wise at first, but who eventually became the worst because of their pride in their intelligence—were not misled by any serpent but by self-love. That is the head of the serpent that the seed of the woman, that is, the Lord, would eventually trample under foot.[213]

[2] Can anyone fail to see on rational grounds that this means more than what is being said in the literal narrative?[214] Can anyone take in the notion that the creation of the world happened the way it is described here? That is why scholars sweat to explain what it says in this opening chapter and finally say that they do not understand it.

Then there are the two trees in the garden or paradise, one of life and one of knowledge, with the second there to make problems; and there is the fact that simply eating from this tree is such an immense sin that not only Adam and Eve but the whole human race as well, as their descendants, became liable to damnation. There is the serpent's ability to mislead them, along with other matters; there is the creation of the wife from her husband's rib; there is their recognition of their nakedness after the fall and covering themselves with fig leaves; there is the provision of leather garments to cover their bodies; and there is the stationing of the cherub with a flaming sword to guard the path to the tree of life.[215]

[3] These are all images used to describe the establishment of the earliest church, its state and its change, and eventually its demise. You may find explanation of the secrets of them all, secrets contained in that spiritual meaning that is in the details, in the volumes on Genesis and Exodus published in London under the title *Secrets of Heaven*.

We may conclude, then, that the tree of life in Genesis means the Lord as to his divine providence, and that the tree of knowledge means humanity as to its own prudence.

242　　2. *Their first son, Cain, killed his brother Abel, and God did not dissuade him by talking with him beforehand, but simply cursed him after the fact.* Since Adam and his wife mean the earliest church, as just noted [§241], Cain and Abel as their first sons mean the two essential qualities of that church, love and wisdom, or charity and faith. Abel means love and charity, and Cain means wisdom or faith, particularly wisdom separated from love or faith separated from charity. When faith has been separated, wisdom tends not only to reject love and charity but to destroy them, killing its own brother.

It is reasonably well known in Christian circles that this is what faith does when it is separated from charity—see *Teachings for the New Jerusalem on Faith*.[216] [2] The curse of Cain is about the spiritual state that people who separate faith from charity, or wisdom from love, arrive at after death. However, in order to prevent the death of wisdom or faith, a mark is placed on Cain so that no one will kill him [Genesis 4:15]. This is because love cannot exist without wisdom, or charity without faith.

Since the meaning of this is very much like the meaning of eating from the tree of knowledge, it follows right after the description of Adam and his wife. People who have separated faith from charity are wrapped up in their own intelligence; while people who have faith because of their caring have a gift of intelligence from the Lord and are in sympathy with divine providence.

243　　3. *The Israelites worshiped a golden calf in the wilderness and acknowledged it as the God who had led them out of the land of Egypt, while God was watching from nearby Mount Sinai and doing nothing to prevent it.* This happened in the wilderness of Sinai near the mountain. The fact that Jehovah did not dissuade them from this outrageous worship is in keeping with all the laws of divine providence, both those already mentioned and those that will follow. They were allowed this evil to keep them all from destruction. That is, the Israelites had been led out of Egypt in order to portray the Lord's church, and they could not portray it until Egyptian idolatry had been uprooted from their hearts. This could not be accomplished unless they were given room to act out what was in their hearts and get rid of it because of severe punishment.

Further meanings of this worship, including the threat of total rejection and the raising up of a new nation by Moses, may be found in the discussion of Exodus 22 *[32]* in *Secrets of Heaven* [10393–10512], where these subjects are discussed.

4. Because David had taken a census of the people, a plague was sent and thousands of people died; and God did not send Gad the prophet to announce the punishment beforehand but only after the fact. Various thoughts and ruminations about this may occur to people who resolutely deny divine providence. They may ask particularly why David was not warned in advance and why the people were punished so severely for David's transgression.

The reason he was not warned in advance comes under laws of divine providence already presented, especially the two[217] explained in §§129–153 and 154–174. The reason the people were punished so severely for the transgression of their king (seventy thousand were struck by the plague) had to do not with the king but with the people, since it says, "Jehovah became more angry with Israel, so he prompted David against them by saying, 'Go, number Israel and Judah'" (2 Samuel 24:1).

5. Solomon was allowed to start idolatrous worship. This was in order that he might provide an image of the Lord's kingdom or the church in all the religions of the whole world, since the church established among the people of Judah and Israel was a representative church. This means that all the laws and statutes of that church were images of spiritual principles of the church, its inner reality. The people themselves represented the church, their king represented the Lord—David the Lord who was to come into the world, and Solomon the Lord after his coming. Since after the transformation of his human nature the Lord had power over heaven and earth (as he himself says in Matthew 28:18), Solomon as an image of him is portrayed in impressive splendor and had more wisdom than all the other kings on earth. He built the temple as well, and particularly allowed and initiated the religions of many nations, which provides an image of the various religions in our own world. His seven hundred wives mean much the same, as do his three hundred concubines (see 1 Kings 11:3), since a wife in the Word means the church and a concubine means a religion.

This enables us to see why it fell to Solomon to build the temple, which means the divine human nature of the Lord (John 2:19, 21) as well as the church, and why he was allowed to initiate idolatrous worship and marry so many wives.

In *Teachings for the New Jerusalem on the Lord* 43, 44, you may see that in many passages in the Word David means the Lord who was to come into the world.

6. Many of the kings after Solomon were allowed to profane the temple and the holy practices of the church. This was because the people portrayed the church, and the king was their head. It was also because the people of

Israel and Judah were a kind of people who could not represent the church for very long. At heart, they were idolaters. Because of this, they gradually drifted away from their representative worship by so misconstruing everything the church stood for that ultimately they destroyed it. This was portrayed by the way the kings profaned the temple and by their idolatry; and the actual ruin of the church was portrayed by the destruction of the temple itself, the carrying off of the people of Israel, and the Babylonian captivity of the people of Judah.

That was the reason, and anything that happens for some reason happens under divine providence, under one of its laws.

247   7. *That nation was allowed to crucify the Lord.* This was because the church in that nation was in ruins, so much so that it not only did not recognize and believe in the Lord but actually felt hatred toward him. Still, everything they did to him was under the laws of his own divine providence. On the passion of the cross as the last temptation or the last battle, by which the Lord completely defeated the hells and completely transformed his human nature, see *Teachings for the New Jerusalem on the Lord* 12–14 and *Teachings for the New Jerusalem on Faith* 34–35.

248   So far, I have been explaining the instances listed in §236 above, instances from the Word that materialists may use to support their reasoning against divine providence, because as already noted [§235] anything such people see or hear or read they can use as arguments against it. However, relatively few people justify their rejection of divine providence by passages from the Word. Most of them draw on what meets their eyes; and it is the list of these in §237 that will now be explained in the same way.

249   1. *Everyone who worships self and the material world instead of divine providence feels justified in this on seeing so many irreligious people acting out their irreverence in so many ways even as they boast about it, and still not seeing any kind of punishment from God because of this.* All instances of irreverence and of boasting about it are instances of permission whose reasons are laws of divine providence. All of us are free, perfectly free, to think whatever we wish, whether against God or for God. People who oppose God in their thoughts are rarely punished in this world, because they are always susceptible to reformation. They are punished in the spiritual world, though. This happens after they die, when they can no longer be reformed.

[2] We can see that laws of divine providence cause these instances of permission if we recall the laws already presented and look at them closely, as follows. We should act in freedom and in accord with reason

(§§71–97 *[71–99]*). We should not be compelled by outside forces to think and intend and so to believe and love in matters of our religion, but we should guide ourselves and sometimes compel ourselves (§§129–153).[218] Our own prudence is nothing. It only seems to be something, as it should. Rather, divine providence is all-inclusive because it extends to the smallest details (§§191–213). Divine providence focuses on eternal matters, and focuses on temporal matters only as they coincide with eternal ones (§§214–220). We are not granted inner access to the truths that our faith discloses and the good effects of our caring except as we can be kept in them to the end of our life (§§221–233).

[3] It will also become clear that the reasons behind instances of permission are the laws of divine providence from the principles about to be presented as follows. Evils are allowed for the sake of the goal, which is salvation [§§275–284]. Divine providence is constantly just as much with the evil as with the good [§§285–307]. And lastly, the Lord cannot act contrary to the laws of his divine providence, because to do so would be to act contrary to his divine love and his divine wisdom and therefore contrary to himself [§§331–340].

If we put these laws together, they can show us the reasons why acts of irreverence are allowed by the Lord and not punished when they happen in our thoughts and are rarely punished even when they are intended and therefore in our volition but are not acted out.

However, every evil entails its own punishment. It is as though there were engraved on the evil the punishment that the unbeliever will suffer after death.

[4] What has just been presented will serve to explain the following other instances cited in §237 as well. *People who worship themselves and the material world feel justified in their denial of divine providence when they see the success of manipulation, plots, and deceit even against people who are devout, fair-minded, and honest, and when they see injustice defeating justice in legal and business affairs.*

All the laws of divine providence are needed. Since they are the reasons things like this are allowed, we can see that if we are to live human lives, to be reformed and saved, the only way the Lord can keep us from such actions is indirectly. For people who realize that all kinds of murder, adultery, theft, and perjury are sins, this is accomplished through the Word, specifically through the provisions of the Ten Commandments. For people who do not realize that they are sins, civil laws and a fear of their penalties serve as means. Other means are moral laws including our fear of losing reputation, rank, and profit. The Lord uses these means to lead evil people, but he prevents them only from actions, not from think-ing about acting or wanting to act. The Lord uses the other means to lead good people not only away from the actions but also away from thinking about acting and wanting to act.

250   2. *People who worship themselves and the material world instead of di-vine providence feel justified when they see irreligious people raised to high rank, getting positions of power in government and the church,*[219] *amply sup-plied with wealth, and living in ostentatious luxury, while people who wor-ship God are living in disgrace and poverty.* People who worship themselves and the material world think that rank and wealth are the highest possi-ble joys, the only possible joys, joy itself. If they think at all about God because of their first childhood religion, they call these things divine blessings; and as long as they have no higher aspirations than this, they believe that God exists and worship him. However, there is something hidden in their worship that they themselves do not know about, an as-sumption that God will keep raising them to higher honor and greater wealth. If they do achieve this, their worship tends more and more into superficiality until it drifts away, and eventually they trivialize and deny God. They do the same if they lose the respect and wealth on which they have set their hearts.

In that case, what are rank and wealth but problems to these evil peo-ple? [2] They are not problems to the good, because they do not set their hearts on them. They focus rather on the service or the good that respect and wealth can help them accomplish. Only people who worship them-selves and the material world, then, can reject divine providence on see-ing that irreverent people are given high rank and wealth and get positions of power in the state and the church.

Further, what is higher or lower rank; what is more or less wealth? Is it really anything but something we imagine? Is one person more con-tented or happier than the other? Look at a government official or even a monarch or emperor. After a few years, does their rank not become sim-ply commonplace, something that no longer brings joy to the heart, something that can even seem worthless? Are people of high rank any happier on that account than people of lower rank, or even than people of no rank at all, like commoners or their servants? These can be even happier when things go well for them and they are content with their lot. What troubles the heart more, what is more often wounded, what is more intensely angered, than self-love? This happens whenever it is not given the respect to which, at heart, it raises itself, whenever things do not turn out the way it wills and wishes.

If rank is not a matter of substance or service, then, what is it but a concept? Can this concept have a place in any kind of thinking except thinking about oneself and the world, and precisely in the thought that the world is everything and eternity is nothing?

[3] I need now to say something about why divine providence allows people who are irreligious at heart to be raised to high rank and to become wealthy. Irreverent or evil people can be just as useful as devout or good people. In fact, they can be more ardent about it because they are focused on themselves in the good they do and regard advancement as intrinsically useful. The stronger their self-love grows, then, the more intense is their passion for service for the sake of their own renown. Devout or good people do not have this kind of fire unless it is subtly fueled by rank. So the Lord controls people of high rank who are irreligious at heart through their concern for their reputation. He inspires them to do what is good for the commonwealth or the country, for the community or the city in which they live, and also for their own fellow-citizens or neighbors. This is the Lord's government, his divine providence, with people like this. The Lord's kingdom is in fact an organized realm of constructive activities;[220] and where there are only a few individuals who perform service for the sake of service, he works things out so that people who worship themselves are raised to the higher offices where they are inspired to do good by their own love.

[4] Imagine some hellish country on earth (though there is no such thing), where nothing but self-love held sway, where self-love itself was the devil. Would everyone not do more constructive things because of the fire of self-love and the radiance of his or her own renown than people did in any other country? While all of them mouthed off about the public good, they would have their own good at heart. All of them would be turning to their leader in order to be promoted, each one wanting to be the greatest. Can people like this see that God exists? They are enveloped by smoke like a burning building, and no gleam of spiritual truth can get through to them with its light. I have seen this smoke surrounding a hell made up of people like this.

Light your lantern[221] and ask how many people there are in quest of high office in today's countries who are not loves for themselves and the world. Will you find fifty in a thousand who are loves for God?[222] And only a few of those will be looking for high office. Given the fact, then, that so few are loves for God and so many are loves for themselves and the world, and given the fact that these latter kinds of love inspire more acts of service with their fires than loves for God do with theirs, how can people justify their beliefs by the fact that more evil people than good people are eminent and wealthy?

[5] These words of the Lord lend their support: "The lord praised the unjust steward because he had acted prudently, for the children of this generation are more prudent than the children of light in their generation. So I tell you, make friends for yourself of the mammon of unrighteousness, so that when you lose it they may accept you into eternal tents" (Luke 16:8, 9).

The earthly sense of this is obvious. In its spiritual meaning, though, the mammon of unrighteousness means those insights into what is true and good that evil people have and that they use solely for gaining rank and wealth for themselves. It is these insights with which good people or children of light make friends, and which accept them into eternal tents.

The Lord tells us that there are many people who are loves for themselves and the world and few who are loves for God when he says, "Wide is the gate and broad is the way that leads to destruction, and there are many who go in through it; but tight and narrow is the way that leads to life, and there are few who find it" (Matthew 7:13, 14). On rank and wealth as either curses or blessings, and for whom, see §217 above.

251   3. *People who worship themselves and the world justify their rejection of divine providence as well when they think that wars are permitted, in which so many people are killed and their wealth plundered.* It is not because of divine providence that wars happen, because wars are inseparable from murder, plunder, violence, cruelty, and other appalling evils that are diametrically opposed to Christian caring. However, it is absolutely necessary that they be permitted, because since the earliest people, the times meant by Adam and his wife (see §241 above), our life's love has become basically a love of controlling others, ultimately everyone, and of gaining possession of the world's wealth, ultimately all of it. These two loves cannot be kept in chains as long as it is the intent of divine providence that we act freely and rationally, as already explained in §§71–97 *[71–99]*. There is also the fact that if it were not for this permission, the Lord could not lead us out of our evil, so we could not be reformed and saved. That is, unless evils were allowed to surface, we would not see them and therefore would not admit to them; so we could not be induced to resist them. That is why evils cannot be suppressed by some exercise of divine providence. If they were, they would stay closed in, and like the diseases called cancer and gangrene, would spread and devour everything that is alive and human.

[2] From birth, each of us is like a little hell in constant conflict with heaven. The Lord cannot rescue any of us from our hell unless we see

that we are in it and want to be rescued. This cannot happen unless there are instances of permission that are caused by laws of divine providence.

This is why there are lesser and greater wars, the lesser ones between property owners and their neighbors and the greater ones between the rulers of nations and their neighbors.[223] The only difference between the lesser and the greater ones is that the lesser ones are limited by national laws and the greater ones by international laws. There is also the fact that in both cases the participants want to violate the laws, and that the lesser ones cannot, but the greater ones can, though still not beyond the bounds of possibility.

[3] There are several reasons hidden in the treasury of divine wisdom why the greater wars, with all their inevitable murder, plunder, violence, and cruelty, are not suppressed by the Lord, acting on the monarchs and leaders, either at the outset or while the wars are in progress. They are suppressed only at the end, when the power of one side or the other has become so weak that there is a threat of extinction. Some of these reasons have been revealed to me, and one of them is that all wars, regardless of the civil issues involved, portray states of the church in heaven and are corresponding images.[224] This was true of all the wars described in the Word, and it is true of all wars today. The wars described in the Word are the ones the Israelites waged with various nations such as the Amorites, the Ammonites, the Moabites, the Philistines, the Syrians, the Egyptians, the Chaldeans, and the Assyrians. When the Israelites, portraying the church, departed from their precepts and laws and fell into the evils meant by these nations (each of the nations the Israelites went to war with portrayed some particular kind of evil), then they were punished by that nation. For example, when they profaned the holy practices of the church by committing gross idolatry they were punished by the Assyrians and Chaldeans, because Assyria and Chaldea stand for the profanation of what is holy. For the meaning of the wars with the Philistines, see *Teachings for the New Jerusalem on Faith* 50–54 *[49–54]*.

[4] Wars in our own times, wherever they occur, portray the same kind of things. Everything that happens in this physical world is in response to something that is happening in the spiritual world, and everything spiritual involves the church. In this world, no one knows what countries in Christendom are the equivalents of the Moabites and the Ammonites, the Syrians and the Philistines, the Chaldeans and the Assyrians, and the other nations against whom the Israelites waged war, but their equivalents do exist.

We in this physical world are absolutely incapable of seeing what the quality of the earthly church is, and which are the particular evils it has given way to, for which it is suffering the punishments of war. This is because all that show in this world are outward matters that do not constitute the church. We can see them in the spiritual world, though, where the inner realities are visible that the real church is concerned with. All the people there form alliances in keeping with their states. Their conflicts in the spiritual world correspond to our wars; and both are correspondingly governed by the Lord according to his divine providence.

[5] Spiritual-minded people realize that the Lord is governing wars in this world by his divine providence, but materialists do not, except when a holiday is declared because of a victory. Then they may get down on their knees and thank God for giving them victory; and they may have said a few prayerful words before the battle began. When they come to their own senses, though, they credit the victory either to their leader's skill or to some decision or event in the middle of the battle, something that they did not think about at the time, but that led to the victory.

[6] On the fact that divine providence, called "luck," is at work in even the smallest, most trivial details, see §212 above. If you recognize divine providence in these matters, you must surely recognize it in affairs of war. In everyday language, we refer to a war's progress and serendipitous events as "the fortunes of war." This is divine providence, especially in the decisions and planning of the leaders, even if at the time and afterwards they attribute everything to their own prudence.

But they may do this if they want to, since they are in complete freedom to think in favor of divine providence or against it, in favor of God or against him. However, they might know that no trace of their decisions or planning comes from themselves. It all comes either from heaven or from hell—from hell by permission, and from heaven by providence.

252   *4. People who worship themselves and the world justify their rejection of divine providence when they base their thinking on the observation that victories come to the prudent side and sometimes not to the just side. It does not matter, either, whether an officer is a person of integrity or not.* The reason it seems as though victories come to the prudent side and sometimes not to the just side is that we judge by appearances. We lean toward one side rather than the other, and we justify the side we prefer by rationalizations. Then too, people do not know that the rightness of a cause is spiritual in heaven and earthly in this world, as has just been explained, and that these two levels are united by a connection between things past and things to come, a connection known only to the Lord.

[2] The reason it makes no difference whether the leader is a person of integrity or not is the same as the reason argued in §250, namely, that evil people are just as useful as good people and because of their fire are more avid than good people. This is true especially in wars because evil people are more skilled and ingenious than good people in devious strategizing, and because of their love for glory they find more pleasure in murdering and plundering people they recognize and identify as enemies. Good people have only care and passion for protecting, and rarely any care and passion for aggression.

It is much the same with spirits of hell and angels of heaven. Spirits of hell attack, and angels of heaven protect.

We may conclude, then, that it is appropriate for all to protect their country and their fellow citizens against invading enemies, even using evil officers; but it is not appropriate to make enemies for no cause. When the cause is one's own glory, that is essentially diabolical, since it comes from self-love.[225]

Up to this point I have been explaining the instances listed in §237 that strict materialists use to justify their opposition to divine providence. Now I need to explain the ones about the religions of many nations that follow in §238, which also serve strict materialists as arguments against divine providence. These people say at heart, "How can there be so many contradictory religions rather than one worldwide, true religion when the goal of divine providence is a heaven from the human race [as explained in §§27–45 above]?"[226]

Please listen, though! No matter what religion people are born into, people can all be saved if they believe in God and live by the precepts of the Ten Commandments—not to kill, not to commit adultery, not to steal, and not to commit perjury, because to do so would be contrary to their religion and therefore contrary to God. They have a fear of God and a love for their neighbor, a fear of God because they think that committing these acts is against God and a love for their neighbor because murder, adultery, theft, perjury, and coveting their neighbor's house and spouse are against their neighbor. Because these people turn to the Lord during their lives and do no harm to their neighbors, they are led by the Lord; and people who are so led are also taught about God and their neighbor according to their religions. This is because people who live this way want to be taught, while people who live otherwise do not. Further, people who want to be taught are taught by angels after death, when they become spirits, and gladly accept the kind of truths we find in the Word. On this subject see the material in *Teachings for the New Jerusalem on Sacred Scripture* 91–97 and 104–113.

253

254   1. *Strict materialists justify their rejection of divine providence when they look at the religious practices of various peoples. There are some with no knowledge of God at all, some who worship the sun and the moon, some who worship images and statues.* People who use this as a source of arguments against divine providence do not know the secrets of heaven, the innumerable secrets of heaven of which we know scarcely one. One of them is that we are not taught directly from heaven but indirectly (see §§154–174 above). Since we are taught indirectly, and since the Gospel could not be brought to everyone in the whole world by missionaries, while some religion could be carried by various means even to people in the remote corners of the world, this has therefore been accomplished by divine providence. That is, people do not simply originate a religion by themselves, they learn from others (who learned it from the Word either directly or by transmission through others) that there is a God, that there is a heaven and a hell and a life after death, and that we must worship God in order to be blessed.

[2] On the way religion has been transplanted throughout the world from the ancient Word and then from the Israelite Word, see *Teachings for the New Jerusalem on Sacred Scripture* 101–103; and on the fact that if it were not for the Word no one would know about God, heaven and hell, or life after death, let alone about the Lord, see §§114–118 of that work.

Once a religion has taken root, the Lord leads its people by the laws and principles of that religion. Further, the Lord makes sure that in every religion there are laws like those of the Ten Commandments, stating that we are to worship God, not to profane his name, to observe holy days, to honor our parents, not to murder, not to commit adultery, not to steal, and not to commit perjury. Any people that regards these laws as divine and lives by them because of its religion is saved, as stated in §253 above. Most of the peoples remote from Christianity regard these not as civil laws but as divine laws and keep them sacred. In *Teachings about Life for the New Jerusalem Drawn from the Ten Commandments*,[227] from beginning to end, it shows that we are saved by living according to these laws.

[3] Another of heaven's secrets is that in the Lord's sight the angelic heaven looks like a single person whose soul and life is the Lord, and that the form of this divine person is human in every respect, not only as to its outer members and organs but also as to its inner members and organs, which are abundant, and even as to its skin, membranes, cartilage, and bones. In this person, though, all these components are not material but spiritual; and the Lord has arranged that even people

whom the Gospel has not reached, people who simply have some religion, can have a place in that divine person who is heaven. They can make up the parts we call skin, membranes, cartilage, and bones, and they are as full of heavenly joy as anyone else. It makes no difference whether their joy is like that of angels in the highest heaven or like that of angels in the lowest heaven, since all the people who get to heaven attain the highest joy of their hearts. They could not bear anything higher or they would suffocate.

[4] It is like a farmer and a king. A farmer can have his highest joy when he is dressed in new clothes of plain wool and sits down at a table where there is some pork, a joint of beef, some cheese, and some beer and mulled wine. He would be profoundly uncomfortable if he were dressed up like a king in purple, silk, gold, and silver and confronted with a table where there was a feast of all kinds of rich delicacies and fine wine. We can see, then, that there is heavenly happiness for the last as well as for the first, all on their own level. So there is happiness for people outside Christendom, if they simply abstain from evils as sins against God because evils are against their religion.228

[5] There are a few people who know nothing whatever about God. You may see in *Teachings for the New Jerusalem on Sacred Scripture* 116 that if they have lived moral lives, after death they are taught by angels and accept something spiritual in their moral life. Much the same is true of people who worship the sun and the moon and believe that God is there. That is all they know, so it is not charged to them as a sin. After all, the Lord says "If you were blind," that is, if you did not know, "then you would have no sin" (John 9:41).

There are many people, though, who worship images and statues, even in the Christian world. This really is idolatry, but not for all of them. For some, the statues serve to awaken thoughts of God. It is from an inflow from heaven that people who believe in God want to see God; and since some of them cannot raise their minds above the sensory level the way deeper, spiritual people can, they awaken their thought with a statue or image. If people who do this are not worshiping the statue as God, and if they live by the laws of the Ten Commandments for religious reasons, they are saved. [6] We can see from this that because the Lord wants to save everyone, he makes sure that all of us can have our places in heaven if we live well.

Heaven is like a single person in the Lord's sight, and therefore heaven corresponds to the human overall and in every detail, with people there who are equivalent to our skin, membranes, cartilages, and bones:

see *Heaven and Hell* 59–102 (published in London in 1758) and *Secrets of Heaven* 5552–5564 *[5552–5569]*, as well as §§201–204 above.

255   2. *Strict materialists justify their rejection of divine providence when they see that Islam has been accepted by so many empires and nations.* The fact that this religion has been accepted by more nations than Christianity can be a real problem for people who give thought to divine providence and also believe that we cannot be saved unless we have been born Christian, born, that is, where the Word is and people therefore know about the Lord. Islam presents no problem, though, to people who believe that divine providence is over everything. They try to discern where it is, and they find it. It is because of divine providence that Islam recognizes the Lord as the Son of God, the wisest of mortals, and a supreme prophet, one who came into the world to teach us. Most of them regard him as greater than Muhammad.[229]

[2] To make it abundantly clear that this religion was prompted by the Lord's divine providence in order to eliminate the idolatrous practices of many nations, I need to lay things out in sequence, so I shall start with the origins of idolatry.

Before Islam, the worship of idols was widespread over the whole world. This was because the churches that existed before the Lord's coming were "symbolic churches." The Israelite church was like this, with its tabernacle, Aaron's garments, its sacrifices, all the furnishings of the temple in Jerusalem, and its laws. All of these were symbolic. Further, for our early ancestors the knowledge of correspondential relationships, which are also symbolic, was the essential knowledge of the sages. It was especially developed in Egypt, and was the basis of their hieroglyphs. On the basis of this knowledge they understood the meaning of all kinds of animals and all kinds of trees, as well as the meaning of mountains, hills, rivers, and springs, of the sun, the moon, and the stars. It was because their worship was symbolic, wholly made up of correspondences, that they conducted their worship on mountains and hills and in groves and gardens. That is why they regarded springs as holy and turned their faces toward the sun in reverence to God. Particularly, it is why they made statues of horses, cattle, calves, and sheep, even of birds, fish, and snakes, and set them up in their houses and elsewhere in patterns that embodied the spiritual characteristics of the church that they reflected or symbolized. They put similar images in their temples to call to their minds the holy things that they symbolized.

[3] In later times, when the knowledge of correspondential relationships had been forgotten, their descendants began to worship the images

as holy in and of themselves. They did not realize that their ancestors had not seen anything holy about them, but saw them simply as symbolizing and therefore pointing to something holy by virtue of their correspondence. This was how the idolatry started that was to fill the whole world, including Asia, its surrounding islands,[230] Africa, and Europe.

In order to uproot all these idolatrous practices, under the auspices of divine providence a new religion developed[231] that was appropriate to the character of people of the Near East. In this religion there would be material from both Testaments of the Word to teach that the Lord had come into the world and that he was the greatest prophet, the wisest of all, and the son of God. The agent of this was Muhammad, which is why the religion is called Muhammadanism.[232]

[4] This religion, which as just noted was suited to the character of the people of the Near East, was awakened under the Lord's divine providence in order to counter the idolatrous beliefs of so many people and to give them some awareness of the Lord before they entered the spiritual world. This religion would not have been accepted by all these nations, it would not have been able to uproot their idolatrous practices, unless it had been made concordant with and suitable to the mental concepts and the lives of all these people.

The reason they did not recognize the Lord as the God of heaven and earth was that the people of the Near East believed in God as the Creator of the universe and could not grasp the idea that he had come into the world and taken on a human nature. Actually, Christians cannot grasp this either, so in thought they separate his divine nature from his human nature, associate divinity with the Father in heaven, and do not know what to do with the humanity.

[5] We can see from this that Islam too was started under the guidance of the Lord's divine providence and that all its adherents who believe in the Lord as the Son of God and live by the laws of the Ten Commandments (which they also have) by abstaining from evils as sins, come into a heaven called the Islamic heaven. This heaven is divided into three heavens, the highest, the intermediate, and the lowest. Muslims who believe that the Lord is one with the Father and is the only God come into the highest; people who give up polygamy and live with one wife come into the second; and people who are starting on this path come into the first.

There is more on this in my *Supplements on the Last Judgment and the Spiritual World* 68–72, where Muslims and Muhammad are discussed.

3. *Strict materialists justify their rejection of divine providence when they see that Christianity is restricted to that smaller part of the inhabited world*

256

that we call Europe, and even there is divided. The reason Christianity is found only in that smaller part of the habitable world called Europe is that it is not suited to the character of people of the Middle East the way Islam is, Islam being a kind of compound religion, as already noted [§255]. Any religion that is not suitable is not accepted. For example, a religion that prohibits marrying more than one wife will not be accepted but rejected by people who have been polygamists for centuries; and the same principle applies to other practices mandated by Christianity.

[2] It does not matter whether a larger or a smaller part of the world accepts a religion as long as there are people who have the Word, since there is still light from them to people who are outside the church and do not have the Word. This has been explained in *Teachings for the New Jerusalem on Sacred Scripture* 104–113. Strange as it may seem, wherever the Word is read reverently and the Lord is worshiped because of the Word, the Lord is present along with heaven. This is because the Lord is the Word, and the Word is that divine truth that makes heaven what it is. This is why the Lord says, "Wherever two or three are gathered in my name, I am there in their midst" (Matthew 18:20). This can be done with the Word by Europeans, then, in many places in the habitable world, because Europeans are in business all around the world and are either reading the Word or teaching from it everywhere. It may seem as though I am making this up, but it is true.

[3] The reason Christianity is divided is that it is based on the Word, and the Word is composed entirely of correspondential imagery. For the most part, these images are semblances of truth that contain hidden genuine truth. Since the church must necessarily derive its teaching from the literal meaning of the Word, and that meaning is of this nature, it is inevitable that there should be quarrels and arguments and dissent in the church especially about the interpretation of the Word, though not about the Word itself or the divine nature of the Lord himself. It is universally believed that the Word is holy and that the Lord is divine, and these two beliefs are essential features of the church. This means that people who deny the Lord's divine nature, the ones called Socinians, are excommunicated by the church, while people who deny the holiness of the Word are not even considered Christians.

I may add at this point something striking about the Word, something that points to the conclusion that inwardly the Word is divine truth itself, and that at its very heart it is the Lord. [4] When spirits open the Word and rub it against their face or clothing, then simply from this touch their faces or clothing glow as brightly as the moon or a star.

Everyone they meet can see this. This is a witness to the fact that nothing in the world is more holy than the Word.

On the Word being composed entirely of correspondential imagery, see *Teachings for the New Jerusalem on Sacred Scripture* 5–26; on the need to draw and corroborate the teaching of the church from the literal meaning of the Word, see §§50–61 of that work; on the fact that it is possible to get heresies from the literal meaning of the Word but harmful to validate them, see §§91–97; and on the church being derived from the Word, with its quality determined by its understanding of the Word, see §§76–79.

4. *Strict materialists justify their rejection of divine providence by observing that in many nations where Christianity is accepted, there are people who claim divine power for themselves and want to be worshiped as gods and who call upon the dead.* They[233] do actually say that they are not claiming divine power and wanting[234] to be worshiped as gods, but they still say that they can open and close heaven, forgive or bind sins, and essentially save or damn people, and this is strictly divine doing. The only goal of divine providence is our reformation and salvation. This is what it is constantly working for with each one of us. Salvation comes only through belief in the divine nature of the Lord and a trust that he saves us when we live by his commandments. [2] Can anyone fail to see that this is the Babylon described in the Book of Revelation[235] and the Babel that we find throughout the prophets? We can see that it is the Lucifer[236] of Isaiah 14 if we read verses 4 and 22 of that chapter. It says in verse 4, "You will proclaim this parable about the king of Babel," and goes on to say, "I will cut down the name and remainder of Babel" in verse 22. This makes it very clear that "Babel" there is "Lucifer" when it says, "How have you fallen from heaven, Lucifer, child of the dawn. And you said in your heart, 'I will scale the heavens, I will raise my throne above the stars of God and sit on the mountain of the meeting in the northern regions; I will rise above the heights of the clouds, I will be like the Most High'" (verses 12, 13, 14).

It is widely recognized that they call upon the dead and pray for their help. We refer to this as invocation because the practice was established by the Papal Bull that confirmed the decisions of the Council of Trent, where it states explicitly that they are to be invoked.[237] Is anyone unaware that we should pray only to God and not to any dead mortal?

[3] Now, though, I need to explain why the Lord let things like this happen. There is no denying that it was for the sake of the goal, our salvation. We know that there is no salvation apart from the Lord;

257

and because this is true, it was vital that the Lord be preached from the Word and that the Christian church be established by this means. This called for leaders who would do this with passion, and the only ones available were people who would preach with the kind of flaming passion that comes from self-love. It was primarily this fire that roused them to proclaim the Lord and preach the Word. It is because their initial state was like this that Lucifer is called "the child of the dawn" in verse 12.

However, once they realized that they could use the holy nature of the Word and the church to gain power, the self-love that had at first roused them to proclaim the Lord broke loose from within and eventually rose to such a height that they transferred all of the Lord's divine power to themselves, leaving nothing unclaimed. [4] This could not be prevented by the Lord's divine providence, because if it had been, they would have preached that the Lord was not God and that the Word was not holy, and would have become Socinians or Arians, thereby destroying the whole church. The church, though, despite the quality of its leadership, did survive among its subject people. All the people of that religion who turn to the Lord and abstain from evils as sins are saved; so they make up many heavenly communities in the spiritual world. It has also been provided that one of these nations should not accept the yoke of this kind of control, because they regarded the Word as holy. These noble people are the French.[238]

But what has happened? [5] When self-love has promoted its power all the way to the Lord's throne, has removed him from it and set itself there, then the only thing that can happen is that the other love, the Lucifer, will profane everything that has to do with the Word and the church. To prevent this, the Lord in his divine providence made sure that they would distance themselves from worship of him; invoke the dead by praying to their statues, kissing their bones, and kneeling at their tombs; prohibit the reading of the Word; ascribe holiness to a Mass that ordinary people do not understand; and sell salvation for cash. They were allowed to do this because otherwise they would have profaned the holy nature of the Word and the church. As explained in the preceding section, we cannot profane what is holy unless we know about it.

[6] To prevent the profanation of the Most Holy Supper, it has happened under the Lord's divine providence that they have divided it. They give the bread to the congregation and drink the wine themselves. The wine in the Holy Supper means what is holy and true, while the bread means what is holy and good. When they are separated, the wine means

truth profaned and the bread means what is good adulterated. Particularly, they have made the Supper physical and material and focused on it as the primary feature of religion.

Anyone who looks closely at these individual items and weighs them in some mental enlightenment can see the marvelous workings of divine providence in protecting what is holy in the church and in saving everyone who can be saved, virtually snatching from the flames everyone who is willing to be rescued.

5. *Strict materialists justify their rejection of divine providence when they see that there are some professing Christians who place salvation in particular words that they think about and say, and attach no value to the good things that they do.*[239] I have explained in *Teachings for the New Jerusalem on Faith* that this is what people are like who make nothing but faith the basis of salvation, not a caring life, and especially who separate faith from charity. I also noted there [§§44–68] that these people are meant in the Word by the Philistines, the dragon, and goats.

[2] The reason a teaching like this is permitted under divine providence is to prevent the profanation of the divine nature of the Lord and the holy nature of the Word. The Lord's divine nature is not profaned when salvation is thought to consist of saying, "May God the Father have mercy for the sake of his Son who suffered the cross and made satisfaction for us," because this is addressing not the divine nature of the Lord but his human nature, without believing that it is divine. There is no profanation of the Word, either, because no attention is paid to the passages that speak of love, caring, doing, and works. They say that all of these are included in their statement of faith. People who advocate this belief say to themselves, "Since the law does not condemn me, neither does evil; and since any good that I myself do is not good, that does not save me." So they are like people who do not know anything true from the Word, which means that they cannot profane it.

However, the only people who really advocate this belief are the ones who are caught up in pride in their own intellect because of their self-love. At heart, they are not even Christians, though they want to appear to be.

I need now to explain that the Lord's divine providence is constantly at work to save people for whom faith separated from charity has become a theological principle. [3] Under the Lord's divine providence, even though this kind of faith has become a theological tenet, everyone knows that this kind of faith does not bring salvation. Salvation requires a caring life in which faith participates. All the churches where this theology is accepted teach that there is no salvation unless we examine ourselves, see our sins, admit them, repent, and refrain from the sins and begin a new life. This is the urgent preface read to all who come to the Holy Supper, together with the statement that unless they do so, they mingle the sacred and the profane and consign themselves to eternal damnation. In England they even say that unless they do so the devil will enter into them as he did into Judas and destroy them, soul and body alike. We can see from this that everyone in churches where faith alone is accepted is still taught that we should abstain from evils as sins.

[4] Not only that, everyone who is born Christian knows that we are to abstain from evils as sins, because the Ten Commandments are placed in the hand of every boy and every girl and taught them by their parents and teachers. Further, all the citizens of the realm, especially commoners, are questioned by priests as to their knowledge of Christian theology solely on the basis of their recitation of the Ten Commandments from memory and warned that they should do what the Commandments say. At such times, the religious authority never tells them that they are not under the yoke of this law[240] or that they cannot obey it because they cannot do anything good on their own.

The Athanasian Creed is accepted throughout Christendom, and people believe what it says at the end, that the Lord is going to come to judge the living and the dead and that then those who have done what is good will enter into eternal life and those who have done what is evil will enter into eternal fire.[241]

[5] In Sweden, where a theology of faith alone is accepted, it is clearly taught that there is no such thing as faith separated from charity or from good actions. We find this in an "Added Reminder" inserted in all Psalters under the title "Obotfertigas foerhinder," or "Obstacles or Obstructions to the Impenitent." It says there, "People who are rich in good actions thereby show that they are rich in faith, because when faith is a saving faith, it works through charity. There is no faith that justifies us by itself, apart from good actions, just as there is no good tree without good fruit, no sun without light and warmth, no water without moisture."

[6] I include these few things to show that even though a theology of faith alone may be accepted, the good effects of our caring are taught everywhere—that is, good actions. This happens under the Lord's divine providence so that the common people will not be led astray by this faith.

I have heard Luther (having talked with him several times in the spiritual world) totally disclaiming faith alone. He has said that when he decreed faith alone, an angel of the Lord warned him not to. However, he thought to himself that if he did not reject works,[242] there could be no separation from Catholic theology, so in spite of the warning he insisted on it.

6. *Strict materialists justify their rejection of divine providence by noting* **259** *that there have been many heresies in Christendom and that there still are— those of the Quakers, for example, and the Moravians and the Anabaptists, among many others.* The thought may occur that if divine providence were over every least detail and did have as its goal the salvation of everyone, it would have made sure that there was one true religion throughout the whole world, one religion undivided, and certainly not torn apart by heresies. Use your reason, though, and think as deeply as you can. Can we be saved if we are not first reformed? After all, we are born immersed in love for ourselves and the world; and since these loves have within themselves no trace of love for God or love for our neighbor except for selfish reasons, we are also born involved in all kinds of evil. What trace of love or mercy is there in these loves? Does it matter to them if we cheat others, or slander them, or harbor murderous hatred toward them, or seduce their spouses, or torture them in order to get even? Our basic agenda is to be the greatest of all and to take possession of everyone's wealth. This means that we see others as insignificant in comparison to ourselves, as worthless. Can people like this be saved? First they need to be led out of their evils and thereby reformed. I have already offered abundant evidence that that this can be done only within the limits of the many laws of divine providence.[243] For the most part, these laws are unknown even though they are matters of divine love and divine wisdom alike, laws the Lord cannot violate because to do so would be to destroy us rather than to save us. [2] Review the laws already presented and compare them, and you will see.

Consider, then, that according to these laws there can be no inflow directly from heaven, only indirectly through the Word, through teaching, and through sermons. Add the fact that in order to be divine the Word had to be composed entirely of correspondential imagery. It then follows that disagreements and heresies are inevitable. Permitting them is quite within the laws of divine providence. Not only that, once the church itself has taken matters of intellect alone to be essential to it— matters of belief, that is, and not matters of volition and therefore of life—and once these matters of life are not essential to the church, then our discernment leads us into utter darkness. We wander around like blind people, bumping into everything and falling into pits. It is our volition that must see in our discernment and not our discernment in our volition, which is the same as saying that our life and its love must lead our discernment to think, speak, and act, and not the reverse. If it were the other way around, then a discernment motivated by evil love, actually by diabolical love, would seize on anything our senses offered and demand that our volition do it. This shows where dissent and heresy come from.

[3] However, provision is still made that all of us can be reformed and saved no matter what heresy we may adopt intellectually, as long as we abstain from evils as sins and do not justify our heretical distortions. This is because our volition is reformed by our abstaining from evils as sins, and through our volition our discernment is reformed. Then for the first time it emerges from darkness into light.

There are three essential principles of the church: belief in the divine nature of the Lord, belief in the holiness of the Word, and the life that we call "charity." For each of us, our faith is determined by that life that is charity; our recognition of what that life must be comes from the Word, and reformation and salvation come from the Lord.

If these three principles had functioned as the essential principles of the church, then intellectual dissent would not have divided it. It would only have varied it the way light varies the colors of beautiful things, and the way different gems make up the beauty of a royal crown.

260   7. *Strict materialists justify their rejection of divine providence when they see the continued survival of Judaism.* They observe that after all these centuries the Jews have still not been converted even though they live among Christians, and that in keeping with the prophecies in the Word they do not confess the Lord and recognize him as the Messiah who, in their minds, will lead them back into the land of Canaan. They remain steadfast in their denial, and yet they prosper. However, people who think along these lines and therefore raise doubts about divine providence are not aware that "the Jews" in the Word means all the people who are part of the church and believe in the Lord, and that "the land of Canaan" where it promises to lead them means the Lord's church.

[2] The reason they are steadfast in their denial of the Lord is that given their own nature, if they were to accept and believe in the Lord's divine nature and the holy attributes of the church, they would profane them. This is why the Lord said of them, "He[244] has blinded their eyes and hardened their heart so that they will not see with their eyes

or understand with their heart and turn, and I heal them" (John 12:42 *[12:40]*; Matthew 13:14; Mark 4:12; Luke 8:10; Isaiah 6:9, 10). It says "so that they will not turn, and I heal them," because if they did turn and were healed, they would commit profanation, and the law of divine providence given in §§221–233 above is that the Lord does not grant us deeper access to the truths that our faith discloses and the good effects of our caring except as we can be kept in them to the end of our life; and if we were granted access, we would profane these holy things.

[3] The reason that the Jewish people has been cared for and spread around much of the world is for the sake of the Word in its original tongue.[245] They revere this more than Christians do; and the Lord's divine nature is present there in every detail. It is actually divine truth united to divine good, emanating from the Lord. As a result, the Word is a union of the Lord and the church and a presence of heaven, as explained in *Teachings for the New Jerusalem on Sacred Scripture* 62–69. The presence of the Lord and heaven takes place wherever the Word is read reverently. This is the purpose of divine providence for which the Jews are maintained and spread over much of the world.

For their lot after death, see *Supplements on the Last Judgment and the Spiritual World* 79–82.

That covers the instances listed in §238 that strict materialists use or may use to justify their rejection of divine providence. Next we turn to the ones listed in §239. These too may serve materialists as arguments against divine providence; and they may cross other minds as well and raise doubts. They are the following.   **261**

1. *Doubts about divine providence may be raised by the fact that all Christendom worships one God in three persons, which is really three gods. Up to the present time they have not realized that God is one in person and in essence, containing a trinity, and that this God is the Lord.* Anyone who thinks rationally about divine providence may say, "Are not three persons three gods when each person by itself is God?" Can anyone think anything else? Does anyone think anything else? Athanasius himself could not think anything else, so the Creed that bears his name says, "Although Christian truth requires us to acknowledge each individual Person as God and Lord, still Christian faith forbids us from saying or naming three gods or three Lords." This can only mean that we are supposed to believe in three gods and Lords but that we must not say or name three gods and three Lords.   **262**

[2] Is there any way we can see one God unless that God is one person as well? Someone may suggest that we can see this if we think that the three have a single essence; but does anyone, can anyone see this as saying any more than that they are of one mind, that they agree? There are still three gods.

If we think more deeply, we ask ourselves how a divine essence that is infinite can be divided, and how it can beget another divine essence from eternity and then bring forth another that emanates from both of them.

If someone says that we are to believe it but not think about it, can we really help thinking about what we are supposed to believe? What else is the basis of that acknowledgment that is faith in its essence? Is not thinking about God and about the three Persons the source for Socinianism and Arianism, which are uppermost in more hearts than you might believe? What really makes the church is a faith in one God and that this one God is the Lord. The divine trinity is within that God. This you may find presented in *Teachings for the New Jerusalem on the Lord,* from beginning to end.

[3] But what do people think about the Lord these days? Do they not think that he is God and Human, God from Jehovah the Father who begot him, and Human from the virgin Mary who bore him? Does anyone think that the God and the Human in him, his divine nature and his human nature, are one person, and that they are actually just as "one" as soul and body are one? Is anyone aware of this? Ask the church's learned theologians and they will tell you that they do not know this. Yet it is part of the theology of the church accepted throughout Christendom, as follows: "Our Lord Jesus Christ, the Son of God, is God and Human; and even though he is God and Human, still there are not two but one Christ. There is one because the Divinity took a human nature to itself, so it is absolutely one. There is a single Person because just as soul and body make a single human, so God and Human make a single Christ." This is from the Athanasian Faith or Creed.

The reason people do not know what the Creed is saying is that when they have read it they have been thinking about the Lord not as God but only as human.

[4] If you ask them whether they know how he was conceived, whether it was by God the Father or by his own divine nature, they will answer that it was by God the Father. This is what the Bible says. Are he and the Father not one the way soul and body are one? Can anyone think that he was conceived by two deities? And if he was conceived by his own divine nature, then he would be his own father.

If you then go on to ask, "What is your concept of the Lord's divine nature and of his human nature?" they will tell you that his divine nature came from the essence of the Father, that his human nature came from the essence of his mother, and that his divine nature is with the Father. Then if you ask, "And where is his human nature?" they will have no answer for you. In their concept, they have separated his divine nature and his human nature, making the divine equal to the divine nature of the Father and his human nature like that of any other human. They do not realize that this is separating the soul from the body; and they do not see the contradiction involved, that this would have his rational self born from his mother alone.

[5] This ingrained concept that the Lord's human nature was like that of any other human has made it almost impossible for a Christian to be induced to think about a *Divine Human* nature, even given the statement that his soul or life from conception was and is Jehovah himself.

Organize your propositions now and think hard. Is there any God of the universe other than the Lord alone, in whom is that essential, originating divine nature called the Father, the divine human nature called the Son, and the emanating divine nature called the Holy Spirit? This makes God one in person and in essence, and this God is the Lord.

[6] If you insist on saying that the Lord himself named the three in Matthew—"Go out and make disciples of all nations, baptizing them in the name of the Father, the Son, and the Holy Spirit" (Matthew 28:19)—he said this in order to let them know that now that he was glorified the Trinity was within him, as we can see from the verses immediately before and after this command. In the verse just before he says that he has been given all power in heaven and on earth, and in the verse just after he says that he will be with them even to the close of the age. So he is talking about himself alone, and not about some trio.

[7] But let us return to divine providence, to why Christians have been allowed to worship one God in three persons—that is, three gods—and why it has not yet been known that God is one in person and in essence, containing a trinity, and that this God is the Lord. We are responsible for this situation, not the Lord. The Lord teaches these things clearly in the Word, as you can tell from all the passages collected in *Teachings for the New Jerusalem on the Lord*.[246] Further, the theology of all churches teaches that his divine and his human natures are not two but one person, united like soul and body. But the church has separated the divine from the human and equates the divine nature with the divine nature of Jehovah the Father and the human nature with that of anyone

else. [8] The church has done this primarily because from the start it has strayed into a Babylon that has transferred divine power to itself.[247] In order to call it human power rather than divine power, though, they have made the Lord's human nature like that of anyone else. Then later, at the Reformation, when faith alone was accepted as the sole means of salvation ("faith alone" meaning that God the Father should have mercy on us for the sake of the Son), there was no other way to view the Lord's human nature. This was because we cannot approach the Lord and in full sincerity recognize him as the God of heaven and earth unless we are living by his commandments. In the spiritual world, where we are all constrained to say exactly what we think, people cannot even say the name "Jesus" unless they have lived Christian lives on earth. This is under his divine providence, to prevent the profanation of his name.

263   For a clearer view of all this, I may add some material presented at the close (§§60–61) of *Teachings for the New Jerusalem on the Lord,* as follows.[248]

It is quite clear from many things that the Lord said that God and Human in him are not two but are one, as the theology says, and are completely one, like soul and body. He said, for example, that the Father and he are one [John 10:30], that whatever belongs to the Father is his and that whatever belongs to him is the Father's [John 16:15], that he is in the Father and the Father in him [John 14:10], that everything has been given into his hand [John 3:35], that he has all power [Matthew 28:18], that he is God of heaven and earth,[249] that everyone who believes in him has eternal life [John 3:15], and that the wrath of God rests on everyone who does not believe in him.[250] He says further that both the divine and the human have been raised up into heaven,[251] and in regard to both he is sitting at the right hand of God (that is, he is omnipotent),[252] and more passages from the Word about his divine human nature that have already been cited in abundance. All of this material bears witness to the fact that God is one in both person and essence, containing a trinity, and that this God is the Lord.

[2] The reason this information about the Lord is only now being made public is that it was foretold in chapters 21 and 22 of the Book of Revelation that a new church would be established at the close of the former one, a church in which this would be fundamental. This church is what "the New Jerusalem" means in those chapters, where no one will enter except those who recognize the Lord as the God of heaven and earth, which is why that church is called "the Lamb's bride."[253]

I am able to proclaim that the whole heaven believes in the Lord alone and that anyone who does not believe this is not allowed into heaven. Heaven is heaven because of the Lord. It is this belief, held in love and in faith, that puts us in the Lord and the Lord in us, as he tells us in John: "In that day you will know that I am in my Father, and you in me, and I in you" (John 14:20); and "Abide in me, and I in you. I am the vine, you are the branches; all who abide in me, and I in them, bear abundant fruit, for without me you cannot do anything. Whoever does not abide in me is cast out" (John 15:4, 5, 6; 17:22, 23).

[3] The reason this has not been seen in the Word before is that if it had been seen any earlier it would not have been accepted. The last judgment had not yet been completed; and until that happened, hell was stronger than heaven. We are in the middle, between heaven and hell; so if we had seen this any earlier, the devil—hell, that is—would have snatched it from our hearts and would have profaned it as well.

This state of hell's power was shattered by the Last Judgment, which has now been completed. Once that was done, in other words now, anyone who wants to be enlightened and wise can be.

2. *Doubts about divine providence may be raised by the fact that until now people have not known that there is spiritual meaning in the details of the Word and that this is the basis of its holiness.* It may raise doubts about divine providence when people ask, "Why is this only being revealed now? And why is it happening through this particular individual, and not through some prominent clergyman?" Whether it is some prominent clergyman or some prominent clergyman's servant, though, is up to the Lord. He knows the nature of each.

There are two reasons, though, that this meaning of the Word has not been revealed earlier. The first is that if it had been revealed earlier, the church would have profaned it, and in so doing would have profaned the very holiness of the Word; and the second is that the genuine truths that constitute the Word's spiritual meaning could not be revealed until the Last Judgment had been completed and the new church meant by the Holy Jerusalem was being founded by the Lord. But let us look at these separately.

[2] (a) *The Word's spiritual meaning was not revealed earlier because if it had been, the church would have profaned it, and in so doing would have profaned the very holiness of the Word.* Not long after the church was begun it turned into a Babylon, and later it turned into a Philistia.[254]

Babylon does actually recognize the Word, but it looks down on it. They[255] say that the Holy Spirit gives just as much inspiration to the members of its supreme council as it did to the prophets. They recognize the Word because the papacy was founded on the Lord's words to Peter,[256] but they still look down on it because it does not agree with them. That is why they have taken it away from the people and hidden it in monasteries, where there are few who actually read it. So if the spiritual meaning had been revealed, where the Lord and all angelic wisdom are present, they would have profaned the Word not only as it is in its outermost form, in what we find in the literal meaning, but in its deepest meanings as well.

[3] Philistia too (meaning faith separated from charity) would have profaned the Word's spiritual meaning, because as already noted [§258] it puts salvation in some words that we are to think about and say and not in good deeds that we are to do. So it attributes the power to save to something that has no such power. Particularly, it creates a gap between our intelligence and what we are to believe. For people like this, what becomes of the light that the spiritual meaning of the Word is in? Does it not turn into darkness? And when the outer meaning is turned into darkness, what else can happen to the spiritual meaning? Does anyone who has decided on faith separated from charity and on justification by that kind of faith want to know what a good life really is, what love for the Lord and our neighbor are, what caring and its good effects are, what good actions are, what "doing" is—actually what faith is in its essence, or any of the real truth that constitutes it? Such people write volumes, and all they do is prove what they call faith, claiming that all the things I have just listed are inherent in that faith.

We can see from this that if spiritual meaning had been disclosed earlier, it would have turned out as described by the Lord's words in Matthew, "If your eye had been evil, your whole body would have been full of darkness. So if the light that is in you is darkness, what a darkness!" (Matthew 6:23). In the Word's spiritual meaning, "the eye" means our discernment.

[4] (b) *The genuine truths that constitute the Word's spiritual meaning could not be revealed by the Lord until the Last Judgment had been completed and the new church meant by the Holy Jerusalem was being founded by the Lord.* The Lord foretold in the Book of Revelation that after the Last Judgment had been completed genuine truths would be disclosed, a new church would be begun, and spiritual meaning would be disclosed. On the completion of the Last Judgment, see what is presented in the

booklet *Last Judgment* and in its supplement.²⁵⁷ This is the meaning of the heaven and earth that will pass away (Revelation 21:1). The disclosure of genuine truths is foretold by these words in the Book of Revelation, "The one sitting on the throne said, 'Look! I am making all things new!'" (Revelation 21:5). See also Revelation 19:17, 18; 21:18–21; and 22:1, 2. On the need for a revelation of the Word's spiritual meaning, see Revelation 19:11–16. This is the meaning of the white horse on which was seated the one called "The Word of God," the Lord of Lords and King of Kings. On this, see the booklet on *The White Horse*.²⁵⁸ On the holy Jerusalem meaning a new church that the Lord would begin, see *Teachings for the New Jerusalem on the Lord* 62–65, where this is explained.

[5] We can see, then, that the Word's spiritual meaning was to be revealed for a new church that would recognize and worship the Lord alone and would keep his Word holy, loving divine truths and rejecting any faith that is separated from charity. There is more about this meaning of the Word, though, in *Teachings for the New Jerusalem on Sacred Scripture* 5–26 and following. There the nature of the spiritual meaning is discussed in §§5–26. Its presence throughout the Word and in every detail is discussed in §§9–17; the spiritual meaning as the reason that the Word is divinely inspired and holy in every word, in §§18–19; why the spiritual meaning has as yet been unknown and was not revealed earlier, in §§20–25; and the granting of the spiritual meaning, from now on, only to people who have genuine truths from the Lord, in §26.

[6] We can therefore tell that it is under the Lord's divine providence that the spiritual meaning has been hidden from the world until this present age, and has been kept safe in the meanwhile among angels, who draw their wisdom from it. This meaning was known and cherished by the people of very ancient times, the ones who lived before Moses; but since their descendants took the correspondential relationships that were the sole basis of their Word and therefore of their religion and diverted them to various forms of idolatry (and to magic in Egypt), that meaning was closed off under the Lord's divine providence, first among Israelites and later among Christians, for the reasons just given. Only now is it being opened for the Lord's new church.

3. *Doubt about divine providence may be raised by observing the igno-*
rance of the fact that the essence of the Christian religion is to abstain from evils as sins. I have explained in *Teachings about Life for the New Jerusalem,* from beginning to end, that this is the essence of the Christian religion; and since a faith divorced from charity does nothing but prevent it from being accepted, that topic was dealt with as well. We can say that people

have not known that abstaining from evils as sins is the essence of the Christian religion, because hardly anyone does know, and yet everyone does know, really (see §258 above). The reason hardly anyone knows, still, is that faith separated [from charity] has blotted it out. This theology claims that faith alone is what saves us, not any good work or goodness effected by our caring. It claims that we are no longer under the yoke of the law[259] but are in freedom. People who keep hearing this stop thinking about any evil life they may be leading or any good life. We are all inclined by nature to embrace this belief; and once we have done so, we no longer think about the state of our lives. This is the reason for our ignorance.

[2] I have been shown this ignorance in the spiritual world. I have asked more than a thousand newcomers from our world whether they knew that abstaining from evils as sins was the essence of religion, and they have told me that they did not, that this was something new that they were hearing for the first time. They had heard, though, that they could do nothing good on their own and that they were not under the yoke of the law. When I have asked whether they knew that they should examine themselves, see their sins, repent, and then begin a new life, and that otherwise their sins were not forgiven, and that if their sins were not forgiven they would not be saved, noting that they had been told this loud and clear every time they came to the Holy Supper, they have answered that they had not noticed this. All they had really heard was that they were being granted forgiveness of sins through the sacrament of the Supper and that their faith would take care of everything else without their knowing about it.

[3] I have said repeatedly, "Why have you taught your children the Ten Commandments, if it is not so that they would know which evils are the sins that they should abstain from? Is it just that they should know this and believe it, and not do anything about it? So why are you telling me that this is something new?" The only answer they have had is that they knew but did not know. They never thought about the sixth commandment when they were committing adultery or about the seventh when they were engaged in surreptitious theft or fraud, and so on, let alone about the fact that such actions are against divine law and therefore against God.

[4] When I have recited any number of statements from the teachings of the church, along with their scriptural basis, statements that abstaining and turning from evils as sins is the essence of the Christian religion and that our faith depends on the extent to which we have abstained and turned from them, they have been silent. The truth of the matter was proved to them, however, when they saw that they were all

being examined in terms of their lives and judged by what they had done, no one being judged by a faith separated from life, because in all cases their faith depended on their life.

[5] It is under a law of divine providence that Christendom is so largely ignorant of this. We are all left to act in freedom and rationally (see above, §§71–99 and 100–128). The law also applies that no one is taught directly from heaven but indirectly through the Word and through teaching and preaching from it (see §§154–174). This ignorance is also under all the laws of permission, which are also laws of divine providence. There is more on these in §258 above.

4. *Doubts about divine providence may be raised by observing the widespread ignorance of the fact that we go on living as individuals after death, and also observing that this has not been disclosed before.* The reason for this ignorance is that deep inside everyone who does not abstain from evils as sins there is a secret belief that we do not go on living after death and that therefore it does not matter whether you say that we go right on living after death or that we are resurrected on the day of the Last Judgment. If some belief in resurrection does occur, people say to themselves, "I am no worse than anyone else. Whether I go to hell or to heaven, I will have plenty of company."

But everyone who has any religion at all has an instinctive realization that we do live as individuals after death. The belief that we live as souls and not as individuals is not held by any people except those who have been deluded by their own intelligence. The following observations show that everyone who has any religion at all has this instinctive realization that we live as individuals after death.

    1. Everyone thinks this when dying.

[2] 2. All who deliver eulogies over the dear departed raise them into heaven and describe them as among the angels, as talking with them and sharing their joy. Sometimes these speakers even deify the dead.

[3] 3. The common people all believe that if they have lived well, then when they die they will enter a heavenly paradise and be clothed with white robes and enjoy eternal life.

[4] 4. Clergy all say something like this to the dying; and they believe it while they are saying it—unless they happen to be thinking about the Last Judgment.

[5] 5. All believe that their [deceased] children are in heaven and that after their own death they will see the [deceased] spouse whom they love. No one believes that these dear ones are

274 260

ghosts or, even worse, that they are disembodied minds floating around the universe.

[6] 6. No one raises any objections when something is said about the lot and state of people who have crossed from time to eternal life. I have told any number of people that this was the lot and state of one individual or another and I have never heard anyone reply that their state was nothing at this point and would not be anything until the Last Judgment.

[7] 7. When people see paintings or statues of angels, they believe that this is what they look like. No one thinks then that angels are bodiless spirits or breezes or clouds the way some scholars describe them.

[8] 8. Catholics believe that their saints are real people in heaven and that other people are somewhere else as well. Muslims believe this about their deceased; Africans especially do so; and so do most peoples. How can it be different for Protestants who know this from the Word?

[9] 9. This universal instinctive realization leads some people to strive for deathless fame, so that they translate their instinct into a form that makes them powerful heroes in times of war.

[10] 10. I have asked around in the spiritual world whether everyone has this instinctive realization and have discovered that it is there in the spiritual concepts of everyone's inner thinking, but not in the more material concepts of everyone's outer thinking.

We can tell from this that we need have no doubt about the Lord's divine providence because of the thought that it is only now being disclosed that we live after death. That is only our sensory self talking, the self that wants to see and touch in order to believe. People who cannot think on a higher level than that are in total darkness about the actual state of their lives.

Evils Are Permitted for a Purpose: Salvation

IF we were born loving, as we were when we were created, we would **275** not be prone to any evil. We would not even know what evil is, because if we have not been drawn to evil and therefore are not inclined to evil, there is no way we can know what it is. If we were told that one thing or another was evil, we would not believe that it was possible. This is the state of innocence that Adam and his wife Eve were in; the nakedness that did not embarrass them portrayed that state. Familiarity with evil after the fall is meant by eating from the tree of the knowledge of good and evil.

The love we were created with is a love for our neighbor that makes us as generous with our neighbor as we are with ourselves, and even more so. We find ourselves full of the joy of that love when we do something good for others, very much the way parents feel toward their children.

This love is truly human. There is something spiritual within it that makes it different from the earthly love that the lower animals have. If we were born loving like this, we would not be born into the darkness of ignorance the way all of us are nowadays, but into some light of knowledge and intelligence; and before long we would actually be informed and intelligent. At first we would go on all fours like animals, but would have an inborn urge to walk on our feet, because even though we were on all fours we would not be looking down toward the ground, but forward toward heaven; and we would be straightening up so that we could look upward.

However, when our love for our neighbor turned into love for ourselves and this love grew stronger, then our human love turned into an **276** animal love and we became animals instead of humans. The only difference was that we could think about what our bodies were sensing and tell one thing from another rationally and could be taught and become civic and moral people and eventually spiritual people. That is, as already noted [§275], we do have a spiritual nature that distinguishes us from the lower animals. That nature enables us to learn what is evil and good on the civic level, what is evil and good on the moral level, and even, if we are willing, what is evil and good on the spiritual level.

Once love for our neighbor had changed into love for ourselves, we could no longer be born into the light of knowledge and intelligence but only into the darkness of ignorance. This is because we were born into that lowest level of life that we call sensory and bodily. We are led from there into the deeper functions of our earthly mind by being taught, always with spirituality close at hand. We shall see later[261] why we are born into that lowest level of life that we call sensory and bodily and therefore into the darkness of ignorance.

[2] Everyone can see that love for our neighbor and love for ourselves are opposing loves. Love for our neighbor wants to do good to everyone, while love for ourselves wants everyone to do good to us alone. Love for our neighbor wants to serve everyone, and love for ourselves wants everyone to be our servants. Love for our neighbor sees all people as our family and friends, while love for ourselves sees all people as our slaves, and if people are not subservient, it sees them as our enemies. In short, it focuses on ourselves alone and sees others as scarcely human. At heart it values them no more than our horses and dogs, and since it regards them as basically worthless, it thinks nothing of doing them harm. This leads to hatred and vengeance, adultery and promiscuity, theft and fraud, deceit and slander, brutality and cruelty, and other evils like that. These are the evils to which we are prone from birth.

To explain that they are permitted for the purpose of salvation, I need to proceed in the following sequence.

1. We are all involved in evil and need to be led away from it in order to be reformed.
2. Evils cannot be set aside unless they come to light.
3. To the extent that our evils are set aside, they are forgiven.
4. So evil is permitted for the purpose of salvation.

277a [262]   *1. We are all involved in evil and need to be led away from it in order to be reformed.* It is well known in the church that we all have an inherited evil nature and that this is the source of our obsession with many evils. This is also why we can do nothing good on our own. The only kind of good that evil can do is good with evil within it. The inner evil is the fact that we are doing it for selfish reasons, and solely for the sake of appearances.

We know that we get this inherited evil from our parents. Some do say that it comes from Adam and his wife, but this is wrong. We all get it by birth from our parents, who got it from their parents, who got it from theirs. So it is handed down from one to another, growing greater and stronger, piling up, and being inflicted on the offspring. That is why there is nothing sound within us, why everything in us is so evil. Does anyone feel that there is anything wrong with loving oneself more than others? If not, then who knows what evil is, since this is the head of all evils?

[2] We can see from much that is common knowledge in our world that our heredity comes from our parents, grandparents, and great-grandparents. For example, we can tell what household and larger family and even nation people belong to simply from their faces; the face bears the stamp of the spirit, and the spirit is determined by our desires of love. Sometimes the face of an ancestor crops up in a grandchild or great-grandchild. I can tell simply from their faces whether people are Jewish or not, and I can tell what family group others belong to. I have no doubt that others can do the same.

If our desires of love are derived and passed down from our parents in this way, then it follows that their evils are as well, since these are matters of desire.

I need now to state where this similarity comes from. [3] For all of us, the soul comes from the father and simply puts on a body in the mother.[263] The fact that the soul comes from the father follows not only from what has just been said but also from a number of other indications. One of these is the fact that the baby of a black or Moorish man by a white or European woman will be born black, and the reverse.[264] In particular, the soul dwells in the semen, for this is what brings about impregnation, and this is what the mother clothes with a body. The semen is the elemental form of the father's characteristic love, the form of his dominant love and its immediate derivatives, the deepest desires of that love.

[4] In all of us, these desires are veiled by the decencies of moral life and the virtues that are partly matters of our civic life and partly matters of our spiritual life. These make up the outward form of life even for evil people. We are all born with this outer form of life. That is why little children are so lovable; but as they get older or grow up, they shift from this outer form toward their deeper natures and ultimately to the dominant love of their fathers. If the father was evil, and if this nature is not somehow softened and deflected by teachers, then the child's love becomes just like that of the father.

Still, evil is not uprooted, only set aside, as we shall see below [§279]. We can tell, then, that we are all immersed in evil.

No explanation is necessary to see that we need to be led away from our evils in order to be reformed, since if we are given to evil in this world, we will be given to evil after we leave this world. This means that if our evil is not set aside in this world, it cannot be set aside afterwards. The tree lies where it falls; and so too our life retains its basic quality when we die. We are all judged according to our deeds. It is not that these deeds are tallied up but that we return to them and behave the same. Death is a continuation of life, with the difference that then we cannot be reformed.

All our reformation is thorough—that is, it includes both first things and last things.[265] The last things are reformed in this world in harmony with the first ones. They cannot be reformed afterwards, because the outermost things of our lives that we take with us after death become dormant and simply cooperate or act in unison with the inner ones.

278a [266] 2. *Evils cannot be set aside unless they come to light.* This does not mean that we have to act out our evils in order to bring them to light but that we need to look carefully not only at our actions but also at our thoughts, at what we would do if it were not for our fear of the laws and of ill repute. We need to look especially at which evils we see as permissible in our spirit and do not regard as sins, for eventually we do them.

It is for this self-examination that we have been given discernment, a discernment separate from our volition, so that we can know, discern, and recognize what is good and what is evil. It is also so that we can see what the real nature of our volition is—that is, what we love and what we desire. It is to enable us to see this that our discernment has been given both higher and lower thought processes, both more inward and more outward thought processes. It is so that we can use the higher or more inward thoughts to see what our volition is up to in our lower or outer thoughts. We see this the way we see our face in a mirror; and when we see and recognize what a sin is, then if we want to and ask the Lord for help, we can stop intending it, abstain from it, and later act against it. If we cannot go through this process easily, we can still make it happen by trying to go through it so that finally we reject that evil and detest it. Then for the first time we actually sense and feel that evil is evil and good is good.

This is what it means to examine ourselves, to see and acknowledge our evils, and to confess them and then refrain from them. However, there are so few who know that this is the essence of the Christian religion (because the only people who do so are ones who have charity and faith and are led by the Lord and do what is good in his strength) that I need to say something about the people who do not do this and still think that they are religious. They are (a) people who confess that they are guilty of all sins but do not look for any single sin in themselves; (b) people who for religious reasons do not bother to look; (c) people who for worldly reasons do not think about sins and therefore do not know what they are; (d) people who cherish their sins and therefore cannot know what they are. (e) In all these cases, the sins do not come to light and therefore cannot be set aside. (f) Finally, I need to expose a previously unrecognized reason why evils could not be set aside apart from this examination, this bringing to light, this recognition, this confession, and this resistance.

These items need to be looked at one at a time, though, because they   **278b** are the basic elements of the Christian religion on our part.

(a) *They are people who confess that they are guilty of all sins but do not look for any single sin in themselves.* They say, "I am a sinner! I was born in sins; there is no soundness in me from head to toe! I am nothing but evil! Gracious God, look on me with favor, forgive me, purify me, save me, make me walk in purity, in the way of the righteous," and the like. Yet they do not look into themselves and therefore do not identify any particular evil; and no one who does not identify an evil can abstain from it, let alone fight against it. They think that they are clean and washed after these confessions when in fact they are unclean and unwashed from their heads to the soles of their feet. This blanket confession is nothing but a lullaby that leads finally to blindness. It is like some grand generalization with no details, which is actually nothing.

[2] (b) *They are people who for religious reasons do not bother to look.* These are primarily people who separate charity from faith. They say to themselves, "Why should I ask whether something is evil or good? Why should I ask about evil when it does not damn me? Why should I ask about goodness when it does not save me? It is my faith alone, the faith that I have thought about and proclaimed with trust and confidence, that justifies me and purifies me from all sin; and once I have been justified I am whole in God's sight. Of course I am immersed in evil, but God wipes this away the moment it happens so that it is no longer present," and more of the same sort.

Can anyone whose eyes are open fail to see that these are meaningless words, words that have no content because they have no worth in them? Anyone can think and talk like this, and can do so "with trust and confidence," when thinking about hell and eternal damnation. Do people like this want to know anything further, whether anything is really true or good? As to truth, they say, "What is truth other than whatever reinforces my faith?" As to goodness, they say, "What is good other than what I have because of my faith? In order to have it within me, though, I do not need to do it as though I were doing it myself, because that would be for credit, and good done for credit is not truly good." So they skip over the whole subject so completely that they do not know what evil is. What will they look for and see in themselves, then? What is their state but a fire of obsessions with evil that is confined within them, devouring the inner substance of their minds and destroying everything right up to the door? All they are doing is guarding the door so that no one can see the fire; but the door is opened after death, and then everyone can see.

[3] (c) *They are people who for worldly reasons do not think about sins and therefore do not know what they are.* These are people who love the world above all and will not give a hearing to any truth that might deflect them from the false principles of their religion. They say to themselves, "What do I care about this? This is not the way I think." So they reject it as soon as they hear it; or if it does get through at all, they suppress it. They do much the same thing when they hear sermons, retaining only a few words and no substance.

Since this is how they treat truths, they do not know what good is, since the two act in unison; and there is no way to identify evil on the basis of any good that is not based on truth. All they can do is call evil "good" by rationalizing it with their distortions.

These are the people meant by the seeds that fell among thorns. The Lord said of them, "Other seeds fell among thorns, and the thorns grew up and choked them. These are people who hear the Word, but the cares of this world and the deceptiveness of riches choke the Word so that it becomes unfruitful" (Matthew 13:7, 22; Mark 4:7, 14 *[4:7, 18, 19]*; Luke 8:7, 14).

[4] (d) *They are people who cherish their sins and therefore cannot know what they are.* These are people who believe in God and worship him with the usual rituals and yet rationalize for themselves that some evil that is a sin is really not a sin. They camouflage it with disguises and cosmetics that conceal how grotesque it is; and once they have accomplished this they cherish it and make it their friend and constant companion.

I have said that these people believe in God because only people who believe in God are capable of regarding evil as sin: all sin is sin against God.

But some examples may make this clear. When people who are bent on profit make different kinds of cheating permissible by inventing ratio-

nalizations, they are saying that an evil is not a sin. People who rationalize taking vengeance on their enemies are doing the same thing, as are
people who rationalize plundering people who are not their enemies in
times of war.

[5] (e) *In these cases, the sins do not come to light and therefore cannot be
set aside.* Any evil that is not brought to light feeds on itself. It is like fire
in wood buried in ashes. It is like poison in a wound that has not been
lanced; for any evil that is shut away keeps growing and growing until
everything has been brought to an end. So to prevent any evil from being
shut away, we are allowed to think in favor of God and against God, in
favor of the holy practices of the church or against them, without being
punished for it in this world.

The Lord speaks of this in Isaiah:

> From the soles of the feet to the head there is no soundness; there is
> wound and scar and fresh beating, not squeezed out or bound up or
> anointed with oil. Wash yourselves, purify yourselves. Take away the
> evil of your deeds from before my eyes. Stop doing evil, learn to do
> good. Then if your sins have been like scarlet, they will be white as
> snow; if they have been ruddy as a purple robe, they will be like wool.
> If you refuse and rebel, you will be devoured by the sword. (Isaiah 1:6,
> 16, 18, 10 *[1:6, 16, 17, 18, 20]*)

"Being devoured by the sword" means being destroyed by our malicious
distortions.

[6] (f) *There is a previously unrecognized reason why evils could not be
set aside apart from this examination, this bringing to light, this recognition, this confession, and this resistance.* I have already mentioned [§§62,
65, 217] that heaven overall is arranged in communities according to
[people's desires for what is good, and that hell overall is arranged in
communities according to] desires for what is evil that are opposite to
those desires for what is good.[267] As to our spirits, each of us is in some
community—in a heavenly one when our good desires are in control,
and in a hellish one when our evil desires are in control. We are unaware
of this while we are living in this world, but in spirit that is where we
are. We could not go on living otherwise, and that is how the Lord is
guiding us.

If we are in a hellish community, the only way the Lord can lead us
out is under the laws of his divine providence. One of them says that we
must see that we are there, must want to get out, and must ourselves

make an effort with what seems to be our own strength. We can do this while we are in this world but not after death. Then we stay forever in the community we joined in this world. This is why we need to examine ourselves, see and acknowledge our sins, repent, and remain constant for the rest of our lives.

I could support this with enough experience to warrant complete belief, but this is not the place to bring in proofs from experience.

279 3. *To the extent that our evils are set aside, they are forgiven.* One currently popular misconception is that our evils are taken from us and discarded when they are forgiven, and that the state of our life can be changed instantly, even totally reversed, so that we become good instead of evil. This would be leading us out of hell and transporting us instantly into heaven, all by some direct mercy of the Lord.

However, people who hold this kind of belief or thought have no idea whatever of what evil and good really are or what the state of our own life is. They are utterly unaware that the feelings of our volition are simply shifts and changes of state of the purely organic[268] substances of our minds, that the thoughts of our discernment are simply shifts and changes of their forms, and that memory is the ongoing effect of these changes. This enables us to see clearly that evil can be taken away only gradually and that the forgiveness of evil is not the same as its removal. This, though, is presenting the ideas in condensed form. If they are not explained at greater length, they can be recognized but not grasped; and if they are not grasped, that is like a wheel that we turn by hand.[269] I need to explain these propositions, then, one at a time in the order just given.

[2] (a) *One currently popular misconception is that our evils are taken from us and discarded when they are forgiven.* I have been taught in heaven that no evil that we are born with or that we ourselves adopt by our behavior is taken completely away from us. Evils are set aside so that they are no longer visible. Like so many other people in this world, I used to believe that when our evils are forgiven they are thrown away just as dirt is rinsed and washed away from our faces by water. That is not what it is like with our evils or sins, though. They are all still there, and when they are forgiven after we have repented, they are moved from the center to the sides. Whatever is in the middle is right in front of our eyes and seems to be out in broad daylight. What is off to the sides seems to be in the shade, or at times, even in the dark of night. Since our evils are not taken completely away, then, but are only displaced or put off to the side, and since

we can be transported from the center to the boundaries, it can happen that we once again get involved in evils we thought we had left behind. It is part of our own nature that we can move from one desire to another, and sometimes into an opposite one. This means that we can move from one center to another. A desire determines our center as long as we are caught up in it. Then we are absorbed in its pleasure and its light.

[3] There are some people who are raised into heaven by the Lord after death because they have lived good lives but who bring with them a belief that they are free and clean from sins and therefore wholly without guilt. At first they are given white robes that reflect this belief, since white robes portray a state of having been purified from evils. Later, though, they begin to think the way they did in the world, to think that they have been washed clean from all evil; so they boast that they are no longer sinners like everyone else. It is almost impossible to separate this from a kind of mental "high" that includes a measure of looking down on others. So at this point, in order to free them from the faith they imagine they have, they are sent down from heaven and back into the evils they had fallen prey to in the world. This shows them that they have inherited evils that they had not known about before. This brings them to admit that their evils have not been taken away from them but only set aside, and that they themselves are still unclean, and in fact nothing but evil; that it is the Lord who is protecting them from their evils and keeping them focused on those good qualities; and that all this seems to be their own doing. Once this has happened, the Lord brings them back up into heaven.

[4] (b) *A second popular misconception is that the state of our life can be changed instantly, so that we become good instead of evil. This would be leading us out of hell and transporting us instantly into heaven, all by some direct mercy of the Lord.* This is the misconception of people who separate charity from faith and attribute salvation to faith alone. That is, they think that the mere thought and utterance of a statement of that faith, performed with trust and confidence, will justify and save them. Many of them also think that this can happen instantaneously, either before the hour of death or as it approaches. They cannot avoid believing that the state of our life can be changed in an instant and that we can be saved by direct mercy. We shall see in the last section of this book, though, that the Lord's mercy does not operate in this direct way, that we cannot become good instead of evil in an instant and be led out of hell and transported into heaven except by the ongoing efforts of divine providence from our infancy to the end of our lives.[270]

At this point we may rest the case simply on the fact that all the laws of divine providence are aimed at our reformation, and therefore at our salvation, which means inverting the hellish state into which we are born into its opposite, a heavenly state. This can be done only gradually as we move away from evil and its pleasure and move into what is good and its pleasure.

[5] (c) *People who hold this kind of belief have no idea whatever of what evil and good really are.* They do not really know that evil is the pleasure we find in the urge to act and think in violation of the divine pattern, and that goodness is the pleasure we feel when we act and think in harmony with the divine pattern. They do not realize that there are thousands of individual impulses that go to make up any particular evil, and that there are thousands of individual impulses that go to make up any particular good tendency. These thousands of impulses are so precisely structured and so intimately interconnected within us that no single one of them can be changed without changing all the rest at the same time.

If people are unaware of this, they can entertain the belief or the thought that an evil that seems to be all by itself can be set aside easily and that something good that also seems to be all by itself can be brought in to replace it. Since they do not know what good and evil are, they cannot help thinking that there are such things as instantaneous salvation and direct mercy. The last section of this book will show that this is not possible.

[6] (d) *People who believe in instantaneous salvation and direct mercy are utterly unaware that the feelings of our volition are simply changes of state of the purely organic substances of our minds, that the thoughts of our discernment are simply changes and shifts of their forms, and that memory is the ongoing effect of those changes and shifts.* Once someone mentions it, everyone will realize that feelings and thoughts can happen only with substances and their forms as subjects. Since they happen in our brains, which are full of substances and forms, we say that these forms are purely organic. If we think rationally, we cannot help laughing at the wild idea that feelings and thoughts do not happen in substantial subjects but are breezes affected by warmth and light, like illusions seen in the air or the ether. In fact, thought can no more happen apart from its substantial form than sight can happen apart from its substantial form, the eye, or hearing from its ear, or taste from its tongue.[271] Look at the brain and you will see countless substances and fibers, and nothing there that is not structured. What need is there of more proof than this visual one?

[7] Just what is this "feeling," though, and just what is this "thought"? We can figure this out by looking at the body overall and in detail. There are many internal organs there, all set in their own places, all carrying out their functions by shifts and changes in their states and forms. We know that they are occupied with their tasks. The stomach has its task, the intestines have theirs, the kidneys have theirs, the liver, pancreas, and spleen have theirs, and the heart and lungs have theirs. All of them are inwardly activated solely for their tasks, and this inward activation happens by shifts and changes of their states and forms.

This leads us to the conclusion that the workings of the purely organic substances of the mind are no different, except that the workings of the organic substances of the body are physical and the workings of the organic substances of the mind are spiritual. The two act as a unity by means of responsiveness [to each other].[272]

[8] There is no way to offer visual evidence of the nature of the shifts and changes of state and form of the organic substances of the mind, the shifts and changes that constitute our feelings and thoughts. We can see them in a kind of mirror, though, if we look at the shifts and changes of state of our lungs in the acts of speech and singing. There is a parallelism, since the sounds of speech and song as well as the differentiations of sound that make the words of speech and the melodies of song are produced by the lungs. The sound itself answers to our feeling and the language to our thought. That is what causes them; and it is accomplished by shifts and changes of the state and form of the organic substances in our lungs, from the lungs into the trachea or windpipe in the larynx and glottis, then in the tongue, and finally in our lips.

The first shifts and changes of state and form of sound happen in the lungs, the second in the trachea and larynx, the third in the glottis by opening its aperture in various ways, the fourth by the tongue by touching the palate and teeth in various places, and the fifth by our lips through taking different shapes. We can see from this that both the sound and its modifications that constitute speech and song are produced solely by sequential and constant shifts and changes in the states of these organic forms.

Since the only source of sound and speech is our mental feelings and thoughts—that is where they come from, and there is no other source—we can see that the feelings of our volition are shifts and changes of state of the purely organic substances of our minds, and that the thoughts of our discernment are shifts and changes of the forms of those substances, just the way it happens in our lungs.

[9] Further, since our feelings and thoughts are simply changes of state of the forms of our minds, it follows that our memory is nothing but their ongoing effect. It is characteristic of all the shifts and changes of state in organic substances that once they have been learned they do not disappear. So the lungs are trained to produce various sounds in the trachea and to modify them in the glottis, articulate them with the tongue, and shape them with the mouth; and once these organs have been trained to do these things, the actions are ingrained and can be repeated.

Material presented in *Divine Love and Wisdom* 119–204 *[199–204]* shows that the shifts and changes in the organic substances of the mind are infinitely more perfect than those in the body. There it is explained that all processes of perfection increase and rise by and according to levels. There is more on the subject in §319 below.

280 Another popular misconception is that when sins have been forgiven they are also set aside. This misconception is characteristic of people who believe that their sins are forgiven through the sacrament of the Holy Supper even though they have not set them aside by repenting from them. It is characteristic also of people who believe they are saved by faith alone or by papal dispensations. They all believe in direct mercy and instant salvation.

When the sequence is reversed, though, it is true: when sins have been set aside, they are forgiven. Repentance must precede forgiveness, and apart from repentance there is no forgiveness. That is why the Lord told his disciples to preach repentance for the forgiveness of sins (Luke 24:27) and why John preached the baptism of repentance for the forgiveness of sins (Luke 3:3).

The Lord forgives everyone's sins. He does not accuse us or keep score. However, he cannot take our sins away except by the laws of his divine providence; for when Peter asked him how many times he should forgive someone who had sinned against him, whether seven was enough, he said that Peter should forgive not seven times but seventy times seven times (Matthew 18:21, 22). What does this tell us about the Lord, who is mercy itself?

281 4. *So the permission of evil is for the purpose of salvation.* We know that we are quite free in our thinking and intentions, but are not free to say and do whatever we think and intend. We can be atheists in our thoughts, denying the existence of God and blaspheming the holy contents of the church's Word; we can even want to destroy them utterly by what we say and do; but civil and moral and ecclesiastical laws hold us back. So we indulge in these ungodly and criminal practices in our thoughts and our wishes and even in our intentions, but still not in our actions. People who are not atheists are still quite free to harbor any number of evil thoughts, thoughts about cheating, lust, vengeance, and other senseless things, and even act them out at times.

Is it credible that if we did not have this complete freedom we would not only be beyond salvation but would completely perish? [2] Listen to the reason. We are all immersed in many kinds of evil from birth. They are in our volition, and we love whatever is in our volition. That is, we love all the intentions that come from within; and we intend whatever we love. This love of our volition flows into our discernment and makes itself felt there as pleasure. It moves from there into our thoughts and into our conscious intentions. So if we were not allowed to think the way the love of our volition wants us to, the love that is within us by heredity, that love would stay closed in and never come out where we could see it. Any such hidden love for evil is like an enemy plotting against us, like pus in a sore, like a toxin in the blood, and like an infection in the chest. If they are kept hidden, they hasten us to our end.

On the other hand, when we are allowed to think about the evils of our life's love even to the point of wanting to act them out, they are healed by spiritual means the way a life-threatening illness is cured by physical means.

[3] I need to explain what we would be like if we were not allowed to think in keeping with the pleasures of our life's love. We would no longer be human. We would have lost the two abilities called freedom and rationality that are the essence of our humanity. The pleasures of those loves would take control of the inner reaches of our minds so completely that the door would be opened wide. We then would not be able to avoid talking and acting in similar fashion, displaying our madness not only to ourselves but to the whole world. Eventually we would not know enough to cover our private parts. It is to keep this from happening that we are allowed to think about and to intend the evils we have inherited, but not to utter and do them. In the meanwhile, we learn civic, moral, and spiritual principles that also work their way into our thinking and displace these insane principles. The Lord heals us by this means, though only to the extent that we know how to guard the door, and not unless we believe in God and ask for his help to resist our evils. Then to the extent that we resist them, he does not let them into our intentions, and eventually not into our thoughts.

[4] We do therefore have a freedom to think as we wish, in order that our life's love may come out of hiding into the light of our discernment; otherwise we would have no knowledge of our evil and could not abstain from it. It would then follow that the evil would gain strength within us to the point that there was no space for recovery within us and, since the evil of parents is passed on to their progeny, hardly any space for recovery in any children we might beget. The Lord makes sure, however, that this does not happen.

282 The Lord could heal everyone's discernment and make us incapable of thinking evil, capable only of thinking good. He could do this by various fears, by miracles, by messages from the dead, and by visions and dreams. However, healing only our discernment is healing us only superficially. Our discernment and its thought processes are the outside of our life, while our volition and its desire is the inside of our life. This means that healing only our discernment would be curing nothing but the symptoms. The deeper malignance, closed in and with no way out, would first devour what was nearest to it and then what was farther away until finally everything was dying. It is our volition itself that needs to be healed, not by our discernment flowing into it but by being taught and encouraged by our discernment.

If our discernment alone were healed we would be like an embalmed body or a corpse bathed in fragrant perfumes and roses. Before long the perfumes would draw forth from the body such a stench that none of us could put our nose anywhere near it. That is what it would be like for heavenly truths in our discernment if the evil love of our volition were repressed.

283 As already noted [§281], the purpose of letting us think about our evils even to the point of intending them is so that they can be displaced by civic, moral, and spiritual principles. This happens when we consider that something is in opposition to what is lawful and fair, what is sincere and decent, what is good and true, and therefore what is peaceful, happy, and blessed in our lives. The Lord heals the love of our volition by these three sets of principles as means, using our fears at first but our loves later.

Still, our evils are not taken away from us and discarded, they are only displaced and relegated to the sides. Once they are there and goodness is in the center, the evils are out of sight, since whatever is in the center is right in front of our eyes, visible and perceptible. We need to realize, though, that even though goodness may be in the center, this still does not mean we are devoted to it unless the evils that are off to the sides are tending downward and outward. If they are turned upward and inward they have not been displaced, because they are still trying to get back to the center. They are tending and turned downward and outward when we are abstaining from our evils as sins, and even more so when we find them distasteful. Then we are condemning them and consigning them to hell, which turns them in that direction.

Our discernment can accept what is good and what is evil, what is true and what is false, but our essential volition cannot. This must be focused on what is evil or what is good and not on both, because our volition is our essential self. It is where our life's love is. In our discernment, what is good and what is evil are kept apart like an inside and an outside, so we can be inwardly focused on evil and outwardly on good. However, when we are being reformed, the goodness and the evil are brought face to face. Then a clash occurs, a battle that is called a temptation if it is severe. If it is not severe, though, it happens like the fermentation of wine or beer. If the goodness wins, then the evil and its distortion are moved to the sides much as dregs settle to the bottom of the bottles. The goodness comes to be like a wine that has become vintage wine after fermentation, or beer that has become clear. If the evil wins, though, then the goodness and its truth are moved to the sides and become murky and dark like half-fermented wine or half-fermented beer.

284

The comparison with fermentation is based on the fact that in the Word, yeast means the falsity that comes from evil, as it does in Hosea 7:4; Luke 12:1; and elsewhere.[273]

Divine Providence Is for Evil People and Good People Alike

285 WITHIN each of us, good and evil alike, there are two abilities. One of them makes up our discernment and the other our volition. The ability that makes up our discernment is our ability to differentiate and think, so we call it "rationality." The ability that makes up our volition is our ability freely to do these things—think, and therefore speak and act as well—as long as they do not violate our reason or rationality. Acting freely is doing whatever we want to whenever we want to do it.

These two abilities are constant. They are unbroken from beginnings to endings overall and in detail in everything we think and do. They are not intrinsic to us but are in us from the Lord. It therefore follows that when the Lord's presence is in these abilities it is a presence in details as well, even in the very smallest details of our discernment and thought, of our volition and desire, and therefore of our speech and action. Take these abilities out of any least detail and you could not think it or speak of it like a human being.

[2] I have already offered abundant evidence that it is by virtue of these two abilities that we are human, that we can think and talk, that we can sense what is good and discern what is true not only in civic and moral issues but in spiritual ones as well, and that we can be reformed and regenerated—in short, it is by virtue of these two abilities that we can be united to the Lord and therefore live forever. I have also explained[274] that not only good people but evil ones as well have these two abilities. Since these abilities are given us by the Lord and we are not to claim them as our own, we are not to claim anything divine as our own either, though something divine can be attached to us so that it seems to be ours. Since this divine gift to us is in the smallest details of our nature, it follows that the Lord is in control of these smallest details in evil people as well as in good people; and the Lord's control is what we call divine providence.

286 Now since it is a law of divine providence that we can act freely and rationally (that is, availing ourselves of the two abilities called freedom and rationality), and since it is also a law of divine providence that whatever we do seems to be done by us and therefore to be ours, and since we can infer from these laws that evils have to be permitted, it follows that we can misuse these abilities. We can freely and rationally justify anything we please. We can take anything we please and make it rational, whether it is inherently rational or not. This leads some people to say, "What is truth? Can't I make anything true that I choose? Isn't that what the world does?" People do this by rationalizing if they can.

Take the most false proposition you can and tell clever individuals to justify it, and they will. For example, tell them to prove that we are nothing but animals, or that the soul is like a spider in its web, controlling the body by its filaments, or that religion is nothing but a restraint, and they will prove whichever you choose so that it actually seems true. Nothing could be easier, because they cannot identify an appearance or a false proposition that is taken in blind faith to be true. [2] This is why people cannot see the truth that divine providence is at work in the smallest details of everyone's discernment and volition, the smallest details of everyone's thoughts and impulses (which amounts to the same thing), in evil and good people alike.

The main thing that misleads them is that this seems to make the Lord responsible for evil when in fact no trace whatever of evil comes from the Lord. It all comes from us through our accepting as fact the appearance that we think, intend, talk, and act autonomously, as we shall shortly see. To make it clear, I need to proceed in the following sequence.

1. Divine providence is at work in the smallest details everywhere, not only with the good but with the evil as well; but it is not in their evils.

2. Evil people are constantly leading themselves into evils, and the Lord is constantly leading them away from evils.

3. The Lord cannot fully lead evil people away from their evils and guide them in what is good as long as they believe that their own intelligence is everything and that divine providence is nothing.

4. The Lord controls the hells by means of opposites. As for evil people who are still in this world, he controls them in hell as to their deeper natures, but not as to their more outward natures.

1. *Divine providence is at work in the smallest details everywhere, not only with the good but with the evil as well, but it is not in their evils.* I have already explained[275] that divine providence is in the smallest details of our thoughts and desires, which means that we cannot think or intend anything on our own. Everything we think and intend, and therefore

everything we say and do, is the result of an inflow. If it is good, something is flowing in from heaven; if it is bad, something is flowing in from hell. In other words, if it is good it is flowing in from the Lord, and if it is bad it is flowing in from our own sense of self-importance.

I do realize, though, that all this is hard to grasp because it differentiates between what flows in from heaven or from the Lord and what flows in from hell or from our own sense of self-importance, and at the same time it says that divine providence is at work in the smallest details of our thoughts and desires to the point that we cannot think or intend anything on our own. Since I am saying that we can think and intend from hell, or from our sense of self-importance, there does seem to be a contradiction. However, there is none, as we shall see below [§294], once a few points are prefaced that will shed some light on the matter.

288 All of heaven's angels admit that no one can originate a thought, that all thinking comes from the Lord, while all the spirits of hell claim that thought cannot originate in anyone but themselves. Actually, these spirits have been shown any number of times that none of them are originating their own thoughts, that they cannot, and that it is all flowing in, but to no effect—they are unwilling to accept it.

However, experience will teach first of all that even for spirits in hell, every bit of thought and feeling is flowing in from heaven. The problem is that the inflowing good is being turned into evil in hell, and the truth is being turned into falsity. Everything becomes its opposite. This is how it was shown to me. Something true from the Word was let down from heaven and taken hold of by people in the upper levels of hell. They sent it on down to the lower hells all the way to the lowest. Step by step along this path the truth turned into falsity, finally into a falsity absolutely opposite to the truth. The people who were changing it thought they themselves were thinking up this falsity. That was all they knew, and yet the falsity was that truth flowing down from heaven on its way to the lowest hell, that truth falsified and distorted. Three or four times I have heard of this happening. The same thing happens to what is good. When this flows down from heaven it is turned step by step into the evil that is opposite to it.

This has enabled me to see that when what is true and good emanates from the Lord and is taken up by people who are devoted to what is false and evil, it is changed. It takes on another form so completely that its original form can no longer be seen. That is just what is going on with all who are evil, because in spirit they are in hell.

I have often been shown that no one in hell originates a thought. **289** They all depend on others around them, who again are not originating their thoughts but depend on still others. Thoughts and desires move from community to community in a pattern without people realizing that they are not thinking autonomously.

Some individuals who believed that they thought and intended autonomously were assigned to a particular community. They were cut off from communication with those neighbors to whom their thoughts usually spread and were held where they were. Then they were told to think differently from the way the spirits of that community were thinking, to force themselves to think along contradictory lines; but they admitted that it was impossible for them. [2] This has happened to any number of people, including Leibniz.276 Even he was convinced that no one thinks independently, only from others, who in turn are not thinking independently. We are all thinking as a result of an inflow from heaven, and heaven depends on an inflow from the Lord.

Some people who have thought deeply about this have declared that it is so stunning that hardly anyone could be compelled to believe it, it is so contrary to the way things seem. However, they could not deny it, because it had been fully demonstrated. Still, in their wonderment they claimed that it meant that they were not to blame for thinking evil and that it seemed as though evil came from the Lord. They did not understand how the Lord alone could work things out so that we all think differently, either. These three issues need to be unfolded next.277

I need to add the following to the experiences already cited. When **290** the Lord first allowed me to talk with spirits and angels, this secret was immediately made known to me. I was told from heaven that, like others, I believed that I was thinking and intending on my own, when in fact nothing was coming from me. If it was good, it was coming from the Lord, and if it was bad, it was coming from hell. I was shown this at first hand by having various thoughts and desires imposed on me so that eventually I could feel and sense it.278 So later, as soon as anything evil impinged on my volition or anything false on my thoughts, I asked where it was coming from and was shown. I was also allowed to talk with the people it came from, to rebut them, and to make them go away. This meant that they took their evil and falsity back and kept it to themselves, no longer instilling anything of the sort into my thoughts. This has happened thousands of times; and I have been in this state now for a number of years and still am to the present time.279 Nevertheless, I seem to myself to be thinking and intending on my own just like everyone else, with no difference at all. It seems like this to everyone because of the Lord's divine providence, as explained at the appropriate point above.[280]

Some newly arrived spirits were bewildered by my state. It looked to them exactly as though I was not thinking or intending anything on my own, and that I was therefore like something empty. However, I explained the mystery to them. I added that I was thinking more deeply and sensing what was flowing into my more outward thinking, seeing whether it was coming from heaven or from hell, rejecting the one and accepting the other. It still seemed to me as though I was thinking and intending on my own, just like them.

291   It is not entirely unknown in this world that everything good comes from heaven and everything evil from hell. Everyone in the church knows it. Is there anyone who has been ordained into the ministry who does not teach that everything good comes from God and that we cannot gain anything that is not given us from heaven?[281] Ministers teach also that the devil puts evils into our thoughts and leads us astray by prompting us to do them. So the ministers who believe they are preaching with holy zeal pray that the Holy Spirit will teach them and guide their thoughts and their speech. Some of them say they have a sense of being led. When their sermons are praised they answer devoutly that they have not been speaking from their own resources but from God.

So too, when they see people speaking and behaving well they describe them as led to it by God, and conversely when they see people speaking and behaving badly, they describe them as led to it by the devil. Everyone knows that this is how people talk in the church, but who really believes it?

292   Everything we think and intend and therefore everything we say and do flows in from the only fount of life; and yet that one fount of life, the Lord, is not the cause of our thinking things that are evil and false.

There are enlightening parallels in the physical world. Warmth and light radiate from its sun, and these two flow into all the subjects and objects[282] that we see with our eyes, not only good subjects and beautiful objects, but also bad subjects and ugly objects; and they bring forth different effects in each. They flow not only into trees that bear good fruit but into trees that bear bad fruit, flowing into the actual fruit itself and helping it to develop. They flow into the good seed and into the weeds,[283] into useful, healthful shrubs and into harmful, toxic shrubs. Yet it is the same warmth and the same light; and there is no cause of evil in it, only in the subjects and objects that receive it.

[2] The same can be said of the warmth that hatches the eggs of owls[284] or vipers and the eggs of doves, beautiful birds, and swans. Putting both kinds of egg under a hen and her warmth, which in and of itself is harmless, will hatch them. What does this warmth have in common with these evil and noxious creatures?

The same applies to the warmth that flows into swamps, manure, decay, and decomposition and into things that are winelike, fragrant, sparkling, and alive. Can anyone fail to see that the cause is not in the warmth but in the receptive subject?

The very same light, too, makes beautiful colors when it flows into one object and unpleasant colors when it flows into another. Actually, it is displaying itself and glowing in bright objects and dimming itself as objects become blacker, darkening itself.

[3] The same thing happens in the spiritual world. There are also warmth and light there from its sun, which is the Lord, flowing from him into their subjects and objects. The subjects and objects there are angels and spirits, specifically their processes of volition and discernment. The warmth there is the radiating divine love and the light there is the radiating divine wisdom. They are not responsible for the fact that different people receive them differently, for the Lord says, "He makes his sun rise on the evil and the good and sends rain on the righteous and the unrighteous" (Matthew 5:45). In its highest spiritual meaning the sun means divine love and the rain means divine wisdom.

I may add what angels think about volition and intelligence. It is their opinion that none of us has even a grain of volition or prudence that is actually ours. If there were such a grain in anyone, neither heaven nor hell could stand and the whole human race would perish. The reason they give is that heaven and hell are made up of millions of people, all the people who have been born since the creation of the world. Heaven and hell are arranged from top to bottom in a design that makes each a unity, heaven a beautiful person and hell a grotesque person. If there were a single grain of volition or intelligence that belonged to anyone, that unity would not be possible. It would be torn apart, and with it would go the divine form that can stand and endure only when the Lord is absolutely everything, and everything else is absolutely nothing.

Another reason they give is that thinking and intending autonomously is divinity itself, while thinking and intending from God is humanity itself. Divinity itself cannot be claimed by any of us: that

293

would mean that we would be God. Remember this; and if you want to, you will find it corroborated by angels when you arrive in the spiritual world after you die.

294   I mentioned in §289 above that when some people were shown convincingly that we do not think on our own but receive thoughts from others, all of whom in turn are not thinking on their own but from an inflow from the Lord, in their wonderment they claimed that it meant that they were not to blame for doing evil[285] and that it seemed as though evil came from the Lord. They did not understand how the Lord alone could work things out so that we all think differently, either.

Since these three thoughts are bound to occur to people who think about effects as coming solely from effects and not from causes, I need to pick these up and look at them in terms of causes.

[2] *First, it meant that they were not to blame for doing evil.* If everything we think is flowing in from others, it does seem as though the blame rests on those others as the source. However, the real blame rests on us who accept what is flowing in, since we accept it as our own. That is all we know and all we want to know. We all want to be our own people and find our own way. Particularly, we want to think our own thoughts and make our own decisions. This is the essence of that freedom we enjoy that seems to be our very own. If we knew, then, that what we are thinking and intending was flowing in from someone else, we would feel caught and caged, no longer under our own control, and all the joy would go out of our lives. Eventually, our very humanity would go, too.

[3] I have often seen this demonstrated. When some individuals were allowed to feel and sense that they were being led by others, their rage blazed up so that they could no longer think straight. They said that they would rather be chained and imprisoned in hell than not be allowed to think what they wanted to think and intend what they were thinking. They called this restriction having their life itself bound, which was harsher and more intolerable than being bound physically. They did not say the same about being restrained from saying and doing what they were thinking and intending, because what held them in check was the pleasure of civil and moral life, and this made the restraint easier to bear.

[4] Since we do not want to know that others are leading us to think what we think, then, but want to think on our own and believe that we do, it necessarily follows that we ourselves are to blame and cannot avoid that blame as long as we are in love with our own thinking. If we are not in love with our own thinking, though, we extricate ourselves from our engagement with these others. This happens when we realize that

something is evil and want therefore to abstain and refrain from it. Then the Lord rescues us from the community that is focused on this evil and moves us to a community that is not. However, if we recognize that something is evil and do not abstain from it, then we are held responsible for it and become guilty of that evil.

Whatever we believe we are doing autonomously, then, is said to come from us and not from the Lord.

[5] *Second, it therefore seemed as though evil came from the Lord.* This can seem as though it follows from what I said in §288, namely, that in hell, the goodness that flows in from the Lord is turned into evil and the truth into falsity. Surely, though, anyone can see that the evil and falsity do not come from what is good and true and therefore from the Lord. They come from the receiving subject or object that is focused on what is evil and false and that distorts and inverts what it is receiving, as has been amply demonstrated in §292. I have already explained several times [§§15, 204, 286] how the evil and falsity in us originate.

There have been experiments in the spiritual world with people who believed that the Lord could take the evils out of evil people and replace them with good qualities, thereby taking all hell into heaven and saving everyone. You may see that this is impossible, though, at the end of this book [§§331–340] where I deal with instant salvation and direct mercy.

[6] *Third, they did not understand how the Lord alone could work things out so that we all think so differently.* The Lord's divine love is infinite, and his divine wisdom is infinite, and infinite forms of love and infinite forms of wisdom radiate from the Lord and flow into everyone in heaven and everyone in hell. From heaven and hell they flow into everyone in the world. This means that none of us can lack the ability to think and intend, since infinite forms are everything infinitely.

The infinite things that radiate from the Lord flow in not only in a general way but in full detail, since divinity is all-inclusive because of those smallest details, and the divine smallest details are what we call "the totality," as already explained [§202]. Further, every divine detail is also infinite.

We can tell from this that it is the Lord alone who makes each one of us think and intend in keeping with our own natures and in keeping with the laws of his providence. I have explained in §§46–69 and in *Divine Love and Wisdom* 17–22 that everything that is in the Lord and that radiates from the Lord is infinite.

2. Evil people are constantly leading themselves into evils, and the Lord is constantly leading them away from evils. It is easier to understand how

295

divine providence works with good people than to understand how it works with evil people. Since this latter is our present concern, I shall proceed in the following sequence. (a) There are countless elements in every evil. (b) Evil people are constantly and intentionally leading themselves deeper into their evils. (c) For evil people, divine providence is a constant permission of evil with the ultimate goal of constantly leading them out. (d) The Lord does this leading out of evil in a thousand ways, some of them quite mysterious.

296   For a clear sense and grasp of the way divine providence works with evil people, I need to explain these statements in the order in which they are listed.

(a) *There are countless elements in every evil.* Every evil looks to us like a simple unit. That is how we see hatred and vengefulness, theft and fraud, adultery and promiscuity, pride and arrogance, and the like. We do not realize that there are countless elements in every evil, more than there are fibers and vessels in the human body. An evil person is a miniature form of hell, and hell is made up of millions of individuals, each one in a form that is human even though it is grotesque. All the fibers and all the vessels in that person are inverted. Essentially, a spirit is an evil that looks to itself like a single entity, but there are as many elements in it as there are compulsions that arise from it. We are all our own good or our own evil from our heads to the soles of our feet. So if evil people are like this, we can see that each one is an evil made up of countless different things that are distinct varieties of evil, things we refer to as the compulsions of that evil.

It then follows that if we are to be reformed, the Lord has to repair and turn around all these elements in the sequence in which they occur, and that this cannot be accomplished except by the Lord's divine providence working step by step from the beginning of our lives to the end.

[2] In hell, every compulsion to evil looks like a vicious animal when it is made visible, like a dragon, for example, or some kind of poisonous snake, or some kind of owl,[286] and so on. This is what the compulsions of our own evil look like when angels see them. All these forms of compulsion have to be turned around one at a time. The task is to take people who in spirit look like gargoyles or devils and turn them around to look like beautiful angels, and each single compulsion has to be turned around so that it looks like a lamb, a sheep, a dove, or a turtledove. This is what the desires for good of angels in heaven look like when they are made visible. Changing a dragon into a lamb or a serpent into a sheep or

an owl into a dove can only happen gradually, by uprooting the very seed of the evil and planting good seed in its place.

This has to be done in the way a scion is grafted onto a tree that is nothing but some roots and a trunk. Even so, the branch that has been grafted gets some sap from the old root and turns it into good, juicy fruit. The scion that is to be grafted has to be taken from the Lord, who is the tree of life. This is the intent of the Lord's words in John 15:1–7.[287]

[3] (b) *Evil people are constantly and intentionally leading themselves deeper into their evils.* We say they are doing this intentionally because everything evil comes from us. We turn the goodness that comes from the Lord into evil, as already noted [§294]. The basic reason evil people lead themselves deeper into evil is that they are making their way farther and farther into hellish communities, getting in deeper and deeper as they intend and do what is evil. This increases their pleasure in evil as well, and it takes possession of their thoughts to the point that nothing feels more gratifying. Furthermore, when we have made our way farther and deeper into hellish communities, we are wrapped up in chains, so to speak, though as long as we are living in this world, we do not feel them as chains. They feel like soft linen or slender threads of silk that we like because they caress us. After death, though, the softness of the chains turns hard, and the caresses start to chafe.

[4] If we consider theft, robbery, plunder, vengeance, domineering, profiteering, and the like, we can recognize this growth of the pleasure we find in evil. Do not the people who are committing these evils feel surges of pleasure as things go well and as obstacles to their efforts vanish? It is well known that thieves get such pleasure from theft that they cannot stop stealing; and strange as it sounds, they love one stolen coin more than ten coins freely given. It would be the same for adulterers if things were not so arranged that the power to commit this evil decreases as it is abused. Still, though, for many people the pleasure of thinking and talking about it is still there, and if nothing else, there is the insistent urge to touch.

[5] What people do not realize is that this is happening because they are making their way farther and farther, deeper and deeper, into hellish communities as they commit these evils intentionally and consciously. If the evils occur in our thoughts only and not in our volition, we are not with the evil in some hellish community yet. We enter such a community when the evils are in our volition as well. If at that time we are also conscious that this evil is against the laws of the Ten Commandments, and if we regard these laws as divine, and still deliberately do it, this

sends us down so deep that the only way we can be rescued is by active repentance.

[6] We need to realize that all of us, in spirit, are in some community in the spiritual world, in a hellish one if we are evil, and a heavenly one if we are good. Sometimes we are even visible there when we are deep in meditation.[288] Further, just as sound and speech spread through the air in the physical world, desire and thought spread out in the communities in the spiritual world. There is a correspondential relationship here because desire answers to sound and thought to speech.

[7] (c) *For evil people, divine providence is a constant permission of evil with the ultimate goal of constantly leading them out.* The reason divine providence is a constant permission for evil people is that nothing can come out of their life except evil. Whether we are devoted to good or evil, we cannot be devoted to both at the same time, or even alternately, unless we are lukewarm.[289] It is not the Lord who lets evil living into our volition and from there into our thought, it is we ourselves; and this is called permission.

[8] Now since everything evil people intend and think is a matter of permission, the question arises as to what divine providence is in this situation, the providence that we say is at work in the smallest details within all of us, evil and good alike. Divine providence consists of the fact that it is constantly allowing things to happen for a purpose and is permitting only things that serve that purpose, nothing else. It is constantly examining the evils that are allowed to emerge, separating them, purifying them, banishing the ones that do not suit its purpose, and lifting them away in ways we cannot see. This is going on primarily in our deeper volition and secondarily in our deeper thought. Divine providence is also constantly at work to see that we do not welcome back into our volition the things that have been banished and lifted from us, because everything we accept into our volition becomes part of us. Things we have accepted in thought but not in volition, though, are separated and sent away.

This is the constant effort of the Lord's providence for evil people— as just noted, a constant permission with a view to constant rescue.

[9] We know very little about this because we do not feel it. The main reason we do not feel it is that our evils are inherent in the cravings of our life's love, and we do not feel these as evil but as pleasant. No one pays them any heed. Do we pay any attention to the pleasures of our love? Our thoughts drift along in them like a little boat in the current of a river. We sense them like a breath of fragrant air that we breathe in

deeply. All we can do is sense a little of them in our outer thought, but we still take no notice of them there unless we have a clear knowledge of what evil is. There will be more on this later, though [§298].

[10] (d) *The Lord does this leading out of evil in a thousand ways, some of them quite mysterious.* I have been shown only a few of these, and only some of the commonest ones at that. What happens is that pleasures of our compulsions, of which we are utterly unaware, are emitted in close-knit groups into the inner thought processes of our spirit and from there into its outer thought processes. There they take on the guise of a kind of feeling that something is gratifying or pleasing or desirable. These inner pleasures mingle there with our lower and sensory pleasures. In this arena there are means of separation and purification and routes of dismissal and relief. The means are primarily the pleasure we find in contemplation, thought, and reflection for various purposes that are constructive; and there are as many purposes that are constructive as there are elements and details of our various jobs and offices. There are also just as many constructive purposes as there are attractive thoughts about how we can seem to be civic-minded and moral individuals and spiritual individuals—as well as some unattractive ones that intrude themselves. Because these pleasures are effects of our love in our outer self, they serve as means by which the pleasures of the compulsions to evil of our inner self can be separated, purified, excreted, and withdrawn.

[11] For example, take dishonest judges, who see money or cronyism as the goals or functions of their office. Inwardly, they are constantly focused on these goals, but this comes out in an effort to act competently and fairly. They find a constant pleasure in pondering, thinking, reflecting, and intending ways to bend, turn, adapt, and finagle the legal system so that their decisions seem to conform to the laws and to mimic justice. They are not aware that this inner pleasure is made up of plots, pretences, deceit, undercover theft, and much more of the same kind, and that a pleasure comprising all these pleasures of obsessions with evil is the controlling element in everything that goes on in their outward thinking where they find pleasure in seeming to be fair and honest.

The inner pleasures are allowed to come down into the outer ones and mingle there the way food is churned in the stomach. That is where they are separated, purified, and withdrawn. This applies, though, only to the more serious pleasures of our compulsions to evil. [12] For evil people, only this separation, purification, and withdrawal of the more serious pleasures from the less serious ones is possible. For good people, however, there can be a separation, purification, and withdrawal of the less serious evils as well as the more serious ones. This is accomplished by means of the pleasures of our attraction to what is good and true, what is fair and honest, pleasures that we experience to the extent that we see our evils as sins and therefore abstain from them and turn away from them, and even more if we actively fight against them. These are the means the Lord uses to purify everyone who is being saved. He also purifies our evils by outward means that have to do with our reputation and respect and sometimes our finances. Even so, the Lord is planting in these means the pleasures of desires for what is good and true that guide and adapt them so that they become pleasures of a love for our neighbor.

[13] If we were to see the pleasures of our compulsions to evil in some kind of visible form or feel them clearly with any other sense, we would see and sense that there are so many that they cannot be delimited. Hell in its totality is nothing but a form of all our compulsions to evil; and in hell there is no single compulsion to evil that is exactly like any other. There cannot be one exactly like another to eternity. We know almost nothing about these countless elements, let alone how they are connected; and yet in his divine providence the Lord is constantly letting them come forth so that they can be withdrawn, doing this in a perfect pattern and sequence. An evil person is a miniature hell, and a good person is a miniature heaven.

[14] There is no better way to see and be assured that the Lord accomplishes this withdrawal from evils in a thousand ways, some most mysterious, than to look at the mysterious workings of the soul in the body. Here are some that we know about.

We know that when we are going to eat something we look at it, smell it, want it, taste it, break it up with our teeth, and use our tongues to send it down the esophagus into the stomach. However, there are mysterious workings of the soul of which we are totally unaware because we do not feel them. The stomach churns the food it has received, breaks it down and sorts it out with its secretions—that is, digests it—and assigns the elements to the appropriate open pores and veins that take them in, carrying some elements off into the blood, some into the lymphatic vessels, and some into the lacteal vessels of the mesentery, while some are sent down into the intestines. Then the chyle that comes from its reservoir in the mesentery is brought down through the thoracic duct into the vena cava and from there into the heart, and from the heart into the lungs. From there it passes through the left ventricle of the heart into the aorta, and from there through the whole branching system into the organs of the whole body. Material is also brought to the kidneys, in both of which there take place separation, purification, and withdrawal from the blood of elements that are not suitable. Allow me to leave out how the heart sends the blood that has been purified in the lungs up to the brain, which it does through the carotid arteries, and how the brain sends energized blood back into the vena cava just above the place where the thoracic duct injects the chyle, and from there back to the heart.

[15] These are some of the mysterious workings of the soul in the body, and there are many others. Most people are unaware of them, and people who are not trained in anatomy know nothing about them. Yet things like this are going on in the deeper reaches of our own minds, since nothing can happen in the body unless it comes from the mind. The mind is our spirit, and the spirit is just as much a person as we are. The only difference is that the things that happen in the body happen on the physical level and the things that happen in the mind happen on the spiritual level. There is a perfect parallelism.

We can see from this that divine providence works in a thousand ways, some most mysterious, in each of us, and that its constant effort is to purify us. This is because it is focused on the goal of saving us; and all that is required of us is that we set aside the evils in our outer self. The Lord takes care of the rest, if we ask.

3. *The Lord cannot fully lead evil people away from their evils and guide them in what is good as long as they believe that their own intelligence is everything and that divine providence is nothing.* It seems as though we can lead ourselves away from evil if we only think that it is against the common good, impractical, and against national and international law. Evil people can do this just as well as good people if by birth or by training they are the kind of people who can think to themselves with analytic and rational clarity. However, we still cannot lead ourselves away from evil.

297

This is because while the Lord gives the ability to understand and appreciate things abstractly to everyone, evil and good alike (as already noted any number of times [§§86, 96, 99, 223, 285]), such understanding still does not enable us to lead ourselves away from evil. Evil is a matter of our volition, and our discernment does not flow into our volition except to give it light, to illuminate it, and to instruct it. If the warmth of our volition (that is, our life's love) is hot because of obsessions with evil, it is cold toward any desire for what is good. This means that it does not accept the light, but reflects it back, or stifles it, or turns it into evil by inventing some distortion. Winter sunlight, which is just as bright as summer sunlight, does the same thing when it flows into frozen trees.

However, it will be easier to see this in the following sequence. (a) When our volition is devoted to evil, our own intelligence sees nothing but falsity. It neither wants to see anything else nor is able to. (b) If our own intelligence does see anything true at such times, it either turns away or falsifies it. (c) Divine providence is constantly making sure we see what is true and giving us a desire to both appreciate it and accept it. (d) In this way we are led away from evil not by ourselves but by the Lord.

298 These items need to be explained in sequence, though, so that whether rational people are evil or good, whether their light is winter sunlight or summer sunlight, they will see them in the same colors.

(a) *When our volition is devoted to evil, our own intelligence sees nothing but falsity. It neither wants to nor is able to see anything else.* I have often been shown this in the spiritual world. When we become spirits, which happens after death, all of us take off our physical bodies and put on spiritual ones. We are then led alternately into our two basic states of life, the outer one and the inner one. When we are in the outer state we talk and act rationally and wisely just like any rational and wise individual in this world. We can tell others a tremendous number of things about moral and civic living. If we were ministers, we can teach about spiritual living as well. However, when we leave that outer state and come into the inner one, when the outer one becomes dormant and the inner one is awakened, then if we are evil people it is a different scene. We become sense-centered instead of rational, and insane instead of wise. Our thinking is prompted by the evil of our volition and its pleasure, which means that we are thinking with our own intelligence. We cannot see anything except what is false or do anything except what is evil. We believe that malice is wisdom and that craft is prudence. Our own intelligence convinces us that we are demigods, and our whole mind is thirsty for appalling skills.

[2] I have seen this kind of insanity any number of times. I have also seen people shift back and forth between these two states two or three times in a single hour, which enabled them to see and recognize their insanity; but they still did not want to stay in their rational and moral state. Of their own accord they turned back to their inner sensory and insane state. They loved it more than the other because that was where they found the pleasure of their life's love.

Who would think that evil people are like this under the surface and that they experience such a metamorphosis when they go within? This experience alone shows what our own intelligence is like when its evil intent is in control of our thinking and actions.

It is different for good people. When they shift from their outer to their inner state, they become even wiser and more decent.

[3] (b) *If our own intelligence does see anything true at such times, it either turns away or falsifies it.* We have both an emotional and a cognitive sense of identity.[290] Our emotional sense of identity is evil and our cognitive sense of identity is the falsity that it prompts. The first is what is meant by "the will of man" and the second by "the will of the flesh" in John 1:13.[291]

Essentially, our voluntary side is a love for ourselves and our cognitive side is a pride born of that love. They are like two married partners, and their marriage is called the marriage of what is evil and what is false. Every evil spirit is consigned to this marriage before entering hell; and once people are there they do not know what is good, since they call their evil good and experience it as pleasant. They turn away from truth as well and do not want to see it. This is because they see the falsity that agrees with their evil the way the eye sees beauty, and they hear it the way the ear hears harmony.

[4] (c) *Divine providence is constantly making sure we see what is true and giving us a desire to both appreciate it and accept it.* This happens because divine providence is acting from the inside and flowing through to the outside, from the spiritual level into things in our lower self. Then it enlightens our discernment with heaven's light and gives life to our volition with heaven's warmth. Essentially, heaven's light is divine wisdom and heaven's warmth is divine love; and nothing can flow in from divine wisdom except what is true, and nothing can flow in from divine love except what is good. This is how the Lord gives our discernment a desire to see what is true and to appreciate and accept it; and this is how we become human not only as to our outer face but as to our inner one as well.

Is there anyone who does not want to seem like a rational and spiritual individual? Is anyone not aware of the desire to be regarded by others as truly human? If we are rational and spiritual only in outward form, then, and not inwardly as well, are we human? Are we anything but an actor on the stage or an ape with an almost human face? Does this not show that we are human only when we are inwardly as human as we seem to others? If we recognize the one kind of humanity, we must recognize the other.

The only thing our own intelligence can do is adopt a human form outwardly, but divine providence can adopt one inwardly and give us an outward form through the inner. When this is done, then we not only look human, we are human.

[5] (d) *In this way we are led away from evil not by ourselves but by the Lord.* The reason we can be led away from evil when divine providence enables us to see what is true and gives us a desire for it as well is that truth points out and indicates things. When our volition does these things, it unites with truth and transforms it to something good within itself. It becomes a matter of its love, and whatever is a matter of love is good. All our reformation is accomplished by means of truth and not apart from it, since in the absence of truth our volition stays dedicated to evil. If it does look to our discernment it is not taught anything. Instead, its evil is justified by falsities.

[6] As for our intelligence, it seems to be ours, really to belong to us, whether we are good or evil. Good people are kept in a state of acting from their intelligence as though it belonged to them, just as evil people are. If we believe in divine providence, though, we are kept from evil; but if we do not believe, we are not kept from it. When we recognize that an evil is a sin and want to be kept from it, we believe; when we do not recognize and want this, we do not believe. The difference between the two kinds of intelligence is like the difference between something we believe to be inherently real and something we believe is not inherently real but which still seems to be. It is like an outer surface that does not have an inner substance consistent with it, and an outer surface that does have such an inner substance. So it is like the speech and actions of mimes and actors who play the parts of royal and noble persons on the one hand, and the royals and nobles themselves on the other. The latter are the same inwardly as they are outwardly. The others have only the outward guise, and when they lay that aside we call them comics, actors, and impersonators.

299 4. *The Lord controls the hells by means of opposites. As for evil people who are still in this world, he controls them in hell as to their deeper natures, but not as to their more outward natures.* People who do not know what heaven and hell are like have no way whatever of knowing what the human mind is like. Our mind is our spirit, the spirit that lives after death. This is because the whole form of our mind or spirit is like the form of heaven or hell. There is no difference whatever except that the one is immense and the other minute, or that the one is the model and the other the impression. As far as our minds or spirits are concerned, then, we are either a miniature heaven or a miniature hell, a heaven if we are being led by the Lord and a hell if we are leading ourselves.

Since I have been allowed to know what heaven is like and what hell is like, and since it is important that we know our nature as to mind or spirit, I want to offer a brief description of each.

All the people who are in heaven are simply desires for what is good and the consequent recognition of what is true; and all the people who are in hell are simply obsessions with evil and the consequent illusions of falsity. These are arranged on each side so that the obsessions with evil and illusions of falsity in hell are exactly opposite to the desires for what is good and recognition of what is true in heaven. So hell is under heaven and diametrically opposed to it, as diametrically opposed as two people lying in opposite directions or stationed foot to foot, one upside down, and both united at the soles of their feet, heel against heel. Sometimes hell can be seen in this kind of location or direction relative to heaven.

The reason is that for people in hell, obsessions with evil constitute the head, and desires for what is good constitute the feet, while for people in heaven desires for what is good constitute the head, and obsessions with evil constitute the soles of the feet. This means that they are opposites of each other.

To say that there are desires for what is good and therefore recognition of truth in heaven, and that there are obsessions with evil and therefore illusions of falsity in hell, is actually to say that there are spirits and angels of this quality, because we are all our own desire or our own obsession. Heaven's angels are their own desires and hell's spirits are their own obsessions.

The reason heaven's angels are desires for what is good and a consequent recognition of truth is that they are receptive of divine love and wisdom from the Lord, and all desires for what is good come from divine love, and all recognition of truth comes from divine wisdom. On the other hand, the reason all spirits of hell are obsessions with evil and consequent illusions of falsity is that they are wrapped up in their self-love and in their own intelligence, and all obsessions with evil come from self-love, and all illusions of falsity come from our own intelligence.

The arrangement of desires in heaven and of obsessions in hell is astonishing: only the Lord knows it. In each case, they are differentiated into genera and species and so coordinated that they act as a unit. Since they are differentiated into genera and species, they are divided into larger and smaller communities; and since they are coordinated so as to act as a unit, they are coordinated the way everything in a person is. As a result, heaven in its form is like a beautiful person whose soul is divine love and wisdom, or the Lord. Hell in its form is like a grotesque person whose soul is self-love and self-intelligence, or the devil. There is actually no "Devil" who is the sole lord in hell; that is a name for self-love.

303   For a better understanding of what heaven and hell are like, substitute "pleasures in what is good" for "desires for what is good" and "pleasures in evil" for "obsessions with evil." After all, there is no desire or obsession that does not have its pleasures: in each case, it is the pleasures that provide the life. They are differentiated and united just the way desires for what is good and obsessions with evil are differentiated and united, as already described [§302]. Every angel in heaven is filled with and surrounded by the pleasure of his or her particular desire. So too, a shared desire fills and surrounds every community in heaven, and the pleasure shared by all, the most pervasive pleasure, fills and surrounds heaven as a whole. In the same way, every spirit in hell is filled with and surrounded by the pleasure of her or his particular obsession, a shared pleasure fills and surrounds every community in hell, and the shared pleasure of all, the most pervasive pleasure, surrounds hell as a whole.

Since heaven's desires and hell's obsessions are diametrically opposed to each other, as already noted [§300], we can see that heaven's pleasure is so painful in hell that people there cannot bear it, and conversely that hell's pleasure is so painful in heaven that people there cannot bear it. This gives rise to hostility, repulsion, and separation.

304   Since these pleasures constitute the life of each individual and of everyone in general, they are not sensed by the people who have them;[292] but the opposite ones are sensed when they come near. This happens especially when they are turned into odors. Every pleasure has a corresponding odor, and in the spiritual world it can be turned into its odor. When this happens in heaven, a shared pleasure smells like a garden, varying depending on the scents of the particular flowers and fruits it contains. A shared pleasure in hell smells like stagnant water into which different kinds of sewage have been discharged, varying depending on the particular stenches of the decaying and putrid matter in it.

I have been shown how people feel the pleasure of each particular desire for what is good in heaven and the pleasure of each obsession with evil in hell, but it would take too long to present that now.

305   I have heard any number of newcomers from our world complain that they did not know that their lot in life would depend on the desires of their love. They said they had not thought about them in this

world, let alone about the pleasures associated with them. They had loved whatever gave them pleasure and had simply believed that our lot depended on what we thought intellectually, especially what we thought in matters of devotion and therefore of faith.

However, they were told that if they had wanted to, they might have known that an evil life is unwelcome in heaven and displeasing to God, but welcome in hell and pleasing to the devil. By the same token, a good life is welcome in heaven and pleasing to God, but unwelcome in hell and displeasing to the devil. By the same token, evil is inherently foul smelling and good is inherently fragrant. Since they could have known this if they had wanted to, why had they not abstained from evils as hellish and demonic, and why had they approved of them simply because they felt good? Since they now knew that the pleasures of evil had such an acrid smell, they could also know that they could not come into heaven smelling like that.

When they had been given this answer, they made their way to people who were devoted to the same kinds of pleasure, because that was the only place where they could breathe.

Given this picture of heaven and hell, the nature of the human mind is clear. As already stated [§§296, 299], our mind or spirit is either a miniature heaven or a miniature hell. Its contents are simply desires and the thoughts that they prompt, differentiated into genera and species the way heaven is differentiated into larger and smaller communities and united so that they act as a unity. The Lord oversees our desires and thoughts in the same way that he oversees heaven and hell. **306**

On the human being as either a miniature heaven or a miniature hell, see *Heaven and Hell* 51–87 [51–86] (published in London in 1758).

We may turn now to the basic proposition that the Lord controls the hells by means of opposites, and that with evil people who are still in this world, he controls them in hell as to their deeper natures, but not as to their more outward natures. **307**

As to the first, that *the Lord controls the hells by means of opposites,* I explained in §§288–289 that heaven's angels do not get their love and wisdom, or desire for what is good and resultant thought about what is true, from themselves, but from the Lord. I noted that the goodness and truth flow from heaven into hell, and that the goodness there is turned into evil and the truth into falsity because the inner reaches of people's minds there are turned in the opposite direction. Since everything in hell is the opposite of everything in heaven, it follows that the Lord is controlling the hells by means of these opposites.

[2] Second, the reason that *with evil people who are still in this world, the Lord controls them in hell* is that as to our spirits we are in the spiritual world, each in some community. We are in a hellish community if we are evil, and in a heavenly community if we are good. Since our minds are inherently spiritual, they can be with spiritual people only, people we will join after death. I have also mentioned and explained this above [§§298, 299].

We are not located there the way spirits are who have been enrolled in a community, though. We are in a constant state of reforming, so depending on our life and the way it changes, the Lord moves us from one community in hell to another if we are evil, while if we are allowing ourselves to be reformed, he leads us out of hell and up into heaven. There too, we are moved from one community to another. This goes on until we die, at which point we are no longer transferred from community to community, because we are no longer in a state of reforming. Instead, we settle in the one where our life places us; so when we die, we are enrolled in our own location.

[3] Third,[293] *the Lord controls evil people in this world one way as to their inner natures and another way as to their outer natures.* The Lord controls the inner levels of the mind as just described, but he controls the outer levels in the world of spirits that is halfway between heaven and hell. This is because most of us are not the same outwardly as we are inwardly. Outwardly we can impersonate angels of light even though inwardly we may be spirits of darkness. As a result, our outer and inner natures are controlled differently; the outer are controlled in the world of spirits and the inner are controlled either in heaven or in hell as long as we are in this world. Consequently, when we die we arrive first in the world of spirits and are conscious in our outer nature. We lay that nature aside in the world of spirits, and once we have done so we are taken to the place where we are enrolled.

On the world of spirits and its nature, see *Heaven and Hell* 421–535 (published in London in 1758).

Divine Providence Does Not Charge Us with Anything Evil or Credit Us with Anything Good; Rather, Our Own Prudence Claims Both

ALMOST everyone believes that we think and intend autonomously **308** and therefore talk and act autonomously. Can we on our own believe anything else when the appearance is so convincing that it scarcely differs at all from really thinking, intending, speaking, and acting autonomously? Yet this is impossible.

In *Angelic Wisdom about Divine Love and Wisdom,* I explained that there is only one life and that we are life-receivers.[294] I also explained that our volition is a receiver of love and our discernment is a receiver of wisdom, and that these and nothing else are the life that we receive.[295] Further, I explained that by creation, and under divine providence constantly since then, life seems to be within us exactly as though it belonged to us, as though it were ours, but that this is only the way it seems in order that we may be receivers.[296] In §§288–294 above I have explained that the source of our thinking is not in ourselves but in others, whose source is again not in themselves. It all comes from the Lord, whether we are evil or good. Further, this is recognized in the Christian world, especially by people who not only say but even believe that everything good and true comes from the Lord, which includes all wisdom and therefore faith and charity. They also believe that everything evil comes from the devil or from hell.

[2] The only conclusion we can draw from all this is that everything we think and intend is flowing into us, and since all speech flows from thought like an effect from its cause, and all action similarly flows from volition, everything we say and do is flowing in as well, albeit secondarily or indirectly. No one can deny that everything we see, hear, smell, taste, and feel is flowing in. What about the things we think and intend, then? Can there be any difference except that what flows in from the physical world flows in through our outer or physical sensory organs, while what flows in from the spiritual world flows in through the organic substances of our inner senses or our minds? In other words, just as the organs of our outer or physical senses are attuned to material objects, the organic substances of our inner senses or our minds are receptive of spiritual objects.

Since this is our actual state, what is our "self"? Our "self" is not really one or another kind of receiver, since it is nothing but the quality of its own receptivity. It is not some aspect of life that is actually ours. When we say "the self," no one hears anything but a being that lives on its own and therefore thinks and intends on its own. Yet it follows from what has just been said that there is no such self in us and that there cannot be.

309 Allow me, though, to pass on something I have heard from people in the spiritual world. These were people who believed that their own prudence was everything and that divine providence was nothing. I told them that nothing is really ours unless we want to call "ours" the fact that we are one kind of subject or another, or one kind of organ or another, or one kind of form or another—that no one has any "self" as people usually understand the word "self." It is only a kind of attribute. No one actually has the kind of self that is usually meant by the term. These people who credited everything to their own prudence (we could even call them overly invested in their own image)[297] flared up so violently that fire came from their nostrils. "You're talking paradoxes and madness," they said. "Surely this would reduce us to nothing, to emptiness. We would be some idea or hallucination, or some sculpture or statue."

[2] All I could say in response was that the real paradox and madness was believing that we are the source of our own life and that wisdom and prudence do not flow into us from God but are within us, believing that this is true of the good that comes from caring and the truth that comes from faith. Any wise person would call this claim madness, and it leads into a paradox as well. Further, this is like people who are living in someone else's house, with someone else's possessions, and convincing themselves that they own them as long as they are living there. Or they are like trustees and stewards who claim as their own everything that actually belongs to their superior, or like the servants to whom the Lord gave greater or lesser sums[298] for business but who claimed them as their own instead of rendering an account of them and therefore acted like thieves [Matthew 25:14–30; Luke 19:12–27]. [3] These are the people we could describe as out of their minds, as nothing and empty. We could also describe them as strict idealists,[299] because they do not have within themselves that goodness from the Lord that is the actual substance of life, so they have no truth either. They could also be called dead, then, and nothing, and empty (Isaiah 40:17, 23, and elsewhere).[300] They are makers of idols, sculptures, and statues.

There is more on this below, though, which will be presented in the following sequence.

1. What our own prudence is and what the prudence is that is not our own.

2. On the basis of our own prudence, we adopt and justify the conviction that we are the source and the locus of everything that is good and true as well as of everything that is evil and false.

3. Everything we adopt and justify becomes virtually a permanent part of us.

4. If we believed that—as is truly the case—everything good and true comes from the Lord and everything evil and false comes from hell, then we would not claim the goodness as our own and make it self-serving or claim the evil as our own and make ourselves guilty of it.

1. *What our own prudence is and what the prudence is that is not our own.* People are devoted to their own prudence when they convince themselves that the way things seem is the way they really are, and particularly when they accept as truth the appearance that their own prudence is everything and that divine providence is nothing but a generality; though as already explained [§201], no such generality could exist without being made up of specifics. They are then caught up in illusions as well, since any appearance that we take to be truth becomes an illusion. Further, to the extent that they justify themselves with illusions, they become materialists to the point that eventually they believe only what they can apprehend with one of their physical senses. They rely primarily on sight because it especially interacts with our thinking. Ultimately they become sense-centered; and if they come down decisively in favor of the material world and against God, they close off the inner levels of their minds and put a kind of veil in the way. From then on, they think underneath this veil, as though nothing above it existed. The ancients called sense-centered people like this "serpents of the tree of knowledge." In the spiritual world they say that as they become fixed in their opinions, people like this close the deeper levels of their minds all the way to the nose. The nose means our sense of what is true, and that sense is lacking.

Now I need to describe what these people are like. [2] They are exceptionally adroit and shrewd, ingenious debaters. They call their ingenuity and shrewdness intelligence and wisdom and see no evidence to the

310

contrary. They look on people who differ from them as simple and stupid, especially if those people revere God and acknowledge divine providence. In the deeper principles of their minds—which they themselves know very little about—they are like the people called Machiavellians, people who trivialize murder, adultery, theft, and perjury as such.[301] If they do argue against such crimes, it is only to be careful that their actual nature does not become obvious.

[3] As far as our life in this world is concerned, the thought that it might be different from that of animals never crosses their minds. They think of our life after death as a kind of living mist that rises up out of the corpse or the tomb and then sinks back down and dies. This insanity leads to the belief that spirits and angels are made of air. Any of these materialists who are obliged to believe in eternal life believe that this is what our souls are like. This means that our souls do not see, hear, or speak, that they are blind, deaf, and mute. All they do is think in their own bit of air. "How could the soul be anything more?" materialists ask. "Aren't the outer senses dead along with the body? We won't get them back until our souls are reunited with our bodies." They cling to these conclusions because they can think about the state of the soul after death only in physical terms, not in spiritual terms. Without their physical concepts they would have lost their belief in eternal life.

They particularly justify their own self-love, calling it the fire of life and the spur to the various useful activities in the state. This makes them their own idols; and their thoughts, being illusions based on illusions, are false images. Since they approve of the pleasures of their obsessions, they are satans and devils. We call them satans because they inwardly justify their obsessions with evil, and devils because they act them out.

[4] I have also been shown what the shrewdest sense-centered people are like. Their hell is deep down at the back, and they want to be unnoticed. So it looks as though they are flying around like ghosts (which are their hallucinations). They are called demons. Once some of them were let out of hell so that I could find out what they are like. They promptly attached themselves to my neck just below the base of my skull and from there moved into my feelings. They did not want to enter my thoughts, and adroitly evaded them. They altered my feelings one at a time, shifting my mood imperceptibly to its opposite, into obsessions with evil; and since they were not touching my thoughts at all, they would have distorted and inverted them without my noticing it if the Lord had not prevented it.

[5] That is what becomes of people who in this world do not believe there is any divine providence, and who pay close attention to others only to find out what their urges and desires are and in this way influence them until they have complete control over them. Since they do this so subtly and shrewdly that others are not aware of it, and since they keep the same nature after death, as soon as they arrive in the spiritual world they are dismissed into this hell. In heaven's light they seem to have no noses, and strange as it may seem, even though they are so shrewd, they are still more sense-centered and superficial than anyone else.

It is because the ancients called sense-centered people "serpents" and because people like this are more deft, shrewd, and clever at debating than others that it says, "The serpent was made shrewd beyond every beast of the field" (Genesis 3:1) and, "The Lord said, 'Be prudent as serpents and simple as doves'" (Matthew 10:16). So too the dragon, who is also called the old serpent, the devil, and satan [Revelation 20:2], is described as "having seven heads and ten crowns, and on the heads seven diadems" (Revelation 12:3, 9). The seven heads mean shrewdness, the ten horns the power of persuasion by distortions, and the seven diadems the holy values of the Word and the Church profaned.

Given this description of our own prudence and of people who believe in it, we can see the nature of the prudence that is not our own and of the people who believe in it. That is, the prudence that is not our own is the prudence people have who do not convince themselves that they are the source of their intelligence and wisdom. They say, "How can people be the source of their own wisdom? How can they do what is good with their own strength?" and when they say it they see within themselves that it is true. Inwardly, they think and believe that other people share this belief, especially educated people, because they do not see how anyone can only think more superficially.

311

[2] Since they are not subject to illusions because of any rationalizations of appearances, they both know and feel that murder, adultery, theft, and perjury are sins, and they therefore abstain from them. They know and feel that malice is not wisdom and that shrewdness is not intelligence. When they hear clever arguments based on illusions, they shake their heads and laugh to themselves. This is because there is no veil between their inner and outer processes, or between the spiritual and the earthly levels of their minds, the way there is in sense-centered people. As a result, they are open to an inflow from heaven that enables them to see things like this more deeply.

[3] They talk more simply and candidly than others and see wisdom as a matter of life rather than of conversation. They are relatively like lambs and doves, while people devoted to their own prudence are like wolves and foxes. Or again, they are like people who live in a house and see the sky through their windows, while people devoted to their own prudence are like people who live in a basement and see nothing through their windows but what is underground. Or again, they are like people standing on a mountain watching people devoted to their own prudence wandering around in the valleys and in the forests.

[4] This shows that a prudence that is not our own is a prudence that comes from the Lord. Outwardly, it looks like our own prudence, but it is totally different inwardly. Inwardly, the prudence that is not our own looks human in the spiritual world, while our own prudence looks like a statue that seems to be alive, solely because people with this prudence still have rationality and freedom, or the ability to discern and to intend and therefore to talk and act. These abilities enable them to pretend to be human. The reason they are statues like this is that what is evil and false is not alive. Only what is good and true is alive; and since they know this rationally—otherwise they would not put on the pretense—they have some lifelike humanity in their statues.

[5] Can anyone fail to realize that our real quality is our inner quality, and that therefore a real person is one whose inner quality is what he or she wants people to see outwardly, and that a statue is someone who is human only outwardly and not inwardly? Think the way you talk—in favor of God, in favor of religion, in favor of justice and honesty—and you will be human. Then divine providence will be your prudence, and you will see in others that their own prudence is insanity.

312   2. *On the basis of our own prudence, we adopt and justify the conviction that we are the source and the locus of everything that is good and true as well as of everything that is evil and false.* Let us try an argument by analogy, an analogy between what is good and true on the physical level and what is good and true on the spiritual level. We begin by asking what is true and good to our eyesight. To our eyes, is not something true when we call it beautiful, and good when we call it pleasing? We do feel pleasure at beautiful sights. What is true and good to our hearing? Is not something true when we call it harmonious and good when we call it sweet? We feel soothed by harmonious sounds; and it is much the same with our other senses. This shows what truth and goodness are on the physical level.

Now think about what is true and good on the spiritual level. Is spiritual truth anything but what is beautiful and harmonious in spiritual events and objects? Is spiritual good anything but what is pleasing and sweet in our sense of that beauty and harmony?

[2] Let us see, then, whether we can say anything about one that we cannot say about the other, anything about the spiritual that we cannot say about the physical. We say of what is physical that the beauty and pleasure in the eye are flowing in from the objects of vision, and that the harmony and sweetness in the ear are flowing in from the instruments. What else is true of the organic substances of our minds? We say that things are happening within these mental substances but that things are flowing into our physical organs; but if we ask, "Why are we saying that things are flowing in?" the only answer is that there seems to be a distance involved. Then if we ask, "Why are we saying that things are happening inside?" the only answer is that there is no perceptible distance involved. That is, it is the appearance of distance that inclines us to believe one thing about what we think and feel, and something else about what we see and hear.

All this collapses, though, when we realize that spirit is not involved in distance the way the material world is. Think of the sun and the moon or of Rome and Constantinople. Is there any distance between them in your thought? There is none as long as the thought is not tied to the experiences we have through sight and hearing. Then why do you convince yourself that what is good and true and what is evil and false are within you, not flowing in, simply because there is no perceptible distance involved in your thinking?

[3] I may add here an experience that is quite common in the spiritual world. One spirit can instill her or his own thoughts and desires into another spirit, and the other spirit is totally unaware that the thought and desire are not arising spontaneously. In the spiritual world they call this thinking in someone else or thinking from someone else. I have seen this a thousand times, and even in the hundreds of times I have done it the appearance of distance was clearly evident. However, as soon as people realized that someone else was instilling these thoughts and feelings, they became resentful and turned away, recognizing still that the distance would not have been perceptible in their inner sight or thought unless it had been unveiled to their inner sight or eye, so to speak. This enabled them to recognize that it was flowing in.

[4] I may append to this experience something that happens to me every day. Evil spirits are often inserting evil and false elements into my thoughts, things that seem to me to be within and from myself, as though I myself were thinking them. However, since I have realized that they were evil and false, I have asked who was inserting them. They have

been unmasked and driven away, and they were at a considerable distance from me.

This shows that everything evil is flowing in with its falsity from hell, and that everything good is flowing in with its truth from the Lord, and that both seem to be within us.

313 As for the nature of people who are devoted to their own prudence and the nature of the people who have a prudence not their own and are therefore conscious of divine providence, this is described in the Word by Adam and his wife Eve in the garden of Eden where there were the two trees, one of life and the other of the knowledge of good and evil, and by their eating from this latter tree. You may see in §241 above that in the inner or spiritual meaning Adam and his wife Eve serve to denote and describe the earliest church of the Lord on our planet, one that was finer and more heavenly than the ones that followed it. As for the meaning of other elements of the story, [2] the garden of Eden means the wisdom of the people of that church; the tree of life means the Lord in particular respect to divine providence; and the tree of knowledge means humanity, particularly in respect to our own prudence. The serpent means our sensory level and sense of autonomy, which is essentially our self-love and our pride in our own intelligence, and therefore the devil and Satan. Eating from the tree of knowledge means claiming what is good and true as our own, believing that they do not come from the Lord and therefore belong to the Lord, but come from us and therefore belong to us. Since what is good and what is true are elements of Divinity within us, goodness means everything that has to do with love, and truth means everything that has to do with wisdom. So if we claim these as our own, we cannot help but believe that we are like God. That is why the serpent said, "On the day you eat from it, your eyes will be opened and you will be like God, knowing good and evil" (Genesis 3:5). This is what people do who are in hell because of their self-love and consequent pride in their own intelligence.

[3] The curse imposed on the serpent means the curse of any love and intelligence we claim as our own; the curse imposed on Eve means the curse of our emotional sense of identity; and the curse imposed on Adam means the curse of our cognitive sense of identity.[302] The thorns and thistles that the earth would sprout mean what is wholly false and evil; the expulsion from the garden means the loss of wisdom; the guarding of the way to the tree of life means the Lord's protection of the holy values of the Word and the church from any violation; the fig leaves that covered their nakedness mean moral truths that concealed the activities of their

own love and pride; and the leather garments in which they were later clothed mean the appearances of truth that were all they had.³⁰³

This is what these items mean on the spiritual level; but anyone who wants to do so may stay with the literal meaning. Just be aware that this is what it means in heaven.

We can tell what people who are deceived by their own intelligence are like if we look at what they imagine when deeper judgment is called for, what they imagine about inflow, for example, about thought, and about life.

314

When it comes to *inflow,* they think backwards.³⁰⁴ They think that our eyesight flows into the inner sight of our minds, our discernment, and that the hearing of our ears flows into our inner hearing, which is also our discernment. They do not see that our discernment is flowing from our volition into our eyes and ears and is not only making them sensitive but is using them as its instruments in the physical world. Since this is not the way things seem, they do not see it. Even if you tell them that the physical does not flow into the spiritual but the spiritual does flow into the physical, they will still think, "What is the spiritual except a purer form of the physical? If the eye sees something beautiful and the ear hears something harmonious, doesn't it seem as though the mind—which is discernment and volition—is pleased?" They do not realize that eyes do not see on their own, tongues do not taste on their own, noses do not smell on their own, and skins do not feel on their own. It is our mind or spirit that is sensing in those organs and is being affected by them according to its own nature; and even so, our mind or spirit is not sensing these things on its own, but from the Lord. Any other notion is based on appearances, and if they are accepted as true, it is based on illusions.

[2] As for *thought,* they say that it is some change effected in the air, varied according to the objects we perceive, and reinforced by habit. This means that the concepts of our thoughts are likenesses that we see in the air like phenomena in the sky, and that our memory is the slate on which they are recorded.³⁰⁵ They do not realize that our thoughts take place in substances that are intricately organized, just as our sight and hearing take place in their organs. They should look at the brain, and they would see a wealth of substances like this. Injure them and you go out of your mind; destroy them and you die. On the nature of thought and memory, see the end of §279 above.

[3] Their only concept of *life* is that it is something that nature does, something that makes itself felt in various ways, just as a living body

moves itself organically. If you say that this means nature is alive, they deny it and say that nature only makes things live.[306] If you ask them whether this means that life vanishes when the body dies, they answer that life remains in that bit of air called the soul. If you ask what God is in this case, whether he is life itself, they have no reply and do not want to express what they are actually thinking. If you ask whether they will agree that divine love and wisdom are life itself, they answer, "What is love? What is wisdom?" This is because they cannot see in their illusions what love and wisdom are or what God is.

I include this to show how we are deceived by our own prudence, since we base all our conclusions on appearances and therefore on illusions.

316 [307]   The reason our own prudence convinces and assures us that everything good and true comes from us and is within us is that our own prudence is simply our cognitive sense of identity, flowing from our self-love, which is our emotional sense of identity.[308] Our sense of autonomy inevitably lays claim to everything. It cannot rise above this. Whenever we are being led by the Lord's divine providence, though, we are lifted out of our sense of autonomy and see that everything good and true comes from the Lord. We even see as well that whatever is in us from the Lord always belongs to the Lord and is never ours.

If we believe anything else, we are like people who have been given responsibility for an owner's assets and insist that they belong to us or claim them as our own. This makes us thieves rather than stewards. Further, since our sense of self is nothing but evil, we plunge the owner's assets into our own evil, where they are devoured the way pearls are when they are thrown into a manure pile or into acid.

317   3. *Everything we adopt and justify becomes virtually a permanent part of us.* Many people think that we cannot see any truth except as we can support it with data, but this is not so. We cannot see what is right and useful in civic and economic matters of the country and the state unless we know a host of regulations and protocols; we cannot do the same in legal affairs unless we know the laws, and in material subjects such as physics, chemistry, anatomy, engineering, and the like unless we are skilled scientists. However, in matters that are purely rational, moral, and spiritual, truths can be seen simply in their own light provided a decent education has made us rational, moral, and spiritual individuals. This is because as far as our spirits are concerned—and it is our spirit that thinks—we are in the spiritual world. We are among people there who are in a spiritual light that enlightens the deeper levels of our own discernment and, so to speak, gives direction, since in its essence spiritual light is the divine truth of the Lord's divine wisdom. It is the reason we can think analytically, decide what is fair and proper in legal matters, and see what is honorable in moral matters and good in spiritual matters. We can also see a great deal that is true that lapses into darkness only because of distortions that have been accepted as truths. We see this truth very much the way we see people's moods in their faces and sense their feelings from their tones of voice, using only the knowledge we are born with. Given the way the inflow happens, why should we not be able to see at least to some extent the deeper processes of our lives, which are spiritual and moral, when there is not a single animal that does not know from its inflow what it needs to know, its physical needs? Birds know how to build nests, lay eggs, hatch their chicks, and recognize their own foods, and there are other wonders that we call "instincts."

Now, though, I need to say how our state changes as a result of our justifications and the convictions that they yield, in the following sequence. (a) There is nothing that we cannot rationalize, and we can rationalize falsity more easily than truth. (b) Once we have justified what is false, we cannot see what is true; but once we have justified what is true, we can see what is false. (c) Our ability to justify whatever we please is not intelligence. It is only cleverness, which even the worst of us may have. (d) There is a kind of intellectual justification that is not volitional as well, but all our volitional justification is intellectual as well. (e) Our justification of what is evil, both volitionally and intellectually, is what makes us believe that our own prudence is everything and that divine providence is nothing. Intellectual justification alone does not do this, however. (f) Anything that we have justified both volitionally and intellectually lasts forever, but not what we have justified only intellectually.

[2] (a) As to the first point, that *there is nothing that we cannot rationalize, and we can rationalize falsity more easily than truth,* is there anything that we cannot justify? Especially when atheists can "prove" that God is not the creator of the universe, but that Nature is her own creatress; that religion is nothing but chains for simple people and commoners; that we are animals and die the way they do? And especially when they can prove that there is nothing wrong with adultery or with surreptitious theft, fraud, and deceptive plots, and that shrewdness is intelligence and malice is wisdom? We all justify our own heresies. Are there not volumes full of proofs of the two primary heresies in Christendom?[309] Make up ten heresies, as obscure as you like, ask clever people to prove them, and they will prove them all. If you then look at them solely

on the basis of their proofs, will you not be seeing false things as true? Given the fact that anything false may shine in our earthly self because of its superficialities and illusions, while truth shines only in our spiritual self, we can see that what is false is easier to prove than what is true.

[3] Let me offer an example to show that anything false and anything evil can be justified to the point that what is false seems to be true and what is evil seems to be good. Let us prove that light is darkness and that darkness is light. Can we not ask what light really is? Is it anything but what we see in our eyes because of their state? What is light to a closed eye? Do not bats and owls have eyes, and do they not see light as darkness and darkness as light? I have heard that some people have sight like this, and they say that hellish people see each other even though they are living in darkness. Do we ourselves not have light in our dreams at midnight? Does this not mean that darkness is light and that light is darkness?

We can answer, though, "What are you talking about? Light is light the way truth is truth, and darkness is darkness the way falsity is falsity."

[4] For another example, let us prove that crows are white. Can we not say that a crow's blackness is simply shadow that is not its real being? Its feathers are white inside, and so is its body. These are the substances that it is actually made of. Since its blackness is a shadow, it becomes white when it gets old. I have seen crows like this. What is blackness, essentially, if not whiteness? Grind up black glass and you will see that the powder is white. This means that if you call a crow black, you are talking about its shadow and not about its real self. We can answer, though, "What are you talking about? This would mean that all birds are white."[310]

I offer these examples, even though they are irrational, to show that we can "prove" the falsity that is opposite to what is true and the evil that is opposite to what is good.

[5] (b) *Once we have justified what is false, we cannot see what is true; but once we have justified what is true, we can see what is false.* Everything false is in darkness and everything true is in the light. We cannot see anything in darkness, so we do not know what anything is unless we feel it. It is different in the light. That is why falsities are called "darkness" in the Word, and why it describes people who believe falsities as walking in darkness and the shadow of death [Psalms 23:4; Isaiah 9:2; 50:10; 59:9; John 12:35]. By the same token, truths are called "light" in the Word, so it describes people who believe truths as walking in the light [Isaiah 2:5; John 11:9; Revelation 21:24] and as "children of light" [John 12:36].

[6] There are many indications that once we have justified what is false, we cannot see what is true; but once we have justified what is true, we can see what is false. Can anyone see anything that is spiritually true without being taught by the Word? Would there not be nothing but darkness that can be dispelled only by light from the Word, and then only for people who are willing to be enlightened? Are there any heretics who can see their errors unless they are open to real truth from the church? Until they are, they cannot. I have talked with people who had convinced themselves of faith separate from charity, asking whether they had seen how much it says in the Word about love and caring, about works and deeds, and about keeping the Commandments, to the effect that people who kept them were blessed and wise and that people who did not were stupid. They have told me that when they read such things, all they could see was that they were about faith, so they skipped over them as though their eyes were closed.

[7] People who have convinced themselves of falsities are like people who see streaks on a wall, and when they do so in the evening shadows, they see the streaks in their imagination as a rider or some other human figure, an optical illusion that disappears when daylight shines in. Can anyone feel how spiritually filthy adultery is who does not feel the spiritual purity of chastity? Can anyone feel the cruelty of vengefulness who is not engaged in doing good out of love for his or her neighbor? Is there an adulterer or anyone eager for vengeance who does not ridicule the people who call these pleasures hellish—the people who say that the pleasures of marriage love and love for their neighbor are heavenly? The list could go on.

[8] (c) *Our ability to justify whatever we please is not intelligence. It is only cleverness, which even the worst of us may have.* There are people who are brilliant at justifying things who do not know anything true. They can still justify both truth and falsity. Some of them say, "What is truth? Is there any such thing? Anything is true if I make it true." In this world, these people are considered intelligent, but they are nothing but whitewashers.[311] The only people who are intelligent are the people who can tell that a truth is true and who corroborate this by a constant awareness of truths. It is hard to tell the two kinds of person apart because it is hard to tell the difference between the light of rationalization and the light of a genuine sense of truth. It can seem as though the things we see in the light of rationalization are being presented in the light of a genuine sense of truth; and yet the difference is like the difference between a deceptive light[312] and real light. In the spiritual world, that deceptive light turns

into darkness when real light shines in. It is the light that many people in hell live in; and when they are let out into real light, they cannot see a thing. We can see from this that the ability to justify whatever we please is only cleverness, which even the worst of us may have.

[9] (d) *There is a kind of intellectual justification that is not volitional as well, but all our volitional justification is intellectual as well.* Some examples may serve to illustrate this. There are people who firmly believe in faith separated from charity but who live caring lives. In general, there are people who firmly believe in a false theology but do not live by these false beliefs. They are people who engage in intellectual justification but not volitional justification along with it. However, people who justify a false theology and live by it are engaged in both volitional and intellectual justification. This is because our discernment does not flow into our volition, but our volition does flow into our discernment.

This enables us to see what malicious distortion is and what distortion is that is not malicious, to see that nonmalicious distortion can be united to what is good, but that malicious distortion cannot. This is because nonmalicious distortion is distortion in our discernment but not in our volition, while malicious distortion is distortion in our discernment because of malice in our volition.

[10] (e) *Our justification of what is evil, both volitionally and intellectually, is what makes us believe that our own prudence is everything and that divine providence is nothing. Intellectual justification alone, however, does not do this.* There are many people who inwardly are convinced of their own prudence because of the way things seem in this world but who still do not deny divine providence. Their conviction is intellectual only. If they also deny divine providence, though, they are engaged in volitional justification as well. This attitude and bias are found primarily among people who deify the material world and themselves.

[11] (f) *Anything that we have justified both volitionally and intellectually lasts forever, but not what we have justified only intellectually.* Anything that is only in our discernment is not within us but outside us. It is only in our thought, and nothing really comes into us and becomes part of us except what is welcomed by our volition. This becomes part of our life's love. The next section will explain that this stays with us forever.

319 The reason that everything we have justified in both our volition and our discernment stays with us forever is that we are our own love, and love is the substance of our volition. Or it is because we are our own good or our own evil, since everything good in us is a matter of love, and the same is true of everything evil.

Since we are our own love, we are also the forms of our own love and can be called organs of our life's love. I explained in §279 above that our feelings and consequent thoughts are changes and variations of the state and form of the organic substances of our minds. Now I need to explain the nature and quality of those changes and variations.

We can get a relative concept of them from our heart and lungs. Their changes are alternating expansions and compressions, or dilations and contractions. In the heart we call them systole and diastole, in the lungs they are our breathing, the alternating stretching and restraining, or the parting and squeezing, of their lobes. These are the changes and variations of the states of our heart and lungs. Similar things happen in the other organs of our bodies, and quite similar things in their parts, the parts through which our blood and life fluid[313] is accepted and circulated.

[2] Much the same happens in the organic forms of the mind, which as already noted [§279] are the subjects of our feelings and thoughts. The difference is that their expansions and compressions, their alternating motions, are relatively so much more perfect that there is no way to describe them in the words of ordinary language. Only the words of spiritual language are adequate, and these necessarily sound like whirlpools spiraling in and out like endless twisted coils joined together in forms that are wonderfully receptive of life.

[3] Now, though, I need to state what these purely organic substances and forms are like in evil people and in good people. In good people, the spirals face forward and in evil people they face backward. When they spiral forward they are turned toward the Lord and are open to the inflow from him. When they spiral backward they are turned toward hell and are open to its inflow. It is important to realize that to the extent that they are turned backward they are open behind and closed in front, and that conversely, to the extent that they are turned forward they are open in front and closed behind.

[4] This shows what kind of form or what kind of organ an evil person is and what kind of form or organ a good person is—they are turned in opposite directions. Further, since once a direction is established it cannot be twisted back the other way, we can see that we keep forever the orientation we have when we die. It is our volition's love that determines this direction, or that turns us forward or backward; for as just noted, each of us is her or his love. That is why after death we all follow the path

of our love—to heaven if we have loved what is good and to hell if we have loved what is evil. We find no rest until we arrive in the community where our own dominant love is; and strange as it may sound, we all know the way. It is as though we were following a scent.

320   4. *If we believed that—as is truly the case—everything good and true comes from the Lord and everything evil and false comes from hell, then we would not claim the goodness as our own and make it self-serving or claim the evil as our own and make ourselves guilty of it.*[314] However, this contradicts the belief of people who have convinced themselves of the appearance that wisdom and prudence come from themselves and do not flow in according to the way their minds are structured (see §319 above). For this reason, it needs to be explained; and to do that clearly, I shall use the following sequence. (a) If we convince ourselves of the appearance that wisdom and prudence come from ourselves and are therefore within us as our own possessions, it necessarily seems to us that if this were not the case we would not be human at all, only animals or statues; and yet the truth is just the opposite. (b) It seems as though it would be impossible to believe and think in accord with the truth that everything good and true comes from the Lord and everything evil and false from hell, when in fact to do so is truly human and angelic. (c) Believing and thinking like this is impossible for people who do not acknowledge the Lord's divine nature and who do not acknowledge that evils are sins; but it is possible for people who acknowledge these two facts. (d) If we make these two acknowledgments, we simply reflect on the evils within ourselves and, to the extent that we abstain and turn from them as sins, throw them back into the hell they came from. (e) This means that divine providence does not charge anyone with evil or credit anyone with good. Rather, our own prudence makes each of these claims.

321   But these need to be explained in the order just given.

(a) *If we convince ourselves of the appearance that wisdom and prudence come from ourselves and are therefore within us as our own possessions, it necessarily seems to us that if this were not the case we would not be human at all, only animals or statues; and yet the truth is just the opposite.* A law of divine providence says that we are to think in apparent autonomy and act prudently in apparent autonomy but are to recognize that this comes from the Lord. It follows that if we do in fact think and act in apparent autonomy and also recognize that it is coming from the Lord we are human, but that we are not human if we convince ourselves that everything we think and do comes from ourselves. Nor are we human if we simply wait for something to flow in because we know that wisdom and prudence come from God. In this case, we are like statues, while in the former case we are like animals.

Clearly, if we wait for something to flow in, we are like statues. If all we can do is stand or sit motionless, hands hanging down, eyes either closed or open without blinking, neither thinking nor breathing—how much life do we have then?

[2] We can also see that if we believe that everything we think and do comes from ourselves, we are not all that different from animals. After all, we are then thinking solely with our earthly mind, the mind that we have in common with animals, and not with our spiritual rational mind, which is our truly human mind. It is this latter mind that realizes that only God thinks autonomously and that we think from God. Then too, the only difference our earthly mind can see between us and animals is that we talk and animals make noises. It believes that death is the same for both.

[3] Something more needs to be said about people who wait for something to flow in. The only people of this kind who actually receive anything are the few who deeply long for it. They occasionally receive a kind of answer through a vivid impression or a subtle voice in their thinking, but rarely through anything obvious. In any case, what they receive leaves them to think and act the way they want to and the way they can. If they act wisely they become wise, and if they act stupidly they become stupid. They are never told what to believe or what to do; otherwise their human rationality and freedom would be destroyed. That is, things are managed so that they act freely and rationally, and to all appearances, autonomously.

If some inflow tells us what to believe or what to do, it is not the Lord or any angel of heaven who is telling us but some fanatical spirit, perhaps Quaker or Moravian,[315] and we are being led astray. Everything that flows in from the Lord flows in by an enlightenment of our understanding and by a desire for what is true, actually through the desire into the enlightenment.

[4] (b) *It seems as though it would be impossible to believe and think in accord with the truth that everything good and true comes from the Lord and everything evil and false from hell, when in fact to do so is truly human and truly angelic.* It seems possible to think and believe that everything good and true comes from the Lord as long as we say no more than that. This is because it is in accord with the official faith,[316] and we are not allowed to think to the contrary. However, it seems impossible to think and believe that everything evil and false comes from hell, because if we

believed this we would not be able to think at all. Still, we seem to think for ourselves even if it is coming from hell, because the Lord provides that no matter where our thinking is coming from it seems to be happening within us and to be ours. Otherwise, we would not live like humans. We could not be led out of hell and led into heaven—that is, reformed, as I have explained so often already [§§96, 114, 174, 210]. [5] So too, the Lord provides that we realize and therefore think we are in hell if we are bent on evil and that our thoughts are coming from hell if they come from evil. He also enables us to think of ways that we can get out of hell and not accept thoughts from hell but instead come into heaven and there think from him. He also gives us a freedom to choose. We can therefore see that we can think what is evil and false in apparent autonomy; and we can also think in apparent autonomy that one thing or another is evil and false. We can think that this autonomy is only the way things seem, and that otherwise we would not be human.

It is essentially human and therefore angelic to base our thoughts on the truth; and the truth is that we do not think on our own but that the Lord enables us to think, to all appearances autonomously.

[6] (c) *Believing and thinking like this is impossible for people who do not acknowledge the Lord's divine nature and who do not acknowledge that evils are sins; but it is possible for people who acknowledge these two facts.* The reason it is impossible for people who do not acknowledge the Lord's divine nature is that it is only the Lord who enables us to think and to intend, and if we do not acknowledge the Lord's divine nature, in isolation from him we believe that we are thinking on our own. The reason it is also impossible for people who do not acknowledge that evils are sins is that their thoughts are coming from hell, and all the people there believe that they are doing their own thinking.

We can tell from the abundance of material presented in §§288–294 above that this is possible for people who acknowledge these two facts.

[7] (d) *If we make these two acknowledgments, we simply reflect on the evils within ourselves and, to the extent that we abstain and turn from them as sins, throw them back into the hell they came from.* Is there anyone who does not know—or who cannot know—that what is evil comes from hell and what is good comes from heaven? Can anyone, then, fail to see that we abstain from hell and turn away from it to the extent that we abstain and turn away from evil? On this basis, can anyone fail to see that we intend and love what is good to the extent that we abstain and turn away from evil, and that in fact the Lord releases us from hell to that same

extent and leads us to heaven? All rational people can see this provided they know that hell and heaven exist and know where evil and good come from. If, then, we reflect on the evils in ourselves, which is the same as self-examination, and abstain from them, then we extricate ourselves from hell, turn our backs on it, and make our way into heaven where we see the Lord face to face. We may say that *we* are doing this, but we are doing it in apparent autonomy, and therefore from the Lord.

When we acknowledge this truth from a good heart and a devout faith, then it is subtly present from then on in everything we seem to ourselves to be thinking and doing, the way fertility is present in a seed at every step until the formation of a new seed, or the way there is pleasure in our appetite for the food that we realize is good for us. In a word, it is like the heart and soul of everything we think and do.

[8] (e) *This means that divine providence is not charging anyone with evil or crediting anyone with good. Rather, our own prudence is making each of these claims.* This follows from everything that has just been said. The goal of divine providence is goodness. That is what it is aiming at in everything it does; so it does not credit anyone with goodness, because that would make our goodness self-serving; and it does not charge anyone with evil, because that would make us guilty of evil. We make both of these claims out of our own sense of independence, because this sense of ours is nothing but evil. The claim to independence of our volition is self-love, and the claim to independence of our discernment is pride in our own intelligence; and that is where our own prudence comes from.

Everyone Can Be Reformed, and There Is No Such Thing as Predestination

SOUND reason tells us that everyone is predestined to heaven and no one to hell. We are all born human, which means that we have the image of God within us. The image of God within us is our ability to discern what is true and to do what is good. Our ability to discern what is true comes from divine wisdom and our ability to do what is good comes from divine love. This ability is the image of God; it is enduring with everyone who is whole and is never erased. It is why we can become civic, moral individuals; and if we can become civic and moral individuals, we can become spiritual individuals, since civic and moral life is receptive of spiritual life. We are called civic individuals if we know and abide by the laws of the country we are living in.[317] We are called moral individuals if we make habits and virtues of these laws and live by them for rational reasons.

[2] Next I need to say how civic and moral living is receptive of spiritual living. Live by these laws not only as civic and moral laws but also as divine laws and you will be a spiritual person.

There is hardly a nation so barbaric that it does not have laws forbidding murder, promiscuity with other people's spouses, theft, perjury, and violation of the rights of others. Civic and moral individuals keep these laws in order to be or to seem to be good citizens; but if they do not regard them as divine laws as well, they are civic and moral individuals only on the earthly level. On the other hand, if they do regard them as divine laws, they become civic and moral spiritual individuals.

The difference is that in the latter instance they are not just good citizens of their earthly kingdom, they are good citizens of the kingdom of heaven as well; in the former instance they are good citizens of their earthly kingdom but not of the kingdom of heaven. It is the good they do that makes the difference. The good that worldly civic and moral individuals do is not intrinsically good because they themselves and the world are at its heart. The good that civic and moral spiritual individuals do is intrinsically good because the Lord and heaven are at its heart.

[3] This shows that since we are all born capable of becoming civic and moral individuals on the earthly level, we are also born capable of becoming civic and moral individuals on the spiritual level. All we have to do is acknowledge God and not do evils because they are against God, and do what is good because that is for God. Doing this enables the spirit to enter into our civic and moral acts, and they come to life. Otherwise there is no spirit in our acts, and they are not alive. This is why worldly people are called "dead" no matter how civic and moral their behavior is, while spiritual people are called "living."

[4] Under the Lord's divine providence, every nation has a religion, and the first principle of every religion is a recognition of the existence of God. Otherwise we cannot call it a religion. Every nation that lives by its religion—that is, that does not do evil because it is against its God—is given a spiritual element within its worldly life.

Imagine hearing non-Christians say that they do not want to do some evil thing because it is against their God. Is there anyone who would not say inwardly that these people are saved? Nothing else seems possible; that is what sound reason tells us. Conversely, suppose some Christian says, "One evil or another does not matter to me. What is this business about saying that it's against God?" Is there anyone who would not say inwardly that this person is not saved? It seems impossible; that is what sound reason tells us. [5] If this individual says, "I was born Christian, I was baptized, I have confessed the Lord, read the Word, and taken the Holy Supper," does all this matter if this individual has a craving for murder and revenge, for adultery, surreptitious theft, perjury, lies, and all kinds of violence, and does not regard them as sins? Are people like this thinking about God or about some eternal life? Do they think that they exist? Surely sound reason tells us that people like this cannot be saved.

I make these statements about Christians because non-Christians pay more attention to God than Christians do, because their religion is in their life.

I need now to say more about this, though, in the following sequence.

1. The ultimate purpose of creation is a heaven from the human race.
2. Consequently, under divine providence everyone can be saved; and everyone is saved who believes in God and lives a good life.
3. It is our own fault if we are not saved.
4. This means that everyone is predestined to heaven and no one to hell.

1. *The ultimate purpose of creation is a heaven from the human race.* I have explained in *Heaven and Hell* (published in London in 1758)[318] and earlier in the present work [§27] that heaven is made up solely of individuals who have been born as people on earth; and since these are the only inhabitants of heaven, it follows that the ultimate purpose of creation is a heaven from the human race.

I explained in §§27–45 above that this is the purpose of creation, but this will become even clearer from the following details. (a) Everyone is created to live forever. (b) Everyone is created to live forever in a blessed state. (c) This means that everyone is created to go to heaven. (d) Divine love cannot do otherwise than intend this and divine wisdom cannot do otherwise than provide for this.

324 Since this also shows us that divine providence is a predestination only to heaven and that it cannot be changed into anything else, I need to show at this point that the ultimate purpose of creation is a heaven from the human race, and I need to do so in the order just proposed.

(a) *Everyone is created to live forever.* In parts 3 and 4 of *Divine Love and Wisdom,* I explained that we have three levels of life called earthly, spiritual, and heavenly, and that these levels are active in each one of us. I also noted that there is only one level of life in animals, a level like the lowest level in us, the one called earthly. It then follows that unlike animals, we can have our life so lifted toward the Lord that we enter a state in which we can discern things that come from divine wisdom and intend things that come from divine love, and in this way can accept something divine. If we can accept what is divine to the extent that we see and sense it within ourselves, then we must necessarily be able to be united to the Lord and to live forever because of this union.

[2] What would the Lord have been doing with all this creating of a universe if he had not made images and likenesses of himself with whom he could share his divine nature? Otherwise, it would only have been making something so that it existed and did not exist, or so that it happened and did not happen, and doing this only so that he could simply watch its permutations from far away, watch its ceaseless changes like something happening on a stage. What divine purpose would there be in all these changes unless they were serving subjects who would accept something divine more intimately, who would see and sense it? Since Divinity has inexhaustible splendor, would it simply keep it all to itself? Could it keep it all to itself? Love wants to share what it has with others, to give to others all that it can. What about divine love, then, which is infinite? Can it first give and then take back? Would this not be giving something that was bound to perish—that was intrinsically nothing, since it would become nothing when it perished? There is no real "is" involved in that. Divinity, though, gives what truly is, or what does not cease to be. This is what is eternal.

[3] To enable us to live forever, what is mortal is taken from us. That mortal part is our material body, which is taken from us by death. This lays bare what is immortal about us, which is our mind, and we then become spirits in human form. Our mind is that kind of spirit.

The sages and wise ones of old saw that our mind could not die. They asked how a spirit or a mind could die when it could be wise. Hardly anyone nowadays knows the ancients' deeper concept of the matter, but it was a concept from heaven that resulted in their general sense that God is wisdom itself, that we share in that wisdom, and that God is immortal or eternal.

[4] There is also something I can say from experience, because I have been allowed to talk with angels. I have talked with some who lived many centuries ago, with some from before the Flood and some from after it, with some from the time of the Lord, with one of his apostles, and with many who lived in subsequent centuries. They all looked like people in the prime of life and told me that the only thing they knew about death was that it was damnation.

When people who have lived good lives get to heaven, they all enter the young adulthood of their earthly lives and keep it forever, even though they had been old and debilitated in the world. Women, even women who had become old and frail in the world, return to the flower of youth and beauty.

[5] We can see from the Word that we live forever after death, in passages where life in heaven is called eternal life. See, for example, Matthew 19:29; 25:46; Mark 10:17; Luke 10:25; 18:30; John 3:15, 16, 36; 5:24, 25, 39; 6:27, 40, 68; 12:50. Or it is simply called "life," as in Matthew 18:8, 9; John 5:40; 20:31. The Lord told the disciples, "Because I am alive, you will also live" (John 14:19), and he said of the resurrection that God is God of the living and not God of the dead, and that they could no longer die (Luke 20:36, 38).

[6] (b) *Everyone is created to live forever in a blessed state.* This is a corollary, since the One who wants us to live forever wants us to live in a blessed state as well. Otherwise, what would eternal life be? Love always wants what is good for others. Parents' love wants what is good for their children; a groom's or husband's love wants what is good for his bride or wife; our love in friendship wants what is good for our friends; so why not divine love? Further, what is goodness if it is not pleasing, and as for divine good, what is it if it is not eternal bliss? We call things good because of the pleasure or blessedness they provide. We do refer to things that we are given or own as "good," but unless they give us pleasure, it is a barren kind of goodness that is not really good at all. We can see, then, that eternal life is eternal blessedness as well.

This state of humanity is the ultimate goal of creation, and the Lord is not to blame if only the people who get to heaven enjoy it. That is our own fault, as we shall shortly see.

[7] (c) *This means that everyone is created to go to heaven.* This is the ultimate goal of creation. The reason not everyone gets to heaven, though, is that people immerse themselves in pleasures of hell that are

contrary to the blessedness of heaven. People who do not enjoy heaven's bliss cannot enter heaven because they cannot stand the place.

When we arrive in the spiritual world, no one is forbidden to come up to heaven, but if we enjoy the pleasures of hell, then as soon as we get to heaven our hearts pound, we struggle for breath, our life starts to ebb away, we are in pain, tortured, and we writhe like snakes next to a flame. This happens because opposites actively oppose each other.

[8] Even so, since we were born human, which provides us with the ability to think and intend and therefore to talk and act, we cannot actually die. Since we are unable to live with others unless their life pleasures are like ours, we are remanded to the company of such people. This means that if we have enjoyed the pleasures of evil, we are sent off to our own kind, as we are if we have enjoyed the pleasures of what is good. In fact, we are all allowed to enjoy the pleasure of our own evil, provided only that we do not make trouble for people who enjoy the pleasure of what is good. However, since evil cannot help but make trouble for the good because of its inherent hatred for everything good, we are sent away to keep us from doing actual harm and sent down to our places in hell, where our pleasure turns into displeasure.

[9] All this does not cancel the fact that by creation and therefore by birth we have the inherent possibility of getting to heaven. All the people who die in early childhood go to heaven. They are raised and taught there the way we are in this world. They absorb wisdom because of their desire for what is good and true, and they become angels. People who are raised and taught in this world could do the same, since what is in little children is also in them. On little children in the spiritual world, see *Heaven and Hell* 329–345 (published in London in 1758).

[10] The reason it is different for so many people in the world is that they love that first level of life called "earthly."[319] They do not want to let go of it and become spiritual—left to itself, this earthly level of life has no love for anything but ourselves and the world. It stays glued to our physical senses, which take center stage in this world. In contrast, the spiritual level of life has an inherent love for the Lord and heaven and also for ourselves and the world. God and heaven come first, though, as primary and definitive, while our selves and the world come second, as tools or servants.

[11] (d) *Divine love cannot do otherwise than intend this and divine wisdom cannot do otherwise than provide for this.* In *Divine Love and Wisdom*, there is ample evidence that the divine essence is divine love and wisdom.[320] I also explained in §§358–370 of that work that the Lord

forms two vessels in every human embryo, one for divine love and one for divine wisdom. The vessel for divine love is for what will be our volition, and the vessel for divine wisdom is for what will be our discernment. This means that each of us has been given the inner ability to intend what is good and to discern what is true.

[12] Since the Lord has put these two human abilities in us at birth, and since the Lord is therefore within us in those abilities as his gifts, we can see that his divine love can intend only that we come into heaven and enjoy eternal blessedness there. We can also see that divine wisdom can provide only that this happen.

However, since the Lord's divine love wants us to feel that heaven's blessedness within us is our own, and since this cannot happen unless we feel absolutely as though we are doing our own thinking and intending, talking and acting, we can be led only in ways that follow the laws of the Lord's divine providence.

2. *Consequently, under divine providence everyone can be saved; and everyone is saved who believes in God and lives a good life.* What has just been presented shows that everyone can be saved. There are people who think that the Lord's church exists only in the Christian world because only there is the Lord known and only there is the Word found. Still, there are a good many people who believe that the church of God is wider, spread out and scattered through all regions of the world, even among people who do not know about the Lord and do not have the Word. They say that it is not these people's fault and that they cannot help being ignorant. It would fly in the face of God's love and mercy if anyone were born for hell when we are all equally human.

[2] Since many Christians (though not all) have a belief that there is a wider church called "a communion," it follows that there must be some very general principles of this wider church that comprises all religions, so that they do make up one communion. We shall see that these most general principles are belief in God and living a good life, in the following sequence. (a) Belief in God brings about God's union with us and our union with God; and denial of God brings about severance. (b) Our belief in God and union with him depend on our living a good life. (c) A good life, or living rightly, is abstaining from evils because they are against our religion and therefore against God. (d) These are the general principles of all religions, through which everyone can be saved.

We need to look at these one at a time and expand on them.

(a) *Belief in God brings about God's union with us and our union with God; and denial of God brings about severance.* Some may believe that people who do not believe in God can be saved just like people who do, provided they lead moral lives. "What does belief accomplish?" they say. "Is it anything but a thought? I could easily believe in God if I knew for certain that God actually existed. I have heard about him, but I haven't seen him. Show me, and I'll believe." Many people who deny the existence of God talk like this when they are given space to argue freely with someone who does believe in God.

But I shall illustrate the fact that belief in God unites and denial of God separates by sharing what I have learned in the spiritual world. If people there think about others and want to talk with them, they are immediately present. This is taken for granted there and never fails. The reason is that there is no distance in the spiritual world the way there is in this physical world, but only an appearance of distance.

[2] Then too, just as thinking about others, together with some awareness of them, causes presence, so a feeling of love for them causes union. This is what makes people accompany each other and converse amiably along the way, live in the same houses or in the same community, meet with each other often, and work on tasks together. The opposite happens, too, if people do not love each other, and even more so if they dislike each other. They do not see each other or get together. They are as far from each other as their lack of love or their active dislike. If by any chance they do meet, that meeting triggers the dislike, and they vanish.

[3] These few examples show what makes for presence and what makes for union in the spiritual world. Specifically, presence comes from remembering others and wanting to see them, and union comes from a feeling that arises from our love.

The same holds true for everything in our minds. There are countless elements there, all arranged and united in accord with our feelings, or the way one element loves another. [4] This union is spiritual union; and it works the same in widely inclusive instances and in individual ones. The source of this spiritual union is in the union of the Lord with the spiritual world and with the physical world, again in inclusive and in individual instances. We can see, then, that to the extent that we believe in the Lord and think about him on the basis of what we understand, the Lord is present, while to the extent that we believe in him on the basis of a loving feeling, the Lord is united with us. Conversely, to the extent that we do not believe in the Lord, the Lord is absent; and to the extent that we deny him, we are separated from him.

[5] A result of union is that the Lord turns our faces toward him and then leads us; and a result of separation is that hell turns our faces toward it and leads us. So all the angels of heaven face toward the Lord as the sun, and all the spirits of hell face away from the Lord. This shows what belief in God does and what denial of God does.

Further, people who deny God in the world deny him after death. They are inwardly structured as described in §319; and the structure adopted in this world remains forever.

[6] (b) *Our belief in God and union with him depend on our living a good life.* Everyone who knows anything religious can know about God. People can talk about God from this knowledge or from memory, and some of them can even think intelligently about God. If they do not live good lives, though, this brings only a presence. They are still perfectly capable of turning away from him and turning toward hell, which they do if they live evil lives.

Heartfelt belief in God, though, is possible only for people who live good lives. Depending on those good lives, the Lord turns them away from hell and toward himself. This is because it is only they who actually love God. They love the divine values that come from him by living them. The divine values that come from God are the commandments of his law. These commandments are God, since he is the divine nature that emanates from him. This is also loving God, which is why the Lord said, "Whoever does my commandments is the one who loves me, but whoever does not do my commandments does not love me" (John 14:21–24 *[14:21, 24]*).

[7] This is why there are two tablets of the Ten Commandments, one for God and the other for us. God is constantly at work to enable us to accept the things that are on his tablet. However, if we do not do the things that are on our tablet, we are not open to the heartfelt acceptance of the things that are on God's tablet; and if we are not open to them, we are not united. As a result, the two tablets are united as a single one and are called "the tablets of the covenant," and "covenant" means "union."

The reason our belief in God and union with him depend on our living good lives is that good lives are like the goodness that is in the Lord and that therefore comes from the Lord. So when we are engaged in living good lives, the union is accomplished. The opposite happens with people living evil lives. Then there is a rejection of the Lord.

[8] (c) *A good life, or living rightly, is abstaining from evils because they are against our religion and therefore against God.* There is ample support

for the proposition that this is a good life, or living rightly, in *Teachings about Life for the New Jerusalem,* from beginning to end. I would add only this, that if you do all the good you can, if you build churches and decorate and fill them with your offerings, if you devote your wealth to hospitals and hospices, if you give alms every day, if you help widows and orphans, if you faithfully attend divine worship, even if you think, talk, and preach about these things in all apparent sincerity, and still do not abstain from evils as sins against God, all these good deeds are not really good at all. They are either hypocritical or self-serving, because there is still evil within them. Our life is in absolutely everything that we do, and good deeds become good only by the removal of evil from them.

We can see from this that abstaining from evils because they are against our religion and therefore against God is leading a good life.

[9] (d) *These are the general principles of all religions, through which everyone can be saved.* Belief in God and refusal to do evil because it is against God are the two elements that make a religion a religion. If either is lacking, we cannot call it a religion, since believing in God and doing evil are mutually contradictory, as are doing what is good and not believing in God. Neither is possible apart from the other.

The Lord has provided that there should be some religion almost everywhere and that everyone who believes in God and does not do evil because it is against God should have a place in heaven. Heaven, seen in its entirety, looks like a single individual, whose life or soul is the Lord. In that heavenly person there are all the components that there are in a physical person, differing the way heavenly things differ from earthly ones.

[10] We know that there are within us not only the parts formed as organs from blood vessels and nerve fibers—the forms we call our viscera. There are also skin, membranes, tendons, cartilage, bones, nails, and teeth. They are less intensely alive than the organic forms, which they serve as ligaments, coverings, and supports. If there are to be all these elements in that heavenly person who is heaven, it cannot be made up of the people of one religion only. It needs people from many religions; so all the people who make these two universal principles of the church central to their own lives have a place in that heavenly person, that is, in heaven. They enjoy the happiness that suits their own nature. On this subject, though, there is more in §254 above.

[11] We are assured that these two principles are basic to every religion by the fact that these two principles are what the Ten Commandments teach, and they were the basis of the Word. They were given from

Mount Sinai by the very voice of Jehovah and written on two tablets of stone by the finger of God. Then they were placed in the ark named for Jehovah and constituted the Holy of Holies in the tabernacle and the very center of the temple in Jerusalem. Everything else was holy simply by being there. We are told a great deal more about the Ten Commandments in the ark in the Word: see the passages collected in *Teachings about Life for the New Jerusalem* 53–61, to which I may add the following.

We are told in the Word that the ark containing the two tablets with the commandments written on them was captured by the Philistines and set up in the shrine of Dagon in Ashdod. Dagon fell to the ground before it, after which his head and his hands were found lying apart from his body on the threshold of the shrine. Because of the ark, the people of Ashdod and Ekron by the thousands were plagued by hemorrhoids, and their land was ravaged by mice. Then, on the advice of their leaders, the Philistines made five golden hemorrhoids and five golden mice and a new cart. They put the ark on the cart with the golden hemorrhoids and mice beside it and sent the ark back to the Israelites drawn by two cows that lowed along the way, in front of the cart. The Israelites sacrificed the cows and the cart (1 Samuel 5 and 6).

[12] Now let us see what all this means. The Philistines meant people who believe in faith separated from charity. Dagon portrayed that system of belief. The hemorrhoids that afflicted them meant earthly loves, which are unclean when they are separated from spiritual loves; and the mice meant the destruction of the church by distortions of the truth. The new cart on which they sent back the ark meant a new teaching, though on the earthly level, because a chariot in the Word meant a teaching derived from spiritual truths. The cows meant good earthly feelings, the golden hemorrhoids earthly loves purified and made good, and the golden mice the destruction of the church taken away by goodness (gold in the Word means what is good). The lowing of the cows along the way pointed to the difficulty of turning the obsessions with evil of our earthly self into good desires, and the sacrifice of the cows and the cart meant that the Lord was appeased. [13] This is what this story means spiritually. Put it all together into a single meaning and see how it can be applied.

On the meaning of the Philistines as people who believe in faith separated from charity, see *Teachings for the New Jerusalem on Faith* 49–54; and on the ark meaning the holiest values of the church because it contained the Ten Commandments, see *Teachings about Life for the New Jerusalem* 53–61.

327   3. *It is our own fault if we are not saved.* Even on first hearing it, any rational person accepts the truth that evil cannot come from what is good, and that good cannot come from what is evil, since they are opposites. This means that nothing but good comes from what is good, and nothing but evil comes from what is evil. Once we admit this truth, we also admit that good can be turned into evil, not by the goodness itself but by the evil that receives it. Every form changes what it receives into something of its own nature (see §292 above).

Since the Lord is goodness in its very essence, or goodness itself, then, we can see that evil cannot flow from the Lord or be brought forth by him, but that it can be turned into evil by a recipient subject whose form is a form of evil. In respect to our claim to autonomy, we are this kind of subject. This apparent autonomy of ours is constantly receiving good from the Lord and constantly changing it to suit the nature of its own form, which is a form of evil. It therefore follows that it is our own fault if we are not saved.

Evil does come from hell, of course, but since our insistence on autonomy accepts evil as its own and thereby incorporates it into itself, it makes no real difference whether you say that the evil is from ourselves or that it is from hell. I need to say, though, where this incorporation of evil has come from, even to the point that religion itself is dying. I will do so in the following sequence. (a) Every religion eventually wanes and comes to completion. (b) Every religion wanes and comes to completion by inverting the image of God within us. (c) This happens because of the constant increase of hereditary evil from generation to generation. (d) The Lord still provides that everyone can be saved. (e) He also provides that a new church will take the place of the earlier one that has been razed.

328   These items need now to be presented in their sequence.

(a) *Every religion eventually wanes and comes to completion.* There have been several churches[321] on our planet, one after the other, since wherever the human race exists there is a church. As already noted, heaven, which is the ultimate goal of creation, comes from the human race, and no one can get to heaven without the two universal principles of the church, belief in God and leading a good life (see §326 above). It follows that there have been churches on our planet from the earliest times all the way to the present day.

These churches are described in the Word, though only for the Israelite and Jewish church[322] are we given historical accounts. There were several churches before them, but these are described only by the names of some people and nations and a few facts about them.

[2] The earliest church, the very first, is described by Adam and his wife Eve. The next church, called the early church, is described by Noah, his three sons, and their descendants. This was extensive, and spread through most of the nations of the Near East:323 the land of Canaan on both sides of the Jordan; Syria; Assyria and Chaldea; Mesopotamia; Egypt; Arabia; and Tyre and Sidon. They had an early Word that is discussed in *Teachings for the New Jerusalem on Sacred Scripture* 101–103. The existence of the church in these kingdoms is witnessed by various statements about them in the prophetical books of the Word.

This church changed significantly with Eber, though, who marks the beginning of the Hebrew church. This was the point at which sacrificial worship was established. From the Hebrew church, the Israelite and Jewish church was born, formally established for the sake of the Word that would be authored in it.

[3] These four churches are meant by the statue that Nebuchadnezzar saw in his dream, with its head of pure gold, its chest and arms of silver, its belly and thighs of brass, and its legs and feet of iron and clay324 (see Daniel 2:32, 33). This is exactly what is meant by the Golden, Silver, Bronze, and Iron Ages mentioned by ancient authors.325 It is well known that the Christian church followed after the Jewish church.

We can also see from the Word that each of these churches declined to its close, called a "consummation," with the passage of time. The consummation of the earliest church, brought about by eating from the tree of knowledge (meaning pride in our own intelligence) is described by the Flood [Genesis 3:6; 7:10–24]. [4] The consummation of the early church is described by the destruction of the nations mentioned in the historical and prophetic books of the Word, and especially by the Israelites' expulsion of the inhabitants of the land of Canaan.326 The consummation of the Israelite and Jewish church is meant by the destruction of the temple in Jerusalem, by the carrying off of the people of Israel into permanent captivity and of the nation of Judah into Babylon, and ultimately by the second destruction of the temple and Jerusalem and the scattering of the people.327 This consummation is foretold in many passages in the prophets, and in Daniel 9:24–27.328

The Lord describes the eventual total destruction of the Christian church in Matthew 24, Mark 13, and Luke 21, but the consummation itself is found in the Book of Revelation.

This shows that with the passage of time the church wanes and reaches its consummation, as does its religion as well.

[5] (b) *Every religion wanes and comes to completion by inverting the image of God within us.* We know that we were created in the image of

God and after the likeness of God (Genesis 1:26), but what is this image and what is this likeness of God? Only God is love and wisdom. We are created to be recipients of both, so that our volition may be a recipient of divine love and our discernment a recipient of divine wisdom.

I have already explained [§324] that we have these two recipient vessels in us from birth, that they are what make us human, and that they are formed within us in the womb. Our being images of God is our being open to divine wisdom, and our being likenesses of God is our being open to divine love. This means that the vessel we call "discernment" is the image of God and the vessel we call "volition" is the likeness of God. This then means that since we have been created and formed to be vessels, it follows that we have been created and formed to have our volition accept love from God and our discernment accept wisdom from God. We do in fact accept them when we believe in God and live by his commandments. We do this to a lesser or greater extent, though, depending on what we know about God and his commandments from our religion. Specifically, our acceptance depends on what truths we know, since truths are what tell us what God is and how we are to acknowledge him, what his commandments are and how we are to live by them.

[6] God's image and likeness in us have not been actually destroyed, but they have been virtually destroyed. They are still there, innate within those two abilities called freedom and rationality that I have already said so much about. They become virtually destroyed when we make the vessel of divine love—our volition—a vessel for self-love and make the vessel of divine wisdom—our discernment—a vessel for our own intelligence. By so doing we invert the image and likeness of God. We turn the vessels away from God and toward ourselves. This is why they are closed on top and open on the bottom, or closed in front and open behind, even though they were created open in front and closed behind. Once they are opened and closed in this inverted fashion, then the vessel of love, our volition, is open to an inflow from hell or from our own sense of self-importance, as is the vessel of wisdom, our discernment. This has led to the birth in our churches of the worship of particular people in place of the worship of God, and a worship based on teachings of falsity rather than on teachings of truth, the latter from our own intelligence and the former from our love for ourselves.

We can see from this that in the course of time a religion will wane and come to its conclusion by inverting the image of God within us.

[7] (c) *This happens because of the constant increase of hereditary evil from generation to generation.* I have already stated and explained [§277]

that we do not inherit evil from Adam and his wife Eve because they ate from the tree of knowledge; instead evil is gradually handed down and transplanted from parents to children, and so by constant increase gets worse with each generation. When this cumulative evil becomes strong enough among the majority, it spreads evil to even more people by its own momentum, since in every evil there is a compulsion to mislead, in some cases blazing with a rage against everything good, and so there is a consequent infectious evil. When this gets control of the leaders, managers, and chief representatives in the church, its religion is corrupted. Its means of healing, its truths, become defiled by distortions. This leads to an ongoing destruction of what is good and an abandonment of truth in the church until finally it is brought to its close.

[8] (d) *The Lord still provides that everyone can be saved.* The Lord provides that there will be some religion everywhere, and that in every religion there will be the two elements essential to salvation: belief in God, and not doing evil because it is against God. The other matters of intellect and thought, what we call the elements of faith, are offered to different people according to the way they live, since they are optional elements as far as living is concerned. If they are put first, we still do not receive life until we live them.

The Lord also provides that everyone who has led a good life and has believed in God will be taught by angels after death. Then people who have been devoted to the two essential principles of religion in the world accept the truths of the church as they are presented in the Word and recognize the Lord as God of heaven and of the church. They accept this more readily than Christians who have brought with them from the world a concept of the Lord's human nature as separated from his divine nature. The Lord has also provided that all the people who die in early childhood are saved, no matter where they were born.

[9] We are all given the means of amending our lives after death, if we can. The Lord teaches and leads us through angels, and since by then we know that we are living after death and that heaven and hell are real, we accept truths at first. However, if we have not believed in God and abstained from evils as sins in the world, before long we develop a distaste for truths and back away. If we have professed these principles orally but not at heart, we are like the foolish young women who had lamps but no oil. They begged others for oil and went off to buy some, but still they were not admitted to the wedding [Matthew 25:1–13]. The lamps mean the truths that our faith discloses and the oil means the good effects of our caring.

This shows that under divine providence everyone can be saved, and that it is our own fault if we are not saved.

[10] (e) *He also provides that a new church will take the place of the one that has been razed.* This has been going on from the earliest times: once a church has been razed, a new one succeeds the former one. The early church followed the earliest church, the Israelite or Jewish church followed the early one, and after that came the Christian church. After it there is going to be still another new church, the one foretold in the Book of Revelation. That is the meaning of the New Jerusalem coming down from heaven [Revelation 21:2, 10].

For the reason the Lord provides a new church to take the place of an earlier one that has been razed, see *Teachings for the New Jerusalem on Sacred Scripture* 104–113.

329   4. *This means that everyone is predestined to heaven and no one to hell.* I have explained in *Heaven and Hell* 545–550 (published in London in 1758) that the Lord does not throw anyone into hell, but that spirits throw themselves in. That is how it is with everyone who is evil and cynical after death. It is much the same with people who are evil and irreligious in this world, except that in this world they can be reformed; they can embrace and absorb the means of salvation, which they cannot do after they leave this world.

The means of salvation boil down to these two, that we are to abstain from evils because they are against the divine laws in the Ten Commandments, and that we are to acknowledge that God exists. We can all do this, provided we do not love what is evil. The Lord is constantly flowing into our volition with the power to abstain from evils and into our discernment with the power to think that God is real. However, no one can do one of these things without doing the other as well. They are united the way the two tablets of the Ten Commandments are united, the one being for the Lord and the other for us.[329] From his tablet, the Lord is enlightening and empowering everyone, but we accept that power and enlightenment only as we do what is on our tablet. Until we do that, it is as though the two tablets were lying face to face and closed with a seal; but as we do what is on our tablet, they are unsealed and opened.

[2] What are the Ten Commandments nowadays but a closed booklet or leaflet opened only by the hands of children and youths? Try telling people of mature years that they should not do something because it is against the Ten Commandments—who actually cares? Of course, if you say that they should not do something because it is against divine laws

they may listen. But the Ten Commandments *are* divine laws. I have checked this out with any number of people in the spiritual world, people who sneered when I talked about the Ten Commandments or the catechism. This is because the second tablet of the Ten Commandments, our tablet, tells us that we are to abstain from evils; and if people do not abstain from them, whether because they are irreligious or because their religion says that works[330] do nothing for our salvation, only faith, they feel smug on hearing talk of the Ten Commandments or the catechism. It is like hearing about some children's book that is no longer of any use to them.

[3] I mention this to show that none of us is unfamiliar with the means by which we can be saved, or the power, if we want to be saved. It follows from this that everyone is predestined to heaven, and no one to hell.

However, since for some people a belief in predestination to nonsalvation, which is damnation, has taken over, and this belief is vicious, and since it cannot be dispelled unless reason sees its insanity and cruelty, I need to deal with the matter in the following sequence. (a) Any predestination but predestination to heaven is contrary to divine love and its infinity. (b) Any predestination but predestination to heaven is contrary to divine wisdom and its infinity. (c) It is an insane heresy to believe that only those born in the church are saved. (d) It is a cruel heresy to believe that any member of the human race is damned by predestination.

To show how vicious belief in predestination is, at least as predestination is commonly understood, I need to pick up these four propositions and support them.

330

(a) *Any predestination but predestination to heaven is contrary to divine love, which is infinite.* I explained in the book on *Divine Love and Wisdom* that Jehovah or the Lord is divine love and that this love is infinite and is the essential reality of all life,[331] as well as that we are created in the image of God after the likeness of God.[332] Since (as already noted [§328]) we are all formed by the Lord in the womb in this image after this likeness, it follows that the Lord is the heavenly Father of us all and that we are his spiritual children. "Father" is in fact what Jehovah or the Lord is called in the Word, and "children" is what we are called in the Word. So it says, "Do not call your father on earth your father, for one is your Father, the one who is in heaven" (Matthew 23:9). This means that he alone is our Father in respect to our life, while our earthly fathers are fathers only as to the clothing of life, the body. This is why no one is called father in heaven but the Lord. We can also see in many passages of the

Word that we are called his children and are said to have been born from him if we have not inverted that life.[333]

[2] We can tell from this that divine love is in all of us, the evil and the good alike, and that therefore the Lord who is divine love must treat us with as much love as an earthly father treats his children—with infinitely more love, in fact, because divine love is infinite. Further, he can never withdraw from anyone, because everyone's life comes from him. It does seem as though he withdraws from evil people, but it is the evil who are withdrawing: he is still lovingly leading them. So the Lord says, "Ask and it will be given to you, seek and you will find, knock and it will be opened to you. Who among you will give a stone if his son asks him for bread? If then you who are evil know how to give good gifts to your children, how much more will your Father who is in the heavens give good things to those who ask him?" (Matthew 7:7–11); and again, "Because he makes his sun rise on the evil and the good and sends rain on the just and the unjust" (Matthew 5:45). It is also recognized in the church that the Lord intends the salvation of all and the death of none.

This enables us to see that predestination to anything but heaven is contrary to divine love.

[3] (b) *Any predestination but predestination to heaven is contrary to divine wisdom, which is infinite.* It is through its divine wisdom that divine love provides the means by which we can all be saved; so to say that there is a predestination to anywhere but heaven is to say that divine love cannot provide the means of salvation. Yet we all do have the means, as just explained, and these come from divine providence, which is infinite.

The reason some of us are not saved is that divine love wants us to feel heaven's happiness and bliss in ourselves. Otherwise it would not be heaven for us; and this feeling cannot happen unless it seems to us that we are thinking and intending on our own. If it were not for this appearance, nothing could be given to us, and we would not be human. This is the reason for divine providence, which is the result of divine wisdom stemming from divine love.

[4] Still, this does not negate the truth that we are all predestined to heaven, and none to hell. This truth would be negated, though, if the means of salvation were lacking. However, I have already shown [§§326, 329] that we are all given the means of salvation, and that the nature of heaven is to provide a place there for all who lead good lives, no matter what their religion may be.

We are like the earth. It brings forth all kinds of fruit: this ability is what makes it the earth. The fact that it brings forth bad fruit does not negate its ability to bring forth good fruit; though it would negate it if it could bring forth only bad fruit. We are also like an object that changes the light rays that strike it. If we offer only ugly colors, that is not the fault of the light. The light rays can also be changed into attractive colors.

[5] (c) *It is an insane heresy to believe that only those born in the church are saved.* People born outside the church are just as human as people born within it. They come from the same heavenly source. They are equally living and immortal souls. They have religions as well, religions that enable them to believe that God exists and that they should lead good lives; and all of them who do believe in God and lead good lives become spiritual on their own level and are saved, as already noted [§326].

Someone could point out that they have not been baptized. But baptism saves only people who have been spiritually washed, that is, regenerated. Baptism serves as a symbol and reminder of this. [6] Someone could point out that they do not know the Lord, and that apart from the Lord there is no salvation. But no one is saved because of knowing about the Lord. We are saved because we live by his commandments. Further, the Lord is known to everyone who believes in God because the Lord is the God of heaven and earth, as he tells us in Matthew 28:18 and elsewhere.[334]

Particularly, people outside the church have more of a concept of a personal God than Christians do; and people who have a concept of a personal God and lead good lives are accepted by the Lord. Unlike Christians, they believe in God as one in both person and essence. Further, they think about God as they lead their lives. They treat evils as sins against God; and people who do this are thinking about God as they lead their lives.

Christians get the commandments of their religion from the Word, but not many of them actually take any commandments of life from it. [7] Catholics do not read it,[335] and Protestants who believe in faith separated from charity pay no attention to what it says about life, only to what it says about faith. Yet the whole Word is nothing but a theology of life.

Christianity is found only in Europe. Islam and other non-Christian religions are found in Asia, the Indies, Africa, and America; and there are ten times as many people in these latter parts of the world as there are in the Christian part of the world—and relatively few of these latter people make their religion a matter of their lives. What could be more insane than to believe that these and only these individuals are saved, and that the others are damned, that heaven is ours by right of birth and not by conduct of life? That is why the Lord says, "I tell you that many will come from the east and from the west and will recline with Abraham and Isaac and Jacob in the kingdom of the heavens, while the children of the kingdom will be thrown out" (Matthew 8:11, 12).

[8] (d) *It is a cruel heresy to believe that any member of the human race is damned by predestination.* It is cruel, that is, to believe that the Lord, who is love itself and mercy itself, would allow such a vast number of people to be born for hell, or that so many millions would be born damned and doomed, that is, born devils and satans. It is cruel to believe that in his divine wisdom the Lord would not make sure that people who lead good lives and believe in God would not be cast into the flames and into eternal torment. After all, the Lord is the Creator and Savior of us all. He alone is leading us, and he does not want anyone to die; so it is cruel to believe and think that such a multitude of nations and people are by predestination being handed over to the devil as prey under the Lord's own guidance and oversight.

The Lord Cannot Act Contrary to the Laws of Divine Providence, Because to Do So Would Be to Act Contrary to His Own Divine Love and His Own Divine Wisdom, and Therefore Contrary to Himself

331 I explained in *Angelic Wisdom about Divine Love and Wisdom* that the Lord is divine love and divine wisdom and that these two are reality itself and life itself, the source of the reality and life of everything.[336] I also explained that what emanates from him is of the same nature, that, for example, the emanating divine nature is actually himself. Divine providence is first and foremost among the things that emanate from him. It is constantly focused on its goal, the purpose for which the universe was created. The working and progress of this purpose, through its means, is what we mean by "divine providence."

[2] Since divine providence is the Lord, then, and since it is the first and foremost thing that emanates, it follows that for the Lord to act contrary to the laws of his divine providence would be to act contrary to himself.

We can also say that the Lord is providence just as we can say that the Lord is the design, since divine providence is the divine design as it relates specifically to our salvation. Further, just as there is no design without its laws (the laws actually define it) and every law is a design because its source is the design, it follows that just as God is the design, he is also the law of his design. We must then say the same of his divine providence, that just as the Lord is his providence, he is also the law of his providence. We can see from this that the Lord cannot act contrary to the laws of his divine providence, because to do so would be to act contrary to himself.

[3] Further, there is no such thing as doing something unless it affects some subject and does so through some means. Unless a deed affects some subject and does so through some means, it does not happen. We are the subject of divine providence; its means are the divine truths that provide us with wisdom and the divine generosity[337] that provides us with love. It is through these means that divine providence accomplishes its purpose, which is our salvation, since anyone who intends to accomplish a purpose intends the means as well. So when the "intender" does accomplish the purpose, it is through means.

These matters will become clearer, though, when we go through them in the following sequence.

1. The working of divine providence for our salvation starts with our birth and lasts to the end of our life and then on to eternity.
2. The working of divine providence is constantly done through means, out of pure mercy.
3. Instant salvation by direct mercy is impossible.
4. Instant salvation by direct mercy is the flying fiery serpent in the church.[338]

1. *The working of divine providence for our salvation starts with our birth and lasts to the end of our life and then on to eternity.* I have already explained [§323] that a heaven from the human race is the purpose of the creation of the universe and that in its working and progress this purpose

is the divine provision for our salvation. I have also explained that all the things outside us, all the things that are useful to us, are secondary purposes of creation. In summary, these are all the members of the three kingdoms: animal, plant, and mineral.[339] If these all constantly function according to the laws of the divine design established at the very beginning of creation, then surely the primary purpose of creation, the salvation of the human race, must constantly function according to its laws, which are the laws of divine providence.

[2] Just look at a fruit tree. See how it is first born from a tiny seed as a delicate sprout, how this gradually develops into a trunk that sends out branches, how these are covered with leaves, and how it then produces flowers, bears fruit, and sets new seeds in the fruit that provide for its endless future. It is the same for all shrubs and all the meadow grasses. Every least thing involved in this process is constantly and wonderfully moving from its purpose to its goal according to the laws of its design. Why should the primary purpose, a heaven from the human race, be any different? Can there be anything in its process that is not going on at every instant in accord with the laws of divine providence?

[3] Since there is this relationship between our life and the growth of a tree, we may draw a parallel or comparison. Our early childhood is like the delicate sprout of the tree emerging out of the ground from its seed. Our youth and young adulthood are like that sprout growing into a trunk with slender branches. The earthly truths that we all take in at first are like the leaves that cover the branches—this is exactly what "leaves" mean in the Word. Our first steps into the marriage of what is good and what is true, the spiritual marriage, are like the flowers that a tree brings forth in spring, and the spiritual truths are the petals of the flowers. The beginnings of the spiritual marriage are the fruit in its early stages. The spiritual benefits—good deeds done from a caring spirit—are like the fruit, and are what "fruit" means in the Word. The propagation of wisdom from love is like the seeds whose fertility makes us like a garden and paradise.[340] In the Word, we are in fact described as trees, and our wisdom, which arises from love, is described as a garden. This is exactly what the Garden of Eden means.

[4] Actually, we are bad trees right from our seed, but we are granted a scion or graft from shoots taken from the tree of life, through which the sap rising from our old roots is changed into a sap that brings forth good fruit.

I offer this comparison to show that if the process of divine providence is so unfailing in the growth and reproduction of trees, it must by all means be unfailing in our own reformation and regeneration. We are far more important than trees, as the Lord said: "Are not five sparrows sold for two little coins? Yet not one of them is left forgotten in the presence of God. No, even the hairs of your head are all numbered. Therefore do not be afraid; you are much more important than sparrows. Then too, who of you can with care add a cubit to his or her stature? So if you cannot do the least, why are you anxious about the rest? Look at the way the lilies grow. If God so clothes the grass in the field that is there today but is thrown into the oven tomorrow, how much more [will he clothe] you, O people of little faith?" (Luke 12:6, 7, 25, 26, 27, 28).

The premise is that for our salvation, divine providence begins at our birth and continues to the end of our life. To understand this, we need to realize that the Lord knows the kind of person we are and the kind of person we want to be and therefore the kind of person we will be. Further, he cannot deprive us of the freedom of our volition if we are to be human and therefore immortal, as amply explained above;[341] so he foresees what our state will be after death and provides for it from our birth all the way to the end of our life. He does this for evil people by both allowing and constantly leading them away from their evils, and for good people by constantly leading them to what is good. So divine providence is constantly at work for our salvation; but it cannot save more of us than want to be saved. We want to be saved if we believe in God and are led by him, and we do not want to be saved if we do not believe in God and we lead ourselves. In the latter case, we are not thinking about eternal life or salvation, while in the former case we are. The Lord sees all this and still leads us, doing so under the laws of his divine providence, laws he cannot violate because that would be to violate his divine love and his divine wisdom, and therefore himself.

[2] Since he foresees everyone's state after death and foresees our place as well—in hell for people who do not want to be saved and in heaven for people who do—it follows that, as just stated, he provides places for the evil by permitting and leading them away and for the good by leading them to their places. It follows also that if this were not being done constantly for everyone from birth to the end of life, neither heaven nor hell would endure. Without this foresight and providence, that is, there would be neither a heaven nor a hell, only confusion. (See §§202–203 above on the fact that we are all provided with places by the Lord in his foresight.)

[3] To illustrate this by a comparison, if an archer or musketeer were to aim at a target and a straight line a mile long were drawn behind the target, then if the aim were off just a hair, at the end of that mile the arrow or ball would have strayed far from the line behind the target. That

333

is what it would be like if the Lord did not have his eye on eternity at every moment, every least moment, in his foresight and provision for everyone's place after death. The Lord does this, though, because to him the whole future is present, and to him everything present is eternal.

On the fact that divine providence focuses on what is infinite and eternal in everything it does, see above, §§46–69 and 214 and following.

334 I have also said that the working of divine providence continues forever, because all angels grow more perfect in wisdom forever. Each of us does so, though, on whatever level of desire for what is good and true we had when we left this world. This is the level that is perfected to eternity. Anything beyond this level is outside an angel, not within, and whatever is outside cannot be developed within. This is the meaning of the good measure, pressed down, shaken, and overflowing, that would be poured into the laps of people who forgave others and were generous to them (Luke 7:37, 38 *[6:37, 38]*), people who are living good and caring lives.

335 2. *The working of divine providence is constantly done through means, out of pure mercy.* Divine providence has both means and ways.[342] The means are what serve to make us human and grow in perfection in discernment and volition. The ways are the manners in which these processes happen.

The means that serve to make us human and grow in perfection in discernment are summed up in the word "truths." They become concepts in our thinking, and we refer to them as facts in our memory. Essentially, they are the thoughts that give rise to what we know.

All these means are spiritual in and of themselves, but since they occur in our earthly concerns, they seem to be earthly because of this covering or clothing, which is earthly and even physical. They are infinite in number and infinite in variety. There are some less simple and some more simple; some less complex and some more complex; some less imperfect and some more imperfect; and some less perfect and some more perfect. There are means for giving form and completeness to our life on the civic, earthly level, for giving form and completeness to our life on the moral, rational level, and for giving form and completeness to our life on the spiritual, heavenly level.

[2] These means occur in sequence, one kind after another, from infancy to the last stage of our life, and then on to eternity. They intensify as they follow each other, with the earlier ones being means to the later ones. All the steps become part of whatever takes shape, like intermediate causes, because every effect of them, every final result, is active

and therefore becomes a cause. So the subsequent ones are means in the sequence. Further, since this process goes on to eternity, there is no last or final step that closes the sequence. That is, just as eternity is without end, so wisdom that increases to eternity has no end. If there were an end of wisdom for the wise, that would be the end of their pleasure in wisdom, which consists of its endless increase and fertility. It would therefore be the end of the joy of their life. In its place would come a pleasure in their brilliance, and there is no heavenly life in this alone. The wise would no longer be young; they would seem to age, and eventually to become decrepit.

[3] Although the wisdom of the wise does increase forever in heaven, angelic wisdom never approaches divine wisdom closely enough to touch it. It is rather like a straight line drawn next to a hyperbola, constantly approaching but never touching; or we might think of the squaring of a circle.343

This shows what is meant by the means that divine providence uses to make us human and to bring us toward perfection in discernment, and shows that the general term for them is "truths." There are the same number of means by which we are given form and completeness in volition, but the general term for these is "good." It is from these latter that we have love, while the former means provide us with wisdom. The union of these two kinds of means makes us human because the nature of that union determines our own nature. This union is what we refer to as "the marriage of goodness and truth."

As for the ways divine providence works with its means, and uses them to form us and bring us toward perfection, they are infinite in number and infinite in variety as well. There are as many of them as there are actions of divine wisdom, prompted by divine love, for our salvation; as many therefore as there are things that divine providence does in keeping with its laws, as already discussed.

336

I have already shown [§§164, 180, 296] that these ways are deeply hidden by comparing them with the way our souls work within our bodies, ways we know little or almost nothing about—how our eyes, ears, nostrils, tongue, and skin register sensations, for example, how our stomach digests, our mesentery produces chyle, our liver works on our blood, our pancreas and spleen purify it, our kidneys separate it from contaminating fluids, our heart gathers it in and sends it out, our lungs cleanse it, and our brain refines it and gives it new life, along with countless other processes, all subtle, whose depths our science can scarcely plumb.

We can see from this that we are even less able to plumb the depths of the subtle workings of divine providence. It is enough that we know its laws.

337 344 The reason that everything divine providence does is done out of pure mercy is that the divine essence is pure love. This is what is working through divine wisdom, and this working is what we call divine providence.

The pure love is pure mercy (a) because it is at work with everyone in the whole world, and by our nature we are all incapable of doing anything on our own; (b) it is at work with the evil and the unjust and with the good and the just alike; (c) it is leading people who are in hell and rescuing them from it; (d) it is constantly struggling with them in hell and fighting for them against the devil, that is, against the evils of hell; (e) that is why it came into the world and underwent temptations even to the final one, the suffering on the cross; (f) it is constantly at work to make the unclean clean and the insane sane, so it is constantly laboring out of pure mercy.

338 3. *Instant salvation by direct mercy is impossible.* I have just explained that the work of divine providence for our salvation begins at our birth and continues until the end of our life and then goes on to eternity, and that this work is constantly being done out of pure mercy and through means. It follows that there is no such thing as instant salvation or direct mercy.

However, there are many people who do not think about church matters or religious matters with discernment. They believe that they are saved by direct mercy and that salvation therefore happens instantaneously; yet the opposite is true; and this is a destructive belief. For these reasons, it is important to lay the matter out in its sequence. (a) Belief in instant salvation by direct mercy is based on the state of our earthly natures. (b) This belief comes from an ignorance of our spiritual state, which is completely different from our earthly state. (c) If we look more deeply into the teaching of all the churches in the Christian world, they deny instant salvation by direct mercy; and yet nominal members of the church are sure of it.

[2] (a) *Belief in instant salvation by direct mercy is based on the state of our earthly natures.* In our earthly consciousness, all we know from our normal state is that heavenly joy is like earthly joy, that it flows in and is received in the same way. For example, it is what happens when poor people become rich and change from the depressed mood of poverty to the happy mood of wealth, or when menial individuals become respected

and move from scorn to honor; it is like people going from the sorrow of a wake to the joy of a wedding. Since these moods can change in a single day, and since people have no different concept of our state after death, we can see why they believe in instant salvation by direct mercy.

[3] In this world, there can be a large gathering in one civil community, all happy together even though they are all different in character. This happens in our earthly state because the outward face of one individual can adjust to the outward face of another no matter how different they may be inwardly. Looking at this earthly state, people conclude that salvation is simply admission to the company of angels in heaven and that admission is by direct mercy. So they believe that heaven can be granted to evil and to good people alike, and that they will then relate to each other the way they do in the world, except that everyone will be full of joy.

[4] (b) *This belief comes from an ignorance of our spiritual state, which is completely different from our earthly state.* There is a great deal of information in the preceding pages about our spiritual state, our state after death. I have explained that each of us is her or his own love and that none of us can live anywhere but with people whose loves are like ours, and that if we do visit others, we cannot breathe in our own life. This is why after death we all begin to associate with people whose loves are like ours. We recognize them as relatives and friends; and strange as it may seem, when we meet and see them it is as though we had known them from childhood. It is our spiritual likeness and friendship that causes this.

Not only that, within our own communities we can live only in our own house. We all have our house in that community, which we find ready for us as soon as we join the community. We can get together with others outside the house, but we can settle down only in our own. Beyond this even, when we are in someone else's quarters we can sit only in our own place. If we sit anywhere else it is as though our minds failed and we could not speak. Remarkably, when we enter a room, we know where we belong. The same holds true in churches and wherever people gather in groups.

[5] We can see from this that our spiritual state is totally different from our earthly state. Essentially, we cannot be anywhere but where our dominant love is. That is where the delight of our life is, and we all want to be where the delight of our life is. Our spirit cannot be anywhere else because it constitutes our life, our very breathing, and the beating of our hearts. It is different in this earthly world. Here our outward nature is

trained from early childhood to pretend with our faces, speech, and body language to pleasures that are not the ones we are feeling inwardly. As a result, we cannot draw conclusions from people's moods in this world about their state after death, since their state after death will be a spiritual one. That is, they will not be able to live anywhere except in the pleasure of the love they have acquired by the way they lived in this world.

[6] This makes it abundantly clear that none of us can be admitted to that pleasure of heaven that is commonly known as heavenly joy if we enjoy the pleasures of hell, which is the same as saying that we cannot enjoy what is good if we enjoy what is evil. This becomes even clearer when we realize that after death no one is prevented from coming up into heaven. We are shown the way and given the resources, and we are let in. However, [if we enjoy evil] when we get to heaven and breathe in its pleasure, we begin to have such chest pains, heart pangs, and dizziness that we writhe like a snake next to a fire. Then with faces turned away from heaven and toward hell, we run away headlong, finding no rest until we are in the community of our own love. This shows that no one can get to heaven by direct mercy, and particularly that it is not simply a matter of being let in, as many people in this world presume. So there is no instant salvation, because this would presuppose direct mercy.

[7] There have been people who had believed in instant salvation by direct mercy in the world and who, once they had become spirits, wanted their hellish or evil pleasure to be transformed by divine omnipotence and divine mercy into heavenly or good pleasure. Since they craved this intensely, permission was granted for angels to do it. The angels took away their hellish pleasure. However, since this was the pleasure of their life's love, since it was their life, in fact, they lay there as though they were dead, senseless and motionless. No life could be breathed into them except their own because all the elements of their minds and their bodies had been turned backwards and could not be turned around again. So they were revived by letting the pleasure of their life's love back in. Later they said that in this more inward state they had felt something profoundly threatening and terrifying, something they did not want to talk about.

So in heaven they say that it is easier to change an owl into a turtledove or a snake into a lamb than to change a hellish spirit into an angel of heaven.

[8] (c) *If we look into the teaching of all the churches in the Christian world, they deny instant salvation by direct mercy; and yet nominal members of the church are sure of it.* If we look deeply enough, we find that the

theologies of all our churches teach how to live. Does any church have a theology that does not tell us we should examine ourselves, see and admit our sins, confess them, repent of them, and then lead a new life? Is anyone allowed to take the Holy Supper without this warning and this command? Investigate the matter, and you will be assured.

Does any church have a theology that is not based on the Ten Commandments? The laws of the Ten Commandments are laws of life.

Is there anyone in the church who has a little of the church within who does not admit, on hearing it, that we are saved if we lead good lives and damned if we lead evil lives? That is why the Athanasian Creed (which is accepted theology throughout the Christian world) says that "the Lord will come to judge the living and the dead, and then those who have done good things will enter into eternal life, and those who have done evil things into eternal fire."

[9] We can see from this that if we look deeply enough, we find that the theologies of all our churches teach how to live; and since they teach how to live, they teach that our salvation depends on how we live. Our life is not breathed into us in an instant but is formed gradually, and is reformed as we abstain from evils as sins—specifically, as we see what is a sin, recognize it, admit it, and then do not intend it, and therefore refrain from it, and also as we know the means that relate to knowing God. By these two means our life is formed and reformed, and they cannot just be poured into us in an instant. Our inherited evil, which is essentially hellish, has to be banished first, and goodness, which is essentially heavenly, planted in its stead. Because of our inherited evil we are like owls as to our discernment and snakes as to our volition, while if we have been reformed we are like doves as to our discernment and sheep as to our volition. This means that instant reformation and consequent salvation would be like the instant transformation of an owl into a dove and a snake into a sheep. Can anyone who knows anything about human life fail to see that this could not happen unless the nature of the owl and the snake were taken away and the nature of the dove and the sheep implanted?

[10] We also know that everyone who is intelligent can become more intelligent and that everyone who is wise can become more wise. That is, our intelligence and wisdom can increase; and for some people it[345] does increase from early childhood right to the end of life, with individuals becoming steadily more and more perfect. Why should this not be even more true of spiritual intelligence and wisdom? This rises by two levels above earthly intelligence and wisdom, and as it rises it becomes angelic

and inexpressible. I have already noted [§335] that for angels it keeps growing forever. Can anyone fail to grasp the notion that it is impossible for something that keeps becoming more perfect forever to become perfect in an instant?

339   We can now see that everyone who thinks about salvation on the basis of life has no thought of instant salvation by direct mercy. The thought is rather of the means of salvation, the means in and through which the Lord works according to the laws of his divine providence, through which we are therefore led by the Lord out of his pure mercy.

However, people who do not think about salvation on the basis of life add the "instant" component to salvation and the "direct" component to mercy. This is what people do who separate faith from charity—charity is a way of living—and make attaining faith instantaneous, an event that occurs at the last hour of dying, if not before. It is also what people do who believe that forgiveness of sins without repentance is absolution from sins and therefore salvation, and who then take the Holy Supper. This also applies to people who trust the indulgences issued by monks and their prayers for the departed and the dispensations given by a power some claim to have over human souls.

340   4. *Instant salvation by direct mercy is the flying fiery serpent in the church.* The flying fiery serpent means an evil bright with hellfire like the evil meant by the flying fiery serpent in Isaiah: "Do not be happy, all Philistia, because the rod that strikes you has been broken, for a snake will come out from the root of the serpent, whose fruit is a flying fiery serpent" (Isaiah 14:29). This kind of evil is on the wing in the church whenever it believes in instant salvation by direct mercy, because this (a) leads to the destruction of religion, (b) makes people feel safe, and (c) blames God for damnation.

[2] As to the first, (a) *that this leads to the destruction of religion,* there are two things that are essential to and omnipresent in religion: belief in God, and repentance. These two are empty for people who believe they are saved by mercy alone, no matter what kind of life they lead. For what more is needed except to say, "God, have mercy on me!" When it comes to everything else that has to do with religion, these people are in darkness and love their darkness. On the first essential of the church, belief in God, all they think is "What is God? Who has seen him?" If you say that God is real and that God is one, they say that God is one. If you say that there are three, then they say that there are three, but that the three are to be called "the One." For them, that is belief in God.

[3] As for the second essential of the church, repentance, these people give it no thought. This means that they give no thought to any sin and eventually do not know that anything is a sin. They hear and absorb with delight the statement that the law does not condemn them because as Christians they are not under the yoke of the law.[346] All you have to do is say, "God, have mercy on me for the sake of your Son," and you will be saved. For them, this is a life of repentance.

But if you take repentance away, which is the same as removing life from religion, what is left but the phrase, "Have mercy on me"? That is why all they can say is that salvation happens the moment these words are spoken; if not earlier, then at the time of death. What is the Word, then, but a dim and enigmatic message from the tripod in the cave or like an unintelligible answer from some oracular idol?[347] In short, if you take repentance away, which is the same as removing life from religion, what are we but an evil thing bright with hellfire, or a flying fiery serpent in the church? For without repentance, we are devoted to evil, and evil is hell.

[4] (b) *Belief in instant salvation from nothing but pure mercy makes us feel that our lives are safe.* The feeling that our lives are safe comes either from the belief of irreligious people that there is no life after death or from the belief of people who separate life from salvation. These latter do believe in eternal life, but they still think, "I can be saved whether I lead a good life or an evil one, because salvation is a matter of pure mercy, and God's mercy is universal because he does not will the death of anyone." If the thought crosses their minds that they need to ask for this mercy in the approved words of the faith, they may think that if they do not do it earlier, they can do this just before the hour of death approaches. People who live in this sense of safety all think nothing of adultery, fraud, injustice, violence, slander, and vengeance. Rather, they lose control of themselves in these actions, body and soul. They have no idea what a spiritual evil is or what obsession with it is. If they hear anything about it from the Word, it is rather like something that falls on a bony surface and bounces off, or like something that falls into a ditch and oozes away.

[5] (c) *By this kind of belief, God is blamed for damnation.* If God can save everyone out of pure mercy, is there anyone who cannot draw the conclusion that God is to blame, not we, if we are not saved? If you say that the means of salvation is faith, is there anyone who cannot be given this faith, since it is nothing but a thought that can be poured in

whenever our spirits are withdrawn from the world, and done so with confidence? People can also say, "I cannot acquire anything by myself"; so if something is not given and someone is damned, then that damned individual can only think that the Lord is to blame because he could have saved but did not want to. Would this not be calling him merciless? Not only that, in the heat of this belief the damned may say, "Why can we see so many damned in hell when the Lord could save them all in an instant out of pure mercy?" and a good deal more of the same, all of which can only be called appalling indictments of Divinity.

This now serves to show that a belief in instant salvation out of pure mercy is the flying fiery serpent in the church.

[6] Forgive me for adding the following to fill out the rest of the page.

By special permission, some spirits came up from hell and said to me, "You have written a great deal that the Lord has given you. Write something from us as well."

I answered, "What should I write?"

They said, "Write that every spirit, whether good or evil, has his or her own delight—a delight in goodness for the good and a delight in evil for the evil."

I asked, "What is your delight?" They said that it was a delight in adultery, theft, fraud, and lying. I went on to ask, "What are these delights like?" They said that others experienced them as stenches from excrement, foul odors from corpses, and the reek of stale urine. I said, "And do you find them pleasant?" They said that they were absolutely delightful. I said, "Then you are like filthy beasts that live in substances like these."

They said, "If we are, we are, but to our nostrils, these scents are delightful."

I asked, "What else do you want me to write?"

They said, "Write this: that we are all allowed to live in our own delights, no matter how filthy they are, as some would say, as long as we do not harass good spirits and angels. But since we cannot help harassing them, we are driven off and cast into hell, where we suffer terribly."

I said, "Why do you harass good people?" They answered that they could not help it, it was as though a rage came over them when they saw angels and sensed the divine aura around them. I said, "This makes you like wild animals." When they heard this, a rage came over them that looked like blazing hatred, and to prevent them from doing any harm, they were taken back into hell.

On the way pleasures are sensed as odors and as stenches in the spiritual world, see §§303–305 and 324 above.

THE END

NOTES & INDEXES

Notes

Notes to §§1–26

1. In Swedenborg's works, "the Lord" refers to Jesus Christ as God. A core concept in Swedenborg's theology is that there are not three persons in the Trinity; there is one person, whose soul is the unknowable divine, whose human manifestation is Jesus Christ, and whose spirit (or influence) is holy. Of the many names and terms from philosophical and biblical backgrounds that Swedenborg uses to denote God (the Divine Being, the Divine, the Divine Human, the One, the Infinite, the First, the Creator, the Redeemer, the Savior, Jehovah, God Shaddai, and many more), the most frequently occurring term is "the Lord" (Latin *Dominus*), a title rather than a name, meaning "the one in charge," and referring to Jesus Christ as the manifestation of the one and only God. For Swedenborg's brief explanation of his reasons for using "the Lord," see his 1749–1756 work *Secrets of Heaven* 14. [JSR]

2. Swedenborg here refers to *Divine Love and Wisdom* (1763), published immediately before the present work, *Divine Providence* (1764). The two works form a pair. See the translator's preface pages 1–4. [JSR]

3. Citations of Swedenborg's works refer to section numbers. For conventions used in marking additions and corrections to this text, see page 39. [JSR]

4. Following a Christian practice of his times, Swedenborg often used "Jehovah" as a rendering of the tetragrammaton, יהוה *(yhvh),* "YHWH," the four-letter name of God in Hebrew Scriptures. A complex set of circumstances gave rise to the name "Jehovah." The Hebrew alphabet originally consisted only of consonants. It was not until the eighth century of the Common Era that a complete system of diacritical marks for vowel notation was developed. When for any reason the consonantal text was held not to be suitable for reading as it stood, the vowels of an approved reading would be added to the consonants that stood in the text, whether the number of syllables in the two words matched or not. Since the sanctity of the name of God, YHWH, was felt to preclude its being pronounced, the word אֲדֹנָי *(Ădōnāi),* "Lord," was regularly substituted, and to indicate this, vowels closely resembling those of the name Adonai were added to YHWH: YeHoWaH. This combination of consonants and vowels was transliterated into Latin as "Jehovah." (Some English Bibles since then have adopted the name "Jehovah" while others have rendered the term as "Lord," so capitalized.) The currently accepted scholarly reconstruction of the original pronunciation of the name is "Yahweh": see *Theological Dictionary of the Old Testament* under "YHWH." As others have done, Swedenborg relates the name YHWH or Jehovah to the concept of being or "is-ness" in his 1771 work *True Christianity* 19:1; see also §9:2–3 there. [GFD]

5. This is the same work previously alluded to in this section as *Divine Love and Wisdom* (see also note 2). Although the long version of the title used here better represents the full title of the published work, Swedenborg himself often cites the work using the short title, which is generally used in this edition as well. [JSR]

6. As noted in the translator's preface (page 5), Swedenborg follows the practice of presenting his arguments in series of numbered propositions throughout the book. [GFD]

7. The Latin terms here translated "volition" and "discernment" are *voluntas* and *intellectus,* traditionally translated "will" and "understanding" (or "intellect"). Each term has two basic meanings. "Volition" means both the faculty of will or intention that enables us to make choices and also the actual exercise of that faculty in deciding on a given course of action. Likewise "discernment" means both the mental faculty that enables us to think, reason, and know and also the exercise of that faculty in an act of judging or perceiving. Swedenborg regards volition and discernment as the two primary characteristics of humanity. [JSR]

8. Swedenborg, like such thinkers as Benedict de Spinoza (1632–1677) and Gottfried Wilhelm Leibniz (1646–1716), found his view of the cosmos profoundly influenced by the hidden worlds made visible by the microscope. For a useful account of the impact of the microscope on seventeenth- and eighteenth-century thought, see Wilson 1995. [GRJ]

9. The Latin phrase here translated "enduring is a constant coming into being" *(subsistentia est perpetua existentia)* was a common theological maxim (see *Secrets of Heaven* 3483:2, 5084:3; see also Swedenborg's 1768 work *Marriage Love* 380:8; and his 1769 work *Soul-Body Interaction* 4). Swedenborg frequently built on it (see *Secrets of Heaven* 775:2, 3648:2, 4322, 4523:3, 5116:3, 5377, 6040:1, 6482, 9502, 9847, 10076:5, 10152:3, 10252:3, 10266; see also Swedenborg's 1758 work *Heaven and Hell* 106, 303; and *Divine Love and Wisdom* 152; *Soul-Body Interaction* 9:1; *True Christianity* 46, 224:1). The notion is referred to as a commonplace in part 5 of *Discourse on Method* by the French philosopher René Descartes (1596–1650): "It is an opinion commonly received by the theologians, that the action by which [God] now preserves [the universe] is just the same as that by which He at first created it" (Descartes [1637] 1952, 55). Elsewhere Descartes offers this explanation: "The present time has no causal dependence on the time immediately preceding it. Hence, in order to secure the continued existence of a thing, no less a cause is required than that needed to produce it at the first" (Descartes [1641] 1952, 131). Catholic philosopher Thomas Aquinas (1224 or 1225–1274) makes a similar statement about all "creatures," that is, created things: "The being of every creature depends on God, so that not for a moment could it subsist [have independent existence], but would fall into nothingness were it not kept in being by the operation of the Divine power" (*Summa Theologiae* 1:104:1; translation in Aquinas 1952). In support of his position, Aquinas in turn cites another Church Father, Gregory the Great (540–604), specifically his *Moralia in Job* (Ethical Disquisitions on Job) 16:37; he is probably thinking of Gregory's statement there that "All things subsist in him [God]. . . . No created thing avails in itself either to subsist or to move." This Scholastic theory of perpetual creation is also discussed by the Anglo-Irish philosopher George Berkeley (1685–1753) in his work *The Principles of Human Knowledge* (Berkeley [1710] 1952, §46). [JSR, SS]

10. The Latin philosophical terms here translated "reality" and "manifestation" are *Esse* and *Existere,* the infinitive of the verbs "to be" and "to stand forth," "be actualized" used as nouns. The first refers to underlying existence, the second, to actualization. In *True Christianity* 21 Swedenborg correlates the terms with substance and form. [JSR]

11. Swedenborg is using "form" (Latin *forma*) to refer to the shape of concrete things,

not to abstract "Platonic" forms. The connection between form and unity is simple. Many bricks become one house when they are given the form of a house. Many flowers become a bouquet when they are given the form of a bouquet. See also note 144 below. [GRJ]

12. On Swedenborg's use of the term "substance" see note 144 below. [SS]

13. Swedenborg uses the word "church" (Latin *ecclesia*) in a variety of meanings. Sometimes it refers to a religious approach in the abstract, whether that occurs in an individual or in a group large or small; sometimes it refers more concretely to local or national Christianity, to all Protestantism, or even to Christianity as a whole; sometimes it applies more broadly to all believers on earth of whatever faith; and sometimes it is used historically to mean the core religious approach of a given age or era through which heaven was connected with humankind, of which there have been five in sequence: the earliest (or "most ancient") church, the early (or "ancient") church, the Jewish church, the Christian church, and the new church (see Swedenborg's 1758 work *Last Judgment* 46 and notes; see also §328 below and *True Christianity* 760, 762, 786). Presumably Swedenborg is here using the term broadly to mean all believers of whatever faith. [JSR]

14. Swedenborg's use here of the singular verb *est* ("is") is striking, and undoubtedly represents his insistence that love and wisdom are only apparently separate entities. He used a singular verb similarly in the passage cited here (*Divine Love and Wisdom* 40), as well as in *Divine Love and Wisdom* 89, 146, and 400. [GFD]

15. The Latin phrase here translated "wholly 'itself' and unique" is *Ipsum et Unicum*, literally, "what is itself and what is unique." [GFD]

16. The work mentioned here was published by Swedenborg in 1758. [JSR]

17. Among the many thinkers Swedenborg might have in mind in this passage was the German philosopher Leibniz. Philosophers previous to Leibniz had theorized that the universe was built up of indivisible material atoms. Leibniz criticized this type of theory by declaring that although the material atom might be thought to be perfectly "simple," that is, noncompound, indivisible, it was in fact infinitely subdivisible. The only truly "simple" thing was a metaphysical or spiritual atom. To designate this atom he adopted the term *monad* (from the Greek μόνας *[mónas]*, "unit," "single thing"); the word had been used frequently in the European philosophical tradition, for example by Nicholas of Cusa (1401–1464) and Giordano Bruno (1548–1600). From these "infinite and dimensionless points" emerged "dimensional forms" (as Swedenborg expresses it here). But Leibniz and his followers were not the only targets of Swedenborg's critique: he is clearly referring to his own efforts to develop an atomic theory in his 1734 scientific treatise *Principia Rerum Naturalium* (Basic Principles of Nature = Swedenborg [1734] 1988). His basic building block there was not a monad but a "first" or "natural" point "produced by motion from the Infinite" (Swedenborg [1734] 1988, 1:2:4). He described it in almost the exact terms used in the present passage—as something "so very simple that nothing could be more so" (Swedenborg [1734] 1988, 1:2:8). [GFD, SS]

18. This passage offers a formulation of the *holographic model* of the universe, the notion that each part includes or represents the whole. See Dole 1988, 374–381. Another such formulation can be found in the *Monadology* of Leibniz: there Leibniz theorizes the existence of the monad, a kind of indivisible, metaphysical atom of which the universe is composed (see note 17 just above and note 276 below). Each monad is

ultimately a microcosmic representation of the entire universe from a particular point of view (Leibniz [1720] 1968, §§62–63, 66), and thus of God, who is "the monad of monads" (see Leibniz [1720] 1968, §83). [SS]

19. This statement of Swedenborg's intentions must be taken as a generalization to which there will be numerous exceptions. [GFD]

20. This is a major theme in part 1 of *Divine Love and Wisdom*, and is clearly assumed in §§3–4 of the present work. [GFD]

21. "The Word" (Latin *Verbum*) refers to the Bible and denotes it as truth revealed by God. It was the common term for the Bible in the Lutheran tradition in which Swedenborg was raised. He indicates elsewhere, however, that by "the Word" he means a smaller set of books of the Bible than are found in the complete Lutheran Bible, specifically the works that he identifies as having a spiritual meaning throughout, namely the Pentateuch (Genesis, Exodus, Leviticus, Numbers, Deuteronomy), some other historical books (Joshua, Judges, 1 and 2 Samuel, 1 and 2 Kings), the Book of Psalms, the major and minor prophets (Isaiah, Jeremiah, Lamentations, Ezekiel, Daniel, Hosea, Joel, Amos, Obadiah, Jonah, Micah, Nahum, Habakkuk, Zephaniah, Haggai, Zechariah, Malachi), the Gospels (Matthew, Mark, Luke, John), and the Book of Revelation. For further discussion, see his *Secrets of Heaven* 10325, and his 1758 works *New Jerusalem* 266, and *White Horse* 16. It should be noted that in his last work, *True Christianity,* he seems to use the term in the full Lutheran sense, including passages from the epistles of the apostles among citations from "the Word." For his explanation as to why he did not generally include the works of the apostles and Paul in "the Word," see his letter to Gabriel Beyer (April 15, 1766), cited in Acton 1955, 612–613. [GFD, JSR]

22. The concept of "correspondence" presented in Swedenborg's works is briefly defined in *Divine Love and Wisdom* 71 as "the mutual relationship between spiritual and earthly things." In its full formulation, it holds that there are two separate universes, one spiritual and one physical, that are related to each other through similarity but not through any shared matter or direct continuity. We human beings bridge the two worlds by having both a spiritual aspect and a physical aspect. In Swedenborg's terminology, the mutual relationship between our volition and discernment (see note 7 above), which are spiritual, and our heart and lungs, which are physical, can be called a "correspondence," and these faculties and organs themselves can also be called "correspondences." [JSR]

23. A concrete example might be the giving of a gift to a loved one who has recently graduated. On an inner level the idea is born when a feeling of love and a desire to congratulate the loved one (which are related to love or goodness and occur in the faculty known as volition) come together with a knowledge of the loved one's tastes and preferences (which is related to wisdom or truth and occurs in the faculty known as discernment). A marriage of affection and information is necessary to give birth to the plan. As the plan then shifts into actualization, the two sides are again involved, but not apparently at the same time. The faculty of discernment and wisdom is first called on to make lists, selections, and arrangements; then finally in the act itself of giving the gift, the love becomes activated as it finds expression in an actual benefit to the other person and its desire to congratulate is fulfilled. Love and wisdom are together on the inside throughout the process, but are apparently separate on the outside at different phases. [JSR]

24. The Latin words here translated "Form is the one and only source of quality" are *ex forma et non aliunde est omne quale,* literally, "from form and not from anywhere else

is all quality." The word *non,* "not," is omitted in the first edition, which would yield the obviously erroneous sense "from form and from anywhere else is all quality." [GFD]

25. The Latin word here translated "earthly" is *naturalis,* traditionally translated "natural." In Swedenborg's terminology, the adjective "earthly" may denote a range of things from what is purely physical and material to what is earthly in the minds or preoccupations of angels and spirits, nonmaterial beings. [JSR]

26. The Latin word here translated "facades" is *apparentia,* literally, "appearances." [GFD]

27. The allusion is to 2 Corinthians 11:13–14, where Paul describes false apostles as "transforming themselves into apostles of Christ; and no wonder, for Satan himself is transformed into an angel of light." [GFD]

28. Most of the summary statements in this section reflect slight variations in wording from the original material in *Divine Love and Wisdom.* In the very last instance, that of §431, the summary accurately reflects the substance of the section referred to, but is not drawn from its wording. [GFD]

29. "Works" means actions, particularly as reflections of one's inner morality and spirituality. When the term appears elsewhere in Swedenborg's works it generally refers to the longstanding debate between Catholics and Protestants over the extent to which "works" or upright, moral actions are necessary for the individual's salvation. For further information, including Swedenborg's position on works, see note 134 below. [JSR]

30. Swedenborg appears here to contradict himself; he says that an evil person can do no harm whatever to good people, and then immediately admits that harm does in fact happen to good people. Statements he makes elsewhere suggest a possible reconciliation: although evil wishes constantly to destroy goodness, it can actually only assault itself in others. The evil traits all of us have inherited and most of us have acted upon make us vulnerable to assault. Even when we are assaulted, however, we are not actually damaged on a spiritual level; only as much evil is allowed to affect us as could be spiritually beneficial to us, depending on our choice of response. See §77 below and *Secrets of Heaven* 59:2, 6489, 6574, 6724:2, 9330:2; *True Christianity* 123:6. For the unintended benefits that evil provides to others, see §§21–26 below. [JSR]

31. See note 27 above. [GFD]

32. See, for example, Matthew 22:1–14 and 25:1–13. [GFD]

33. Swedenborg frequently uses the word "church" (Latin *ecclesia*) to denote the whole religious ethos and practice of a given people or era. See note 13 above. [GFD]

34. The work mentioned here was published by Swedenborg in 1763. It is referred to in this edition by the short title *Sacred Scripture.* [JSR]

35. In this passage Swedenborg's verbs emphasize both the completed disruption of the marriage of goodness and truth in the past and the ongoing disruption of that marriage in the present: "have broken . . . and still do," "have become opponents, and continue to be so." Swedenborg may intend both tenses to apply to the same people, indicating that once such a decision is made, it is made over and over again; but it is more likely that he intends the different tenses to apply to two distinct groups: evil spirits in hell, who have already made their decision, as opposed to evil people who are still in this world or in the world of spirits, whose decision is not yet finalized. Compare the mention in §27:2 just below of "people who have become angels and are becoming angels." [JSR]

Notes to §§27–45

36. The work mentioned here was published by Swedenborg in 1758. [JSR]

37. The work mentioned here was published by Swedenborg in 1763. It is referred to in this edition by the short title *Supplements.* [JSR]

38. The Latin phrase here translated "totally present" is *in suo Esse,* literally, "in its to be," meaning in its being or "is-ness," its true underlying identity. [GFD]

39. This theme is developed in striking fashion in §§191–213 below. [GFD]

40. The use of the word "soul" in this sentence is not strictly metaphorical. Swedenborg notes elsewhere that the soul of any particular thing can be defined as its innermost element (see Swedenborg's unpublished manuscript of 1759, *Revelation Explained* [= Swedenborg 1997a] §313:14); that nothing can exist unless it has a soul; and that the essence of anything is called its soul (*Revelation Explained* [= Swedenborg 1997a] §1206:2). This concept of soul is a strikingly different from other concepts in the Western philosophical tradition. For example, Swedenborg speaks of the "vegetative soul"— the essence or soul of a plant—as the function to which the plant gives form; that is, as its useful function (*Divine Love and Wisdom* 61; see also his 1745 work *Worship and Love of God* 24; *Revelation Explained* [= Swedenborg 1997a] §§1214:2 and 1214:4; and his unpublished manuscript of 1762–1763, *Sketch for Divine Love* [= Swedenborg 1997b] §10:3 = §27). Clearly, as in this passage, his definition of soul depends on the final cause, or purpose, of the plant as seen in the entirety of the Divine pattern. By contrast, the concept of the vegetative soul developed by the Greek philosopher Aristotle (384–322 B.C.E.) is defined in terms of the three basic faculties of plant nutrition, growth, and reproduction (*On the Soul* 413a, 415a). [SS]

41. On the nature of apparent space in the spiritual world, see *Heaven and Hell* 17, 85, and especially 191–199. [GFD]

42. Once again, the wording of several of the propositions referred to varies in the respective passage in *Divine Love and Wisdom.* [GFD]

43. This is explained more fully in *Divine Love and Wisdom* 184. [GFD]

44. The Latin phrase here translated "from the other side" is *ab extra,* literally, "from the outside." The context suggests that it means "the farther side," from the Lord's point of view. [GFD]

45. Although Swedenborg sometimes briefly follows the general Christian view of his times in referring to "the Devil" as if there were a single evil force opposite God, doing so even in his third of five tenets for the new church (see Swedenborg's 1769 work *Survey* 43; see parallel passages at *Survey* 117; *Marriage Love* 82:1; and *True Christianity* 3:2), in fuller discussions elsewhere he asserts that there is no such thing: "the Devil" is a collective term for hell (see *Secrets of Heaven* 251:2; *Heaven and Hell* 311, 544). Nor is there one supreme "Satan." Swedenborg does, however, speak of two classes of people in hell called "satans" and "devils" or "demons." The distinction is outlined in *Heaven and Hell* 311:2 and *Divine Love and Wisdom* 273. In general, "devils" are associated with demonic loves and "satans" with maliciously distorted thoughts, or "devils" with love for oneself and "satans" with love for the world. Swedenborg consistently describes "devils" or "demons" as more profoundly pernicious than "satans." [GFD, JSR]

46. On Swedenborg's view of Satan, see note 45 just above. [JSR]

47. See, for example, *Heaven and Hell* 191–199. [GFD]

48. The Latin word here translated "the material world" is *natura,* literally, "nature," a term used in a fairly broad variety of meanings in Swedenborg's works. [JSR]

49. The phrase "falling star" is here used by Swedenborg in the poetic sense that is common today (*True Christianity* 759:2). It was surmised at least as early as Aristotle that stars were enormous bodies that we see from an immense distance (*On the Heavens* 2:8). The notion of stars as the centers of individual solar systems was popularized by the French writer Bernard le Bovier de Fontenelle (1657–1757) in his *Entretiens sur la pluralité des mondes* (Conversations on the Plurality of Solar Systems, 1686). For Swedenborg's knowledge of stars, see *True Christianity* 770 and especially *Secrets of Heaven* 9441: "It is known in the learned world that every star is like a sun in its own place." [GFD, SS]

50. There is no direct evidence linking the twelve steps mentioned here and the twelve steps to recovery from alcoholism outlined by William G. "Bill" Wilson (1895–1971) in *Alcoholics Anonymous* ([Wilson] 2001, 59–60). However, some connection has been suspected, based on the fact that his wife, Lois Burnham Wilson (1891–1988), was raised a Swedenborgian and thus may have been familiar with the passage. See Wilson 1979, 2. [JSR]

51. The pairing of life and wisdom rather than love and wisdom is noteworthy. Swedenborg does explicitly mention levels of wisdom in §34 above, and while the phrase "levels of life" does not occur in either of the sections cited, it is noted in §32:3 that the opening of the levels depends on the way we live. [GFD]

52. For Swedenborg's view of "the devil" see note 45 above. [JSR]

53. The Latin here translated "in a garbage dump" is *in putoribus,* "in places that smell terrible." [GFD]

54. The allusion is presumably to Galatians 5:1, "It is for freedom that Christ has freed us, so stand firm and do not let yourselves be weighed down by the yoke of bondage," and 5:18, "If you are led by the spirit, then you are not under the law" (see also Romans 6:14). [GFD]

55. See especially §§129–153. [GFD]

Notes to §§46–69

56. On Swedenborg's use of the term "essence" see note 144 below. [SS]

57. The idealists here referred to are members of a school of philosophy that either minimizes or denies the reality of the material world. Idealism has a long history that continues to the present day. Its roots can be traced in philosophers usually classified in other schools, such as Plato (427–347 B.C.E.) and several of the Scholastics; an undisputed adherent would be Swedenborg's contemporary, George Berkeley (1685–1753). Swedenborg refers here to those proponents of idealism who hold the view that whatever exists does so primarily or exclusively through our own mental constructs. Few if any idealists, however, actually maintain that we as observers do not exist. [GFD, SS]

58. The assertion that everything "is real, and is not just an image of reality" is another refutation of the beliefs of the idealists just mentioned. Berkeley (see note 57 above) does seem a likely target; he asserts that the "supposed originals or external things" of the world are only sense-derived ideas, which are "the pictures and representations" of those things (Berkeley [1710] 1952, §8). In all fairness to Berkeley, however, it should be noted that while he denied that we can infer the independent existence of objects from our perception of them, he also argued that they do actually exist when outside our perception, because God continues to perceive them (Berkeley [1710] 1952, §§6, 48). [GFD, SS]

59. Swedenborg does not here deny that space and time in the material world are real; he asserts only that in the material world the appearance of space and time is relative to our inner states. In the spiritual world, however, space and time are nothing but the appearance of inner spiritual states. [GRJ]

60. The three figures mentioned here, John Calvin (1509–1564), Martin Luther (1483–1546), and Philip Melanchthon (1497–1560), were all major Protestant reformers. Calvin and Luther were the founders of the two principal branches of Protestant Christianity; Melanchthon was Luther's faithful colleague and collaborator, as well as the author of the first systematic treatise of reformed theology, *Loci Communes Rerum Theologicarum* (Common Theological Topics, 1521, with many subsequent editions; see Melanchthon [1543] 1992) and of the first Protestant manifesto, the *Augsburg Confession* (1530; = [Melanchthon] [1530] 1901). The former treatise was later eclipsed by Calvin's *Institutes of the Christian Religion* (1536; 2nd ed., 1559; = Calvin [1559] 1987). On Luther, see Brecht 1993a, 1993b, and 1994; on Calvin, see Bouwsma 1988 and McGrath 1990; on Melanchthon, see Manschreck 1958. For Swedenborg's interactions with them in the spiritual world, see *True Christianity* 796–798. [GRJ]

61. The allusion is to 1 Corinthians 12:3, "No one can say that Jesus is the Lord except by the Holy Spirit." [GFD]

62. See part 4 of *Divine Love and Wisdom*, particularly §§310–318. [GFD]

63. On reproduction as the imitation of eternity, see Plato *Symposium* 207a–208b; and Aristotle *On the Soul* 2:3–4 and *On the Generation of Animals* 2:1. [GRJ]

64. For more on the distinction between spiritual and heavenly angels, see *Heaven and Hell* 29–40. [GFD]

65. The Latin word here translated "direct contact" is *adjunctio,* literally, "a joining or binding to." The word emphasizes that angels sense their union with God as a connection between separate entities (themselves and God) rather than an actual merging or blending. [JSR]

66. The Latin phrase here translated "people who are engaged with divinity" is *qui in Divino sunt.* Since this is the only occurrence of this phrase in Swedenborg's theological works, it is possible that a word or phrase has dropped out and that Swedenborg intended a phrase that occurs more frequently, such as "people who are engaged with divine goodness and truth." [GFD]

67. The Latin words here translated "millions" are *myriades myriadum,* literally, "ten thousands of ten thousands," an idiom intended to convey not mathematical precision but simply an inconceivably great number. [GFD]

68. An explanation of this point is offered in *Last Judgment* 12 as follows: "In the most perfect form, the more participants there are, the more there is a shared tendency toward unity. The tendency and the unity are strengthened with numbers because each element is given its place as a welcome link between two or more, and everything that is given such a place serves to strengthen and unite." The perfection of a form comes not only from the sheer number of components but also from the variety among those components; see *Heaven and Hell* 56, and §4:4–5 above. [GFD]

69. This point is developed more fully in §§191–213 below, in the context of a discussion of human prudence. [GFD]

70. By "corresponds" Swedenborg means "corresponds to the function of a given organ or part of the body." For detailed information about the correspondences of the

various parts of the body, see the references to *Secrets of Heaven* in *Divine Love and Wisdom* 377; for an overview, see Worcester 1931. [GFD]

Notes to §§71–99

71. Swedenborg's discussion of the philosophical commonplace that humans can reason and animals cannot is unique in the form it takes, if not in its conclusion. For representative passages from the classical authors and Scholastics on the gap between animals and humans with respect to rationality, see Aristotle *Metaphysics* 1:1; *History of Animals* 1:1; *Politics* 7:13; and Aquinas *Summa Theologiae* 1:79:1, 2:1:50:4. On the contrast with respect to freedom as well, see the physician Galen (129–about 200 C.E.) *On the Natural Faculties* 1:12; and Aquinas *Summa Theologiae* 2:1:13:2. For representative passages from Enlightenment thinkers, see the discussion in Descartes [1637] 1952, 59–60 and the views of English philosopher John Locke (1632–1704) in Locke [1690] 1952, 145. The opposite view, called animalitarianism, is discussed by Lovejoy and Boas 1935, 389–420, specifically as it appears in ancient times. Among Enlightenment thinkers, the Scottish philosopher David Hume (1711–1776) maintains some skepticism about the superior rationality of humans (Hume [1748] 1952, 487–488), as does the French philosopher Julien Offray de La Mettrie (1709–1751; see notes 143 and 306 below). [SS]

72. See especially *Divine Love and Wisdom* 236–240. [GFD]

73. The Latin word here translated "our sense of who we are" is *proprium,* an adjective used as a noun to mean "what is our own." Since Swedenborg insists that in the last analysis nothing is really "our own," *proprium* more precisely denotes what we claim as our own. Swedenborg uses the Latin term with a wide range of meanings that extend from a healthy sense of self to an evil preoccupation with self; see, for example, *Secrets of Heaven* 141, 1937, and 5660. [GFD]

74. The Latin word here translated "becoming part of our sense of who we are" is *appropriare,* which by its etymology might be translated as "attaching to our *proprium,*" our sense of ourselves. [GFD]

75. See especially §293. [GFD]

76. See §§308–321, and also §§79–81. [GFD]

77. The reference is to the extended treatment of the interaction between volition and discernment under the image of the interaction between heart and lungs, beginning at §394 and continuing through §431, which indicates that volition initiates and discernment responds, rather than the reverse. [GFD]

78. Luke 6:45 reads "Good people bring forth what is good from the good treasure of their hearts, and evil people bring forth evil from their evil treasure. The mouth speaks out of the overflow of the heart." [GFD]

79. Swedenborg frequently specifies these fears, characteristically including fear of losing our reputation, respect, position, wealth, and life (see, for example, *Secrets of Heaven* 81:3, 1077, 1944:2, and 2126; *Heaven and Hell* 257 note e, 508:5, 559, and 573; *True Christianity* 400:7). *Secrets of Heaven* 6914:3 adds to the usual list a fear of being sent to hell. [GFD]

80. The work mentioned here was published by Swedenborg in 1763. It is referred to in this edition by the short title *Life.* [JSR]

81. The Latin words here translated "born" and "regenerated" are closely related: *generari* and *regenerari*. [GFD]

82. The Latin title given in the first edition here reads simply *Doctrina Novae Hierosolymae*, "Teachings for the New Jerusalem." In 1763, the year before he published the present work, Swedenborg published three works with titles that begin with these words: *Teachings for the New Jerusalem on the Lord, Teachings for the New Jerusalem on Sacred Scripture,* and *Teachings for the New Jerusalem on Faith.* They are referred to in this edition by the short titles *The Lord, Sacred Scripture,* and *Faith.* From the topic and the section numbers cited it is clear that *Faith* is the work he intended to cite here. [GFD]

83. The Latin phrase here translated "the greatest good there is" is *summum bonum,* literally, "highest good," a term commonly used in philosophy to denote the one good that should be chosen in preference to all others. See, for example, the Roman philosopher Cicero (106–43 B.C.E.): "The thing that is the highest, ultimate, or final good (the Greeks call it the *telos*) is that which is not a means to anything else, but to which all else is a means" (*On Ends* 1:42). [GFD, SS]

84. There is no §84 in the first edition. [GFD]

85. Without the material added here in brackets from the previous sentence, the logical connection in the sentence is uncharacteristically obscure. [GFD]

86. This subject is developed in somewhat more detail in §109 below. [GFD]

87. The Latin word here translated "visible individual" is *persona,* which originally meant "mask" and came to mean "an individual." Here it seems to carry some of its original connotation of the exterior representation of a person. [GFD]

88. Swedenborg fairly often mentions that one tablet of the Ten Commandments relates to God and the other to us (*Life* 62; see also Swedenborg's 1766 work *Revelation Unveiled* 490; *True Christianity* 285, 287). In a passage he never published Swedenborg gives a more specific delineation: the first three commandments pertain to God; the last six commandments pertain to us; and the fourth commandment is a kind of bridge connecting the two tablets and their areas of relevance (*Revelation Explained* [= Swedenborg 1997a] §1026:3). [JSR]

89. The Latin word here translated "perceptions" is *cognitiones,* which in Swedenborg's works means "data," "known facts," or "items of knowledge about interior things." The translation "perceptions" is based on the assumption that words such as this, which are compounded from the Latin root *gnoscere,* "to find out," regularly refer to experiential knowledge as opposed to theoretical or second-hand knowledge. [GFD]

90. On Abraham, see Genesis 18, especially verses 2 and 22; on Hagar, see Genesis 21, especially verse 17; on Gideon, see Judges 6, especially verses 12, 14, and 16. [GFD]

91. For the preceding discussion, see §§87–94. In the following pages, the propositions presented in §§100–128, 129–153, and 154–174 deal with specific aspects of the subject. [GFD]

92. Although "immortality" and "eternal life" might seem synonymous, in the Protestant tradition of Swedenborg's times "immortality" meant permanent existence, of whatever quality, whereas "eternal life" meant the blissful afterlife enjoyed only by the blessed. Compare §322:3 below, where worldly people are called "dead" and spiritual people "living." [GFD]

93. Swedenborg here seems to suggest that in later sections of this work (Latin *in sequentibus,* literally, "in the following [sections]") he will disclose many reasons why

people who are capable of attaining true rationality and freedom fail to do so. The end of the section immediately following (§99) implies but one reason: failure to abstain from evils as sins. The promised disclosure of many reasons is apparently unfulfilled. [JSR]

94. On "demons" (also called "devils") and "satans," see note 45 above. [JSR]

95. Other contexts make clear that by "state of life" Swedenborg here means the state of one's inner life, not one's physical or social condition. [JSR]

Notes to §§100–128

96. On "the yoke of the law," see note 54 above. [GFD]

97. See §106 below. "Our life's love" (Latin *amor vitae*) may be thought of as our central motivation or reason for being. Compare *Secrets of Heaven* 8855: "We have as our goal whatever we love above all. We are focused on that in everything else. It is in our intentions like the hidden current of a river that carries us here and there even when we are doing something else, because that is what is making us live." [GFD]

98. The "life's love" (see note 98 above) is here seen as the end or ultimate purpose of our actions; it gives rise to a lesser love—a love of the means that conduce to that end. The complete sequence would be: (1) the focus on one's life's love—for example, teaching; (2) the development of means toward bringing about that love, such as acquiring an education and practicing instruction; (3) the engendering of a secondary love that focuses on those means—for example, love of learning and of interacting with young people; (4) the eliciting of our pleasure and of memories that reinforce our movement toward our life's love. Compare *Worship and Love of God* 48: "[The understanding faculties of the mind] began to see love as the end, and everything else as means leading to that end, though they still loved everything else on account of that end; for they saw the end as present in the means." [SS]

99. Swedenborg presumably has in mind *Divine Love and Wisdom* 369. [GFD]

100. The Latin terms here translated "purpose, means, and result" are *finis, causa,* and *effectus,* traditionally translated as "end, cause, and effect." [GFD]

101. In Swedenborg's young adulthood, he lived under and eventually developed a fairly close relationship with Sweden's charismatic King Carl (Charles) XII (1682–1718), who pushed Sweden to new heights and then brought it to the brink of ruin by his unrelenting obsession with conquest. This made a strong impression on Swedenborg, as is evidenced by extensive comments in his unpublished diary of 1745–1765; see especially *Spiritual Experiences* (= Swedenborg 1889b) §§4748, 4751. [GFD]

102. The first edition reads "Jesus" for "John." [GFD]

103. Swedenborg's intention is to point out that Protestant theologians believe Romans 3:28 refers to the "laws" given by God known as the Ten Commandments, whereas actually it refers to the rituals set out in the first five books of the Bible. In the time of Paul these books were known collectively as "the Law," from the Hebrew תּוֹרָה *(tôrā),* "Torah." (See, for example, Matthew 22:40, where what we now call the Old Testament or the Hebrew Bible is referred to in full as "the Law and the Prophets.") The books of "the Law" were attributed to Moses (as in Luke 24:27), and included detailed prescriptions for sacrificial ritual, personal cleanliness, and diet, as well as for ethical behavior. If Paul had been writing in Hebrew, the confusion over the meaning of

the word "law" could not have arisen, because he would have used the unambiguous term "Torah." But he was writing in Greek, and thus naturally adopted the word for Torah used in the standard Greek translation of the Hebrew Bible familiar to him, νόμος *(nómos),* "law." Unfortunately, the Greek term is susceptible to misinterpretation. There can be little doubt, however, that when Paul wrote *nómos* in Romans he was referring to the Torah, not the Ten Commandments. It would be appropriate therefore to translate the phrase in Romans 3:28 as "the works of the Law" (the capital letter designating the title of the written works) or, unambiguously, as "the works of the Torah." A paraphrase of the entire verse would then read: "We are justified by faith apart from the rituals prescribed in the Torah." [GFD]

104. Swedenborg may have in mind here the passage called the "hymn to love," 1 Corinthians 13:1–13. [GFD]

105. Swedenborg may here be thinking of Romans 2:5–10; but there is no lack of passages where Paul insists that Christians should not do evil. [GFD]

106. The term *natural moralism* (and its synonym, *ethical naturalism*) is extremely vague; a natural moral code can be very broadly defined as "a moral code that conforms with nature" (see Lovejoy and Boas 1935, 451–456). In most cases, natural moralism rests on the idea that one should live as people did in the supposedly Golden Age before civic life developed (see note 181 below); but some influential thinkers have seen the *natural* life of humankind as consisting of engagement in *civilized* interaction. For example, in a well-known passage Aristotle declares, "The state is a creation of nature, and the human being is a political animal. . . . A social instinct is implanted in all humans by nature" (*Politics* 1:2; translation in Aristotle 1952, 446). During the Enlightenment, this view was seconded by thinkers such as Anthony Ashley Cooper, 3rd Earl of Shaftesbury (1671–1713); see Willey 1961, 67–70. The program of natural moralism also took on energy from the hurricane brewing over the separation of church and state during the Enlightenment (for an overview, see Cassirer 1951, 160–182); if the religious basis of morality and civil behavior was to be dispensed with, another had to be found to take its place. [SS]

107. Priapus, a Greek and Roman god of fertility, is depicted in classical art as a grotesque and obscene male figure. [GFD]

108. Throughout his theological works, to mentions of "abstaining from evils" Swedenborg often adds the phrase "as sins." The material he points to here, *Life* 108–113, especially 111, gives the reason for his emphasizing abstaining from evils *as sins.* It asserts that many people abstain from evils for various worldly and personal reasons; but abstaining from evils is only effective in bringing transformation on a spiritual level when those evils are seen as sins, as actions or attitudes that are wrong before God, not just questionable to the public eye. [JSR]

109. Here Swedenborg is speaking of what later came to be known as the unconscious or subconscious mind. [GRJ]

110. The Latin phrase here translated "in all the elements" is *in omnia,* literally, "into everything"; it occurs three times in this sentence. There seems to be no concise English way to convey the idea of "working from the outside to make something happen from the inside" that is expressed by this simple phrase in its context. [GFD]

111. The work mentioned here was published by Swedenborg in 1763. It is referred to in this edition by the short title *The Lord.* The passages referred to are §§21, 34:3, and 35:2. [JSR]

112. The Latin phrase here translated "the divine Being" is *Divinum Esse,* literally, "the divine 'to be.'" The Latin term *Esse* is the infinitive of the verb "to be" used as a noun. It is a common philosophical and theological term for basic existence or "is-ness" as an attribute. [GFD]

113. This concept is developed in considerable detail elsewhere. See, for example, *Heaven and Hell* 59–67 and the material from *Secrets of Heaven* extracted in Swedenborg 1984. [GFD]

114. See especially §201. [GFD]

115. See especially *Divine Love and Wisdom* 209–216. [GFD]

116. The "first things" mentioned here are infinite divine qualities in God. The "last things" are material substances of the physical world. As Swedenborg explains elsewhere, by "becoming flesh" God became present and powerful on the physical level in a new way (*Sacred Scripture* 99; *True Christianity* 109). [JSR]

117. See Revelation 1:11, 17; 2:8; and 22:13. [GFD]

118. See note 29 above. [JSR]

Notes to §§129–153

119. This seemingly definitive generalization followed immediately by a contradiction of it is worth noting. Compare *Heaven and Hell* 256, which first indicates that spirits cannot talk to us from their own memories, and then suggests that when they do, it causes our sensation of déjà vu. These and other such sweeping statements, then, may well be rhetorical devices intended to stress the importance of the principle expressed rather than careful, literal statements to which there are no exceptions. [GFD]

120. The Latin word here translated "second-hand belief," *persuasio,* is regularly used by Swedenborg to denote something that is believed on grounds other than its own merits. For an instance of this usage, see *Faith* 11. [GFD]

121. The relationship between our reading of the Word "from the outside" and the Lord's acting from the inside is explored in some detail in §172 below. See especially subsection 6 there. [GFD]

122. Here Swedenborg affirms one of the central innovations of Protestantism: the claim that miracles have ceased. [GRJ]

123. The Latin phrase here translated "the Reed Sea" is *mare Suph,* a name adopted directly from the Hebrew יַם־סוּף (*yam-sûp̄*), which means "the Sea of Reeds." While its precise location is debated, it has traditionally been identified with the Red Sea, and the phrase is usually so translated. [GFD]

124. By "evil people" Swedenborg means "people who are involved in evil," not "people who are intrinsically and unavoidably evil." The divine ability to save everyone and the universal human faculty of freedom to respond are centerpieces of Swedenborg's theology (see for example §§322–330 below). [JSR]

125. For more on how the Word is all about the Lord, see *The Lord* throughout. [JSR]

126. This passage in Matthew concerns an unclean spirit that temporarily leaves someone but then later "moves back in," bringing along seven worse spirits. [GFD]

127. In the first edition, this and the following section are both numbered 134. [GFD]

128. Where the translation reads "Zechariah 1:18, 20, 21; 2:1 and following," the first edition cites Zechariah 2:1, 3, and following. This is due to a significant difference between Latin and English Bibles in the versification of Zechariah 1 and 2. Zechariah 2:1, 3 in Latin Bibles is Zechariah 1:18 and 20 in English Bibles. The following verses that include mention of a man with a measuring line in his hand occur in Zechariah 2:4 and following in Latin Bibles, which is Zechariah 1:21 and 2:1 and following in English Bibles. [JSR]

129. The Latin phrase here translated "spirits who inspire deceptive passions and visions" is *spiritus enthusiasticos, & visionarios,* literally, "enthusiastic and visionary spirits." The Greek roots of "enthusiastic" signify "god-filled," and in ancient times an enthusiast was someone ecstatic or possessed by a god. By the time of the Enlightenment, however, "enthusiasm" had come to mean a deep belief that relies not on reason or logic but on a conviction that God has communicated truth directly to the believer. Many thinkers of the Enlightenment had a deep horror for such belief; the label "enthusiast" was a devastating charge to fling against an opponent. They saw it as rampant in faiths such as Quakerism, in which adherents base their actions on the "leading" of an "inner light" (see note 212 below). The foremost denouncer of enthusiasm was Locke, who devoted the entirety of chapter 19 of his *Essay Concerning Human Understanding* to the topic. There he asks rhetorically, "How do I know that God is the revealer of [a given proposition] to me; that this impression is made upon my mind by his Holy Spirit; and that therefore I ought to obey it?" He insists on the necessity of ascertaining through reason "that God is the revealer of [a given proposition], and that what I take to be a revelation is certainly put into my mind by Him, and is not an illusion dropped in by some other spirit" (Locke [1690] 1952, 4:19:10). [GFD, SS]

130. By the word "now" here Swedenborg presumably means since 1757, the year when he witnessed the Last Judgment in the spiritual world (see *Last Judgment,* especially §45). Swedenborg reports that the Last Judgment involved a major reordering of that world. [GFD]

131. Swedenborg elsewhere asserts that these conversations with spirits and angels were more or less constant or ongoing (*Secrets of Heaven* 4923:2, 6200:1; *Divine Love and Wisdom* 355; *Marriage Love* 419; *True Christianity* 281:1; compare *Secrets of Heaven* 227; *Marriage Love* 326:1; *True Christianity* 157:1, which suggest that his experience of both worlds may have been intermittent at times). The "many years" were roughly twenty by this point. In a work published in the previous year, he gave the length of time as "nineteen years" (*Divine Love and Wisdom* 355). The exact length of time is difficult to determine for various reasons, one of which is that, although he had visions of Christ in 1744 and 1745, Swedenborg's spiritual awakening seems generally to have been a gradual process occurring between 1743 and 1745 rather than a momentary initiation. The most detailed account of his revelatory commission is found in Acton 1927; for a briefer overview, see Rose 1988. [GFD, JSR]

132. This statement seems to contradict Swedenborg's reports elsewhere of conversations with angels, in a number of which the angels do explain theological matters (see, for example, *True Christianity* 25–26, 385, 624, 661–662) and tell how they understand the Word (see, for example, *Secrets of Heaven* 8011). The contradiction is not easy to resolve, but the following sentence here suggests that Swedenborg means he was able to detect and experience the direct influence of the Lord in whatever medium it was using. [GFD]

133. This point is developed at some length in *Divine Love and Wisdom* 410. [GFD]

134. Swedenborg uses the phrase "by faith alone" to refer to the Protestant conception of salvation in his day, which Swedenborg rejects for two reasons. First, as an inner transformation, faith is merely a change in our faculty of discernment, whereas what is more fundamental is a transformation of our character and our core values, which are a matter of the faculty of volition. Second, no inner transformation is complete until it gives rise to concrete works of charity. To this extent, Swedenborg agrees with the Catholic doctrine of the necessity of works (see also note 29), but he criticizes Catholicism insofar as it makes these works merely external and mechanical and therefore divorced from inner spiritual transformation. Swedenborg wishes to fuse inner spiritual transformation—the transformation of character, not just belief—with concrete works of charity. [GRJ]

135. The Latin word here translated "rulers" is *plutones,* the plural of *Pluto,* a byname for the god who ruled over hell in Greek mythology. [GFD]

136. The Latin phrase here translated "imagined or illusory guilt" is *conscientiae spuriae & falsae,* literally, "consciences illegitimate and false." *Conscientia* here seems clearly to intend the negative function of conscience, namely the inner conviction of guilt. [GFD]

137. See, for example, *Heaven and Hell* 528. [GFD]

138. The suggestion here that some people are reformed in the spiritual world after death seemingly contradicts the statement in §17 above that we cannot be reformed or regenerated after death. The contradiction is more verbal than substantive, however, since it is clear that the "reformation" intended here is the process of bringing our outer natures into accord with our inner intentions, which involves no fundamental change in those inner natures. [GFD]

139. Swedenborg probably here has in mind the picture of the New Jerusalem as the bride in Revelation 21:2 and 9, and may also be thinking of the use of the image of adultery in the Book of Hosea. These basic themes are found a number of times in the theological works; see *Heaven and Hell* 384 and Swedenborg's footnote h there, which gives numerous cross-references to the topic of adultery as it appears in *Secrets of Heaven.* [GFD]

140. See part 3 of *Divine Love and Wisdom,* especially §§236–255. [GFD]

141. The work mentioned here was published by Swedenborg from 1749 to 1756. [JSR]

142. See, for example, *Secrets of Heaven* 3147 and 10243. [GFD]

Notes to §§154–174

143. Swedenborg here describes a notable trend in some eighteenth-century philosophic thought, in which nature was no longer seen as a means employed by God to work his will but as an object of quasi-religious reverence in itself, displacing God entirely. For a discussion of this trend, see Willey 1961, 155–167. Such atheism was to be found primarily among the French *philosophes;* the chief atheists among them included Julien Offray de La Mettrie; Denis Diderot (1713–1784); Claude-Adrien Helvétius (1715–1771); Paul-Henri Dietrich, Baron d'Holbach (1723–1789; see note 168 below); and Nicolas-Antoine Boulanger (1722–1759). Slightly younger followers of the atheist movement were editor Jacques-André Naigeon (1738–1810), poet Pierre-Sylvain

Maréchal (1750–1803), astronomer Joseph-Jérôme Le François de Lalande (1732–1807), and his student, the astronomer, mythologist, and ex-priest Charles François Dupuis (1742–1809). [SS]

144. Essence, substance, and form are technical terms stemming from ancient Greek philosophy. They were adopted by medieval Scholastic philosophers and were widely used in various senses by Enlightenment philosophers as well. Often equated with one another, even by the Scholastics, in most uses their definitions overlap. Furthermore, each of these terms could be further specified; for example, the Scholastics distinguished at least ten different types of essence. Therefore the precise sense in which Swedenborg is using these terms may not be documentable. Rather than relying on the reader to understand arcane Scholastic distinctions, however, he generally uses terms in their immediate and commonsense meanings. His definition of essence probably agrees with the chief definition of the term in Scholastic philosophy, where it appears as "the inherent principle by which a thing is what it is." Aquinas (see note 9) gives as an example the humanity of human beings; he follows other medieval philosophers in equating essence with another technical term, *quiddity,* the "whatness" of a thing (*On Being and Essence* 1). Substance, in Swedenborg's use, seems equivalent to what we would call a material. By "form" Swedenborg is likely dispensing once again with Scholastic subtleties and referring approximately to the shape of a physical thing, as determined by the essence that informs the substance of which the thing is made. Thus just below (§157:4) he notes that "substance is nothing apart from form," that is, a material thing must have a physical shape. Finally, it is important to bear in mind that Swedenborg speaks of substance and form as belonging not only to the material world, but to the spiritual world as well, where their analogues have similar effects (for an example, see note 271 below; see also *Divine Love and Wisdom* 91, 257). For Swedenborg's discussion of these terms, see his unpublished work *Ontology* (Swedenborg 1901). For further information, see Brown 1919, 398–413. [SS]

145. This is the basic theme of part 2 of *Divine Love and Wisdom.* See especially §§89–92 and 151–156 there. [GFD]

146. See especially *Divine Love and Wisdom* 4, 55–60. [GFD]

147. See especially *The Lord* 29–54. [GFD]

148. See §§33:4, 49, 51 above; also see *Divine Love and Wisdom* 69–72. [GFD]

149. See *Divine Love and Wisdom* 319–326 and especially *Heaven and Hell* 59–77. The topic is suggested in §124 above, but it receives no explicit treatment until §§201–204 below. [GFD]

150. See *Divine Love and Wisdom* 113–118, §28 of the present work, and *Heaven and Hell* 7–12. [GFD]

151. See §§29, 31 above and *Heaven and Hell* 101; also see the references in note 150 just above. [JSR]

152. Swedenborg here refers to the complex and circuitous route by which fat is digested. Unlike digested sugars and proteins, which are absorbed by the blood vessels of the small intestine and delivered directly to the liver, fat is absorbed by lymphatic capillaries (lacteals) in the lining and turned into a milky substance called "chyle." The chyle then moves sluggishly through a dense network of mesenteric lymph vessels, not by action of the heart, but passively, by external muscular activity and a series of one-way valves. It is collected first "into its reservoir," the cisterna chyli, and transported

upwards from there via the large thoracic duct, which empties its contents into the left brachiocephalic vein, just above the heart. In this way, fat initially bypasses the liver and instead first enters the bloodstream to be presented to the liver in a diluted state for processing. See also §296:14 below. For more on how spirits go through a chylelike process as they are absorbed into heaven, see *Secrets of Heaven* 5173–5174. For Swedenborg's presentation and discussion of contemporary views on the mesentery and lacteals, see his 1744–1745 work *The Soul's Domain* (= Swedenborg [1744–1745] 1960) §§141–157; on the thoracic duct and lymph vessels, see §§158–170. [RPB, GMC]

153. See §157:7 above. This is also the starting point and in a sense the main theme of *Divine Love and Wisdom*. [GFD]

154. Swedenborg uses this combination to denote the level of mind that is focused on matter. [GFD]

155. The "world of spirits" (Latin *mundus spirituum*) is a technical term in Swedenborg's usage throughout his works (see especially *Heaven and Hell* 421–431). It refers to the region "halfway between heaven and hell" in which people spend their "halfway state after death" before going to either heaven or hell (*Heaven and Hell* 422). The world of spirits is not to be confused with the spiritual world *(mundus spiritualis),* although the former is part of the latter. When he refers to the spiritual world Swedenborg means heaven, the world of spirits, and hell (*Divine Love and Wisdom* 140). [JSR]

156. See §§86 and 109 above for statements concerning the rational ability belonging to evil people. [GFD]

157. See *Sacred Scripture* 100 and 53–56. [GFD]

158. The frequent association of "the Word" with "sermons" (see §§17, 131, 233:7) may reflect a belief that in an age when literacy was far from universal, religious life was not solely for the literate. [GFD]

159. See §§166–168 above, and *Divine Love and Wisdom* 83–172. [JSR]

Notes to §§175–190

160. Swedenborg is here taking notice of a lively debate about the nature of causation that ensued primarily during the early and middle Enlightenment period (about 1640 to 1750). The increasing strength of materialism during this period led thinkers to see a distinct disconnection between things spiritual and things material. By the end of this debate, many philosophers believed that whatever God's causative powers might be, they were distinct from causation as it took place in matter; in other words, the spiritual simply did not affect the material (see Clatterbaugh 1999, 208). Hume, for example, refused to grant God any role in causation on the grounds that we are "ignorant of the manner or force by which a mind, even the supreme mind, operates either on itself or on body [matter]" (Hume [1748] 1952, 57). He further claimed that "any thing may produce any thing. Creation, annihilation, motion, reason, volition; all these things may arise from one another, or from any other object we can imagine" (Hume [1739–1740] 1902, 173, as quoted in Clatterbaugh 1999, 199). For more on theories of causation during this period, see Clatterbaugh 1999. The prerequisite for any discussion of the notion of causation in Swedenborg is Woofenden 1970 (= Woofenden 1990–1991). [SS]

161. This is the general subject of §§71–99; §96 focuses particularly on the issues raised here. [GFD]

162. See, for example, §116. [GFD]

163. The passage cited here, Luke 12:14–48, includes a story of a wealthy farmer who is anxious to hoard all the crops harvested in a bumper year, not realizing he is about to die; an admonishment not to worry about food and clothing and to consider how even the ravens and lilies are taken care of; and a reminder to be like servants awaiting their master's return at an unknown hour. [GFD]

164. The parallelism between the list of things we do and the preceding list of "inner workings" is informative. The first list brings in a female perspective when it mentions "our wombs," while the second list brings in a male perspective when it mentions "impregnating our wives." This juxtaposition of seemingly mutually exclusive contexts reinforces the notion that Swedenborg had both sexes in mind when he used the Latin term *homo*, meaning "a human" or "humankind," which is the term here translated "we." [GFD, JSR]

165. There is no §188 in the first edition. [GFD]

166. This is central to the argument of the next major section. It will be introduced as the fourth proposition in §192 and treated at greater length in §§201–203. [GFD]

167. See §§62, 64, 65 above. There are many references to the universal human form of heaven (Latin *maximus homo*) in *Secrets of Heaven*. See §1274 there for a general article on the subject; and see *Heaven and Hell* 59–67 for a somewhat more extended description. This is, however, apparently the first mention in a published work that hell looks like a single grotesque person. (For an earlier mention that was written but not published by Swedenborg, see *Revelation Explained* [= Swedenborg 1997a] §1224:4.) The concept is repeated later in *True Christianity* 68. [GFD]

168. The success of scientists such as Isaac Newton in discovering "constant and reliable laws" at first led Enlightenment philosophers to an enthusiastic reaffirmation of the power of God. (For a representative overview of this trend in England, see Porter 2000, 130–138.) Some thinkers, however, being inclined toward materialism for other reasons, made use of the notion of immutable scientific law to dispense with divine providence altogether. This school reached its fullest form shortly before and after the time of publication of *Divine Providence*, in the writing of the German-born French philosopher Paul-Henri Dietrich, Baron d'Holbach (1723–1789). In *Système de la nature, ou des lois du monde physique et du monde moral* (The System of Nature, or On the Laws of the Physical World and the Moral World; see d'Holbach 1770; = d'Holbach [1770] 1999), d'Holbach declared: "Instead . . . of seeking outside the world . . . for beings who can procure him a happiness denied him by Nature, let man study this Nature, let him learn her laws. . . ." (part 1, chapter 1, quoted in Durant and Durant 1965, 703). See also the chapter aptly titled "Newton's Physics without Newton's God" in Gay 1969, 140–150. [SS]

Notes to §§191–213

169. See §§13 and 106 of the present work and *Divine Love and Wisdom* 1–3, 363–368. [GFD]

170. The general topics listed here are implicit throughout the treatment of freedom and rationality in §§71–99 of the present work and explicit in §74. It is introduced in *Divine Love and Wisdom* 1–6 and is a major theme throughout the work. [GFD]

171. This image is developed in detail in *Divine Love and Wisdom* 394–431. [GFD]

172. The Latin word here translated "impulses" is *affectiones,* traditionally translated "affections," elsewhere also rendered "desires." The word is a noun derived from the verb *afficere,* which means "to act upon," "to produce an emotional effect upon," "to move." "Impulses" is here chosen to convey this sense of motivation. *Divine Love and Wisdom* 410–412 discusses the relationship of our impulses or desires to our life's love. [GFD]

173. It may be worth remembering that such situations, which are now the stuff of fiction, were quite real in Swedenborg's world. On his first voyage to England, for example, the ship on which he was sailing was not only boarded temporarily by privateers, but also later mistakenly assumed to be privateering itself by the British navy, which fired on it (Sigstedt 1952, 19). [GFD]

174. The allusion is to John 3:27. [GFD]

175. Our acting freely and rationally is the subject of §§71–99. The particular image of standing idly and waiting for inflow recurs, with further elaborations, in §§210:1 and 321:1 below. Previous to *Divine Providence,* Swedenborg had used the image in various forms in *Secrets of Heaven* 1712, 5660:2, 8176, and 10299:4; and *Life* 107. Later he used it again in *True Christianity* 356. [GFD]

176. Here Swedenborg alludes to the distinction between general providence (God's framing of the basic laws of the universe) and particular providence (God's concern with every detail of the universe) as formulated by the French philosopher Nicolas de Malebranche (1638–1715). In what follows, Swedenborg emphatically rejects Malebranche's denial of particular providence and affirms that God's providential concern extends to every sparrow. For more on this topic, see the introduction. [GRJ]

177. "The laws of permission" here refer to the divine laws that govern how and when evil is allowed or permitted to occur, called "permission" rather than "providence" because God does not will or cause evil. [JSR]

178. See *Divine Love and Wisdom* 11 and §124:2 of the present work. [GFD]

179. The point is made explicitly in §96 of the present work, and is implicit in *Divine Love and Wisdom* 425. [GFD]

180. See especially *Divine Love and Wisdom* 4. [GFD]

Notes to §§214–220

181. The Golden Age was a common topic in ancient Greek and Roman literature (see, for example, Hesiod *Works and Days* 109–126; Vergil *Eclogues* 4; Ovid *Metamorphoses* 1:89–112). According to classical authors, during this age the gods kept company with humankind, food was readily available, people dwelt happily in small, anarchic communities, and technology was nonexistent. Swedenborg discusses the Golden Age in several of his works, including *Worship and Love of God* 1–2; *Secrets of Heaven* 1551:1, 5658:2, 10160:2; *Heaven and Hell* 115; and *Marriage Love* 75. For background and for discussion of the echoes of classical authors in the language Swedenborg uses in these descriptions, see Frazier 1998. For treatment of the Golden Age and other primitivistic themes in ancient times, see Lovejoy and Boas 1935; in medieval times, Boas 1948. [SS]

182. See John 12:31; 14:30; and 16:11. [GFD]

183. The shift from plural ("the loves") to singular ("which is") is surprising. [GFD]

184. The two types of causes mentioned here were part of a vast system of categories of causation developed by Scholastic philosophers, building on the basic causes, four in

number, described by Aristotle. In the Scholastic system *principal cause* is a cause that works through the power of its own form so that the result is in some way like itself (the humanness of a painter painting a portrait might be an example). The *instrumental cause* is an instrument or tool that serves another cause (the hand with which the painter works, for example). The novel point that Swedenborg is making is that good people actually use wealth and fame as instruments to help them do good in the world. This view stands in strong contrast to the ascetic classical and Christian traditions, which saw wealth and fame (at least in theory) as evils to be avoided. [SS]

185. The assertion that judges, officials, and kings exist to serve others is in agreement with major concepts in Enlightenment thought such as freedom, equality, natural law, and the social contract. (On these trends see, for example, Hazard 1963, 172–188; Gay 1969, 326–343.) Increasingly during this era, political thinkers saw the state as existing to serve the people, an idea that stood on its head the time-honored notion of society as an inevitable hierarchy in which social inferiors rightfully served their superiors. Eventually this revolution in thought led to literal revolutions in the American colonies of Britain and in France. However, unlike the Enlightenment political philosophers whose thinking underlay these revolutions—for example, Locke, Montesquieu (1689–1755), and Jean-Jacques Rousseau (1712–1778)—Swedenborg bases his very modern view of the purpose of civil administration and executive power exclusively on moral and religious considerations. He does not dispense with social hierarchy itself—it even exists in heaven (*Heaven and Hell* 213, 215, 217–219); but he sees its elements, whether upper or lower, as existing to serve the whole. [SS]

186. In fact all evil spirits in the hells appear upside down to angels (*Secrets of Heaven* 9128:3; *Revelation Explained* [= Swedenborg 1997a] §1143:4; compare *Revelation Unveiled* 655:6). For a somewhat comical description of how this appears, see *Marriage Love* 79:3; for a rather gruesome description, see *Worship and Love of God* 75. [JSR]

187. See especially *Divine Love and Wisdom* 5. [GFD]

188. The Latin phrase here translated "whether they are true or not" is *num ita sit*, literally, "whether so it is." There are some seventy instances of this phrase in the published theological works; in the vast majority of these cases, it is clear that Swedenborg holds a negative view of the people asking the question. Apparently Swedenborg identifies this phrase with the academic stance of rigorous skepticism, as is perhaps clearest in *Secrets of Heaven* 2718, 4214; *Heaven and Hell* 183; and *True Christianity* 333. One alternative to asking "whether something is so" would be to simply accept it out of naive credulity. The present passage, however, effectively rules that alternative out. Though people described here do not ask the question, they do not need to do so: "They see within themselves, from the Lord," whether something is true or not. According to *Secrets of Heaven* 4214, it is also possible to see whether something is true "from what is good" *(ex bono)*. [GFD]

189. While the subject of service has been touched on a number of times, this particular point has not yet been made explicitly; though it is certainly implicit in §215. It is treated at some length in *Heaven and Hell* 485–490. [GFD]

190. The shift to the past tense here is probably due to the implicit circumstance that after death these individuals no longer have any wealth and resources to focus on. [GFD]

191. On this passage in Luke, see note 163 above. [GFD]

Notes to §§221–233

192. Jesuits are members of the Catholic Society of Jesus, founded in 1540 by Ignatius Loyola (1491–1556). In Swedenborg's time the Jesuits suffered a reputation for duplicity and deceit, particularly in Protestant lands. [GRJ]

193. See note 27 above. [GFD]

194. The allusion is to Revelation 20:12, where the dead are judged by having their "books" opened and compared with "the book of life." See also Revelation 3:5; 13:8; 20:15; 21:27; 22:19; and Psalms 69:28. [GFD, JSR]

195. The necessary negative is missing from the Latin of the first edition. [GFD]

196. Following a long-standing Christian tradition, Swedenborg referred to the Hebrew Scriptures as "the Old Testament." [JSR]

197. The Pharisees are the precursors of Rabbinical Judaism. They emerge as an identifiable sect in the third century B.C.E. Swedenborg uses them as an example because Jesus condemned them as intellectually dishonest hairsplitters who observed the law in letter but not in spirit. [GRJ]

198. In the traditional lore of Christianity, Lucifer came to be thought of as an angel who rebelled against the Lord and was cast out of heaven, marking the beginning of evil in what had been a perfect world. Swedenborg rejects this notion out of hand. See note 45 above. [GFD]

199. The plural "their" presumably refers to "the people meant by Lucifer." [GFD]

200. Socinians were followers of Faustus Socinus (1539–1604) and his uncle Laelius Socinus (1525–1562), who denied the divinity of Christ. Arians were followers of Arius, a fourth-century priest who denied that Christ was of the same substance and essence as God. [JSR]

201. The Latin word here translated "turning" is *conversio*. Most often, Swedenborg uses it to refer to a turning of our attention toward the Lord rather than to the more fundamental change of direction meant by "conversion" in contemporary religious parlance. The present passage may or may not be an exception to this. [GFD]

202. Matthew 13:13 reads, "The reason I speak to them in parables is so that they will not perceive when they see or listen or understand when they hear." The verses immediately following this one cite Isaiah 6:9–10 to the same effect. [GFD]

203. See especially §§102–113. [GFD]

Notes to §§234–274

204. On the "laws of permission" see note 177 above. [JSR]

205. The criticisms cited as examples here are typical of those leveled at the Bible by Deists, theists, and atheists during the Enlightenment. (Both Deism and theism during this period can be defined roughly as a belief in God based on inborn knowledge, reason, and experience, without acceptance of revelation or traditional religion.) One of the foremost of such critics was the French philosopher Pierre Bayle (1647–1706), particularly in his *Dictionnaire historique et critique* (Historical and Critical Dictionary, 1697, with a second, definitive edition dated 1702). As a Fideist ("faith-ist"), Bayle believed that humankind must have blind faith in God, and he did not hesitate to point out inconsistencies in all matters besides blind faith on which believers might base their religion; this included both dogma and literal interpretation of the Bible. In England

his criticism was seconded by the Deists Matthew Tindal (1657–1733), Thomas Woolston (1669–1733), and John Toland (1670–1722). Though the uproar started by the Deists in England had quieted by around 1740, their works, along with those of Bayle, continued to serve atheists and theists throughout Europe as a gold mine of biblical inconsistencies. Under editor Denis Diderot (1713–1784), the French writers of the *Encyclopédie* (Encyclopedia, 1751–1772), in company with the *philosophe* Voltaire, obliquely ridiculed the Bible by making just such objections as Swedenborg lists here. This critical movement continued in Germany, and oddly enough, eventually led to a form of biblical criticism less intrinsically hostile to religion. For a summary of this entire movement, see Hazard 1963, 59–73. [SS]

206. The Latin here translated "the wisest people" is *sapientissimus,* literally, "the wisest one," singular; but the following plural verb requires a plural subject, and the plural, *sapientissimi,* is used in the restatement of this proposition in §241 below. [GFD]

207. On Solomon, see 1 Kings 11:1–8. In the narrative of events after the early Jewish nation was divided into two kingdoms, all the kings of Israel (the northern kingdom) are accused of continuing Jeroboam's sin—the establishment of temples in Bethel and Dan—though this is not explicitly associated with the worship of other gods. Some kings, however, are accused of open idolatry: see 1 Kings 16:25–26; 22:53; 2 Kings 3:2–3; 21:2–7, 21; 23:32, 37; 24:3, 19. [GFD]

208. For explicit references to crucifixion, see Matthew 27:35; Mark 15:24; Luke 23:33; and John 19:18. [GFD]

209. The Latin phrase here translated "getting positions of power in government and the church" is *fieri magnates et primates,* literally, "becoming magnates and primates." Both terms indicate high rank; the first is more commonly associated with the state and the second with the church. [GFD]

210. It may be noted that in eighteenth-century Europe, as in earlier times, looting by victorious soldiers was routine, and was considered virtually part of the compensation for military service. [GFD]

211. Swedenborg here as elsewhere uses one of the usual Latin designations for Islam, *Religiosum Mahumadanum,* literally, "the Muhammadan religion." Current thinking about words such as *Muhammadan* and *Muhammadanism* is that they may give the false impression that Muhammad is an object of worship. Wherever possible, this misleading designation has been replaced by the more accurate term "Islam," in accordance with the principle that the term customary in Swedenborg's time should be translated with the term customary at the present. For an exception, see §255:3 and note 232 below. [GFD]

212. Quakerism, founded in England by George Fox (1624–1691) in the mid-seventeenth century, was a radically egalitarian revival movement that laid special stress on openness to the immediate presence of the Holy Spirit. The Moravian church had its roots in a reform movement in Bohemia in the fourteenth century, an attempt to return to the simplicity of the apostles. After a protracted eclipse, it was revived in the early eighteenth century under the leadership of Count Nikolaus von Zinzendorf (1700–1760). It had strong Pietist tendencies—that is, it emphasized a relationship with God on the personal, as opposed to institutional, level. The Anabaptist movement began in Switzerland in the sixteenth century as a radical revivalism and took various forms in different regions of the Continent. [GFD]

213. The allusion is to Genesis 3:15. [GFD]

214. The Latin phrase here translated "what is being said in the literal narrative" is *quae historice ibi in littera memorata sunt,* literally, "the things that are there recorded historically in the letter." Swedenborg is clearly using *historice,* "historically," in the broad sense of "in past-tense narrative," without commitment to its historical accuracy. [GFD]

215. These allusions summarize the narrative from Genesis 2:15 through 3:24. [GFD]

216. See especially *Faith* 44–48. [GFD]

217. The first edition's phrasing here is nonsensical: *est secundum leges . . . imprimis contra binas* literally means "is according to laws . . . especially against the two." Clearly the text should read *est secundum leges . . . imprimis secundum binas,* literally, "is according to laws . . . especially the two," a correction originally suggested by editor Samuel H. Worcester in Swedenborg [1764] 1889a. [GFD]

218. The first edition reads "§§154–174" here, suggesting that the printer inadvertently skipped over part of the text he was meant to print, from the citation "§§129–153" now supplied, through the law discussed in §§154–174, namely, "It is a law of divine providence that we should be led and taught by the Lord, from heaven, by means of the Word, and teaching and preaching from the Word, and that this should happen while to all appearances we are acting independently." [GFD]

219. On the phrase "getting positions of power in government and the church," see note 209 above. [GFD]

220. The Latin phrase here translated "organized realm of constructive activities" is *regnum usuum,* traditionally translated "a kingdom of uses." The phrase suggests a realm characterized or even constituted by constructive activities that are so arranged as to be supportive of each other. [GFD]

221. This may be an allusion to Diogenes the Cynic (about 412–about 321 B.C.E.), the Greek philosopher. He is reported to have gone about in broad daylight with a lantern "looking for a [true] human being" (Diogenes Laertius *Lives of Eminent Philosophers* 6:41). [GFD]

222. These references to people as being "loves for themselves and the world" or "loves for God" are an unusual and striking reflection of the principle that the love is the essential person. See especially §§13 and 199. [GFD]

223. In the eighteenth century, continental Europe was divided into a vast number of territories, the "descendants" of the fiefs of feudalism; they ranged in size from major kingdoms to substantial estates to villages. Many of them had their own armies. Although Swedenborg's statement was and remains universally applicable, it is worth remembering that at the time he was writing, Europe was just subsiding into peace after the convulsion of the Seven Years' War (1756–1763), which pitted France, Austria, Saxony, Sweden, and Russia against Prussia and Hanover. (Britain also fought France, though primarily overseas in the Americas and India.) [GFD, SS]

224. Swedenborg seems here to be using "heaven" in a broader sense than usual to mean the spiritual world in general, since heaven itself is characterized by peace (see *Heaven and Hell* 284–290). The statement here that "all wars . . . portray states of the church in heaven and are corresponding images" does not mean that actual wars occur in heaven but that conflicts on earth reflect spiritual conditions in the church in the spiritual world. [GFD]

225. Swedenborg may well have had Sweden's King Carl (Charles) XII in mind with this postscript, having seen the disastrous results of Charles's ambitions early in his own career. See also note 102 above. [GFD]

226. The text in square brackets here was written by Swedenborg. [JSR]

227. The first edition here cites this title erroneously as *Teachings of the New Jerusalem Drawn from the Ten Commandments*. The version of the title given here instead is from the title page of the work itself. [GFD]

228. It should be noted that quite often Swedenborg describes non-Christians as being more deeply religious than Christians. Particularly striking is the story in *Marriage Love* 103–114 in which an African delegation receives a prize for the deepest understanding of the origin of marriage love after various delegations from Christian European countries have offered their opinions. [GFD]

229. Misinformation regarding Islam was rampant in Europe from the time of its founder, Muhammad (about 570–632); Swedenborg here seems to have fallen victim to it. The Qur'an explicitly denies that Jesus was the Son of God in many passages, especially Surah 5:75 and following, which not only calls those who believe such things infidels, but offers several arguments against the idea that God could have a son at all. Though Islam does accept the miracle of the virgin birth as a special sign from God to humankind (Surah 19), the result of that birth is acknowledged only to be a child without a human father, not necessarily an offspring of God. Furthermore, any connection of Jesus with God in the role of his Son is strictly ruled out by the fact that one of the greatest crimes in Islam is to equate anything or anyone with God, since God is the greatest of all; this is the crime of شرك *(shirk),* "association." Islam does teach that Jesus was one of many prophets who were precursors to Muhammad, and it could be said that it even teaches that Jesus was the greatest of these *pre-Islamic* prophets; but Muhammad has a distinct status as the Messenger or apostle of the one God, Allah, and no Muslim could regard Jesus as "greater than Muhammad." Some do believe that Jesus will come again at the end of time as a special sign from God; but this assertion is found only in other works of Islamic literature, not in the Qur'an. [GMC]

230. Swedenborg normally uses the Latin proper noun *Asia* (here in an adjectival form as *Asiaticum*) to mean what we now commonly refer to as "the Middle East": see, for example, *Secrets of Heaven* 10177:10; *Heaven and Hell* 327; *Sacred Scripture* 21; *True Christianity* 202; and §328:2 of the present work. Here, however, the reference to "surrounding islands" suggests that it refers more broadly to the Asian continent including India and the islands of the East Indies (see also *Sacred Scripture* 105:3). [GFD]

231. The Latin word here translated "developed" is *auspicor,* which by virtue of its relationship to *auspicium,* "omen," suggests a beginning under good omens or divine favor. There are only three other instances of this verb in Swedenborg's theological works. Two are the repetitions of this paragraph in *Marriage Love* 342:4 and *True Christianity* 833:4; the third is in *Secrets of Heaven* 2516:2. The point being made in this latter instance is that no doctrinal system of faith can be "launched" or founded on reasoning based solely on sensory information; here again the connotation of divine favor is clearly appropriate. [GFD]

232. On the expression "Muhammadanism," see note 211 above. Very slightly revised versions of this account of the origin of Islam may be found in *Marriage Love* 342 and *True Christianity* 833; on its accuracy, see note 229 above. [GFD]

233. It is noteworthy that the people meant by "they" here are not explicitly identified in this section, although it becomes clear from the fuller description that follows, especially from the mentions of a papal bull, the Council of Trent, and Mass, that

Swedenborg is alluding to Roman Catholics. Later in this passage Swedenborg specifies that he means its leadership rather than its laity, and points out that there are many heavenly communities of Catholics in the spiritual world. [GFD]

234. A grammatically necessary negative has been omitted here in the Latin. [GFD]

235. The equation of the Catholic Church with the Babylon of the Book of Revelation 14:8; 16:19; 17:5; 18:2, 10, 21 (and other passages) was taken largely for granted in eighteenth-century Lutheran thought. [GFD]

236. The Latin *Lucifer* means "the light-bearer" and was the classical name for the planet Venus as the morning star. [GFD]

237. The Council of Trent, which was called for the purpose of church reform in response to the Protestant Reformation, was held from 1545 to 1563. Among the many measures passed was one in 1562 authorizing masses to be said in honor of the saints. The relative authority of the council and the pope was very much at issue, so complete assurance of the validity of the council's conclusions was not attained until Pius IV (1499–1565) confirmed them in the "Profession of the Tridentine Faith" in 1564. [GFD]

238. Swedenborg is probably alluding to the conflict between King Philip IV of France (1268–1314) and Pope Boniface VIII (1235–1303) about whether the Catholic Church and its officers were subject to civil law and whether its properties and incomes were subject to taxation. The king established his rights by imprisoning the pope. From 1305–1378, the papal court resided in Avignon, in the south of France, under the control of the French monarchy. [GRJ]

239. Here Swedenborg is discussing the Protestant doctrine of justification by faith alone, not by "works." See notes 29 and 134 above. [GRJ]

240. On "the yoke of the law," see note 54 above. [GFD]

241. Swedenborg gives the full text of the Athanasian creed in *The Lord* 56. It is striking that while the creed begins by saying that preserving the faith is absolutely necessary to salvation and then presents a complex doctrine of the Trinity at considerable length, it concludes with this simple statement. [GFD]

242. See notes 29 and 134 above. [JSR]

243. There are five laws of divine providence that are clearly labeled as such in their headings; they are discussed in §§71–99, 100–128, 129–153, 154–174, and 175–190. Three other headings that are discussed in §§191–213, 214–220, and 221–233 are not initially labeled as laws of divine providence but are later referred to as such (§249:2). The last of these, §§221–233, is also referred to as a law of divine providence in §§221, 232, and 260:2. In addition to these eight laws, some other statements are briefly referred to as laws of divine providence, such as our not knowing the future (§179), our apparently leading ourselves (§202:3), our needing to see that we are in hell, to desire to leave, and to try to leave (§278b:6), our being allowed our evils so that we can be led out of them (§286:1), and our thinking and acting seemingly on our own and yet needing to acknowledge that these abilities come from God (§321:1). [JSR]

244. The word "he" here refers to God. [JSR]

245. Swedenborg is referring to the role of Jews as the preservers of the Hebrew Scriptures and teachers of the Hebrew language. [GRJ]

246. See especially §45 of that work. [GFD]

247. This is a reference to the Catholic Church; see note 235 above. [GRJ]

248. In the first edition, the material indented below is marked off by quotation marks at the beginning of each line of text. This is characteristic of the typography of the period. Significant variations from the original passage are pointed out in the following notes. Minor variations in punctuation and capitalization are not noted. [GFD]

249. This is presumably a further reference to Matthew 28:18, where Jesus states that all power in heaven and earth has been given to him. [GFD]

250. See John 3:36. Swedenborg apparently added this item when he copied the material from *The Lord*. [GFD]

251. This is presumably a reference to the Ascension (see Mark 16:19; Luke 24:51), although the passages describing it contain no explicit references to Jesus' divinity or humanity. [GFD]

252. Mark 16:19. Again, the verse contains no explicit mention of Jesus' divinity or humanity. [GFD]

253. This mention of the church as the Lamb's bride is not in the text of *The Lord*. [GFD]

254. Babylon refers to the Catholic Church, Philistia to the Protestant (see note 235 above). [GRJ]

255. "They" here refers to leaders of the Catholic Church. [GFD]

256. The reference is to Matthew 16:18: "You are Peter, and on this rock I will found my church." (The name *Peter* is derived from the Greek word πέτρος *(pétros)*, "rock.") [GFD]

257. The books referred to here are *Last Judgment* and *Supplements*. [JSR]

258. The work mentioned here was published by Swedenborg in 1758. It is referred to in this edition by the short title *White Horse*. [JSR]

259. On "the yoke of the law," see note 54 above. [GFD]

260. The section numbering here skips from 265 to 274. The continuity of the subject matter indicates that no text has been omitted. [GFD]

Notes to §§275–284

261. Unless he is referring to the vaguely relevant material in §277a, Swedenborg's promise to explain later why we are born on the lowest level of life goes apparently unfulfilled. [GFD]

262. In the first edition, this section and the following one are both numbered 277. [GFD]

263. The view that in conception the father contributes the spiritual or formal element of the offspring while the mother contributes only the material element dates back at least as far as Aristotle (*Generation of Animals* 1:20–22). See also Lacus Curtius Pliny (Pliny the Elder, 23/24–79 C.E.) *Natural History* 7:15. This view was widely accepted until the late Renaissance and continued to be a live option in debates about generation well into the eighteenth century. See also Pinto-Correia 1997. [GRJ]

264. By "the reverse" Swedenborg means that the baby of a white man and a black woman will be white. These erroneous statements need to be set in the context of an almost complete lack of genetic science at the time. For example, more than a hundred years would pass after this statement before Gregor Mendel (1822–1884) first published his findings that both male and female parents contribute genetic traits and that these are either dominant or recessive (Mendel [1865] 1946). Yet even given the contemporary

lack of genetic understanding, these examples are surprising for two reasons: they imply a belief that along with the soul, the physical characteristics of race are also inherited from the father and not the mother; and they suggest as well that although Swedenborg was a man of the world who had by this point made eight lengthy journeys abroad, he had apparently not had many opportunities to see children of interracial couples. [JSR]

265. By "first things" and "last things" that are affected by our reformation, Swedenborg means our inner desires and thoughts (first things) and our outer actions and words (last things). [JSR]

266. In the first edition, this section and the following one are both numbered 278. [GFD]

267. The bracketed material, clearly necessary to the sense of the passage, is missing from the Latin of the first edition. Presumably the printer's eye skipped down from one phrase on one line to a similar phrase on the next line of Swedenborg's fair copy. [GFD]

268. The Latin word here translated "organic" is *organicus,* the meaning of which includes the notions "living" as well as "structured," or "organized." [GFD]

269. Although the type of wheel meant by "a wheel that we turn by hand" is not specified here, context suggests that it would usually be driven by some force much stronger than the human hand. It may refer to a waterwheel in a mill (compare *True Christianity* 576) or a wheel of a carriage (compare *Secrets of Heaven* 8215). Since Swedenborg had been an engineer and inventor (see text and illustrations at Kirven and Larsen 1988, 17; and Brock 1988, 481), he may have had some more specific type of wheel, cog, or gear in mind here. In any case the implication is that not much progress will be made without explaining these ideas or propositions at greater length. [JSR]

270. See §§331–340. Calling attention to this conclusion this far in advance suggests that it embodies a main purpose of the book. [GFD]

271. Swedenborg's description of the connection between thought and materiality is unique. This can be seen by contrasting it with that of Descartes, who believed in two kinds of substance, an intelligent substance ("soul") and a substance that has dimension (or "extension") in physical space. He declared that the thinking part of a human being is "entirely and absolutely distinct" from the body (Descartes [1641] 1952, 98). By contrast, Swedenborg insists that thinking requires the organic forms that can be seen in the body, though "the workings of the organic substances of the mind are spiritual" (see §279:7 below). Even after death, thinking continues only because the human soul possesses a bodily form with the requisite organic components for thought to occur (*Secrets of Heaven* 444). For further discussion see *Heaven and Hell* 432–444. [SS]

272. Swedenborg here refers to the notorious "mind-body problem" that is still debated by philosophers: How can an apparently nonphysical entity, the soul or mind, interact with a physical entity, the body? Aristotle and the Scholastic philosophers argued that there is some *physical inflow* by which a material component of external objects flows into the body and then into the soul. However, after René Descartes, writing in the early 1600s, drew an absolutely exclusive distinction between mind or soul and things that have dimension or extension in three-dimensional space, this theory was felt to be untenable (see note 271 just above, and Leibniz [1710] 1959, 1 §59). In search of a solution to the dilemma to which Descartes had given new urgency, Cartesians such as Arnold Geulincx (1624–1669) suggested the theory of *occasionalism.* This hypothesis holds that it is God who both makes us think and brings about the physical actions that

we seem to perform as a result of thought. (The theory takes its name from the notion that God uses the "occasion" of the body to create the mind's attitudes.) Leibniz advanced another, similar theory, which holds that God does not act to make us think and move in each instance, but instead has established the harmony of all future mental and physical activity at the beginning of the world. Like occasionalism, this theory, called *preestablished harmony,* denies a cause-and-effect connection between thought and physical action. Still another theory, championed by Swedenborg, is that of *spiritual inflow.* It reverses the direction of Aristotelian and Scholastic physical inflow on the grounds that pure, refined, spiritual things must by nature flow into grosser, impure, physical things. Swedenborg's summary of the theory at this point in the text is much abbreviated; for more details, see the two works he wrote on the topic, a work written about 1734 that he did not publish, *Soul-Body Mechanism* (= Swedenborg 1992) and the privately distributed *Soul-Body Interaction* (1769). See also §314 below and note 304 there. [SS]

273. Hosea 7:4 reads, "They are all adulterers, like a heated oven. Once the dough has been kneaded, the baker does not stir the fire until the dough is leavened." Luke 12:1 reads, "He began to say to his disciples, 'Beware of the yeast of the Pharisees, which is their hypocrisy.'" [GFD]

Notes to §§285–307

274. See §§70–99 above, especially §96. [GFD]

275. See §§285 and 286 just above; also see §§212, 240. [JSR]

276. Philosopher and mathematician Gottfried Wilhelm Leibniz is a major figure of the Enlightenment; among his many accomplishments was the invention of the differential and integral calculus at the same time as, but independently of, Isaac Newton. He developed a philosophical theory of the workings of the universe whose most memorable feature, presumably the feature at issue here, was the positing of elementary metaphysical particles called "monads" (see notes 17 and 18 above). Each monad reflects the entire universe in microcosm but none actually communicates with any other; the appearance of communication between these independent units is simply a side effect of the unity of the universe that is reflected in each independent monad. Swedenborg, by contrast, maintains that communication between souls is not incidental appearance, but the direct result of a shared divine inflow. See also note 272 above. [GFD]

277. For a discussion of each of the three issues just mentioned here in the text, see §294 below. [JSR]

278. For a more detailed description, see Swedenborg's unpublished manuscript of 1745–1747, *The Old Testament Explained* (= Swedenborg 1927–1951) §943, which also occurs as *Spiritual Experiences* (= Swedenborg 1998) §5a. [GFD]

279. See note 131 above. [GFD]

280. See especially §210. [GFD]

281. The reference is to John 3:27, where John the Baptist is asked about the fact that Jesus is baptizing and replies, "No one can receive anything except what is given from heaven." [GFD]

282. It is not clear what difference Swedenborg intends between "subjects" and "objects" here. Elsewhere he sometimes uses "subjects" to refer to people and "objects" to things (see for example *True Christianity* 43:2). Here, however, both subjects and

objects are things, and later on in the section both subjects and objects are people. The underlying Latin words *(subjectum, objectum)* are philosophical and logical terms with a wide range of meanings, some of which overlap as "recipients of some action or influence." Here Swedenborg is generally portraying both subjects and objects as recipients of what flows in from God or the sun, yet he does seem to intend some differentiation in which subjects apparently relate to volition and are good or bad, whereas objects relate to discernment and are beautiful or ugly. [GFD]

283. The Latin word here translated "weeds," *zizanias,* has been translated "tares" in traditional English Bibles. The allusion is to the parable in Matthew 13:24–30. [GFD]

284. The Latin words here translated "owls" are *ulula, bubo,* two kinds of nocturnal bird, both of which we now know as owls but which were apparently considered in Swedenborg's time to be categorically different. The two terms appear as separate items in other general lists in §296:2 below and in *Divine Love and Wisdom* 338, 339; *Revelation Unveiled* 757:4; and *True Christianity* 78:5, 531. Lexicographers generally render them both as "owls," although *ulula* is sometimes specified as a "screech owl" while *bubo* is a "barn owl" or "tawny owl." [GFD, JSR]

285. When this statement was originally made in §289:2 it read "thinking evil" rather than "doing evil." [GFD]

286. The Latin words here translated "or some kind of poisonous snake, or some kind of owl" are *vel sicut basiliscus, vel sicut vipera, vel sicut bubo, vel sicut ulula,* literally, "or like a basilisk, or like a viper, or like an owl, or like an owl." On these two types of owl see note 284 just above. [GFD]

287. John 15:1–7 is the section of the Last Supper discourse that presents the image of the Lord as the vine, the Father as the vinedresser, and disciples as branches. [GFD]

288. See *Heaven and Hell* 438. [GFD]

289. The allusion is to Revelation 3:15–16, where the letter to the church in Laodicea begins, "I know your works, that you are neither cold nor hot. I wish that you were either cold or hot. However, since you are lukewarm and neither cold nor hot, I am about to spit you out of my mouth." [GFD]

290. The Latin phrases here translated "emotional sense of identity" and "cognitive sense of identity" are *proprium voluntarium* and *proprium intellectuale,* traditionally translated "a voluntary proprium" and "an intellectual proprium." These phrases may best be equated with what we describe colloquially as "how we feel about ourselves" and "what we think of ourselves." For more on the meaning of the Latin term *proprium* see note 73 above. [GFD]

291. John 1:12–13 reads, "But to all who accepted him, to all who believed in his name, he gave power to become children of God who were born not of blood or of the will of the flesh or of the will of man, but of God." [GFD]

292. Presumably people do not sense the pleasures that constitute their life because those pleasures are usually constant and pervasive. A change from them registers much more clearly. [GFD]

293. The first edition here reads *Quartum,* "fourth." [GFD]

Notes to §§308–321

294. See *Divine Love and Wisdom* 1–6. [GFD]
295. See *Divine Love and Wisdom* 360. [GFD]

296. See *Divine Love and Wisdom* 115–116. [GFD]

297. The Latin phrase here translated "overly invested in their own image" is *proprietarii in imagine sua,* literally, "proprietaries in their own image." *Proprietarii,* "proprietaries," were in general people who held ownership in a thing. In its specific application to monks who held property after taking a vow of poverty, the term acquired connotations of an ownership that was self-serving and in violation of rules; ultimately it came to be applied to any people guided by self-interest. Here the term also puns on the word *propriae,* "their own," in the preceding clause. The phrase *in imagine sua,* "in their own image," alludes to and plays against the statement that God created humankind "in his own image" (Genesis 1:27). In a darker sense an *imago,* or "image," refers to an empty reflection or an idol; see, for example, the statement below in the same section that such people are (figuratively) "makers of idols, sculptures, and statues." [JSR, SS]

298. The Latin phrase here translated "greater or lesser sums" is *talenta & minas,* literally, "talents and minas." A talent was a unit of weight and money used in ancient Greece, Rome, and the Middle East. At different times and places, it ranged from 57 to 88 pounds of gold, silver, or copper, roughly the equivalent of twenty years' wages for a laborer. A mina was a sixtieth of a talent, or roughly four months' wages. [JSR]

299. On idealists, see note 57 above. [GFD]

300. Isaiah 40:17, 23 reads: "All nations are like nothing before him, and they are reckoned by him to be less than nothing and empty. He causes the princes to be nothing; he makes the judges of the earth like something empty." [GFD]

301. Niccolò Machiavelli (1469–1527) was a Florentine statesman and writer. In works such as *Il principe* (The Prince, 1513), he proposed what he saw as realistic solutions for the dire political chaos of the Italy of the early *cinquecento.* "A prince," he says, "cannot observe all those things which are considered good in men, being often obliged, in order to maintain the state, to act against faith, against charity, against humanity, and against religion" (Machiavelli [1513] 1950, 65). The classic analysis of his work is that of the British historian Thomas Babington Macaulay (1800–1859), who concludes that "the peculiar immorality which has rendered *The Prince* unpopular . . . belonged rather to the age than to the man, that it was a partial taint, and by no means implied general depravity" (Macaulay [1827] 1914, 30). Whatever extenuation may be granted by an objective view of Machiavelli's works, in the centuries immediately after his death his name became synonymous with the cynical and amoral use of power. [SS]

302. On "emotional sense of identity" and "cognitive sense of identity," see note 290 above. [GFD]

303. For a more detailed verse-by-verse presentation of the interpretation summarized here, see *Secrets of Heaven* 6–63, 73–165, 190–313. [GFD]

304. Here Swedenborg is referring to the physical inflow doctrine associated with Aristotle, the Scholastics, and John Locke and contrasting it to his own spiritual inflow doctrine. See note 272 above. [GRJ]

305. Swedenborg is here drawing a composite portrait of various psychological and epistemological theories rather than depicting a single school. The Scholastic philosophers maintained that understanding was formed by a kind of image sent forth from the thing understood (a so-called *intelligible species;* see, for example, Aquinas *Summa Theologiae* 1:85:2). Similarly, the British philosopher Thomas Hobbes (1588–1679) maintained that "the thoughts of man . . . are everyone a *representation* or *appearance,* of some quality or other accident [attribute] of a body without [outside] us" (Hobbes

[1651] 1939, 131). Locke held that the mind is essentially a passive mirror that reflects what is before us (Locke [1690] 1952, 2:1:25); he also compared it to "white paper, void of all characters" until sensory experience writes on it (Locke [1690] 1952, 2:1:2; see Aristotle *On the Soul* 3:4; Aquinas *Summa Theologiae* 1:72:2). Hume emphasized habit or custom in the thought process: "All belief of matter of fact or real existence is derived merely from some object, present to the memory or senses, and a customary conjunction between that and some other object" (Hume [1748] 1952, 5:2:38). [SS]

306. Swedenborg seems to be referring generally to atheists who claimed that life was only a mechanical effect of nature. The foremost exemplar of this belief was Julien Offray de La Mettrie (1709–1751), in his book *L'Homme Machine* (Man as Machine; La Mettrie 1748 = La Mettrie [1748] 1994); for a brief sketch of his career, see Durant and Durant 1965, 617–622. On atheism in general during the Enlightenment, see note 143 above. [SS]

307. There is no §315 in the first edition. [GFD]

308. On "cognitive sense of identity" and "emotional sense of identity," see note 290 above. [GFD]

309. By "the two primary heresies in Christendom" that have been voluminously proved Swedenborg presumably means the Catholic belief that the pope is the vicar of Christ and possesses the power to open or close heaven to people and forgive their sins (see *Secrets of Heaven* 9410:2), and the Protestant belief that faith alone saves and that good actions are unnecessary and even detrimental to salvation (see *Revelation Unveiled* 537). [GFD]

310. The medieval *disputatio*, "disputation," a system of education by debate, was still utilized in universities in Swedenborg's time, and Swedenborg is known to have participated in it (Broberg 1988, 284). In these disputations, a student defending a point of view would first entertain objections to it; he would then attack the objections and thus vindicate the proposed thesis. Written Scholastic argumentation assumed the same pattern. Students were also required to argue for or against propositions at the whim of their professor; and in some cases, scholars themselves called for *quaestiones quodlibetales*, "questions on any topic you like" (Colish 1997, 272), which inevitably led to showcase defenses of absurd positions. Implicit in these educational methods was the notion that an able scholar should be able to prove anything true. For a detailed argument of this kind, "proving" that crows are white, see *True Christianity* 334:5; compare *Marriage Love* 233:4, and *Revelation Explained* (= Swedenborg 1997a) §824:2. [JSR, SS]

311. The Latin phrase here translated "whitewashers" is *incrustatores parietis*, literally, "coaters of a wall." It suggests that these are people who can cover up any evil and make it seem like good. The translation derives from the parallel seen in the English expression "whitewashing," meaning to cover up a crime. Also see Matthew 23:27. [JSR]

312. The Latin phrase here literally translated "deceptive light" is *lux fatuus*. It refers to a phenomenon now known by another Latin name, *ignis fatuus*, literally, "deceptive fire," a glow seen over swamps at night, sometimes attributed to the decay of organic material. It was apparently a significant or at least a proverbial hazard in early times, as travelers could easily be misled by it, and many Enlightenment writers used it as a metaphor for delusion. It is also referred to as a "will-o'-the-wisp." [JSR]

313. The Latin phrase here translated "life fluid" is *succus animalis*, literally, "fluid of the soul." It occurs only here in the theological works, though *succus* ("fluid" or "juice") appears several times without *animalis* ("of the soul"). Swedenborg's use of singular

verbs with the joined terms here translated "blood" and "life fluid" suggests the possibility that he regards the two as synonymous. However, it is also possible that he only groups them together on the grounds that these fluids are commonly mingled. That is, he may be using the phrase *succus animalis* in order to avoid the term *spiritus animalis,* usually translated "animal spirit(s)," but literally meaning a highly refined fluid associated with the soul, which he saw as mingling with the blood. The term *animal spirits* was widely employed by other philosophers (Odhner 1933, 218–223), and in one instance in Swedenborg's scientific works it is possible to detect an aversion to it on his part (*Dynamics of the Soul's Domain* [= Swedenborg [1740–1741] 1955] §1:37). He may have feared that his own unique use of the term would be misunderstood, and so have chosen "fluid" here rather than "spirits." For a discussion of the term *animal spirits,* including references to its occurrences in Swedenborg's scientific works, see Odhner 1933; for a translation of Swedenborg's unpublished work on the topic, see Swedenborg 1917. [GFD, SS]

314. For an earlier statement of this principle, see *Heaven and Hell* 302. [GFD]

315. On Quakers and Moravians see note 212 above; on Quakers and fanaticism (also called enthusiasm) see note 129 above. [JSR]

316. The Latin phrase here translated "the official faith" is *fidem Theologicam,* literally, "the theological faith." The following clause makes it clear that it refers to the theological principles to which the faithful are required to subscribe. [GFD]

Notes to §§322–330

317. The addition of the phrase "of the country we are living in" is significant. Europeans had an ongoing fascination with the wide variation in cultures they encountered during the centuries of exploration after 1492. (For sketches of the effects of this interest, see Porter 2000, 354–363, and Hazard 1963, 4–9.) This cultural variation suggested to some that cherished European beliefs and institutions rested only on arbitrary tradition, and so was often used by those arguing against Christianity. Here Swedenborg reasserts the uniformitarian principle that the necessity of honoring the image of God within oneself, doing good to others, and thus being a "civic" individual is independent of local tradition and applicable in all cultures. [SS]

318. See *Heaven and Hell* 311–317. [GFD]

319. See note 25 above. [JSR]

320. See *Divine Love and Wisdom* 28–33. [GFD]

321. On the meaning of "church" in this context, see note 13 above. [JSR]

322. The dual designation "Israelite and Jewish" refers to Judaism as recorded in the Hebrew scriptures. The two names are presumably based on the names of the two kingdoms of the Holy Land in ancient times (975–721 B.C.E.): Israel, or the northern kingdom; and Judah, or the southern kingdom. When Swedenborg refers to "the Israelite *or* Jewish church" at the end of the present section, it suggests that the two names are alternative designations for the same entity. [GFD]

323. The Latin phrase here translated "the nations of the Near East" is *Regna Asiae,* literally, "the kingdoms of Asia." Swedenborg's use of the term *Asia* to mean the Near East is illustrated by the list of nations that follows (see also similar lists in *Secrets of Heaven* 10177:10; *Heaven and Hell* 327; *Sacred Scripture* 21; *True Christianity* 202). [GFD]

324. By "legs and feet of iron and clay" Swedenborg means "legs made of iron and feet made of iron mixed with clay." See *Secrets of Heaven* 1326:2, 2162:3, 3021:8, 10030:2–5; *Marriage Love* 78:1. [GFD]

325. On the Golden Age see note 181 above and the references cited there. The Silver, Bronze, and Iron Ages were progressively more degenerate ages that according to classical mythology followed the ideal and primitive Golden Age. [GFD]

326. The stories of the conquest of the Promised Land occupy much of the Book of Joshua and substantial parts of 1 and 2 Samuel. In the Bible books ascribed to the prophets, there are frequently oracles predicting the destruction of various enemies of Israel, perhaps the best known being the sequence in the first two chapters of Amos. [GFD]

327. For the exile of Israel, see 2 Kings 17:5–6. The fall of Jerusalem, destruction of the temple, and exile to Babylon are described in 2 Kings 25. The Bible gives no historical account of the destruction of the second temple (70 C.E.) and accompanying razing of Jerusalem and Diaspora; Swedenborg's reference is presumably to Jesus' prediction of the destruction of the temple (see Matthew 24:2; Mark 13:2; Luke 21:6). [GFD]

328. Although Swedenborg seems here to distinguish between Daniel and the prophets, he shows elsewhere that he definitely considered Daniel to be a prophet (see for example *The Lord* 28). [JSR]

329. See note 88 above. [JSR]

330. See notes 29 and 134 above. [JSR]

331. See *Divine Love and Wisdom* 1–6. [GFD]

332. See *Divine Love and Wisdom* 358. [GFD]

333. See, for example, Matthew 5:9; Luke 6:35; John 1:12–13; 3:3–8. [GFD]

334. See the extensive collection of citations in *The Lord* 29–36, especially those in §32. [GFD]

335. Swedenborg here echoes a common contemporary (and still persisting) Protestant opinion that Catholics do not read Scripture, based presumably on the Catholic Church's former use of Bibles written in Latin, a language that many in the church could not read or understand. [JSR]

Notes to §§331–340

336. See *Divine Love and Wisdom* 28–33, 55–60. [GFD]

337. The Latin word here translated "generosity" is *bona*, literally, "good things." [GFD]

338. The allusion is to Isaiah 14:29: "Out of the serpent's root will come a viper, and its offspring will be a flying fiery serpent." See also *True Christianity* 487:4. [GFD]

339. There is no previous reference to this subject in *Divine Providence*, but it is covered in *Divine Love and Wisdom* 65–68. [GFD]

340. As he often does elsewhere, Swedenborg is presumably here using "paradise" in its original meaning of "a park." [GFD]

341. See for example §§74–77. [GFD]

342. In this section and the next Swedenborg differentiates "means" and "ways." The "means" (Latin *media*) may be compared to tools used by an agent, while the "ways" (Latin *modi*) may be compared to the ways in which the agent uses the tools. [GFD]

343. Swedenborg, though by all accounts a solidly trained practical mathematician, rarely utilizes mathematical comparisons of this type. A hyperbola is a geometrical

figure that can be described in nontechnical terms as the outline of an hourglass. A line (called the asymptote) can be drawn at a slant through the narrow neck of the hourglass shape such that though it approaches nearer and nearer to both the upper and lower curves as it extends to infinity, it never touches them. The squaring of the circle was one of three classic mathematical problems dating from Greek antiquity. It required one to construct a square equal in area to a given circle using only an unmarked straight edge and compasses. Its solution, though avidly pursued by amateurs to this day, was from an early period widely believed by experts to be impossible. It was not until 1882 that the German mathematician C.L.F. Lindemann (1852–1939) finally proved it so. See Beckmann 1971, 37, 49–50, 172–182. [SS]

344. Here the first edition reads 327. [GFD]

345. "It" refers here to intelligence and wisdom (Latin *intelligentia & sapientia*) as a single entity. In fact, Swedenborg treats "intelligence and wisdom" as singular throughout this brief discussion. [GFD]

346. On "the yoke of the law," see note 54 above. [GFD]

347. The "tripod in the cave" is a reference to the tripod at the oracle of the Greek god Apollo at Delphi in ancient times. The Pythia, or priestess of Apollo, was suspended in a seat from this tripod when delivering prophesies. The messages of ancient oracles in general were ambiguous and notoriously susceptible to misinterpretation. [GFD]

Works Cited
in the Notes

Acton, Alfred. 1927. *Introduction to the Word Explained.* Bryn Athyn, Pa.: Academy of the New Church.

———. 1955. *The Letters and Memorials of Emanuel Swedenborg.* Vol. 2. Bryn Athyn, Pa.: Swedenborg Scientific Association.

Aquinas, Thomas. 1952. *Summa Theologiae.* Translated by the Fathers of the English Dominican Province and revised by Daniel J. Sullivan. Vols. 19–20 of *Great Books of the Western World.* Chicago: Encyclopedia Britannica.

Aristotle. 1952. *Politics.* Translated by Benjamin Jowett. In volume 9 of *Great Books of the Western World.* Chicago: Encyclopedia Britannica.

Bayle, Pierre. 1697. *Dictionnaire historique et critique.* 2 vols. Amsterdam: Reinier Leers. 2nd. ed., 1701, 4 vols., Rotterdam: Reinier Leers.

Beckmann, Petr. 1971. *A History of Pi.* New York: St. Martin's.

Berkeley, George. [1710] 1952. *The Principles of Human Knowledge.* In vol. 35 of *Great Books of the Western World.* Chicago: Encyclopedia Britannica.

Boas, George. 1948. *Primitivism and Related Ideas in the Middle Ages.* Baltimore: Johns Hopkins University Press.

Bouwsma, William James. 1988. *John Calvin: A Sixteenth-Century Portrait.* New York: Oxford University Press.

Brecht, Martin. 1993a. *Martin Luther: The Preservation of the Church, 1532–1546.* Translated by James L. Schaaf. Minneapolis: Fortress Press.

———. 1993b. *Martin Luther: His Road to Reformation, 1483–1521.* Translated by James L. Schaaf. Minneapolis: Fortress Press.

———. 1994. *Martin Luther: Shaping and Defining the Reformation, 1521–1532.* Translated by James L. Schaaf. Minneapolis: Fortress Press.

Broberg, Gunnar. 1988. "Swedenborg and Uppsala." Translated by Gunilla Stenman Gado. In *Emanuel Swedenborg: A Continuing Vision.* Edited by Robin Larsen. New York: Swedenborg Foundation.

Brock, Erland J. 1988. "Mining and Engineering in Swedenborg's Time." In *Emanuel Swedenborg: A Continuing Vision.* Edited by Robin Larsen. New York: Swedenborg Foundation.

Brown, Reginald W. 1919. "The Fundamental Concept of Substance, and of Its Form and Activity." *The New Philosophy* 22:398–413.

Calvin, John. [1559] 1987. *Institutes of the Christian Religion.* Edited and translated by Tony Lane and Hilary Osborne. Grand Rapids, Mich.: Baker Book House.

Cassirer, Ernst. 1951. *The Philosophy of the Enlightenment.* Princeton: Princeton University Press.

Clatterbaugh, Kenneth. 1999. *The Causation Debate in Modern Philosophy, 1637–1739.* New York: Routledge.

Colish, Marcia L. 1997. *Medieval Foundations of the Western Intellectual Tradition, 400–1400.* New Haven: Yale University Press.

Descartes, René. [1637] 1952. *Discourse on the Method of Rightly Conducting the Reason.* Translated by Elizabeth S. Haldane and G.R.T. Ross. In vol. 31 of *Great Books of the Western World.* Chicago: Encyclopedia Britannica.

———. [1641] 1952. *Meditations on First Philosophy.* Translated by Elizabeth S. Haldane and G.R.T. Ross. In vol. 31 of *Great Books of the Western World.* Chicago: Encyclopedia Britannica.

Diderot, Denis and Jean Le Rond d'Alembert, eds. 1770–1775. *Encyclopédie ou Dictionnaire raisonné des sciences, des arts et des métiers.* 3rd ed. Livourne.

Dole, George F. 1988. "An Image of God in a Mirror." In *Emanuel Swedenborg: A Continuing Vision.* Edited by Robin Larsen. New York: Swedenborg Foundation.

Durant, Will and Ariel Durant. 1965. *The Age of Voltaire.* New York: Simon and Schuster.

Fontenelle, Bernard le Bovier de. [1686] 1990. *Conversations on the Plurality of Worlds.* Translated by H. A. Hargreaves. Berkeley, Ca.: University of California Press.

Frazier, Scott I. 1998. "Echoes from the Past: A Look at Classical Influences within Swedenborg's 'Golden Age.'" *Scripta: Bryn Athyn College Review* 1:27–44.

Gay, Peter. 1969. *The Enlightenment: An Interpretation.* New York: Norton.

Hazard, Paul. 1963. *European Thought in the Eighteenth Century from Montesquieu to Lessing.* Translated by J. Lewis May. Cleveland: World.

Hobbes, Thomas. [1651] 1939. *Leviathan.* In *The English Philosophers from Bacon to Mill.* Edited by Edwin A. Burtt. New York: Modern Library.

Holbach, Paul-Henri Dietrich, Baron d'. 1770. *Système de la nature, ou des lois du monde physique et du monde moral.* London.

———. [1770] 1999. *The System of Nature.* Adapted from the original translation by H. D. Robinson, introduction by Michael Bush, translation of Greek and Latin by Alistair Jackson. Manchester: Clinamen.

Hume, David. [1739–1740] 1902. *A Treatise of Human Nature.* Edited by L. A. Selby-Bigge. 2nd ed. rev. by P. H. Nidditch. Oxford: Clarendon.

———. [1748] 1952. *Concerning Human Understanding.* Edited by L. A. Selby-Bigge. In vol. 35 of *Great Books of the Western World.* Chicago: Encyclopedia Britannica.

Kirven, Robert H. and Robin Larsen. 1988. "Emanuel Swedenborg: A Pictorial Biography." In *Emanuel Swedenborg: A Continuing Vision.* Edited by Robin Larsen. New York: Swedenborg Foundation.

La Mettrie, Julien Offray de. 1748. *L'Homme machine.* Lyde.

———. [1748] 1994. *Man a Machine; and, Man a Plant.* Translated by Richard A. Watson and Maya Rybalka. Introduction and notes by Justin Leiber. Indianapolis: Hackett.

Leibniz, Gottfried Wilhelm. [1710] 1959. *Théodicée.* In *Opera Philosophica Quae Exstant Latina, Gallica, Germanica Omnia.* Edited by Johan Eduard Erdmann. Facsimile edition. Aalen: Scientia.

———. [1720] 1968. *The Monadology.* In *The Monadology and Other Philosophical Writings.* Translated by Robert Latta. Oxford: Oxford University Press.

Locke, John. [1690] 1952. *Essay Concerning Human Understanding.* In vol. 35 of *Great Books of the Western World.* Chicago: Encyclopedia Britannica.

Lovejoy, Arthur O. and George Boas. 1935. *Primitivism and Related Ideas in Antiquity.* Baltimore: Johns Hopkins University Press.

Macaulay, Thomas Babington. [1827] 1914. "Machiavelli." In *Critical and Historical Essays.* Vol. 2. New York: E. P. Dutton.

Machiavelli, Niccolò. [1513] 1950. *The Prince and the Discourses.* New York: Random House.

Manschreck, Clyde L. 1958. *Melanchthon, the Quiet Reformer.* New York: Abingdon Press.

McGrath, Alister E. 1990. *A Life of John Calvin: A Study in the Shaping of Western Culture.* Cambridge, Mass.: Basil Blackwell.

[Melanchthon, Philip]. [1530] 1901. *Die unveränderte Augsburgische Konfession.* Leipzig: A. Deichert.

———. [1543] 1992. *Loci Communes.* Translated by J.A.O. Preus. St. Louis: Concordia.

Mendel, Gregor. [1865] 1946. *Experiments in Plant Hybridisation.* Cambridge: Harvard University Press.

Odhner, Hugo Lj. 1933. "The History of the 'Animal Spirits,' and of Swedenborg's Development of the Concept." *The New Philosophy* 36:218–223, 234–249.

Pinto-Correia, Clara. 1997. *The Ovary of Eve: Egg and Sperm and Preformation.* Chicago: University of Chicago Press.

Porter, Roy. 2000. *The Creation of the Modern World: The Untold Story of the British Enlightenment.* New York: Norton.

Rose, Donald L. 1988. "The Pivotal Change in Swedenborg's Life." In *Emanuel Swedenborg: A Continuing Vision.* Edited by Robin Larsen. New York: Swedenborg Foundation.

Sigstedt, Cyriel Odhner. 1981. *The Swedenborg Epic: The Life and Works of Emanuel Swedenborg.* New York: Bookman Associates, 1952. Reprint, London: Swedenborg Society.

Swedenborg, Emanuel. [1764] 1889a. *Sapientia Angelica de Divina Providentia.* Edited by Samuel H. Worcester. London: Swedenborg Society.

———. 1889b. *The Spiritual Diary of Emanuel Swedenborg.* Vol. 4. Translated by George Bush and James F. Buss. London: James Speirs.

———. 1901. *Ontology.* Boston: Massachusetts New-Church Union. Undated facsimile reprint, Bryn Athyn, Pa.: Swedenborg Scientific Association.

———. 1917. *The Animal Spirit.* [Translated by Hugo Lj. Odhner.] *The New Philosophy* 20:114–130.

———. 1927–1951. *The Word Explained.* 10 vols. Translated and edited by Alfred Acton. Bryn Athyn, Pa.: Academy of the New Church.

———. [1740–1741] 1955. *The Economy of the Animal Kingdom.* 2 vols. Translated by Augustus Clissold. London: W. Newbery, H. Bailliere; Boston: Otis Clapp, 1845–1846. Bryn Athyn, Pa.: Swedenborg Scientific Association. A more accurate translation of the title of this work is *Dynamics of the Soul's Domain.*

———. [1744–1745] 1960. *The Animal Kingdom.* 2 vols. Translated by J.J.G. Wilkinson. London: W. Newbery, 1843–1844. Bryn Athyn, Pa.: Swedenborg Scientific Association. A more accurate translation of the title of this work is *The Soul's Domain.*

———. 1984. *Emanuel Swedenborg: The Universal Human and Soul-Body Interaction.* Edited and translated by George F. Dole. New York: Paulist Press.

———. [1734] 1988. *The Principia; or, The First Principles of Natural Things.* 2 vols. Translated by Augustus Clissold. London: W. Newbery, 1846. Bryn Athyn, Pa.: Swedenborg Scientific Association.

————. 1992. *On the Mechanism of the Soul and the Body.* Edited by Alfred Henry Stroh. 2nd ed. edited and rearranged by William Ross Woofenden. Bryn Athyn, Pa.: Swedenborg Scientific Association.

————. 1997a. *Apocalypse Explained.* 6 vols. Translated by John C. Ager, revised by John Whitehead, edited by William Ross Woofenden. West Chester, Pa.: Swedenborg Foundation.

————. 1997b. *On Divine Love and Divine Wisdom.* Translated by John C. Ager, revised by John Whitehead, edited by William Ross Woofenden. In vol. 6 of *Apocalypse Explained.* West Chester, Pa.: Swedenborg Foundation.

————. 1998. *Emanuel Swedenborg's Diary, Recounting Spiritual Experiences.* Vol. 1. Translated by J. Durban Odhner. Bryn Athyn, Pa.: General Church of the New Jerusalem.

Theological Dictionary of the Old Testament. 1986. Edited by G. Johannes Botterweck and Helmer Ringgren, translated by John T. Willis. Vol. 5. Grand Rapids, Mich.: William B. Eerdmans.

Willey, Basil. 1961. *The Eighteenth Century Background.* London: Chatto and Windus, 1940. Boston: Beacon Press.

Wilson, Catherine. 1995. *The Invisible World: Early Modern Philosophy and the Invention of the Microscope.* Princeton: Princeton University Press.

Wilson, Lois Burnham. 1979. *Lois Remembers.* New York: Al-Anon Family Group Headquarters.

[Wilson, William G.]. 2001. *Alcoholics Anonymous: The Story of How Many Thousands of Men and Women Have Recovered from Alcoholism.* 4th ed. New York: Alcoholics Anonymous World Services.

Woofenden, William Ross. 1970. *Swedenborg's Philosophy of Causality.* Diss. St. Louis University, St. Louis. Ann Arbor: University Microfilms.

————. 1990–1991. "Swedenborg's Philosophy of Causality." *The New Philosophy* 93.1–94.4.

Worcester, John. 1931. *Physiological Correspondences.* Boston: Massachusetts New-Church Union.

Index to Preface, Introduction, and Notes

The following index, referenced by page number, covers material in the translator's preface, the introduction, and the scholars' notes. References to the Bible in this material are listed under the heading "Scripture references." (References to the Bible that appear in the translation proper are treated in a separate index.)

Index to Scriptural Passages in *Divine Providence*

The following index refers to passages from the Bible cited in the translation of *Divine Providence*. The numbers to the left under each Bible book title are its chapter numbers. They are followed by verse numbers with the following designations: bold figures designate verses that are quoted; italic figures designate verses that are given in substance; figures in parenthesis indicate verses that are merely referred or alluded to. Biblical references that are enclosed in brackets indicate allusions in the text for which the present edition provides references. The numbers to the right are section numbers in *Divine Providence;* subsection numbers are separated from section numbers by a colon. (Passages from the Bible cited in the preface, introduction, and scholars' notes can be found under the heading "Scripture references" in the separate index of those elements.)

Table of Parallel Passages

The following table indicates passages in *Divine Providence* that parallel passages in Swedenborg's other theological works. The table draws on John Faulkner Potts's *Swedenborg Concordance* (1902, London: Swedenborg Society) 6:859–864, and on the table of parallel passages in Emanuel Swedenborg, *Delights of Wisdom Relating to Married Love*, translated by N. Bruce Rogers (1995, Bryn Athyn, Pennsylvania: General Church of the New Jerusalem).

Reference numbers in this table correspond to Swedenborg's section numbers; subsection numbers are separated from section numbers by a colon.

Divine Providence	**Parallel Passage**
197:2	*Marriage Love* 354; *True Christianity* 663:2–4
236	*True Christianity* 479
255	*Marriage Love* 342
263	*The Lord* 60, 61
318:3, 4	*Marriage Love* 233:3, 4; *True Christianity* 334:3–5
340:6, 7	*Marriage Love* 461:7, 8; *True Christianity* 570:7

Index to *Divine Providence*

The following index covers the translation of *Divine Providence*. For references to passages from the Bible and to topics treated in the preface, introduction, and scholars' notes, see the separate indexes to those elements.

Reference numbers in this index correspond to Swedenborg's section numbers in *Divine Providence;* subsection numbers are separated from section numbers by a colon.

A

Aaron, garments of, 255:2

Abandonment, of truth in the church, 328:7

Abel
killed by Cain, without divine providence preventing it, 236, 242
meaning love and charity, 242

Abraham
seeing angels completely filled with the Lord's divine nature, 96:6
speaking to the rich man in hell, 100:2

Abscesses, causing physical death if not healed, 112:2

Absence from the Lord, 326:4–5

Absolution from sins, 339

Absorption in evil, still permitting entrance of truth without profanation, 233:7–8

Abstinence from evils, 210:2
as the essence of religion, 239, 265, 278a
good loves drawing us to that extent, 61
as they are against God, the meaning of living rightly, 326:8
as they come from devils, 33:3–4, 258:3

Academics. *See* Educated people

Acceptance
of love and wisdom from God, 328:5
by us, the intention of the Lord, 96:5

Acid, dissolving pearls thrown into, 316

Acknowledgment of our evils
as the essence of religion, 239, 265
needed for us to discard our sins, 321:7

Acknowledgment of the Lord. *See also* Admission
how everything good and true comes from him, 91:1–2
and later turning away from divine things, 226
needed for us to discard our sins, 321:7

needed for us to understand truth and goodness, 321:6
uniting with our volition, 231:1
from wisdom, a kind of knowing coming from our belief system, 91:2

Action. *See also* Deeds
in accord with freedom and reason, a law of divine providence, 71–99, 178:1
apparently on our own, 174:2
based on our ability called freedom, 15
being free but irrational, or rational but not free, 78:2
as earthly, 71
given us by the balance between heaven and hell, 23
the intention for, requiring love to produce, 3:1
labor ceasing if intention is taken out of it, 3:2
the Lord's presence in the details of, 285:1
not from force acting on its own, 3:3
our ability of, coming only from something higher, 88
our freedom of, 23, 73:1
our limited awareness of its complexity, 199:3
the purpose, means, and result of, 108:1
seeing evil in and ceasing, 20, 101:2
in the spiritual world, thoughts coming out as, 29:1

Actors. *See also* Appearances
all of us, in how we wish to be seen, 298:4
going through the motions of religious practices, 222:2
not the real thing, 298:6
portraying monarchs, emperors, even angels, 224:1, 298:6
wearing royal robes until the play ends, 217:7

The Father *(continued)*
    the Lord from eternity, 157:9, 330:1
    never withdrawing from anyone, 330:2
    those believing he has mercy for the sake of
        his Son, 221
    turning to for repentance, 122
Fear
    able to occupy our outer thought processes,
        139:2
    capable of healing our discernment, but
        only superficially, 282
    of God, 136:9, 140
    never occupying our inner thought
        processes, 139:2
    taking away our freedom and rationality,
        139:1
    used by the Lord at first to heal the love of
        our volition, 283
Feces, 164:7
Feebleminded people, real freedom and ratio-
    nality impossible for, 98:2
Feelings. *See also* Emotional states
    accounting for human attraction and dis-
        like, 326:2–3
    all flowing into the physical world from the
        spiritual, 308:2
    of being caught and caged, 294:2
    beyond description, 39:1
    coming from pleasurable thoughts, 199
    each having its own thought, 194, 198
    every bit of flowing in from heaven, 288
    of goodness, as what pleases, 195:3
    hearing in people's voices, 317
    making themselves known through a sense
        of pleasure and gratification, 198
    origins of, 279:6–9, 319:1–2
    our not controlling the skin in, 180:8
    resting in what is good and true, 157:6
    seeing our own, 16
    sounds corresponding with, 194
    spirits present with us and sharing, 50:2
    variety of, 56:2
    of the workings of divine providence not
        reaching us, 175–190
The feet
    activated by the mind to walk, 181:1
    our inborn urge to walk upright upon, 275
Fellow citizens, desiring the good of, 220:11
Fermentation
    means by which purification can promote
        the union of goodness and truth in us,
        25, 284

separating things that do not belong to-
    gether and uniting things that do, 25
from things that are evil and false being in-
    jected into communities, 25
Fertility. *See* Fruitfulness; Reproduction;
    Seeds
Fibers. *See* Motor fibers; Nerve fibers
    all inverted in an evil person, 296:1
    bodily forms organized from, 180:2
Fig leaves, 313:3
Figurative language, of the Word, 241:1
Filthy beasts, 340:6
Filthy things
    appealing to evil people, 40
    exciting our physical fibers, 38:1–2
    hells overflowing with, 38:2
Finite beings
    Divinity having an infinite regard for every-
        thing in, 53:3
    it seeming to them that the Infinite is
        within them, 54
    unable to grasp the infinite, 46:1, 53:3
Finite things
    bearing no ratio to infinite things, 32:3,
        54
    everything created being, 52
    infinity only able to focus on what is infi-
        nite from itself in, 52–54
    unable to contain the infinite, 54, 219:2
Fire, 140
    burning more intensely the more it is fed,
        112:2
    coming from the nostrils, 309:1
    of life, justifying self-love as, 310:3
    of life, love being like, 167
    the sun as nothing but, 3:2
    of unseen inward obsessions with evil,
        278b:2
    in the Word, evils compared to, 112:2
Fireplace
    in darkness, people building, 206:3
    light in the middle hell like, 167
The first and only substance
    being the basis of everything, 6:1, 157:4
    being the sun of the spiritual world, 5:1,
        157:4
    coming from the sun of the spiritual world,
        6:1
First Being
    a gathering at the boundaries of everything
        coming from, 124:4
    source of everything created, 56:1, 157:5

Human beings *(continued)*

who exist solely for the sake of self and the
world, 14:1

who have become angels and are becoming
angels, a heaven made up of, 27:2

who have been saved, making up images of
what is infinite and eternal, 60–63

who have ceased being human, 231:7

who love evil and discern falsity, hell originating from, 27:1

who love good and discern truth, heaven
originating from, 27:1

who neglect reflecting on evil, 101:1–2

who would join the Lord in heaven, the
universe created for, 27:2

whom the Lord can lead to heaven, 67–68

in the Word, not receiving or doing anything on their own, 88:2

worshiping, 136:9, 328:6

Human body. *See* The body

Human form

all parts of making up an inclusive entity
acting as a single whole, 124:2, 201–203

both heaven and hell in, 204

every desire for what is both good and true
being like, 66

Human mind. *See also* Reflective moods; Spiritual mind; Thinking; Thoughts

activating the body in its outward functions, 181:1

also existing in our spirit, 296:15

being locked into the earthly, 147

being our spirit that lives after death, 196,
299

circle of love occurring in all the functions
of, 29:3

complete freedom of, 129:1

compulsions of evil obsessing the deeper
levels of, 38:1

constant preoccupation with purposes,
means, and results, 178:2

grasping truths, depending on its own state,
14:2

not sensing things on its own, but from the
Lord, 314:1

not thinking or intending on its own, 88

organic forms of, 319:2

pleasures of, prompting physical pleasures,
38:1

shifts and changes in, 202:3

of a spiritual person, 124:1–2

state of depending on the body, 142:1

that has lost its bearings, seeing imaginary
visions, 134a:3

three levels of, 75:1

understood only by those knowing what
heaven and hell are like, 299

what it is in us that thinks, 196

workings of similar to those of the body,
181:2

Human nature

from creation, enabling closer and closer
union with the Lord, 32–33

incapable of doing anything on its own, 337

that we have from birth, able to be opened,
32:1, 83

Human prudence. *See* Prudence

The Human-born One, John receiving the divine vision of, 134a:3

Humanity

emanating divinity accomplishing the marriage of the good and the true within,
58

everyone desiring the appearance of true,
298:4

foreknowledge destroying our essential, 179

forming a heaven from, the goal of divine
providence, 27–45, 202:1–2, 323–324

governed by the Lord, from himself, 163,
203:1

heaven and hell coming from, 204

intention of divine providence to save, focusing only on what is infinite and eternal from itself, 55–59

in its prudence, tree of knowledge as, 241:3

our rationality and our freedom giving us,
16

people believing that it is their own wisdom
and prudence that give them their, 321:1–3

things that are both good and true giving us
our, 16

The humble, raising up of, 183:4

Husbands

wanting what is best for their wives, 324:6

in the Word, term for the Lord, 8

Hyperbola, straight line approaching, but
never touching, 335:3

Hypocrisy, 150:1, 224:1

based on misuse of our abilities of freedom
and rationality, 15

Biographical Note

EMANUEL SWEDENBORG (1688–1772) was born Emanuel Swedberg (or Svedberg) in Stockholm, Sweden, on January 29, 1688 (Julian calendar). He was the third of the nine children of Jesper Swedberg (1653–1735) and Sara Behm (1666–1696). At the age of eight he lost his mother. After the death of his only older brother ten days later, he became the oldest living son. In 1697 his father married Sara Bergia (1666–1719), who developed great affection for Emanuel and left him a significant inheritance. His father, a Lutheran clergyman, later became a celebrated and controversial bishop, whose diocese included the Swedish churches in Pennsylvania and in London, England.

After studying at the University of Uppsala (1699–1709), Emanuel journeyed to England, Holland, France, and Germany (1710–1715) to study and work with leading scientists in western Europe. Upon his return he apprenticed as an engineer under the brilliant Swedish inventor Christopher Polhem (1661–1751). He gained favor with Sweden's King Carl (Charles) XII (1682–1718), who gave him a salaried position as an overseer of Sweden's mining industry (1716–1747). Although he was engaged, he never married.

After the death of Carl XII, Emanuel was ennobled by Queen Ulrika Eleonora (1688–1741), and his last name was changed to Swedenborg (or Svedenborg). This change in status gave him a seat in the Swedish House of Nobles, where he remained an active participant in the Swedish government throughout his life.

A member of the Swedish Royal Academy of Sciences, he devoted himself to scientific studies and philosophical reflections that culminated in a number of publications, most notably a comprehensive three-volume work on mineralogy (1734) that brought him recognition across Europe as a scientist and philosopher. After 1734 he redirected his research and publishing to a study of anatomy in search of the interface between the soul and body, making several significant discoveries in physiology.

From 1743 to 1745 he entered a transitional phase that resulted in a shift of his main focus from science and philosophy to theology. Throughout the rest of his life he maintained that this shift was brought about by Jesus Christ, who appeared to him, called him to a new mission, and opened his perception to a permanent dual consciousness of this life and the life after death.

He devoted the last decades of his life to studying Scripture and publishing eighteen theological titles that draw on the Bible, reasoning, and his own spiritual experiences. These works present a Christian theology with unique perspectives on the nature of God, the spiritual world, the Bible, the human mind, and the path to salvation.

Swedenborg died in London on March 29, 1772, at the age of eighty-four.